Elder Law Answer Book

Second Edition

This new edition of the *Elder Law Answer Book* replaces the prior edition and its supplements. Please discard the previous edition and its supplements.

Elder Law Answer Book

Second Edition

Robert B. Fleming

ASPEN
PUBLISHERS

1185 Avenue of the Americas, New York, NY 10036
www.aspenpublishers.com

This publication is designed to provide accurate and authoritative information in regard to the subject matter covered. It is sold with the understanding that the publisher is not engaged in rendering legal, accounting, or other professional services. If legal advice or other professional assistance is required, the services of a competent professional person should be sought.

— From a *Declaration of Principles* jointly adopted by
a Committee of the American Bar Association and
a Committee of Publishers and Associations

A Wolters Kluwer Company
www.aspenpublishers.com

Printed in the United States of America

ISBN 0-7355-3888-3

1 2 3 4 5 6 7 8 9 0

About Aspen Publishers

Aspen Publishers, headquartered in New York City, is a leading information provider for attorneys, business professionals, and law students. Written by preeminent authorities, our products consist of analytical and practical information covering both U.S. and international topics. We publish in the full range of formats, including updated manuals, books, periodicals, CDs, and online products.

Our proprietary content is complemented by 2,500 legal databases, containing over 11 million documents, available through our Loislaw division. Aspen Publishers also offers a wide range of topical legal and business databases linked to Loislaw's primary material. Our mission is to provide accurate, timely, and authoritative content in easily accessible formats, supported by unmatched customer care.

To order any Aspen Publishers title, go to *www.aspenpublishers.com* or call 1-800-638-8437.

To reinstate your manual update service, please call 1-800-638-8437.

For more information on Loislaw products, go to *www.loislaw.com* or call 1-800-364-2512.

For Customer Care issues, please call 1-800-234-1660, fax 1-800-901-9075, or email CustomerCare@aspenpublishers.com.

Aspen Publishers
A Wolters Kluwer Company

SUBSCRIPTION NOTICE

This Aspen Publishers product is updated on a periodic basis with supplements to reflect important changes in the subject matter. If you purchased this product directly from Aspen, we have already recorded your subscription for the update service.

If, however, you purchased this product from a bookstore and wish to receive future updates and revised or related volumes billed separately with a 30-day examination review, please contact our Customer Service Department at 1-800-234-1660, or send your name, company name (if applicable), address, and the title of the product to:

Aspen Publishers
7201 McKinney Circle
Frederick, MD 21704

Preface

The very nature of elder law makes production of *Elder Law Answer Book* a challenge and, ultimately, a rewarding experience. With practice areas ranging from age discrimination and nursing home rights, to Medicaid and other public benefits programs, to traditional estate planning and administration, the scope of many elder law practices is very broad indeed. This single volume includes detailed information about each of those disparate, but frequently related, aspects of elder law practice. The question-and-answer format of this book makes it possible to cover the broad field of practice in an intelligible manner, providing precise guidance on the most common concerns of practitioners.

Reflecting the diversity of elder law, this book is divided into separate parts for each of the broad practice areas included in many practices. Each part is further divided into chapters covering individual practice topics. Topics covered include:

- *Medicaid and long-term care planning.* The federal/state Medicaid program is bewilderingly complex, and even seasoned practitioners are likely to get lost in its rules. Although ostensibly subject to federal guidelines, the program is administered quite differently in each state, and the state variability increases over time. This volume summarizes the rules, pointing out significant state variations in the context of the individual principles. The usefulness of long-term care insurance is also discussed, including specific suggestions both for review of insurance contracts and for consideration of the value of insurance for individual clients.

- *Estate planning.* Many elder law practitioners are uncomfortable with tax-driven estate planning concepts and approaches. The principal techniques are explained in plain language, together with the appropriate situation for implementation of each approach. Even as the significance of tax-driven estate planning diminishes with the increase in the size of estates avoiding any federal taxation, the complexity of planning for larger estates is compounded by the certainty of change. Non-tax planning considerations are also explored, as are the usefulness, design and administration of powers of attorney.

- *Guardianship and conservatorship.* Although state variations in this area of the law are profound, there are a number of common themes, and procedures are often similar. Residency requirements for surrogates, court processes, inventory and accounting requirements and limitations on the powers of guardians and conservators are all described.

- *Probate and trust administration.* An explanation of the need for probate proceedings and demystification of the process itself will help in explanations to clients. Different administration requirements for trusts and probate proceedings are described, as well as methods of avoiding the probate process entirely.

- *"Special Needs" trusts.* Though a growing portion of many elder law practices, special needs trust planning and administration remain unfamiliar territory for many elder law attorneys. Questions about the propriety of special needs trusts for particular clients, language necessary to effect special needs provisions, tax treatment of trusts and other administrative concerns are covered in depth.

- *Medicare.* Although nearly all seniors rely on Medicare for most of their medical care, few practitioners are sufficiently familiar with the operation, limitations and entitlements of that program. A thorough discussion of the program will help guide the practitioner through clients' problems and needs.

- *Patient autonomy and the right to die.* Constitutional and statutory provisions governing the right of a client to direct the withholding or withdrawal of medical care are described, and suggestions made for particular documents and approaches.

- *Ethical issues.* Elder law practitioners daily navigate an ethical minefield. Questions about conflicts of interest, multiple representation, duties to report client misconduct and other ethical issues are analyzed and suggestions offered for resolution of the ethical problems which do arise.

- *Practice management.* Technology (including computers and software) has revolutionized the practice of law, especially in elder law and estate planning. Business development, once anathema to lawyers, is now a requirement for survival. Questions and answers about practice development and management, including uses of technology, are offered, with particular emphasis on the characteristics which make an elder law practice unique.

Age discrimination, veteran's and Railroad Retirement benefits, nursing home rights, and other topics encountered by elder law attorneys (albeit less frequently) are also explained. A growing area of practice for many elder law attorneys—the rights of grandparents and other family members to visitation with and/or custody of minor children—is also addressed and discussed.

The Elder Law Answer Book is intended for several audiences. Lawyers looking for answers to frequent questions about elder law issues somewhat outside their usual area of practice should be able to find those answers here. Sometimes lawyers with another practice focus have no desire to practice elder law, but find that elder law issues persist among their clients; this book should help those lawyers answer clients' questions (and direct those clients to appropriate resources) without requiring that they become elder law practitioners. Many non-lawyers deal with elder law issues, including accountants, brokers, financial planners, geriatric case managers, guardians and conservators, medical personnel, social workers, discharge planners, and others. They will find that this volume explains concepts clearly and concisely. Elder law constantly attracts new practitioners who come to the practice from such disciplines as estate planning, benefits law, and family law, and from public practices and legal aid organizations. For these attorneys, *Elder Law Answer Book* will serve as a solid introduction to their new practice area. Even seasoned elder law practitioners should find help with aspects of the practice they do not regularly encounter.

One principal goal throughout this book has been to make explanations comprehensible. In other words, every effort has been made to retain the use of the English language and to avoid legalese, circumlocution, and jargon. That approach, coupled with the question-and-answer format, should make the material understandable to the clients of elder law practitioners as well.

Another main purpose has been to give real-world relevance to the questions and answers. To that end each chapter concludes with a set of examples drawn from personal practice experience and discussions with practitioners. These are intended to consolidate and focus the information in each chapter into one or more scenarios of the sort that practitioners of all experience levels have encountered (or will encounter) in actual practice. While individual questions can often be answered in a few sentences, those reality-based scenarios should help place many answers in better context.

The question-and-answer format of *Elder Law Answer Book* is uniquely helpful to an understanding of elder law issues. Although other reference books are invaluable resources for analyzing the law, it is often difficult to understand the interrelationship of legal principles and to integrate concepts from a recitation, albeit orderly, of the relevant points. My personal attraction to this format is entirely practical; from my own real-world experience with other volumes in the *Answer Book* series I can report that it is truly wonderful to find my precise question asked and answered in a few sentences. I hope to provide other readers with that same satisfaction.

Elder law is rapidly evolving, both in terms of styles of practice and in the substantive law. The Foster Care Independence Act of 1999, for example, reinstated transfer penalties for Supplemental Security Income (SSI) and subtly altered the landscape of special needs trusts. Despite that change, the use of special needs trusts has grown tremendously in recent years, with an accompanying growth in interest among elder law practitioners. On the practical side, technology and other practice management issues have also seen dramatic changes in past years.

While the national legal community initiates a discussion of "multi-disciplinary practices," elder law attorneys across the country have pioneered the use of staff social workers and accountants and important and valuable linkages with medical, case management, insurance, and other professionals. Litigation-based ethical rules about governing representation of multiple clients are strained by both traditional estate planning and newer elder law client scenarios.

It has been a challenge to try to address the volume of material and pace of change inherent in a modern elder law practice. The future of elder law is uncertain, and the practice may appear very different in a few short years. In addition to the certainty of change, however, there is another certainty: the world is aging, and the legal problems faced by elders grow more numerous and more complex every day. Along with tremendous new demands on an already overburdened long-term care system, the future holds new medical technology that may extend life while challenging individual concepts of quality of that life. New family dynamics, already a hallmark of the past half-century, will further change the needs and care options of the next generation of seniors. Government benefit programs, which are strained financially and administratively, must be adapted in coming decades; increased emphasis on in-home care may reduce the strain on those programs or, paradoxically, may increase that strain. Abolition of the federal estate tax, often suggested as a popular measure, may lead to reintroduction of the concept of "carry-over basis" for capital gains tax purposes. In other words, the tools described in this volume, though the best available today, will have to be adapted for future elders.

Robert B. Fleming
Lisa Nachmias Davis
September 2003

About the Authors

Robert B. Fleming is a partner in the Tucson law firm of Fleming & Curti, P.L.C., with a practice limited to guardianship, conservatorship, estate planning, and probate. His interest in this area was developed while serving as the Pima County Public Fiduciary for five years prior to starting his current practice. Mr. Fleming has been selected as a fellow of both the American College of Trust and Estate Counsel and the National Academy of Elder Law Attorneys, and regularly writes and lectures on elder law issues. He is a past Chair of the State Bar of Arizona's Mental Health and Elder Law Section and Probate and Trust Section; he has also served as a Member of the Board of Directors of the National Academy of Elder Law Attorneys. At different times he served as President of both the Pima County Bar Association (he is now a member of the Board of Directors of that association) and the Young Lawyers Section of the State Bar of Arizona (he no longer qualifies to be a member). He was named as a delegate to the 1995 White House Conference on Aging and was a member of the Arizona State Legislature Committee on Health Care Powers of Attorney, Living Wills and Advance Directives in 1991. Mr. Fleming is the webmaster for his firm's extensive website at *www.elder-law.com,* and writes a weekly newsletter distributed by e-mail from that website. He is a member of the Southern Arizona Estate Planning Council, the Pima County Bar Association and the State Bar of Arizona. Mr. Fleming received his J.D. at University of Arizona School of Law and his B.S. at Utah State University.

Lisa Nachmias Davis is a senior associate in the Connecticut firm of Tyler, Cooper & Alcorn. She practices primarily in the areas of elder law, estate planning, estate administration, and the law of nonprofit organizations. She is a frequent speaker on topics in these areas. She maintains a website, www.sharinglaw.net, that has become a widely used resource for elder law attorneys in Connecticut and elsewhere. With Edward Dale (now of AARP) she developed the website www.CTElderLaw.org that is now maintained by Connecticut Legal Services, and the site includes her contributions on the topics of Living Wills, Powers of Attorney, and Funeral Planning. She has also created the website for the South Central Connecticut Agency on Aging, where she serves as a member of the Board of Directors. She serves on the Executive Committee of the Connecticut Bar Association Elder Law Section; as a member of the American Bar Association Real Property Probate and Trust Law Section and the New Haven County Bar Association; and as a member of the National Academy of Elder Law Attorneys. She is a professional member of the National Alliance for the Mentally Ill and PLAN (Planned Lifetime Assistance Network) of Connecticut. Since 1998, Ms. Davis has also been a co-director of the Yale Law School Nonprofit Organization Law Clinic, teaching students how to represent nonprofit organizations. Ms. Davis received her B.A. in history, magna cum laude, from Yale College in 1982 and her J.D. from The Yale Law School in 1990, after which she served as law clerk to the late Justice David M. Shea of the Connecticut Supreme Court.

Acknowledgments

For this Second Edition of The Elder Law Answer Book, I owe a huge debt of gratitude to Lisa Nachmias Davis, an excellent and eloquent elder law practitioner from New Haven, Connecticut. Ms. Davis has agreed to take on the responsibility of co-authoring future updates and editions of the Answer Book, and much of this Edition reflects her expertise in both legal and editorial duties. The Second Edition simply would not have been completed without her efforts. Thanks also should go to Lisa's law firm, Tyler Cooper & Alcorn, for its willingness to allow her the time necessary for this rewrite; I know that I should also thank her family for their forbearance during the writing process.

For the First Edition and the annual updates issued since, I have thanked a number of contributors including Victoria Blair, Elizabeth Smith and Carolyn Robinson. Each of them did substantial work on the writing and rewriting of both questions and answers. Reflecting back on their collective contributions makes me wonder exactly what role I took in preparation of what is known in my home and office as "the book."

Lisa has asked that I particularly mention thanks to her clients for making the elder law practice a meaningful way of life. That seems to me to be appropriate for my practice as well as for hers, and the fact that I am prepared to steal her expression of thanks should give some indication of how willing I have been to take credit for her work throughout this book.

Robert Fleming
Tucson, Arizona
September 2003

How to Use This Book

Elder Law Answer Book integrates the most current information regarding the various areas of elder law including estate planning, retirement planning, medical and long-term care planning, and fiduciary administration into a single-volume reference. It is designed for attorneys and other professionals who need quick and authoritative answers to help them work within the complex programs and to comply with the multitude of legal, tax, and, regulatory provisions.

The author writes in straightforward language, avoiding technical jargon as much as possible. Citations of authority are provided throughout the volume and will serve as research aids for those who wish to pursue particular items in greater detail.

The question-and-answer format helps to clarify for the reader the important issues in this complex area and offer a clear and useful guide to understanding the many areas of law that comprise elder law. This format enables the reader to focus rapidly on particular problems.

Numbering System: The questions are numbered consecutively within each chapter (e.g., 1:1, 1:2, 1:3).

List of Questions: The detailed List of Questions that follows the Table of Contents in the front of this book helps the reader locate areas of immediate interest. This list serves as a detailed table of contents that provides both the question number and the page on which it appears.

Index: The index is a further aid to locating specific information. All references in the index are to question numbers rather than page numbers.

Contents

Part I Establishing and Managing an Elder Law Practice

Part III Fiduciary Administration

List of Questions

Part I Establishing and Managing an Elder Law Practice

Chapter 1 Practice Considerations

Characteristics of the Elder Law Practice

Office Design and Accommodating the Elder Client

Attorney Fees and Billing

Law Practice Management

Evaluating the Practice

Practice-Related Issues

Chapter 2 Ethical Issues in Client Representation

Overview

Representing Married Couples and Families

Dealing with the Incompetent Client

Conflicts of Interest

Fiduciary Representation

Practical Ethical Questions

Part II Estate and Retirement Planning

Chapter 3 Retirement Planning

Overview

Information Gathering

ERISA

Qualified Plans

Vesting Requirements

Participation and Nondiscrimination Requirements

Plan Terminations

Rollovers and Termination of Employment

Types of Qualified Retirement Plans

Simplified Employee Pension Plan (SEP)

Savings Incentive Match Plan for Employees (SIMPLE Plan)

Individual Retirement Accounts

Spousal Rights

Distributions

Minimum Required Distributions

Beneficiaries

Roth IRAs

Nonqualified Plans

Tax Issues in Retirement Planning

Practice-Related Issues

Chapter 4 Non-Tax Aspects of Estate Planning: Wills, Trusts, and Other Transfers of Property Upon Death

Overview

Wills

Who Should Make a Will

Will Clauses and Distribution Provisions

Requirements for a Valid Will

Personal Representative

Types of Wills

Probate

Joint Tenancy

Joint-Name Bank Accounts

Requirements for a Valid Trust

Using Trusts to Protect Assets

Trustees

Other Resources

Practical Estate Planning Problems

Chapter 5 Estate Planning

Overview

Estate and Gift Tax Basics

Gift Tax

Gift Tax Planning

Education IRAs or "Coverdell Accounts"

529 Plans

Estate Tax

Overview of Estate Planning Techniques

Marital Deduction Planning

Charitable Gift Planning

Life Insurance as an Estate Planning Tool

Valuation Discounts as an Estate Planning Tool

Generation-Skipping Tax Planning

Practice-Related Issues

Chapter 6 Post-Mortem Estate Planning

Overview

Post-Mortem Tax Reporting

Estate Tax Elections and Valuations

Income Tax Elections

Deduction of Administrative Expenses

Disclaimers

Post-Mortem Retirement Account Planning

Post-Mortem Reformations and Other Fixes

Practice-Related Issues

Part III Fiduciary Administration

Chapter 7 Probate and Trust Administration

Overview

When Are Probate Proceedings Required?

Personal Representative

Principles of Estate Distribution

The Probate Process

Estate Administration

Claims Against the Estate

Estate Distribution and Closing

Trust Administration

Practice-Related Issues

Chapter 8 Will and Trust Contests

Wills: Validity and Challenges

Trust Challenges

Practice-Related Issues

Chapter 9 Guardianship and Protective Proceedings

Overview

Selection or Appointment of a Guardian or Conservator

The Appointment Process

Powers and Duties

Practice-Related Issues

Chapter 10 Powers of Attorney

Overview

Durable Power of Attorney

Health Care Power of Attorney

Attorney-in-Fact

Designation and Qualifications

Duties and Powers

Refusal to Honor Power of Attorney

Termination and Revocation of Power of Attorney

Practice-Related Issues

Part IV Paying for Medical and Long-Term Care

Chapter 11 Long-Term Care Options

Overview

Home Care

Continuing Care Retirement Communities

Congregate Living and Adult Care

Assisted Living

Skilled Nursing Facilities and Nursing Homes

Hospice Care

Practice-Related Issues

Chapter 12 Paying Privately for Long-Term Care: Long-Term Care Insurance

Overview

Purchase of Long-Term Care Insurance

Long-Term Insurance Policy Provisions

Tax Issues

Part A Benefits

Inpatient Hospital Care

Skilled Nursing Facility Care

Home Health Care Services

Hospice Care

Part B Benefits

Medicare+Choice Program

Medigap Insurance

Medicare Appeals Process

Practice-Related Issues

Chapter 14 Medicaid Benefits

Overview

General Eligibility Requirements

Income Eligibility

Resource Eligibility

Spending Down

Asset Transfers

Liability for Eligibility-Related Asset Transfers

Asset Transfer Techniques

Medicaid Trust Planning

Estate Recovery

Medicaid Planning-Related Practice Issues

Chapter 15 Social Security

Overview

Eligibility

Retirement Benefits

Disability Benefits

"Ticket to Work" Program

Appeals

Survivor's Benefits

Dependent's Benefits

Application for Benefits

Receipt of Benefits

Practice-Related Issues

Chapter 16 Other Benefit Programs

Supplemental Security Income

Veterans Benefits

Railroad Retirement Benefits

Practice-Related Issues

Part V Health Care Decision-Making and Protection of the Elderly

Chapter 17 Special Needs Trusts

Overview

Self-Settled Special Needs Trusts

Third-Party Special Needs Trusts

Distributions from Special Needs Trusts

Taxation

Trust Administration

Practice-Related Issues

Chapter 18 Patient Autonomy and Self-Determination

Overview

Informed Consent

Right to Refuse Medical Treatment

Advance Directives

Language of Directives

Enforcement

Practice-Related Issues

Chapter 19 Elder Abuse, Neglect, and Exploitation

Overview

Reporting Requirements

Recognizing Abuse or Neglect

Responsibilities in Cases of Abuse, Neglect, or Exploitation

Remedies

Remedies

Older Workers Benefit Protection Act

Practice-Related Issues

Chapter 21 Grandparents' Rights

Grandparent Visitation Rights

Grandparent Caretakers

Part I

Establishing and Managing an Elder Law Practice

Chapter 1

Practice Considerations

Elder law is a growing practice area—some might say specialty—nationally. The growth of elder law has primarily been fueled by a rapid growth in the older segment of our population, coupled with the increasingly complex tax, medical, and social issues they face. Elder law attorneys tend to be sole practitioners, small law firm members, or boutique specialty practice members. The type of practice, and the lawyers drawn to it, lends itself to a more casual and friendly (and less adversarial) office structure. Both new lawyers assaying their practice choices and existing lawyers who are unhappy with their current practices are considering changing to the elder law field, and many are taking the steps to make the transition. This chapter discusses what an elder law practice is, and distinguishes it from other practice areas; how to develop an elder law practice; and law practice issues including office design, attorney fees and billing, law practice management, and computer software and technology for the elder law office. It is intended to provide insight into these issues, and suggestions for both new and existing elder law practitioners as they develop their practices.

Characteristics of the Elder Law Practice

Q 1:1 What is elder law?

Elder law began to develop as a practice focus in the early 1980s. Recognizing that their practices focused on similar topics, most of which did not fit well into existing specialty areas, a number of individuals from different states began to meet regularly to discuss the emerging practice area.

A common observation among these practitioners was that their clients were predominantly older, or were the children of older parents seeking assistance with the elders' legal problems. From this observation grew the use of the term "elder law," even though innovators realized that the term was imprecise. Many of the common legal problems of the elderly are shared by younger clients who may be disabled, or poor enough to qualify for government assistance, or terminally ill, or wealthy enough to require tax planning assistance despite their age. Still, most elder law clients tend to be older, and many elders tend to share similar legal problems.

Today, elder law is a much better recognized area of practice. Usually, elder law attorneys focus their practices in a handful of areas. Those focus areas typically include long-term care planning, guardianship and conservatorship, advance medical directives, and the more traditional trust and estate planning. Other elder law attorneys spend considerable time dealing with Medicare and other government benefits, abuse, neglect, and exploitation issues, age discrimination, charitable giving, probate administration, and a host of other practice areas.

Of course, elderly individuals can have any sort of legal problem, and a practice devoted to serving the elderly is likely to be quite diverse; however, most elder law attorneys will find that they concentrate their practices in a few substantive areas, or even in one area alone.

Q 1:2 How are elder law clients different from other clients?

Because elder law attorneys primarily serve the elderly and disabled, their clients will obviously be older than the clients of most general practitioners. Some of their clients are, however, younger family members concerned about a parent's legal problems (or the problems of another elderly relative or friend). In addition, many legal problems commonly encountered by the elderly are also concerns for the disabled (for problems such as long-term care and advance medical directives) or minors (in conservatorships of the estate). As a result of these factors it cannot truly be said that all elder law attorneys' clients are elderly; many of them are young.

Elder law clients may present with a single legal problem, not realizing that multiple issues are actually involved. For example, a client may request assistance with estate planning without realizing he or she should be considering the need for long-term care insurance, or the need to plan for eligibility for public assistance with long-term care. Conversely, a client may request information about the availability of public assistance with the long-term care of a spouse without realizing that the spouse's illness requires rethinking of the client's own estate planning. Similar multiple-issue circumstances might occur for children planning for their parents' long-term care, or parents seeking information about care of disabled children.

Q 1:3 Are there generalizations that can safely be made about the characteristics of elder law clients?

Because most clients of an elder law attorney are older, they will have had some common life experiences. Many clients will have been born (or begun adulthood) before the onset of the Great Depression. Clients tend to be the parents or grandparents of the Baby Boom generation. They are the first generation to have been guaranteed Social Security throughout their work lives, and they are now collecting on that guarantee. They were usually raised in a smaller town than they now live in, and may have a stronger sense of public correctness or propriety than their younger counterparts.

It is, of course, dangerous to generalize; however, over time, the elder law attorney will observe that his or her clients are prompt to a fault (many will arrive early for their appointments, and some will conduct "dry runs" to the office days in advance to make sure they can arrive in time). They will be attuned to value and may even engage in comparison-shopping and/or negotiating of the fee, but they will expect to pay for professional services and will intend to pay at the time of delivery of those services (or in advance). They will appreciate informality and personal touches, but will also respond instinctively to being addressed more formally and expect appropriate deference. They will frequently be more interested in the attorney's personal life, family, and hobbies than other clients, and will be on the lookout for common backgrounds, avocations, or contacts.

Many of the elderly and disabled will also have some physical and/or mental impairment. Often they will recognize the impairment, but frequently they will deny its existence (or minimize its impact). Gentle and indirect attempts to deal with those impairments will make the attorney-client relationship easier.

Q 1:4 What sorts of legal issues regularly arise in an elder law practice?

Legal problems faced by the elderly and disabled are wide-ranging; however, most practitioners who consider themselves elder law attorneys focus much of their professional energy in a handful of areas. A few practice in most or all of those areas, while others may limit themselves to only one, or even to a subset of one. The most common practice areas for elder law attorneys include, in no particular order:

1. Long-term care planning, including advice regarding long-term care insurance and the availability of Medicaid;
2. Guardianship of the person and conservatorship of the estate;
3. Estate planning, including more advanced tax planning issues;
4. Probate (or other procedures required on a person's death), including will contests, and questions relating to the administration of trusts;
5. Planning and implementation of "living wills" and other advance directives and health care rights;

6. Caring (and providing) for disabled children, including special needs trusts; and
7. Access to Social Security, Medicare, and health benefits or insurance.

Less frequently, but often enough to require familiarity with the legal issues, an elder law attorney might be asked for advice regarding:

1. Access to veteran's benefits, railroad retirement benefits, public housing benefits, and other benefit programs less widely available than Social Security and Medicare;
2. Age discrimination;
3. Nursing home rights and procedures, including discharges from nursing home care, quality of care, patient's rights to privacy and association, and similar problems;
4. Dissolution of marriage (or separation) where one spouse is physically or mentally disabled;
5. Guardianship of grandchildren or even great-grandchildren, and visitation rights of grandparents, as family life tends to become more fragmented and nontraditional domestic arrangements proliferate;
6. Elder abuse, not infrequently at the hands of spouses or caretaker children; and
7. Exploitation of elderly clients and efforts to recover lost assets.

Even as the practice of law becomes more specialized, the issues commonly seen in an elder law practice seem to multiply over time. As a result many elder law practitioners choose to "specialize" in only one or two of the individual areas described here.

Q 1:5 Is it possible to specialize in elder law, and does it make sense to do so?

Although the legal profession is primarily regulated by state bar associations, state supreme courts, and other state-level organizations, the national tendency has been to recognize elder law as a distinct specialty practice. In fact, the National Elder Law Foundation (1604 N. Country Club Road, Tucson, AZ 85716, (520)

881-1076) conducts a certification process and conveys the designation of Certified Elder Law Attorney (CELA). The program has been accredited by the American Bar Association, and is formally recognized in a small number of states, including Alabama, Ohio, and Tennessee. Another handful of states (notably including Florida, which adopted a separate elder law specialty designation in 1998) include elder law as one of the state-designated specialty areas of practice. On either the national or state level, certification will require a minimum number of years of practice, a concentration in elder law, and a certification examination.

Some state bar associations prohibit the use of specialty bar designations without specific approval of the program. Many critics believe that those limitations are unlikely to be enforceable if ever tested against federal constitutional free speech protections, but that may be slight consolation to the prospective respondent in a state disciplinary proceeding.

Q 1:6 Whether a lawyer seeks certification as a specialist or not, is it important to focus one's practice in an area such as elder law?

It is of course possible to practice elder law as part of a larger scope of practice. In fact, because "elder law" tends to be defined by clients rather than legal issues, the "specialty" is necessarily a sort of general practice. The development of elder law is in many ways analogous to the growth of gerontology in the medical field; in both cases, the practitioner is required to maintain familiarity with a broad base of issues, and to adapt those to an older clientele.

In an era of specialization, there is much to be said, however, for focusing one's practice in a defined area. Not only does this reduce the amount of time required to maintain currency in the area of law practiced, but it also permits concentration of practice development energy, office design, and staff selection and training. Most practitioners who begin to practice in elder law seem to gravitate to the area; in addition to administrative and financial rewards, the limited practice simply seems to be more enjoyable.

Q 1:7 Can an elder law practice be incorporated into an existing general practice?

A general practitioner, or an attorney with a different practice concentration, will likely be able to learn and practice elder law as well. There is little that is so arcane or difficult to master about elder law that it should discourage an interested practitioner. The office structural accommodations and the investment in learning (and keeping current in) technical government program rules and requirements may, however, make it difficult to maintain an elder law practice at the same time as a more general practice.

To the extent that elder law issues can be delegated to one attorney (or a few attorneys) in a larger office, the problem of keeping current can be minimized; however, some practice areas might not coexist well with an elder law practice, and so it might be difficult to maintain an elder law section in a firm otherwise devoted to criminal law or antitrust litigation, for example.

The obvious connection for an elder law practitioner is to either practice in estate planning or develop an association with someone who does. By offering tax planning advice alongside long-term care planning, the attorney or firm can offer a range of services to clients from very poor to very wealthy. Many of the estate planning lawyer's clients will also have problems with (or questions about) guardianship and conservatorship, advance medical directives, and many of the other areas of elder law practice. Typically estate planning clients will also be older, making their office visits and physical accommodations more consistent with those of the elder law attorney.

Q 1:8 How does an estate planning attorney typically deal with elder law issues?

Many current elder law practitioners began their professional careers as more traditional estate planning attorneys. Increasingly often, estate planning clients ask questions about long-term care for themselves, or planning for disabled children. Estate planning attorneys sometimes think of themselves as tax experts, and overlook the importance of care issues in the client's plan; however, estate planning attorneys more often find themselves drawn to the care concerns of clients.

Estate planning is presently undergoing a rapid change, with pressure on law firms from financial planners, accountants, "boutique" practices, and even computer software. For many, an increased focus on care concerns helps differentiate them in the estate planning field, and provides greater job satisfaction even as it improves the bottom line.

Q 1:9 What different approaches to practice organization have been successfully implemented in elder law practices?

Some of the areas of elder law practice lend themselves particularly well to the use of legal assistants and support staff. A long-term care practitioner, for example, may be able to use support staff to collect financial information from the client and to complete Medicaid applications. A guardianship of the person may be managed or overseen by legal assistants or, in some cases, staff social workers.

Because of the nature of elder law clients and their legal problems, it is critically important to collect comprehensive and useful information at the outset of representation. To this end, most practitioners rely heavily on "intake" forms, which should be designed to query the client about obvious issues (are some of a couple's children really children of only one spouse?) as well as less-likely possibilities (are both spouses U.S. citizens?). Even after collection of this detailed information, it is dangerous to rely on the responses from clients; given the high degree of reticence, the occasional confusion on the part of clients, and the complexity of legal issues, it is important to check the validity of information provided on intake forms.

Because the contact with clients may be relatively short, an elder law practice is usually a high-volume proposition. This puts a premium on a structured organization, where appointments can be made and confirmed, data collected, and work completed efficiently and on time. It also places a premium on office automation and the efficient use of technology.

Precisely because of the high volume and short average client contact time, an elder law practice must depend on an efficient "tickler" system. Usually such systems are automated, and may be a part of the firm's calendaring program, but even the nonautomated practitioner must develop a reliable method of keeping track of the status of many cases at one time.

Notwithstanding the high volume of a typical elder law practice, the age and social background of clients will require that staff be friendly and personable. Perhaps more than other clients, elder law clients will appreciate birthday reminders, recognition of family relationships, and other personal touches. This reality argues for thoughtful staff selection, clear delegation of client contact responsibilities, and low staff turnover. Given the high volume of clients, the last may be both especially important and especially difficult to achieve.

Q 1:10 How many and what kind of support staff should an elder law attorney expect to employ?

Attorneys in some practice areas expect to have a ratio as low as one staff member to every two attorneys. Across practice areas, the ratio is probably about one to one. For an elder law practitioner, the ratio may be three staff members to each attorney. In fact, the ratio may be even higher if the practice is heavily concentrated in such areas as Medicaid applications (which may utilize many application preparers) or guardianship (which may require case managers or social workers).

Even an elder law practice devoted to nearly traditional litigation or estate planning work may find it important to have a higher staff/lawyer ratio because of the nature of the clientele. Not every elder law attorney will utilize nonlawyer staff members so extensively, but with the use of social workers (common as regular paid staff members in elder law practices), legal assistants, Medicaid workers, and other paraprofessionals, some elder law attorneys have as high a staff to lawyer ratio as is seen in any practice area.

Because the elder law practice focuses on a type of client as much as on a kind of law, the personalities of office staff can be more important than in other practice types. Older clients usually enjoy personable, outgoing staff members; an ability to work and communicate with elderly clients is obviously an important plus. Efficiency, accuracy, and competence remain essential employee traits, but a willingness to chat and a friendly demeanor should be equally prized.

Q 1:11 What kinds of lawyers are drawn to elder law?

In early reports compiled by the National Academy of Elder Law Attorneys (NAELA), as many as half of current elder law practitioners received training through either a local legal services organization or some other governmental (or quasi-governmental) experience. Another significant percentage were drawn to elder law as a result of the perceived mistreatment of (or difficulty of arranging treatment for) a close family member, usually a parent. A growing number of elder law attorneys began their professional careers as more traditional estate planners, and have gradually come to emphasize elder law issues.

A large number of elder law attorneys are sole practitioners or in small firms. A small percentage practice in mid-sized or larger law firms—this trend mirrors the national tendency toward smaller and "boutique" firms in a number of practice areas. Those elder law attorneys in larger law firms tend to be part of the firm's estate planning department.

Q 1:12 What special training is required for elder law practitioners, and where is it available?

An elder law practitioner must maintain proficiency in relevant areas of the law. Because of the age of the elder law attorney's clients, it is also important to be aware of and able to deal with the problems and characteristics of aging. Training should include not just legal seminars, but also social awareness, an understanding of physical and mental limitations, and familiarity with the shared experiences that strongly affect seniors' approach to problems and choices. College-level gerontology courses, values-development training sessions, and public policy lectures are all useful in developing a thoughtful approach to client concerns. Empathy training, in which the participants are given an opportunity to learn what it is like to navigate modern life with hearing and visual impairments, is an excellent way to develop better appreciation for and understanding of elderly clients. Remember that the two great events that shaped the current senior generation—the Great Depression and World War II—were more than just historical events to older clients, and that learning more about them can improve the ability to relate to those clients. As a wonderful side benefit, starting a conversation with an older client about an area of mutual interest can be a pleasant, effective way to learn more about those historical events.

Familiarity with diseases common to the elderly, their treatment, and the side effects of treatment, is an essential component of the training for an elder law attorney. This background can be helpful in making judgment calls concerning a client's capacity, susceptibility to influence, and future needs. To the extent that the elder law attorney also deals with the problems of disabled family members or clients, he or she will also benefit from medical knowledge in that area. A social work or nursing background would be an asset to any elder law attorney. In short, although no one needs to be a doctor or nurse first to make a good elder law attorney, exposure to these disciplines will add value to your elder law practice.

One of the most difficult areas of the law for the new elder law practitioner is the law of entitlement benefits. Each state has its own specific rules. The rules can be confusing, hard to locate, and harder to understand, and the programs are numerous and ever-changing. It is not enough to learn the basic federal law of the Medicaid program; the attorney who has a "little knowledge" in this technical area can do a client great harm. The learning curve is long and steep. The new practitioner of elder law should seek out and study the core "source material," the statutes, regulations, and manuals that apply in his or her state, and should attend continuing legal education programs before attempting to advise a client on issues that relate to entitlement benefits.

In addition to social, historical, and values-based training, a general familiarity with the relevant medical issues; and initial training in benefits law, an elder law attorney must keep current in all of the facets of this specialized area of law. With the growth of elder law as a practice area, state and local bar associations (and private continuing education providers) have begun to offer often-excellent continuing legal education (CLE) programs. The national seminars conducted by the National Academy of Elder Law Attorneys (NAELA) are another excellent training opportunity. NAELA presents an annual symposium (geared to beginning and intermediate-level practitioners) in the spring, and an institute (geared to more advanced practitioners) each fall. For several years, before each symposium NAELA has offered a separate one-day seminar on the basics of elder law. NAELA materials and presentations are uniformly excellent. Recent themes have included estate and income tax issues, litigation and law office management, and extensive information about public benefits planning.

Q 1:13 Where is specialized training in elder law provided?

At least two organizations offer specialized elder law programs on a national basis. The University of Denver Law School (located at 7039 East 18th Ave., Denver, CO 80220, (303) 871-6000) and Stetson University College of Law (1401 61st St. South, St. Petersburg, FL 33707-3246, (727) 562-7800) present annual one-day (or two-day) intensive elder law programs. A number of state bar associations also regularly conduct elder law programs with nationally recognized presenters, usually as a result of active elder law sections. Notable are regular programs presented by the Florida State Bar Association ((850) 561-5844), New Jersey State Bar Association ((732) 249-5000), North Carolina State Bar Association ((919) 677-0561), and Massachusetts State Bar Association ((978) 744-4166).

One annual program deserves special mention. For the past several years, NAELA has conducted an unusual program in Dallas. Called "The Unprogram," this three-day session brings practitioners of different levels of sophistication together in a relatively unstructured format. Rather than lectures by recognized experts, the Unprogram relies on the experiences and expertise of the participants themselves. Sessions are conducted in small groups of six to fifteen, with topics selected by participants at the time of the program. Vigorous (and enlightening) discussions might focus on computer software, cutting-edge techniques for obtaining Medicaid eligibility, real-world problems with administering guardianships and conservatorships, or whatever topic is of interest or concern to a particular attendee. Such seminars often provide an extraordinary opportunity to resolve actual practice dilemmas and share trade secrets with other participants. The Unprogram is currently open only to NAELA members and, in most states, will not qualify for mandatory continuing legal education credits (since it does not have traditional presenters or written materials).

Q 1:14 How does the "informal network" among elder law attorneys work?

Practitioners new to the elder law field uniformly remark on one of the most salient characteristics of elder law attorneys: They are extraordinarily helpful to and supportive of their fellow practitioners. Membership in organizations such as NAELA and state bar elder law sections is almost always an entree into an open and supportive circle of like-minded professionals who will be willing to share information, forms, and experiences. Attendance at a national elder law program (or a few programs), whether sponsored by NAELA or other organizations, will almost always lead to professional assistance and counseling as well as lasting personal friendships.

Q 1:15 What is the National Academy of Elder Law Attorneys, and how is it important to the elder law practitioner?

NAELA was formed in 1986 with a core of about three dozen members from around the country. The organization was first envisioned as a result of several meetings of the principals at American Bar Association meetings over a few years, and the surprise most of them felt at finding lawyers with similar practices from other states. Since that time, the organization has grown to about 3,000 lawyers, with representatives in every state.

Membership in NAELA confers a number of important benefits:

1. Information about (and reduced rates to attend) three national seminars each year, which are consistently among the best continuing legal education programs available to elder law attorneys.
2. Newsletters and "special interest group" (SIG) participation which help keep the lawyer current in the area, and within sub-specialties of elder law.
3. Participation in an extraordinary e-mail list, where more than 500 participants share information, practical experiences, and tips, and answer questions for one another with an exceptional openness and spirit of cooperation. If this list were the only benefit of NAELA membership, it would be worth the membership dues.

4. Access to other members, both as resources and as referral sources.

Q 1:16 Where can elder law attorneys obtain forms, materials, and more information?

As interest in elder law has grown, the number of elder law publications has increased. There are several national sources of practice forms and materials. Notable entries include:

1. Begley & Jeffreys, Representing The Elderly Client: Law and Practice (Aspen Law and Business/Panel Publishers 1999)
2. Regan, Gilfix, Morgan & English, Tax, Estate & Financial Planning for the Elderly: Forms & Practice (Matthew Bender 1999)
3. Frolik & Brown, Advising the Elderly or Disabled Client (RIA 2000)
4. Margolis, The ElderLaw Forms System (Aspen Law & Business 1999)
5. Margolis, The ElderLaw Forms Manual (Aspen Law & Business 1999)
6. The Elder Law Portfolio Series (looseleaf) (Aspen Law & Business 1995)

NAELA offers a free weekly e-mail update on news, cases, and opinions concerning elder law issues. The same weekly bulletin is also available to non-members by subscription. NAELA members can access the archives of the NAELA e-mail discussion group from the NAELA website.

In addition, periodicals such as *Aging News Alert* (CD Publications) and *Bifocal* (ABA Commission on Law and Aging) are invaluable sources of regular news and updated information on elder law issues. Several elder law practitioners offer free web- or e-mail-based newsletters that provide current news and case law development information. For examples, visit *www.elder-law.com* or *www.tn-elderlaw.com*.

Finally, an excellent way to stay current with medical developments that may affect the attorney's analysis of client needs and capacities is to become a member of organizations such as the Alzheimer's Association or the National Alliance for the Mentally Ill.

These organizations have regular newsletters as well as valuable internet resources and online support groups to provide non-legal information.

Developing a Practice

Q 1:17 How can a new elder law attorney establish a practice?

It is difficult to break into any area of practice, including elder law; however, the lawyer who wishes to start an elder law practice has several advantages over other focused practitioners. Client communication skills are perhaps more important in elder law than in other fields of law, so a lawyer who is genuinely interested in elderly clients may be better able to develop a clientele than can a new practitioner in other areas of law. Relevant training in medicine, nursing, social work, or other non-legal areas will likely be more useful in an elder law practice than in most other practice fields. The fact that sole practitioners and small firms dominate the elder law field also makes it easier for a solo attorney to develop an elder law practice. Most important of all for the new practitioner is that elder law attorneys, as a group, tend to be more helpful and supportive of new elder law practitioners than is seen in other practice areas.

To become known as an elder law attorney, it helps to volunteer time to local organizations dealing with related issues (such as Alzheimer's and Parkinson's associations and the area agency on aging). Offering to speak to those groups' members, or to answer legal questions for staff members, can help to build a solid reputation as a qualified and concerned practitioner. Similarly, offering to speak to social workers and other hospital employees, nursing home staffs (and residents and family members), and other professional and public groups can help build a positive reputation in the field. Making individual contacts with care managers, accountants, financial advisors, and other professionals can develop a source of referrals. Many attorneys are interested in some aspects of the elder law practice; offering to speak at bar association seminars can help promote their expertise in the area. Many larger employers offer retirement counseling sessions to employees who may be within a few years of retirement age and will welcome estate planning and long-term care planning presentations from a local attorney.

Presentations and publications (including an internet presence) geared to the elderly and children of the elderly can develop prospects directly. In short, there are numerous opportunities for a motivated practitioner to establish a reputation and both a client base and a referral base from public presentations on elder law issues.

Q 1:18 Is there a typical progression of elder law practice development?

Because a large portion of most elder law practices is devoted to long-term care planning, the most common introduction to the elder law field is probably through that avenue. In other words, most existing elder law attorneys first developed a reputation in long-term care planning, and began development of the practice largely in that arena.

For those elder law attorneys who learned their craft in public practice (whether government, legal assistance, or law school work), learning the long-term care system is sometimes easier. Although that system is often arcane and counterintuitive, it can be professionally rewarding for precisely that reason. In most communities, it is a niche practice, and a legal area that is usually underserved.

Q 1:19 What existing practices lend themselves to an elder law focus?

An existing estate planning practice is easily adapted into an elder law practice. Less obvious practice connections can, however, be made. A family law practitioner, for example, might choose to focus on the problems of the elderly in dissolution proceedings, which would necessitate familiarity with long-term care issues. A bankruptcy attorney might make a logical transition to counseling older clients with debt problems, which could lead to expertise (and a reputation) in pension counseling. Employment law can give way to an age discrimination practice. Because of the very diversity of elder law sub-topics, many existing practices can be adapted to an elderly clientele.

Q 1:20 Should an attorney focus on one (or a few) of the practice areas within the field of elder law?

Elder law can be a broadly based practice. It encompasses arcane tax rules, and equally arcane Medicaid eligibility rules. It can be practiced in probate courts, trial courts, regulatory agencies, and offices. Not surprisingly, many elder law attorneys focus on narrow specialties within the larger elder law field.

Such super-specialization has obvious benefits. Economies of scale, simplification of staff training and continuing legal education for the lawyer, and comfort with the substantive areas all argue for narrowed practice focus. On the other hand, many lawyers enjoy a broader practice, and there is nothing impossible about keeping up with more than one legal topic in the elder law field.

Those considering narrowing the elder law focus should first take stock of their present circumstances. Does one area seem to predominate in the practice already? Is there one topic or area more enjoyable or rewarding than others? If the answer to these questions is yes, a more narrow practice focus may be warranted. Although it may be painful, many lawyers report that the practice actually becomes busier and more profitable when a decision is made to drop one or more kinds of work; the administrative overhead required to remain competent in multiple areas of practice can quietly consume surprising amounts of time and profit.

Q 1:21 Should a new elder law attorney select a mentor, and if so, how?

As noted above, the practice of elder law requires a thorough understanding of extremely arcane, obscure, and confusing entitlement programs that are available in a particular locality. It is almost impossible to learn even the minimum necessary to assist a client without having either an experienced mentor or an array of helpful colleagues upon whose experience the new practitioner may draw. Fortunately, because the elder law practice tends to be so strongly collegial, a new attorney will most likely be able to find support and assistance from more experienced colleagues. Most state bar associations (and not a few local bar associations) have an elder law section or committee; involvement in those organizations is an obvious way to make connections with practitioners in the same community.

Offering to help with cases or research in return for periodic consultations may provide an entree into an existing and successful practice. In fact, simply asking an existing attorney to act as mentor may be the most obvious and successful approach. If this seems too burdensome, having a group of colleagues to whom one can put questions (one hopes, in exchange for advice and assistance on matters in which you may have expertise) should help.

A continuing relationship with an established elder law attorney can be valuable in a number of ways. Sole practitioners particularly need some form of periodic validation, or a check on their approach to legal issues, because they typically do not have access to partners and associates for legal discussions. New techniques can be shared, and the usefulness of regional or national educational programs enhanced, by regular professional contact. Because of the high volume of many elder law practices, such associations also have great value as referral sources, for either office overflow or conflict situations.

Finally, internet discussion groups can serve in lieu of a more personal mentoring experience. The NAELA discussion group mentioned in Q 1:16 provides one such opportunity. The local NAELA chapter or bar association elder law section may have established an online discussion group. If one does not exist, it can be started with minimal effort at any time. Not only does such a device provide a forum for questions, and a means to raise standards of practice in the locality, but also it may enable the new practitioner to identify those colleagues who are indeed experts to whom one may regularly turn for reliable advice.

Q 1:22 How can an attorney determine whether there is any market for elder law services?

Despite the growth in elder law practices in the past decade, in most areas the elderly population remains underserved. Even communities with several active elder law practitioners may have plenty of market room for new elder law attorneys.

One way to test the market is to ask existing practitioners. Despite the perception that they may have a vested interest in minimizing market prospects, the same collegiality that makes elder law practitioners so pleasant to work with might make their expressed opinions valuable, genuine, and even insightful.

Surveying other attorney contacts might also be helpful. Ask family lawyers, for example, whether they have one or a handful of attorneys to whom they regularly refer elder law issues, and whether they could add to that list. Similarly, approach personal injury lawyers, bankruptcy practitioners, and others.

Not only lawyers need to make referrals to elder law attorneys. Consult hospital discharge planners, nursing home social workers, nurses, and even physicians and psychologists about whether they feel a need to develop a referral list. Incidentally, expect some of those contacts to ask about your willingness to provide continuing professional education, or in-service training, on legal topics; you are likely to find that there is an extraordinary demand for information about elder law topics among nonlawyer professionals.

Q 1:23 What referral sources are particularly likely to be useful to an elder law attorney?

Although referral sources will vary tremendously from attorney to attorney, some generalizations can be made about the possible sources of new elder law clients. Referral sources include:

1. *Other attorneys.* Many attorneys (perhaps most) are loath to get involved in elder law issues. As a consequence, lawyers often make the best referral sources for the elder law practitioner. This is particularly true of attorneys who practice in fields that do not deal with issues of aging, such as personal injury, domestic relations, bankruptcy, and real estate law. Even many estate planning attorneys choose not to get involved in long-term care issues, and can be an excellent referral source for an elder law attorney eager to work on long-term care planning but unlikely to take estate planning work from the referrer.
2. *Social workers, hospital discharge planners, nursing home administrators, geriatric care managers, and other social service/medical workers.* Elder law issues frequently arise in the context of family medical and social emergencies. Hospital staff, doctor's offices, and nursing home administrators can be among the most regular referral sources.

3. *Organizations.* Local support groups, organizations focusing on specific diseases, government agencies, and quasi-government groups all maintain contact with attorneys familiar with elder law issues. Most such organizations prefer to give clients a choice of three or more names, so even a new elder law attorney should be able to get some referrals from organizations. Of course, it helps if the local branch of the Alzheimer's Association, the state adult protective services (or similar agency), the local area agency on aging, and other groups are familiar with the lawyer's philosophy and practice; an appropriate comfort level is most easily achieved if the lawyer volunteers time and energy working with the organizations, speaking to member and support groups, and cheerfully answering the occasional legal question from staff members.
4. *Individuals.* Not only clients and former clients, but neighborhood activists, senior volunteers, and other individuals can be valuable sources of referrals in the senior community, and often turn into clients in their individual capacities.

Although elder law has been a widely recognized practice area for over a decade, there is still plenty of room for growth in this area of the law. Many options are open for someone just beginning an elder law practice or trying to build on an existing practice. Before developing a marketing strategy, or setting up an outreach program, the elder law attorney might be well-advised to consider which of the many prospective referral sources is being targeted, whether other attorneys, social service and medical providers, individuals, or other professional groups.

Q 1:24 What are some good ways to generate referrals from other attorneys?

To reach other attorneys who might make referrals, offer to present continuing legal education programs for related legal professionals. A presentation to personal injury lawyers on Medicaid eligibility and how personal injury settlements can affect future eligibility, or on the use of special needs trusts in settling personal injury actions, can simultaneously improve the level of practice among the personal injury bar and spread the presenter's name as one familiar with this area of law. Some suggested CLE topics are:

1. Concerns about how parents use a minor's personal injury settlement proceeds. Too often, personal injury lawyers believe that their responsibility (and liability) ends with the settlement, and that they have no continuing liability for the possible misdeeds of the parent/conservator.
2. Dealing with the aging spouse, possibly with diminished capacity, in divorce proceedings. Determining what effect the division of marital property may have in future long-term care financing considerations is not familiar territory for most domestic relations lawyers.
3. Hospital and medical staff liability for failure to comply with advance directives. Most hospital lawyers are familiar with the issues and concerns, but may not have considered the value or importance of outreach efforts, ethics committees, careful documentation, and family mediation.
4. The interface of probate and bankruptcy courts. Bankruptcy practitioners may not be familiar with the creditor's claims procedures in probate, or the effect of one spouse's death on the debts of the other spouse. The ability to discharge liability for breaches of fiduciary duty is of obvious importance to both kinds of lawyers.
5. A general overview of government benefit programs, and particularly long-term care. The confusing nature of government programs discourages not only clients and prospective applicants, but also fellow lawyers who might start with the notion that a poverty-based program should not be too difficult to understand.

Q 1:25 What are some good ways to elicit referrals from social service and medical providers?

Social service and medical providers are often starved for high-quality, accurate legal information. When provided with useful and common-sense general legal advice, they will usually turn into regular referral sources. There are obviously a number of ways to provide such information:

1. Offer continuing education programs for health care providers. Explain advance directives, the providers' duties under state law, and possible liability for ignoring (or following) the

patient's wishes. Most presenters find that health care providers are surprisingly unfamiliar with these legal concepts and issues, so these kinds of venues are particularly appealing. Participants will be so starved for legal information that they will usually be extremely supportive and uncritical, and the questions (though very practical) will be easy to answer. Such presentations help develop speaking skills and are genuinely helpful in countering the poor level of information available to health care workers, and the prevalence of misinformation.

2. Contact individual nursing home administrators and hospital social work departments, and offer to provide "in-service" training. Most facilities mandate a regular program of lunch time (or other one- to two-hour) programs for staff, and will welcome a discussion of legal issues. Expect to present to a small (perhaps 20 or fewer) group of nurses and social workers, but also expect the questions to be practical and the situations to be intensely real-world. Often one or more of the attendees will ask about a specific, current situation, and then refer the family (or the facility) to the elder law presenter immediately after the session. Also expect to have the in-service session taped and reviewed repeatedly over several weeks or months.
3. Newsletters addressed to the health community can be particularly effective. Invite specific legal questions, and offer practical advice. It may take weeks or months to gain name recognition or acceptance for quality advice, but recipients will eventually respond gratefully.
4. Seminars for residents and family members at assisted living centers, nursing homes, and other facilities can be well-received. Although an occasional audience may be full of thoroughly confused patients, there will almost always be a handful of attendees genuinely seeking legal information. Even if there are not, the goodwill developed with the facility's program director will be worth the small investment of time.
5. Speaking to related professional groups can also be rewarding. Insurance salespersons, financial planners, accountants, stockbrokers, and other related professionals also have surprisingly little general information about elder law issues.

Expect that presentations to these groups will lead to requests for reciprocal arrangements: promises of legal referrals in exchange for making insurance or accounting referrals to the requesting party. Before embarking on such a relationship, be comfortable with the competence and integrity of the other professional involved.

Q 1:26 What are some good ways to generate individual prospects?

Individual prospective clients can be the most difficult to reach. Experienced elder law practitioners disagree widely on the effectiveness of outreach efforts, but tend to agree that clients and prospective clients appreciate candid, useful advice and answers to at least occasional real-world questions. Some ways to reach individual clients include:

1. *Traditional advertising programs, ranging from telephone listings to newspaper and radio advertising.* Some practitioners insist that telephone listings are too easily lost in the crowd of advertisements, while others maintain that the telephone book remains the most steady and reliable source of new clients. Some elder law practitioners have experimented with regular weekly radio shows devoted to elder law issues, while others have reported success with shared radio shows (perhaps rotating through six or seven legal specialty areas on a set schedule).
2. *Newsletters.* Like health professionals, individuals tend to be starved for reliable legal information. The glut of information currently available in some ways only tends to exacerbate the problem—whereas it was once difficult to get any information, it is now difficult to assess the quality of the information pouring into the client's mailbox, computer, and through other sources. It may take time to develop a reputation for accurate and reliable newsletters, but the reputation will be increasingly valuable over that time.
3. *Websites.* Recent years have seen steady growth in the use of computers among the elderly. Perhaps more importantly, the children of the elderly are often the motivating factor in seeking legal advice, and they tend to be quite computer-savvy. While opinions differ on the profitability of internet

websites, the fact remains that it is a relatively inexpensive way for the new elder law practitioner to establish a niche and simultaneously build some public credibility.

4. *Public seminars.* Entire national organizations have been built on the simple premise that the public is starved for reliable information. Offer a public seminar on estate planning, long-term care planning, or medical decision-making, and expect a substantial crowd to attend. Often, these work best if they are co-sponsored by a charitable community organization or an institution; do not be shy about contacting various organizations to see if they are interested in promoting such a presentation. Be prepared to provide useful information and hand out explanations. Many of the attendees will have gone to several competing presentations, and will be looking for the one presenter who seems to speak to them most directly. Do not be surprised if a client shows up months or even years after such a presentation; it is an easy way for the timid prospective client to seek general legal information without having to make an early commitment to one professional. Most seminar presenters indicate that the current "hot" topic is living trusts, with nursing home expenses closing in rapidly. If this is true in your area, you may wish to advertise the presentation with references to either or both of these topics, and then be sure to provide accurate, timely, and informative advice on the advertised topics. To reach an elderly audience, schedule the presentation for late morning or late afternoon, offer refreshments, and hold the seminar in an attractive (but easily accessible) location. To reach an audience of professionals or the working children of the elderly, schedule the presentation for an evening or weekend, unless the presentation is being held at a place of business.

Q 1:27 Which other professional groups are commonly seen as referral sources for elder law attorneys?

Most successful elder law practices rely on regular referrals from a wide variety of sources. Obviously, the particular emphasis of a given practice might direct the choice of referral sources, but categories might include:

1. *Financial sources.* Stockbrokers, accountants, and financial planners are often interested in learning more about legal issues and improving their ability to benefit clients. Individuals may also be interested in developing a reputation of working well with elderly clients. Exclusive referral arrangements may be problematic—it is probably preferable to give clients several names of prospective accountants from which they might choose, both to minimize the appearance of endorsing one candidate and to encourage the client to make a thoughtful choice. If, for example, three accountants see occasional referrals from the elder law practice, that practice will probably be one of three names regularly provided to their clients as elder law referrals.
2. *Medical sources.* Physicians have busy schedules and are difficult to reach as a source of referrals. Even so, elder law practitioners may need to refer clients to doctors with gerontology training or experience. If possible, meet some of the leading local practitioners of gerontology in order to determine the best referrals. At the same time, if an attorney becomes known in the community as an elder law attorney, referrals may come from the doctor's office (nurse, physician's assistant, or nurse practitioner) even if they do not come from the doctor herself. Specialty practices may keep on file a list of practitioners and once an attorney is on that list, referrals can become automatic.
3. *Nursing and social work.* One of the best referral sources can be a hospital discharge planner; develop a relationship with one, two, or the entire local professional organization. They will appreciate not only referrals, but also a willingness to provide in-service training (as described previously) and to answer occasional small legal questions. Similarly, nursing home social workers will be glad to direct clients to experienced attorneys who can process the Medicaid application efficiently to prevent any gap in coverage.
4. *Bank and clerical workers.* With the increase in reports of exploitation of the elderly, some positive response may come from contacts in the banking industry.
5. *Adult protective services (APS).* Most APS offices have rules that either prohibit referrals to lawyers or require that referrals be given to at least three names. Strive to be one of the

three names regularly mentioned. APS workers, like others in the social service field, are starved for legal information, and eager to develop contacts with lawyers.

Q 1:28 How might an elder law attorney work with other attorneys?

In addition to the value of mentoring and other collegial contacts with elder law attorneys, there is a tremendous opportunity for practice development among other attorneys not practicing in elder law. Personal injury attorneys are frequently unsophisticated about the nature and administration of special needs trusts, or even conservatorships. Estate planners are often disinclined to learn government benefit eligibility rules. General practitioners should be aware of the need to make referrals when a particular case requires a more specialized practitioner. Nearby rural practitioners also may need to make referrals to a specialist from time to time. Conversely, an elder law attorney may develop contacts by making referrals to other attorneys. For example, an elder law practitioner may want to refer matters out when they involve divorce, complex litigation, income tax, or criminal matters. Develop relationships with as many of these practitioners as possible, and offer to provide a service that they need —the follow-up for their clients who otherwise will not be well served.

Q 1:29 How might an elder law attorney work with other professionals?

Though overused, the term "holistic" is often applied to the elder law practice. In large part, that is because elder law attorneys tend to look at family dynamics, medical care, personal and religious values, individual and family wealth, and program availability as well as more traditional legal issues. In order to develop any level of sophistication in such diverse (and not necessarily law-related) fields, the elder law attorney must work closely with other professionals.

Most clients will already have established relationships with doctors and other medical treatment professionals, religious advisers, bankers, insurance agents, stockbrokers, and other professionals. The elder law attorney may need to have regular contact with some or all of the members of the client's professional "team." Remembering that the confidentiality concerns of lawyers are of a higher order than for most of those other professionals, it may nonetheless be important to be able to share information among those contacts. Where such a professional team is missing a critical member, the elder law attorney should counsel the client regarding the need for assistance, and help the client locate an appropriate contact.

Although the client remains at the center of the relationship, the elder law attorney will frequently act as a *de facto* leader of the professional team. This status can make the work of the attorney both challenging and rewarding.

Q 1:30 What communication tools have been successfully employed by other elder law attorneys?

In a world of internet access, e-mail, fax machines, and other instant communication systems, the elder law practice often straddles the technological fence. On the one hand, the nature of a high-volume practice makes it necessary to have a firm grasp of the ability of technology to assist in getting work done. On the other hand, the clientele of an elder law attorney is less likely to be technologically savvy than is the average law office client.

While e-mail and fax communication are experiencing exponential growth, they remain little-used by most elders. That circumstance should be expected to change, both as the technology becomes ubiquitous and as the relatively savvy "baby-boomers" join the ranks of the elderly. For the moment, though, an elder law attorney should be prepared to communicate by e-mail and fax, especially with out-of-state children, but also expect to conduct most communications with elders themselves by postal mail, telephone, and in person. (Hearing difficulties may make telephone communications as difficult as e-mail.)

Nearly all legal practice management texts reiterate the same commonly understood truth: Regular contact is the surest way to satisfy clients and avoid malpractice, ethical complaints, and disgruntled customers. An elder law attorney's "tickler" system should remind the attorney to make some kind of contact periodically with the client, even though little may be happening at the moment.

For many clients the problem may be less how to communicate than how to limit the constant demand for information. Clear billing practices may help encourage the client to wait for developments, or collect questions into a single periodic visit or telephone call; however, for most clients the judicious and thoughtful use of support staff is the most efficient way to ensure sufficient communication without encouraging excessive and counterproductive contacts.

Remember that most of the clients of an elder law attorney grew up before (and during) World War II, and they may remember (even if only idyllically) a slower paced, more gentle and personable time. They may be more responsive to the personal relationship (the same staff person should ideally do most or all of the work on one client's case, and make all the personal contacts) and eager to have both professional and human contacts (encourage staff to ask about the client's well-being, and to discuss shared personal interests, though not to excess—be careful about leaving the client with the impression that he or she is being billed for personal calls).

Although personal contact is valuable, whether by telephone or in person, written communication is also important. Remember that elderly clients may require more than one review before feeling comfortable with legal alternatives, and that written explanations can be reviewed at the client's leisure. Written confirmation of telephonic discussions can be useful to both the lawyer and the client. On the other hand, it is unwise to rely on disclaimers and lengthy technical explanations to "cover yourself." The client's attention may fade with an explanation that goes on for more than a few pages. Written explanations will not speak for themselves and should be discussed.

Even though the client base may not be particularly technology-savvy, encourage those clients with e-mail or facsimile access to utilize that technology. Both can be timesaving devices for the lawyer, and allow much more rapid responses to the client. The client who is the child or grandchild seeking legal assistance in dealing with an elder may be more likely to have access to technology, and may be more comfortable using it.

Q 1:31 How can an elder law attorney maintain contact with existing clients?

Many elder law attorneys take the view that they continue to represent their clients actively even after an estate plan is prepared, or the public benefits application is successfully completed. Consider periodic follow-up letters to clients, explaining what changes have occurred in law or practice (or explaining that no changes have occurred, if that is the case). Clients will respond favorably both to suggestions that they need to update their legal work and to reassurances that they need not take any action at present.

Some elder law practitioners regularly send "thank you" cards to clients who refer new clients, and holiday, birthday, or anniversary cards to all clients. Computerized case management software makes it possible to add such personal touches even to a volume practice, but a simple card file and efficient secretary may serve just as well.

Newsletters are a useful way of maintaining client contact. While the expense and time involved in preparing monthly, quarterly, or even annual newsletters may be substantial, clients will once again appreciate being kept informed. With careful use of case management software, newsletters can be tailored to specific client populations (e.g., estate planning clients can be updated on tax law changes, while public benefits clients are updated on long-term care conditions in the community).

Newsletters can be expensive to prepare and deliver, but the costs can be pared somewhat. Circulate a periodic newsletter by facsimile machine, or enclose it in monthly billing statements; even if the newsletter does not reach all clients, it is surprising how often requests are made to add a client or former client to the distribution list. By all means keep copies of newsletters in the front office, so clients can peruse past issues.

One dilemma an elder law practitioner may face is how to maintain contact with existing clients without creating an expectation that the attorney will always keep them up-to-date with changes in the law. "Why didn't you tell me?" could be the first step to a malpractice claim. There is no easy solution. Don't forget to include easy-to-understand and easy-to-read disclaimers in all written material. If possible, each stage of representation should end with a gentle "closing letter" that warns the client not to treat the communiqués as proof that the attorney has assumed the responsibility for their legal needs in perpetuity.

Q 1:32 What may an attorney do in recognition of a referral from a client, personal contact, or other professional?

When a lawyer receives a referral, whether from a client or another professional, it indicates confidence in his or her personal and professional skills. It is only natural to want to thank the referrer. It is also good business practice; it both lets the referring party know the contact was made (which may be particularly important when the referral is from a fellow professional) and reinforces positively the confidence demonstrated by the referral.

Ethical rules may prohibit disclosure of even the fact of referral. Before formally acknowledging the referral, it is wise to ask the permission of the client; consider placing a request for permission to contact the referrer right in the intake forms for the client to approve. Once the client's approval is obtained, it is both good business and good human relations to send a card, or even a token of appreciation, to the referring party.

Some successful elder law attorneys do make small (and it is important that they be small) gifts to regular referral sources. One firm has a court runner hand deliver a tin of premium cookies to each referrer. Another maintains a supply of chocolate presented in a small box with the firm's logo for each referral. Yet another firm gives monogrammed robes, totes, or stadium blankets as gifts to the firm's best referral sources each holiday season. Many firms give a single token, such as a holiday food basket, to those referrers who have made more than a minimum number of referrals each year. Most firms at least recognize a referral with a simple, professional, but personalized "thank you" card. And the mutual exchange of lunch dates can serve both as a thank you and as a way for each of you to evaluate the other as an appropriate source of help for your clients.

Q 1:33 How can repeat business be encouraged?

Periodic newsletters can maintain contact with existing clients, and should result in repeat business from some of the same clients. Particularly when there have been important changes in estate tax laws, Medicaid laws or regulations, or state advance directive laws or practices, for example, such a newsletter can help generate repeat contacts with existing clients.

Some firms keep more personal and individual contact. For example, one prominent elder law firm sends an annual letter to estate planning clients, reminding them what year they last changed their estate planning documents, reassuring them that there have been no significant changes in the law governing their estate plan (or alerting them to any changes, if there have been any), and inviting them to make contact if their circumstances have changed in any important way. Such a letter reinforces the client's view that the firm continues to represent him or her, and encourages future contacts to make appropriate changes. Although the mechanics of setting up such a system can be daunting, the reward (in terms of both client satisfaction and future business) is substantial.

A poorly maintained client database can, however, do as much harm as good. Sending a newsletter to Mr. and Mrs. Jones three months after Mr. Jones' death will not endear the sender to the family. Sending three copies of the newsletter to Mr. and Mrs. Fredericks, Harvey and June Fredericks, and Ms. June Fredericks, will make the sender about as popular as the average mail-order company. Here, technology can be a friend or can bury the user in unwanted detail. Whatever method is adopted, be sure to review the mailing list as a whole to reduce the odds of such problems.

Office Design and Accommodating the Elder Client

Q 1:34 How should an elder law attorney deal with physical barriers in the office?

Although elder law is not necessarily a disability-oriented practice (healthy seniors abound, and many practitioners regularly represent the younger, more physically able children of seniors), it is critical that the practitioner's office be accessible. Wheelchair accessibility is important, but so is walker accessibility—although a ramp may be easy to navigate in a wheelchair, especially a motorized wheelchair, it may be difficult for a senior to negotiate with a walker. Longer ramps should have attractive and inviting places to sit and rest. Doorway thresholds should be minimized, and doors should be wide enough to accommodate wheelchairs, a senior, his or her walker, and a caregiver simultaneously. Door handles should be lever-type, so that arthritic hands are able to open the door more easily. In short, more attention should be paid to the ergonomics of the elder law practice than is required in most other professional offices.

Doorways and stairs are not the only physical barriers to easy access for the elderly. Seating should be firm enough to permit an easy exit, but not uncomfortably hard. Chairs and couches should be high enough to reduce the risk of falls (either while sitting or while getting up from the seat), and should usually have arms (to make it easier to get out of the seat). The waiting area, as well as the office or conference room where meetings take place, should be neat, quiet, and professional, although sterility should be avoided. As a group, seniors will appreciate tasteful references to family, hobbies, and personal interests; pictures of children and mementos can be a spark to revealing (and wonderfully entertaining) discussions of the senior client's own life experiences.

Elderly clients will frequently be concerned about their ability to locate the lawyer's office. In fact, it is common for clients to make a "dry run" to the office, just to make sure they can locate it. Elder law clients are famous for arriving half an hour to an hour early for their appointments, and usually give concern about locating the office (or uncertainty about traffic conditions) as the reason for the early arrival. Having an easily located office can ease these client anxieties. Make sure signs offer directions and mark entrances plainly. Prepare maps to be mailed out with appointment confirmation notices.

Parking can be both a physical barrier (handicapped parking is a must) and a psychological barrier (plainly marked, easily accessible parking with sufficient space for large cars and plenty of turning room are required).

It is not easy for most people who have no significant physical limitations to recognize the barriers inadvertently placed in the way of clients with physical or mental limitations, and there is no relevant training offered in most law school curricula. It may be appropriate to have the office evaluated by an appropriate professional in accessibility issues.

It may not be possible to select the optimum location for an elder law practice. If the setup is less than ideal, be helpful, flexible, and humorous. Make sure to point out the problems ahead of time and suggest ways to cope with them. Be ready to make home visits, schedule appointments at the most convenient time for those who will assist the client, or have a staff member waiting curb-side to assist the client entering the office. Make jokes about remaining impediments so it is clear that the building, not the client, is at fault for any difficulties that have been experienced.

Q 1:35 Should home visits be encouraged or even permitted?

Nearly all elder law practitioners make occasional home visits. Clients can become bedridden or at least find mobility difficult. The practitioner should develop a set of guidelines about when home visits will be made, whether there will be an extra charge (and whether it will be based on distance, time, or the simple fact that the lawyer is out of the office), and how the home visit option will be offered to the client. Many elder law attorneys add a separate (usually flat) charge for home visits; many report that clients who profess to be completely unable to get to the office are much more mobile once the charge is explained. An experienced practitioner will recognize that immobility is not synonymous with incapacity, and that homebound seniors often have serious legal problems.

A benefit of the "house call" is the additional insight it may provide into the client's capacity, emotional state, and physical needs. The elder law attorney's job is not case assessment, but observations of the home environment may make an attorney better able to help a client. Home visits may prove especially valuable in learning about the family dynamics. If there is anything to hide, it will be harder to hide it at home, where the guard is down. Another benefit often cited as an outgrowth of home visits is that clients' neighbors and family members may meet the visiting attorney and become clients themselves.

Q 1:36 How might an elder law attorney deal with a client's visual impairment?

Many elderly clients are unable to see clearly, with some attempting to minimize their visual impairment. Rather than wait for the client to admit to poor vision, the attorney should assume there may be a problem and act accordingly. Several easy steps will assist in dealing with elderly clients:

1. *Arrange the office so that the client never looks toward windows or bright lights.* While it may be esthetically pleasing to have windows open to a garden or atrium, the glare may make it difficult for clients to see the attorney or to read documents. Utilize strong lighting, but keep the source of light behind the client. Never place the lawyer's desk or chair in front of a window.
2. *Use a large or bold computer font for documents, at least selectively.* If clients seem to have difficulty reading drafts, reprint them in a larger size font. If the problem occurs with some regularity, consider switching fonts (or font sizes) to a more readable choice. Although the fonts ordinarily set as defaults in most word processing programs are quite readable, they are smaller and more compactly arranged than many fonts and may not be the best choice for clients with slight visual impairments.
3. *Offer to read documents, or to review them after the client has read them.* Whenever possible, read aloud and explain key passages whether or not you are asked to do so. Do not assume that just because you have given the client printed documents with enough lead time to permit reading, they have necessarily read the documents. Elderly clients will frequently assure the lawyer that they have read drafts, even though they have not been able to do so. The tendency of clients to minimize their visual problems is ordinary human nature, and requires an elder law attorney to discuss actual content with clients before accepting assurances that they have read and understood drafts (or final documents).
4. *Be careful about relying on technology that may not be understandable or useful to clients.* Visual aids, such as spreadsheets and flowcharts, may confuse some clients even if they help others. Computer demonstrations and videotapes can, however, be very useful practice tools.

Q 1:37 How might an elder law attorney deal with a client's hearing impairment?

Many elderly clients have difficulty hearing; many of those either deny their limitations or seek not to call attention to the hearing deficits. It is insufficient simply to ask whether the client hears adequately, as most clients will answer in the affirmative whether or not they actually can hear well enough to understand the discussion. It is also inadequate to look for visual and social cues, as individuals with progressive hearing loss usually develop social mechanisms to mask their disability.

To ensure that clients actually hear and understand, it may be useful to ask them to repeat important points. This can be done without appearing to challenge the client; after covering three planning choices, for example, the attorney might ask the client to explain in his or her own terms which choice he or she favors, and why. If the client responds that "the last one" sounds good, follow-up questions might elicit whether the client actually heard the options and the competing considerations.

Simple interview techniques can enhance the likelihood that the client can hear and understand the conversation. Always meet clients in a well-lit room, and face the clients as nearly head-on as possible. The attorney should also avoid holding files, papers, or books in front of his or her face, as facial features can be an important clue for the hearing-impaired listener. In addition, even people without lip-reading training or ability often have a natural ability to use visual cues to "sound out" the words. Speak slowly and distinctly, and somewhat louder than casual conversation. At the same time, do not appear to be condescending to the client, or too obviously responding to the perception of hearing impairment. Use body language to provide additional visual cues whenever possible.

Although it is often a good technique to involve staff members in client interviews, develop a clear understanding with staff about who will present material to the client. A free-flowing, give-and-take conversation between two people can be especially difficult for the hearing-impaired client to follow; make sure that transitions between staff members are clear, and that cues are provided to let the client know when it is time to attend to another speaker. If two staff members' voices are in opposite registers (one soprano and the other tenor, for example), experiment with switching roles in the interview process—frequently, someone with a hearing impairment will have a markedly easier time hearing at one end of the audible range than the other.

Repeat important concepts without using the exact same terms, structure, or intonation. Repetition is important not only for the hearing-impaired client, but also for the client of diminished (or diminishing) capacity; often the elderly client will be both. When counseling multiple family members, do not speak solely to the client without a hearing impairment. It frequently happens that a husband and wife have worked out a system (after long years of practice) whereby both appear to follow the conversation, but one repeats the information to the other, hearing-impaired, spouse later; legal issues are too complex, the number of choices too numerous, and the consequences too severe to allow the professional discussion to be "interpreted" in this fashion.

Make hearing assistance devices available for clients, but do not expect them to be utilized frequently. Simple earphone-based amplifiers can be purchased at electronics stores for less than $20, and can really be helpful for the client willing to admit to a hearing impairment. Have the devices not only available but conspicuously so, and offer to set them up if the client appears to be having any difficulty following the conversation. Because people seem to be sensitive about even the appearance of hearing impairment, do not expect the client to respond eagerly; if the client declines the assistive device, or tries it and then sets it aside, do not try to insist on its use.

Q 1:38 Should a family member help translate for a hearing impaired client?

Family members are often willing, even eager, to help "translate" for a hearing-impaired client, but do not usually allow this. Although they may have worked out complex (and difficult to reproduce) patterns of communication, they may also filter out some of what should be conveyed to the client. They also may subtly redirect the flow of the discussion, and make it awkward to discuss their role (and the roles of absent family members) candidly in the legal process under discussion.

Attorney Fees and Billing

Q 1:39 How may an attorney set fees for his or her services?

There are a number of widely practiced methods of setting legal fees, each with its own benefits and limitations. The most common fee structures are the traditional hourly fee and flat fees, but value billing, blended fees, transaction fees, minimum and maximum fees, and other arrangements are frequently used.

A competent client and his or her lawyer are generally free to negotiate any fee arrangement that they choose, subject primarily to the lawyer's ethical obligation not to charge an unreasonable fee. That basic principle may not apply in guardianship, conservatorship, and probate proceedings, or in any negotiation with a client who is incompetent (or, at least in some states and circumstances, even "vulnerable"). In those cases, fees must usually be "reasonable," and that term is most often defined as the amount of time reasonably spent, multiplied by a reasonable hourly rate. In other words, in fiduciary work the hourly fee is most common.

Although bar association-sponsored "minimum fee schedules," once commonplace, have been abandoned in light of modern antitrust limitations, one vestige of the set fee remains in many states. Statutory fee schedules in probate proceedings (and, less commonly, in guardianship and/or trust proceedings) may be effective for both fiduciaries and their counsel. Statutory fee schedules are usually expressed as presumptively reasonable fees, or occasionally as maximum fees; in practice such schedules tend to be treated as an absolute fee mandate. It is probably also fair to observe that such statutory fee schedules almost always result in higher average fees than those for comparable work in jurisdictions with no statutory schedule.

In setting fees, the lawyer should be guided by general ethical principles. Ethical Rule 1.5 of the American Bar Association's Model Rules of Professional Conduct, the most widely adopted expression of ethical standards, spells out the criteria to be used in evaluating the reasonableness of fees from an ethical perspective:

1. The time and labor required, the novelty and difficulty of the questions involved, and the skill requisite to perform the legal service properly;
2. The likelihood, if apparent to the client, that the acceptance of the particular employment will preclude other employment by the lawyer;
3. The fee customarily charged in the locality for similar legal services;
4. The amount involved and the results obtained;

5. The time limitations imposed by the client or by the circum stances;
6. The nature and length of the professional relationship with the client;
7. The experience, reputation, and ability of the lawyer or lawyers performing the services; and
8. Whether the fee is fixed or contingent.

Q 1:40 How may an attorney bill for staff services?

Staff time is generally billed (if at all) on an hourly basis, at a substantially lower hourly rate than the lawyer's. Although the relationship of a staff member's fee to the lawyer's fee will obviously vary depending on the training and experience of both workers, it is reasonably common for experienced legal assistants' services to be billed at about half (or slightly less) of a principal lawyer's rate.

Of course flat fees may obviate the need for separate billing rates for nonlawyer staff members. If the same fee will be charged regardless of who does the work or how long it takes, there is no need to set a rate for each individual member of the office team.

An increasingly common approach is to establish a so-called "blended" rate. Under this approach, the entire representation is billed at a fixed hourly rate, regardless of who performs the work. This mechanism is partially intended to reduce the client's resistance to the lawyer's higher hourly fee, while at the same time encouraging the client to make contact with the staff member who would ordinarily be viewed as having the highest "value."

"Transactional" billing also blurs the distinction between lawyer and staff rates. If most of the individual office tasks carry a flat rate (by transaction), the law firm is encouraged to become more efficient (using technology and good office practice), and to shift work to the lowest-paid employee capable of performing each task. Transactional billing has attained widespread respectability, and is increasingly likely to be accepted even by courts supervising the determination of "reasonable" fees.

Q 1:41 Should an elder law attorney charge on a flat fee, hourly, or other basis?

Flat and hourly fee structures each have their advantages and disadvantages. A fee structure that benefits the lawyer may work to the disadvantage of the client, and vice versa. The ideal approach is to figure out a fee structure that benefits both client and lawyer.

A comparison of the benefits and disadvantages of hourly and flat fee systems should include the following observations about the benefits of each of the two most common choices:

Hourly fees	*Flat fees*
Widely recognized and accepted by courts and clients	Encourages lawyer efficiency
Rewards lawyer properly for more difficult (and therefore time-consuming) matters	Provides client reasonable certainty of final cost
Encourages clients to take responsibility for more management of the matter (and less contact with lawyer)	Makes client more willing to contact lawyer (or office) to check on status of matter and effect of decisions

To decide which fee system to choose, or whether to experiment with transactional fees, blended fees, value billing, or other systems, the lawyer will need to assess local community practice, state ethical and court views of the alternatives, client response, and office setup. The correct answer to the dilemma is seldom clear; it may be reasonable to experiment with different approaches, or to offer clients an option in each case.

In general, flat fees are more commonly employed in estate planning and long-term care planning matters, and hourly fees are more common in guardianship, litigation, and other, similar kinds of cases. This division is frequently dictated by local court practice or statutes requiring the "reasonableness" of fees to be tested against time spent on the matter, but flat fees may be approved even in those cases if time records are sufficiently detailed to permit the lawyer to demonstrate the amount of work and time actually expended.

One important situation that may require not only a flat fee, but also a nonrefundable fee paid in advance, is the request for assistance with a Medicaid application. Unless there is a family member willing to assume the burden of the attorney's fee, the attorney is asking to be paid by someone who is on the threshold of insolvency. If the attorney is not paid ahead of time, he or she may not be paid at all. And uncomfortable as it may feel, it is important to ask for a nonrefundable payment that is *not* held in a trust account. The Medicaid agency may treat that retainer as an amount held in trust for the client and available for nursing home costs. Even if there is a family member to pay the fee, such as the spouse, the attorney's fee should be paid *before* any agency assesses available assets. The attorney will want to be paid from the assets that the agency will otherwise require to be spent, *not* from the funds being set aside for a spouse.

Q 1:42 What is meant by "value billing" and how might it be an important idea in an elder law practice?

"Value billing" is a concept that was sketched out in the 1980s in response to growing dissatisfaction with hourly billing. The central concept is stunningly direct: Rather than focus on the cost to the lawyer of delivering services, focus instead on the value to the client of receiving those services. This approach is not, as is commonly (and incorrectly) assumed, the same thing as "transactional" billing; in true value billing, the lawyer and client together determine the fee by calculating the benefit to the client. In fact, value billing was first introduced by insurance, corporate, and institutional clients who sought to reduce substantially the total cost of legal fees.

Value billing, at least as originally conceived, is simply flat fee billing with the added requirement that the flat fee reflect the value of the services. Few firms today actually practice value billing methods, although many firms insist that they do.

What most lawyers think of as value billing is really transactional billing. In the latter type of system, the lawyer establishes the price for each of the component tasks involved in representation. In a guardianship context, for example, the lawyer might set one fee for preparing and filing a petition, another fee for appearing in court, and yet another for preparation of the inventory. In this manner, the client can be reasonably sure of the final bill, while the lawyer continues to be paid for individual services (such as telephone calls, or extra hearings occasioned by the client's failure to comply with instructions) that can make representation much more complicated for the lawyer.

Value billing is *not* the same as billing on a percentage basis, however. A few attorneys have argued that the money "saved" with appropriate tax or asset protection planning, should be the basis of the fee. Most attorneys, however, express concern that such practices will be found unethical. With estate or asset protection planning, there is no way to determine what has been "saved" until the planned-for occasion occurs. Until then, the "savings" is simply hypothetical.

Value billing, transactional billing, and flat fee billing share one key component. In each system, the lawyer is rewarded for efficiencies (whether they come from automation, delegation systemization, or specialization) by continuing to collect the same fee even though the amount of work may diminish with each repetition. Value billing (but not flat fees or transactional billing) also has the advantage of placing the client's perceived benefit at the center in setting fees. All three systems share the advantage (to the client) of reasonable certainty about the final cost of the representation.

Q 1:43 How can an attorney determine whether his or her fees are both fair and competitive?

It can be difficult to compare fees with other practitioners. This is especially true in smaller venues and specialized practices; colleagues are usually also competitors, and may be reluctant to share such information. Depending on the context, discussions about fees could violate antitrust laws.

Over time, a lawyer should be able to gauge how his or her fees compare to those of other practitioners in the same community. There may be a number of ways to collect more concrete information, ranging from asking clients about their previous experiences, to reviewing court filings and benefits applications (on shared cases, at least), to checking competitor's websites. A more direct approach might be to ask clients whether they are comfortable with the firm's fees, the method of determining those fees, and the quality of bills actually produced.

Law Practice Management

Q 1:44 What should an elder law attorney look for in employees?

As in any legal practice, an elder law attorney's employees must be professional, competent, and trustworthy. Employees must be pro-active and "take ownership" of client's cases for there to be any efficiency gain in using employees to gather information, carry out plans, and follow up, rather than the attorney doing the work. Because of the special characteristics of clients and their common legal problems, a number of other attributes are important as well:

1. *Discretion.* Many elder law clients will be making their first contact with an attorney. Many will believe, even though they may not say so, that there is something shameful or embarrassing about their need for legal assistance. It may be important to be keep the very fact of their visit confidential. At the same time, clients' stories are often touching or humorous, and the temptation to discuss clients outside the office can be strong. Even as the attorney encourages warmth and human empathy in employees, strict confidentiality is imperative.
2. *Empathy.* A friendly, outgoing, and engaging employee can be not only a great asset to the practice, but also a real source of future referrals. If clients feel warmly received, and that employees are genuinely interested in their circumstances and personal lives, they will refer their friends and associates more readily.
3. *Honesty.* Many elder law practices deal not only in confidences, but also in money and assets. Guardianship and conservatorship, probate, and even long-term care planning create innumerable opportunities for the dishonest employee to steal from clients (or the lawyer), to form outside relationships with clients for their own benefit, or to otherwise profit improperly.

Some elder law attorneys regularly administer personality profile tests to prospective employees. Background and reference checks are a must. Most important is that the employee can make clients comfortable and relate to them professionally but personally. It should be obvious that training and periodic reminders are necessary to maintain a professional image and practice.

Q 1:45 Should an elder law practice project a professional or a friendly image?

Both. Elderly clients are particularly responsive to personal, friendly touches, including pictures of family members on the wall, indicators of hobbies, travel, or other personal passions, and similar personalizing touches. Do not hesitate to describe personal history, family relationships, hobbies, and passions with clients; they will not only appreciate the friendly contact, but will also respond with their own, related experiences and passions. The information will cement the personal relationship and also strengthen the ability to serve the client professionally. A better understanding of the client's history will permit the lawyer to explore unexpected information (the ability of a child to manage money, the source of assets that have since appreciated in value, the significance of family heirlooms, or even the relationship of client and family). It will also provide an opportunity to reinforce the important elements of the legal representation with the individual client. Not least importantly, it will also make the client into a real human person, with ambitions, hopes, and fears, recognizable and memorable to the lawyer and staff.

At the same time, it is important to maintain a professional image. Clients, even though they may be much older than the lawyer, have come to the office seeking professional advice, and expect to be dealing with an authority figure. A messy office, a haphazard scheduling system, or a shabby or tasteless interior can drive away clients (and diminish referrals). The client engaging an attorney for an adversarial matter will want to feel confident that the attorney will impress the opposition and be tough as well as kindly. Remember also that the client is more interested in his or her own situation than the attorney's and may later resent office time spent hearing about the attorney's own child care or family problems. Strive for a balance between warm and homey on the one hand, and crisp and professional on the other.

Q 1:46 What techniques help the practitioner maintain the right image?

Techniques used by successful elder law attorneys to maintain the proper balance between personal and professional range from simple and obvious to subtle and psychological. A sampling of ideas suggested by other attorneys:

1. *Place family members' pictures prominently in the office.* In addition to being a pleasant reminder of family life, the pictures can generate conversations with clients about family, and the interests and occupations of spouses and children. There is likely to be a connection ("What does your husband teach? What a coincidence!"), and, if nothing else, family discussions lead nicely into an exploration of the client's relationship with his or her own children (or other family members). It is a good idea to choose pictures that show family members engaged in their favorite sports or hobby, or their occupation.
2. *Arrange the office (or conference room) to minimize the lawyer/client dichotomy.* Some attorneys utilize a round conference table for client meetings—that way the contact can be a discussion rather than a lecture or a quiz. One practitioner notes, however, that a small, round dining table, while it makes the clients feel more at home and at ease, also gives them a clear view of the notes the attorney is taking—be careful that those notes are not unflattering or too cryptic. Another practitioner swears by his practice of having no table between him and clients at all; he meets clients with his back to his desk and nothing between him and the clients. This can create a challenge for note taking, too, because it will require a lapboard or clipboard of some kind, but clients may feel more involved in the interview process and more comfortable in a homelike setting.
3. *Select office furniture that resembles home furniture.* One practitioner took a cue from home visits; whenever she went to the client's home, she was inevitably shown to the dining table for the discussion of legal problems. When she decorated her office, she tried to reproduce that comfortable homelike feeling, using dining room table and chairs in the

conference room, and matching dining room chairs in the lobby.

4. *Surprise clients with personal touches.* One law firm buys bagels and fixings every Friday, and clients who schedule appointments on that day are treated to a delightful bagel buffet. As the practice has grown, clients learn to request Friday appointments; those who are "in the know" feel more of a connection to the law firm, and the real cost of this apparent largesse is actually quite modest. Another firm purchased a bread-making machine, and regularly bakes bread in the office. The bread making cycle takes several hours, so relatively few clients end up sharing in the product, but the smell is wonderful, and clients are delighted to be let in on the office's practice. A simpler version of the same sort of hospitality: Always offer coffee, tea, water, or cold drinks to clients, and use dishes (and coasters) that remind them of home settings.

Q 1:47 What issues are important to clients when they visit an elder law office?

In addition to the legal issue that brought the client into the office, he or she is likely to have a number of other concerns. The cost of the representation, the confidentiality of the conversations, the likelihood that the client will be "passed on" to other lawyers or even legal assistants, the professional tenor of the office, and the credentials of the lawyer will all be of concern to the client. All of those concerns should be allayed in the initial interview, by discussing legal fees (and securing a signed fee agreement), and by providing information about the firm, the lawyer(s) who will actually work on the case, and office practices about confidentiality. Additionally, any staff members who will work on the client's case should be introduced to the client at the initial meeting, and the client encouraged to make contact directly with the staff person.

Q 1:48 How can the attorney collect the information necessary to advise clients properly?

A comprehensive intake questionnaire is vitally important in any elder law practice. Some attorneys prefer to go through the questionnaire with the new client, asking questions and filling out the form;

most attorneys would argue that such a practice is time-consuming and, ultimately, expensive for the client. Far more common is the use of a standard questionnaire, mailed out to clients in advance of the meeting. A sample estate planning questionnaire is included as Appendix A; obviously, the questionnaire can be made more comprehensive or more concise, and can be changed appropriately for a single person. A similar questionnaire should be developed for other practice areas.

Several difficulties arise in the use of intake questionnaires. One common concern is that clients will simply not complete the questionnaire, and may in fact cancel their appointment when faced with the daunting task of collecting so much personal information. As a result, it can be a difficult balancing act to achieve thoroughness without attempting to exhaust all possible permutations. An abbreviated "issue-spotting" questionnaire might be sent for completion prior to the meeting, with the attorney asking more detailed questions in person. A gentle reminder of one's hourly rate, and the time that can be saved by providing complete information, will also work wonders. Experience will help determine which questions must be asked in every case, and which can be handled by casual follow-up questions in the office interview.

Some clients will inevitably fail to complete the questionnaire. When that happens, some elder law attorneys simply refuse to meet with the client until the forms are completed. Others delegate staff members to meet with the client and go through the form, trying to collect as much information as possible before the meeting with the attorney. Still other attorneys choose simply to go through the form with the new client, and anticipate that some initial interviews will take longer as a result. In any event, it is certainly good practice to offer staff member assistance in completing the form, as a way of minimizing the client's resistance to the concept; in practice, the offer of staff assistance will probably not be taken by too many clients.

Finally, the questionnaire may be one area in which family assistance to the client may be encouraged. The questionnaire demands facts and figures, not subjective impressions. Ask the wavering client whether a copy should be sent to the assisting child.

Q 1:49 What is a "tickler" system, and why is it important?

Every law practice requires a mechanism to make sure critical dates are not overlooked, work is completed in a timely fashion, and contacts with clients and others involved in the legal matter are maintained in a timely fashion. Before the advent of computers, the most common mechanism was a paper-based "tickler" system. In such a system, each time a task is completed for a client a slip of paper (or card) is prepared describing the next task and its due date. This slip of paper is placed in a calendar file for the date by which it should be completed. So long as every active file has at least one tickler slip in the calendar file, it is easy to ensure that the file continues to move through the lawyer's office; all that is required is for the lawyer (or staff) to pull out the tickler slips each morning, distribute them appropriately, and require that the appropriate staff person complete that task, update the slip or card, and place it back in the calendar file for a new date.

There are a number of shortcomings to the paper-based tickler system. If a given slip or card is lost or misfiled, it is easy to "lose" the file itself—even if it is exactly where it belongs in the filing cabinet. To protect against this problem, it is necessary to review all currently active files manually on some regular basis to ensure there is at least one pending tickler slip. It is also inevitable that the tickler cards will begin to pile up on staff members' desks, and it is difficult to maintain the priorities of innumerable slips of paper.

With the advent of computers, the paper-based tickler system has become obsolete; however, it is important to understand the purpose of such systems in order to utilize computerized tickler systems effectively. A well-constructed (and maintained) system should make it easy to ensure that every file has a pending update, to prioritize the updates on some basis, and to ensure that uncompleted tasks remain active on the appropriate staff member's to-do list. Even better, the system should permit supervisors periodically to review the status of tickler items for other staff members, and even automatically generate due dates and task descriptions as much as possible.

Q 1:50 How important is computerization in managing an elder law practice?

As has been previously observed, elder law tends to be a high-volume practice. Even though the range of practice topics is tremendous, most elder law attorneys tend to focus on one or a few of those topics. Given these dynamics, both delegation and automation are vital to the survival and growth of most elder law practices.

Computerization has dramatically changed the practice of law generally, but perhaps nowhere as dramatically as in elder law. Software exists to automate document preparation, calculate taxes and public benefits, and even manage cases and case flows. Of course, time and billing software, word processing programs, and office management systems exist in abundance for all types of law practices and, indeed, all businesses.

Q 1:51 What computer hardware should an elder law attorney expect to purchase?

Every lawyer, and particularly every elder law attorney, should expect to use and be proficient with computers. This means that a computer should sit on every desktop in the office, and staff should be expected to prepare documents, maintain calendars, update and manage cases, take and receive telephone messages, and complete all sorts of other tasks on those computers.

In order for computerization to be maximally effective, an office network is essential. Any office with two computers should expect to have them hooked together and communicating. This will require not only a machine on each desk, but also the equipment (e.g., computer cards and cables) necessary to create a network with shared resources and information.

Recent rapid increases in the pace of hardware development have resulted in a dramatic reduction in the cost of hardware and the failure of most software packages to take full advantage of hardware capabilities. This, in turn, simplifies the process of purchasing new office computers; there is little gain in productivity by purchasing the fastest, most powerful system currently on the market, and substantial savings to be realized by purchasing the second (or third) most powerful offering.

Even as the lawyer chooses to save costs by purchasing less-powerful computers, there are several areas in which the rules are reversed. In general, more money should be spent on these items:

1. *Monitors*. Larger monitors are easier to work with, and make staff and lawyers happier with their worklife. For now, 17" or 19"monitors seem to be the standard in new purchases; larger monitors are available, but they tend to be space-hogging behemoths that completely dominate most offices. LCD (liquid-crystal display) panels are often not much more expensive than comparable CRT (cathode ray tube) displays. An LCD panel will typically have a usable area about the same size as a CRT described as two inches larger, i.e., a 17" LCD panel is roughly comparable to a 19" CRT monitor). Expect the comparative cost of LCD panels to continue to drop in the near future. In addition to space savings, LCD panels generate less heat and, for most people, less eyestrain.
2. *Storage devices*. Not too long ago, hard disks with 20 megabytes (MB) of storage and floppy disks with 360 kilobytes maximum were industry standards. Few people could imagine a world in which those numbers were inadequate. Today, even a simple word processing program might require 50 MB of space on the hard drive, and individual files can easily exceed the capacity of even high-density floppy drives. Four to six gigabyte hard disks are standard. The removable Zip™ drive is already being replaced by CD-RW drives that allow the user to "burn" an entire CD of data. CD-RW disks may only be read in CD-RW drives, but CDR disks (without erase or rewrite capability) should be readable from any CD-ROM drive. In fact, even that technology may soon be eclipsed by ready availability of DVD burners that permit several times as much material as a typical CD to be put on a single disk. For the time being any newly purchased machine should have the largest affordable hard drive and at least one CD-ROM or DVD rewritable drive. Floppy drives are still useful for some limited purposes, and it is probably too soon to abandon them entirely.
3. *Memory*. Random access memory (RAM) prices have been low for an extended period. Just as memory storage require-

ments have grown, so too have RAM requirements; any new machine should have a minimum of 256 MB of RAM.

4. *Connectivity.* Handheld organizers (like the Palm™ or Windows CE™ machines), network printers, and multi-purpose machines (fax, photocopier, scanner, and printer all in one) are extremely useful. Make current purchases with them in mind; one or all of them are sure to be added shortly after the initial hardware investment.

Q 1:52 How should a lawyer work with computers?

Any modern law practice requires the active use of computers by lawyers as well as support staff. The complexities of practice, competition from other lawyers and nonlawyers, the increasing sophistication of clients, and the ubiquitousness of the internet compel not only the active use of computers, but also a broad understanding of the possibilities and capabilities of technology generally and computers in particular. Because of the usual case loads involved in an elder law practice and the arcane nature of statutory and regulatory provisions, that basic principle is even more apparent in the elder law practice than in many other legal fields.

The lawyer who proudly proclaims unfamiliarity with technology is doomed to professional extinction. Every lawyer should have a computer on his or her own desktop, and should be proficient at word processing and legal research. Office calendars and to-do lists should be maintained on the computer, even if old habits require that the calendar be printed out periodically. The lawyer should be capable of checking the calendar and updating appointments and projects. Time and billing should be completed on the computer, rather than on paper sheets or slips to be entered later by a clerical staff member.

In the mid-1980s, the fax machine became an office essential. E-mail has already established itself as the fax machine of this decade. Clients, family members, and colleagues will increasingly expect lawyers to have ready access to e-mail, and to communicate quickly and effectively through this new medium.

During the past decade, legal research has moved out of books and onto CD-ROM disks. Indeed, many legal research sources have taken the next step and are now more easily available on the internet. Both CD-ROM and internet research ultimately require the lawyer to be personally familiar with computers and able to work through their particular logic. Lawyers who were trained on proprietary paper "digests" (such as the Decennial Digest used by an earlier generation of lawyers) learned not only how to use the available research systems but also their limitations. Similarly, a modern lawyer must not only be proficient at computerized research, but also recognize the limitations of the medium. All of these proficiencies require regular hands-on use by the lawyer, working at the lawyer's own desktop.

Q 1:53 How important is it to network office computers?

One of the most astonishing synergies evident in the technological revolution of the past two decades has been the value of office interconnectedness. In the law (or business) office setting, computer networks were originally seen as useful for sharing files among various users. By networking some or all of the office's computers, it became possible not only to share files, but also to ensure that the most recent version of any file was the only one available to users. The office computer network promised to simplify greatly document management.

With widespread implementation of office networks comes less obvious, but even more powerful, efficiency. Suddenly, it became possible via computer networking to deliver phone messages to the staff member's desk immediately and even permit the staff member to review the message while still on the telephone with someone else. It also became simple to archive telephone messages, search them by first or last name or subject matter, and group them by subject matter for later review (as in a fee contest or disciplinary proceeding). No longer is it necessary to save box after box of duplicate phone message slips, or to search manually through five or six books looking for the evidence of a telephone call two years before.

Networks also made possible all sorts of other technological advances. Time and billing records can be kept in a central computer file, with each staff member updating the billing records directly; with this approach, no clerk is required to enter time slips manually at the end of each month. Calendars cannot only be kept on the computer, but multiple calendars can be reviewed and updated by some or all of the other employees in the office. Financial records can be kept on one computer, but reviewed by anyone else in the office; most programs and the networks themselves can be configured to limit access to selected individuals, or to those who possess a password.

Modern software choices will allow most or all of the computers on an office network to access a central CD-ROM (or a bank of CD-ROM drives) for legal research. It is even relatively simple and inexpensive to configure a network to share access to the internet through one portal. The combination makes it possible to do online research from any desktop in the office.

Even a two-computer office will have substantial efficiency improvements if those two computers are networked. The return on investment in network hardware (most operating systems have fully usable network capabilities built right in without requiring additional enabling software) is immediate and impressive. Any law office that has not yet networked its various computers should complete this project as its next technological step forward.

Q 1:54 What types of software are important for an elder law practice?

Any elder law attorney should have, install, and use the following kinds of software:

1. *Word processing.* Once a software field filled with programs and innovators, the word processing market has been reduced to Corel's WordPerfect and Microsoft Word. Word's market share is steadily gaining, but WordPerfect's last market niche is the legal business. Ideally, be familiar with both—WordPerfect because it is arguably a better program, Word because clients will have Word and will only be able to view Word attachments.
2. *Presentation software.* Obliquely related to word processing is presentation software such as Microsoft PowerPoint and Corel's Presentation. These programs allow you to develop slides that may be printed onto transparencies for use with an overhead projector, or more effectively, shown directly from a laptop by using a connected projector. Slides may also be used for smaller client presentations, with the clients posi-

tioned to view the laptop screen. These programs are also helpful tools for preparing outlines.

3. *Time and billing.* Sage's Timeslips is the most commonly used entry in this legal-niche software category, but PCLaw, Jr. from Alumni Computer Group has its partisans and substantial market share. Other programs in this category include Client Project from Micro Billing Systems, Inc.; RTG Bills from RTG Data Systems; and TimePro from TimePro Legal Software, Inc. For the more computer-literate elder law attorney, one choice might be to utilize Microsoft's Access database and customize a time-and-billing system. One brand-new option is Billing Matters, a product fully integrated with DataTXT's Time Matters case management software (see below) but also available as a standalone time and billing program. Billing Matters has the potential to eclipse the competition, but has not yet seen adequate exposure to the marketplace to determine whether it will meet that potential.

4. *Case management.* Recent developments in this software category have made case management software almost essential to office productivity. Capable case management programs merge the ability to keep track of clients and other contacts, cases, word processing and other computer files, calendars and to-do lists, and telephone and e-mail messages all in one place. Case management has become the front-end software through which most other software packages are accessed. At the same time, the word processing, billing, and other software entries are indexed and linked on the basis of dates (date of creation, due date, review date, etc.), contacts (clients, vendors, opposing attorneys, etc.), cases, and tasks. Most case management programs were designed for litigators, and the paradigm of adversary relationships make them less useful for the elder law practitioner. Two programs that stand out for their ease of use and ability to adapt to a consultative practice are DataTXT's TimeMatters and Gavel and Gown's Amicus Attorney. Although not specifically designed for the legal field, and much less for elder law attorneys, Microsoft's Outlook is worth consideration, if for no other reason than its connectability.

5. *E-mail.* By far the most popular source of internet connections is America Online (AOL), which provides its own proprietary software for sending, receiving, and archiving e-mail messages. For those not using AOL, the most popular software choices are Microsoft's Outlook (or Outlook Express), Eudora ProMail from Qualcomm Inc., and freeware offering Pegasus Mail. Those happy with Netscape as a browser may also want to use Netscape's messenger program. Version 7.0 is an improvement over earlier versions. Modern case management programs (like Time Matters and Amicus Attorney, described above) include e-mail clients as part of the program; this permits incoming and outgoing e-mails to be automatically connected to the appropriate contact or case, improving the ability to find all the documents and activities related to a particular case or client in one place. One notable downside of Outlook is its susceptibility to viruses, not due to any inherent flaw in the program, but because its use is so widespread that virus- or worm-generators will look for the Outlook mailbox when spreading their infections.
6. *Internet browsers.* Despite an abundance of early program choices, the field has been left almost entirely to Microsoft's Internet Explorer and Netscape Navigator. Some sites can only be viewed on Explorer. Conversely, sites designed for Navigator may have formatting problems when viewed in Explorer. Ideally, you will want to have both available, even though you prefer one or the other for regular use.
7. *Document assembly.* Lawyers generally, and elder law attorneys particularly, recycle phrases, clauses, and whole documents endlessly. Automating that process is both time-consuming and labor-intensive (it almost requires active involvement by one or more lawyers), but is nonetheless immensely rewarding, both personally and financially. Both WordPerfect and Word have tremendous document assembly abilities built into their word processing software. More usable (but still difficult to master) stand-alone programs are available, but the market leader by far is HotDocs from Matthew Bender.
8. *Number processing.* Lawyers who will be managing assets in a fiduciary capacity, planning for Medicaid eligibility, or pre-

paring tax returns will need, at a minimum, a spreadsheet program such as Microsoft Excel or Corel QuattroPro, and probably a financial management/check-writing program such as Quicken or Quickbooks (or PCLaw, Jr. for legal-specific use). Z-calc is an add-on to Excel that includes estate planning computations, such as annuity or income factors. An attorney whose practice is weighted towards estate administration may decide to explore the many software packages for tax-return preparation, a topic beyond the scope of this volume. At the very least, an attorney should be able to utilize the computational features built into the table functions of Word and WordPerfect.

9. *Publishing in print and on the internet.* Most attorneys may prefer to keep it simple and produce newsletters and handouts using ordinary word processing programs. If one is up to the challenge, however, desktop publishing software such as Microsoft Publisher can create a very professional product. Similarly, attorneys who want to try their hands at a website may be able to get by with FrontPage or FrontPage Express (bundled with various iterations of Microsoft Office products) or Netscape Page Composer (bundled with the Netscape browser), but the ambitious may want to explore Dreamweaver or other web design programs.

Q 1:55 Which categories of software are more important, and in which order should software be acquired?

By far the most extensively used software in most law offices (whether elder law or otherwise) is word processing software. Time, billing, and accounting software are nearly as essential. While e-mail and internet browser software are not as critical, the software comes bundled with most new computers (at no additional cost), and is easy to acquire for older machines.

Once critical functions are under control, the attorney should look to the software categories that facilitate office efficiency and quality control. Case management is probably the next area to be tackled, followed by document assembly. Meanwhile, consideration should be given to legal research needs and the acquisition of appropriate books, CD-ROM products, and online access.

Q 1:56 How can an attorney select among competing software packages?

The following factors should be considered in selecting software:

1. *Cost.* Competing software packages can have extraordinarily divergent price tags. Factor in the need for new, faster, or more capable hardware (or software upgrades in related packages), and the costs can be even more disparate. Of course one should not purchase on the basis of price alone; there is plenty of inexpensive but unusable software on the market. On the other hand, cost of software is often unrelated to the usefulness, ease of use, or features of competing programs.
2. *Familiarity.* If the entire office staff is accustomed to one word processor or case management program, do not lightly change the software they know and like. Such a change can lead to lost productivity (which should be temporary, but can be substantial), loss of employee morale and dedication, and discouragement of office standardization.
3. *Training requirements.* Few lawyers acknowledge the need for formal, professional training in software use. Training may be widely available, but be sure the trainers have experience with the particular needs (and uses) of law offices. Some training must be onsite (particularly on software that is not widely available, or that is highly legal-specific), but do not hesitate to send staff to a computer workshop where each person can work on a separate computer while watching the instructor's directions on an overhead screen. Even highly proficient employees should be considered for training sessions; modern software is so complex that few regular users tap anything like the full potential of the software. Besides, most employees will view such training programs as valuable employee benefits, and productivity (and office morale) will climb almost immediately.
4. *Market share.* In choosing competing software packages, consider leaning toward the program with the larger market share. This is particularly worth considering where the market leader is extremely dominant. While no one wants to contribute to (or back) Goliath against the more appealing

David, there are several practical reasons to consider going with the crowd. There will almost certainly be better and more numerous training opportunities for a widely used program. Support groups, online user groups, and publications are more likely to be devoted to the market leaders. Later new programs (or categories) will be more likely to support (or import data from, or work with) the market leader than a capable but little-used niche program.

5. *Legal specificity.* Although there is a sound argument for choosing the generic market-leading program, there is also something to be said for the program that has been prepared (or is customizable) with the legal practice in mind. This is even more true when the program is easily adaptable to a consultative (as opposed to adversary) legal practice like elder law.

Q 1:57 Should elder law practitioners have their own websites?

Use of the internet to locate and communicate with professionals of all types is increasing. Despite the fact that consumers of elder law services tend to be less web-aware than most other groups (they are, after all, generally older and frequently retired), internet connectivity is growing among the population of elder law clients as well. In addition, most elder law attorneys find that many of their clients are the younger, actively working, and internet-connected children of senior citizens.

While every elder law attorney should establish some internet presence, it does not necessarily follow that every practitioner needs to develop a website. There is an abundance of elder law information online already, and a new website focusing on elder law topics must distinguish itself from existing entries. Most practitioners who maintain active websites indicate little business is directly produced by their online offerings. While the existence of a website may be a powerful tool for validating the lawyer's expertise in the eyes of existing or new clients, it is unlikely to generate substantial business unless a strong investment and commitment to web development is undertaken.

NAELA membership offers an easy alternative to a private website. For a small fee, the NAELA member can use a form-filler program to construct a personal web page that acts as an online resume to be viewed by referral sources and clients alike.

Evaluating the Practice

Q 1:58 How can an attorney help ensure consistent quality in the practice?

Modern law offices must recognize that the legal profession is also a business. In an increasingly competitive professional environment, lawyers must be prepared to do what they do well, and to convince clients (and the public) that they provide additional value over the sometimes similar services offered by accountants, financial planners, bankers, stockbrokers, insurance agents, and independent paralegals.

Outside of the legal profession, American business has for two decades focused increasing attention on the need for customer satisfaction as the best indicator of business success. The legal profession has been relatively slower to measure clients' views of the outcome of representation.

Some firms address this shortcoming directly, routinely asking clients to complete an "exit interview." This is an opportunity not only to gauge the success of the representation, but also to test the client's view of that success (lawyers often forget that clients may not view a "successful" outcome in the same manner, or even as the same success, as the lawyer). Not insignificantly, this is also an opportunity to demonstrate to clients a genuine interest in their view of legal services provided, and to build client loyalty over time.

In the typical busy elder law practice, it is difficult to stop other, "more productive" work in order to interview clients and former clients. Whether such reviews are to be undertaken on all clients or only a sampling, they will take place only if made part of standard procedure and staff are convinced of the utility of the exercise. Before making a decision to interview clients or former clients, it is also important to commit to making the appropriate changes if their answers indicate a need for change.

There are other methods of improving both consistency and quality. Implementing a document assembly system and updating it regularly will help ensure that the work product of the office has a professional look and reflects current law and approaches. Regular, formal employee reviews help maintain professional standards and focus on needed office changes. Periodic office retreats and regular staff meetings provide an opportunity to let staff members become involved in improving quality and consistency. The precise mix of these techniques, and the relative success of each, will depend on the commitment of both lawyers and staff, as well as the personalities, strengths, and weaknesses of individual office members. Do not be afraid to try one or more, adapt the approach as necessary, and abandon it if it has not proved helpful.

Q 1:59 How should employees be evaluated?

Formal written evaluations should be required for all businesses, whether large or small. Most firms conduct evaluations in connection with an annual salary review, either on the anniversary date of each employee's hiring or on an annual schedule shared by the entire office (or groups of employees). The senior staff member supervising the employee's work should oridnarily undertake the evaluations: usually the proprietor or a partner, but occasionally an associate attorney or, rarely, a senior legal assistant or office manager. One useful tool to make the evaluation process easier: Ask the employee to prepare a brief self-evaluation and use that as the basis for the supervisor's evaluation. Either require employees to complete formal self-evaluation forms, or simply ask them to write a letter describing their own strengths and weaknesses.

Larger offices, and those more committed to client satisfaction, may involve other staff members and even clients in the evaluation process. Although such approaches can be problematic (sometimes leading to long-term staff disagreements, or difficult client relationships), they can also be productive if undertaken professionally. Also consider implementing a reverse review process, by which employees can describe the office's (and managers') strengths and weaknesses, and suggest methods for overcoming the weaknesses.

Employee evaluation, hiring, and firing are also fraught with peril. The employer risks claims of violating age, sex, and race discrimination laws, labor laws, or privacy rights, to say the least. Safe and effective employee management is a topic requiring an entire treatise of its own. It is a good idea for the new employer to attend at least one seminar in employment law in order to minimize problems.

Q 1:60 What choices are available for long-range planning?

In recent years, American businesses have developed a fascination with long-range business planning. As a result, professional consultants abound, university courses proliferate, and even software packages have been developed to build a professional "mission statement" and/or long-range plan. Although there may be some dispute about the value of formal long-range planning as actually undertaken by most businesses, there can be little doubt that some form of planning for future growth and development is valuable and important.

Long-range planning should involve the entire office staff (and maybe selected or core clients). In order to be effective and responsive to changing circumstances, it should be periodically reviewed and revised. It is unhelpful to have the two senior partners of a small law firm meet for two days, prepare a "plan," and deliver it to staff members as received wisdom. The process should be thoughtful and should involve at least one extended session for the entire staff, away from office telephones and messages. It should be repeated every year or two to maintain the currency of the plan.

Q 1:61 What approaches have other lawyers used effectively to balance practice and life?

Lawyers and many other professionals now place increasing emphasis on the need to balance personal and professional lives. This is usually manifested as a desire to work fewer hours, or to work part-time from home. Such arrangements may be a virtual necessity to the lawyer with child care responsibilities, even if daycare or other arrangements are usually available. Many lawyers aspire to such arrangements, but it can be a challenge to implement them successfully.

Begin by setting appropriate expectations. It may be possible to work one day (or its eight-hour equivalent) from home as a substitute for office time, but do not expect to work one fewer day per week, from any site, yet continue to earn the same salary and get the same amount of work done. Those professionals who believe they will get more work done from home, free of the distractions of the office and having no need to undergo the daily commute, may be in for an unhappy surprise. The eight hours of billable work achieved from home may consume twelve of your waking hours. By the same logic, while you may be able to achieve a reasonable amount of working time when working from home, it is nearly impossible to achieve a high-intensity work schedule if you have family commitments. Rather than setting alternative work arrangements expecting no change in productivity or profitability, enter into the arrangement realizing the limitations on productivity and income. The challenge then is to maximize what can be accomplished within these limitations.

There is only one way simply to work fewer days than a standard five-day workweek, whatever the work location. Schedule one day per workweek out of the office, and actually stick to the schedule. Clients can be trained to work around this revised schedule. If the goal is a genuine three-day weekend, or an undisturbed Thursday golf game, do not make exceptions for important clients or emergencies; all clients quickly become important and all their problems emergencies. If you choose to select a regular day off, be mindful of the practical realities. Although a three-day weekend is a pleasant concept, it may be unrealistic (depending on the type of office maintained) to be unavailable for three days in a row. If this is the case, consider trying a midweek day off, instead. If the goal is to have more time to complete personal tasks and errands, or to have an occasional day with the family, Tuesday through Thursday may be perfectly fine days for those purposes.

To ease into a day off more slowly, start with a half-day off. Many lawyers find the four-and-a-half-day week gives them plenty of time to feel refreshed and relaxed in the practice. If taking a half-day per week, make sure to take the morning off; otherwise, it may be impossible to get out the door and the half-day off will become two stolen hours at the end of an occasional day.

If the goal is not to minimize work time, however, but to generate flexibility for child care or other responsibilities, you will find that flexibility is a two-way street. If the flexibility to leave the office at 2:00 P.M. for music lessons is important, you may have to be sufficiently flexible to make a home visit on Saturday afternoon. The downside is a blurring of the line between worktime and playtime.

The upside is that your home experiences may enrich your professional practice, and the "intrusion" of your profession into your home life may allow your family to understand better why your profession is important to you.

Whether or not this kind of flexibility is a real necessity, it is unquestionably a convenience if you live in parts of the country where weather wreaks havoc with the best laid plans. Fortunately, modern technology makes it possible to consider getting work done productively from home. To make maximum use of the technology, have a high-speed computer link between home and office. Fortunately, the proliferation of DSL (digital subscriber line) technology and cable modems make high-speed access a possibility in most areas of the country, and they are becoming more economical. As of this writing, such access costs about $50 per month, with $200 or so for modems and another $200, if needed, for a home network link. With such a connection, you can e-mail office staff, share word processing files (including editing done on a home machine), review and update office calendars and to-do lists, and basically conduct the practice as if physically sitting at the office desk. Without a high-speed connection, however, this is almost impossible. With advanced telephone technology, whether use of voicemail or reliance on a cell phone, even clients who call the office need not know calls are being answered from home. Legal research can be conducted ever more easily over the internet or by using CD-ROMs mounted on a home machine. With a comprehensive document scanning, fax, and file management system, even correspondence and pleadings will be available for review and use from home. The only things missed will be the daily commute, access to the physical (paper) files, and face-to-face contact with employees.

Practice-Related Issues

Q 1:62 What typical practice considerations might arise regularly in an elder law practice?

A few illustrations of typical practice consideration issues might help bring the practice area into a little sharper focus. These questions are intended to be both illustrative and largely rhetorical:

1. *Client capacity to draw a will.* The attorney has been contacted by an elderly individual and persuaded to go to the client's home to draw up a will. Although the client sounds lucid on the telephone, it becomes clear during the home visit that the client does not have sufficient capacity to make a will. Is it reasonable for the attorney to charge for the visit?

   Most attorneys would be uncomfortable taking a fee from someone who may not have a full understanding of the transaction. More important, the conscientious attorney should undertake at least a minimal investigation to satisfy himself that a client as incapacitated as this one is in a safe environment. Does the client live alone, and does the home appear clean and well-maintained? Who takes care of the client's bills? The attorney who is concerned that the client may be in a vulnerable situation should initiate contact with family members or with adult protective services. The attorney may end up representing the client in contexts other than preparation of a will, such as guardianship and conservatorship proceedings, for which a fee can be charged.

2. *The family translator.* An adult child brings her mother to the attorney's office to have a simple will and general durable power of attorney drawn up. Ordinarily the attorney would meet at least briefly with the mother by herself to determine capacity and whether she is being made to do this against her will; however, the mother speaks only Polish, and the daughter has come along to serve as translator. Does the attorney have any choice but to include the daughter in all the conversations?

   The ideal solution, of course, is to have a disinterested translator participate. The reality is that the family may not want to pay for a professional translator, and may not want neighbors or friends who speak the language to know their private business. If the mother's wishes are merely to mirror intestate succession laws in her will, the attorney may risk relying on the daughter as translator. As a safety precaution, and with the permission of the mother, the attorney should contact her other children; if there is undue influence, the siblings would be the ones most likely to make such allegations. The siblings might also confirm the approximate wealth of the mother; if there is sufficient money to justify paying for a translator, and if the attorney feels there may be some family dysfunction, he or she should insist on hiring a professional translator.

3. *Reduced fee arrangement.* The attorney is contacted by a client who says that she desperately needs to draw up a will because she is having life-threatening surgery in a week, but cannot afford the full fee for a will. The attorney suspects there may be no surgery, but has no way of determining this. Should the fee be reduced?

   The attorney may wish to determine whether the client's will has any special provisions or merely follows the intestate succession laws; if the latter, the client may be relieved to find that if she dies without a will, it doesn't mean that the state will take her money (a common assumption). Most attorneys are willing to do simple wills at a reduced fee or *pro bono* on occasion, not only for the "warm fuzzies" but also because one never knows when such a good deed will lead to a worthwhile referral.

Chapter 2

Ethical Issues in Client Representation

Two ethical considerations generally arise in any elder law practice. First, elderly (and disabled younger) clients can be mentally impaired, or so physically impaired as to be vulnerable even if not incompetent[1]; even fully competent clients may be statistically more likely to become incompetent in the not-too-distant future. Second, elder law attorneys are frequently consulted by family members (or friends) "on behalf of" an elderly person. Both of these circumstances lead to possible confusion about the identity of the lawyer's client, and what duties the lawyer owes to that client, or to other third persons. This chapter will discuss common ethical problems that arise in elder law practice including conflict of interest, confidentiality, client competency, and fiduciary representation. These situations are as difficult to resolve, as they are frequent of occurrence. This chapter should be seen as no more than a starting point in analyzing these issues.

[1]In many states, the traditional term "incompetent" has been replaced by "incapacitated" or "incapable," or more specifically, "incapable of" followed by a statutory listing of activities for which a person is not capable of acting without a surrogate. The shorthand "incompetent" may not be a legal term, but is used here to describe a person who has been adjudicated incapable of making decisions regarding his or her care and assets.

Overview

Q 2:1 What are the most common ethical problems faced by an elder law attorney?

Ethical problems in an elder law practice can and do run the gamut from lawyer competence (Ethical Rule 1.1 of the Model Rules of Professional Conduct) to the duty to report misconduct of other attorneys (Ethical Rule 8.3); however, elder law attorneys generally deal with three main ethical issues:

1. *Conflicts of interest*. Ethical rules prohibit a lawyer from representing two clients with competing interests unless two requirements are met. [ABA Model Rule 1.7] First, the lawyer must reasonably believe that the conflict will not actually work to the detriment of either client. Second, the lawyer must obtain an affirmative and informed consent to the representation (or continued representation) from both affected clients. Although a family may appear at the lawyer's office for consultation on legal issues that they see as common to the entire family, the lawyer must first determine whether the interests of the various family members are (or might become) divergent, and then determine whether each potential client understands that conflict or potential conflict and actually consents to the multiple representation. Alternatively, the lawyer may represent only one family member; it is then imperative to communicate that limited representation clearly to all present and to advise the unrepresented family members that they might require outside legal help. This process is difficult in practice—most laypersons fail to appreciate the importance or logic of ethical rules, and will persist in their belief that the entire group is securing legal advice for their common interests and good.
2. *Potential (e.g., future or perceived) conflicts of interest*. Even though current conflict of interest issues may be resolved, the

elder law attorney can frequently confront problems later. If, for example, an elderly client has the attorney prepare a durable power of attorney, it is logical for the named agent to contact the same lawyer later, after the client/principal has become incompetent. The lawyer will now be faced with a new dilemma: Can he or she give advice to the agent, or might that advice conflict with the duty to the original client? Does the answer change if the agent clearly consults the lawyer only in his or her capacity as agent? Is it sufficient to have the client/principal consent to such potential conflicts at the time the power of attorney/agency agreement was drawn up? Does it matter if, for example, the agent has been given a power to make gifts, and is now considering embarking on a gifting program for tax or long-term care planning? If the named agent contacts the principal's attorney just to get clarification of the language of the document, the attorney can comfortably answer such questions and still feel he or she is acting on behalf of the client/principal. The attorney should, however, be cautious about actively assisting the agent with actual transactions, particularly with gifting and compensation. Prior consent by the principal during capacity may offer the attorney some protection, but the attorney will probably not be privy to sufficient information to determine whether the agent's activities may in fact harm the principal. Because there is certainly the appearance of a conflict, the attorney may also be vulnerable to claims made by heirs of the estate after the principal's death.

3. *Confidentiality.* Estate and personal planning require that the attorney gather extensive information about the client's background, family situation, financial status, and wishes. Although the information must, of course, be kept confidential in most circumstances, it will frequently be necessary to reveal some portion of the information in order to help effect the client's wishes. This circumstance is complicated by the fact that the client is frequently either noncommunicative or deceased when the issues arise.

Q 2:2 Are there special ethical problems for attorneys who work in larger firms?

In addition to conflict of interest rules applying to the individual lawyer, most states (and the Model Rules of Professional Conduct) prohibit other firm members from undertaking representation that would be impermissible for any one member of a firm. This rule is no different for larger firms or elder law attorneys. The high volume of clients in most elder law practices, coupled with the larger number of clients in larger firms, places a practical premium on computerized conflict checking in those larger firms. Of course, even a smaller firm must have and utilize some regular form of conflict checking, and this task is especially suited to computerization. One qualification: The Model Rules, at least, prohibit a firm member from "knowingly" representing a client when another firm member would be prohibited from doing so. This safe haven should not be seen as encouragement to avoid efficient conflict checking systems.

The finer points of the rules of professional conduct do permit representation in some situations that may cause concern. Model Rule 1.9 prohibits representation that is adverse to a *former* client only in a "substantially similar" matter. The large firm's prior representation of a nursing home in a real estate matter may not preclude the firm's attorneys from representing a resident alleging mistreatment, assuming any information received in the real estate matter remains confidential. This being said, as a practical matter the larger firm will not welcome representation of one of many smaller, poorer clients against corporations that are likely to be more potentially remunerative clients over the long haul. To practice elder law in the larger firm, the elder law attorney must be sensitive to these dynamics and willing to turn some matters over to colleagues elsewhere.

Q 2:3 How do the Model Rules of Professional Conduct apply to an elder law practice?

The Model Rules of Professional Conduct promulgated by the American Bar Association have been adopted in some form in most states. The predecessor rules, the Model Code of Professional Conduct, based on an essentially similar analysis of ethical concerns, remain in effect in other states. Both sets of rules (but particularly the Model Rules) have frequently been criticized for several reasons.

Critics point out that the entire framework of the Model Rules is predicated on an adversarial legal practice; in other words, litigators wrote the Model Rules, and they assumed that most legal representation involved a client seeking legal advice about a discrete problem with an opponent. Elder law attorneys are more often asked to provide consultation, that is, to act as legal counselors as much as, or even more than, advocates.

A second criticism of the Model Rules of Professional Conduct is that they express a paternalistic attitude toward clients with limited competence or, indeed, toward clients who simply disagree with their lawyers. Elder law attorneys frequently find themselves trying to help clients get as close to their legal goals as possible, in the face of family, medical, religious, or social concerns about the propriety or advisability of the clients' chosen course of action.

Notwithstanding these concerns, most lawyers are bound by the Model Rules of Professional Conduct. Any challenge to the ethical propriety of the elder law attorney's course of action (or refusal to act) will be judged by those rules, as applied by a panel of lawyers dominated by the same kind of litigators who drafted the rules.

Q 2:4 What do the Model Rules require when a client has diminishing capacity?

In February 2002, the American Bar Association House of Delegates adopted numerous revisions to the Model Rules following a five-year review by a commission nicknamed "Ethics 2000." The revisions include changes that address the ethical problems involved in dealing with clients that have "diminished capacity." In general, the revised Model Rules give attorneys more flexibility in taking action to protect clients even if this requires a breach of confidentiality, but, at the same time, the revisions emphasize both the importance of employing the least restrictive alternative and the importance of putting the client's interests first. The full model rules can be found online at *http://www.abanet.org/cpr/mrpc/mrpc_home.html.*

A key change adopted by the ABA in February 2002 was the new version of Model Rule 1.14, which addresses the "Client with Diminished Capacity" (previously entitled, "Client Under a Disability").

The new Rule recognizes that "disabled" is nondescriptive in most cases, and shifts its coverage to representation of clients with "diminished capacity." It repeats the original mantra that the lawyer shall "as far as reasonably possible, maintain a normal client-lawyer relationship" with a disabled client (see Q 2:14), which presupposes an existing relationship, rather than the situation that confronts the elder law attorney whose entirely new client appears to suffer from diminished capacity.

Q 2:5 What do the Model Rules permit when a client has diminished capacity and the attorney is concerned about the client's best interests?

Revised Rule 1.14 permits an attorney to commence a "protective proceeding" (petition seeking appointment of a protective fiduciary such as a guardian or conservator) against the client:

> Rule 1.14(b) When the lawyer reasonably believes that the client has diminished capacity, is at risk of substantial physical, financial or other harm unless action is taken and cannot adequately act in the client's own interest, the lawyer may take reasonably necessary protective action, including consulting with individuals or entities that have the ability to take action to protect the client *and, in appropriate cases, seeking the appointment of a guardian ad litem, conservator or guardian.* [Emphasis added]

However, this option is considered only after the attorney has tried other less restrictive measures. Official comment [5] states: "Such measures could include: consulting with family members, using a reconsideration period to permit clarification or improvement of circumstances, using voluntary surrogate decision-making tools such as durable powers of attorney... ."

Rule 1.14 does not directly explain how the attorney's commencement of such a proceeding can square with Rule 1.7, which prohibits representing a party adverse to a client. The Wingspan recommendations (see Q 2:7) deal with this circumstance by stating that the attorney may seek the appointment of a guardian but may not represent the third party seeking to be appointed. The distinction would seem to be a situation in which the attorney takes the adverse action directly (filing the petition) as compared with representation of an adverse party.

One problem with this resolution arises in the situation in which well-meaning, non-abusive family members ask for advice about an older parent whose capacity is diminished but who may yet be capable of executing documents. An alternative to a conservatorship proceeding would be the older person's voluntary delegation of powers by a durable power of attorney. This alternative is quicker, less expensive, and more dignified than a court proceeding. Of course, the lawyer will point out that unless the client has the capacity to execute the power of attorney, the document is invalid, and the notary or other official should not take the client's legally required acknowledgment. If, however, the principal becomes the attorney's client as a result of the document preparation, and matters break down thereafter, the attorney will appear to breach Rule 1.7 if he or she assists the family (who approached the attorney in the first place) in the ensuing conservatorship proceeding should the principal refuse to execute the durable power of attorney. (The lawyer would, however, be able to assist with a voluntary conservatorship or guardianship proceeding in which the petitioner is the client.)

When approached, the attorney must use good judgment, and refrain from establishing an attorney-client relationship with the older person until it seems clear that there will not be an adversarial proceeding. For example, the attorney may advise family members to talk things over with the elder person first before the attorney will be willing to assist in any capacity and even advise that, once the process of working on a durable power of attorney has begun, the attorney will be precluded from assisting should a court proceeding become necessary. In theory, this issue might be resolved by a preliminary "get acquainted" meeting in which the attorney decides whether the older person, or the family, should be the client, but this won't help if the attorney's duty to the "prospective client," under Rule 1.18, precludes use of confidential information against the impaired client in a protective proceeding. Another solution is to assume the worst and make it clear from the start that the attorney represents the family. If the "impaired" person turns out to be agreeable to (and arguably capable of executing) a durable power of attorney, the attorney can then either refer the impaired person to separate counsel who will prepare the document, or the attorney can prepare the document making clear that he or she does so on behalf of the family and simply making sure that the impaired person is aware of the right to independent counsel (see Q 2:12). It isn't clear how realistic that right may be if the person is indigent, however.

Q 2:6 How do the Model Rules address the issue of confidentiality when a client has diminished capacity?

The other important rule at issue in this situation is Rule 1.6, which addresses the attorney's duty of confidentiality to an existing client. Rule 1.6 provides:

> (a) A lawyer shall not reveal information relating to the representation of a client unless the client gives informed consent, the disclosure is impliedly authorized in order to carry out the representation or the disclosure is permitted by paragraph (b).
>
> (b) A lawyer may reveal information relating to the representation of a client to the extent the lawyer reasonably believes necessary:
>
> (1) to prevent reasonably certain death or substantial bodily harm;
>
> (2) to secure legal advice about the lawyer's compliance with these Rules;
>
> (3) to establish a claim or defense on behalf of the lawyer in a controversy between the lawyer and the client, to establish a defense to a criminal charge or civil claim against the lawyer based upon conduct in which the client was involved, or to respond to allegations in any proceeding concerning the lawyer's representation of the client; or
>
> (4) to comply with other law or a court order.

Rule 1.14 now makes explicit a limited exception to 1.6 where a protective proceeding seems necessary:

> Information relating to the representation of a client with diminished capacity is protected by Rule 1.6. When taking protective action pursuant to paragraph (b), the lawyer is impliedly authorized under Rule 1.6(a) to reveal information about the client, but only to the extent reasonably necessary to protect the client's interests.

Unanswered is whether the fiduciary, once appointed, may waive the client's confidentiality rights in order to obtain information that might assist the fiduciary in acting in a protective capacity.

Q 2:7 What other resources and commentaries address ethics in the context of an elder law practice?

The American College of Trust and Estate Counsel (ACTEC) Commentaries on the Model Rules of Professional Responsibility [American College of Trust and Estate Counsel, 3d Edition, 1999] were written with regard to the traditional role of trust and estate lawyers as family counselors and the generally nonadversarial nature of this area of practice. Because a trust and estate practice is similar to an elder law practice in many ways, the ACTEC Commentaries provide excellent guidance to the elder law attorney, including proper explanation of fiduciary duties to the client(s), representation of co-fiduciaries, communications with nonclient beneficiaries, notice of acts or omissions of the fiduciary client, fee arrangements with nonclient entities (such as third-party fiduciaries or family members), and issues surrounding gifts to the attorney (such as bequests in a will). The Commentaries can be found online at *http://www.actec.org/pubInfoArk/comm/toc.html.*

Presumably ACTEC will issue commentaries on the revised Rules as they are adopted in more states.

Another important new reference is the recommendations of the Second National Guardianship Conference known as "Wingspan." This Conference, which took place in December 2001, brought together judges, attorneys, and other experts to make recommendations regarding the practice of guardianship law nationwide. The Conference recommendations include the following:

> 62. A lawyer petitioning for guardianship of his or her client *not* (a) be appointed as the respondent's counsel, (b) be appointed as the respondent's guardian ad litem for the guardianship proceeding, and (c) seek to be appointed guardian except in exigent or extraordinary circumstances, or in cases where the client made an informed nomination while having decisional capacity.
>
> 63. The lawyer for a client with diminished capacity not attempt to represent a third party petitioning for guardianship over the lawyer's client.

The Wingspan recommendations may be found online at *http://www.law.stetson.edu/lawrev/abstracts/PDF/31-3 Recommendations.pdf.*

Q 2:8 Are written retainer agreements required in every case?

The revised Model Rule 1.5(b) requires that

> the scope of the representation and the basis or rate of the fee and expenses for which the client will be responsible shall be communicated to the client, preferably in writing, before or within a reasonable time after commencing the representation, except when the lawyer will charge a regularly represented client on the same basis or rate. Any changes in the basis or rate of the fee or expenses shall also be communicated to the client.

This is a change from earlier versions that made such communications "preferable" but not required. If not yet required in every state, presumably it will be required, and, in any event, the value of a written memorialization of the scope of representation and fees cannot be overstated.

Some lawyers prepare written "fee agreements" and secure the client's signature. Others prefer to memorialize the representation agreement by an engagement letter that may not be signed by the client, but instead will be provided under circumstances that should make the letter's receipt capable of proof if required (such as including in the letter the requirement of a retainer or asking for other documents to be returned). Such an engagement letter should spell out the same limitations on the representation, costs, and expectations. Those preferring the engagement letter approach fear that requiring a signed agreement will impair the client's confidence by implying an adversarial relationship between attorney and client. More practically, the forgetful client may never sign, or procrastinate, leaving the representation in limbo when important action is required immediately. Ideally, however, a letter should be signed, especially when any significant work will be undertaken, and especially when time permits.

Any retainer agreement or engagement letter should include provisions that:

1. Identify the client or clients;
2. In the case of multiple clients, describe the potential for conflicts of interest and the steps the lawyer will take if and when conflicts arise;
3. Describe the scope of the representation;

4. Secure the client's consent (when there will be multiple clients) to sharing of information gathered in communications with each client; and
5. Set out the fee agreement, including a description of hourly rates or any other mechanism used to establish fees.

A sample retainer agreement for a single client can be found in Appendix B.

Representing Married Couples and Families

Q 2:9 What problems typically arise when representing married couples?

Although married couples may not appreciate the potential for conflicts of interest, joint representation is rife with opportunities for such conflict. Conflicts can arise in any number of contexts, including:

1. *In estate planning or long-term care planning, one spouse can be disproportionately wealthier than the other.* In this situation there may be good tax or planning reasons to either maintain the separate nature of assets or transfer them to joint or community ownership. Although this may pose no problem so long as the couple remains married, any transfers may have a serious effect on future separation, divorce, or support proceedings. The elder law attorney counseling the married couple on how to title assets must be careful to provide information about all of the consequences of the proposed course of action.
2. *Modern "blended" families can present special problems.* Clients' interests in protecting assets for one another may be tempered by a desire to retain the assets within the owner's family; it may be difficult to construct an equitable distribution of property where the goals of the owner are so disparate, and each spouse may wish to approach the problem differently. A candid discussion of the merits of each proposed course of action is made more difficult by the presence of one of the potential beneficiaries of each proposed distribution, and it is made even more difficult by the client's recognition that the next (or previous) discussion will focus on that beneficiary's plans for the same distribution issues.

3. *Long-term care planning may be facilitated by transfers of all assets to the community spouse (and away from the ill spouse).* While this undoubtedly benefits the community spouse, and arguably benefits the community itself, it can hardly be said to benefit the ill spouse. The elder law attorney who meets with both spouses and represents the couple may have a difficult time explaining to the ill spouse why the transfer is beneficial; alternatively, he or she may have a difficult time explaining to either spouse why the ethical concerns are so strong.
4. *The attorney representing a couple may collect information, perhaps from only one spouse, that might materially affect the other spouse's plans.* For example, one spouse might inform the attorney, in confidence, that he or she has a child from a former marriage (or out of wedlock) who has never been disclosed to the other spouse. The lawyer then must balance competing obligations: maintain the confidentiality of communications with one client/spouse while providing all relevant information to the other client/spouse.
5. *Even though conflicts may not occur at the initial representation, later problems might arise.* After estate planning has been completed for a couple, one spouse might later contact the attorney about the effect of transferring assets out of joint tenancy, or into the name of a new beneficiary; does this create a duty to alert the other client/spouse of the possibility of economic injury caused by the client/spouse initiating the contact?

Q 2:10 What steps should the elder law attorney take to minimize problems inherent in representing married couples?

Some state disciplinary systems require affirmative disclosure of the potential for conflicts and written waivers before a lawyer begins representing a married couple. While this level of formality is not ethically required in most jurisdictions, it is nonetheless advisable to deal with the potential conflict in writing at the initiation of the representation. Clearly, if the interests of the spouses are materially adverse, then counsel should not represent both spouses.

When securing waivers from married couples, two different approaches can be considered. After the possible conflict has been raised, the lawyer can ask that both spouses waive the confidentiality of lawyer/client communications as between the spouses. In other words, any information that comes to the lawyer can immediately be shared with both spouses, and the duty to keep clients informed of relevant information is given supremacy. This statement can be explained, or included in the engagement letter or fee agreement in a manner that will prevent the statement from being overlooked. In the second, less frequently practiced, approach, confidentiality is identified as the more important concern; each client/spouse waives the lawyer's duty to disclose information imparted to the lawyer by the other client/spouse confidentially, and the lawyer advises both clients that such a development would require withdrawal from representation of either spouse. If spouses do not want confidences disclosed to each other then the attorney must represent them separately rather than jointly; however, this approach is rife with conflict and the attorney may be forced to withdraw from representation of one or both spouses.

A few lawyers advocate an even more stringent approach, refusing to represent married couples. In this view estate planning and long-term care planning are not unlike negotiation of a prenuptial agreement; in each case the couple is actually resolving competing and occasionally adverse interests, and separate counsel is required. Arguably, this conclusion is not changed by the coincidence (common though it might be) that both parties intend the same result, at least initially.

Q 2:11 How can the attorney consistently and accurately determine who is the client in each representation?

It is important to remember two points: A lawyer may have formed an attorney-client relationship even before the attorney intends to, or before legal advice has actually been offered, and one important determinant of the existence of an attorney-client relationship is the reasonable expectation of the "client" that such a relationship has been formed. In other words, it is both easy and common to develop an attorney-client relationship before the lawyer has decided that he or she knows who the client is (or should be), and even before the lawyer has decided to take on anyone as a client. It is also easy to establish multiple attorney-client relationships inadvertently in a short span of time.

In first meetings with clients and prospective clients, it is imperative that the elder law attorney clearly communicate his or her intentions and expectations at the outset. If two or more generations of a family show up for an initial interview, many attorneys feel it is preferable to meet first with the person to be represented, and only then to have contact with the other family members only after obtaining approval to do so from that client. Some attorneys will meet with the family group first on the theory that the older person may be more comfortable that way and is unlikely, as a practical matter, to want the entire meeting to be private. (Official Comment [3] to ABA Model Rule 1.14 asserts that the attorney-client privilege should not be waived by meeting in a group in this fashion, but state law interpretations of privilege will vary.) However, these attorneys will still insist on a private meeting with the client alone, once everyone has gotten acquainted, the facts and issues are on the table, and the attorney has had a chance to assess the family dynamics. Certainly, the private meeting is essential whenever the discussion relates to disposition of the older party's assets. Whatever the order of events, counsel must explain to the other family members the limitations of counsel's representation and should confirm that they understand those limitations. Family members will, of course, routinely acquiesce in such a relationship while continuing to believe the entire family is being represented; the limited nature of that representation should be repeated each time the elder law attorney deals with them, and each contact with the family should be routinely documented in writing.

In determining who the client actually is, the elder law attorney must consider not just his or her own objective view of the representation but also the views of the client and others with whom the attorney has had contact. Factors that might gauge the reasonableness of a nonclient's view that the attorney represents (or has represented) him or her include:

1. Who paid the attorney's fee?
2. Who made the initial contact with the attorney's office, and what did they describe as the reason for their visit?
3. With whom has the attorney primarily dealt in the course of his or her representation? Who has corresponded with the attorney's office, and what is the tone of their letters or telephone messages?

4. Who, if anyone, has met privately with the attorney and provided confidential information?
5. Who benefits from the course of action suggested by the attorney?
6. What written evidence is there of the nature and scope of the representation? Is there a written retainer agreement? An engagement letter?
7. Which, if any, of the individuals with whom the lawyer has dealt has a reasonable belief that the lawyer represents him or her?

For more guidance in evaluating client conflict situations common in elder law practices, consider Fleming & Morgan, *Lawyers' Ethical Dilemmas: A "Normal" Relationship When Representing Demented Clients and Their Families*, 35 Ga. L. Rev. 735 (2001).

Q 2:12 Is it permissible to prepare documents for someone the lawyer has never met?

This issue arises frequently in an elder law practice. An individual, often an adult child with an elderly parent, may contact an attorney and request that the attorney prepare, for example, a power of attorney, or a new will, for the parent. The attorney may be told that the parent is too ill, or too unsophisticated, or too far away, to come to the attorney's office, but the child assures the lawyer that he or she knows what the parent wants, and will take the document to the parent for signature. Besides, because the document will require witnesses and notary, there is no possibility that the child will be able to secure a coerced or forged signature.

This scenario should be resisted in every instance. There is no positive goal served by the attorney's decision not to meet with the parent before preparing documents (or at the very least, at the planned time of execution), and there is tremendous opportunity for mischief, abuse, and even malpractice claims and ethical complaints. Though no ethical rule expressly prohibits the practice, it surely falls below the standard of ethical practice in every legal community, and the potential for misrepresentation, coercion, and outright fraud should be apparent.

Consider the usual reasons given for such an arrangement:

1. *The parent is too far away.* Surely there is an experienced attorney nearer to the parent. If the parent is actually in a different state, the attorney should be even warier about preparing documents, which may have an unintended effect, or may fail to comply with the law of the state of execution.
2. *The parent is too ill.* This should set up red flags more aggressively than any other suggestion. An ill principal/testator is an opportunity for undue influence, and the attorney surely has an affirmative ethical duty to meet with the real client, determine what the client wants, and establish to the attorney's own satisfaction that the client's wishes are not the product of undue influence. To do less is no benefit to either the parent/client (whose legitimate, informed, and competent wishes could be thwarted by the failure of the attorney to document that they are in fact legitimate) or the child/client (whose ability to prevail in subsequent proceedings may be affected in the same way, or whose inclination to commit fraud and abuse could be enabled by the attorney's actions). A single visit to the home, hospital, or nursing home may completely resolve the objection that the client is too ill to attend to the legal concerns.
3. *The parent is too unsophisticated.* It is the attorney's duty to inform the unsophisticated client. It is more important to determine the unsophisticated client's true wishes in any event, because such clients are peculiarly susceptible to exploitation.

Consider also the potential for conflict of interest in such an arrangement. No thoughtful attorney can doubt that the parent, if he or she is competent, will view the attorney as his or her attorney; any tribunal asked to pass on the attorney's behavior after the fact is likely to view the representation in the same way. Preparing documents for one client (the child) to have another client (the parent) sign without any legal explanation, or even the opportunity to ask questions, is an invitation to disabling conflicts and ethical disaster.

In *Tetrault v. Mahoney, Hawkes & Goldings* [425 Mass. 456, 681 N.E.2d 1189 (1997)], an attorney prepared a will, trust, and deed at the request of a stepson of the testator. After the death of the testator several beneficiaries brought suit against the attorney alleging, among other things, that the attorney had a duty to meet with the testator personally to discuss the testator's assets, holdings, and options. Although it upheld the trial court's dismissal of the complaint, the Massachusetts Supreme Judicial Court made clear that the attorney's behavior was unacceptable:

> Our conclusion does not mean that we approve of the professional conduct of the lawyers in this case. To fail to meet with a client for whom one is drafting a will is certainly poor professional practice for "[a]n attorney owes to a client, or a potential client, for whom the drafting of a will is contemplated, a duty to be reasonably alert to indications that the client is incompetent or is subject to undue influence and, where indicated, to make reasonable inquiry and a reasonable determination in that regard." [citing Logotheti v. Gordon, 414 Mass. 308, 311 (1993)]

More recently, in *Keatinge v. Biddle* [2002 Me. 21, 789 A.2d 1271 (2002)], an attorney who prepared a series of documents subsequently executed by the client wound up with a $600,000 jury verdict for breach of the attorney-client relationship.

In a few situations it may be permissible to prepare the document in absentia, although it is almost never appropriate to both prepare the document and arrange for execution without meeting the client. It is possible to prepare a durable power of attorney that excludes any self-dealing or self-donative provisions or, in the alternative, a document that permits limited gifting, and bring the documents to a face-to-face meeting where the client can decide which course to pursue. Suppose the elder client is a nursing home resident and the attorney has seen the physician's reports stating that the client requires constant care and cannot return home. The attorney has also seen the bank statements and is persuaded that the client is impoverished. The durable power of attorney will be a convenience to the family who must attend to the Medicaid application, spending down the few assets that remain. Odds are high that the attorney will recommend that the documents be executed, and the client will want to execute the documents. Even then, it is important to meet the client and ascertain not what he ought to want, but what he actually does want. No matter how sensible the course of action, if the client prefers that the son in Massachusetts act as his agent rather than the daughter next door, that is his privilege.

The point here is that there are rarely only two impossible choices: on the one hand, multiple visits and delayed document preparation that will cause trouble, annoyance, and expenses, or on the other hand, abdication of the duty towards the client.

Q 2:13 What problems arise when representing multiple generations of the same family, and how can these be resolved?

One of the best indications that representation is successful is when clients refer family and friends to the lawyer for legal representation. When the family members so referred are also named as fiduciaries and beneficiaries of the initial client's estate plan, however, the possibilities for conflicts of interest should be apparent.

Sometimes multi-generational conflicts will be relatively benign. If the lawyer has represented parents in estate planning and long-term care planning, later preparation of the children's wills and trusts should not be too problematic. Where the lawyer first represents the children, and parents then consult the same lawyer about the possibility of transferring property into the children's names, the conflict possibilities are more apparent. If the suggestion to transfer assets to the children's names comes from the lawyer (even though appropriate because of the parent's tax or long-term care situations), the conflict becomes even more problematic.

For instance, an attorney may find herself in an untenable position if she represents both the principal and the agent in a "half a loaf" gifting program established to qualify the principal for Medicaid benefits. (See chapter 16 for a discussion of Medicaid.) Under this scenario, a portion of the principal's assets is set aside for the principal's care and the rest is gifted to beneficiaries (usually the children). The attorney who represents the principal only would advocate for a greater sum to be set aside for the principal so that all eventualities and emergencies would be covered. The attorney for the children would push for larger gifts, and try to eliminate any risk that at the end of the three-year Medicaid lookback period there would be a sum left over that would have to be spent. Thus the attorney representing both generations has an inherent conflict, even when ending up with the same figures that opposing counsel would have reached through negotiation.

In the Medicaid scenario, the solution is to make clear from the outset whose interests are represented in the engagement. As a matter of policy, most elder law attorneys will state that they represent the elder principal in any matter that involves planning or recommendations concerning the elder's assets. If someone from the younger generation seeks advice, he or she can seek independent advice on what the plan entails, but not assistance in "inducing" the older family member to change plans. The second part of the solution is to phrase all recommendations with reference to the risks and benefits to the older person. For example, larger gifts may leave the older person at risk if the children die, divorce, or are subject to claims of creditors. The elder may still choose to take that risk, but it should be quite clear who the attorney represents.

The same problems can arise when the context is not Medicaid, but federal estate tax planning. Estate tax savings benefit the family, not the client. Annual gifts may make tax sense if the goal is estate tax savings, but the attorney must be certain that this is the client's goal, not the goal of the younger family members.

Dealing with the Incompetent Client

Q 2:14 What ethical problems arise when dealing with the incompetent or marginally competent client?

For centuries, the legal system has dealt with incompetence paternalistically. Although "acting in the best interest" of disabled clients sounds initially like an unassailable approach, it fails to consider either the client's current or previously expressed wishes. A growing recognition of the importance of individual autonomy, even for incompetent or marginally competent individuals, has shifted the emphasis of lawyers and courts over the past few decades. Increasingly, the lawyer is required and encouraged to advocate for the wishes of the disabled client, and courts are encouraged to balance those wishes against subjective notions of what would be in the client's "best interests."

In the ethical arena, this dichotomy is expressed in Ethical Rule 1.14 of the Model Rules of Professional Conduct. That provision requires that "the lawyer shall, as far as reasonably possible, maintain a normal client-lawyer relationship with the client," but also expressly permits the lawyer to "seek the appointment of a guardian or take other protective action with respect to a client, only when the lawyer reasonably believes that the client cannot adequately act in the client's own interest." Unfortunately, this expression of the dual approach provides little concrete guidance, and leaves the lawyer in the position of deciding when his or her role should shift from advocacy to protection. This duality is somewhat ameliorated by revisions to Model Rule 1.14 proposed by the ABA's Commission on Evaluation of the Rules of Professional Conduct (see Q 2:5).

The Wingspan Conference (see Q 2:7) addressed squarely the "best interests" versus "zealous advocate" roles of the attorney for a client with impaired capacity. The prevailing view that is growing in recognition is that the lawyer's role is to pursue the client's expressed wishes, rather than best interests. The guardian *ad litem*, or court-appointed representative, may advocate for "best interests."

Some state statutes complicate this result further, by requiring the attorney (at least in guardianship and conservatorship matters) to file a written report outlining the attorney's findings regarding the client's "best interests." Sometimes a similar result is reached by conferring on the attorney for an allegedly disabled person all the rights and duties (whatever they may be) of a guardian *ad litem*. Although more modern approaches abandon this inappropriate and conflict-ridden duality, some states have not yet moved in that direction. When confronted with such a statutory requirement, the lawyer must carefully analyze ethical duties, and may frequently conclude that it is impermissible, statutory duties notwithstanding, to take a formal legal position that opposes the client's instructions to the lawyer. This can be especially difficult for the attorney who has been appointed by a judge to fill these competing roles, in part because the costs will be born by the court when the client is indigent. It may be possible to act as attorney for the impaired client making it clear that the views expressed are those instructed by the client and *not* necessarily the client's best interests, thereby leaving it to the judge to appoint a separate guardian *ad litem*. (The new Rule 1.14 would permit the attorney to suggest to the judge that a guardian *ad litem* be appointed.) Conversely, the guardian *ad litem*, appointed as such, may coincidentally be an attorney; the attorney who will be reporting on the "best interests" of a proposed ward must take special care not to indicate (or even infer) that he or she will be acting as the lawyer for the proposed ward (see Q 2:25).

Q 2:15 How can an attorney be sure that an elderly client is sufficiently competent to conduct legal business?

Many elderly clients (and not a few younger ones) may exhibit some limitations in their ability to process legal information and make informed decisions. This is particularly an issue in estate planning, where the soundness of the client's mind is a central question. However, this issue arises frequently in other elder law practice areas, including long-term care decisions (where one choice may be to gift substantial portions of the client's assets to family members or friends) and general legal representation (where the ability of the client to understand and accept settlement offers, or to participate in litigation, may be at issue). It may be uncomfortable (not to mention expensive and time-consuming) to try to administer a competence screening tool in every case, but the elder law practitioner must be constantly alert for signs of limited comprehension or capacity.

Q 2:16 What tests are available to determine competency?

Most elder law attorneys are not trained as psychologists, physicians, or therapists and therefore may not have the background or skills necessary to formally administer an evaluative tool. Nonetheless, every elder law attorney should be familiar with some of the most widely used competency screening tools, if only to understand the psychiatric reports that make reference to these tests:

1. The Folstein mini-mental status exam. The Folstein mini-mental or MMSE as it is usually known, was first published (and is copyrighted) by M.F. Folstein. [S.E. Folstein & P.R. McHugh, *"Mini-Mental State": A Practical Method for Grading the Cognitive State of Patients for the Clinician*, 12 J. Psychiatric Res. 189–198 (1975)] The MMSE takes about ten minutes to administer, and tests memory, language and spatial skills, and the ability to understand information, alter it, and repeat it to the interviewer. Scores in the MMSE range from 0–30, with scores below 24 generally regarded as abnormal, although patients with less education tend to score lower than better-educated patients with similar mental deficits.
2. The Short Portable Mental Status Questionnaire (the SPMSQ) is based on Dr. Folstein's work and was first published in

1975. [E. Pfeiffer, *A Short Portable Mental Status Questionnaire for the Assessment of Organic Brain Deficit in Elderly Patients*, J. Am. Geriatrics Soc. 23(10):433–441(1975)] The SPMSQ is a 10-item test that primarily assesses orientation to time and place and general and personal knowledge. The only question testing reasoning ability requires the patient to count backwards from 100 by sevens ("serial sevens").

3. "Legal Capacity Questionnaire," published by A.C. Walsh, M.D., B. Brown, Esq., K. Kaye, Psy.D. & J. Grigsby, Ph.D. [A.C. Walsh, M.D., B. Brown, Esq., K. Kaye, Psy.D. & J. Grigsby, Ph.D., Mental Capacity: Legal and Medical Aspects of Assessment and Treatment, 2d Ed. (1994), and B.B. Brown, *Determining Clients' Legal Capacity*, 4 Elder Law Rep. 1 (Feb. 1993)] The "Legal Capacity Questionaire" asks that the lawyer read a "client passage" to the client. The client passage contains fairly simple legal concepts. Following the reading of the passage there are three sections containing questions. These sections are: Natural Objects of Bounty (i.e., "Are you married?" "What is your spouse's name?" "Do you have any children?"); Kind and Character of Property (i.e., "True or False—Real Estate is known as land" "Which of the following would not be considered property: Car, clothes, books, friendship"); and Nature and Effect of Estate Planning (True or False—If you die without a will, any vehicles you may own will be automatically given to the United States Postal Service).

Q 2:17 Is consent required prior to administering a test of competency?

If normal questions are asked to ensure the client understands his or her options and the consequences of those options, then no client consent is necessary. These questions are merely an implicit test of competency. However, if an elder law attorney wishes to utilize a formal screening test (like one of those described in Q 2:16), client consent is crucial. Obtaining consent is not only ethical, it preserves the client's privacy and demonstrates the attorney's intent to protect the client's interests. If the client is unable to consent, the elder law attorney should determine when a legally authorized surrogate is available for consent. A surrogate may be in place through a durable power of attorney or power of attorney for health care, or by operation of law under a state default surrogate law for health care decisions. Under ABA Model Rule of Ethical Procedures 1.14, an attorney may have to assume the decision-making role as a protective action.

Q 2:18 What can an attorney do to optimize communication with a client who may be incompetent?

A lawyer for an incompetent client might take several practical steps in an attempt to maintain or establish a "normal" client-lawyer relationship. Even incompetent clients must be advised about their legal status and consulted about their wishes. The immediate problem facing the lawyer is how to communicate with an incompetent client. The attorney may take some practical steps in the effort to maintain a normal relationship:

- Speak slowly and distinctly, and avoid jargon. Stay in the client's line of sight, and make eye contact.
- Repeat critical information two or more times, using different words. Written material may help (at least with the moderately incompetent), though well-meaning family members and others may intercept correspondence and share it with others, or filter it through their own views of the legal and family issues.
- Make multiple contacts, varying the time of day, the circumstances, and even the location of the conversation. At least some contacts should be made in the client's home where he or she may be more comfortable. An exception to this would be in cases of moderately incompetent clients who may concentrate better when they are taken to the office and made to understand the importance of the visit. Different incompetent clients respond better at different times; some may be clearer early in the morning, others just after or before a meal, and still others at another time of day. For example, many Alzheimer's patients "sundown," that is, the symptoms of the disease become more pronounced as the day progresses.
- Make the substantive portion of the interviews as private as possible. It may be necessary to involve family members in the initial stages of the visit to ease the client's anxiety, but most of the substance of the interview should be outside the presence

of family members, caregivers, or other interested persons. If the contact is in the client's home, family members and caregivers should clearly move outside the range of hearing, so that the client understands that they will not be eavesdropping on the conversation.

- Ask for and accept the client's direction on legal matters. Rather than suggesting the "correct" answer, ask open-ended questions. When using yes/no questions, repeat the question in slightly different terms more than once, in a manner that requires the client to give both "yes" and "no" answers to be consistent. Many dementia patients will simply answer "yes" to any question, so avoid couching all questions in such a manner that consistent "yes" answers create a false impression of capacity and/or direction.

Q 2:19 Could a client be deemed incompetent only in certain situations and what can be done to determine and handle such a situation?

Competence can be a shifting concept. Although a client may not be competent to conduct some kinds of legal business, he or she may be able to do other things. Similarly, a client who is not clearly competent at one time of day, or in the presence of one staff person, or in a particular setting, may be capable of signing if moved to a different setting, visited at another time, or removed from the presence (and influence) of a staff member or family member. Plan on visiting the marginally competent client more than once and testing for consistency of opinions.

One might take a number of steps to help determine whether a client really understands the legal issues and choices in question. Begin the contact with nonlegal issues, to get the client focused on the conversation. Ask about family, or about events from the distant past, as a way of testing the client's memory subtly. Make sure that questions are posed so that the "correct" answer is sometimes affirmative and sometimes negative. Ask for the client's open-ended response, but not with such vague questions ("Is there anything else I've missed?") that the client will use conditioned social responses. Remember that social conditioning will permit an incompetent client to give perfectly correct responses to a wide variety of questions without truly understanding the issues presented.

It can often be helpful to seek assistance from medical and psychological professionals, both in determining the client's capabilities and in working around limitations. In appropriate cases, involve the treatment professional in the interview process, and consider using a helpful medical expert as a witness to the client's competence and wishes. If nothing else, a medical or psychological evaluation from about the same time as the legal representation may help protect the client's wishes from later challenges by disgruntled family members, government officials, or disciplinary personnel.

In all dealings with clients of diminished capacity, remember that the lawyer's ethical rules require that the client be treated (as nearly as possible) as if the disability did not exist. [ABA Model Rule 1.14] In other words, communicate the effect of the client's choices fully, without controlling or directing the client's selections, and be prepared to answer questions both honestly and candidly. Treat the marginally competent client with respect, dignity, and patience. Rather than dismiss the client as incompetent to complete the legal task, remember that even marginally competent clients deserve full representation, and the best possible shot at having their legitimate legal wishes carried out. They deserve an attorney's capable and complete representation as much as fully competent clients do.

Q 2:20 Can a client be competent for some functions, but be incompetent to perform other functions?

Yes. First, it is important to remember that "competency" or "capacity" is both a medical concept and a legal concept. The evaluative tools may permit a medical analysis that does not square with the legal distinctions.

Legally, there are different levels of competency for different functions. An individual may be able to grasp the basics of a will and be able to name his or her heirs ("testamentary capacity"), but the mechanics of a trust may be completely beyond his or her ability to understand. Does this mean that the client can execute a will but not a trust into which the will pours? Section 601 of revised Uniform Trust Code will apply to the establishment of a revocable trust the same reduced standard of "testamentary capacity" used to test the capacity to execute a will, but it is not yet the law in most states.

Most attorneys do not look for a high level of capacity when preparing a health care power of attorney, but the witnesses may have to state that the signatory had capacity or was able to "understand the nature and consequences of health care decisions."

Caution must be exercised with financial powers of attorney, but that may vary depending on the powers conferred and the stakes involved. Even if the client demonstrates a trusting attitude toward the proposed agent, financial powers of attorney are commonly abused and the attorney may be especially vulnerable if there is evidence that the client was even partially incapacitated at the time the document was signed. On the other hand, if there is little or no possibility of self-dealing or diversion of the principal's dispositive wishes, because the principal is impoverished already or the document has controls built in, and the principal understands and approves of the identity of the agent, should the attorney require the principal to have the full capacity to understand contracts, as case law may require?

An excellent discussion of different levels of legal "capacity" for different tasks and situations may be found in an article by Charles P. Sabatino, former president of NAELA and chair of the ABA Commission on Law and Aging (formerly, Commission on Legal Problems of the Elderly), *Assessing Clients with Diminished Capacity*, Bifocal (2002). The article recommends, in effect, that the capacity requirement depend in part not on legal technicalities, but on the level of risk to the client's interests and wishes. The lower the risk, the lower the capacity threshold.

Q 2:21 Can a lawyer who represents an impaired client act on behalf of the client?

The attorney must make every effort to determine the client's wishes as the client in his or her incapacitated state expresses them. The attorney may also wish to interview friends and family members to get some sense of the client's wishes prior to incapacity. Most jurisdictions subscribe to one of two theories applied to representation of the incapacitated client. The first, the "best interests" rule, calls for the attorney to weigh all evidence fully before determining independently what is best for the client.

> **Example 2-1.** The client may suffer from dementia and be in denial about his or her need for surgery. The attorney may decide not to object on the client's behalf to emergency proceedings that would authorize the surgery.

Many jurisdictions believe the "best interests" theory patronizes the client and encourages the attorney to be the factfinder instead of the advocate. They use the "substituted judgment" approach instead, following the client's wishes as closely as possible even if they are clearly not in the client's best interests. Proponents of the substituted judgment theory argue that the client's side will be appropriately represented in adversarial proceedings and the judge, commissioner, or other factfinder will usually rule for whatever is in the client's best interests anyway. *Matter of M.R.* [135 N.J. 155, 177, 638 A.2d 1274 (1994)] is an excellent review of the role of an attorney for a client with diminished capacity, in connection with a guardianship proceeding in which the ward wished to contest the guardian's placement decision. In that case the court noted:

> A declaration of incompetency does not deprive a developmentally disabled person of the right to make all decisions. The primary duty of the attorney for such a person is to protect that person's rights, including the right to make decisions on specific matters. Generally, the attorney should advocate any decision made by the developmentally disabled person. On perceiving a conflict between that person's preferences and best interests, the attorney may inform the court of the possible need for a guardian *ad litem*.

Q 2:22 What should the attorney do when a client's capacity appears to be borderline?

This situation frequently arises with regard to a decedent's testamentary capacity when a will is being contested. An attorney can represent a client who has borderline testamentary capacity and evidence of the client's capacity should be preserved. In addition to meeting with the client, counsel should do a capacity assessment and, if the client's competency is marginal, a professional should evaluate the client.

Because will contests frequently revolve around the decedent's capacity, and because most elder law attorneys do hundreds of wills, they should include in the file some notes about the client's capacity or lack of it. If, in the course of meeting with the client, the attorney senses that there may be a problem with capacity, the attorney should order an assessment by the client's treating physician or, preferably, a psychiatrist or psychologist. The assessment and evaluation should be made part of the client's file. Some attorneys choose to videotape an interview with the client during which testamentary wishes are discussed, to serve as additional evidence in the event of a will contest. Open-ended questions should be asked of the client, such as: "Why are we meeting here in my office today? What is it that you wish to accomplish through preparation of a will? Do you own property? How much money do you have? Who do you wish to inherit this money and property?" Of course, the attorney notes, evaluation by a professional, and videotape could end up proving the incapacity of the decedent and thus compromising the attorney. The videotape option is the most risky, as even a competent person can appear odd or confused under the stress of a camera.

Q 2:23 Can the lawyer who believes the client cannot manage his or her own affairs seek the appointment of a guardian *ad litem*?

Yes. Model Rule 1.14 provides: "A lawyer may seek the appointment of a guardian or take other protective action with respect to a client only when the lawyer reasonably believes that the client cannot adequately act in the client's best interest." The lawyer's determination that his or her client is so impaired as to require initiation of a guardianship or conservatorship inevitably leads to ethical conflicts. Except in those rare cases where the client acknowledges a need for protective proceedings, this conflict is irresolvable.

Even though ethically permitted to initiate proceedings, a lawyer may attempt to find alternate ways to resolve the dilemma, and should decline any further involvement in the proceedings (except to be available as a witness, at least as to those matters not covered by the attorney-client privilege). While the attorney may act on his or her own volition, it is good practice to seek medical advice before seeking the appointment of a guardian. The lawyer should not attempt to be appointed as the guardian, unless there are exigent circumstances, and should not represent a third party seeking such appointment over the client's expressed objections regardless of what the lawyer thinks of the client's capacity at the time the objections are made.

Although this problem arises infrequently, it is a relatively more common occurrence for elder law attorneys, who deal with marginally competent clients on a regular basis.

Q 2:24 What is the lawyer's duty when retained as counsel to the guardian?

When an attorney is asked by a family member to represent the person who will be appointed guardian for the incompetent person, the attorney-client relationship will be between the attorney and the guardian (see Q 2:26). An attorney who represented the incompetent person prior to the appointment of the guardian represents both the client (in the client's fiduciary capacity) and the incompetent person; however, the attorney who represents only the fiduciary still has a derivative duty toward the incompetent person and has a duty to prevent or rectify any misconduct on the part of the guardian. [See Comment 4 to ABA Rule 1.14] In *Fickett v. Superior Court* [558 P.2d 988 (Ariz. App. 1976)], a claim was made against the attorney for a guardian of the estate on the basis that the attorney owed a duty to the ward herself. Although the trial court granted summary judgment in favor of the attorney, that award was overturned by the Court of Appeals and the case remanded for a determination as to the attorney's liability.

Q 2:25 What is the lawyer's obligation when appointed as a guardian *ad litem*?

In many states, lawyers are still appointed as a guardian *ad litem* in guardianship and conservatorship proceedings. (See chapter 10.) The original language of the Uniform Probate Code (UPC), for example, provided that if an attorney were to be appointed to represent any unrepresented person against whom a guardianship was sought, the attorney would "have all the powers and duties of a guardian *ad litem*." [UPC 1990, § 5-303(C)] The current draft revisions to that section delete the reference to the powers and duties of a guardian *ad litem*. [UPC 1998 (Draft), § 5-303(b)] Note that in both versions of the UPC, appointment of an attorney is included in alternative provisions, that is, the National Conference of Commissioners on Uniform State Laws has taken no position on whether appointment of counsel should be mandatory in every guardianship proceeding. Regardless of the statutory scheme in any state, the client with diminished capacity is entitled to meaningful legal representation, especially in a proceeding as formal as guardianship or conservatorship. [*In re Lee*, 132 Md. App. 696 (2000)]

One problem is that no one seems to be clear what powers and duties a guardian *ad litem* has or should have. The growing consensus is that the guardian *ad litem* is something other than the alleged incompetent's advocate or advisor, and may have a duty to advocate for the client/ward's "best interests" instead of his or her wishes. Where the lawyer attempts to act as both guardian *ad litem* and advocate for the client, there may be an insuperable conflict between the roles.

As a constitutional matter, persons alleged to be incompetent should have a right to counsel, and that right should be meaningful. The nature of the attorney-client confidential relationship is to encourage the full discussion of legal options and strategies, without fear that the client's opinions or statements will one day be used as part of the legal proceedings themselves, to show the client's inability to manage personal affairs, his or her delusions, or other limitations. The lawyer should consider the attorney-client relationship paramount and reject the "powers and duties of a guardian *ad litem*" where necessary to effect the attorney-client relationship. It may even be necessary to seek the appointment (by the court) of a separate guardian *ad litem* in some cases, although modern commentators question the need for a formal advocate for the potential ward's best interests, because that is the province of the court itself.

Conflicts of Interest

Q 2:26 Can conflict of interest problems be adequately addressed by securing waivers from clients?

Many elder law attorneys deal with conflicts of interest by routinely securing waivers from clients, ostensibly permitting the lawyer to continue representation, or advise other parties, even after a conflict has been determined. In analyzing the validity of this approach, two observations must be made:

1. *Not all conflicts of interest can be waived.* The ethical rules recognize that not all conflicts of interest can be waived, even by fully informed and competent clients. Before a waiver can be effective, the lawyer must also determine that the continued representation "will not adversely affect the relation-

ship with the other client." [ABA Model Rule 1.7] In other words, actual conflicts may not be waived.

2. *Waivers must be informed.* It is insufficient to secure a general waiver of all present and potential conflicts, unless the conflicts have been described and the risks and advantages of the joint representation discussed. It is difficult to imagine (and even harder to document) a discussion of all possible future conflicts, and so a general waiver should not be viewed as comforting protection for the lawyer. Furthermore, waivers executed by clients at a time when they can barely imagine misbehavior or questionable behavior by, or even the possibility of disagreement with, their chosen fiduciaries can hardly be effective at a distant future date when the offensive behavior occurs.

Q 2:27 May an attorney who determines that a conflict of interest has arisen continue to represent any of the parties?

Ethical rules on conflicts of interest prohibit the lawyer from representing clients where the interests of other clients or former clients will be materially affected. [ABA Model Rule 1.7] Consequently, whenever a conflict of interest actually arises between two clients (except where adequately waived by both), the lawyer is precluded from representing either client and must withdraw from representation altogether.

Q 2:28 What requirements exist for the separation of client funds and accounting for their management?

Ethical rules clearly and unequivocally require that funds belonging to clients (or third parties) be maintained separately from the lawyer's own funds. [ABA Model Rule 1.15] Although many states have adopted mandatory interest on lawyers trust account (IOLTA) rules, those rules are almost always limited to circumstances where the interest earned on separate client funds would be expected to be minimal. Otherwise, a client's assets should be held in a separate income-producing account.

Some states' ethical rules may limit the range or type of investments that may be chosen by lawyers for their client trust accounts.

Because elder law attorneys frequently act as fiduciaries (either for clients or for beneficiaries who are not clients), the fiduciary duty to comply with appropriate investment rules should override any trust account ethical limitations.

Where an elder law attorney acts as a fiduciary, he or she will be bound by all appropriate state and common-law rules. Ordinarily, those rules (prohibiting, for example, self-dealing, improper investments, or withdrawal of unreasonable fees) will be at least as strict as ethical proscriptions.

Fiduciary Representation

Q 2:29 May an attorney or the attorney's family members be a beneficiary of a client's estate plan?

Although state ethical proscriptions may vary (and the rules have varied over time), the most common current rule is that expressed by the Model Rules of Professional Conduct. A lawyer is prohibited from preparing a will, trust, or other instrument that benefits the lawyer, the lawyers parent, child, sibling, or spouse, unless the lawyer is related to the client for whom the document is prepared. [Model Rule 1.8] In some jurisdictions, including California and Texas, the proscription is against a lawyer preparing any will or trust by which he or she, or a member of his or her family, would receive more than an intestate share of the client's estate.

Note that the rule does not prohibit the lawyer from being a beneficiary of a client's estate, but only from preparing an estate plan by which he or she unduly benefits. This should not be taken as permission to encourage a client to make such a disposition; good ethical practice requires the lawyer actively to discourage clients from leaving property to the lawyer or the lawyer's family members. On those rare occasions when clients insist on benefitting the lawyer or family, such clients should be encouraged to make contact with a disinterested attorney for consultation about their estate plan.

Q 2:30 May an attorney agree to act as executor or other fiduciary for a client or former client?

Nothing in the Model Rules of Professional Conduct prohibits a lawyer from drafting an instrument that names himself or herself as personal representative, trustee, or other fiduciary, or as attorney for the fiduciary; however, drafting an instrument that purports to require the fiduciary to retain the drafter or his or her firm as counsel is both unseemly and ineffective, and should be avoided. More problematic is the practice of naming the drafting lawyer as the fiduciary.

For clients who genuinely have no other reasonable choices to act as fiduciary, or where the client makes the request on his or her own initiative, most lawyers are comfortable with drafting an instrument naming the lawyer as fiduciary. Frequently, in order to minimize any appearance (or the reality) of improper suggestions, concerned lawyers will strongly suggest that clients name another person as fiduciary, and use the lawyer only as alternate fiduciary. In either case, the lawyer should ensure that the client truly has a good reason for taking what should be an unusual step, that the client is fully advised of the alternatives, costs, and drawbacks of naming the lawyer, and that the choice is unquestionably the client's decision. All of this should be documented in the lawyer's file. In short, the practice should be uncommonly employed.

Q 2:31 What problems arise in the successive representation of principals and their fiduciaries?

Quite frequently the agent named in a durable power of attorney (or the successor trustee of a revocable living trust) will ask the attorney who prepared the document for legal assistance in implementing the grantor's asset management plan. Some elder law attorneys (perhaps most) would argue that the drafting lawyer is the obvious choice to help ensure that the original client's intentions are properly construed and carried out. The potential for conflict of interest in this situation is particularly unsettling. If the agent ever self-deals, disobeys the principal's directions, or otherwise breaches his or her fiduciary duty, the lawyer will probably be conflicted from representing either the original client or the fiduciary client. If the principal decides to revoke or modify the fiduciary relationship, the lawyer is probably precluded from advising and assisting the original client, or from continuing to represent the fiduciary client. Given the potential for problems, many elder law attorneys decline to represent fiduciaries in connection with the administration of estate plans they have drafted, and instead maintain that the only role they will accept is the continued representation of the original client, the principal. Others will expressly state in the engagement letter that the client is the principal, that they will advise the agent or fiduciary only to the extent consistent with the principal's expressed wishes or best interests (or to the extent not inconsistent with the principal's best interests), and that in the event of any conflict, the attorney reserves the right to cease representation of the agent but to continue representation of the principal.

Q 2:32 Are there different considerations when acting as agent, guardian/conservator, or trustee for a living client (or living former client)?

A fiduciary for a living client (or former client) has the same ethical concerns whether acting as executor, personal representative, or trustee. Two other issues make acting as fiduciary easier in some ways and more problematic in others.

On the one hand, a living client may be competent—or at least competent enough to understand what steps the lawyer is taking on his or her behalf. Where a competent client asks his or her lawyer to act as fiduciary, and is capable of overseeing the lawyer's actions, there is a much lower risk of misunderstanding or injury to the client. Such a client/principal may lose competence later (and, incidentally, become suspicious or otherwise more difficult to correspond with); careful practice would suggest the value of identifying an alternate to whom the lawyer will account in the event of future incompetence.

On the other hand, handling the affairs of a living client significantly expands the responsibility of the lawyer/fiduciary. Where financial concerns will predominate in handling the estate or trust of a deceased client, a living client's health and well-being will be intimately affected by the lawyer's actions. Acting as guardian of the person, trustee of a living client's trust, or agent under a durable power of attorney for the client creates the potential for catastrophic failure. Consequently, ethical rules require the lawyer so employed to have and utilize the special skills and staffing necessary to manage the personal affairs of such clients effectively.

Q 2:33 When an attorney represents a fiduciary, does he or she also owe a duty to the beneficiary?

Elder law practitioners frequently represent individuals (or organizations) who act as guardian, conservator, executor, trustee, or in another fiduciary capacity. Where the client is a fiduciary, the attorney may have ethical duties not only to the principal client, but also to the beneficiary (or principal) of the fiduciary. This relationship is sometimes described in terms of an attorney-client relationship between the fiduciary's lawyer and the beneficiary, and sometimes as a separate obligation that rises to nearly the level of the lawyer's duty to the fiduciary client. In at least one reported case in this connection, the court went so far as to observe that "[i]n fact, we conceive that the ward's interests overshadow those of the guardian." [Fickett v. Superior Court of Pima County, 27 Ariz. App. 793, 558 P.2d 988 (1976)]

Q 2:34 May the beneficiary bring a negligence action against the lawyer representing the fiduciary?

In some states the concept of "privity of contract" may insulate the lawyer from a negligence action brought by the beneficiary of a fiduciary relationship, though even existing law in those states must be viewed cautiously. The developing view is clearly that a balancing of interests is required in determining whether to impute liability for failure to discover or prevent the fiduciary's misbehavior. For instance, in *Fickett v. Superior Court of Pima County* [27 Ariz. App. 793, 558 P.2d 988 (1976)], the Arizona Court of Appeals ruled that an attorney can be held liable for the actions of a fiduciary following examination of factors such as the following:

1. The extent to which the fiduciary's behavior was intended to affect the beneficiary;
2. The foreseeability of harm;
3. The degree of certainty that the beneficiary actually suffered harm;
4. The closeness of the connection between the lawyer's behavior (or failure to discover or prevent the behavior of his or her client);

5. The moral blame to be attached to the lawyer's behavior or failure; and

6. The public policy interest in preventing future harm.

Lawyer liability for negligence is not the same thing as ethical responsibility. Ethical Rule 4.1(b) of the Model Rules of Professional Conduct instructs that "a lawyer shall not knowingly . . . fail to disclose a material fact to a third person when disclosure is necessary to avoid assisting a criminal or fraudulent act by a client, unless disclosure is prohibited by ER 1.6." Ethical Rule 1.6, in turn, requires that client confidences be maintained, except in narrow circumstances—one of those exceptions arguably applies to fiduciary misbehavior. Ethical Rule 3.3(a)(2) directs that "a lawyer shall not knowingly . . . except as required by applicable law, fail to disclose a material fact to a tribunal when disclosure is necessary to avoid assisting a criminal or fraudulent act by the client."

This circular series of ethical requirements and proscriptions is difficult to apply concretely to cases of fiduciary misbehavior. Arguably, the lawyer's ethical duty may be different in cases where court accounting or reporting is required (such as in guardianship, conservatorship, or probate proceedings), because a client's misbehavior must be disclosed in order to avoid committing a fraudulent act (the misbehavior itself may, of course, have been fraudulent). By this rationale, the fiduciary's lawyer must ethically maintain his or her client's confidence despite the effect on beneficiaries in the case of trustees and agents under durable powers of attorney.

The lawyer may become aware of the fiduciary client's misbehavior through some means other than the clients confidential communications. In such a case, the ethical rules would seem to permit, if not require, disclosure to the appropriate court or to the beneficiaries themselves.

All of this analysis is further complicated in the states that mandate reporting of abuse, neglect, or exploitation of elderly or vulnerable adults. In at least some states, the mandatory reporting law may be viewed as overriding ethical limitations; in other words, failure to report a fiduciary client's misbehavior might amount to a criminal act under some circumstances.

Q 2:35 What steps should an elder law attorney take when he or she learns that a fiduciary client has breached his or her fiduciary duty?

In those cases where the lawyer has determined that his or her duty to disclose fiduciary misbehavior outweighs duties owed to the client, the misbehavior must be promptly communicated to the appropriate court, agency, or individual(s). Communicating the information to an incompetent beneficiary is inadequate to discharge that duty. Typically, reports of the misbehavior will be made to a court supervising the administration of the fiduciary relationship, to duly appointed representatives (e.g., a guardian or conservator) of the victim, to the state's adult protective services (or similar agency), or to law enforcement officers.

Where a report of client misbehavior has been made, the lawyer must next consider whether he or she must discontinue representing the client. If the lawyer determines that ethical duties prohibit disclosure of the misbehavior, he or she must still assess whether to continue representing the client. Withdrawal should be considered where:

1. The client refuses to follow the lawyer's advice to acknowledge the misbehavior.
2. The lawyer would otherwise be required to participate in filing a false or misleading report with the court or other tribunal.
3. The lawyer's continued involvement in the case could lead to additional losses or injury to the beneficiary.

Withdrawal as counsel may, if there are pending court proceedings, require the approval of the court. The lawyer should then file a formal motion to withdraw, indicating that the reason for the withdrawal cannot be disclosed, and give notice to all interested parties. If no court proceedings are pending, the lawyer's withdrawal from representation should be communicated to the beneficiaries or other interested persons, along with the suggestion that they may wish to seek their own independent legal advice. Some lawyers may feel comfortable suggesting to the appropriate court that it may be necessary to appoint counsel for incompetent beneficiaries, without disclosing the reasons for such an appointment.

Practical Ethical Questions

Q 2:36 How might ethical questions actually arise in an elder law practice?

Illustrations of common ethical dilemmas may help to focus attention on how the problems described in this chapter may develop in the real practice of elder law.

1. *Client capacity to execute a power of attorney.* An elderly individual contacts the attorney by phone and asks to make an appointment. After a few minutes of discussion on the phone, the attorney realizes that the client is having trouble collecting her thoughts and keeps forgetting the words for things—for instance, it appears that she wants her daughter to help her with her financial affairs, but she cannot think of the term "power of attorney." Should the attorney prepare a power of attorney for this person? Should he contact the daughter for information-gathering purposes?

   Any client who initiates communication with the attorney and can get across the gist of what she wants probably has sufficient capacity to sign a power of attorney. The attorney should make a note in the file of the circumstances of retainer, and may wish to suggest to the client that she undergo a mental status assessment around the time of the signing of the documents to support her capacity. Some individuals who have suffered strokes have some expressive aphasia (inability to retrieve words), but are fully competent to understand the implications of documents such as powers of attorney. As always, the client should weigh such factors as the potential for challenge from other family members.

2. *Removal of co-guardian.* Some months ago the attorney represented a mother and daughter in their petition for co-guardianship of the father. At the time of the petition and hearing they were in total agreement as to his care and housing. Now the attorney gets a call from the daughter, stating that the local Medicaid agency has cut off benefits to her father because it discovered her mother did not declare some of the father's pension income when applying for benefits on his behalf and has been keeping the money for herself. The

daughter wants the mother removed as co-guardian. What should the attorney do?

The attorney has an ethical duty to withdraw from representation of both co-fiduciaries because of the conflict. There is an interesting twist here: The parties will probably not be able to retain separate counsel unless they pay out of their own pockets, because Medicaid does not allow attorney fees to be paid out of the recipient's share of the cost. The attorney may wish to meet with the co-fiduciaries, explain the nature of the conflict and the attorney's duty to withdraw, and try to work out an agreement that would hopefully benefit the ward as well. A follow-up letter explaining the conflict and the co-fiduciaries' options should be mailed to them immediately.

3. *Trouble with a prior attorney.* A client comes to the attorney and asks him to amend his will, living trust, and powers of attorney. The attorney who prepared the original documents is named the personal representative, sole trustee, and agent on these documents. The client just read in the newspaper that this attorney was indicted on drug charges, and the article mentions that his license was suspended in another state because of theft from clients' accounts to support his cocaine habit. The new attorney amends the documents and sends the client on his way. He suspects that there may be many more clients of the indicted attorney whose bank accounts are vulnerable (and may already have been rifled). Does he have an ethical obligation to report his suspicions, and to whom does he report them?

   ABA Model Rule 8.3 states that if an attorney learns that another attorney has violated the ethical rules in a way that suggests his fitness to practice has been compromised, that information must be reported to the appropriate professional authority. Attorneys are often reluctant to do this, but the preceding facts indicate that time is of the essence. Reporting the violation arguably protects the attorney whose behavior is at issue, because it may stop him from committing additional acts of dishonesty.

Part II

Estate and Retirement Planning

Chapter 3

Retirement Planning

Clients frequently are unfamiliar with pension rights, and private retirement programs are generally misunderstood or poorly understood by beneficiaries of the programs. Even the ubiquitous individual retirement account (IRA) is the source of much client and public confusion as to the rights of the plan. As a result of the boom in retirement planning in the last two decades, it is increasingly common to see retirees with substantial portions or even the majority of their wealth tied up in retirement plans. Most elderly clients may be past the age when active contributions to retirement plans are an issue, but many will still be employed (or self-employed) and covered by IRAs, Keogh plans, 401(k) and 403(b) plans, and other private pension plans.

Once retirement benefits are in place, particularly when those benefits are in any of the self-directed defined contribution plans, the rules for administration, distribution, and rollover are myriad. This chapter discusses the different types of pension plans and retirement accounts, who can make contributions, how much can be contributed on a tax-deferred basis, and the rules and tax consequences of distributions from these plans.

Inevitably, a situation will present itself that seems to fall outside the basic information included in this chapter. Other resources that may be useful include:

- S. Lockwood, D. Levy & M. Fleisher, *Individual Retirement Account Answer Book, 9th Edition* (Aspen Publishers 2003)

- Natalie Choate, *Life and Death Planning for Retirement Benefits, 5th Edition* (Ataxplan Publications 2003)
- IRS Publication 590
- Final regulations under Code Section 401. [Treas. Reg. § 1.401A-9] An amusingly annotated version is available on the website of attorney Noel Ice (*http://trustsandestates.net*), who can be relied upon to provide copious notes on anything new that is tax-related.

Overview

Q 3:1 What kinds of retirement savings or pension arrangements might an elder law attorney encounter?

When Social Security was established in the 1930s, it was usually described as one leg of a three-legged stool to support retirees. The first leg was supposed to be private savings and accumulated wealth, the second private pension and retirement benefits. The third, and least important leg, was to be the new Social Security plan, which would ensure that even poor retirees would have a minimum level of support.

In practice, the three-legged stool has been thoroughly upset. Most retirement-age seniors depend almost entirely on Social Security, and the private savings rate for American retirees is abysmal. Private pensions, once expected to be the cornerstone of protection for seniors, instead became a relative rarity in the decades after Social Security's introduction.

In the mid-1950s, and largely as a result of collective bargaining, employer pension plans became more commonplace. With changes in the economy, bankruptcy and mergers of major employers, and a change in the way employees viewed their relationship to employers, private pension plans became less stable in the last quarter of the twentieth century. Congressional actions created favorable tax treatment for various kinds of individual retirement accounts and a boom in truly private pensions ensued.

Today, most recent retirees will have some individual retirement accounts (not limited to IRAs) in addition to their Social Security benefits, and may have rights in a private employer-sponsored pension plan as well. Many will have "cashed in" or "rolled over" their employer-sponsored pension benefits, and created an individual retirement account (usually an IRA) with the proceeds.

Q 3:2 What is the elder law attorney's role in interpreting the retirement plan document?

Most elder law attorneys are not particularly adept at investment counseling, and few are skilled at interpreting plan provisions. The primary purpose for reviewing the retirement plan will in most cases be to determine the client's vested interest, make recommendations about changes in beneficiary (if any), and advise the client on the general tax and planning issues involved in the distribution of the plan. In addition, the attorney handling an estate when the decedent owned retirement benefits may need to advise concerning ways to rearrange the disposition through disclaimers to prevent adverse tax consequences. Unless the elder law attorney is adept at investment planning or plan interpretation, those functions are better referred to other skilled members of the estate planning team.

Q 3:3 What is it important for an elder law attorney to know about retirement benefits law and the client's retirement arrangements?

An elder law attorney must have some familiarity with pension issues and the rules governing IRAs, primarily as they relate to the following kinds of work:

1. Helping the client with estate planning, that is, planning how assets will be disposed of at death and what the effect of that disposition may be;
2. In the context of estate administration, helping the family of a deceased client make the most tax-advantaged use of retirement assets; and
3. As part of any asset protection/Medicaid planning strategies, when the client owns an account or is a plan beneficiary.

Q 3:4 When does it make sense to consult with an employee benefits and compensation specialist?

The elder law attorney whose practice includes estate planning (including will and trust preparation) to any significant extent will be expected to have a solid familiarity with the rules that govern retirement beneficiary designations and their income tax consequences. However, when the elder law attorney is uncertain about the plan's terms, the proper beneficiary designation, or the tax or planning effect of current or proposed designations, it may make sense to refer the matter to a specialist for association or review. Of course, this will mean an additional expense and delay for the client, who may choose simply to overlook any possibility of future problems; in such a case, the elder law attorney should advise the client to secure appropriate assistance and carefully document that advice. In smaller (nontaxable) estates with small retirement benefits, it may not make economic sense for the client to analyze thoroughly every possible permutation of the plan or beneficiary designation. If the plan is a large one, however, and the client has authorized the administrator to communicate with the attorney, it may be a good idea to consult with the plan directly to resolve any questions. This may not be a guarantee of results, but it may prove helpful. Always ask for documentation to justify the plan employee's conclusions, however.

Information Gathering

Q 3:5 How can good information be obtained from a client regarding his or her retirement benefits/assets?

An intake interview form can be critically important for collecting preliminary information about retirement assets. Unfortunately, many, perhaps most, clients will be unfamiliar with the differences between pensions, qualified plans, IRAs, and other retirement benefits. Similarly, many clients will be unsure whether a beneficiary designation has been completed or who might be named as beneficiary of the existing plan(s). The intake form will not answer these questions but will target the areas for further investigation, which almost always must be conducted later in the process.

A further complication can be that clients will report their investments without mentioning that some of the investments are held in an individual retirement account. Thus, the client will complete the intake form by listing "Merrill Lynch account - $500,000," without noting that $200,000 of this is held in an individual retirement account. Brokerages confuse matters further by giving the client a statement page listing all assets, combining IRA and non-IRA amounts. Some clients will double up on the reporting, listing assets in the portion designated for IRAs and again as investments. It is important to double-check with clients and ask for statements whenever the amounts involved are significant.

For the simple estate with a small retirement asset component, rough estimates of value, beneficiary designation, and type of arrangement may be sufficient. For larger estates, and particularly taxable estates with substantial qualified retirement plans or IRAs, more detail, usually found only in the retirement plan itself will usually be necessary.

For all plans, it is highly recommended that the attorney obtain an actual copy of the beneficiary form or other proof from the plan sponsor as to the client's beneficiary, as well as any boilerplate provisions that will regulate benefit payout terms and conditions. In this area as in many others, the client cannot be relied upon to report the necessary information correctly.

Q 3:6 How can an employee obtain a copy of the retirement plan or account documents?

The administrator of any qualified retirement plan is required by law to make a copy of the plan available to every participant/owner and is also required to provide a copy to any participant/owner upon request. Most employer-sponsored plans (and especially large plans administered by the employer) will have an office or a contact person at the participant workplace who can provide a copy of the plan to the participant, along with a copy of the current beneficiary designation.

Self-directed plans; IRAs held by banks, brokerage houses, and other institutions; and other plans will be available from the administrator or account custodian as well, although it may take more persistence to locate and secure a copy. For example, if the client has an IRA with a bank custodian, the client (or attorney) will need to contact the bank. Many bank functionaries will be unaware that there is an actual document governing the IRA other than the application form the client signed on opening the account.

If the retirement benefits are a large portion of the client's estate, or if there are unusual planning options under consideration (such as designating a charitable beneficiary, or funding of a trust with plan proceeds), the elder law attorney should request that the client secure a copy of the retirement plan or IRA custodial agreement and the beneficiary designation before drafting the estate plan. Many elder law attorneys would go one step further, and insist that every retirement plan and beneficiary designation should be reviewed, regardless of the size or complexity of the asset or the estate.

In this area as many others, it may be difficult and time-consuming for the attorney to prevail upon the client to obtain these documents. It is often more useful to ask the client to sign a release form that will authorize the administrator not only to provide documents to the attorney, but to discuss the client's plans with the attorney and answer the attorney's questions.

Q 3:7 In what types of retirement plans might a client have accumulated benefits?

Many different types of retirement plans might be available to individual workers. Among the common plans (and types of plans) the elder law practitioner will frequently encounter are:

- Profit sharing plan (see Q 3:30)
- Money purchase pension plan (see Q 3:31)
- Defined benefit pension plan (see Q 3:32)
- Target benefit plan (see Q 3:33)
- Thrift or savings plan (see Q 3:37)
- Section 401(k) plan (see Q 3:38)
- Section 403(b) plan (see Q 3:39)
- Stock bonus plan (see Q 3:34)
- Leveraged employee stock ownership plan (ESOP) (see Q 3:35)
- Keogh plan (see Q 3:40)
- Cash balance plan (see Q 3:41)
- Simplified employee pension IRA (SEP-IRA) (see Q 3:42)
- Savings incentive match plan for employees (SIMPLE) plan (see Q 3:47)

Less frequently, the client may have benefits in any of several other retirement accounts (most nonqualified for income tax purposes, and therefore taxed to the beneficiary at the time of contribution):

- Rabbi trusts (see Q 3:110)
- Secular trusts (see Q 3:111)
- Supplemental executive retirement plans (SERPs) (see Q 3:112)

In addition to the above, all of which require some form of employment or employer sponsorship, there are retirement accounts established completely by individuals:

- Individual retirement account (IRA) (see Q 3:50)
- Roth IRA (see Q 3:95)

ERISA

Q 3:8 What is ERISA?

The Employee Retirement Income Security Act of 1974 (ERISA) radically changed the nature of retirement plan administration. Prompted by the failure of several major employers' retirement plans (most notably Studebaker—when the automaker shut its doors, over 4,000 former employees lost some or all of their pension benefits), Congress acted to preempt state action in the regulation of pension and retirement benefits. At the same time, Congress established the federal Pension Benefit Guaranty Corporation (PBGC).

ERISA establishes minimum requirements for qualified plans in a number of areas, including participation and coverage, vesting, payout rules, and (as of 1984) spousal benefits. ERISA legislation was prepared in both the labor and tax committees in Congress, and is administered by three separate agencies (the Department of Labor, the Internal Revenue Service (IRS), and the PBGC), with the result that ERISA regulations can be exquisitely complicated.

Q 3:9 What retirement arrangements are not covered by ERISA

Not all plans that qualify for favorable tax treatment are covered by ERISA. Governmental plans (those provided by state and local government employers) and plans offered by churches are not required to adhere to ERISA regulations, although they may elect to be covered. "Top-hat" or excess plans (Q 3:112) and "rabbi trusts" (Q 3:110) are not covered by ERISA.

IRAs and Roth IRAs are also not covered by ERISA in that they are not employer-sponsored in any way. The same holds true of IRAs created when a retired employee "rolls over" a qualified plan accumulation into a separate IRA.

Q 3:10 What is ERISA preemption?

ERISA expressly provides that its Title I and Title IV (governing retirement accounts generally and certain types of defined benefit plans specifically) preempt any contrary state laws. This has had a tremendous impact on state laws in a number of contexts, from abrogation of state community property laws [Boggs v. Boggs, 520

U.S. 833, 117 S. Ct. 1954 (1997)] to claims under state law for tortious breach of contract [Pilot Life Insurance Co. v. Dedeaux, 481 U.S. 41, 107 S. Ct. 1549 (1987)] to invalidation of state laws of succession after divorce. [Egelhoff v. Egelhoff, 532 U.S. 141, 121 S. Ct. 1322 (2001)]

Q 3:11 What does it mean for the client if a claim is preempted by ERISA

Before undertaking litigation related to a claim that an employer has broken a promise relating to retirement or other employee benefits, it is vital to understand that many such claims are preempted by ERISA. This does not necessarily leave the client without recourse, but may require (1) exhaustion of administrative remedies provided for in the plan, and ultimately (2) filing suit in federal rather than state court, claiming a breach of ERISA rather than a claim under state law.

Q 3:12 What is the ERISA preemption in the health care context?

Because ERISA preempts any state laws that "relate to any employee benefit plan" [29 U.S.C. § 1144(a)], the scope of preemption has been extended to include even employer-provided health plans, such as insurance coverage or health maintenance organization (HMO) membership. Although the state of the law is in some flux, the doctrine of preemption as it applies to health care benefits has been significantly eroded in recent years. [See Dukes v. U.S. Healthcare, 53 F.3d 350 (3d Cir. 1995); Pacificare of Oklahoma v. Burrage, 59 F.3d 151 (10th Cir. 1995)] This is possible because ERISA states that preemption does not apply to generally applicable state laws that regulate insurance. Nonetheless, ERISA preemption may still bar actions by employees against health care providers for at least some negligence or malpractice claims. Generally, if a complaint alleges a denial of benefits it will be preempted by ERISA. Claims not involving denial of benefits, such as medical malpractice, fraud, or unfair insurance practices, are not preempted.

Qualified Plans

Q 3:13 What is a qualified employee benefit plan?

A qualified plan is one that complies with Internal Revenue Code (Code or I.R.C.) Sections 401 to 417, ERISA, and their various regulations. Qualified retirement plans have special income tax treatment for both the employer and the employee. The tax benefits available to both the employer and the employee are the reason qualified plans are adopted. The employer's contributions to a qualified plan are deductible by the employer at the time the contribution is made [I.R.C. § 404], but do not count as income to the beneficiary until the beneficiary receives a distribution of benefits. [I.R.C. § 402(a)(1)] Furthermore, income continues to accumulate in the qualified plan tax-free until the benefits are distributed (usually at retirement). [I.R.C. §§ 401, 402, 501(a)]

Q 3:14 What conditions must a retirement plan meet to be qualified for favorable tax treatment?

To qualify for favorable income tax treatment, a retirement plan must meet both minimum vesting requirements and nondiscrimination rules.

Vesting Requirements

Q 3:15 What is vesting?

Vesting occurs when the employee's right to receive benefits is irrevocably established. Even if the employee leaves the employer's service, he or she must be entitled to receive benefits upon attainment of normal retirement age. [I.R.C. § 411]

Q 3:16 What are the minimum vesting requirements for qualified plans?

Every covered employee's rights under a plan must vest under one of two approaches. [I.R.C. § 411(a)(2)] The first approach requires that the employee's interest vest completely after five years of service, with no vesting required prior to five years of service. This five-year vesting schedule is known as "cliff vesting." Until 1989, plans were permitted to employ a 10-year cliff vesting period.

Multi-employer plans may still elect to use the 10-year vesting rule.

The second approach, known as graded vesting, requires that 20 percent of the employee's benefit vest after three years of service, increasing by 20 percent per year until the seventh year of service. In other words, the employee with five years of service under a graded vesting plan will be entitled to 60 percent of the full retirement benefit. Graded vesting requires that vesting occur at least as rapidly as the following schedule:

Years of Service	*Percentage vested*
3	20
4	40
5	60
6	80
7	100

Q 3:17 Are there special vesting requirements under certain circumstances?

Certain special circumstances require even more rapid vesting schedules. These circumstances include:

1. If the employee reaches the normal retirement age (which may not exceed age 65) before fully vesting, the plan must provide for 100 percent vesting. [I.R.C. § 411]
2. When 60 percent of plan benefits or contributions go to owners, officers, or highly paid employees, the vesting schedule is shortened. In those circumstances, cliff vesting may not exceed three years, and graded vesting must be completed between years two and six. [I.R.C. § 416(b)]
3. Upon termination, partial termination, or discontinuance of contributions to a retirement plan, the benefits under the plan must fully vest. [I.R.C. § 411(d)(3)]

Participation and Nondiscrimination Requirements

Q 3:18 What nondiscrimination rules apply to qualified retirement plans?

Qualified retirement plans cannot discriminate in favor of highly compensated employees. [I.R.C. § 401(a)(4)] "Highly compensated employees" include those employees who either (1) own a 5 percent or greater interest in the employer, or (2) receive a salary of $80,000 (1996 figure, adjusted for inflation) and are among the top-paid group in the organization. Regulations contain "safe harbors" in plan design, so that plans constructed in accordance with regulations will clearly pass the nondiscrimination tests. [Treas. Reg. § 1-401(a)(4)-2]

Q 3:19 What are minimum participation requirements for qualified plans?

Under the minimum participation requirements, an employer may elect to provide coverage to all employees, but any plan offered to employees must at least cover all employees over age 21 with one year of service with the employer. [I.R.C. § 410(a)(1)(A)] For this purpose, a year of service is defined as a 12-month period (beginning with the employee's first hour of service) during which the employee works for at least 1,000 hours (including some paid leave hours). [I.R.C. § 410(a)(3)] An employee with a break in the first year's service may lose all accrued benefits. [Treas. Reg. § 1.410(a)-7]

In addition, employers may elect not to cover some categories of workers. Any such limitation must not violate the rules against discrimination. [I.R.C. § 410(b)]

Q 3:20 What other important requirements apply to qualified plans?

Qualified plans must also meet requirements relating to plan beneficiaries, distributions during the participant's lifetime, and payments upon the beneficiary's death. These issues are discussed beginning with Q 3:64.

Plan Terminations

Q 3:21 Can a qualified plan be terminated?

A qualified plan may be terminated at any time. The termination is accomplished by adopting resolutions authorizing the termination and filing an application with the IRS. Defined benefit plans must also file an application with the PBGC.

Q 3:22 What happens when a pension plan is terminated?

The major consequence of terminating a plan is that all participant/owners must be 100 percent vested in their account balance or accrued benefits. [I.R.C. § 411(d)(3)(A)] In defined contribution plans, the participant/owner will ordinarily receive whatever assets are held in his or her account. Defined benefit plans, on the other hand, may or may not have sufficient assets to pay all accrued benefits. If there are sufficient assets (or if the employer chooses to pay the shortage into the plan), the employer may purchase an appropriate annuity, or may choose to distribute plan assets to individual accounts for all vested participant/owners. [29 C.F.R. §§ 4041.27(a), 4041.27(c)] If there are insufficient assets and the employer is unable to cover the shortfall, notice must be given to plan participant/owners and the PBGC. The PBGC will then ordinarily cover the plan's liability, with some limitations. Limitations on PBGC coverage include:

1. Increased benefits added to the plan within five years of termination (coverage for these will be phased in over the five-year period);
2. Benefits under plans covering professional corporations with 25 employees or fewer;
3. Disability benefits not already being paid out;
4. Early retirement benefits; and
5. Health insurance or other health benefits paid to retirees.

[ERISA § 4021]

Rollovers and Termination of Employment

Q 3:23 What alternatives are available to a qualified plan participant/owner when he or she terminates employment?

Many defined contribution plans permit the participant to choose complete distribution of retirement assets upon termination of employment, even though the participantt/owner has not yet reached normal retirement age or even early retirement age. The plan may not require the participant/owner to withdraw all benefits if he or she leaves employment before normal retirement age (or age 62, if normal retirement age is younger) and the participant/owner's accrued benefits are over $5,000. Otherwise, the plan may compel a complete distribution. [I.R.C. § 411(a)(11)] If the participant/owner elects not to accept a complete distribution at the time of termination of employment, the plan may require such a distribution later when the participant/owner reaches normal retirement age (or age 62, if normal retirement age is earlier).

An exception to these principles permits the employer to force distribution of smaller retirement plan benefits. Where the participant/owner's accrued benefits are less than $5,000, the plan may compel a full distribution upon termination of employment. [I.R.C.§ 411 (a)(11)]

Q 3:24 When may a plan beneficiary roll plan distributions over into a new qualified plan?

The original plan beneficiary and the surviving spouse of a deceased beneficiary may qualify to roll over plan distributions into a new qualified plan or individual retirement account and continue to defer income taxation of plan benefits. [I.R.C. § 402(c)] In order to qualify for such a rollover, the distribution must *not* be:

1. One of a series of substantially equal periodic (at least annual) payments calculated over the life or life expectancy of the employee and/or his or her beneficiary, or over a specified term of 10 years or more. [I.R.C. § 402(c)(4)(A)]
2. A required minimum distribution commencing at age 70½. [I.R.C. § 402(c)(4)(B)]

3. A return of excess deferrals in a 401(k) plan or excess employee after-tax contributions to a plan. [I.R.C. § 402(c)(2)]
4. A distribution to a non-spouse beneficiary under a QDRO or upon death. [Temp. Treas. Reg. § 1.402(c)-2T, Q&A-10(B); I.R.C. §§ 402(c)(9), 402(d)(4)(H), 402(e)(1)(B)]
5. A distribution specified in IRS regulations. [Temp. Treas. Reg. § 1.402(c)-2T, Q&A-4]

In all other cases, the beneficiary or surviving spouse may elect to roll received benefits over into an accepting plan or an IRA; however, any rollover must occur within 60 days of the distribution and must be in kind (if the distribution was other than cash). [I.R.C. § 402(c)(3)] If the beneficiary actually receives the benefits, he or she will be subject to a 20 percent withholding for federal income taxes, [I.R.C. § 3405(c)] so the beneficiary will have to "contribute" (if only temporarily) the missing 20 percent from other funds. Consequently, it is almost always advisable to arrange any rollover directly from the distributing plan into the transferee plan.

Types of Qualified Retirement Plans

Q 3:25 What are the three general types of qualified plans?

Modern pension and retirement plans are divided into three categories:

1. Defined benefit plans (see Q 3:26);
2. Defined contribution plans (see Q 3:27); and
3. Hybrid plans (see Q 3:28).

Qualified plans include profit-sharing plans, money purchase pension plans, defined benefit pension plans, target benefit plans, stock bonus plans, leveraged employee stock ownership plans (ESOPs), 401(k) plans, thrift or saving plans, Keogh plans, cash balance plans, and simplified employee pension plans (SEPs).

Q 3:26 What is a defined benefit plan?

A defined benefit plan provides the participant/owner with a fixed or defined benefit at retirement. Defined benefit plan benefits paid are set by rules governing the plan itself. Those benefits may vary by the length of employment, the age at retirement, and even the salary level of the worker at retirement (or for a period of time immediately prior to retirement), but the benefits will not vary based on the market performance of pension plan investments or the size or nature of the group covered by the pension plan. Social Security is the classic example of a defined benefit plan, and most governmental and union-sponsored retirement plans tend to be defined benefit plans.

Q 3:27 What is a defined contribution plan?

A defined contribution plan does not promise a fixed or defined benefit upon retirement. Instead, the plan pays benefits based on the size of the plan. The plan size, in turn, is governed by the amount the worker contributed to the plan, the investment experience of the assets, and the length of time the plan assets have been allowed to accumulate and grow. Individual retirement accounts are the classic example of defined contribution plans.

American business has generally moved away from defined benefit plans and toward defined contribution plans over the past several decades. Today, few defined benefit plans operate outside of government agencies and large, heavily unionized corporations. One reason for the shift is that in a defined benefit plan, the employer may be responsible for future shortfalls in plan assets. In other words, the employer bears a substantial portion of the risk of poor investment policies, changes in market pricing, and demographic shifts that might lead to increased pension plan costs. In defined contribution plans, on the other hand, the only risk borne by the employer is the risk of defalcation by plan administrators.

Q 3:28 What is a hybrid pension plan?

A hybrid plan has features of both the defined benefit and defined contribution plans. Taft-Hartley plans (see Q 3:19) are a classic example of hybrid plans. Under a Taft-Hartley plan the employer promises to make a specified contribution to a defined contribution plan; however, no separate account is established for each employee. The plan promises employees a formula benefit upon retirement as does a defined benefit plan.

Q 3:29 What is a multi-employer retirement plan?

While most retirement plans are established and administered by a single employer, some industries have seen industry-wide (or union-wide) plans established by collective bargaining agreements. These retirement plans are sometimes known as Taft-Hartley plans. These plans are created pursuant to the Labor Management Relations Act of 1947 (LMRA), also known as the Taft-Hartley Act, and are usually administered by a joint board of trustees. Minimum vesting requirements are different for collectively bargained multi-employer plans. [I.R.C. § 411]

Q 3:30 What is a profit sharing plan?

A profit sharing plan is a qualified, defined contribution plan that gives the employer the discretion to vary the amount of total contributions each year up to 15 percent of covered compensation earned by the participant/owners in the plan. [I.R.C. § 404(a)(3)] Contributions do not have to be based on profitability [I.R.C. § 401(a)(27)], but must be constructed so as not to discriminate in favor of owners or top executives. [I.R.C. § 410(b)] A profit sharing plan may, however, be "age-weighted," which permits higher contributions (as a percentage of salary) to older employees. [Treas. Reg. § 1.401(a)(4)-2(b)(3)] Such a profit sharing plan will usually disproportionately benefit senior management and company owners.

Q 3:31 What is a money purchase pension plan?

A money purchase pension plan is a qualified, defined contribution plan. In a money purchase pension plan, the employer is required to make annual contributions to the account of each participant/owner at a fixed percentage of compensation. Annual contribu tions are limited to 25 percent of compensation or $30,000 (indexed for inflation) whichever is less. [I.R.C. § 415(c)(1)]

Q 3:32 What is a defined benefit pension plan?

A defined benefit pension plan is a qualified plan that promises a specific benefit on retirement usually based on the number of years of service and the compensation received by the employee. The benefit is normally an annuity. The employer is required to make annual contributions regardless of profits and bears the risk of bad investment returns on pension plan funds. An advantage of a defined benefit plan is that it does not limit the amount of employer contributions; the contribution can be whatever is necessary to fund the projected benefit. Because there is no limit on employer contributions, defined benefit plans are attractive to small employers whose key employees are older and have limited time to save for retirement.

There are three general types of defined benefit pension plans: the fixed benefit plan, flat benefit plan, and unit benefit plan. In a fixed benefit plan, the participant/owner's retirement benefit is calculated according to a formula, usually based on the average (or, in some cases, maximum) salary earned over a period of time, usually the last several years (sometimes the highest-paid years) of employment. Usually, this salary figure is divided by the years of service to determine the average salary figure on which the retirement benefit is based. The figure so calculated is multiplied by a constant to determine the fixed benefit; subsequent cost-of-living adjustments may raise that figure over time.

A flat benefit plan is one in which the retirement benefit is calculated solely based on the participant/owner's salary. Typically, benefits under such a plan are computed by multiplying the employee's average monthly compensation by a fixed percentage, without regard to either length of service or increases in salary level late in the employment cycle.

A unit benefit plan rewards length of service by calculating the retirement benefits based on the average salary multiplied by the years of service. This figure is then multiplied by a constant percentage to determine the monthly retirement benefit.

Q 3:33 What is a target benefit plan?

A target benefit plan is a form of money purchase pension plan that provides for a targeted benefit. The employer is required to make a contribution each year sufficient to keep the plan actuarially sound based on the projected benefit and the demographics of covered employees. Because the actuarial assumptions can be more or less favorable, the actual benefits provided may increase or decrease based on the plan's investment experience. The employer is not required to adjust contributions to account for past investment experience, and so the target benefit plan is treated as a defined contribution plan despite the elements of a defined benefit plan included in its structure. Generally, a target benefit plan will often be constructed to benefit older employees.

Q 3:34 What is a stock bonus plan?

When an employer wishes to encourage employees to invest in the company, and simultaneously to increase the market for the employer's shares, it may offer a profit sharing plan in which the participant/owners have the right to request that contributions be made in shares of the company's stock. These types of plans are qualified, defined contribution plans.

Q 3:35 What is a leveraged employee stock ownership plan?

A leveraged ESOP is a stock bonus or profit sharing plan that meets the requirements of Code Section 4975(e)(7). The main difference between a leveraged ESOP and a stock bonus plan is that a leveraged ESOP may borrow money to buy company stock from the employer or shareholders without violating the prohibited transaction rules. An ESOP is a qualified, defined contribution plan that invests primarily in the employer's securities. [I.R.C. § 4975(e)(7)(A)]

Some of the specific requirements and features of ESOPs include:

1. The plan must permit participant/owners who receive a distribution of stock that is not readily marketable to sell the stock to the employer for fair market value within a specified period of time after distribution. [I.R.C. §§ 4975(E)(7), 409(h)(1)(B)] The plan may require the participant/owner to give the employer a right of first refusal to buy the stock. [Treas. Reg. § 54.4975-7(b)]
2. Each participant/owner or beneficiary must be able to direct the voting of the securities allocated to his or her account.
3. At least 50 percent of the ESOP must be invested in employer securities over the life of the plan. [DOL Ad Op 83-6A, Jan. 24, 1983]
4. Nothing prohibits the use of newly issued securities for funding an ESOP, so that the employer can make contributions without having to raise additional cash.

5. The ESOP is permitted to borrow money to purchase the employers stock, and the employers contributions to the ESOP can then be used to repay the loan. [I.R.C. § 404(a)(9)(A)]

Q 3:36 What are the advantages and disadvantages of ESOPs as retirement plans?

ESOPs permit employees to become at least partial owners of the employer company, and may therefore increase loyalty, productivity, and longevity. Because newly issued stock can be purchased for the ESOP, the employer has an opportunity to "raise" additional cash without immediate tax consequences to either the employer or employees. ESOPs have also become useful tools for resisting corporate takeovers, by creating a class of owners who presumably have common interests with the corporate leaders. ESOPs also give the company a tax deduction without affecting its cash flow.

ESOPs do, however, impose reporting and accounting rules on the employer that resemble public disclosure requirements for publicly traded stocks. Effectively, extensive use of an ESOP can turn a privately held employer into a public entity. Existing shareholders may also see the ESOP as diluting the value of outstanding shares of stock.

ESOPs may also give clients an illusion of retirement security that disappears as suddenly and completely as the value of stock in Enron. Because the ESOP is not diversified, the employee's retirement is always at risk. In some cases, employers may use the ESOP, created to benefit employees, as a means of better deferring their own compensation.

Q 3:37 What is a thrift or savings plan?

A thrift plan (or savings plan) requires the employer to make contributions only if the employee makes contributions from his or her own after-tax income. Because the employee's contributions are not tax deductible (although the employer's contributions are deductible), these plans have declined in popularity. Thrift plans are qualified, defined contribution retirement plans.

Q 3:38 What is a Section 401(k) plan?

A 401(k) plan is a plan permitted by Section 401(k) of the Internal Revenue Code. This type of retirement plan may contain a "cash or deferred arrangement," and the employee may elect to authorize a portion of his or her salary to be contributed to the plan.

The 401(k) plan mixes employer and employee contributions. Employee contributions are pre-tax, so that the employee is not taxed on 401(k) contributions in the year they are made. Section 401(k) plans permit different employees to make different elections as to the amount of contributions, although some highly compensated employees will be limited to the level of contributions elected by other employees. Frequently, employers wishing to favor the highly compensated participant/owners will make employer contributions for other employees to permit the favored participant/owners to make larger contributions. The 401(k) is a qualified, defined contribution plan.

Q 3:39 What is a Section 403(b) plan?

A Section 403(b) plan is a tax-deferred annuity plan that is only available to employees of public schools and tax-exempt educational, charitable, and religious organizations. Although some of the distribution rules vary slightly from those for 401(k) plans, the two types of retirement plans are quite similar. Section 403(b) plans are usually arranged with one or a few private investment organizations (mutual funds, etc.) by each employer, and the participant/owners contribute pre-tax dollars (by salary reduction) to purchase an annuity.

Q 3:40 What is a Keogh plan?

Keogh plans (sometimes also referred to as HR-10 plans) permit unincorporated employers to offer retirement programs that are similar to corporate tax-qualified plans. [I.R.C. § 401(c)] Sole proprietorships and partnerships make extensive use of Keogh plans to provide retirement planning options to employees. Rules governing corporate retirement plans generally also apply to Keogh plans, as do two special rules (which make Keogh plans less attractive to employees):

1. While some qualified plans are permitted to loan money to the plan beneficiary, a Keogh plan may not make such a loan to an owner-employee. [I.R.C. § 401(c)(3)]
2. When calculating the maximum contribution permitted to a Keogh plan, a self-employed individual must take into account all deductions for contributions to any qualified plan. In other words, the total amount that may be contributed to a Keogh plan will be reduced for a self-employed participant/ owner.

A Keogh plan is established by adopting an IRS-approved standard master plan offered by a bank, financial institution, insurance company, or mutual fund, or a plan written to meet specific needs. Once the Keogh plan is established, a trust or custodial account for investments of funds must be established or an annuity contract or face amount certificates from an insurance company must be purchased.

Q 3:41 What is a cash balance plan?

A cash balance plan is a defined benefit plan that has a hypothetical cash balance account (a bookkeeping entry) for each participant/owner. The participant/owner is entitled to a benefit equal to the hypothetical account balance. Each year the account gets credited for employer contributions plus interest at a specified rate.

Simplified Employee Pension Plan (SEP)

Q 3:42 What is a simplified employee pension plan or "SEP"?

A simplified employee pension plan (SEP) is a qualified, defined contribution plan funded through an individual retirement account for each eligible participant/owner, including employees over age $70^1/_2$. [I.R.C. § 408(k)] SEP plans were created in order to reduce the administrative costs of retirement plans, and to make establishment of retirement plans more attractive to employers. Under a SEP arrangement, the employer establishes a written plan (usually using IRS Form 5305-SEP) in conjunction with a financial institution. Each individual participant/owner must also establish an IRA. The employer then makes contributions to individual retirement accounts set up for each employee; for this reason SEPs are sometimes referred to as SEP-IRA plans. The continuing management of the employee's retirement fund can be left to the employee, who may roll over the IRA to a new institution or even withdraw the benefits (and incur the early distribution penalty, if applicable) without affecting the remaining SEP participant/owners. Distributions from SEPs are subject to the same distribution rules that apply to IRAs. Lump-sum distributions are not allowed.

Q 3:43 What contributions can be made to a SEP?

The employer may make an annual contribution to each employee's SEP-IRA up to the lesser of 25 percent of the employee's compensation up to $200,000, or $40,000. [I.R.C. § 402(h)(2)] The employer is not required to make any contribution in any year.

Q 3:44 Who must be covered by a SEP?

Once the employer decides to establish a SEP, most employees must be fully covered. The employer is not required to make any contribution in any year, but if the employer elects to make a contribution it must be apportioned among employees in accordance with their share of the total covered salaries earned during that year. [I.R.C. § 408(K)(3)(C)] Any employee over the age of 21 who has earned more than $450 in three of the immediately preceding five years is entitled to an equal contribution (measured as a percentage of total salary received in the year of the contribution). [I.R.C. § 408(K)(2)]

Q 3:45 What effect does a SEP have on the employee's other retirement planning choices?

Employees who participate in a SEP may contribute up to $3,000 to a regular IRA. The deductible amount is phased out as adjusted gross income (AGI) exceeds $40,000 for single individuals and $60,000 for married couples filing jointly. [I.R.C. §§ 219(g)(1), 219(g)(5)(A)(v)] Contributions in excess of the yearly limitation may be withdrawn without penalty by the due date for filing the tax return and are includible in the employee's gross income.

Q 3:46 What is a salary reduction simplified employee pension?

Prior to January 1, 1997 employers with fewer than 25 employees could adopt a SEP plan that allowed employees to elect to have their salary reduced and the amounts added to their SEP-IRA. [I.R.C. § 408(k)(6)] This type of plan is called a salary reduction SEP or a SARSEP. Employers that adopted a SARSEP prior to January 1, 1997 may continue to contribute to the SARSEP under the pre-1997 rules for all current and new employees. The SARSEP is not available to new employers for plan years beginning after December 31, 1996. The SIMPLE plan has replaced the SARSEP (see Q 3:47).

Savings Incentive Match Plan for Employees (SIMPLE Plan)

Q 3:47 What is a SIMPLE plan?

In 1997, Congress adopted the savings incentive match plan for employees (SIMPLE). [I.R.C. § 408(p)] The SIMPLE is similar to, but even simpler than, a SEP. A SIMPLE plan is an elective salary-reduction arrangement that provides a simplified tax-favored retirement plan for small employers. [I.R.C. § 408(p)] An advantage of a SIMPLE is that it need not comply with the nondiscrimination and "top-heavy" rules that apply to SEPs, and Form 5500 (Annual Return/Report of Employee Benefits) does not have to be filed. A top-heavy plan is a plan in which 60 percent or more of plan assets are allocated to accounts of highly compensated employees.

The SIMPLE plan can be established as either a SIMPLE IRA or a SIMPLE 401(k) plan. The employer must make either vesting matching contributions or nonelective contributions to a SIMPLE IRA. No other employer contributions may be made. SIMPLE IRA contributions, including matching contributions, are immediately 100 percent vested. [I.R.C. § 408(p)(3)]

The SIMPLE plan is available for all employers including partnerships, sole proprietorships, S corporations, and tax-exempt entities that meet plan requirements. The employer may not maintain any other qualified retirement plan in the same year a SIMPLE is maintained, except for collectively bargained plans and certain other arrangements. [I.R.C. § 408(p)(2)(D); Notice 98-4, 1998-2 I.R.B. 26]

In addition, the SIMPLE is not available for employers who employ more than 100 employees who received at least $5,000 of compensation from the employer during the preceding year. [I.R.C. § 408(p)(2)(C)(i)(I)]

Q 3:48 What contributions can be made to a SIMPLE plan?

Annual contributions are capped at $8,000 for 2003 [I.R.C. § 408(p)(2)(A)(ii)] and need not comply with the nondiscrimination and top-heavy rules that apply to SEPs and most other retirement plans. For employers wishing to make larger contributions to their own retirement funds, a SEP or conventional retirement account may be more attractive.

Q 3:49 Can tax-free rollovers be made from one SIMPLE to another SIMPLE or to an IRA?

Tax-free rollovers can be made from one SIMPLE into another SIMPLE. A tax-free rollover can be made from a SIMPLE to a traditional IRA only after two years from the date that the individual first participated in a SIMPLE plan. [Notice 98-4, 1998-2 I.R.B. 25] The two-year period begins to run on the first day on which the employer deposits contributions into the individual's SIMPLE IRA. [Notice 97-6, Q&A I-2, 1997-2 I.R.B. 26] An individual may not transfer or roll over assets from a traditional IRA into a SIMPLE IRA.

Individual Retirement Accounts

Q 3:50 What is an individual retirement account?

The individual retirement account (IRA) was conceived as a universally available retirement savings account, albeit modest in scope. Originally, any individual could make an annual contribution of up to $2,000 (otherwise limited only by the amount of compensation income), [I.R.C. § 219(f)(1)] and could then maintain full control over the investment choices and management of those funds.

Because the IRA contribution yields a tax deduction (as opposed to a reduction of taxable income), and the individual (rather than the individual's employer) establishes the plan, IRAs are not usually viewed as tax-qualified retirement plans in the same way as are traditional pension plans. Nonetheless, many of the same requirements (notably the minimum distribution rules) apply to IRAs, and they can be viewed as a specialized type of qualified, defined contribution retirement plan. This is especially appropriate where the IRA includes (or consists solely of) traditional retirement plan benefits rolled over into the IRA upon retirement or plan termination.

Q 3:51 Who can establish an IRA?

Anyone who receives compensation at some point during the year and who is under age 70½ at the end of the year may establish an IRA. [I.R.C. § 219(d)(1)] Compensation includes wages, salaries, professional fees, commissions, alimony, and earnings from self-employment. [I.R.C. § 219(f)(1)] An IRA can be established even if the individual is covered by another retirement plan; however, if the individual is covered by another retirement plan, deductibility of the IRA contribution may be reduced or eliminated (see Q 3:56).

Q 3:52 How is a traditional IRA established?

A taxpayer generally establishes a traditional IRA by completing IRS Form 5305, Individual Retirement Trust Account, or Form 535-A, Individual Retirement Custodial Account. An IRA can be established and contributions made up to the date for filing the income tax return for the previous year. An individual can therefore establish and make contributions to an IRA as late as April 15 and attribute them to the previous year. [I.R.C. § 219(f)(3)]

Q 3:53 What types of IRAs can be established?

Traditionally, there are two different types of IRAs: contributory and rollover. These IRAs differ only in the source of funding for the account. The SEP-IRA discussed above is an employer-sponsored plan that includes use of an IRA.

In addition, Congress created two specialized types of IRAs, the Roth IRA and the Education IRA, in 1997. The Roth IRA (see Q 3:95) and the Education IRA have different tax rules and effects. The Education IRA, not really a retirement device but rather a mechanism for paying for future educational expenses (usually of children or grandchildren) with tax-favorable treatment, has much less significance in most elder law practices but is discussed in Chapter 5.

A contributory IRA is established by the annual contributions of the plan beneficiary augmented by the growth and income generated by the plan assets. Various rules govern the maximum amount of annual contributions, but contributions may not exceed $3,000 even if those rules are met. [I.R.C. § 219(b)(1)] Contributory IRAs are important, and can grow to significant size over a number of years, but are not usually the central focus of retirement planning and elder law issues.

Rollover IRAs are created by the distribution of qualified pension plan benefits at the time of retirement, termination of employment, plan termination, or death of a participant/owner spouse. In order to avoid the immediate income taxation of qualified plan benefits, the participant/owner (or the surviving spouse) may elect to roll over the plan assets into an IRA and be governed thereafter by the IRA accumulation and distribution rules. Such conversions to an IRA are permissible only upon retirement or termination from employment, or by a spouse upon the death of the participant/owner.

Rollover IRAs can be a significant consideration in estate planning, retirement planning, and long-term care planning. It is increasingly common to find retirees with few liquid assets but hundreds of thousands of dollars invested in rollover IRA accounts. Large retirement plans of any type, but especially large rollover IRAs, can complicate credit shelter estate tax planning, the division of assets to minimize estate tax liability, eligibility for public benefits for either the participant/owner or the nonparticipant/owner spouse, and calculation of future income tax liability issues.

Q 3:54 How much can an indvidual contribute to an IRA?

The maximum annual contribution to a traditional IRA is the lesser of $3,000 or 100 percent of the individual's annual compensation. [I.R.C. § 408(A)(1)] The taxpayer can have more than one IRA (including a Roth IRA), but the overall maximum annual contribution for all the IRAs, regular and Roth combined, is still $3,000. Married couples may contribute a maximum of $6,000, which can be allocated between the spouses as long as neither spouse is credited with more than $3,000. [I.R.C. § 219(c)(2); Prop. Treas. Reg. § 1.219(a)-3(c)] Pursuant to the Economic Growth and Tax Relief Reconciliation Act of 2001 (EGTRRA), the maximum deductible contribution to IRAs is scheduled to increase to $4,000 in 2005 and $5,000 in 2008.

The Job Creation and Worker Assistance Act of 2002 (JCWAA), H.R. 3090, contains several provisions relating to pensions and technical corrections of EGTRRA. Under EGTRRA, an individual age 50 or over may make additional catch-up contributions to certain retirement plans, up to a specified limit. The JCWAA clarifies that the catch-up limit applies to all qualified retirement plans, tax-sheltered annuity plans, SEPs, and SIMPLE plans maintained by the same employer on an aggregated basis, as if all plans were a single plan.

Q 3:55 What is a spousal IRA?

Each spouse, including a homemaker who does not work outside the home, can make a deductible IRA contribution. Prior to 1997, spouses who did not work outside the home could not make deductible IRA contributions in the same manner as their spouses who worked outside the home. Married taxpayers who file a joint return can now contribute up to $3,000 for each spouse, including a nonworking spouse who has no earned income, if the combined compensation of both spouses is at least equal to the contributed amount. [I.R.C. § 219(c)] The spousal IRA is the IRA for the nonworking spouse or the spouse with less than $3,000 of income. The contribution may be a deductible contribution to a regular IRA or a nondeductible contribution to a Roth IRA.

Q 3:56 Are contributions to the IRA always deductible?

Not all contributions to an IRA are deductible. Whether an individual's contributions are deductible depends on whether the individual or spouse is an active participant/owner in an employer-sponsored retirement plan, the modified adjusted gross income of the individual and spouse, and the individual's filing status.

Individuals who are not active participant/owners in qualified retirement plans (and whose spouse is not an active participant/owner) are not subject to any income limits and can deduct the entire contribution to the IRA.

An individual covered by an employer's retirement plan may have the IRA deduction reduced or eliminated depending upon income and filing status. The deduction is phased out for active participant/owners in a qualified employer retirement plan whose adjusted gross income exceeds certain levels. [I.R.C. § 219(g)(2)] Separate rules apply to determine if an employee is an active participant/owner in an employer-sponsored retirement plan. Note that a person will not be considered an active participant/owner in an employer-sponsored retirement plan merely because the spouse is considered one. [I.R.C. § 219(g)(1)]

For tax year 2003, the deduction for employees covered by another retirement plan will decrease for joint filers with an income of $60,000 and will be unavailable if income exceeds $70,000. Single filers for tax year 2003 will be subject to a similar phase-out of the deduction for adjusted gross income over $40,000 with no deductibility for income in excess of $50,000. [I.R.C. § 219(g)(2)(A)] For spouses filing jointly where one spouse is an active participant/owner in a plan and the other spouse is not an active participant/owner, the spouse who is not the active participant/owner can make a deductible IRA contribution up to $3,000. The phase-out range for deductibility is between $150,000 and $160,000 of total income. [I.R.C. § 219(g)(7)]

If the individual's adjusted gross income falls within the phase-out range, the maximum contribution will be the greater of $200 or 20 percent of the amount by which income is less than the higher phase-out figure (e.g., $49,000 for single filers) applicable in each case.

> **Example 3-1.** John and Martha file a joint return for the year 2003. John reports $50,000 of employee income, and Martha reports $18,000 of employee income. John is covered by a retirement plan at his employment, but Martha is not. Each contributes $3,000 to an IRA for 2003. Martha's entire contribution is deductible, because their income is below the $150,000 threshold for married couples and she is not covered by an employer's plan. John, on the other hand, is covered by an employer's plan, and so his income must be compared to the phase-out tables. Because their combined income exceeds $60,000, he is limited to the greater of $200 or 20 percent of the difference between their total income and the maximum phase-out figure ($59,000 in John and Martha's case). In other words, John may deduct only $1,800 of his IRA contribution. He may elect to have the balance returned to him by April 15, 2002, or he may treat it as a nondeductible contribution.

Q 3:57 How are IRA distributions taxed?

Distributions from a traditional IRA are taxed as ordinary income in the year the cash payments are received. [I.R.C. § 408(d)] If the IRA contributions were deductible when made, the distribution is fully taxable; however, distributions are not taxed to the extent they are allocable to original nondeductible contributions. The allocation is based on a ratio of the nondeductible contributions to the total contributions in all of the individual's traditional IRAs.

> **Example 3-2.** George made both deductible and nondeductible contributions to his IRA account over a period of years. By the time of his retirement, 10 percent of the principal balance of his IRA can be attributed to his nondeductible (after-tax) contributions. As he begins to make withdrawals, he will be taxed on 90 percent of each distribution from the plan. In future years, the remaining portion of plan assets attributable to nondeductible contributions will be recalculated based on plan value at the close of the year. [I.R.C. §§ 72(a), 72(b), 408(d)(1)]

Spousal Rights

Q 3:58 What rights does a surviving spouse have in retirement benefits?

ERISA requires qualified plans to provide benefits payable in the form of a qualified joint and survivor annuity (QJSA). [I.R.C. § 401(a)(11)] Under such an arrangement, the participant/owner receives a benefit for life; after the participant/owner's death, the participant/owner's surviving spouse is entitled to receive a lifetime benefit of at least 50 percent of the participant/owner's own benefit. [I.R.C. § 417(b)] The participant/owner may elect to receive benefits under a different structure, but the participant/owner's spouse must sign any waiver of the QJSA. [I.R.C. § 417] Such a waiver must be completed within 90 days of the annuity's starting date. [Treas. Reg. § 1.417(e)-1(b)(3)]

When a plan participant/owner dies before the annuity starting date (one month after retirement), the participant/owner's surviving spouse will be entitled to a qualified preretirement survivor annuity (QPSA). [I.R.C. § 401(a)(11)(A)(ii)] This protection becomes available immediately upon vesting of the participant/owner's interest in the plan. The QPSA must provide a benefit of at least 50 percent of the amount the participant/owner would have received if he or she had retired the day before the date of death, without regard to the participant/owner's age. In other words, the amount is calculated as if the participant/owner was retired, even though he or she could not have qualified for retirement.

IRAs are not subject to ERISA and therefore a surviving spouse may have no right to amounts held in an IRA. Further, many states do not include IRA funds as part of the decedent's estate as to which a spouse may make an election to take a share even if omitted as a beneficiary by the deceased spouse.

Q 3:59 Can spousal rights in qualified plans be waived?

The participant/owner's spouse may waive his or her right to a QJSA or a QPSA. [I.R.C. § 417] The waiver must be in writing, must acknowledge the effect of the waiver, and must be notarized or witnessed by a plan representative. Spousal waiver requirements may themselves be waived if the spouse is found to be incompetent, is legally separated from the participant/owner, or cannot be located. [I.R.C. § 417(a)(2)(B); Treas. Reg. § 1.401(a)-20, Q&A 27]

Q 3:60 Does a divorced spouse have rights in the ex-spouse's retirement benefits?

While Social Security does permit a divorced spouse to make a claim against his or her ex-spouse's "retirement savings," pension benefits do not give a divorced spouse similar rights. However, a divorce decree should take account of these benefits.

Pension benefits ordinarily cannot be assigned, but a qualified domestic relations order (QDRO) may direct payment of plan benefits as alimony, child support, or marital property division to an alternate payee if it meets several criteria. [I.R.C. § 414(p)] A QDRO must include the name and address of the alternate payee and the participant/owner, identify the plan itself, specify the percentage to be paid (or provide a method of determining the amount of payments), and specify the number of payments or period to which the QDRO applies. [I.R.C. § 414(p)(2)]

A QDRO may not provide for additional payments over and above those provided by the plan itself, but may only divide the payments to which the participant/owner would otherwise be entitled. One exception is that if the participant/owner has reached the earliest retirement age under the plan but has not retired, the QDRO may direct payments to the alternate payee. The QDRO may also provide that the former spouse is to be treated as a surviving spouse.

In addition to the assignment of payments under a QDRO, an alternate beneficiary is entitled to be treated as a plan beneficiary. Consequently, an alternate payee is entitled to request information about plan administration.

Distributions

Q 3:61 What are the payout rules for qualified plans?

Unless the participant elects otherwise, qualified benefit plans must begin paying benefits no later than 60 days after the close of the plan year in which the worker reaches normal retirement age and has actually retired. [I.R.C. § 401(a)(14)] "Normal retirement age" can be specified in the plan, but may not be more than 65 years of age. [I.R.C. § 401(a)(14)] While a plan may pay a reduced benefit for earlier retirement, it need not provide for any early retirement benefit. This rule is designed to protect retired workers and thus does not pertain to IRAs. In addition to these rules are the minimum distribution requirements (see Q 3:65).

Q 3:62 May a participant in a qualified plan take early retirement payments?

Whether or not the participant may take payments from a plan (or, for that matter, loans) will depend on the terms of the plan. Even if the Code permits early distributions, the plan may not permit them.

Assuming the plan does permit early payments, the participant must still pay a 10 percent penalty on distributions taken prior to age $59^{1}/_{2}$. The 10 percent penalty on early distributions does not apply to the following types of distributions, however:

1. Rollovers from a qualified plan or IRA into an IRA within 60 days after the date of distribution [I.R.C. § 72(t)(1)];
2. Distributions from a qualified plan or IRA to a beneficiary because of the participant/owner's death [I.R.C. § 72(t)(2)(A)(ii)];
3. Distributions from a qualified plan to a plan participant who separates from service after the year in which he or she reaches age 55 [I.R.C. § 72(t)(2)(A)(v)];
4. Payments from a plan or IRA as part of a series of "substantially equal periodic payments" spread over the participant/owner's life expectancy [I.R.C. § 72(t)(2)(A)(iv)];
5. Distributions based on the participant/owner's total or partial disability [I.R.C. § 72(t)(2)(A)(iii)]; or
6. Distributions to pay medical expenses in excess of 7.5 percent of adjusted gross income (AGI). [I.R.C. § 72(t)(2)(B)]

Q 3:63 Is there a penalty for early withdrawals from an IRA?

Yes. The penalty rules for IRA early withdrawals are similar to the early withdrawal rules that apply to qualified employer retirement plans (see Q 3:62). There is a 10 percent additional tax on distributions prior to age 59½. [I.R.C. § 72(t)(2)(A)(I)] The 10 percent penalty on early withdrawals does not apply to the following distributions:

1. Made after the taxpayer attains age 59½ [I.R.C. § 72(t)(2)(A)(i)];
2. Made to a beneficiary or the taxpayer's estate because the taxpayer has died [I.R.C. § 72(t)(2)(A)(ii)];
3. Part of a series of substantially equal annual payments over the participant/owner's lifetime or life expectancy or the joint lives or life expectancies of the participant/owner and a designated beneficiary [I.R.C. § 72(t)(2)(A)(iv)];
4. Made on account of disability [I.R.C. § 72(t)(2)(A)(ii)];
5. To pay for medical expenses in excess of 7.5 percent of AGI [I.R.C. § 72(t)(2)(B)];
6. To pay health insurance premiums for individuals who are unemployed for more than 12 months [I.R.C. § 72(t)(2)(D)];

7. To pay for qualified higher education expenses for the taxpayer, the taxpayer's spouse, child, grandchild, or spouse's child or grandchild [I.R.C. § 72(t)(7)(A)];
8. For first-time home purchases up to $10,000 [I.R.C. § 72(t)(2)(F)];
9. Transfers to a spouse's IRA incident to divorce [I.R.C. § 408(d)(6)];
10. Made after December 13, 1999, for IRS levies on IRAs. [I.R.C. § 72(t)(2)(A)(vii)]

Minimum Required Distributions

Q 3:64 Do the same rules for minimum required distributions apply to Qualified Plans and IRAs?

Most defined contribution plans are covered by the same minimum distribution rules. Separate rules apply to distributions from ESOPs (see Q 3:94) and no such rules apply to nonqualified plans. The same minimum distribution rules also apply to IRAs, SEPs, Keoghs, and 401(k) and 403(b) plans. [I.R.C. § 4974(b)]

While there are some important distinctions between qualified plans and IRAs when it comes to beneficiaries and distributions, there are far more similarities. The key distinctions to remember are:

1. The ERISA rules on spousal rights to post-death distributions do not apply to IRAs;
2. Recent laws permitting longer deferral of distributions for participants/owners do not apply to IRAs; and
3. Qualified plan accounts and IRAs cannot be combined to meet the various minimum distribution requirements.

Q 3:65 Are there any retirement arrangements to which the minimum distribution rules do not apply?

Nonqualified plans and benefits are not subject to these rules. In addition, some individuals also purchase tax-deferred annuities that may seem like IRAs. Their beneficiary provisions and distribution requirements seem patterned on the IRA regulations. If they are not actually IRAs, however (for example, you notice that the owner is 80 and there is no distribution for 5 years), these new minimum distribution rules do *not* apply. The effect of this may be that the annuity contract seems to have some of the old rules.

Table 3-1. Method for Determining Minimum Required Distributions January 1, 2003, and following

(P = retired participant or IRA account owner)

(All Tables shown in IRS Publication 590; see http://www.sharinglaw.net/elder/MRDTables.pdf)

A. Computing Participant's Distribution When Participant is Living

If NO "DB"	*If all beneficiaries qualify as DB's and at least one beneficiary is NOT spouse*	*If spouse is SOLE beneficiary*
Compute using P's life expectancy using IRS "Uniform Table for Owners"	Compute using P's life expectancy, using IRS "Uniform Table for Owners"	P can choose to either: (1) use IRS "Uniform Table for Owners"
("Uniform Table" is IRS Table III designated for use by "participants or owners"; in reality, this table uses the joint life expectancy of P and hypothetical beneficiary 10 years younger.)		OR (2) if spouse is 10 or more years younger than P, use joint life expectancies of P + spouse redetermined each year (using IRS joint life tables)

Table 3-1. Method for Determining Minimum Required Distributions January 1, 2003, and following (*cont'd*)

B. Participant Dies Before RBD:
Computing Beneficiary's Distribution After P's Death

If NO "DB"	*If all beneficiaries qualify as DB's and at least one beneficiary is NOT spouse*	*If spouse is SOLE beneficiary (no rollover)*
Must distribute ALL by 12/31 of 5th year following year of death, but no need to start sooner. *(Notes: (1) if any beneficiary isn't a DB there is "NO DB." but* *(2) Beneficiaries who are paid off / have accounts segregated by 9/30 following year of death are DISREGARDED).*	Either: (1) Begin by 12/31 following year of death, use DB's life expectancy perIRS "Table for Beneficiaries" for year following year of P's death minus 1 for each year (2) If begin later, then must take ALL by 12/31 of 5th year following year of death *(For multiple-DB accounts, "DB" is DB with shortest life expectancy, but see Note (2), Column 1)*	While spouse is living: (1) zero until year in which participant/owner would have reached 70 1/2; (2) thereafter, spouse's life expectancy in year following death, recalculated each year per IRS "Table for Beneficiaries" After spouse's death: spouse's life expectancy in year of death, minus 1 for each succeeding year.

Table 3-1. Method for Determining Minimum Required Distributions January 1, 2003, and following (*cont'd*)

C. Participant Dies After RBD:
Computing Beneficiary's Distribution After P's Death

If NO "DB"	*If all beneficiaries qualify as DB's and at least one beneficiary is NOT spouse*	*If spouse is SOLE beneficiary (no rollover)*
Begin by 12/31 following year of death, use P's life expectancy perIRS "Table for Beneficiaries" minus 1 for each year. (If begin later, must take ALL by 12/31 of 5th year following year of death *(Notes: (1) if any beneficiary isn't a DB there is "NO DB." but* *(2) Beneficiaries paid off / have accounts segregated by 9/30 following year of death are DISREGARDED).*	Either: (1) Same as if P died BEFORE RBD, or (2) if longer, P's life expectancy per IRS "Table for Beneficiaries" *See Note (2) column 1.*	Either: (1) Same as if P died BEFORE RBD, or (2) if longer, P's life expectancy per IRS "Table for Beneficiaries"

Table 3-1. Method for Determining Minimum Required Distributions January 1, 2003, and following (*cont'd*)

D. Rolling Over: Computing Distributions

If P has NO DB	*If at least one of P's beneficiaries is NOT spouse*	*Spouse is sole beneficiary and rolls over*
N/A (not possible). However, it may be possible to get a ruling that would permit rollover if estate is named, spouse (or trust in which spouse has withdrawal rights) is SOLE beneficiary of estate, and spouse receives ENTIRE account value (not reduced by taxes, expenses etc.)	Spouse can still roll over his/her share PROVIDED other beneficiaries have been paid off before September 30th of year following year of P's death, OR her share is a segregated account. Spouse then applies rules as if she were participant/owner. On spouse's death, spouse's beneficiaries apply rules shown for an owner's beneficiaries.	During spouse's lifetime, distribution computed for spouse using rules for participant/owner. After spouse's death, spouse's beneficiaries apply rules shown for an owner's beneficiaries where owner dies after RBD.

The "Uniform Table" is the IRS table designated for use by "participants or owners," Table I in Publication 590. In reality, this table uses the joint life expectancy of the participant or owner and a hypothetical beneficiary 10 years younger.

Q 3:66 What are the minimum required distribution rules?

Retirement benefits continue to accumulate without current income tax payments, so plan beneficiaries are frequently interested in delaying distributions from the plan as long as legally permissible. However, the favorable tax treatment of retirement plans was not intended to encourage accumulations of wealth or transfers of substantial assets to subsequent generations. In order to prevent indefinite accumulation of retirement wealth, and to ensure that the accumulation and growth in retirement plans is eventually taxed, Congress enacted rules that compel the plan participant/owner to begin withdrawing retirement benefits eventually. The rules require a participant/owner to take at least a minimum required distribution (MRD) beginning at least by a date called the required beginning date (RBD) (See Q 3:68). The IRS temporary regulations implementing these rules since the 1980s were initially very complex but were ultimately simplified greatly by the publication of final regulations effective January 1, 2003. [26 CFR § 1.401(a)(9)-0 et seq.] A summary of the MRD rules may be found in Table 3-1, and the rules are further discussed in this chapter.

Q 3:67 What are the penalties for failure to comply with the minimum distribution requirements, and who is responsible?

Failure to comply can result in a tremendous penalty. In addition to any other tax, there is a 50 percent excise tax payable by the payee on any portion of the minimum distribution not actually distributed. [I.R.C. § 4974]

A retirement plan will not "qualify" for desirable income tax treatment if it does not have provisions that require compliance with these rules. Since an employer will always have to seek IRS approval for a plan ahead of time, it is unlikely that the participating employee will run afoul of these requirements.

However, an IRA custodian is not required to make any payments. Instead, the IRA account owner is required to take a minimum required distribution for each year beginning with the year in which the owner turns $70^1/_2$, with the first payment no later than the required beginning date (see Q 3:68). (The owner should take the first payment during the year he or she turns $70^1/_2$, rather than wait until April 1st, to avoid "bunching" two payments in one year and paying income tax at a higher bracket.) The account owner is entitled to compute the required distribution amount as to the total aggregate individual retirement accounts held by that owner and may take the required minimum distribution from any one or more accounts.

Many clients do not realize that the minimum distributions are their responsibility. Because underdistributions were self-reported, there was a high incidence of noncompliance by IRA owners. EGTRRA now requires the custodian to notify the account owner as to what the required distribution amount would be if that account were the owner's only IRA and to report that amount to the IRS in order to reduce the problem of noncompliance.

Q 3:68 What and when is the required beginning date?

The required beginning date (RBD) for a plan participant who is a 5 percent or more owner of the business is April 1 of the year following the calendar year in which the participant/owner reaches age $70^1/_2$. This means that the 5 percent owner must begin to take minimum required distributions by that date.

The RBD for an IRA account owner is the same—April 1 of the year following the calendar year in which the owner reaches age $70^1/_2$.

For all other participants of qualified plans, distributions must begin by April 1 following the *later of* the calendar year in which the participant/owner (1) reaches age $70^1/_2$ or (2) retires. [I.R.C. § 401(a)(9)(C)]

Q 3:69 What is the importance of the required beginning date?

The RBD used to be a critical date for estate planners. Choices were foreclosed after the RBD, often with disastrous results. Final Regulations issued in April 2002 have made the RBD far less important. Now, the RBD matters only as (1) the date by which distribution must commence to escape penalty and (2) the date before which one should not die without a designated beneficiary [Q 3:76]. New attorneys are thus spared the rush of adrenalin still experienced by those who practiced under the "old rules" when realizing that a client's RBD has passed. Of course, the legacy of the old rules may live on in documents that seem (to younger eyes) peculiarly obsessed with determining beneficiaries and making distribution decisions prior to the RBD.

Q 3:70 What is the required minimum distribution amount during the participant/owner's lifetime?

The required minimum distribution is the minimum amount that the plan participant/account owner must take each year to avoid the 50 percent penalty on undistributed amounts. In general, the required minimum distribution is a portion of the participant/owner's account paid out over the participant/owner's hypothetical life expectancy according to IRS tables. Computation of the amount was very complex under the old rules and is now simplified. Only two methods apply.

The most common method by far applies to everyone who is not married to a spouse more than 10 years younger. During the participant/owner's life, minimum distributions are determined in accordance with the table provided in the regulations, and now made available in IRS Publication 590. Although no longer important, it is interesting to note that the new table effectively gives every participant/owner the benefit of the prior rules' recalculation method based on having a designated beneficiary 10 years younger than the participant/owner, regardless of what beneficiary, if any, the participant/owner may actually have selected. There is no express authority for this in the rules Congress enacted, but the IRS chose to calculate its tables for life expectancies on this basis, apparently to avoid the enormous complications and problems for participants that occurred when more accurate tables were used.

Minimum distributions each year are calculated by dividing the entire qualified plan balance (accumulating multiple plans for purposes of calculation) by the number from the appropriate IRS tables.

Q 3:71 Besides using the standard tables, what is the second method for computing the minimum required distribution during the participant/owner's lifetime?

Under the new regulations, when the participant/owner's spouse is more than 10 years younger than the participant/owner, an alternative minimum distribution calculation method may permit smaller distributions each year. [Treas. Reg. § 1.401(a)(9)-5, A-4(b)] If the younger spouse is the plan's sole beneficiary, minimum distributions are calculated by using the joint life expectancy of the employee and spouse using both of their attained ages in the calendar year of the distribution. This will result in a slower payout.

Beneficiaries

Q 3:72 What happens to retirement plan assets upon the death of the participant/owner?

Assuming that the retirement plan is either a qualified defined contribution plan or an individual retirement account, assets may remain in the plan upon the death of the "participant/owner" (in the case of a qualified plan) or the "owner" (in the case of an individual retirement account). On the participant/owner's death, those assets will pass to a beneficiary. Although some qualified plans and IRAs may designate a beneficiary in the plan documents, the participant/owner is usually permitted to designate a beneficiary of his or her choice. For ERISA plans, however, the default beneficiary is the spouse, and the spouse's consent is required to designate a different beneficiary (see Q 3:58).

Q 3:73 What is a designated beneficiary?

A designated beneficiary is not the same as a beneficiary. A beneficiary is simply the person or entity named as beneficiary of the retirement plan/account in the event of the participant/owner's death. The beneficiary is normally named in a beneficiary designation form completed and signed by the participant/owner (and the participant/owner's spouse if the participant/owner is married and the plan is an ERISA plan). Most qualified plans designate a default beneficiary; for example, many plans provide that if no beneficiary is chosen, then the surviving spouse is automatically named as beneficiary, whereas some IRAs may provide that if no beneficiary is chosen, the estate is the beneficiary.

A designated beneficiary is a beneficiary that is an individual. A charity cannot be a designated beneficiary. An estate cannot be a designated beneficiary. Even a trust cannot itself be a designated beneficiary, but regulations state that, provided the trust meets certain qualifications, the trust beneficiaries will be treated as the designated beneficiaries. Another way of putting all this is that unless the beneficiary is an individual there is no designated beneficiary.

Q 3:74 Does it matter who is the designated beneficiary?

The existence and identity of a designated beneficiary is no longer important during the life of the participant/owner. With the exception of a beneficiary who is a spouse more than 10 years younger than the owner/participant, it makes no difference, during the participant/owner's lifetime, who has been chosen as designated beneficiary.

However, after the owner/participant's death, the identity of the beneficiary chosen is more important than simply identifying to whom the account's assets are paid.

Q 3:75 What is the consequence of having no "designated beneficiary" if a participant/owner dies *after* the required beginning date?

A person might have no designated beneficiary because the named beneficiary is an estate, charity, or nonqualifying trust. A person might also have no designated beneficiary because a beneficiary designation form was not completed and the plan specifies "the estate" as a default beneficiary.

Under the old regulations, if the participant/owner died *after* his or her required beginning date (RBD), usually meaning after retirement, the entire remaining account balance had to be withdrawn (and the income tax paid) in the year after death. Because of the accelerated payout, the entire plan balance was then subject to income taxation.

Under the new final regulations, the results are less dire. If the participant/owner dies *after* his or her RBD "without a designated beneficiary," the account balance may be paid out over the participant/owner's remaining life expectancy using the IRS tables that apply to the life expectancies of *beneficiaries*, not *owners*. [Treas. Reg. § 1.401A(9)-5, 5.5(a), 5.5(c)(3)]

> **Example 3-3.** Faun's qualified plan named no beneficiary, and the plan documents provided that the remaining balance would be payable to her estate. Faun dies in 2002, shortly after her birthday, at the age of 82. Her estate is not concluded by the end of the calendar year following the year of her death, and so there is no designated beneficiary. Application of the minimum distri-

bution table required that Faun withdraw 1/16 of her plan balance in 2002. In 2003, her estate must withdraw 1/15. In 2004, her heirs must withdraw at least 1/14 of the balance, and the denominator of the fraction must be decreased by one each year thereafter.

Q 3:76 What is the consequence of having no "designated beneficiary" if a participant/owner dies *before* the required beginning date?

Under both old and new rules, there is a downside to having no designated beneficiary if the participant/owner dies *before* his or her RBD. In that situation, distribution must be made commencing no later than December 31 of the year following the year of death, and concluding by the fifth anniversary of the death. [Treas. Reg. § 1.401(A)(9)-3, 3.1(a)] This is known as the "five-year rule." [I.R.C. § 401(a)(9)(B)(ii)]

Fortunately, there is also now some leeway in determining whether and when a participant/owner has a designated beneficiary. It may be possible to cure the problem of having no designated beneficiary provided one acts quickly.

See Table 3-1 for further explanation.

Q 3:77 When is the designated beneficiary determined?

Determination of the designated beneficiary is made as of September 30 of the year following the year in which the participant/owner died. [Treas. Reg. § 1.401(a)(9)-4, A-4] This is an important liberalization of the previous rules, which fixed the designated beneficiary as of the year after the participant/owner attains age $70^1/_2$, but slightly less generous than proposed regulations, which permitted determination by December 31. Modification was deemed necessary so that the custodian/administrator could make the required payment in time.

Q 3:78 Can a designated beneficiary be changed?

The beneficiary designation may be changed by the participant/owner at any time. Even after the RBD, the participant/owner may change the beneficiary without affecting required minimum distributions.

After the participant/owner's death, the beneficiaries themselves may not be selected or changed. However, since the designated beneficiary need not be identified until September 30 of the year following the year of the participant/owner's death, it may be possible to change which of these beneficiaries will be identified as a designated beneficiary.

Finally, the beneficiary who continues to receive distributions over his or her lifetime may select a new beneficiary to take distributions upon the first beneficiary's death.

> **Example 3-4.** Donald died on June 30 at age 65, leaving as his only asset an IRA worth $100,000. His beneficiary designation left the IRA as follows: $10,000 to a charity and the balance of his estate in equal shares to his three nephews Hubert, Louis, and Dewlap, ages 40, 35, and 30, respectively. Donald's personal representative/administrator has until December 31 of the year following the year of his death (in Donald's case, 18 months) to make distribution of the $10,000 to the charity and separation of the balance of the IRA into shares for each of the three nephews. Each nephew will then be required to withdraw his share based on his own life expectancy; Dewlap will be able to take advantage of his younger age in scheduling the withdrawals. Under the prior proposed regulations, Donald's entire IRA would have to be distributed (and taxed) within five years, because the charity would "taint" the entire designation. The charity would have the shortest life expectancy (zero).

Q 3:79 Who can change a designated beneficiary?

Most plans and all IRAs permit the participant/owner to choose a beneficiary other than the default set out in the plan document or IRA custodial agreement itself.

If the participant/owner is married and the plan is an ERISA plan, however, his or her spouse will need to consent to the change in beneficiary designation for an ERISA by providing a notarized signature to a consent form on the beneficiary change form. [I.R.C. §§ 401(a)(11), 417(a)(2)] (See Q 3:58.) If the account is an IRA, ERISA does not apply, and no spousal consent is required.

Under the new final regulations, even after the participant/owner's death, the beneficiary taking distribution using his or her life expectancy is entitled to name a successor beneficiary to his or her interest.

It is not clear whether the agent under a durable power of attorney may change a retirement plan/IRA's beneficiary designation. In a recent case involving an agent who created a trust with the principal's funds, the California appellate court held that the agent lacked the power to do so, despite statutory authorization for the establishment of a trust, because there was no authorization in the document for the agent to change the principal's beneficiaries. [Schubert v. Reynolds, (Cal. App. Jan. 10, 2002)] By reverse implication, a power of attorney document *could* specifically authorize such changes. The plan itself, however, might not accept the change. Similarly, it is not clear whether a fiduciary could make changes on behalf of a ward.

Q 3:80 How can a beneficiary be changed?

Practically speaking, beneficiary changes are accomplished by filing a "Change of Beneficiary" form with the plan administrator or IRA custodian. The plan/custodian will usually insist on its own particular form, completed according to whatever formalities it has decided are important. The change will not be accomplished until it has been recorded by the administrator/custodian. This means that it is absolutely critical that the elder law attorney (or client) overseeing such a change ensure that the correct form is used, that delivery can be proven, and that the administrator/custodian actually recorded the change on its records. Unlike insurance companies, plan administrators and IRA custodians may not necessarily send back a stamped or receipted copy of the change. A call to check months later may reveal that the old beneificary is still on the books. While the plan might be liable if it had received the change but failed to track it and made distribution to the wrong person, that sort of problem is never welcome to the client's loved ones trying to pay bills after the client's death.

Plan administrators and IRA custodians are also subject to stringent privacy requirements. The attorney may wish to follow up or have staff follow up to be sure that important changes have been made. This will not be possible without the proper authorizations from the client. Here again, the plan administrator or IRA custodian may have his or her own special authorization or release form. The attorney should ask the client to procure this form or should try to obtain a copy from the plan's website.

Q 3:81 After the participant/owner's death, what is the consequence of having named the spouse as the designated beneficiary?

If the participant/owner's spouse is the designated beneficiary at the time the participant/owner dies, the spouse will usually have two choices. Either the benefits can be paid out over the life expectancy of the spouse [I.R.C. § 401(a)(9)(B)(iv)(II)], or the spouse may elect to receive all plan benefits and roll them over into a new qualified plan or IRA. [Treas. Reg. § 1.401(a)(9)-1] This has the advantage of beginning a new calculation of the RBD and minimum required distribution, as if the retirement account had always belonged to the spouse. (See Table 3-1, fourth row.) Assuming the spouse is younger than the deceased participant/owner, and that continued income tax deferral is the most important consideration, spousal rollover will almost always be the favored option.

Example 3-5. Harry and Martha (ages 74 and 72, respectively) are married, and Harry's qualified plan names Martha as sole beneficiary. Minimum distributions have been taken based on the uniform table. Upon Harry's death, Martha rolls over the remaining plan assets into her own IRA, naming the couple's only daughter Sandra (age 48) as sole beneficiary. Martha's new IRA also has minimum distribution rules (she is over the RBD), but those minimum distributions are calculated based on the IRS table that applies to owners (that is, based on the joint life expectancy of Martha and someone 10 years younger). Upon Martha's death, her daughter Sandra may now continue to take distributions recalculated each year based on her own life expectancy, this time using the table for beneficiaries. The result is the deferral of income tax on most of the qualified plan through Harry and Martha's entire life and well into the next generation.

See Table 3-1 for further explanation.

Q 3:82 Is there a time limit for a spouse to roll over an account into a new spousal rollover IRA?

No. A spouse can elect to roll over into her own spousal rollover IRA at any time.

Q 3:83 What option may a spouse have to further defer distributions?

The spouse may have another option besides making an immediate rollover or immediately taking distribution based on his/her life expectancy.

If the participant/owner dies before reaching his or her required beginning date (RBD), the spouse can elect not to roll over yet, but to let the account continue to be treated as the participant/owner's own account and defer distribution until April 1 of the year following the year in which the deceased participant/owner would have turned 70½. [Treas. Reg. § 1.401(A)(9)-1, C-3(b); I.R.C. § 401(a)(9)(B)(iv)]

At that point, the spouse will probably roll over the account, in order to take distribution using the IRS tables for participant/owners rather than the shorter life expectancy tables the IRS uses for beneficiaries.

If the spouse is older than the participant/owner and has other sources of income this can be very useful. Note that while the spouse is deferring the distributions, the plan may want to re-title the account in the name of the surviving spouse, but it will not be a rollover unless the spouse has specifically elected to roll over.

Q 3:84 What choices do unmarried couples have for selecting retirement plan beneficiaries?

Unmarried couples do not enjoy the benefits of spousal rollover or deferral. The unmarried partner is treated in the same way as any other unrelated beneficiary.

Q 3:85 What is the consequence of naming a nonspouse as the designated beneficiary?

Upon the death of the participant/owner, the nonspouse beneficiary will simply receive the remainder of the plan's assets. The beneficiary may elect, however, to withdraw the plan assets according to the minimum distribution rules (see Q 3:65), and thereby minimize the tax effect of each year's withdrawals. [I.R.C. § 401(a)(9)(B)(iii); Treas. Reg. § 1.401(a)(9)-3] The required minimum distribution amount for the beneficiary will be computed using the beneficiary's life expectancy according to the IRS table for beneficiaries, not owners. [See IRS Pub. 590]

See Table 3-1 for further explanation.

Q 3:86 What is the consequence of naming a trust as the designated beneficiary?

A trust can be named as beneficiary of a qualified plan or IRA, but there may be serious adverse consequences. Unless the trust meets special rules, the participant/owner will be said to have had no designated beneficiary, with all that this implies (See Qs 3:74 and 3:75.)

In order for the IRS to "look through" to the trust's beneficiaries, which are then treated as the designated beneficiaries, a trust must meet the following tests *by September 30 of the year following the participant/owner's death:*

1. The trust must be irrevocable (originally, or by its terms becoming irrevocable upon the death of the IRA owner);
2. The trust beneficiaries must all be individuals;
3. The beneficiaries must be identifiable from the trust instrument; and
4. The trust must be valid under state law.

[Treas. Reg. § 1.401(A)(9)-4]

Further, by October 31 of the year following the year of death, the trustee must either provide a final list of all beneficiaries as of September 30 of the year following the year of death, certified as correct and complete, or provide the custodian or plan administrator a copy of the trust instrument. [Treas. Reg. § 1.401(A)(9)-4, 4.6(b)]

Q 3:87 When can naming a trust as the beneficiary have the same effect as if the spouse were the designated beneficiary?

In order for a trust for the benefit of a spouse to have the same advantages as a spouse (potential for deferred distribution; opportunity to roll over and use the longer participant/owner schedule for distributions) upon the participant/owner's death, the spouse must be entitled to withdraw all of the trust assets.

However, for the trust to be used during the participant/owner's lifetime to defer distribution because the spouse is more than 10 years younger than the participant/owner, the spouse need not be entitled to withdraw. The trustee must simply certify the trust beneficiaries or provide the trust instrument to the plan administrator/IRA custodian, as described in Q 3:86.

Q 3:88 Why would a client want to name a trust as beneficiary of a qualified plan or IRA?

There are two reasons to mix trust planning and retirement beneficiary designations. The client who has established a revocable living trust as a means of avoiding probate, and perhaps controlling the use of funds for the benefit of children, may want to save the costs and possible conflicts inherent in establishing separate trusts for the retirement benefits and nonretirement assets. In other cases, a married client may want to use trust planning to attempt to maximize the credit shelter amount, especially where the retirement accounts are the major part of the estate.

Q 3:89 What happens if the participant/owner names multiple individual beneficiaries?

If there are multiple accounts, with different beneficiaries for each account, the calculation of minimum distributions from each account after the participant/owner's death will be based on the life expectancy of that account's beneficiary.

If there are multiple beneficiaries of a single plan or account, the calculation of minimum distributions after the participant/owner's death will be based on the shortest life expectancy (i.e., that of the oldest beneficiary) of the group.

However, Section 1.401(a)(9)-8 of the final regulations permits the single account with multiple beneficiaries to be divided into separate shares, one for each beneficiary, so that each beneficiary can use his or her own life expectancy. This is allowed provided the division is accomplished by the end of the year following the participant/owner's death.

See Table 3-1 for further explanation.

Q 3:90 What happens if a charity is named as beneficiary of an IRA?

The client who has charitable inclinations would be well advised to consider using qualified plan and IRA assets to satisfy those charitable intentions. Because the beneficiary of a retirement account is responsible for the income tax liability incurred as a result of distributions, and because charitable organizations are exempt from income taxation, more of the account will actually get to the charitable beneficiary than to a non-charitable beneficiary.

> **Example 3-6.** Client has a $100,000 IRA and $100,000 in cash. The client's son is in the 30 percent marginal income tax bracket. If the client leaves $100,000 in cash to charity and the IRA to his son, the son will have to pay $30,000 and get $70,000, whereas charity will get $100,000. Conversely, if the client leaves the $100,00 IRA to charity and $100,00 in cash to the son, each gets $100,000.
>
> Of course, the 30-year old son could have kept the $70,000 in the IRA and taken distributions over his lifetime, reaping the benefits of tax-deferred investing. Arguably, in a bull market with a capital gains tax rate higher than is now in effect, this might make up for the lost $30,000 and even surpass it. Financial planners can project all sorts of things. In most cases, however, the standard advice will be to give the IRA to charity and the cash to the son.

Q 3:91 Are there any problems with naming a charity as a beneficiary of an IRA?

Under the old rules, including a charity as one of several beneficiaries was a recipe for disaster. The old rules would have required payout based on the shortest life expectancy. While one might argue that charities' "lives" are eternal, the IRS has decided that charities have a zero life expectancy. One morsel of charitable intent in a multi-beneficiary designation would taint the entire account and require immediate payout.

All this has changed. Under the new rules, there are two options in this situation:

1. Since the designated beneficiary is not determined until September 30, the charity's share can be paid out before that date in any event and ignored for purposes of determining distributions, or
2. A retirement account naming a charity and one or more individual beneficiaries can be divided into separate accounts prior to the end of the year after the participant/owner's death, and the remaining share(s) (after payment of the charitable portion) can still take advantage of rules permitting the account to be withdrawn over each beneficiary's life expectancy. [Treas. Reg. § 1.401(a)(9)-8 A-3]

Q 3:92 May plan participants and owners withdraw more than the minimum required distribution?

It depends. The law does not prohibit a plan participant/account owner from withdrawing as much as he or she wants. With an IRA, once the owner has passed age 59$^1/_2$, he or she may take withdrawals of any size without penalty and, even after the RBD, may take amounts larger than the required minimum amounts.

However, some qualified plans, even though they are not defined benefit plans, take a paternalistic approach and prohibit participants from taking out more than a certain amount. They may also require employees to "annuitize" the amounts in certain plans, effectively fixing the payout. Many 403(b) plans take this approach. Particularly when Medicaid planning is involved, it is important to know what limitations may be imposed on the participant's ability to cash out (and transfer) account balances, and whether the participant will be required to take an annuity.

When advising a client about the benefits of continued deferral, make sure they determine whether they will still have the flexibility to take out more if needed.

Q 3:93 What happens when a plan participant/owner dies before the required beginning date?

All of the rules described up to this point have involved participant/owners who die after reaching the RBD. When the participant/owner dies before the RBD, different rules apply. With one exception for spouses (see Q 3:83), distribution must be made in one of two ways:

1. Within five years of the date of death, that is, by the last day of the calendar year in which the fifth anniversary of death occurs. [Treas. Reg. § 1.401(A)(9)-3; I.R.C. § 401(a)(9)(B)(ii)] This is the *only* option if there is no designated beneficiary. [Treas. Reg. § 1.401(A)(9)-3, 3.4(a)(2)]
2. Over the life expectancy of the designated beneficiary, provided distributions begin by December 31 of the year following the beneficiary's death. [Treas. Reg. § 1.401(A)(9)-3, 3.3]

Q 3:94 How are distribution rules different for ESOP plans?

An ESOP must provide that, if the participant/owner (and the participant/owner's spouse, if applicable) elects, distributions begin no later than one year after the end of the plan year:

1. In which the individual's employment terminates as a result of reaching retirement age, disability, or death; or
2. That is the fifth plan year following the plan year in which the participant/owner terminates employment for other reasons (unless the participant/owner has resumed employment with the same employer). [I.R.C. §§ 401(a)(9), 409(o)(1)(A), and 409(o)(1)(B)]

Roth IRAs

Q 3:95 What is a Roth IRA?

In 1997 Congress established a new kind of individual retirement account, called the Roth IRA. Beginning with the 1998 calendar year, most taxpayers are permitted to establish these specialized accounts.

Roth IRAs are really quite different from traditional IRA accounts. Annual Roth IRA contributions are not tax-deductible; they are funded with after-tax dollars. On the other hand, distributions from a traditional IRA (even though made according to distribution requirements) are ordinarily taxable income to the beneficiary, while qualified distributions from a Roth IRA are not included in income for tax purposes. In other words, although the Roth IRA provides no tax advantage at the time of establishment, it permits the entire accumulation of income and growth in the investment to avoid income taxation if it is withdrawn according to the Roth IRA rules.

Q 3:96 How does a Roth IRA differ from a traditional IRA?

The significant differences between a traditional IRA and a Roth IRA are:

1. Contributions to a Roth IRA are not deductible.
2. Distributions from a Roth IRA are not includible in gross income.
3. The required minimum distribution rules under Code Sections 408(a)(6) and 408(b)(3) do not apply to a Roth IRA during the lifetime of the owner.
4. Contributions to a Roth IRA can be made if the owner is older than $70^1/_2$.
5. Eligibility to contribute to a Roth IRA is subject to special modified income limits.

Q 3:97 Who may establish a Roth IRA?

After-tax contributions of up to $3,000 per year ($3,500 if age 50 or older) may be made to a Roth IRA by taxpayers with AGIs of less than $95,000 for a single person, or $150,000 for a married couple filing jointly. [I.R.C. §§ 408A(c)(3)(A), 408A(c)(3)(C)] For slightly higher income levels the maximum contribution is reduced, so that no contribution can be made for individuals with AGIs of $110,000 or married couples with AGIs of $160,000.

Example 3-7. Robert, a single man, has an AGI for 2003 of $106,000. He makes no other IRA contribution, and he wishes to establish a Roth IRA. His Roth IRA contribution is limited to $2,190. This is calculated by deducting the phase-out threshold

($95,000) from his AGI, dividing that figure by $15,000 and multiplying the maximum Roth IRA contribution ($3,000 in Robert's case, because he has made no IRA contribution) by the resulting fraction. The maximum contribution amount is then reduced by this figure.

There are no age limits for Roth IRA contributions. Individuals over age 70½, even though they may have begun to receive benefits from other retirement accounts, may contribute to a Roth IRA. [I.R.C. § 408A(c)(4)] Compensation income (generally, wages and salary) must be at least as much as the Roth IRA contribution, so those who are completely retired and have no earned income will be unable to contribute to a new Roth IRA.

Q 3:98 What special distribution rules apply to Roth IRAs?

Roth IRAs have no minimum distribution rules for the plan participant/owner, so the Roth IRA assets can continue to grow without being taxed. On the other hand, distributions are not included in the recipient's gross income for federal income tax purposes if they are qualified distributions (see Q 3:99). In other words, the growth in a Roth IRA is completely exempt from income taxation unlike the growth in a traditional IRA or other retirement account, which is a tax *deferral* mechanism.

Q 3:99 What makes a Roth IRA distribution qualified?

In order to avoid income taxation, a distribution from a Roth IRA must be made at least five years after the first contribution to the Roth IRA *and* be:

1. Made on or after the date the participant/owner reaches age 59½;
2. Made after the participant/owner's death;
3. Attributable to partial or total disability of the participant/owner; or
4. Used for the purchase of a first home and be less than $10,000.

[I.R.C. § 408A(d)(2)(A)]

All other distributions are nonqualified distributions. No qualified distributions can be made from a Roth IRA until 2003 because it would be impossible for anyone to meet the five-year holding period until that year.

Q 3:100 How is the five-year holding period determined?

The five-year holding period begins on the earlier of the first day of the individual's tax year for which the first IRA contribution or conversion was made to any IRA and ends on the last day of the individual's fifth consecutive tax year. [Treas. Reg. § 1.408A.6, Q&A-2] The five-year period is based on the year, not the day. Contributions made between January 1 and April 15 may be made for the current tax year or the previous tax year. The taxpayer must elect the year to which the contribution is to be attributed.

Once the five-year period begins, it begins for the initial contribution as well as all future regular contributions. [I.R.C. § 408A(d)(3)(B)]

Q 3:101 How is a nonqualified distribution from a Roth IRA treated?

Distributions are not qualified if they are taken either within five years of the first Roth IRA contribution or before the participant/owner reaches age 59½, dies, becomes disabled, or purchases a first home. Nonqualified distributions are subject to a 10 percent tax in addition to any income tax due on the proceeds.

Although the 10 percent tax is a significant disincentive to withdrawal, early withdrawals will benefit somewhat from favorable tax characterizations. Unqualified distributions are first characterized as returns of contributions (in other words, the original contribution amount—on which income tax has already been paid—is returned first). [Treas. Reg. § 1.408A-6, Q&A-4] Contrast this to the treatment of regular IRAs, in which the distributions from an account to which after-tax dollars have been contributed will be treated as proportionally taxable and tax-free.

Distributions are treated in the following order:

1. Contributions (nontaxable)
2. First conversion from a non-Roth IRA (taxable portion first)

3. Subsequent conversions from a non-Roth IRA (taxable portion first)
4. Earnings (taxable)

Example 3-8. Beth, age 55, has accumulated $11,200 in her Roth IRA. That balance includes a $2,000 initial contribution, made in 1999, plus earnings on that contribution totaling $200, plus $9,000 rolled over from a regular IRA. The regular IRA, in turn, was established over four years with annual $2,000 nondeductible contributions. If she withdraws money from her Roth IRA this year, the first $2,000 withdrawn will be tax-free (representing contributions for which no deduction was taken at the time). The next $1,000 withdrawn will be fully taxed, as it represents the taxable portion of her IRA rollover. Note, however, that at least a portion of the tax may have already been paid (in connection with the rollover itself). The taxable portion of the distribution will also be subject to the 10 percent tax on nonqualified distributions.

Q 3:102 Are Roth IRAs subject to the 10 percent penalty tax?

A nonqualified distribution is subject to the 10 percent penalty tax unless the distribution is made after age 59½ or meets one of the other exceptions to the penalty. [I.R.C. § 72(t)(2)(A)(I)] The 10 percent distribution penalty also applies to the distribution of nonqualified conversion amounts if the conversion amounts have not been held for five years, and no exceptions apply. The exceptions to the 10 percent premature distribution penalty that apply to traditional IRAs also apply to Roth IRAs (see Q 3:63).

Q 3:103 What minimum distribution rules apply to Roth IRAs?

Although no minimum distribution rules apply to the Roth IRA owner, all of the same rules governing regular IRAs apply to other Roth IRA beneficiaries. In other words, upon the death of the owner, comparable to a death before the required beginning date of an IRA owner, a nonspouse beneficiary will have to withdraw all funds either within five years of death or over the life expectancy of the beneficiary (see Q 3:93). A surviving spouse beneficiary will have the same options as with a regular IRA (see Q 3:81). Remember, however, that qualified distributions (including those made after the death of the Roth IRA owner) will not be included in the gross income of the recipient, so the importance of minimum distribution rules is to limit the continuing tax avoidance of plan growth.

Q 3:104 What is the required beginning date for Roth IRAs?

There is no RBD for a Roth IRA. In other words, the owner can change his or her beneficiary at any time, and thereby change the calculation method for the beneficiary's minimum distributions after the owner's death.

Q 3:105 What is a conversion or rollover Roth IRA?

Money accumulated in a regular IRA can be converted into a Roth IRA. [I.R.C. § 408A(d)(3)] Although the conversion will trigger income taxation of the accumulated IRA, money transferred into the Roth IRA will begin to grow tax-free. In 1998, Congress permitted special treatment for Roth IRA conversions: Taxation of the IRA benefits could be spread over a five-year period (four years plus the year of distribution). Conversions after 1998 will cause full income inclusion in the year of the conversion. [I.R.C. § 408A(d)(3)(F)]

Q 3:106 Should IRA funds be converted to Roth IRAs?

One option provided by the creation of Roth IRAs is to roll over existing IRA funds into a new Roth IRA. This permits future accumulations in the IRA to avoid income taxation (assuming again that Roth IRA distribution rules are followed), but causes the rolled-over assets to incur income taxation in the current year. As previously discussed, for 1998, Congress created a special one-year rule that made conversion more attractive: Taxation of rolled-over IRA benefits could be spread out over a five-year period despite the fact that the entire transaction was concluded in 1998. That special authority was not extended for future years, but it may (depending on the amount and nature of the IRA, the size of the client's estate, and the amount and effect of the income tax liability) still be beneficial in some cases to choose to roll over IRA assets into a Roth IRA.

Although individual circumstances will obviously vary, Roth IRAs should be considered for a number of different types of clients:

1. The client who has already retired but has a long life expectancy can avoid the minimum distribution rules at age $70^{1}/_{2}$ by converting to a Roth IRA.
2. The terminally ill client with an existing IRA naming no beneficiary could use a Roth IRA conversion to permit the designation of a new beneficiary and revision of the minimum distribution rules.
3. The client with insufficient non-IRA assets to fully fund a credit shelter trust might consider conversion to a Roth IRA and use of the Roth IRA to fully utilize the exemption equivalent. While this has the unfortunate effect of requiring earlier payment of income tax, it has the salutary effect of permitting continued tax deferral while still utilizing the exemption equivalent (and avoiding the complicated income in respect of a decedent (IRD) rules—see Q 3:118).

Q 3:107 When planning for retirement, should an individual establish a traditional IRA or a Roth IRA?

Assuming that a given individual is able to make a regular or Roth IRA contribution, the latter will be preferable in most cases. This is true because the Roth IRA permits tax avoidance, rather than simply tax deferral. Recall, however, that Roth IRA contributions are limited to $3,000 per year, so that the value of new (as opposed to rollover) contributions will be slight until several years of contributions have been made.

Nonqualified Plans

Q 3:108 What is a nonqualified plan?

Nonqualified deferred compensation plans are benefit arrangements whose distributions do not receive the favorable tax treatment accorded to qualified distribution plans; however, nonqualified deferred compensation plans are not subject to all of the restrictive funding, vesting, distribution, and reporting requirements that apply to qualified plans.

Q 3:109 Why would an employer and employee consider a nonqualified retirement plan?

Although nonqualified plans are rarely used, there are some limited circumstances in which employers may wish to establish nonqualified plans to provide retirement benefits even though contributions are not deductible to the employer or may be treated as income to the employee. Two of the most common nonqualified plans are the rabbi trust (see Q 3:110) and the secular trust (see Q 3:111).

There are several possible reasons for establishing a nonqualified plan despite the adverse tax consequences, including:

1. ERISA requires spousal consent for changes in qualified retirement plan beneficiaries; because they are not regulated by ERISA, nonqualified plans are not subject to the spousal consent rules.
2. Nonqualified plans can be set up for the benefit of independent contractors, who would not otherwise be covered by qualified retirement plans.
3. Because ERISA regulations are difficult to comply with, nonqualified plans may cost less to administer.
4. Nonqualified plans can be used to provide early retirement incentives to high-income, long-service employees.
5. Most frequently, nonqualified plans can be used to maintain the loyalty and security of key employees. Because such plans are not subject to the dollar limitations imposed on contributions to and benefits payable from qualified retirement plans, key employees participating in nonqualified plans can presumably enjoy large enough account balances to be assured of their own financial security despite future business setbacks, takeover attempts, or disenchantment with management's techniques.

Q 3:110 What is a rabbi trust?

A rabbi trust is usually established as an irrevocable trust, funded over a period of years by an employer, to provide payments to a highly compensated employee upon retirement or death. Rabbi trusts are not qualified retirement plans, and so reporting and vesting requirements of ERISA do not apply, although a simple notice filing may be required at the time of inception of the plan. Typically a rabbi trust is established as a grantor trust, so that the income inside the trust is taxed to the employer. Assets of the trust are reachable by the employer's creditors or in the event of insolvency or bankruptcy of the employer. Because the rabbi trust is not fully vested, it does not provide the same security for the key employee that a qualified retirement plan would provide. It serves primarily to protect the employee against a change of attitude or management that might make continued employment (and participation in retirement plans) untenable. If the employer becomes insolvent, the employee may have a contractual right to claim the deferred compensation but no trust corpus to ensure the availability of funds to satisfy the claim. Rabbi trusts tend to be established for key employees and other highly compensated individuals.

Q 3:111 What is a secular trust?

A secular trust is like a rabbi trust, but the employer's creditors cannot reach the secular trust's assets. Because the employee's interest is vested, secular trusts may actually be subject to ERISA protections and reporting requirements, and the employee will be taxed on the trusts assets as vesting occurs. [I.R.C. § 402(b)] The purpose of a secular trust is usually to provide some protection for the employee in the event of the employer's future insolvency.

Q 3:112 What is a supplemental executive retirement plan?

A supplemental executive retirement plan or top-hat plan is a nonqualified deferred compensation plan. It may be established in addition to a qualified retirement plan, to increase the retirement benefits available to the executive beyond the level permitted by qualified plans. They are frequently used when the executive earns well in excess of the maximum compensation ($160,000 in 1999) for which most retirement benefits may be calculated, or to permit the total plan to discriminate in favor of highly compensated individuals.

Tax Issues in Retirement Planning

Q 3:113 Are retirement benefits subject to estate taxation?

Yes. The value of retirement plan benefits is taxed without any credit for the unpaid income tax liability. [I.R.C. § 2039] The beneficiary of the retirement benefits can, however, receive an income deduction for the estate taxes paid with regard to such benefits. [I.R.C. § 691(c); Treas. Reg. § 1.691(c)-1]

Q 3:114 How does the income tax credit for estate taxes paid on retirement benefits actually work?

At the time estate taxes are paid, the estate computes the difference between (1) the estate tax liability if the retirement benefits were not included and (2) the actual estate tax liability. This difference reflects the marginal tax incurred because the retirement account was included in the estate. The proportionate share of this calculation is then used as a deduction on each distribution of retirement income from the plan. State estate taxes are not included in the computation, which means that the portion of retirement benefits reflecting payment of state estate taxes will also be subjected to income taxation. [Treas. Reg. § 1.691(c)-1(a)]

Q 3:115 How are retirement plan distributions taxed during the life of the plan participant/owner?

Retirement account distributions are ordinary income to the plan participant/owner. In some cases, when partial contributions have been made with after-tax dollars (nondeductible IRA contributions, for example), a portion of the postretirement distribution may actually be a return of those after-tax contributions. In such cases, the retirement distributions will be partially taxable income and partially nontaxable distributions.

In addition, early distributions from qualified plans, IRAs, and 403(b) plans will incur a penalty of 10 percent of the distributed amount. This penalty applies to most distributions made before age $59^1/_2$, although there are several exceptions to that general rule. Note that for this rule $59^1/_2$ means six months after the participant/owner's 59th birthday, not January 1 of the year in which the participant/owner turns $59^1/_2$.

Q 3:116 When are early distributions from qualified plans, IRAs, and 403(b)s not subject to the 10-percent penalty?

Early distributions will not be subject to the 10 percent penalty if they fall within one of 12 classes of exceptions—although not all exceptions apply in the same way to all types of plans. The exceptions include:

1. Distributions that are a "part of a series of substantially equal periodic payments" made at least annually for the life (or life expectancy) of the participant/owner or for the joint lives of the participant/owner and the designated beneficiary. [I.R.C. § 72(t)(2)(A)(iv)] Although this exception may contemplate an annuity purchase, the regulations themselves address calculation of the series of payments to approximate the same result as an annuity.
2. Distributions made to the beneficiary or his/her estate as a result of his or her death. [I.R.C. § 72(t)(2)(A)(ii)]
3. Distributions "attributable to" the total disability of the beneficiary. [I.R.C. § 72(m)(7)] Note that "attributable to" is not defined by the statute or regulations; it could theoretically be necessary to show that the beneficiary needed distributions to pay for necessities.
4. Distributions for medical expenses. This exception does not require that distributions actually pay for medical expenses, but permits reduction of the penalty to the extent that medical expenses exceed 7.5 percent of adjusted gross income. [I.R.C. § 72(t)(2)(B)] Note, however, that the distributions remain taxable and themselves increase the adjusted gross income from which the 7.5 percent limitation is figured.
5. Distributions from a qualified retirement plan or 403(b) plan (but not from an IRA) after the employee has reached age 55 and then experienced a "separation from service." [I.R.C. § 72(t)(3)(A)]
6. Distributions from a qualified retirement plan or 403(b) plan (but not an IRA) made pursuant to a qualified domestic relations order. [I.R.C. § 72(t)(2)(C)]
7. Some stock dividends distributed from ESOPs (but not from other types of plans). [I.R.C. § 72(t)(2)(A)(vi)]

8. Distributions from IRAs (only) used to pay health insurance premiums for an unemployed beneficiary. [I.R.C. § 72(t)(2)(D)]
9. Distributions from IRAs (only) to the extent that they do not exceed the participant/owner's "qualified higher education expenses." [I.R.C. § 72(t)(2)(E)]
10. Up to $10,000 withdrawn from IRAs (only) within 120 days to pay "qualified acquisition costs" of a first home for the participant/owner, a spouse, child, grandchild, or ancestor of the participant/owner. [I.R.C. § 72(t)(8)(A)]
11. Distributions resulting from an IRS levy. [Murillo v. Commissioner, 75 T.C. Memo 1564 (1998)]
12. Distributions made to correct excess contributions to 401(k) plans. [I.R.C. §§ 401(k)(8)(D), 401(g)(2)(C)]

Q 3:117 Who pays the income tax on retirement benefits after the death of the plan participant/owner?

Upon the death of the participant/owner, distributions to the designated beneficiary will be taxed to the recipient as ordinary income. The recipient may, however, have a deduction for estate taxes paid at the time of the participant/owner's death. In order to calculate this effect, the Code implements a concept known as income in respect of a decedent (IRD) (see Q 3:118). [I.R.C. § 691(c)]

Q 3:118 What is income in respect of a decedent?

Income in respect of a decedent (IRD) is any item of gross income that cannot be included in the decedent's final tax return, but to which the decedent had a right and would have received had he or she not died. [I.R.C. § 691(a)] IRD is the tax concept used to effect taxation of plan benefits after the death of the participant/owner. Unlike other assets passing from the decedent to beneficiaries (by will, trust, or beneficiary designation), retirement benefits do not receive a stepped-up basis, and the entire income is taxable to the recipient at the recipient's income tax rates.

Q 3:119 What happens when IRD is paid to a charitable beneficiary?

IRD is taxable to the recipient at the recipient's income tax rates. Although there is no exception for charitable distributions, charities are exempt from payment of income taxes. Consequently, IRD paid to a charitable organization escapes income taxation altogether. For this reason, clients with charitable intentions are often encouraged to name the charity as beneficiary of retirement accounts.

Q 3:120 What is the tax effect of retirement income paid to a trust?

Once again, IRD is taxed at the recipient's tax rates. Because income retained in a trust is taxed at the highest tax rate very quickly, the income tax effect of naming a trust as beneficiary of retirement accounts can be punitive. This is particularly a problem when the trust is intended to be a credit shelter trust. In order to avoid the punitive income tax rates, the trustee would have to make distributions of all retirement income to the trust beneficiary (e.g., the surviving spouse). This would, however, have the effect of moving the credit shelter trust's assets back into the surviving spouse's estate, and defeating the entire purpose of establishing the trust. The alternative is to incur the punitive income tax rates on retirement income distributed to (and held in) the trust.

A further complication arises because "income" for trust accounting purposes is *not* the same as "income" for income tax purposes. All of the IRD will be income for income tax purposes and taxed at ordinary income tax rates. However, under the most recent version of the Uniform Principal and Income Act, which is the law in many states, only 10 percent of the distribution will be considered income for trust purposes. If the trust requires that "all income" be paid to the spouse but principal only paid out for "emergencies," there may be no way to get the IRD out of the trust to escape trust income tax rates. By contrast, the Uniform Trust Code, which has been adopted in only a few states, treats any distribution from an IRA or qualified plan as income. In that situation, the "all income" trust will simply pass through the required minimum distributions to the trust's income beneficiary.

Q 3:121 What is assignment of IRD?

When retirement plan distributions are divided according to a fractional formula for calculating a credit shelter trust or a distribution to a nonspouse, no problems arise as a result of that division: Each recipient pays the tax on the share of IRD actually received.

When the formula for dividing assets is a pecuniary formula, problems can arise. If assets are distributed in kind in satisfaction of a pecuniary formula, the IRS view is that an exchange of assets has occurred, resulting in immediate realization of the income by the estate (or trust). It is not clear whether this principle applies to IRD in the same fashion, but in-kind distributions of IRD in satisfaction of a pecuniary bequest should probably be avoided.

Keep in mind that any pecuniary amount can be converted to a fraction. For example, $25,000 can be converted to a fraction, the numerator of which is $25,000 and the denominator of which is the total value of the account.

Q 3:122 When the beneficiary receives retirement plan benefits as a distribution, is the entire value of the plan benefits taxable in the year of receipt?

Under Code Section 402(d), lump-sum distributions may be eligible for special income tax treatment. The effect of this section may be to permit five-year forward averaging, ten-year forward averaging, or 20 percent capital gains tax methods for spreading the tax effect over a period of years. The rules governing these special-treatment provisions are both complex and regularly changed (both by Congress and the IRS), so a complete description of the effect of Section 402(d) is exceedingly difficult. Special income tax treatment may generally be available when:

1. Distributions are from qualified plans. (IRA, SEP-IRA, and 403(b) distributions do not qualify.)
2. A distribution is made because of the death of the participant/owner-employee, or after the employee reaches age 59½, or because of the employee's separation from service.
3. The participant/owner has actually reached age 59½. (Death benefits paid when the participant/owner died before age 59½ do not qualify.)

4. Special treatment has not previously been used for other distributions.
5. The entire plan balance was distributed in one taxable year.
6. The employee was a participant/owner in the plan for at least five years.
7. The employee has not previously rolled over benefits from the plan.
8. The recipient is an individual, estate, or trust.
9. The recipient elects the special treatment on the appropriate IRS form.

Q 3:123 How are retirement accounts treated when applying for public assistance with long-term care?

Although this subject is treated more fully in the chapter on Medicaid long-term care (see chapter 14), it is important to note that federal regulations mandate that an ineligible spouse's "funds held in individual retirement accounts (IRA), as described by the Code, or in work-related pension plans (including such plans for self-employed individuals, sometimes referred to as Keogh plans)" will not be treated as available to the institutionalized spouse when determining Medicaid eligibility. [20 C.F.R. § 416.1202(a)] Although the federal rule appears to be clear, some states still treat those benefits as available to the institutionalized spouse. On the other hand, some states treat even the institutionalized spouse's qualified plan benefits as unavailable for eligibility purposes.

Q 3:124 How are retirement accounts treated in bankruptcy?

Amounts held in qualified plans are not part of the bankruptcy estate if the participant declares bankruptcy under federal law, because of the ERISA prohibition on assignment. They are also not part of the bankruptcy estate under state law bankruptcy because of ERISA preeemption. However, states differ on whether or not IRAs are immune from creditors' reach in bankruptcy (and from garnishments).

Practice-Related Issues

Q 3:125 What are some of the practical problems that might arise in counseling clients about retirement planning?

Retirement planning is not always carefully considered by lawyers, accountants, financial planners, and clients. It may be necessary to ask probing questions about retirement accounts. Clients are often unaware that there are options to consider, much less that those options may have a significant effect on the beneficiaries of their retirement funds. The designation of beneficiaries on retirement accounts can also dramatically change the minimum distribution rules during the client's life. Few clients appreciate the importance of careful beneficiary designations during their lifetime. The kinds of problems that arise in retirement planning are illustrated in the following examples, one covering beneficiary grandchildren inheriting an estate with a large rollover IRA as half its assets, and another covering a client trying to determine the type of retirement program to establish for her small retail business.

> **Example 3-9.** Clint has a relatively modest estate of $800,000, but half of that is in a rollover IRA. He is single (his wife died several years ago) and 68 years old. His two children are both professionals and have accumulated substantial wealth. Clint is interested in using his estate to provide for the education of his four grandchildren, who range in age from 2 to 22.
>
> Clint could simply leave his entire estate to his grandchildren, and even name them as beneficiaries of his IRA; however, he is likely to have concerns about the ability of at least his younger grandchildren to handle the proceeds. In order to ensure that the money is used for educational purposes, and to distribute it to the grandchildren only after they are able to handle the proceeds, he will probably prefer to establish a trust for their benefit or even separate trusts for each grandchild's benefit.
>
> The IRA presents a special challenge (and two opportunities). Although Clint could name all four grandchildren as beneficiaries, this would cause two problems: an inability to control the use or accumulation of the proceeds (the same problem for the non-IRA benefits described previously) and the necessity of using the oldest grandchild's life expectancy for all distributions. During

Clint's life, the second problem would not be of much concern (even the youngest grandchild will be treated as if he were only 10 years younger than Clint); however, upon Clint's death, the oldest grandchild's life expectancy will dictate the withdrawal schedule unless the account is physically divided into separate accounts for each grandchild.

Given Clint's goals and the size of his IRA, he should probably consider establishing four separate trusts, one for each grandchild. His own will (or trust) could divide his assets into those separate trusts upon his death. Finally, he should divide his IRA and name each trust as beneficiary of one of the four divided IRA accounts.

Given his age and the size of his estate, Clint has only two estate tax concerns to consider: He might die before the credit shelter amount has risen to the level necessary to exempt his estate, or his estate might grow to a taxable size. If he is concerned about either of those possibilities, he might look into lifetime gifts to his grandchildren (or to Crummey trusts for their benefit), a charitable remainder trust (perhaps with a life insurance component for the benefit of his grandchildren) or a family limited partnership or limited liability company to reduce the value of his non-IRA assets.

Example 3-10. Olivia is the owner of a small retail business with four full-time employees and several part-time and seasonal employees. She is beginning to show a profit in her business, and wants to consider establishing some sort of retirement plan for herself and her employees. She seeks advice about which of her various choices she should adopt.

Establishing a retirement plan can be a daunting task. The complexity of plan documents and administration has generated a significant industry of plan salespersons and administrators. Olivia may want to avoid some of those complications by opting for a SIMPLE plan. The chief attractions of the SIMPLE plan are its simplicity and the ability to benefit some individuals disproportionately. The principal drawback is that annual contributions are limited to $8,000 per participant/owner (2003).

Olivia might prefer a SEP. Like SIMPLE plans, SEPs are easy to adopt; the employer need only sign the specimen plan form provided by a mutual fund company, brokerage house, or bank.

Contributions are made into individual accounts for each employee, and the continuing administration of those plans is undertaken by the mutual fund company, brokerage firm, or bank, with no continuing reporting requirements for the employer. The maximum contribution Olivia can make for any employee is 25 percent of their salary. Whatever contribution level she sets must be the same for all qualified employees. Qualified employees are those who are in at least their third year of service. She can make the same 25 percent contribution to her own account, but again she must contribute the same percentage to all qualified employees as she does to her own account. Incidentally, she need not fund her own SEP-IRA at all, if the purpose of the retirement plan is to benefit the employees more than her. Next year, if the business is not as profitable, she can make a smaller percentage contribution to the SEP-IRAs or no contribution at all.

Olivia might choose to establish a Keogh plan for herself and her employees. Permitted contributions will be higher, and the ability to disproportionately benefit herself and highly paid employees will be increased somewhat. The reporting requirements and administration of the plan will create significant additional work for Olivia, however.

Chapter 4

Non-Tax Aspects of Estate Planning: Wills, Trusts, and Other Transfers of Property Upon Death

A key aspect of any estate plan is determining the disposition of an individual's assets after death either by drafting a will and having the property go through the probate process or by relying on alternative means of transferring property through either a trust or joint tenancies. Increasingly, a client's assets are held in a manner that can avoid the probate process, simplify estate planning, or defeat creditors' claims. This chapter covers basic will and trust requirements and discusses the advantages and disadvantages of going through the probate process versus avoiding probate using joint tenancies.

Overview

Q 4:1 What non-tax considerations are important in preparing an estate plan?

In addition to minimization of estate and gift taxes (see chapter 3) and avoidance of probate proceedings, a number of other considerations require attention in preparing and reviewing estate plans for clients. Concern about the possibility of future incapacity, dealing with presently incapacitated spouses, children, and other beneficiaries, and the need to prepare for possible long-term care costs all play an important role in estate planning. The effect of gifts or bequests on the beneficiary should be considered, especially where the beneficiary is disabled or receiving government or other benefits.

Taxes, probate avoidance, and planning for future incapacity have become the three pillars of modern estate planning. Oddly, the original purpose of estate planning—to provide for the orderly transfer of wealth to succeeding generations and to impose such limits or restrictions as the property owner wishes to use to encourage or prevent certain behavior—is often nearly overlooked. To clients, the lawyer's fixation on taxes, probate avoidance, and incapacity may seem somewhat misplaced.

Wills

Who Should Make a Will

Q 4:2 Is it important to make a will?

Failure to make a will does not, of itself, result in increased taxes, lengthier probate proceedings, or higher costs or fees (other than the expense of procuring a bond for the personal representative). In fact, each state government has adopted a structure to decide who will inherit the estate of someone who dies without a will. The law of "intestate succession," which varies slightly from state to state, directs the disposition of property for the decedent who failed to sign a valid will. Usually, spouses inherit all or most of the estate, and if there is no surviving spouse, children (and the descendants of deceased children) usually inherit. In most states, in fact, the law of intestate succession will provide for distribution to the nearest relatives even though they may be as distant as fifth cousins (see chapter 7).

Although there may be some limitations in individual states, it is permissible to change the rules of distribution from the default adopted by the state government. While it may not be possible to disinherit spouses and children completely (the rules will vary by state), the bulk of one's estate can usually be left to one or more persons by executing a valid will.

In addition to changing the default rules of succession, a will can name an executor and a guardian for minor or disabled children. Once again, most states have a default mechanism for making a selection in the absence of a valid will. Finally, a will may provide for waiver of the requirement that the executor post a surety bond to guarantee the faithful performance of his or her fiduciary duties (although some states, such as California, may routinely require a bond in any event).

There are a number of common circumstances where wills are particularly important. For example, in gay, lesbian, and other non-traditional family arrangements (where intestate succession is unlikely to lead to the client's desired result), estate planning becomes more critical. Where second (or subsequent) marriages blend stepchildren (who may be adopted, or even adopted as adults) with "shared" children, it will often be necessary to vary the rules of intestate succession. In some states where intestate succession rules do not seem logical to most clients, a will can be important just to avoid unexpected surprises. For example, in Connecticut, where there are children and a surviving spouse, the surviving spouse is entitled to the first $100,000, but only 50 percent of the balance of the estate. Further, where the decedent is survived by a spouse and parents, but no children, the spouse and the parents divide the balance of the estate between them, 75 percent to 25 percent. It cannot be overstated that when it comes to wills, as with other matters, the elder law attorney must be familiar with his or her own state's peculiarities in order to give competent advice.

Q 4:3 Who should make a will?

Obviously, anyone who wishes a different distribution from that provided for by intestate succession rules will need to make a will. Similarly, if the selection of an executor other than the person who would otherwise have priority is important, a will is required. Parents of minor children should prepare a will to provide for guardians for their children (and any estate that may be left to them). In short, most people should prepare and sign a will, even though they are likely to adopt the default rules as to most questions. If nothing else, the preparation and signing of a will can reassure the signer that the issues have been addressed.

Parents of disabled children have additional reasons to make a will. If no plans are prepared, the disabled child may be the recipient of an inheritance that he or she is incapable of managing and that may interfere with the availability of crucial government benefits. (See chapter 17 for a discussion of special needs trusts.)

Finally, where a couple is concerned about preserving assets against the costs of long-term care for the survivor, whether to protect the survivor or to further other goals such as leaving an inheritance, one method may *only* be achieved through the use of a will: the testamentary special needs trust for a surviving spouse, which is neither counted as an asset to the survivor, nor as a prohibited transfer, should the survivor apply for Medicaid.

Q 4:4 Who should keep the original of a will, and where should it be kept?

Practices differ by location, individual preference of practitioners, and individual client circumstances. Some elder law attorneys prefer to maintain all original documents unless the client specifically requests the originals. Others prefer to release originals to the client unless there is some compelling reason to retain them. Still others make a decision whether to recommend that they retain originals based on the individual facts of each case and decline to adopt a standard approach. Finally, some practitioners advocate creating multiple original documents. Each of these choices has drawbacks.

Retaining originals. The attorney effectively becomes custodian of the documents and must maintain the safety of the documents, an adequate retrieval system, and regular contact with the client. While the last of these has salutary effects as well, it can impose a burden on the attorney to maintain contact whether or not the client cooperates or responds. This choice makes the least sense in a single-person practice. This choice makes the most sense where the firm is large enough to ensure continuity of custody, so that the client who dies 20 years after executing the will can be sure to find the will where it was left. In some states, case law will indicate that the presumption of revocation when a will cannot be found does not arise if the will was not in the client's custody but in custody of the lawyer, which is a legitimate reason to suggest to the client that the will be retained by the attorney.

Releasing originals. The attorney loses control over whether the original documents are safely stored and increases the likelihood they might be inadvertently lost or maliciously destroyed by aggrieved heirs or others, or even that a misplaced will is deemed to be revoked. By releasing the original, the attorney also foregoes an important opportunity for contact with not only the client but also the heirs and devisees.

Individual determination. While it may seem obvious that individual consideration is preferable, failure to adopt a default approach has its own risks. Survivors will not be able to determine easily whether the original is in the lawyer's possession, and unless the lawyer's file is clear (to both the lawyer and to survivors) it may be difficult to determine satisfactorily whether the original was ever in the client's possession. This may not only lead to unhappy devisees, but also to thwarting of clients' testamentary wishes when it is not clear whether a missing document was revoked by the client or misplaced by the attorney. It stands to reason that the client should always be given a copy of the will that clearly states where the original is located.

Multiple originals. Some practitioners argue in favor of multiple originals as a means of resolving the problems inherent in each of the other approaches; however, unless the client clearly understands the existence of an original in the attorney's possession, it is easy for the client's wishes to be thwarted. If the client methodically destroys all originals in his or her possession with the intent to revoke them, the remaining original in the attorney's control may still be admissible as the client's will. For some attorneys, the idea of multiple wills is anathema.

Q 4:5 Are there any other documents that should be prepared when making a will?

Although circumstances may differ and should control which documents will be provided in individual cases, most clients planning their estates will also want to consider making arrangements for their possible future incapacity. Durable powers of attorney are tremendously powerful (and dangerous) instruments, but with appropriate safeguards they will be a part of most clients' estate plans. (See chapter 11 on durable powers of attorney.) Health care directives (whether denominated as living wills, health care proxies, health care powers of attorney, or other names by local law and practice) will also be a part of most clients' estate plans. (See chapter 18 on advance directives and patients' rights to control medical treatment in advance.) In many cases, particularly where tax planning is involved, or disposition complicated, the client will need to execute a "pour-over" trust agreement (see Q 4:36), into which the estate will "pour" by way of a direction in the will itself.

Will Clauses and Distribution Provisions

Q 4:6 What provisions should be expected in most wills?

A will may be as simple as a single-sentence declaration of the disposition of property, coupled with the signature of the testator and two witnesses. More commonly, a will may include provisions nominating an executor (and guardian for minor children), waiving bond for the executor or other fiduciaries, naming alternate fiduciaries, directing the payment of the testator's legitimate bills, specifying which legatees are responsible for which taxes, and providing for distribution of the estate. While it is common to identify the testator's marital status and children (if any), it is not required; the practice grew out of a desire both to demonstrate that the testator was aware of the natural objects of his or her bounty and to defeat claims of putative illegitimate heirs. Similarly, it is not necessary for the will to leave a nominal amount to disinherited children or other relatives; the practice of leaving a dollar (or other token amount) is also an attempt to demonstrate that the testator did not omit the disinherited child out of forgetfulness. A will may also include administrative provisions, such as a description of powers of the executor, although failure to include such a list will not ordinarily limit the powers granted by general law or statutes.

Q 4:7 How should a will be drafted and arranged?

There are as many styles of will drafting as there are attorneys. The approach an attorney adopts may depend upon the relative weights given to the following concepts, which tend to be somewhat inconsistent with one another:

- *Clarity.* A will should be clearly understandable to the person signing it and those who must later interpret it. (This may result in the use of outline formatting, many subsections, and defined terms.)
- *Brevity.* A will should be brief enough for the testator to read it and for the attorney to minimize the drafting errors and proofreading lapses that are more likely to arise with additional length. (This will result in omission of "unnecessary" provisions and little formatting.)
- *Simplicity.* A will should be written with as little legalese, and as few legal references, as possible in order for the person signing it to understand it. (This may mean that legal shorthand is spelled out and technical precision blurred.)
- *Specificity.* A will should be detailed enough, even if that means it is long and complicated, to minimize the chances of a successful perversion of its provisions. (This will result in statements that captions are included for convenience only, that gender-specific pronouns are similarly without meaning, the repetition of statutory interpretations of established terms, and the use of lists.)
- *Completeness.* A will should address everything that will happen upon the testator's death. (This will result in directions as to payment of just debts and taxes, a recitation of fiduciary powers that would be available by law, etc.)
- *Non-redundancy.* A will should not replicate well established legal principles or statutory rules where the jurisdiction in which it will be probated seems fairly certain. (This can result

in problems if the testator moves to another state that has different provisions, or if the parties implementing the will are unfamiliar with the law.)

- *Explanatory.* A will is a person's "last word," and the person may wish to explain the reasons for the disposition. (This will result in descriptive references such as "my beloved wife" or statements that a child is omitted because "otherwise provided for" or "for reasons which he well knows.")
- *Only the necessary.* Including reasons for one's actions is an invitation to a will contest alleging mistakes of fact, undue influence, and the like, so a will might include only the basic facts without further explanation. (This could result in hurt feelings when the omitted child believes the omission is a punishment and may seem too cold and impersonal.)

Similarly, some attorneys prefer to start a will with the "good stuff," the dispositive provisions, and only later spell out provisions of administration, payment of taxes, and the like. Others begin with recitations of facts, so everyone reading the will knows who is who from the start. Others like an orderly disposition, following the likely sequence of events following death, (i.e., payment of debts and expenses, payment of taxes, and only then, distribution). There is no "correct" way to organize and present a will.

Q 4:8 Can a will refer to other documents?

An important distinction between states will be whether and to what extent the will can refer to other documents that are thereby "incorporated" into the body of the will. Many states follow the principle of "no incorporation by reference" unless there is specific statutory authorization. For example, in Connecticut, there is specific authorization to incorporate the terms of the Connecticut Fiduciary Powers Act, but not much else. By contrast, in Florida a testator may state that personal property shall be disposed of as provided in a separate memorandum, and this memorandum, even though not included in the will, is binding on the personal representative. This would not be possible in Connecticut.

It is not uncommon for a drafter to state that the residue passes to a separate trust, and that if the trust does not exist or has dissolved prior to the testator's death, then the provisions of the trust instrument are incorporated into the will and distribution will be made accordingly. In a state that follows the "no incorporation" doctrine, this might result in an intestacy. The anxious drafter must either ensure that the trust does exist, permit it to be established by pour-over upon death (see Q 4:36) and authorize the executor to determine the residuary beneficiaries of the trust and distribute directly to them rather than the trustee, or include in the will an abbreviated set of the trust provisions.

Q 4:9 What is the difference between "give," "devise," and "bequeath?"

Under English common law, real estate was properly the subject of a "devise," while personal property could be included in a "bequest." A "gift" could be of either personal or real property. Furthermore, property could sometimes be classified as mixed real and personal property, which makes such distinctions potentially even more confusing. As a consequence of these arbitrary and historical distinctions, it became common practice to "give, devise, and bequeath all my property, whether real, personal or mixed" (and, for the really thorough, "wheresoever situate"). The distinctions are largely irrelevant today, but they nonetheless live on in testamentary language.

Q 4:10 What is the difference between an "heir" and a "devisee?"

Although property can be devised or bequeathed (depending on its type), the recipient of property passing by will is usually referred to as a "devisee." A person who inherits by intestate succession, on the other hand, is usually identified as an "heir."

Q 4:11 What is an "in terrorem" clause?

As previously noted, many laypersons believe that will contests are much more common than they actually are. In order to prevent a will contest, or to encourage family harmony generally, many clients are interested in providing a penalty for any family member or devisee who seeks to challenge the validity or effect of the client's will. A clause that provides for the disinheritance of anyone contesting the will is usually referred to as an "in terrorem" clause.

Q 4:12 Is an "in terrorem" clause effective to prevent will contests?

Although "in terrorem" clauses are popular (and widely used), their effectiveness is limited by two factors. First, state laws (in some but not all states) disfavor such clauses, at least where there may have been a reasonable basis to challenge the validity of the will. Second, disinheritance may not be much of a deterrent to a family member who has already been substantially or completely disinherited by the terms of the will itself.

In most states a provision purporting to disinherit a will contestant partially or completely will be unenforceable if there is "probable cause" (or some other level of evidence) to support the challenge. The Uniform Probate Code (UPC), for example, provides that a will provision "purporting to penalize an interested person for contesting the will or instituting other proceedings relating to the estate" will be unenforceable "if probable cause exists for that action." [U.P.C. § 2-517] The UPC has been adopted in 18 states, and as of this writing, has been proposed for adoption in Massachusetts as well. The following states are UPC states: Alaska, Arizona, Colorado, Hawaii, Idaho, Maine, Michigan, Minnesota, Montana, Nebraska, New Jersey, New Mexico, North Dakota, Pennsylvania, South Carolina, South Dakota, Utah, and Wisconsin. Of course, that leaves 32 non-UPC states with their own idiosyncratic laws. The UPC and other uniform laws can be viewed online at *http://www.nccusl.org/*. In some states, a separate proceeding may be initiated to determine whether there is a sufficient basis for the challenge. The purpose of such a proceeding is not to determine the validity of the will but to determine whether the potential objector may be permitted to even bring a contest.

On a more practical level, a disinherited child cannot effectively be further penalized for challenging the document that purports to disinherit him or her. In order effectively to prevent will contests, a will should provide for at least a meaningful inheritance for any person who might be expected to initiate a contest and then provide for the loss of that inheritance if that person commences filing any such contest. For the *in terrorem* clause to be effective, the potential challenger must have something worthwhile to lose.

Q 4:13 What provisions should a will make for simultaneous death?

One problem that can arise is the possibility that a testator and his or her devisee might die in a common accident, or close together in time. If this happens, the cost of administering the will may increase because the first decedent's estate must be probated in order to confirm title in the second decedent, and the second decedent's estate must also be probated. Simultaneous death can also frustrate the first decedent's testamentary plans. He or she might wish property to pass to another person if the second decedent happens not to live long enough to enjoy the property, and if no provisions exist to deal with simultaneous death the second decedent's heirs or devisees will acquire the first decedent's property. Determining the order of death can be difficult, particularly in a common accident, and an inability to decide which decedent died first may make the disposition of either or both decedents' property problematic. Finally, although federal estate tax credits are provided for property passing through two estates in quick succession, simultaneous death can result in increased estate tax liability.

In order to protect against the problems inherent in simultaneous death, the will drafter can include a provision requiring the devisees to survive for a specific period of time before inheriting. This requirement might be short enough to prevent problems arising from a common accident (e.g., five, seven, or ten days, "or under such circumstances that it is impracticable to determine the order of our deaths"), or long enough to ensure that no property will pass to a decedent's estate (e.g., until the distribution of the property in probate or for a fixed period approximating the length of probate). For large estates, a provision requiring devisees to survive by 90 days (but no more) permits a gift to "skip" a generation without the imposition of a death tax in the devisee's estate and without imposition of a generation-skipping transfer tax (imposed when gifts of $1 million or more skip generations, under Code Section 2601) on the testator's estate.

Many state probate codes provide for a default provision upon simultaneous death. Under that approach, unless the decedent's will provides otherwise, every devisee must survive the decedent by at least a specified short period, frequently five days. That, for example, is the approach of the UPC, which provides for a 120-hour (five-day) default survivorship requirement in UPC Section 2-702. The portion of the UPC dealing with simultaneous death has also been promulgated as the Uniform Simultaneous Death Act and has been adopted in at least five non-UPC jurisdictions (District of Columbia, Kansas, Kentucky, Ohio, and Virginia). States that have not adopted this rule may provide that the property of each passes as if the devisee had predeceased the testator. [See, e.g., Connecticut General Statutes § 45a-440 ("When the title to property or the devolution thereof depends upon priority of death and there is no sufficient evidence that the persons have died otherwise than simultaneously, the property of each person shall be disposed of as if he had survived, except as provided otherwise in this section.")]

Q 4:14 What is the difference between "per capita" and "per stirpes" distribution?

When the recipient of property under a will (or by intestate succession) dies before the death of the person leaving the property, a determination must be made as to who will receive the property. If the will provides that the deceased devisee's share should lapse, or should be given instead to a substitute devisee, then those instructions will apply; however, where the will or the law of intestate succession direct that the deceased devisee's share should go to his or her descendants, a determination must be made about how to divide the property.

The two most common methods of dividing property among descendants are referred to by the shorthand designations per capita and per stirpes. Per stirpes is Latin for "by way of the stocks" or "stems," and per capita is Latin for "by way of the heads." The difference between the two methods is best illustrated with an example:

> **Example 4-1.** Assume that the testator is survived by a child and two grandchildren who are the children of a predeceased child of the testator. If the will provided for per stirpes distribution, the surviving child would take one half, and each of the grandchildren would take one quarter (i.e., divide the total by the number of "stems" or "stocks," and thus the grandchildren split the share that would have gone to their parent if he or she had survived). If, on the other hand, the will provided for per capita distribution,

then each of the surviving child and the two grandchildren would take one third (i.e., divide the total by the number of heads).

Q 4:15 What is meant by "right of representation"?

Some wills, rather than using the shorthand per capita or per stirpes designations, provide for distribution by "right of representation." In most states, this structure is defined to mean the same thing as per stirpes distribution.

The UPC, in its most recent version, provides otherwise. In UPC Section 2-709, the UPC defines "right of representation" to mean "per capita at each generation." This is a reversal of prior UPC law, which made per stirpes and right of representation synonymous. Rather than risk the possibility of unintentionally changing the client's desired distribution scheme, it is probably advisable either to use the more precise per capita per stirpes language or to spell out the succession provisions in the document itself.

Q 4:16 How is property distributed if there is no will, or if the will does not specify whether per capita or per stirpes distribution is to be used?

Most states also provide for a default choice to be applied in the absence of specific language. Thus, per stirpes distribution will be the distribution mechanism in most states unless the decedent has specifically provided otherwise. Once again, however, the most recent version of the UPC provides for the opposite default provision; UPC Section 2-706 establishes "representation" (synonymous with "per capita at each generation") as the methodology to be used unless the decedent has provided otherwise.

Q 4:17 What are specific, pecuniary, and residuary devises?

A will may provide for the distribution of a specific piece of property, an amount of money, or a portion (or the whole) of the rest of the estate. The first of these ("I hereby devise my 1969 Mustang Convertible to my daughter June") is a specific devise. The second ("I hereby give the sum of $10,000 to my son David") is a pecuniary devise, sometimes referred to as a "pecuniary legacy." After specific and pecuniary devises have been provided for, the will should (but does not always) direct distribution of the remaining property ("I hereby give, devise, and bequeath all the rest and residue of my estate in equal shares to my three children, *per stirpes*") in a residuary devise. The residue might be distributed to a single person or multiple persons, in equal shares or fractional shares.

Failure to include a residuary devise will not invalidate a will, but may result in a "partial intestacy." In that situation, the other provisions will be given effect, and the residue of the estate will pass as if there was no will.

Three problems can arise when making specific devises or bequests:

1. The will disposes of all the property item by item and then makes a residuary bequest—but there is nothing left for the residue. The result may be (a) unintended consequences when the testator actually meant to benefit the residuary beneficiary and (b) problems in getting the taxes and expenses paid when there is no residue left to pay them (requiring "abatement" or reduction of the other bequests).
2. The will makes specific dispositions that are very large and generate taxes which then consume the entire residue. This means the "tax clause" will require attention, as discussed in chapter 5.
3. The will disposes of specific property that cannot be found, or is no longer owned, when the testator dies (see Q 7:38).

Q 4:18 What is the difference between a "fractional share" and a "pecuniary" clause?

Trust or will language pertaining to the distribution of assets typically directs that the distribution be made in "pecuniary," or straight monetary, amounts, or in "fractional shares," by which each beneficiary is assigned a percentage of the assets. For instance, the testator or grantor may provide for "My daughter Annie, $20,000," or "My daughter Annie, thirty percent (30%) of the residuary estate."

Q 4:19 What is a power of appointment?

A power of appointment is a power granted to a person, usually a beneficiary of a trust, that allows that person to alter the arrangements in the document, either by directing the trustee to make distributions to other persons currently (an *inter vivos* power of appointment) or by directing the trustee to alter the disposition upon the beneficiary's death (a "testamentary" power of appointment).

The power may be granted in a very explicit way, by having a clause labeled "Power of Appointment" and saying "Beneficiary X shall have the power to appoint the trust property to such one or more persons as he or she may appoint by an instrument in writing delivered to the trustee during his or her lifetime, or by his or her will duly admitted to probate, in each case by making specific reference to this provision." Alternatively, the power may be included in the dispositive clause of the document, for example, "Upon the death of X, the trust property shall be distributed to such one or more persons as X may direct by specific reference to this provision in his or her last will and testament duly admitted to probate, or if and to the extent such direction is not given, to my issue." Different tax consequences will follow from limitations (or the lack thereof) on the power (see Q 5:40).

If a client is the beneficiary of a trust, it is important to review the trust document to determine (1) whether he or she has a power of appointment, (2) if so, the scope of the power and its tax consequences, and (3) how the power may be exercised in the event that exercise is desirable. Usually, if the client intends to exercise the power, the attorney will include a separate article for that purpose. The reference to the power of appointment will state something like, "Under article 4th of the will of my father, John Jones, dated June 6, 1963, I have the power to appoint property of the trust under article 3rd of such will to and among my issue. I exercise this power of appointment as follows. ..." Many courts have concluded that the "residuary clause" does not operate to exercise a power of appointment and that any clause in a will purporting to exercise a power of appointment must make that fact clear.

If the client is leaving property in trust, especially if the ultimate beneficiaries on a spouse's death are young children, it is often a good idea to give the surviving spouse a power to appoint the property among the children, in order to adjust for future inequities in needs. Particularly important is the power to appoint the property "in such manner, including in trust," to add flexibility that would permit distribution to a special needs trust for a disabled beneficiary rather than requiring the property to be distributed outright.

Q 4:20 What are "special" and "general" powers of appointment?

The distinction between a "special" (also known as "limited") power of appointment, and a "general" power of appointment, can have critical importance for tax purposes, as discussed in chapter 5.

A general power of appointment is defined for federal estate tax purposes as a power to appoint property to any one or more of the powerholder, his or her estate, his or her creditors, and the creditors of his or her estate. Any one of these powers will cause the power of appointment to be a general power for federal estate tax purposes. [Treas. Reg. § 20.2041-1(b)]

A special (or limited) power is any other power of appointment. Some practitioners feel it is sufficient to specify a class of beneficiaries that does not include the prohibited categories, such as "my children" or "my issue." Others, fearful of having the power treated as a general power, and pointing out that a child might be the powerholder's creditor, will specifically exclude the powerholder, his or her estate, his or her creditors, and the creditors of his or her estate.

A general power will also be found if the person alone, or in conjunction with any third party who is not "adverse," has the discretion to direct that property be paid to himself or herself without binding limitations on that discretion known as an "ascertainable standard." "Health, education, maintenance, and support" is one such standard. Another is "health, education, maintenance in reasonable comfort, and support." Although the distinction appears slight, the power to direct property to be paid to oneself for one's "welfare" or "comfort" (not maintenance in comfort, just comfort) or similar phrases, will be treated as holding a power of appointment. [Treas. Reg. § 20.2041-1(c)(2)]

A beneficiary will also be found to hold a general power of appointment if he or she has the power to "remove and replace" another party (usually, the trustee) who has the right to exercise the power in favor of the beneficiary. However, the IRS has conceded that provided the replacement is a truly "independent" person (obviously, other than the beneficiary), defined as one who is neither "related" nor "subordinate" to the removing party as those terms are defined in Code Section 672, the power will not be imputed to the beneficiary with the removal power. [Rev. Rul. 95-58, 1995-2 C.B. 191]

What is the significance of holding a general power of appointment? Property subject to a general power of appointment is included in the estate of the decedent powerholder for estate tax purposes; exercise of the power is a taxable gift by the powerholder for gift tax purposes. However, there are some exceptions: property subject to a general power of appointment that was "irrevocable" on or before October 22, 1942 (i.e., the power was included in a trust that was irrevocable by that date or a decedent's will executed before that date and who died before July 1, 1949), will *not* be taxed as part of the powerholder's estate unless the powerholder exercises the power. [Treas. Reg. § 20.2041-1(e)] It may be very important that the holder of a pre-1942 general power of appointment not exercise the power, and an attorney could commit malpractice by failing to draw this to the testator's attention when preparing a will that exercises the power.

Similar to a general power of appointment is a right to take out, withdraw, or appoint property of a trust to such a degree that one is treated as the owner of the trust. Conversely, the IRS has decided that this power will be considered *de minimis*, and disregarded, when the power extends to property that does not include the greater of 5 percent of the trust property or $5,000. This is known as a "5 & 5 power" and is commonly included in trusts to give the surviving spouse better access to trust funds than if he or she had to depend upon the judgment of the trustee. It is used as a limiting provision whenever a surviving spouse or beneficiary might otherwise be treated as the trust owner, such as a credit shelter trust. However, if the owner dies with such a power still exercisable, that 5 percent will still be included in his or her estate for tax purposes.

Q 4:21 Do adopted or illegitimate children inherit under a will?

The status of adopted children (and, for that matter, illegitimate children) has differed over the centuries and continues to differ on a state-by-state basis. Most states now provide that an adopted child will inherit the same as a child "of the blood." Issues can arise when (1) the state permits adult adoption, so that in some cases an adult child could "adopt" a same-sex partner in order for that partner to have inheritance rights through the child's family, (2) a client distrusts adopted children and only wants to include his or her own adopted children and not adopted grandchildren, or (3) the client is a beneficiary under another party's trust that predated the adoption statute. The solution will depend on state law, but "when in doubt, spell it out," at least when doing the drafting. Similar issues can arise with illegitimate children. Historically, the child born to a mother out of wedlock could inherit from the mother's family, but not the father's unless the father had "acknowledged" paternity. Most states now permit posthumous paternity determinations. A male testator may wish to specify his or her children to dispel any claim of acknowledgment as to future claimants of paternity. A grandparent may not wish property to pass to an illegitimate grandchild based on a belief that the child's other parent would have "bad blood." It is not for the attorney to judge the client's beliefs in this area, although it is good advice to present some scenarios and ask the client to consider what they would want in those situations and whether it would create family acrimony. This is also an area that must be reviewed by the practitioner on a state-by-state basis.

Requirements for a Valid Will

Q 4:22 Who is competent to make a will?

Any competent adult may sign a will. State law will define competence, but the classic formulation under the English common law has been adopted (with some variations) in every state. In order to be adjudged competent to sign a will, the signer (referred to in the law as the "testator") must:

1. Know the natural objects of his or her bounty (i.e., know of and understand the existence of spouse, children, and, where appropriate, grandchildren);
2. Be aware of the nature and extent of his or her estate (although detailed knowledge is not usually required); and
3. Be able to form a donative intent (this requirement is sometimes described as being able to understand the nature of the act of signing a will).

In most states a person will be assumed to have testamentary capacity even though he or she has a guardian. In some states, the appointment of a guardian of the person or estate may create a presumption of incapacity to sign a will, though that presumption may be overcome by an affirmative showing of capacity. A mere diagnosis of a disabling condition, even if the condition demonstrates a diminution of capacity, will not be a disqualifying factor. In other words, even a dementia patient may demonstrate the ability to execute a will, depending on the ability to meet the classic three-part test of testamentary capacity.

Q 4:23 What are the formal requirements for a will to be valid?

Unless the state recognizes oral or handwritten wills, a valid will must be signed by the testator as his or her will and witnessed by two people. "Signature" may include the mark of someone incapable of forming an entire signature.

It is important that the testator state, whether in writing or orally to the witnesses, that the document is the testator's will. Usually this is obvious, but not always. There must be an indication that the testator intended the document to act as a will, (i.e., to actually provide for the disposition of property at death), not only to indicate a wish for such a disposition. Some states permit the testator to direct another person to sign on his or her behalf.

The "two witness" requirement is not universal. Vermont still requires three witnesses [14 Vermont Stat. Ann. § 5], as many states did in past years. Louisiana's statute on "mystic" or "sealed" wills requires three witnesses to the testator's having placed the document in a sealed envelope. [Louisiana Civil Code Article 1584] The witnesses may be required actually to witness the testator's signature, but may be permitted by state law simply to witness the testator's acknowledgment that he or she signed the will. Typically, the witnesses must also sign in the testator's presence and in the presence of each other.

In general, any competent adult can act as a witness. However, only individuals who have no interest whatsoever under the will should act as witnesses. Where an "interested" individual (or his or her spouse) acts as a witness, most states provide that any will provision for the individual's benefit is void unless there are two other witnesses. Depending on the state, this may also apply to provisions appointing an executor, because an executor is entitled to a fee.

Notarization is not required, although some states propose a notarized "self-proving affidavit" that is included with, and follows at the end of, the will (see Q 4:26).

Special issues may arise when the testator is blind or visually impaired, illiterate, or does not speak the language in which the will is drafted. Whether and how the will can be validly executed will vary depending on state law.

Many practitioners require the testator and the witnesses to initial at the bottom of each page as a guard against forgery. Some also require dating of each page, although this can be problematic when someone makes a mistake. Some require that the paragraphs break across page endings, for the same reason. These are not usually legal requirements, but attorney preference, just as some attorneys may require that all parties use the same pen, or a certain type of pen. Similarly, as a guard against claims of "undue influence" some practitioners require that the testator execute out of the presence of any interested party, or insist that the witnesses know the testator personally. It may be useful, in the event of a future will contest, to follow the same ritual every time. On the other hand, it may be necessary to adjust any ritual to accommodate the client's own need and feelings.

Q 4:24 What are the jurisdictional requirements?

Probate proceedings are generally conducted primarily in the state in which the decedent was domiciled at his or her death. The domiciliary jurisdiction (i.e., the state in which the primary probate proceeding is commenced—usually the state of the decedent's death and/or the decedent's residence prior to death) has no authority to administer assets located in other states. Separate ancillary proceedings, referred to as ancillary probate, must be initiated in those states in which properties of the decedent are located. Ancillary administration is usually required only for real estate and certain tangible personal property, because the domiciliary probate state has the ability to direct management and distribution of personal property even if the depository (bank, brokerage house, stock issuer, etc.) is located in another state. This process has been streamlined in states that have adopted the UPC. It is the responsibility of the personal representative to determine not only the location of all the decedent's property, but the applicable state laws if the property is situated out of state.

Q 4:25 Should any special arrangements be made if the client owns property in a foreign country?

International estate planning is not just for rich playboys. Even an elder law attorney whose client base is mostly middle class or those of yet more modest means can expect in his or her lifetime to come across the client with property, usually real estate, in a foreign country. While international estate planning can be a complex topic, involving tax treaties and special U.S. tax rules for nonresident aliens, there are few general points to keep in mind when a client owns real estate in a foreign country:

1. It may be desirable to encourage the client to execute two wills, one disposing of the U.S. estate, and the other, disposing exclusively of the foreign property, prepared by a local attorney in the foreign jurisdiction. In this situation, typically the "exordium" or introductory portion of the will should state that it does not dispose of the property in the other jurisdiction. At the very least, if the clients are elderly, encourage them to develop a legal contact in the foreign jurisdiction with whom there is some ability to communicate in English or another language in which you have fluency. E-mail is also helpful if there are time zone issues that make telephone contact a problem.
2. If executing only one will, determine whether the other country is a signatory to the Convention of October 26, 1973, Providing a Uniform Law on the Form of an International Will, and if so, follow its requirements. In general, the execution requirements are very similar to the most common U.S. procedures; however, the statute requires that each page of the will be numbered and signed by the testator; that an "authorized person" (typically, an attorney licensed to practice in the jurisdiction or a U.S. consul) also sign the will; and that in order to provide "conclusive evidence" of due execution, a certificate must be executed by the authorized person, at the time of execution, attesting to the circumstances of the execution. A will that does not qualify in all respects may also be admitted to probate, but for a signatory nation a will that

follows the Convention *must* be admitted. See Table 4-1 for a list of countries that have signed the convention.

3. Be wary of unforeseen tax consequences in other jurisdictions. Many have an "inheritance tax" structure and will require proof of payment before allowing transfer of title.
4. Consider how the two documents relate when it comes to a source of funds for payment of taxes and expenses. For example, if probate in Germany of a German will is required, and the U.S. will requires the U.S. residue to pay "all" expenses of administration and "all" taxes, do these also cover the German property passing under the German will? Or are there two estates, each with its own residue, each responsible for the expenses and taxes relating to the property in the jurisdiction? This is particularly problematic with large estates.
5. Avoid trusts. Most jurisdictions do not recognize or understand trusts, although they may have arrangements that mimic the benefits of trusts (the usufruct interest in France, for example). When it comes to real estate, keep it simple, name the surviving spouse if at all possible, and see if you can have the client dispose of the property *inter vivos* to children (if allowed—it is not always possible to divest property during lifetime) to avoid the probate issue entirely.

Table 4-1. Countries that Accept International Wills According to the Convention of October 26, 1973, Providing a Uniform Law on the Form of an International Will

States that Signed the Convention:	*States that have Acceded to the Convention*
Iran	Niger
Sierra Leone	Portugal
United States of America	Canada
Laos	Libyan Arab Jamahiriya
Holy See	Yugoslavia

Table 4-1. Countries that Accept International Wills According to the Convention of October 26, 1973, Providing a Uniform Law on the Form of an International Will (*cont'd*)

States that Signed the Convention:	*States that have Acceded to the Convention*
Belgium	Cyprus
Ecuador	Italy
United Kingdom	Slovenia
France	Bosnia-Herzegovina
Russian Federation	
Czechoslovakia	

Source: Official Web Site of the International Institute for the Unification of Private Law (UNIDROIT), *http://www.unidroit.org*.

Table 4-2. Estate and Gift Tax Treaties with Other Nations

Estate tax treaties exist with the following countries:

Australia*	France*	Italy	Sweden*
Austria	Germany*	Japan	Switzerland
Denmark*	Greece	Netherlands	United Kingdom*
Finland	Ireland	Norway	

* Indicates that a gift tax treaty also exists.

Q 4:26 What is a "self-proving affidavit"?

Most states permit the use of a special provision that avoids the necessity of producing witnesses at the time the will is admitted to probate. Typically, the provisions require testimony that the testator and witnesses all sign in one another's presence and the presence of a notary public. Although most states will, by principles of comity, permit probate of a will validly executed in another state according to that state's laws, even when the procedures would not have been valid in the state of probate, it is important that the self-proving affidavit follow the formalities required in the state in which the will is to be probated.

Even if such an affidavit is traditionally executed at the same time as the will and is appended to the will, it does not necessarily need to be executed at the same time as the will. That is, while one may typically want two witnesses as well as the attorney or notary (who will take the oath of the witnesses signing the affidavit), if that is not possible, the two witnesses may later execute the affidavit before a notary who was not present when the will was actually signed.

Personal Representative

Q 4:27 Who can serve as the personal representative of the estate?

Although a personal representative (in many states, the "executor") may be nominated by the decedent's will, the actual appointment of the fiduciary is a court process. Most state statutes permit the court to bypass the nominee in the will for good cause—if, for example, the nominated personal representative has failed to act and the estate has suffered from that failure, or if the nominee has an irreconcilable conflict. Usually there will be a priority list of candidates for the position of personal representative, lead by the decedent's nominee and followed by spouse, children, parents, other heirs, creditors, state agencies, or other interested persons.

A few states require that the executor or administrator (the personal representative appointed when there is no will or no appointment of an executor who is able to serve) be a resident of the state in which the proceedings are initiated. Some states treat executors (of wills) and administrators (of intestate estates) differently, permitting the former to be nonresidents but not the latter. Those states permitting nonresident fiduciaries sometimes require the fiduciary to designate a resident of the state (or the probate judge) as agent for acceptance of service of process. States requiring executors or administrators to be residents include Alabama (as to administrators), Florida (except for certain relatives), Indiana (unless serving jointly with a resident), Kentucky (except for relatives), Nevada (as to administrators), New York (unless serving jointly with a resident),

Ohio (as to administrators), Rhode Island (as to administrators), and Wyoming (as to administrators, and unless serving jointly with a resident).

In most states, a personal representative (or any other fiduciary) can be only (1) an individual, or (2) a corporation "having trust powers" under the state's banking laws (usually a trust company, although there may be other corporations specially granted trust powers). This means that a law firm cannot be a personal representative, although an individual lawyer may be. State law may also permit a charitable corporation to serve as trustee of a trust in which it has a beneficial interest, but not as an executor. State law may also provide that if a bank named as personal representative is "taken over" or otherwise transfers its trust business to a different bank, the new bank will be treated as if named in the first instance.

One or more persons can serve as personal representative. When there are two or more representatives, state law will determine whether each may act independently, or whether consent of all (or a majority) is required. For practical purposes, the court and any brokerage or institution is likely to require that all representatives sign whenever signature on behalf of the estate is required.

Q 4:28 What are the powers of the personal representative?

In order to handle probate affairs with the utmost efficiency, personal representatives are given broad powers in most states with regard to dealings with third persons. The powers conferred in most wills, or bestowed by state law, correspond with the powers given in general durable powers of attorney and trust documents. The personal representative is restricted, by statute and common law, only by his or her fiduciary duties to the estate and to the beneficiaries of the estate.

Some states still require all probate proceedings to be closely supervised by the courts. In such states, the personal representative's powers may be limited to only those specifically conveyed by the order appointing him or her. Sale of property, distribution of assets to heirs or devisees, payment of creditors claims and costs of administration, and even valuation of estate assets may all require prior court approval, often after notice and an opportunity to object afforded to all interested persons, unless such approval is waived in the will itself.

In more modern probate systems, the powers of a personal representative may include the ability to lease or sell realty; to enter into, honor, or refuse contracts; to convert nonliquid into liquid assets; to take possession of property; to make repairs; to vote securities; to borrow money; to sue on behalf of the estate and to defend the estate against claims; and to enter into settlements, all without court approval.

Q 4:29 What are the duties of the personal representative?

The personal representative will owe a duty not only to the estate's beneficiaries, but also to the estate's creditors. These duties also mean liabilities. The estate's creditors will include the IRS, and the representative who distributes the estate assets before receiving approval from the taxing authorities will be personally liable for the taxes due. Similarly, the representative who distributes estate assets before the creditors have been paid, or before the time has passed during which creditors have the right to make a claim, will be liable to the creditors, although the creditors may also have the right to pursue the beneficiaries. Service as personal representative is not without risks, and clients should understand that when appointing a favorite child who may or may not approach the job with the requisite level of conscientiousness.

Types of Wills

Q 4:30 Is an oral will valid?

An oral will, also known as a "nuncupative" will, may be valid in about half of the states. Those states that recognize nuncupative wills typically require that the declarant be a soldier or sailor in actual military service, and limit the effect of the nuncupative will to personal property. States recognizing some form of nuncupative will include:

Alaska	Mariners at sea or soldiers in military service may dispose of personal property within six months of death, if the declaration is reduced to writing within 30 days.

District of Columbia	Mariners at sea or soldiers in actual military service may dispose of personal property by making a declaration before two witnesses during last illness and reduced to writing within 10 days.
Georgia	Anyone may make nuncupative will during last sickness if he or she asks someone to witness the will. It must be reduced to writing within 30 days and proved by two witnesses; probate must be commenced within six months.
Indiana	Valid up to $1,000 of personal property, or up to $10,000 for soldiers in active service in time of war.
Kansas	Valid for personal property if made during last illness, witnessed by two persons and reduced to writing within 30 days.
Louisiana	Requires a public act before a notary public in the presence of three witnesses (or five witnesses if the declarant does not reside in the place of the declaration).
Massachusetts	Soldier in actual military service or mariner at sea may use to dispose of personal property.
Mississippi	Must be during last illness. If bequest exceeds $100, must be proved by two witnesses; death must be within six months of declaration.
Missouri	Valid if made in imminent peril of death and death actually results; two witnesses required; must be reduced to writing within 30 days and probate begun within six months if property exceeds $500.
Nevada	Valid up to $1,000 of personal property if proved by two witnesses and made during last illness.
New Hampshire	Valid up to $100; for larger amounts, requires three witnesses, last illness, and a declaration in declarant's "usual dwelling" (unless taken sick elsewhere and unable to reach home).

New York	Must be made within hearing of two witnesses.
North Carolina	Valid for personal property if made before two witnesses during last illness or imminent peril, and declarant does not survive.
Ohio	Valid as to personal property if made during last sickness, witnessed by two disinterested persons, and reduced to writing within 10 days. Must be submitted to probate within six months.
Oklahoma	Valid where estate does not exceed $1,000, declarant was in actual military service and in contemplation, fear, or peril of death. Two witnesses required.
Rhode Island	Mariner at sea or soldier in actual military service.
South Dakota	Valid up to $1,000 for soldier in actual military service in the field or shipboard, if in contemplation, fear, or peril of death, or in expectation of death from injuries sustained the same day. Must be reduced to writing within 30 days and filed for probate no sooner than 14 days after death and no later than six months after death.
Tennessee	Up to $1,000 of personal property, or up to $10,000 for soldiers in active military service. Requires two disinterested witnesses, must be reduced to writing within 30 days and filed for probate within six months. A nuncupative will may not change or revoke existing written will.
Texas	Personal property only. Must be made at time of last sickness.
Vermont	Up to $200 (except that soldier or sailor may be able to dispose of wages as possible under common law). One witness must reduce the declaration to writing within six days, and filed for probate within six months.
Virginia	Soldier in actual service or mariner or seaman at sea may dispose of personal property.

Washington	Wages or personal property of soldier, sailor, or merchant marine up to $1,000 in value. Must be made in last sickness before two witnesses and reduced to writing; must be filed for probate within six months.
West Virginia	Soldiers in actual military service or seamen at sea may use to dispose of personal property.

Q 4:31 Is a videotaped or audiotaped will valid?

Videotaped or audiotaped wills have not been accepted as valid on their own in any state thus far. Arguments against them include the fact that they can be easily doctored (although the same argument applies to written wills). Witnessing and notary requirements are not easily transferred to a taped vehicle, and they would be cumbersome to manage mechanically in the context of a court proceeding.

Some planners videotape the execution of a written will to demonstrate the competency of the testator at the time of signing. This can be an effective, though not dispositive, way to capture a "lucid moment" of a demented person, for instance. It has been argued that the attorney should videotape *all* will executions, because taping just the questionable ones might just confirm their questionability. If videotaping (whether of an occasional will or all wills) is contemplated, the process should be undertaken, or at least overseen, by a competent professional; poor lighting, meandering conversations, and bad camera angles can combine to make a competent testator look less competent.

Q 4:32 Is a handwritten will valid?

Many states accept what is called a "holographic will," or a will that is written (or, in most states, the "material provisions" are written) *entirely* in the hand of the testator and signed by the testator himself or herself. They do not have to be witnessed or notarized. A challenge to the will may require additional evidence, such as comparison of the handwriting by an expert. Holographic wills may be valid if completed in Alaska, Arizona, Arkansas, California, Colorado, Idaho, Indiana (up to $1,000), Kentucky, Louisiana, Maine, Maryland, Michigan, Mississippi, Montana, Nebraska, Nevada (up to $1,000), New Jersey, New York (during war or while at sea), North Carolina, North Dakota, Oklahoma, Pennsylvania (which does not require witnesses in any event), South Dakota, Tennessee, Texas, Utah, Virginia, West Virginia, or Wyoming.

Even if a state does not itself accept "holographic wills," the state may well accept a holographic will that was executed in a state in which such wills are valid, by principles of comity.

Q 4:33 What is a statutory will, and is it valid?

A statutory will is a preprinted, fill-in-the-blanks, check-the-boxes form. Use of a statutory will is authorized by four states: California, Maine, Michigan, and Wisconsin. A statutory will has the theoretical advantage that it is cheap, simple, and reliable. Practically speaking however, it may not be useful in any but the simplest situation because the forms have limited choices. Furthermore, if the testator makes any attempt to make changes, the form may be negated in its entirety. For reasons such as these, no state has adopted a statutory will since the mid-1980s.

Q 4:34 What is a codicil?

A codicil is an amendment to a will, changing only some of the provisions of the original document. A codicil must usually be executed with all of the formalities of a will. Because the codicil ratifies all of the provisions of the will itself, as modified, the attorney who prepares a codicil may be held responsible for malpractice committed by the drafter of the original will. With the advent of word processing and document assembly techniques, codicils are used less frequently.

Q 4:35 Are there other ways to change a will besides a codicil?

Some clients believe they can change the will by crossing out one provision and inserting something different. This may either be ineffective or at worst may constitute a revocation of the entire will. It is important to advise clients that to change a will, they should execute a codicil or a new will. In dire emergency, where intestacy is preferable to the will and there is no time to make a change, the testator could revoke the will. Methods of revocation are usually specified by statute but typically include burning, tearing in half, or "canceling," but only if actually done by the testator's own hand. A will may also be revoked when specified events occur such as divorce or remarriage; this too varies state to state. If an original will may not be found, in many states a presumption arises that it has been revoked; this is sometimes a reason to store the will with an attorney (see Q 4:4).

It may be possible to "restore " the provisions of a prior will that has been superceded, merely by revoking the intervening will. This is called the "doctrine of relative revocation" and does not apply in every state. The principle behind this doctrine is that any will is preferable to intestacy.

Q 4:36 What is a pour-over will?

As discussed in Qs 4:62 and 4:63, many clients may wish to fund a "living trust" during their lifetimes in hopes of avoiding the expenses and delay of the probate process, which vary considerably from state to state. However, many kinds of assets are cumbersome or impossible to transfer into a trust during one's lifetime, for instance, jewelry, clothing, furniture, artwork, and other property that does not have title requirements. Grantors are notoriously lax about getting all their titled assets into the trust as well. Even if a client does not intend to fund a living trust, the client may prefer that the bulk of the estate plan's dispositive provisions pass through a trust rather than a will, in order to avoid the publicity and accounting requirements of probate.

A pour-over will contains language directing the residuary of the decedent's estate to the trustees of a separate trust instrument, thereby guaranteeing that all the decedent's assets will end up in the control of the trust. Items that have not already been transferred to the trust during the decedent's lifetime must still pass through probate, but once transferred to the trust by the personal representative they will be subject to the terms of the trust. In addition, the testator can accomplish things in the pour-over will that cannot be accomplished in a living trust, such as appointing guardians for minor children and appointing an executor to handle any probate assets. Living trusts should ordinarily be accompanied by a pour-over will, although in some circumstances the grantor's will might simply leave any probate assets, particularly tangible items, directly to beneficiaries. Where the client has not funded a living trust, the pour-over will typically leaves tangible assets directly to beneficiaries, may specifically devise real estate to a surviving spouse, and then "pours" the residue only to the separate trust.

In some states it is important that the trust was executed prior to the will in order that the will's direction to pour over to the trust can be valid. It is common to recite that the trust was executed the same day as, but prior to, the execution of the will. This issue may have been resolved by a statute providing that the bequest is valid so long as the trust is executed the same day as the will. Another issue is whether an "unfunded" trust is valid at all. This, too, may be resolved by statute, but some trusts, to be safe, recite that $10 has been given to the trustee in order to make sure the trust actually exists. Finally, there was concern whether the trust was really "in existence" and thus a genuine beneficiary that could be named, if the grantor, trustee, and lifetime beneficiary were one and the same (a declaration of trust). This too has been resolved in most cases by statute.

Probate

Q 4:37 What is probate?

Probate is the system of court proceedings by which the estate of a decedent is processed and distributed. It usually includes the admission of the will, or, if there is no will, the designation of heirs according to the principles of intestate succession. A personal representative is appointed by the court and is thereby given the authority, pursuant to the terms of the will, to collect and inventory the assets of the decedent, liquidate them if necessary, pay all the debts, taxes, and administrative expenses of the estate, and distribute the net assets to the beneficiaries. (See chapter 7 for a discussion of probate.)

Many states have streamlined their probate procedures to accommodate the administration of small estates or eliminate it altogether, and, if there are no challenges raised, to expedite the process for larger estates. In most states and for most estates, probate is not a particularly burdensome or expensive process. Once the will is admitted and the personal representative appointed, notice to creditors and beneficiaries is required and a period of time designated during which creditors and others can make claims against the estate. Typically this "window" runs for four to six months, which is not an unreasonable delay considering that during the same period of time the personal representative will usually be busy handling estate sales, real estate agents, and tax returns.

In some states, probate is a process that has its own procedures but uses the same court of general jurisdiction used for all routine civil cases. In other states, probate takes place in courts specially designed for such matters. The smaller the court's geographical jurisdiction, and the more specialized the court, the more likely that the process will be simple and quick. Unfortunately, the converse is also true.

Q 4:38 Is probate always required if a decedent owns assets?

No. Most states have a simple procedure for disposing of a person's assets, even though held in sole name, without involving the full probate process. The procedure usually involves filing an "affidavit" that lists assets briefly and states that funeral expenses and creditors have been paid (or asking that they be paid from the funds remaining). The affidavit then either states that there is nothing left, or in some states, requests approval to distribute what remains to the persons named in the will, or who take by intestate succession. This affidavit is filed in the probate court in lieu of administration, and it is the probate court that issues the order for any distribution of funds to pay claims or to distribute to heirs. One way to put this is to say that so long as a decedent owns one dime, there will be some probate involvement, a kind of "mini-probate," but that it will be very simple.

While the 50 states each have additional requirements for making this "mini-probate" available—a common one being that there is no real property held in the decedent's sole name—Table 4-3 provides a quick look at the maximum value permitted for the "affidavit in lieu" process for small estates.

The table is current through March 1, 2002, and attorneys should be aware that states vary on the use of an affidavit or other abbreviated process in lieu of full probate, and those variations may not be adequately captured in this table.

Table 4-3. When is Probate Required?

State	*Probate Required if Gross Probate Exceeds:*	*Probate Required, Without Regard to Column 2, If:*	*Probate Not Required, Without Regard to Column 2 or 3, If:*
Alabama	$3,000		
Alaska	$15,000		
Arizona	$50,000	Estate includes over $5,000 in compensation	
Arkansas	$50,000		
California	$20,000 real property, $100,000 personalty	$20,000 or more net of liens, encumbrances, expenses	Less than $20,000 net of liens, encumbrances, expenses
Colorado	$27,000		
Connecticut	$20,000	Any real estate	
Delaware	$20,000		
District of Columbia	$40,000		
Florida	$25,000 for Summary Administration (but Family Administration may be available if under $60,000)		No administration if nonexempt personal property does not exceed funeral expenses and expenses of last illness; Summary if decedent

Table 4-3. When is Probate Required? (*cont'd*)

State	*Probate Required if Gross Probate Exceeds:*	*Probate Required, Without Regard to Column 2, If:*	*Probate Not Required, Without Regard to Column 2 or 3, If:*
			dead for two years
Georgia	No provision	Always unless (1) intestate and (2) mutual distribution agreed	
Hawaii	$100,000		
Idaho	$25,000		
Illinois	$50,000		
Indiana	$25,000		
Iowa	$10,000, $15,000 or $50,000 depending on who requests		
Kansas	$10,000		
Kentucky	No provision	Always, unless mutual distribution	
Louisiana	$50,000		
Maine	$10,000		
Maryland	$30,000 net of secured debts		Personal representative must post bond if $10,000 or more after expenses

Table 4-3. When is Probate Required? (*cont'd*)

State	*Probate Required if Gross Probate Exceeds:*	*Probate Required, Without Regard to Column 2, If:*	*Probate Not Required, Without Regard to Column 2 or 3, If:*
Massachusetts	Car + $15,000		
Michigan		$15,000 net	
Minnesota	$20,000		
Mississippi	$20,000		
Missouri	$40,000		
Montana	$20,000		
Nebraska	$25,000 less liens		
Nevada	$50,000		
New Hampshire	$10,000		
New Jersey	$10,000 to spouse, $5,000 to heirs		
New Mexico	$30,000		
New York	$20,000	Any real property	
North Carolina	$10,000; $20,000 if passing to surviving spouse only	Any real property	
North Dakota	$15,000		
Ohio	$35,000	(In some circumstances may be up to $100,000)	
Oklahoma	$60,000		

Table 4-3. When is Probate Required? *(cont'd)*

State	*Probate Required if Gross Probate Exceeds:*	*Probate Required, Without Regard to Column 2, If:*	*Probate Not Required, Without Regard to Column 2 or 3, If:*
Oregon	$50,000 personalty, $90,000 real property		
Pennsylvania	$25,000		
Rhode Island	$15,000	Any real property	
South Carolina	$10,000		
South Dakota	$25,000		
Tennessee	$25,000		
Texas	$50,000	Any real property	
Utah	$25,000		
Vermont	$10,000	Any real property	
Virginia	$10,000		
Washington	$60,000		
West Virginia	No provision	No provision	
Wisconsin	$20,000		
Wyoming	$70,000		

Many states also have a procedure for an abbreviated administration. The will is offered for probate, a representative (or if no will, administrator) is appointed, notice is provided to creditors, and many of the other requirements apply, but formal accounting procedures are not required.

Q 4:39 Are there any benefits to using the probate process?

Much has been made of the loss of privacy inherent in probate, yet this may not be a bad thing. Probate helps ensure that those entitled to it will get proper notice, and will have a forum in which to make claims or settle disputes. The personal representative's activities are monitored, and inventories and accountings must either be filed with the court or delivered to the beneficiaries, with proof of delivery filed in court. Beneficiaries of a trust have much greater difficulty challenging the activities of the trustee or getting information about the trust assets. For those with dysfunctional families (particularly when the designated trustee is a step-parent), the need of a beneficiary to file a lawsuit to claim his or her right is often outweighed by the desire for privacy.

In addition to the obvious (property in the sole name of a decedent cannot be transferred to successors without invoking the probate process), there are several reasons a probate proceeding might be seen as beneficial.

In most states, individual creditors may be foreclosed from proceeding with claims more than a year (sometimes two) after the individual's death. But an even shorter statute of limitations applies to probate proceedings. Typically, no claim can be made, even by creditors unknown to the executor or family members, more than four months after newspaper publication of notice to creditors in a probate proceeding. For creditors known to the executor, giving actual notice of the probate proceedings to the creditor can typically start the four-month statute of limitations. Note that any state probate statute purporting to permit preclusion of claims by known creditors who have not received actual notice of the proceedings is probably constitutionally infirm. [Tulsa Professional Collection Services, Inc. v. Pope, 485 U.S. 478 (1988)]

The value of this shortened statute of limitations in particular circumstances has been much debated. Some practitioners argue that the estates of virtually all professional people (doctors, lawyers, architects, accountants, stockbrokers, etc.) should be filed as probates, because the prospect of malpractice claims will otherwise continue to loom over family members (and heirs or devisees) for months or years longer without the probate proceeding. Others counter that the likely interpretation of statute of limitation rules will not preclude an injured client from filing a claim who first discovers the injury later than four months after notice to creditors, and that in any event it may be necessary to give formal notice to anyone who has ever been a client or patient of the deceased in order to secure the protection of creditor claim statutes. While the final resolution may depend on state law, and may vary significantly in different fact situations, it seems safe to assert that a probate proceeding can provide one more (and fairly substantial) barrier to claimants against the estate of deceased professionals.

One other reason for seeking out the probate court bears mentioning. In particular family situations, especially where there is considerable rancor and mistrust, the protection of surety bonds and court accountings might work to the benefit of executors as well as beneficiaries. In most probate-avoidance schemes, the potential liability of the fiduciary may continue for years, or even indefinitely; with proper notice and accounting, the probate process can cut off liability for the fiduciary. Judicious use of surety bonds can simultaneously protect the beneficiaries from loss occasioned by mismanagement of the fiduciary.

Finally, if the estate is large enough to require filing a federal estate tax return (Form 706), it may be necessary that there be a probate estate, with a personal representative, in order to be able to deduct "expenses of administration" on the estate tax return. [See Grant v. Commissioner, 294 F.3d 352 (2d Cir. 2002)]

Q 4:40 What are the drawbacks of probate?

Much is sometimes made of the delay and loss of privacy when an estate must be probated. Another issue can be the expense of court fees and attorneys' fees. Last, and sometimes most important, is the forum it provides to disgruntled family members. In most cases, these considerations will not be of great importance, but in some cases, probate avoidance can be critical to achieving the client's goals.

Delay. As noted, the delays required by the probate deadlines are not very long and not unreasonable given the issues involved such as creditors' claims and tax computations. More pertinent is the supposed delay in getting money out to the family that may require access to the estate assets in order to live. There are two responses to this concern. First, probate and non-probate assets are not mutually exclusive; keep a joint bank account and/or small life insurance policy to provide liquidity. Second, most states permit the surviving spouse to request a "spousal allowance" paid from the estate as an expense of administration during the pendency of probate.

Loss of privacy. Probate records are public records. An inventory of the decedent's property and the dispositive provisions of the will may be pored over by curious eyes for years. Some websites specialize in the wills of celebrities. Presumably a celebrity's affairs will always be public, but for the rest of the world, a pour-over will and trust will take care of most of these concerns. This concern is ameliorated somewhat in many states by provisions permitting inventories and accountings to be sent to interested parties (heirs and devisees) but not filed with the court, but the fact remains that the probate process is more open to public scrutiny than alternatives such as living trusts or beneficiary designations.

Expense. Probate courts charge fees in connection with the probate proceeding, usually some fraction of the estate. If proceedings are complex and require an attorney, the attorney will also charge. What this all means will vary considerably from state to state. In Connecticut, for example, the maximum probate fee, no matter how large the estate, is $12,000. A fee is assessed based on the larger of the inventory, the Connecticut taxable estate, or the federally taxable estate, and is imposed whenever there is any probate filing, including the abbreviated "non-probate" filing to obtain authorization for transfer of a bank account. By contrast, the attorney's fee must be "reasonable" and there is no statutory minimum. In other states, there may be a much higher court fee, the fee may only apply to the probate estate, and the attorney involved in probate may be entitled to a minimum statutory fee no matter how simple the probate process. In short, probate in some states may be an expensive proposition, but not in other states. This is an area that must be examined on a state-by-state basis.

Problems with heirs and creditors. In almost every state a will must be "admitted" after a hearing or the right to request a hearing is made available. The disgruntled, disinherited heir can seize this occasion to bring a will contest. If there is no probate, and the plan is implemented by way of a trust, the disgruntled heir, if not a beneficiary, (1) may have no right to information about the plan in the first place, and (2) if the plan is discovered, will have to bring a suit in a court of general jurisdiction in order to "break" the trust. When it comes to creditors, the probate process provides a convenient forum in which creditors may present claims, and a fiduciary who owes the creditors a duty. By contrast, although the trust is also subject to the claims of creditors, the trustee, who owes creditors no duty, may freely distribute trust assets before claims are presented, and the creditors (like the disgruntled heir) may have more trouble discerning what was in the trust and presenting a claim. Without probate, disgruntled heirs and creditors are put to more effort in challenging the decedent's goals.

Q 4:41 What assets are not subject to probate?

As a general rule, assets held in trust or in joint tenancy with right of survivorship bypass probate proceedings, as do pay-on-death (or transfer-on-death) benefits payable to third parties, as well as life insurance, annuity, or other contractual rights that name beneficiaries on the death of the insured or annuitant. Real estate can "pass" to another person on the death of one owner in the case of joint tenancy or a life estate. In addition, at least one state (Arizona) authorizes a "beneficiary deed" for real estate, which effects the same result as pay-on-death titling does for bank accounts. The Arizona beneficiary deed is fully revocable during the grantor's life (i.e., the beneficiary can be changed or all beneficiaries deleted during the grantor's life, and the beneficiaries gain no interest in the property until the death of the grantor). [Ariz. Rev. Stat. § 33-405(G)] Language to create a "beneficiary deed" can be included in any deed form, and is both straightforward and simple: "I (WE) HEREBY CONVEY TO (GRANTEE) EFFECTIVE ON MY (OUR) DEATH THE FOLLOWING DESCRIBED REAL PROPERTY (property description)."

Q 4:42 Can non-probate assets be reached by creditors or Medicaid's estate recovery efforts?

While non-probate assets transfer directly upon death of the deceased owner (or co-owner), various state statutes may give creditors the power to pursue the recipient of non-probate assets (although not usually life insurance proceeds) to satisfy the deceased owner's debts. As a practical matter, however, creditors may not feel the claim is worth the effort.

In the particular context of Medicaid estate recovery, the federal government has expressly authorized states to consider measures to seek recovery from non-probate assets. Generally speaking, however, state laws giving rights to creditors against non-probate assets require that the creditor locate the asset and initiate the proceeding, that assets so recovered are returned to the decedent's estate for distribution to all creditors in accordance with state law setting priorities for payment, and that the probate assets must be first shown to be insufficient to satisfy the decedent's debts before non-probate assets can be reached. Even where the probate estate is insolvent, the administrative expense in seeking out non-probate assets and obtaining recovery from beneficiaries may be more than it is worth to the Medicaid agency. For all these reasons, actions against non-probate assets remain relatively rare. One cannot be complacent, however; in several recent cases, states have sought to recover against the death benefit of annuities or other resources, and such attempts may increase as states are confronted with shrinking Medicaid budgets.

Joint Tenancy

Q 4:43 What is joint tenancy?

Joint tenancy is commonly used to refer to titles held as "joint tenants with the right of survivorship" (JTWROS). JTWROS is a form of multiple ownership of real or personal property, by which full title passes intact to the survivor(s) on the death of a tenant. The distinguishing characteristic of JTWROS titling is that, upon the death of any joint tenant, the deceased joint tenant's interest in the property automatically passes to the remaining joint tenants. Thus, if three individuals own a piece of real property as joint tenants, they each own an undivided one-third interest and have equal rights to use and possession of the property. Upon the death of one of the three joint tenants, the remaining two automatically own a one-half undivided interest in the property, with each retaining the right to use and possession of that property.

This is not to be confused with "tenancy in common," in which multiple parties may own a share of the property but without the right of survivorship. The share owned by a tenant in common will pass not to the other tenants, but to the decedent's heirs or devisees.

Almost any property can be held in JTWROS form. Real estate, bank accounts, stocks and bonds, and most other properties are routinely titled in joint tenancy, particularly as between spouses. When it comes to the owners' rights during their lifetimes, however, these assets are treated differently. Most states give joint bank account holders the right to use 100 percent of the account assets. The same may or may not be true of securities accounts, and few brokerage accounts allow each joint owner unlimited access to account securities. With JTWROS real estate, the consent of all titleholders is required to convey; however, one joint owner can convey his or her proportionate share to a third party, thereby "breaking" the JTWROS status and converting the title to a tenancy in common. (In one instance known to the author, when a couple cohabiting for 20 years purchased a house as JTWROS, one member of the couple conveyed to a straw party who reconveyed back, in order to sever the joint tenancy and permit the party to leave one share to the couple's child rather than the survivor.)

Q 4:44 What is tenancy by the entirety?

Tenancy by the entirety is a form of property ownership specifically designed for married couples. Its effect upon death is the same as that of joint tenancy with the right of survivorship, with the survivor assuming full title at the death of the first spouse; thus, the transfer bypasses probate. Tenancy by the entirety has generally been abolished in the states that have adopted community property approaches. A number of other (common law) states have also abolished tenancy by the entirety. In some of those states, such as Connecticut, the conveyance to grantees "as tenants by the entirety" does *not* create a tenancy by the entirety, but simply creates a joint tenancy. See, for example, Connecticut General Statutes Section 47-14a.

Q 4:45 What are the advantages of using a joint tenancy?

Joint tenancy can be a very effective means of avoiding the delays and expense of probate. The right of survivorship feature of joint tenancy means that property will pass to the surviving joint tenant(s) automatically, and will not be embroiled in any probate proceedings (or, in most cases—depending on that particular state's law—subjected to the deceased joint tenant's creditor's claims). Perhaps most importantly for many laypersons, there is no need to even consult a lawyer in order to transfer most kinds of property into joint tenancy. Consequently joint tenancy is often the default method of estate planning, particularly for persons of modest means.

Q 4:46 What are the drawbacks to holding property in joint tenancy?

While holding property in joint tenancy can be an effective tool for allowing property to pass unimpeded to a spouse or child and bypasses probate, there are the following drawbacks:

1. Heirs of the decedent tenant lose out completely. For instance, if a husband with children from a former marriage and his second wife own a home in JTWROS, and husband dies first, the second wife gets full title to the home and the children of the first marriage get no share of the home.
2. Joint tenancy can be cumbersome if the tenants divorce or need to sell the property arises—the consent of all joint tenants is needed to sell the property, even if one formerly owned the property as his or her separate property and put the name of the other joint tenant(s) on the deed for convenience or as a gift. (A deed signed by only one party will "sever" the joint tenancy, creating a tenancy in common, and result in a conveyance of only the signatory's interest—not likely to be of interest to a buyer.)
3. Property held in joint tenancy cannot be transferred to a trust and maintain its character. The trust grantor who wishes to better control the distribution of that property must persuade the other tenant(s) to change the ownership of the property.
4. There is no income tax benefit to joint tenancy—in fact, the IRS will deem the property wholly owned by the decedent tenant unless and until the other tenant(s) can prove that *both* the joint tenants acquired the property by gift, devise, or inheritance, or that the survivor financially contributed to the ownership or maintenance of the property. [I.R.C. § 2040]

5. In some states, should one of the joint owners require Medicaid, the state may be able to seek recovery against, or place a lien upon, that owner's share, depending on who the other owners are and whether they live in the property as their "home." Even though the property will pass automatically to the survivors, the lien may survive; even if the lien is supposed to be extinguished, there may be trouble getting the Medicaid agency to remove the lien from the land records.
6. Creating a joint tenancy may subject the property to the claims of the second party's creditors (and self-interested intentions). Although the Uniform Multi-Party Accounts Statute states that joint tenants own jointly held accounts in proportion to their actual contributions (and thus an account ought not to be subject to the claims of a non-contributory tenant), it is not clear whether this will apply to brokerage accounts; at the very least, litigation may be required to prevent the claim. [See, e.g., Deutsch, Larrimore Farnish, P.C. v. Johnson, 2002 Pa. Super. 13 (2001)]

Q 4:47 What are the general tax effects of using joint tenancy?

Property held in joint tenancy will only get a stepped-up basis for the share owned by the decedent, whereas property held in the sole name of the decedent will get a full stepped-up basis. Depending on state law (and the ability of survivors to prove the contributions to the jointly owned property), that may be only a portion of the stepped-up basis. While this will ordinarily not be a concern for bank accounts and money market funds, it may have a tremendous effect on appreciated property; if, for example, a single parent places three joint tenants on the family home, they might enjoy only a one-fourth step-up in the basis on the parent's death (though the more likely result is a full step-up in basis). This could result in a significant tax penalty over the full step-up they would have received if the property had been held outright by the parent—in many cases, the income tax savings alone will easily pay the costs of any probate proceeding.

The effect of this general rule is ameliorated by another rule: jointly held property is presumed to have been beneficially owned entirely by the decedent. In other words, where a parent places his or her children's names on the property "as a convenience" without sale of any interest to the children, upon the parent's death the entire property will be included in his or her gross estate and therefore receive a stepped-up basis. On the other hand, if one of the children should die before the parent, that child's estate will also presumptively include the entire value of the property, resulting in a possible estate tax liability (but an arguable step-up in the basis to the value at the date of the child's death).

The "step-up" problem is less of an issue, however, when the child or other party "added to the deed" also lives in the property. When the property is ultimately sold, provided the seller resided in the property for two of the preceding five years, there will be a capital gains tax exclusion for sale of principal residence (up to the limits allowed, currently $250,000 for a single person, $500,000 for a couple).

Q 4:48 What are the tax effects of using joint tenancy in community property states?

For spouses living in community property states, there is a drawback to using joint tenancy. Community property receives a full step-up in basis on the death of either spouse, while joint tenancy property will (assuming both spouses really owned the property) yield only a half step-up. Thus spouses who have held onto the family homestead for 40 years will have a distinct advantage if they own it as community property; when the first spouse dies, the survivor can sell the home without capital gains tax consequences. Although the surviving spouse may in fact choose to remain in the property for the rest of his or her life, the step-up in basis will at least have the effect of giving the surviving spouse additional flexibility in making financial plans.

Q 4:49 Are there reasons not to use joint tenancy as a means of planning for transfers of property on death?

While the convenience of joint tenancy is hard to ignore, the transfer may have unintended effects. Most laypersons have an imperfect understanding of the interplay among property titles, wills and trusts, and the probate process. It is commonplace for parents, for example, to place property (particularly bank accounts) in joint tenancy with one child, believing that a will effectively directs distribution of the property equally among all children. Many family disputes center around the legal reality that joint tenancy property avoids the probate process, and the instructions contained in the decedent's will, completely.

This problem can be exacerbated in some family situations. For instance, if a husband and wife each have children from a former marriage, holding their property as joint tenants allows the transfer of the assets directly and fully to the surviving spouse with no share going to the separate children of the first spouse to die. Similarly, if a parent owns property in joint tenancy with a child, it should be with the intent that the child gets full title at the parent's death without any obligation to share the property with the other siblings.

It is possible, of course, to avoid the prospect of one child (or the surviving spouse) receiving all property through joint tenancy by simply placing all the intended beneficiaries on the title as joint tenants. This also causes problems. If, for example, a parent transfers property into joint tenancy with several children, the odds increase that one of those children will predecease the parent. Although the parent may intend that the deceased child's share should go to that child's spouse, or children, the nature of joint tenancy will cause the interest to revert to the remaining joint tenants (the parent and the still-living children). Any effort to give an interest to the deceased child's heirs will now probably require unanimity among the remaining joint tenants. In other words, the parent's testamentary intentions are subject to veto by any of the other beneficiaries.

Some clients will add the name of a minor child or grandchild to an account rather than opening a custodial account for the minor. This, too, will cause problems if upon the client's death the minor's property exceeds the statutory maximum for a minor without appointment of a guardian of the estate for the minor.

Joint-Name Bank Accounts

Q 4:50 What are the differences between "POD," "ITF," and "TOD" accounts?

Funds held in a "Payable on Death," or POD account (usually a bank checking account), are owned solely by the decedent during his or her lifetime, and then payable at his or her death to a third party or parties designated by him or her. Most state laws now permit POD accounts at banks, savings associations, and credit unions. An alternative designation is "In Trust For," usually abbreviated as ITF. ITF accounts are sometimes also referred to as Totten trusts, after the famous New York case. [Matter of Totten, 179 N.Y. 112, 71 N.E. 748 (1904)] This form of ownership of a bank account as "A in trust for B" is essentially an implied revocable trust.

Thus, a bank account may be held in the name of "John Jones, POD Dennis Jones" or even "John and Mary Jones, POD Dennis and Diane Jones." In each case, the POD beneficiary has no ownership interest in (or ability to control the use of) the account until the death of the primary account holder, but the account can be transferred automatically on the death of the primary owner(s) without the necessity of probate administration in those states in which it is recognized.

The Uniform Multiple-Person Accounts Act [§§ 12, 1, 8B U.L.A. 178 (1993)] permits POD or ITF designations as described here. The 1989 version of the act has been adopted by nine states or jurisdictions (Alaska, Arizona, Colorado, District of Columbia, Montana, Nebraska, New Mexico North Dakota, and South Dakota). An earlier version of the act, the 1969 version (included in the Uniform Probate Code), was adopted by 18 other states (California, Florida, Georgia, Hawaii, Idaho, Indiana, Kentucky, Maine, Maryland, Minnesota, New Jersey, Oregon, South Carolina, Texas, Utah, Virginia, Washington, and Wisconsin). Although the remaining states have not expressly adopted the Uniform Multiple-Person Account Act, most states have specifically authorized POD or ITF accounts by statute. States recently adopting POD accounts (generally, in 1997) include Massachusetts, Nevada, New Hampshire, and North Carolina. As of 2002, New York and Pennsylvania still do not appear to recognize POD or ITF designations.

"Transfer on Death" (TOD) designations are now permitted by almost all states for stocks, bonds, mutual funds, and brokerage accounts (see Q 4:52). At least one state permits the functional equivalent of TOD/POD titling for real estate. Beginning in 2001, Arizona recognizes a "beneficiary deed" designation, revocable by the property owner during life, which effectively avoids the probate process (see Q 4:41).

Q 4:51 What is the best way to title accounts at banks, savings and loans, and thrift associations in order to avoid the necessity of probate?

Individuals who intend their accounts to bypass probate should make their intent clear to the bank at the time the account is created. Giving another person power of attorney over the account is effective for management of the account during the principal's lifetime, especially during incapacity, but is ineffective as a death transfer. Putting another person's name on the account ("John Doe and Mary Smith") will give both parties access to the account even before the death of the original owner, and will also result in the surviving joint tenant receiving the entire account. If the intent of the account owner is to have complete control of all the funds prior to his or her death, and then have the funds transferred to and available to the survivors immediately after death, then the account should be designated as POD ("payable on death") or ITF ("in trust for") the intended recipient(s). In other words, a more protective (and effective) means of titling the previous bank account would be "John Doe POD Mary Smith." A married couple might even hold an account as "John and Jane Doe JTWROS, POD Mary Smith and Bob Doe." By such an arrangement, the married couple has retained complete control (and the ability to change beneficiaries) over the account during their joint lives, and the surviving spouse retains control after the death of the first spouse. Assuming that the account title is not changed before the death of the second spouse, the couple's two children will receive the account equally, without needing to go through the probate process.

Q 4:52 Are "payable on death" and "in trust for" accounts permitted for stocks, bonds, and brokerage accounts?

Although ITF designations are not available for stocks, bonds, or brokerage accounts, most states permit either POD ("payable on death") or TOD ("transfer on death") accounts. The Uniform TOD Security Registration Act, finalized in 1989, has been adopted by 46 states and the District of Columbia. Only Louisiana, New York, and North Carolina have not yet adopted the Act, and only Louisiana does not recognize the TOD designation at all. The TOD title designation is functionally equivalent to the POD bank account title (see Q 4:50).

It is important to note that the TOD beneficiary remains liable to the estate administrator for expenses, and (depending on which version the state has adopted) may also be liable to creditors to the extent of the property value.

The Uniform TOD Act permits various account titles:

1. "John S. Brown TOD John S. Brown, Jr." (On John S. Brown's death, the securities are automatically transferred to his son, John S. Brown, Jr.)

2. "John S. Brown and Mary B. Brown, JTWROS, TOD John S. Brown, Jr." (John and Mary Brown own the securities jointly, and the survivor will take the entire interest by right of survivorship. On the second death, the securities will automatically transfer to their son, John S. Brown, Jr.)

3. John S. Brown and Mary B. Brown, JTWROS, TOD John S. Brown, Jr. SUB BENE Peter Q. Brown. (Same as item 2, except that if John S. Brown, Jr., is not living at the time of the death of the surviving spouse the securities will automatically go to the "substituted beneficiary" Peter Q. Brown.)

4. John S. Brown and Mary B. Brown, JTWROS, TOD John S. Brown, Jr., LDPS. ("LDPS" stands for "lineal descendants per stirpes"—this titling automatically transfers the securities to John S. Brown, Jr., on the second death but to his descendants if he is not then living.)

Q 4:53 What are the advantages of using TOD and ITF accounts?

Holding bank accounts in joint tenancy with, or as TOD or ITF accounts for, a spouse, child, or other trusted individual can make immediate post-death arrangements much easier. A power of attorney has distinct logistical advantages during one's lifetime, but the power terminates at the death of the principal. A bank account held in joint tenancy with another allows the surviving tenant full access to the account to take care of funeral expenses, utilities, debts, and other expenses in the weeks following the death and before probate is initiated.

Q 4:54 What are the disadvantages of using JTWROS accounts as distinguished from TOD or ITF accounts?

The obvious drawback to joint tenancy titling (as distinguished from TOD and ITF accounts) is that the principal has given immediate ownership of (and access to) property to the joint tenant/recipient. Although few individuals believe their children would steal from them, abuse of joint tenancy accounts is a widespread and, in the view of most professionals, rapidly growing phenomenon. Although many individuals indicate that they are placing a child's name on an account "for convenience," the legal reality is that the joint tenant will usually have unrestricted access to the entire account at any time before the principal's death.

Most state laws direct that assets in jointly held accounts belong to those on the account title in proportion to their contribution to the account. In other words, the parent who places a trusted child's name on a bank account remains the "owner" of the entire account (assuming the child places none of his or her money in the account) and could, in a legal proceeding, presumably establish that ownership against the child. This legal nicety has significance only between the parties: If the child chooses to withdraw the full account, the parent may have a claim against the child but not against the bank or other financial institution.

Even a joint tenant who behaves properly may cause legal problems. In the event of a lawsuit against the noncontributing joint tenant, or a bankruptcy proceeding, for example, the "owner" of the account may be forced to establish ownership by affirmatively showing that the joint tenant did not contribute to the account. While this may be easy to do, it still means the prospect of legal proceedings, expense, and anxiety. If ownership cannot be established, the account may be subjected to the claims against the joint tenant.

Placing property in joint tenancy can also harm the recipient joint tenant if the marriage is dissolved. Although the joint tenancy property will probably not be treated as marital property (and the joint tenant's divorcing spouse therefore will not have any direct claim against the property), it may be treated as an available resource to the divorcing joint tenant. This may result in a reduction in spousal maintenance or child support, or other reductions in the joint tenant's share of marital property.

Q 4:55 Is the creation of a joint tenancy considered a gift?

The creation of a joint tenancy account is not ordinarily considered a gift for tax purposes. Federal estate tax principles include all jointly owned property in the decedent's estate to the extent of the decedent's contribution to the property, and both stepped-up basis and gift tax implications follow the same rule. In other words, establishing a joint tenancy account with a child (or another person) without receiving actual consideration for the transfer does not create a gift for gift tax purposes and does not eliminate the ultimate step-up in basis on the original owner's later death.

However, creation of a joint tenancy may be considered a gift for other purposes, such as the rules relating to transfers by those who later apply for Medicaid. Because the "multiple owner bank account" rules allow the creator of the account to take out all of the account assets, creation of those accounts is not considered a "transfer," but creation of a joint tenancy in real estate, or possibly even securities, may well be considered a gift of one-half of the total.

Q 4:56 Is mental capacity required to create a joint tenancy?

Frequently clients will "add to the title" of bank accounts, securities accounts, and even real estate, as a simple way to avoid probate, and for convenience in the event of their own incapacity. Sadly, these decisions may have unintended consequences when one child entrusted to distribute the property to siblings chooses instead to rely on the letter of the law and keep the jointly titled property, or refuses to consent to the owner's wishes with respect to jointly titled securities. For this reason, there are many cases in which the creation of the joint title is challenged on the basis that the creator lacked capacity or was under undue influence.

In the main, these cases will indicate that creation of a joint tenancy carries a rebuttable presumption that the owner intended to make either a present gift or a testamentary gift to the other party. That presumption may be rebutted by evidence, and in many cases is successfully rebutted. [See, e.g., Bachman v. Reardon, 138 Conn. 665, 667 (1953) (creation of joint tenancy not intended to confer a present gift upon co-owner, but did intend to confer a testamentary gift)] The presumption of donative intent will be enhanced when the joint owner is a "natural object of the donor's bounty," such as a spouse or child. [2 Restatement (Second), Trusts §§ 442, 443]

As to the level of capacity required, the usual standard of capacity for making a gift is "whether, at the time of the transaction, the donor had the ability to understand the nature and effects of his or her act." [38 Am. Jur. 2d Gifts § 13] In addition, "[t]o have the capacity to execute a valid conveyance, the grantor must not only have the ability to transact the ordinary affairs of life and to understand their nature and effect, but also to exercise his will in relation thereto without such will being unduly influenced by another." [Sullivan v. Clear, 101 Conn. 603, 610 (1924)]

Q 4:57 What is a life estate?

Another title arrangement, besides joint tenancy, tenancy in common, and tenancy by the entirety, are title arrangements that provide for a succession of interests: a "life estate" to one party and a "remainder" to another.

The burdens and privileges of a "legal life estate" will be defined by state law. Typically, the burdens include the duty to maintain the property subject to the life estate, to pay real estate taxes and insurance, and to prevent "waste." State law may be less clear on the life tenant's obligations with respect to "improvements" or major capital items with a lifetime that may exceed the life tenant's tenure, such as a new roof, a retaining wall, or a swimming pool. When the capital item is required to prevent waste, the life tenant may be required to seek contributions from the remaindermen, unless the document provides otherwise. The privilege of a life use will be the right to make any use of the property that a tenant in fee could make during the term of the tenancy. This would include the right to all rents from the property. Finally, if property is sold, state law will dictate whether the proceeds are divided between life tenant and remainderman according to their actuarial interests, or whether the life tenant will be entitled to an income interest in the entire proceeds, for life.

The benefit of a life estate in "Medicaid planning" is that the value of property transferred subject to a life estate will be the value of the remainder interest, not the entire property value, which will decrease the penalty applied by the Medicaid agency. Another benefit may be protection of the grantor, who retains a right to life in the property transferred. A third benefit is that the property does receive the full "step up" in basis upon the grantor's death. A fourth benefit is simplicity. The life estate may be conferred in a will or trust, or conveyed as a gift, by deed. The usual approach is to quitclaim to the remainderman "reserving, however, a life estate."

Since title passes at death automatically to the remainderman, the real estate should not be included in the probate estate of the life tenant, and as such, may escape claims of creditors and recoupment demands from Medicaid agencies. These agencies are more or less aggressive about demanding that the life tenant who applies for benefits seek a return on the life estate either by renting, or by a forced sale to the remainderman. More problematic is the likelihood of claim against sales proceeds should the real estate subject to the life estate be sold while the life tenant is receiving Medicaid benefits. Other problems with a life estate include loss of full access to the exclusion from capital gains on sale of a personal residence (which should be allocated actuarially using IRS tables) and the inability of the selling life tenant to use the entire proceeds as a down payment on a retirement community or assisted living facility endowment.

Practitioners have tried to develop ways around the drawbacks of the life estate. Some have created "revocable life estates" where the life tenant can revoke the remainderman's interests. In some states, these may be invalid unless executed with the formalities of a will. Moreover, Medicaid agencies have claimed with success that this arrangement does bring the property into the life tenant's probate estate so that it becomes subject to a recoupment claim.

Similar is the deed with the "power of sale," which states that the life tenant may sell the entire property and keep the entire proceeds.

Others have used "Lady Bird deeds" in which the life tenant has the power to "roll over" the entire sales proceeds into a new piece of real estate in which the life tenant will continue to have a life estate, but any excess must be paid to the remainderman. (When drafting such an arrangement in a will or trust, rather than by conveyance, one may wish to require that life tenant have the right to "roll over" into a retirement community contract or similar arrangement provided the remainderman is named as beneficiary of any amounts recovered at the life tenant's death.) Whether or not this will pass muster is a matter to be reviewed with local title insurance companies. Also, unlike a legal life estate, this will not qualify for a marital deduction, because the spouse does not have unqualified rights to the life use; any amount not expended on the substitute property will go to third parties.

Finally, if the primary concern is protection of the grantor, some practitioners do not reserve a life estate but merely a "right of occupancy." This would not appear to impose burdens or grant additional benefits to the life tenant other than the ability to veto any sale.

Trust

Types of Trusts

Q 4:58 What is a trust?

> An express trust is a fiduciary relationship with respect to property, subjecting the person by whom the property is held to equitable duties to deal with the property for the benefit of another person, which arises as a result of a manifestation of an intent to create it. [1 Restatement of Trusts (2d) § 2]

Thus, a trust is a relationship between trustee and beneficiary with respect to property, the relationship having been established by the transfer, the act of another party, the "grantor" or "settlor." Only a trust permits such a division of title. In its simplest form, a trust is a relationship created by a transfer of assets to one person for the benefit of another (in some circumstances, the two persons can actually be the same person). The recipient, or holder, of the property is the "trustee," and the person for whom the property is held is the "beneficiary." While the trustee is said to hold "legal" title to the property, the beneficiary holds the "beneficial" title. In addition, a trust is one way to provide a succession of interests over time, in the same property. Frequently, one beneficiary is entitled to the use of the property (and the income or some other portion thereof) for life, with another beneficiary to receive the interest after the death of the first beneficiary. In such a case, the lifetime beneficiary is referred to as the "income beneficiary," and the ultimate recipient is the "remainder beneficiary."

In addition to the trustee and beneficiary, another point in the triangle is the transferor of property, the "grantor," "trustor," or "settlor." The choice of terms appears to be largely regional, although the term "grantor" takes on special meaning because of the Internal Revenue Code's use of "grantor trust" as a term with income tax significance. (This book will use all three terms interchangeably.) The Internal Revenue Code, and most cases, understand that it is the party who subjects the property to the trust relationship, not necessarily the party who sets the words of the trust to paper, who is the true "grantor."

However, just as the word "trust" has come to denote in common parlance the trust instrument itself, the paper document or documents setting forth the terms of the relationship, the concept of the "grantor," the party transferring the property, is often confused with the party who executes the paper document that sets forth the terms of the relationship and recites that the signatory is the "grantor."

Q 4:59 What is a revocable trust?

A revocable trust is a trust in which the settlor reserves the right to revoke. Because the settlor retains this level of control over the trust, the assets held in trust will be deemed fully includible in the gross for estate and gift tax purposes, fully subject to the claims of the settlor's creditors, and fully available to the settlor for purposes of determining the settlor's eligibility for entitlement benefits.

Whether and to what extent a power to "amend" a trust's terms, whether held by the settlor or a third party, will cause a trust to be considered "revocable" despite the pronouncement that it is irrevocable, is unclear. Presumably, a limited power of amendment that cannot return the trust property to its original owner need not cause the trust to be considered a revocable trust.

Historically, a trust has been presumed irrevocable unless the power to revoke is expressly reserved. This presumption would be reversed in the Uniform Trust Code.

Q 4:60 What is an irrevocable trust?

An irrevocable trust is a trust that cannot be revoked (or significantly amended) once the trust instrument is signed; thus, the transfer of assets into the trust may qualify as a completed gift of a present interest in property, and the grantor theoretically gives up control of the assets once the transfer is made. By using the trust vehicle rather than making an outright gift, the grantor can dictate in advance, even from the grave, how assets are managed and distributed.

An irrevocable trust may be an effective vehicle when the grantor wishes to protect assets from creditors. Great care must be taken, however, to avoid what could be construed as a fraudulent transfer. Most states have statutes either criminalizing fraudulent conveyances or permitting creditors to avoid such conveyances, or both. The Uniform Fraudulent Transfer Act, for example, makes transfers voidable if they were made "with actual intent to hinder, delay, or defraud any creditor of the debtor." Recently, asset protection devices using a combination of irrevocable trusts and trustees beyond U.S. jurisdiction ("offshore trusts") have begun to fail, in some cases subjecting the settlor to criminal penalties.

Moreover, many states consider a "self-funded" trust to be against public policy to the extent that it could be used to defeat the claims of creditors while at the same time allowing the settlor to benefit fully from the trust property. For example, in *Greenwich Trust Co. v. Tyson* [129 Conn. 211 (1942)], Connecticut's Supreme Court held that such a trust is subject to the claims of the settlor's creditors without regard to the terms of the trust instrument. Similarly, federal Medicaid law treats property held in a trust as fully available to the settlor (or spouse) to the extent that the trustee might, under any circumstances, be able to distribute that property to the settlor (or spouse). [42 U.S.C. § 1396p(d)(3)(B). This statute replaces the earlier "Medicaid qualifying trust statute, (former) 42 U.S.C. § 1396a(k)(2), repealed Aug. 10, 1993, but which applies to trusts established prior to that date. See further discussion in chapter 14.]

Q 4:61 What is the difference between a living trust and a testamentary trust?

A trust established during life is usually referred to as a living trust. Whether or not assets are actually transferred to the trustee to be held pursuant to the terms set out in the trust instrument, the relationship the instrument establishes exists immediately upon creation. The term "living trust" may be used in some regions to refer to a trust that is actually funded by the transfer of property, and the more quaint Latin term *inter vivos* trust (between the living) to refer more broadly to all trust relationships expressed by way of an agreement between living settlor and living trustee, whether or not funded. By contrast, the terms of a testamentary trust are set forth within the text of a will (that speaks at the testator's death), and the transfer of property does not occur until the testator's death. Thus, the testamentary trust has no viability until the death of the testator. Even though the document is signed and witnessed, the trust does not come into existence unless the testator dies without having revoked the will (and it may not even come into existence then, if the testator's will is not submitted to probate, or if there are insufficient assets to fund the trust).

Q 4:62 What are the advantages of executing a revocable living trust agreement?

Living trusts are often (and not completely incorrectly) marketed as estate tax savings devices. However, living trusts do not, in and of themselves, effect any estate or income tax savings. While married couples with combined assets in excess of $1 million usually need a trust to avoid losing certain tax advantages further discussed in chapter 5, they do not necessarily need an *inter vivos* trust agreement, whether funded (a "living trust"), or unfunded. Income taxes will usually be unaffected by living trusts, even most irrevocable living trusts. One exception is that some capital gains tax savings can be accomplished in community property states by treating trust assets as community property (and thereby receiving a full step-up in tax basis on the death of the first spouse), even though the assets might have been one spouse's separate property, or held by the spouses as joint tenants, prior to establishment of the trust.

However, a living trust agreement (funded or unfunded) does have some important advantages.

Clients with real estate in more than one state should seriously consider establishing a revocable living trust. Because the cost of probate will be compounded by the necessity of initiating proceedings in each state where real property is located, the benefit of bypassing probate is more apparent for such individuals. The client with a trust agreement, even a simple one, can avoid the ancillary probate by the simple expedient of executing a deed transferring the real estate to the trustee and recording the deed on the land records.

The funded living trust is appropriate whenever there is a need for management and distribution by a party other than the grantor himself or herself. The advantage of private management may also be useful to those who are not incapacitated, but want to enact a wall of privacy and control between their assets and those who would make demands upon them, such as an abusive or demanding spouse or children. The trustee is the person who can say no to those that prey upon the grantor/beneficiary's good will.

The trust is particularly important, however, when the grantor becomes incapacitated. The trust agreement will permit trust assets to be managed and distributed in accordance with the grantor's wishes even when the grantor becomes incapacitated, without the need for a court-appointed and supervised fiduciary or court proceedings that will be matters of public record. Those who value privacy as a general matter especially favor this aspect. This advantage is available so long as the trust is set up, even if no assets have yet been transferred to the trustee's custody, provided a power of attorney can be used to transfer property to the trust when the time comes.

Thus, the most important advantage to living trusts will often be neither probate avoidance nor tax savings, but the avoidance of court supervision of property at a later date if the grantor should become incapacitated. Even as probate rules have been liberalized in most states, the guardianship and conservatorship process (or guardianship of the person and property, as it is called in some states) has remained procedurally mired in 18th century common law. While this helps provide wonderful protection for incapacitated wards, the cost is extremely high in both financial and emotional terms. For many laypersons, the prospect of submitting their personal and financial affairs to close court supervision is anathema, and a living trust may seem like a fair investment to avoid that possibility. Durable powers of attorney will accomplish much the same result, but suffer from the drawback that many third parties will resist accepting instructions from an attorney-in-fact. Trustees do not encounter such problems and therefore more effectively avoid the necessity of court proceedings.

Living trusts are also often touted as a means of avoiding controversies among the intended beneficiaries of an estate plan. While most states have statutes or case law making trust contests essentially similar to will contests, the practical reality is that the lack of court supervision inherent in trust administration makes it less likely that any beneficiary (or disinherited family member) will institute a legal proceeding to contest the terms or administration of a trust.

For those reasons and others, funded living trusts represent a substantial and growing portion of the estate planning marketplace. In many jurisdictions lawyers routinely discourage the use of living trusts, particularly for clients of modest assets, but the growth of living trusts continues nonetheless. To a considerable extent, that growth is fueled by financial planners, insurance salespersons, accountants, bankers, and others who may have their own vested interest in marketing ancillary services (e.g., life insurance, investment, accounting, or banking services), but the strong public interest in avoiding the probate process is undoubtedly the principal motivating force behind the living trust phenomenon.

Q 4:63 Are there drawbacks to establishing a living trust?

Assuming that the trust is properly drafted and funded, it is difficult to say that a living trust would actually harm any client. There are, however, several drawbacks to the choice of a living trust as an alternative to more traditional estate planning. Chief among these drawbacks are cost and inconvenience.

In most areas and cases, preparation and implementation of living trusts will cost significantly more than preparation of other estate planning documents. A properly drafted living trust will usually be accompanied by a will (probably a pour-over will, which directs that any assets outside the trust be transferred into the trust; see Q 4:36), appropriate powers of attorney, and/or health care directives. In other words, the choice of a living trust will only increase the number (and complexity) of documents that need to be prepared.

The living trust also requires additional steps to complete the planning cycle. In the case of a will (and supporting powers of attorney), planning is complete once the documents are signed; in order to be an effective probate-avoidance mechanism, the living trust must be "funded." That is, all (or most) assets must be transferred into the trust's name in order to avoid having those assets subjected to the probate process despite establishment of the trust. Moreover, all subsequently acquired assets must also be transferred into the trust's name. In most states, married couples routinely establish separate living trusts; in addition to transferring assets into the trusts, such an arrangement requires a division of those assets into appropriate shares before the trust funding is undertaken.

All of this means that the cost of estate planning with living trusts is significantly higher than that of more traditional estate planning. Typically, the cost of preparing and funding a living trust will be at least double the cost of preparing wills for the same client (for some attorneys, 10 to 20 times). While this does not mean the living trust option is too expensive for most clients, it does mean that the decision to utilize living trusts becomes a straightforward cost-benefit analysis: Is the cost (today) of establishing a living trust significantly lower than the cost (at some future date) of probating the estate? Part of that analysis requires consideration of the likelihood of death during the time covered by the current estate plan (most advisers recommend review and revision of estate plans every five or ten years) and the fact that the cost of a living trust will come from the principal's funds, while the cost of probate will come from funds being paid to the beneficiaries.

Finally, transfer of the principal's assets into the trust's name during life may require a substantial investment of time and energy. Remember, in order to be effective, the living trust must not only be funded but it must remain funded for the rest of the principal's life. In other words, the settlor must always remember that newly acquired property must be titled to the trust, and must maintain sufficient records to ensure that titling is accurate for the rest of his or her life. This is particularly frustrating when the trust's assets include securities. Brokerages and transfer agents may require the signatures of all trustees, special trustee affidavits, copies of trust documents, "medallion guaranteed" signatures, and, should there be any change in the trustee's identity, will require everything to be done all over again. As for publicity, in some states transfer of real estate into a trust requires recording of the entire trust document in the land records; the only way around this requirement is yet another document, the "nominee trust," a "straw man" trust of which the real trust is beneficiary or ultimate payee. And all this trouble will be for nothing if the settlor slips up and retains sole title to an asset valuable enough to require probate in his or her state, which may be unavoidable if property such as accrued vacation time or unpaid salary is involved, and if not unavoidable, is very likely for any individual owning an expensive car. (For example, in Connecticut, $20,000 is the minimum amount of personal property for which probate is required.)

While these annoyances may not result in any financial cost, they will make the living trust more than slightly aggravating to administer during the principal's lifetime. In fact, the difficulties encountered in funding and maintaining the living trust are usually the same difficulties encountered later by family members if the principal relies on a will (and the probate process) instead. In other words, in the case of a living trust the principal is effectively administering his or her own probate during life; the same work must be done, but it will be done by the principal rather than the estate's recipients.

Of course, all states are different. In California, for example, where probate can be particularly expensive, there is case law that a simple notarized statement by the settlor that all assets owned or thereafter acquired are assigned to the trust is sufficient to effectuate the transfer and avoid probate, even if the record title to the assets has not been changed. Therefore, living trusts may be very common in states like California, and ultimately so much less costly than probate that they become worth the effort. It is a mistake, however, for practitioners from other states to assume that what works in California works in their states.

One more observation about living trusts is that in some states, where probate is simple and informal, court proceedings may still serve their original purposes of protecting beneficiaries and incapables. Once a trustee is appointed, the trustee is likely to run unencumbered by any oversight. The trustee that "goes bad" can inflict more damage than a court-supervised fiduciary. If the client has any qualms about the choice of fiduciary, therefore, court supervision may be a good thing rather than a bad thing and ultimately cost less than the fees charged by a remote institutional trustee.

Q 4:64 What is the income tax consequence of establishing a grantor living trust?

Remembering that the umbrella term "living trust" is quite broad, there are two basic kinds of trusts established during the life of the grantor for income tax purposes. A "grantor trust" is one in which the grantor has retained a sufficient interest to cause the trust's income to be taxed to the grantor. This includes all revocable trusts (the retention of the power to revoke the trust is itself sufficient to cause inclusion of the income in the grantor's tax return) and some irrevocable trusts, typically life insurance trusts. Simply because the grantor has made the transfer irrevocable, and even if he or she has given up the current right to receive income, the trust will still be a grantor trust if he or she retains the right to direct the ultimate distribution of trust assets.

The effect of grantor trust status is to treat trust income as belonging to the grantor. In the usual revocable living trust situation, this is not a problem; the grantor is not particularly interested in getting rid of income or getting trust assets out of his or her estate before death. In fact, this is usually viewed as an advantage by the trustor(s)—no additional tax filings are required, and the trust assets can continue to utilize the grantor's social security number. In other words, the income tax effect of a revocable living trust is usually negligible. Even for the irrevocable grantor trust, a similar approach may be used, or, alternatively, the trustee will file a blank tax return indicating that all income is reported to the grantor, and then provide the grantor with a statement to enable preparation of the grantor's Form 1040.

The only significant income tax effect is that in community property states the joint grantor trust may be used to obtain the full step-up in basis on the death of the first spouse, while retaining the functional equivalent of a survivorship arrangement.

Q 4:65 What are the tax consequences of establishing a nongrantor living trust?

In a nongrantor trust, income tax follows the income. Distributions are presumed (for tax purposes) to be first of income, then of principal; any distributions to beneficiaries are therefore deductions from the tax liability of the trust, but result in a tax liability to the distributee. This is sometimes stated as "all distributions carry out income." This will be true even if the distributions are for the benefit of the beneficiary, rather than made directly to the beneficiary. The beneficiary of a special needs trust, for example, may have income tax liability for payments made for education, health care, or entertainment, even though no money was actually paid to the beneficiary. This concept is not difficult to grasp, but it does result in reporting "income" (and filing an income tax return) for someone whose income is closely monitored; the trustee should be prepared to explain the nature of the distributions when the government benefits office finally connects the reporting of income for tax purposes.

It must also be kept in mind that "income" will be calculated differently for taxes and for trust accounting. This may result in an income tax liability for some trusts, even though the terms of the trust provide for the distribution of all income.

Q 4:66 Is it preferable for a married couple to prepare separate living trusts or a single, joint living trust?

In community property states, where most married couples already are deemed to be equal owners of nearly all assets held by either spouse, single trusts are commonplace. In those states, married couples generally should execute a single trust if they have shared assets that they wish to leave to the same beneficiaries, and if the value of their assets is not substantial enough to trigger tax consequences.

In both types of states, separate trusts are recommended if the spouses have separate property that they intend to leave to children from former marriages or where there are substantial separate assets.

In the case of separate trusts, a division of assets must be made at the time the trusts are established (and funded). It is usually insufficient to establish only a trust for one spouse, because the credit exemption amount will not be used if the other spouse happens to die first. Because assets must be split at the time of trust establishment, clients must be walked through the process of selecting assets (or dividing those assets they decide to hold in both trusts), and must maintain an appropriate division for the rest of their lives. However, at the time of the first death, no decisions need to be made or effected regarding which assets need to be retitled, and each spouse remains free unilaterally to change the ultimate disposition or other trust terms.

In the case of joint trusts, the decisions about splitting assets can be deferred until the first death. This not only makes establishing the trust easier, but also maintains maximum flexibility to select appreciating assets for one subtrust and income assets for the other, depending on the mix of assets and the surviving spouse's needs at the time of the first death. Because most married couples tend to think of their assets as jointly owned in any event, the joint trust may be easier for the client to comprehend and appreciate.

Q 4:67 What is a joint revocable trust?

A joint revocable trust is a single-document trust created by a married couple. The trust provides two main functions: (1) it simultaneously provides asset management for both spouses during their lifetimes, and (2) it contains the couple's estate plan and all of the instructions for distribution of assets at death. Joint revocable trusts have long been used in community property states, where most assets are ordinarily owned by the community (and therefore beneficially owned by both spouses equally). They have been far less common in common-law states, where concerns over the gifting effect of transferring separate assets to a joint trust have made the joint trust approach less comfortable for practitioners. Because the prior equivalent of $600,000 was so low, and so many estate planning clients had either achieved, or might be expected to achieve, that threshold for the couple's combined assets, it was considered risky indeed to use a joint trust that might muddy the waters of title, in addition to the gift tax concerns that might arise depending upon the trust's terms. As the exemption equivalent rises, however, and the gift tax schemes of all states become tied to the federal exemption amount, joint trusts may become more common.

Q 4:68 Who has control over the joint revocable trust?

Typically each spouse has joint control of and access to the assets placed in the trust. Furthermore, both spouses receive equal shares of trust income and principal for life (or it is paid to the person to whom they direct).

Q 4:69 Can a joint revocable trust be amended?

Although trust terms may differ in each instance, typically the joint trust is fully amendable during the joint lifetime of the spouses. Any amendment will usually require signatures of both spouses, though the trust may provide otherwise (as it might, for instance, if one spouse was facing a high likelihood of incapacitation at the time the trust was established). After the death of the first spouse the trust may become irrevocable (to protect the couple's original distributive plan), partially irrevocable (as it might, for instance, if the joint trust divides into an exemption equivalent trust and a survivor's trust for estate tax planning purposes), or remain fully revocable. The choice of revocability provisions is one to consider with the couple at the time of inception, and will be colored by the couple's estate tax situation, the couple's concern for the surviving spouse's ability to manage marital assets, and any desire to protect the ultimate beneficiaries of the couple's estates.

Q 4:70 What are the advantages of having a joint revocable trust?

In general, joint revocable trusts are simple, short, and understandable. A joint trust is in some cases appealing because it maintains a "joint property ownership" sharing of rights, and reflects the non-legal understanding of most married couples that the assets belonging to either of them (with some exceptions) are really jointly owned. In the case of a combined estate subject to estate tax, the joint trust also avoids any requirement of physically dividing the couple's assets at the time of establishment of the trust; the division can be made at the time of death of the first spouse to die. Financially, the joint trust provides the same benefit as separate trusts prepared for each spouse; avoidance of probate on both the first and second death will save the joint estates whatever it saves based on probate costs in the couple's state of residence.

Q 4:71 What are the disadvantages of having a joint revocable trust?

If a couple's assets are more than the federal estate tax-exempt amount ($1 million in 2002) and those assets are not roughly equally divided between the spouses, there may be some tax consequences to the estate. First, the entire trust could possibly be included in the estate of the first spouse to die (though proper drafting can easily overcome this concern). This may occur even if that spouse did not contribute all or any of the assets to the trust. Second, the entire trust may be included in the estate of the second spouse to die. This is so even if part of the trust was intended to qualify as a unified credit or bypass trust that was not supposed to be included in the estate of the second spouse (again, proper drafting should address this concern in every instance).

Q 4:72 Is it considered a "gift" for gift tax purposes when assets are transferred into the joint trust?

Yes. A spouse may be making a taxable lifetime gift subject to gift tax when he or she transfers assets in his or her own name to a joint trust. In community property states, this can be less of a concern if each spouse is already considered to own a half interest in all assets transferred.

Q 4:73 Can creditors reach the assets in a joint revocable trust?

Ordinarily, yes. Of course, the underlying assets would ordinarily also be reachable by creditors if no trust had been established, and the same state law that makes a joint trust available to creditors will make separate trusts similarly available. The principal difference is between a trust (joint or separate) and the state's treatment of marital property; in community property states it may be possible to avoid liability incurred by one spouse if that liability is not a community debt. More importantly, common-law states that recognize "tenancy by the entireties" may exempt property held in that form from execution by one spouse's creditors, even if the debt was incurred for the benefit of the community. In such a circumstance "tenancy by the entireties" titling may provide more protection against creditors than any trust, joint or separate.

Q 4:74 What kinds of trusts might an elder law attorney encounter or prepare in practice?

Although the revocable living trust currently enjoys tremendous popularity for estate planning, there are any number of variations on the basic theme. Irrevocable trusts are used less frequently, but are an important part of many estate plans. For example, an irrevocable trust may have been established to own or purchase life insurance in order to keep the insurance policy's value out of the taxable estate, or an irrevocable trust (a charitable remainder trust or charitable lead trust) may have been established to take advantage of charitable deductions while avoiding capital gains tax on substantially appreciated property.

Some clients will have more than one kind of trust. The commonly used names for types of trusts are frequently nondescriptive, but among the more common trust types are the following:

- Revocable living (*inter vivos*) trusts
- Credit shelter (or exemption equivalent or "A/B") trusts (see Q 5:65)
- Qualified terminable interest property (QTIP) trusts (see Q 5:71)
- Qualified domestic trusts (QDTs) (see Q 5:63)
- "Crummey" trusts (see Q 5:28)
- Irrevocable life insurance trusts (ILITs) (see Q 5:88)
- Special needs (or supplemental benefits) trusts (see chapter 18)
- Charitable remainder trusts (see Q 5:77)
- Charitable lead trusts (see Q 5:83)
- Grantor retained annuity trusts (GRATs) (see Q 5:101)
- Qualified personal residence trusts (QPRTs) (see Q 5:101)
- "Grantor" trusts (not really a type of trust, but a category for determining the income tax treatment of some trusts) (see Q 4:64)

Although they may have special importance in Medicaid benefit planning (see chapter 16 for a discussion of Medicaid Trusts) rather than general estate planning, the following trust types are also frequently seen:

- "Miller" (or, sometimes, "qualified income") trusts
- "d(4)(A)" trusts (or, sometimes, "payback" trusts)
- Pooled trusts
- Income-only trusts (not to be confused with "qualified income" trusts)

Requirements for a Valid Trust

Q 4:75 What are the formal requirements for a living trust to be valid?

The trust must identify three entities:

1. The grantor (sometimes called trustor or settlor), who creates the trust agreement and whose wishes are expressed in the trust language;
2. The beneficiary, who will immediately or eventually receive income from the trust assets and/or distributions of trust principal; and
3. The trustee, who manages the trust assets and accounts to the grantor and to the beneficiaries.

All three can be the same individual, and multiple parties may fulfill the functions of any of the three parties.

Where the trust is established by an agreement, both the grantor(s) and the trustee(s) must sign, preferably before a notary (witnesses are not usually required). Usually the grantor(s) and the trustee(s) are the same; common practice is to have the signatures separated by role even when that means two signatures from each individual. Alternatively, most states permit a trust to be established by declaration of the trustor(s); in such a case the trustee(s) need not sign. This is usually referred to as a "declaration of trust" because the grantor "declares" that he or she will now be acting as a fiduciary.

Signed acceptance by successor trustees is usually not required, and in fact corporate trustees may delay accepting the responsibility until the death of one or both grantors. Even though corporate trustees may not be required to sign, it is good practice to offer the documents for their signature, as they often will identify problems with the document as drafted, or concerns about future administration, which are much easier to address during the grantor's life and competence. Besides, a corporate trustee will usually insist on reviewing the trust terms before it will agree to serve, and may refuse to serve as trustee of life insurance trusts during the settlor's lifetime. The corporate fiduciary may even insist on an environmental audit before agreeing to serve as trustee of a trust holding certain kinds of real estate. It is better to flush out these problems at the beginning rather than confront them at the time the trust is ready to go into operation.

Clients should be reminded that a trust instrument is almost useless by itself—the assets must be transferred to the trustee in order to "avoid probate" or attain any of the other goals for which the trust is established. This is usually accomplished by changing the record title of the trust property to reflect ownership by the trustee of the trust. Most attorneys take steps necessary to transfer real estate into the trust, and assist clients with transfers of personal property, bank and brokerage accounts, and other investments. However, if the attorney will be doing this personally, rather than using support staff, the attorney should consider the expense involved and offer the client a choice. Another member of the planning "team," such as a financial advisor, may be able to oversee these steps at lower cost.

Q 4:76 How can a living trust be amended?

The provisions of a living trust will ordinarily indicate whether it is amendable and how it can be amended, if at all. At common law, a trust without any express provision for revocation or amendment was deemed to be irrevocable and unamendable, though this result may have been changed in individual states by statute or case law.

Q 4:77 What capacity is required to sign a living trust?

The standard for competency to create and sign a trust agreement may be higher than the standard applying to execution of a will (see Q 4:22). In addition to knowing what he or she has and to whom he or she wishes his or her assets distributed, the grantor must be able to comprehend and express a desire that the assets be entrusted to another for a period of time, ultimately to be distributed to a third party. The Uniform Trust Code provides that the capacity to create and sign a revocable trust is the same as that to execute a valid will. [U.T.C. § 601] As yet, however, only Kansas, Nebraska, and Wyoming have adopted the Uniform Trust Code.

The attorney should take particular care with married couples that both trustors are fully competent and fully involved, even to the extent of interviewing them separately. There must be a clear delineation of community and separate property, and each spouse must understand exactly where his or her trust assets will go. While intestate laws of succession protect the rights of children of former marriages, the complexities of a trust may lead to the inadvertent bypassing of these persons. As with any matter involving a couple, if the attorney senses that one spouse is dictating the terms of the trust and the other seems a little too willing to defer, a separate interview would probably be in order.

Q 4:78 What steps might an individual consider to protect against his or her own future incapacity?

Every trust document should contain some provision for the grantor's incapacity, so that if the grantor lacks the capacity to manage the trust assets or to modify or revoke the trust, the co-trustees or successor trustees can take over some or all of those responsibilities. The tests for determining incapacity may vary; typical language requires written confirmation from two doctors, one of whom is the grantor's treating physician, that the grantor lacks the capacity to continue to manage the trust. Third parties dealing with the successor trustees may (and should) require such documentation before entering into agreements with the successor.

Powers of attorney may be established during the individual's lifetime, in which he or she designates others to take over health care and financial decision-making when he or she is no longer able to do so. A health care power of attorney names an agent who can act for the incapacitated person with regard to housing and health care decisions; usually this person does not have the power or authorization to handle money matters (although a health care power of attorney standing alone may be a sufficient indication of trust for the Social Security Administration to grant the agent payee status). A general durable power of attorney gives the agent the power to handle all the assets of the incapacitated person, including the ability to buy and sell real estate. It is usually effective upon execution; those who do not wish to grant such broad powers right away may opt instead for a *springing* power of attorney, which would take effect upon the incapacity of the principal. As with a trust, language should be incorporated in the *springing* power of attorney that would set the requirements for determining incapacity. If an individual has established an "unfunded" trust, or if any assets remain outside the individual's partially funded trust, a power of attorney should expressly authorize the transfer of the individual's assets to the trustee. (See chapter 10 for a discussion of powers of attorney.)

Using Trusts to Protect Assets

Q 4:79 What standards should a trust set for distributions by the trustee?

Although not technically required for a trust to be valid, a key provision in every trust is the kinds of distributions that must or may be made by the trustee. Options include one or more of the following:

- Required distribution of "income" only (the meaning of "income" then determined by the instrument itself and state law, which may include one or more versions of the Uniform Principal and Income Act; in general, "income" does not include realized capital gains)—this is a mandatory provision that does not require exercise of discretion
- The same, but with discretion to "spray" income among beneficiaries pursuant to a standard
- Discretionary distribution of principal for one beneficiary pursuant to a standard (known as a "principal invasion power")
- Discretionary distributions of principal (the power to "spray" principal) among a class of beneficiaries pursuant to a standard
- Discretionary distribution of income among one or a class of beneficiaries

Where there is no discretion on the trustee's part, limits on who may serve as trustee are fewer, but opportunities for asset protection are less.

Standards to be used for discretionary distributions fall into one or more of the following categories:

- For "support" (making the trust a "support" trust and thus not immune from demands by Medicaid agencies that the trust principal be spent on the beneficiaries' needs)
- Pursuant to an "ascertainable standard" that may, but need not, include the term "support" (see Qs 4:20, 5:66)—this standard is typically used so that a beneficiary may serve as

trustee without the trust property being included in the beneficiary's estate for tax purposes

- "Absolute" discretion, with no objective standard (making the trust a fully "discretionary" trust and likely to be immune from the demands of creditors as a spendthrift trust and possibly, but not necessarily, protected from demands of Medicaid agencies)
- "Absolute" discretion tempered by an instruction not to make distributions that would reduce or replace government benefits (a "special needs trust," as discussed in chapter 17)

Q 4:80 Can trust assets be protected from creditors?

To the extent that a grantor has control over the trust assets, those assets will be considered available to him or her and will thus be vulnerable to creditors. This is true of assets transferred into the standard revocable living trust, as long as one or both grantors is alive (but separate property of one spouse may not be subject to the debt obligations of the other spouse, depending on state law regarding spousal obligations).

A beneficiary of a trust, on the other hand, does not have control over the assets until those assets are actually distributed to him or her. Depending on the terms of the trust and state law, the beneficiary may not have the power to compel distributions provided the trustee has acted in good faith. If the grantor wishes to make sure of this, the grantor will include in the trust instrument language that confirms this, usually called the "spendthrift provision." The language typically states that neither principal nor income from the trust can be anticipated by or assigned to the beneficiary, nor can any creditor of the beneficiary attach it. The creditor cannot in effect "garnish" the trust funds or demand that the trustee pay a judgment to the creditor rather than the beneficiary. A possible exception is the IRS; a recent case holds that the Treasury may be able to levy upon even a spendthrift trust. [Internal Revenue Service v. Orr, 180 F.3d 656 (5th Cir. 1999)] Of course, once the distribution is made, the trust offers no protection to the beneficiary against his or her creditors.

In many—perhaps most—states, the trust will *not* protect the assets from the grantor's own creditors if the grantor is also the beneficiary, if there are any circumstances under which the trustee could make distributions to the beneficiary. Thus, if the trust states that "only income" is payable to the grantor-beneficiary, but not principal, the principal may be immunized. By contrast, if the principal can be paid to the grantor-beneficiary "in the trustee's discretion," principal may be protected in some states, but not in others. [See, e.g., Greenwich Trust Co. v. Tyson, 129 Conn. 211 (1942)]

Q 4:81 How can trusts be used to control distribution of assets to spendthrift or unreliable beneficiaries?

Trusts are the preferred way to control the distribution of assets to unreliable beneficiaries. The trusts can be funded with gift or death transfers; however, if the donor wishes to gain some tax advantage by removing property from the donor's estate, the trust must not be revocable by the donor.

Q 4:82 Are gifts to an irrevocable trust subject to gift tax?

In order for a donor to be able to treat a gift to a trust as excluded from gift tax by virtue of the $10,000 per donor, per donee "annual exclusion" (as of 2003, increased by COLA to $11,000), the trust must be designed to satisfy the requirement that the gift be a gift of a "present interest." This usually means including provisions giving the beneficiary certain rights to withdraw the gift. These are discussed at Q 5:28. While it is possible to limit these rights in order to safeguard some beneficiaries against imprudent withdrawal, it may not be possible to include these rights and at the same time ensure that the beneficiary will be eligible for public or medical assistance benefits. Since in most states no gift tax will actually be payable until the grantor's gifts have reached a total of anywhere from $600,000 to $1 million (with Connecticut being an exception to this statement), it may be preferable to risk the eventual gift tax than to include the withdrawal rights.

Q 4:83 How can trusts be used to distribute assets to a beneficiary who is receiving public benefits or who may require long-term care?

Outright distribution of assets to an individual who is disabled and receiving Supplemental Security income or Medicaid benefits may cause that person to lose the benefits, because the benefits are usually need-based. (On the other hand, Social Security disability income and Medicare are not needs-based and will never be affected.) In certain situations, special needs trusts can be set up that allow recipients to receive goods or services paid for by the trust without jeopardizing their Social Security income or Medicaid benefits, but such trusts must be drawn up with care to conform with state and federal guidelines. Income from the trust must not be considered available to the beneficiary or the income may push the beneficiary over the income limit for the public benefit and disqualify the beneficiary. Funds put into the trust usually cannot be used for anything ordinarily provided by the public benefit programs, such as shelter, food, and health care, without at least some reduction in benefits; rather, the special needs trust will be primarily intended for the recipient's personal use or for special medical or educational needs not provided otherwise. If any potential beneficiary is in this situation (and for the very cautious, if any potential beneficiary ever might be in this situation), trust language should be included that either redirects the beneficiary's share to a separate special needs trust that conforms to state and federal requirements, or disinherits the disabled person altogether. (See chapter 17 for a discussion of special needs trusts.)

Those who anticipate the need for long-term care must also consider state Medicaid regulations, which may place burdensome restrictions on trusts.

1. For instance, if a Medicaid recipient receives an outright gift or inheritance of more than several thousand dollars, he or she would be declared ineligible to receive Medicaid benefits (and in some states, would have to give the state some or all of the inheritance as repayment of his or her accrued "debt" with respect to other benefits than Medicaid). The balance of the gift would then have to be spent down before the recipient could reapply.

2. If a Medicaid applicant's house is not owned directly, but instead is held in a revocable trust, it may no longer be treated as exempt for Medicaid eligibility purposes, and will have to be taken out of the trust before the grantor can receive benefits.

3. The lookback period for transfers from or to a trust is significantly longer than that for regular gift transfers under federal regulations (60 months for trusts, 36 months for individuals). [42 U.S.C. § 1396p] (See chapter 14 for a discussion of Medicaid trusts.)
4. As noted above, trusts in which the Medicaid applicant or spouse retains interests are not protected and are counted as available.
5. A trust for a surviving spouse intended to meet only special needs and not be counted as the spouse's assets *must* be contained within the four corners of a will, not a living trust, in order that it not be counted as "available" to the surviving spouse.
6. In at least one state, Connecticut, an irrevocable trust established for the benefit of an applicant or spouse, in which interest greater than 5 percent is retained, may be entirely terminated upon a request by the state, rendering all assets available. [Conn. Gen. Stat. § 45a-486]
7. Some state courts may decide that it is against public policy to allow any beneficiary of a trust, no matter how restricted, to access government benefits and will impress a repayment lien on a trust the moment the trust beneficiary receives anything of value. [Ohio Rev. Stat. § 1339.51]

Q 4:84 Should a living trust be designated as beneficiary (or alternate beneficiary) of qualified retirement plans and tax-sheltered annuities?

The client may have competing interests in dealing with tax-qualified assets such as retirement accounts and annuities. On one hand, naming the trust as beneficiary ensures that the assets are divided in accordance with the client's then-current wishes, and permits changes to be made in one place to effect the change in all assets. Naming the trust as beneficiary also permits the client to place appropriate limitations on the use of the proceeds, a particularly important issue if the beneficiaries (or some of them) are minors, disabled individuals receiving public benefits, or simply unreliable or spendthrifts.

On the other hand, by naming a trust as beneficiary of tax-qualified assets the client may be giving up flexibility to continue to delay the income taxation of those plan benefits. In addition, the client may be forcing the income tax on those benefits into the highest marginal tax bracket. As a result of these competing interests, it is impossible to generalize about whether the trust should be named as beneficiary.

In most cases married couples will choose to name one another as the primary beneficiary of tax-qualified plans, because of the flexibility afforded to spouses (to roll over plan assets into a new individual retirement account). Married couples may consider naming the trust as alternate beneficiary, both to accomplish the goals described and to permit the surviving spouse to disclaim a portion of the retirement benefits, if appropriate. Such a disclaimer may be useful, for example, fully to fund the credit shelter share of a trust upon the death of the first spouse.

Q 4:85 In community property states, does separate property lose its character when transferred to a joint trust?

Married couples may choose to establish a single joint trust rather than two separate trusts holding their individual assets. In such a case the trust should include provisions confirming that separate and community property will maintain their separate or community character even when transferred to a trust unless the grantors wish to have all property treated as one or the other. A schedule of trust property may be included in the trust agreement, in which the grantors can describe the property as community property or as the separate property of the respective spouses. However it is effected, characterization of the property as separate or community should preserve its treatment under tax rules and the terms of the trust itself.

Often trust assets are removed or added after the execution of the trust agreement. In anticipation of death or incapacity the grantors should take special care to ensure that the successor trustee is given information on how the assets are to be characterized. It is also important that a joint trust agreement or declaration provide for the management and characterization of trust assets as separate or community.

Trustees

Q 4:86 What are the duties of a trustee?

A trustee has several obligations to discharge in administering the trust. Although these duties are owed to the trust itself, they may be enforced in an action by or on behalf of the beneficiaries of the trust. Among the duties of a trustee are the duties to:

1. Carry out the settlor's intent (in accordance with the terms of the trust instrument). Depending on the particular state's laws, this requirement may "trump" most of the others except the duty to act in good faith. The Uniform Trust Code, however, will make some of these duties "non-waivable," whatever the state's case law currently provides. [U.T.C. § 66]
2. Administer the trust solely in the interest of the beneficiary or beneficiaries to the extent not otherwise limited by the terms of the trust instrument, also referred to as the "duty of loyalty." In the trustee's dealings with the beneficiary, the trustee must not be influenced by the interest of a third party. [3 Bogert, Trusts & Trustees, § 543; Restatement § 170, comment]
3. Refrain from self-dealing. The duty of loyalty is exemplified by the duty of the trustee not to engage in "self-dealing" for the trustee's own benefit, potentially at the expense of a beneficiary. [Restatement § 170; Scott § 170] A frequently quoted case is *Meinhard v. Salmon* [249 N.Y. 458, 464, 164 N.E. 545 (1924) (Cardozo, J.)], referring to a fiduciary's duty as "the punctilio of an honor the most sensitive" as the "touchstone."
4. Not to delegate liability (although modern trust law may permit delegation of responsibility as, for example, to an investment adviser).
5. Keep and render clear and accurate accounts. [Restatement § 172, Scott § 172]
6. Keep the beneficiaries informed, when requested. [Restatement § 73, Scott § 173] The best approach is to provide information on a reasonable schedule, and make records and

supporting documentation available for the beneficiary's review.

7. Exercise reasonable care and skill in the administration of the trust, and utilize any special skill used to procure appointment as trustee. [Restatement § 174, Scott § 174]
8. Take control of trust property, and maintain control so as to avoid loss or injury to the trust. [Restatement § 175, Scott § 175]
9. Use reasonable care to preserve trust property from loss or waste. [Restatement § 176, Scott § 176]
10. Take reasonable steps to recover claims due to the trust. [Restatement § 177, Scott § 177]
11. Reasonably defend actions brought against the trust that might result in a loss to the trust. [Restatement § 178, Scott § 178]
12. Keep trust assets separate from the trustee's own property, or the property of other trusts or individuals (duty not to commingle). [Restatement § 179, Scott § 179]
13. Make trust property productive (unless the trust instrument provides otherwise). [Restatement § 181, Scott § 181] By contrast, the proposed Uniform Trust Code would remove this requirement and merely require the trustee to exercise the care of a prudent person. [U.T.C. § 804].
14. Deal impartially with beneficiaries, not favoring individual beneficiaries or classes of beneficiaries (e.g., income versus remainder beneficiaries). [2A A.W. Scott & W.F. Fratcher, The Law of Trusts 4th Ed. (1987); § 183, 1 Restatement (Second) of Trusts]

Q 4:87 What is the "prudent person" rule, and how does it apply to trust administration?

In making investment decisions, a trustee must exercise the same care a prudent person would when investing his or her own property, considering the need for preservation of the estate and the amount and regularity of income to be derived. This broad statement has come to be referred to as the "prudent person" rule, and has been adopted in some form in most jurisdictions.

Q 4:88 What is the "prudent investor" rule, and how does it differ from the "prudent person" rule?

Criticism of the "prudent person" rule has focused on a number of concerns. Although the prudent person rule does not expressly condone review of individual investment decisions without reference to the larger investment strategy of the trustee, in application the effect has often been to isolate individual investments that perform poorly and charge the trustee for mistakes with the benefit of perfect hindsight. The result of that tendency (or perception, at least) has historically been conservative investment strategies and resultant low rates of return. In order to permit a more balanced investment approach, the Restatement of the Law of Trusts (Third Edition, currently under revision and partially published) has adopted a "prudent investor" approach to analyzing the trustee's investment decisions. A number of states have followed suit by explicitly adopting the prudent investor principle. The Uniform Prudent Investor Act incorporates the Restatement approach, and despite having only been released in 1994, by 2002 it had already been adopted in 37 states plus the District of Columbia, excepting only Alabama, Delaware, Florida, Georgia, Kentucky, Louisiana, Mississippi, Montana, Nevada, New York, South Dakota, Texas, and Wisconsin. [See *www.nccusl.org* and *www.fpanet.org/gov/investments/upia071900.cfm*]

Q 4:89 What is the "modern portfolio theory of investment," and how is it related to the prudent investor rule?

Modern portfolio theory proceeds from two premises:

1. Financial markets are efficient; therefore, the price of an asset is directly related to its expected total return and volatility; and
2. Diversification of assets reduces volatility.

With those two concepts in mind, modern portfolio theory directs the investor to determine an appropriate mix of asset types, considering the portfolio's tolerance for risk and the desired rate of return. Once the asset mix is determined, investments should be diversified in order to approximate that asset mix. As individual assets (or funds) increase and decrease in value, some adjustment may be necessary (either of the asset mix or the underlying assumptions), but the basic approach will not change with fluctuations in the marketplace or in the actual assets.

The modern portfolio theory approach is greatly facilitated by the prudent investor rule's abandonment of individual after-the-fact investment reviews. Rather than focus on the performance of individual holdings, the prudent investor rule encourages the trustee (and any court asked to pass judgment on the trustee's performance) to consider the larger investment picture and the importance of diversification.

Q 4:90 Who should act as trustee of a trust?

Often the grantor(s) will serve as the initial trustee(s) of the trust, in order to work with the trust and determine personally its efficacy. For unfunded trusts, the surviving spouse may be named the sole trustee during lifetime and after death. In the case of married couples establishing a joint trust, the surviving spouse often continues to serve as trustee of the trust and/or any subtrusts created at the death of the first spouse to die, and only when the survivor dies or becomes incapacitated does the successor trustee step in. The successor can be a family member, a trusted third party, or a corporate trustee.

Naming family members as trustee (or successor trustee) will usually lower the cost of administration (most family members do not charge fees as trustee, and even if they do they are likely to charge considerably less than professional trustees) and help ensure that personal and family issues receive adequate consideration. Many clients will feel strongly that family members should be able to handle family financial business, and if the ultimate beneficiaries are also the trustees, the client may correctly observe that the only person hurt by any failure of a family trustee is the same family member.

To counterbalance the positives inherent in naming family members as trustees, there are of course some negatives. Family may not be particularly adept at handling financial matters, particularly if the second generation has had less money than the client's generation (which is the normal circumstance). Family members may disagree, even when clients believe that no disagreement is possible. Family members are more likely to misappropriate trust assets than are professional trustees, and every practitioner has stories of seemingly reliable trustees who abuse the trust placed in them by clients when establishing a trust.

The grantors may wish to designate two or more beneficiaries as co-trustees of the trust, so that they can monitor one another's behavior. This is not always advisable—if there is dysfunction among family members, the co-trustees may be unable to work with each other and the management and distribution of trust assets will be significantly hampered.

Q 4:91 Should the attorney act as trustee?

One choice of professional fiduciary available to clients is the attorney. Although serious ethical questions may need to be considered, most states permit individual attorneys to act as trustee without having to register (or be regulated) as a trust company. Setting aside the ethical concerns, there are disadvantages and advantages to both the trustor and the attorney if the attorney is selected as trustee.

From the trustor's perspective, the attorney trustee is likely to be somewhat more skilled at management of trust assets than most family members, and somewhat less likely to misbehave. At the same time, the attorney/trustee will usually be less expensive than a corporate trustee. On the other side of the issue is the same problem with naming any individual as trustee: The future availability, capability, and even fee structure of an individual trustee is unknown. At least with a corporate trustee the trustor has the ability to look at decades of experience, and to generalize about the likely future structure and behavior of the entity.

From the attorney's perspective there are also positives and negatives to acting as trustee. Fiduciary work is predictable and reliable, and so long as the beneficiaries are not in conflict or making unreasonable demands, is seldom stress-inducing or confrontational. It also requires the attorney to rethink office structure, staffing patterns, training, and emphasis. The attorney-trustee must be familiar with investment principles and money management, and may even need to register with state and federal agencies as if he or she were a financial planner or adviser. Although the work is usually low-stress, when errors do occur they tend to be of high magnitude, and close supervision and careful systems design are essential.

Q 4:92 Is a corporate trustee the best choice?

Not necessarily. Corporate trustees may refuse to become trustees of trusts with assets deemed too minimal, and grantors may wish to do some research on typical corporate trustee fees before designating them in their trust instruments. There is an argument that corporate trustees have a built-in conflict, because their employers benefit to the extent that they can hang on to the assets of the trust. Some trustors prefer that level of conservatism, especially when the trust beneficiaries tend to be irresponsible, but a family member or friend will probably have a much better understanding of the needs of the beneficiaries.

Corporate trustees may also be limited by their parent firms as to how the trust assets are to be invested. Banks often have a single national pooled fund for assets of all trusts (or all trusts under a certain figure, such as $2 million), which may or may not be sufficiently diversified or well-suited for certain assets. The trustees may be unable to take advantage of investment opportunities in their own communities. Again, the trustor may prefer this level of conservatism rather than risk having a family member invest all the assets frivolously.

Q 4:93 How do the powers of a trustee differ from those of a personal representative?

Generally the testator/grantor wants to give each fiduciary broad powers in order to carry out the wishes in the will/trust instrument, although both are restricted to the extent that their activities cannot be self-serving, but must be directed solely for the benefit of the beneficiaries. However, while the personal representative's duties are finite, the trust might be managed by a trustee for years, even decades; accordingly, the grantor must take care to ensure that the trustee can do almost anything the grantor can do, other than amend or revoke the instrument itself.

For example, most trusts will include powers to purchase or sell real estate, to borrow or loan money, to purchase stocks or bonds, and to exercise the powers associated with those actions (voting shares of stock, purchasing insurance, etc.). Failure explicitly to include those powers will probably not be fatal, as broad general powers are implied (unless specifically excluded) by either common law or statute in most states.

Some powers may not be assumed in practice. As an illustration, although broad powers to purchase, hold, and encumber stocks and bonds may be included in the trust document or the state's general law governing trusts, many brokerage houses will refuse to authorize margin purchases or hypothecation unless those powers are specifically described. Of course, many trust settlors will specifically wish to exclude those powers.

Q 4:94 Can the trustee of a trust be replaced?

The trust instrument may provide for a mechanism to remove a trustee and name a successor. Frequently, the trustor retains that power; sometimes the beneficiary (or a majority of the beneficiaries, acting together) is given the power to change trustees. (Removal powers for a surviving spouse may need to be limited for tax reasons discussed in chapter 5; see also Q 4:20.) If no provision for a change of trustees is included in the trust instrument, or if the conditions for a change of trustee have not been met, it may still be within the discretion of a court of competent jurisdiction to determine that a change in trustees would be in the best interests of the trust itself, or of some or all of the beneficiaries, and to remove and replace the trustee.

Because *inter vivos* trusts are ordinarily not subjected to the control of a court, an interested person (e.g., a beneficiary, a trustee, a trustor, or a creditor) would have to bring an action in the appropriate court to gain authority over the trust. Usually, the domicile of a trust (and therefore the state or territory having jurisdiction over the trust's administration) is the same as the domicile of the trustee. When there are two or more trustees, the state of residence of each trustee may have jurisdiction over the trust's administration. The state in which a beneficiary, or even most or all of the beneficiaries, resides, or the state in which the trustor resided or resides, will not necessarily have any jurisdiction over the trust. Although the trust may include language directing that it will be governed by the state in which it was executed (or some other state), jurisdiction will still lie with the trustee's domiciliary state, which would then have to apply the law specified by the trust.

Other Resources

Q 4:95 What are a practitioner's other resources when dealing with wills, trusts, and other means for the transfer of property?

Trust, estate, and property law have a long and fascinating history. While it is obviously important to become familiar with the state statutes in this area, to the extent that statutes are skimpy the practitioner should recognize that much of the law would be found in published case law. To the extent that the state's case law is also inadequate, however, the practitioner should be familiar with the established treatises, which include:

- Restatement (2nd) of Trusts, and as it is completed, the 3rd Restatement.
- Scott on Trusts (commonly referred to as such although it now has many other authors).
- Bogert on Trusts and Trustees (not used as often as Scott).
- For those whose states have adopted the various Uniform Laws dealing with trusts, the official comments of the Uniform Laws Commissions. These are available in the published volumes of Uniform Laws Annotated, and also online at *http://www.nccusl.org/*.

Practical Estate Planning Problems

Q 4:96 What practical and ethical issues commonly arise in estate planning and administration?

A variety of practical and ethical problems commonly appear in this area of elder law. The rest of this chapter covers such problems, which may arise in situations such as the following:

1. Incomplete knowledge of the whole family picture;
2. Possible incompetence of the client;
3. Using the attorney as agent or using corporate trustees;
4. Use of a nonstandard "will";
5. Equalizing pay-on-death benefits; and

6. Anticipated dissension among beneficiaries.

Q 4:97 What practical and ethical issues can arise when the entire family picture of an elder law client is unknown?

The following examples may identify some such concerns.

1. *Unexpected existence of progeny.* The attorney gets a call from an angry individual who identifies herself as the child of the attorney's client who recently passed away. She has just discovered two documents: the title to her mother's home, which states that the home was held in joint tenancy with the caller's brother; and a letter from the attorney to the client recommending the transfer to joint tenancy to avoid probate. The attorney realizes he had not known about the daughter's existence when he wrote the letter, but does not remember if this was because the client purposefully did not tell him or if he did an inadequate job of intake. Is the attorney in trouble? Is there a way to ensure this does not happen?

   The attorney's best defense against problems of this type is prevention. Adequate intake, coupled with thorough file documentation, is the key to establishing the client's wishes and the attorney's successful protection of those wishes. Contemporaneous notes and correspondence to (and from) the client are especially valuable in subsequent attempts to reconstruct the events.

   The attorney is not, however, a guarantor of the client's wishes. If the client does not provide complete information after the attorney makes reasonable efforts to collect it (and to explain to the client why it is important), the attorney cannot be charged with omniscience. Failure to provide complete information may, in fact, be the result of client incapacity; while a good elder law attorney should be skilled at recognizing those problems, he or she should not be expected to serve as a psychologist or diagnostician. Adequate intake efforts and careful documentation will not only help document the attorney's actions months or years later, but will also help reveal the client's shortcomings if that is the cause of the failure.

2. *Benefit cutoffs.* The daughter of a recently deceased client calls the attorney in tears and says she just found out that

under the terms of the decedent's will, which the attorney had prepared, the caller's brother gets half the $60,000 estate. Unfortunately the brother is disabled and was receiving government benefits, but with his newfound inheritance his benefits have been cut off. What questions should the attorney ask? What advice should he give?

Once again, adequate intake is critical. If the client knew of the son's disability and public benefits, and knew there were ways to protect the continued benefits from loss despite the son's receipt of an interest from the estate, he or she would probably have arranged for the estate to pass subject to an appropriate trust (see chapter 17 on special needs trusts). Failure to offer that option may have been the attorney's fault if he or she did not make adequate inquiry.

There may still be steps to take to minimize the problems caused by loss of benefits. Purchase of a home, an exempt vehicle, household effects, or medical equipment may permit the immediate resumption of benefits. Other steps may be available depending on the family situation, the amount remaining in the disabled brother's name, and the precise nature of the suspended public benefits. Among the likely solutions: The court (either through the pending probate proceeding or in a separate guardianship/conservatorship action) might be asked to create an appropriate special needs trust and direct the transfer of the assets into the trust. It is critical at this juncture that the elder law attorney not compound the problem by making snap decisions about how to rectify the situation.

Q 4:98 What practical and ethical considerations are involved in drafting or determining the validity of a will?

The following examples may occur when drafting or probating the will of a client.

1. *Capacity to make a will.* Client A is bipolar and alcoholic, and has been living on the streets most of his adult life. He wanders into the downtown Legal Aid office and states that he wishes to make a will leaving his backpack and its contents to his drinking buddy. Client B has been diagnosed with dementia, Alzheimer's type, and has become obsessive about

the making of a will. She knows that she wants her caretaker daughter to get everything, but is incapable of providing information about her assets, including whether she owns the home she lives in and the size of her bank accounts. Is either client capable of making a will?

Assessing the competence of a client to make a will is a problem regularly faced by elder law attorneys. While few attorneys have specific training in formal evaluative techniques, it is important to remember that the test of competence is not clinical, but functional.

The attorney might view his or her goal as any one of three possibilities, or (most likely) a combination of all three:

a. Carry out the legitimate wishes of the client to the best of the lawyer's ability.

b. Ensure that the "right" result is obtained, considering high-minded concepts of justice and personal autonomy.

c. Always be able to defend successfully any estate planning documents the attorney prepares.

The difficulty should be obvious: If the lawyer is interested in client autonomy, and the client has strong (but peculiar or unusual) wishes, it will occasionally be necessary to prepare documents for marginally or questionably competent clients. Few practitioners would decide that either Client A or Client B should be foreclosed from carrying out their wishes. That leads to the conclusion that the lawyer's job is to ascertain whether the client is really competent, and to help ensure that the client's wishes are actually carried out (i.e., that the estate planning documents are capable of being successfully defended).

While multidisciplinary evaluations may be invaluable in guiding the lawyer (and providing the background to later defend the client's estate plan), the central questions will be about the client's capacity to make a will at the time the will is made. Unless the physician, psychologist, and therapist are going to be present at the time of the signing of the will in each case, it becomes the lawyer's job to make sure any evaluation relates appropriately in time and substance to the execution of documents. That will often require multiple interviews (to establish that the client's wishes are fixed and consistent), detailed questioning, and adequate documentation (to protect the admissibility of the lawyer's contemporaneous impression).

Despite the oddity of their living arrangements and wishes, nothing in the facts described for Client A or Client B suggests that either is incapable of making a will. It then becomes the lawyer's job to make sure the will each signs actually reflects his or her intentions, and is defensible in any later proceeding. The mere fact that a contest is unlikely (as, for example, in the willing of Client A's backpack) does not diminish the lawyer's obligation to treat the client professionally and with dignity.

2. *Holographic will.* A terminally ill man handwrites a letter to his daughter, stating that he wants to leave everything in equal proportions to her and her brother, but that he does not want any of his estate to go to a younger daughter who is on drugs. He suggests that the brother may be a better choice for personal representative (which the daughter says is based on his old-fashioned perceptions about men being more capable with finances). Does this constitute a holographic will? If not, does the document have any other use?

   If a written document is presented purporting to be a will, the attorney may need to determine first its validity as a will. The letter is probably not a proper will, even in a state that recognizes holographic wills—it only expresses the author's intent to make a will. Such a writing may form the basis of a family agreement, if all family members decide to honor his wishes (however, it is unlikely the daughter on drugs will go along with this, when under intestate succession laws she would likely get a full third of the estate). In this case, the letter may be submitted as evidence for the court to consider in appointing a personal representative.

3. *Equalizing pay on death benefit.* A couple retains an attorney to do their wills and health care powers of attorney. This is a second marriage for both, but it has lasted 20 years; they each have two children from former marriages. During the interview the couple reveals that after attending a seminar on probate avoidance, they have put their home and all their bank accounts in joint tenancy with right of survivorship, and designated each other as beneficiaries for their stockholdings.

The children have not been named secondary beneficiaries, but the spouses have promised each other that the survivor of them will make sure that all the children benefit at the survivor's death. What advice should the attorney give?

Pay-on-death benefits are contractual, and are not subject to wills, probate, or the intestate succession laws. Under this scenario, *all* the assets will go to the surviving spouse, who is then under no legal obligation to leave any of the children anything. The survivor may marry again and leave his or her estate to the new spouse, or may decide to leave all the money to Greenpeace. Wills are not necessarily the best protection either, as the spouses may again agree to leave everything to each other and the survivor may then amend his or her will to leave the estate to beneficiaries other than the children.

The attorney should advise the couple of the worst-case scenarios, then suggest that the spouses provide for their own children at the first death, either in the will or through pay-on-death benefits such as life insurance policies. The attorney should also explain to the couple the pitfalls of owning a home in joint tenancy when there are children of a former marriage. A popular solution is a trust (whether in the will, or a separate document) that gives the surviving spouse the right to all income from the trust, principal if needed, and then leaves the remainder to the testator's or trustor's children. A similar arrangement can provide for the house, perhaps a form of "life use" for the survivor that will enable him or her continued ability to deduct property tax payments. The couple may decide to "risk" the children losing any inheritance with respect to the house, but to protect their interests in other funds—a compromise solution.

4. *Anticipation of dissension among the beneficiaries.* There are clients who have a realistic idea of how their children will behave during probate proceedings and ask the attorney drafting the will how they can forestall any complications.

   A favorite device is the "in terrorem" clause, which states that any beneficiary who challenges the will loses all claim to any distribution from the will. These are completely ineffective against valid objections to the will, for instance if there is good evidence that the testator was demented or coerced at the time of execution, but they can prevent frivolous (or even questionable) challenges. They are only effective if the prospective challenger does receive a benefit under the will or trust so that there is actually something to lose should the clause take effect.

Although the testator has the right to do anything he or she wants with his or her estate, the attorney should try to discourage using the will to punish the children. Equal distribution is almost impossible to challenge in court, but the exclusion of a child from a will for any reason might generate a challenge to the probate proceedings and will certainly polarize the family for years to come. Unequal distribution is most easy to defend when it is obvious from the children's circumstances that some were more in need than others.

Although he or she has no obligation to do so, the testator can be encouraged to discuss his or her wishes with the children beforehand to see how they react. Their reaction may be surprising. Allowing the children themselves to "elect" the personal representative might prevent a potential fight over the testator's choice of personal representative. The attorney could well end up doing the probate, so she should do what she can to assist the testator in forestalling post-mortem disputes.

Q 4:99 What practical and ethical considerations apply where the attorney is asked to serve as agent or a corporate trustee is used?

The following examples serve to illustrate the special considerations that could arise where the attorney is asked to serve as agent or a corporate trustee is chosen.

1. *Attorney as agent.* The client has no spouse or children, but likes the idea of planning for possible future incapacity by signing a financial power of attorney so that "those nosy courts won't get involved and tell the whole world that I've lost my marbles." He likes and trusts the attorney, and asks him to be the agent. The attorney likes the client, who does not have a large estate. Should he go along with the client's wishes?

While there is a natural inclination to try to solve clients' problems by whatever means may be available, taking on fiduciary responsibility for a client should not be approached lightly. Fiduciary duties are extensive and offer tremendous opportunities for the lawyer to expand personal liability beyond acceptable levels. Furthermore, even if the lawyer is prepared to accept those responsibilities, it may be economically infeasible to manage a small estate for a fee. In other words, most attorneys (even those with extensive fiduciary practices) inevitably advise clients to seek alternatives before relying on the lawyer as fiduciary.

Once the lawyer has agreed to act as fiduciary, problems of conflicting interests arise. In order to resolve those problems comfortably, the attorney may be wise to insist that the client secure separate (independent) legal advice before executing any document naming him as fiduciary. If the client insists, at the very least the attorney should counsel the client to include alternative agents, perhaps with the power to remove the attorney.

2. *Corporate trustee.* The surviving grantor of a joint revocable trust, who is the income beneficiary of the decedent's trust established by the bank trustee after the husband's death, is in a nursing home selected by the bank trustee. The grantors' daughter, who visits her mother twice a week, is unhappy with the selection and wishes her mother to be moved to a more expensive nursing home (which is also located somewhat closer to the daughter's home). She also wishes to be reimbursed for her expenses in visiting her mother, and in fact has been lobbying for a small salary for her services performed on behalf of her mother, such as taking her on day trips and advocating on her behalf with the health care providers (but the nursing home staff say she is a pain in the neck). There are three other children, all of whom live out of state. The corporate trustee balks at the daughter's suggestions, and the daughter calls an attorney. What questions should the attorney ask?

   Corporate trustees are by nature cautious, and conflicts can easily arise between family members, who want the very best for the surviving spouse (or at least say they do), and the trustee, whose focus will be on conservative management of assets. The daughter and her attorney should make another pass at the trustee, but their best option will be to discuss the matter with the other beneficiaries. A family agreement would go far to persuade the trustee of the merits of the extra care (and would reduce its liability risk), especially because a family who can agree on a care plan for their mother can also agree on the removal of a trustee.

Chapter 5

Estate Planning

Estate and gift tax considerations have been the major factor shaping estate planning decisions in the past several decades. However, in fact most Americans now have little reason for concern about the prospect of owing taxes at death. With the federal tax exemption equivalent amount now $1,000,000, and scheduled to increase progressively to $4,000,000 with ultimate repeal in 2010, few decedents' estates face any federal tax liability. Even if the full repeal never is completed, it is unlikely that the exemption will ever fall below $1,000,000 and may well be fixed at a higher number such as $2,000,000. Moreover, under federal law, the exemption has applied to asset transfers made during one's lifetime as well as those made at death using a "unified system." This has meant that those not expecting to pay estate taxes at death did not have to be concerned about gift taxes during lifetime. This will change when the estate and gift tax exemptions part company in 2004, but the gift tax exemption will be fixed at $1,000,000, still beyond the reach of many.

Why make the effort to understand these tax regimes, then? Leaving aside the possibility that one may encounter wealthy clients with obviously taxable estates and would prefer not to refer them to others, there are also those times when clients who seem to live modestly find themselves unexpected millionaires. In the late 1990s, before the steep stock market declines, many professionals saw their humble retirement funds zoom into the millions; localized real estate booms can cause the vacation cottage to be valued as if it were a palace; and an old family business or farm with hard assets like land or machinery could turn out to be an "estate" incurring more tax than cash on hand with which to pay.

This chapter discusses the exclusions, exemptions, and deductions available to ease the tax burden including the unified credit exemption equivalent, referred to above, and the marital deduction, which allows assets to pass tax-free to the donor's or decedent's spouse. For those whose estates are valued at (or might reach) taxability, there are a number of estate planning choices to consider. Estate and gift tax basics are also discussed, as are the most commonly used estate planning approaches, including lifetime gifts, marital deduction planning, charitable giving, life insurance, and valuation discounts.

It is important for the beginner or general practitioner to recognize that some of the techniques described in this chapter are considered "complex" estate planning and it is advisable to do further study or obtain an expert's review before undertaking such techniques alone. Helpful resources include:

- William D. Mitchell, Estate & Retirement Planning Answer Book (4th Ed.), Aspen Publishers.
- BNA Tax Management Portfolio Series (available on disk or in multiple spiral volumes)—although expensive, if one were to choose a single resource for tax information, this would be the one; it may be available in a law library near you.
- Jeffrey N. Pennell, A. James Casner, Estate Planning (6th Ed.) (Aspen Publishers).
- Howard M. Zaritsky, Tax Planning for Family Wealth Transfers: Analysis with Forms (RIA) (other titles also useful).
- For charitable planning: Conrad Teitell, Deferred Giving; also Portable Planned Giving Manual (and many other titles), published on Mr. Teitell's own label, Taxwise Giving (www.taxwisegiving.com).

- Archives of the discussion groups ABA-TAX and ABA-PTL (see www.abanet.org).

Overview

Q 5:1 What are the major estate planning approaches during phase-in of the federal estate tax repeal?

The major estate planning approaches include:

1. *"Bypass" planning.* Gifts or bequests to spouses are tax-free regardless of value, so it is simple (from a tax perspective) to leave a decedent's entire estate to the surviving spouse. By this method, any tax liability will be due only at the second death. But there are good reasons to "bypass" some of the marital deduction and incur at least some tax liability on the first spouse's death, if for no other reason than to utilize the full exemption equivalent amount for each spouse. Thus, a couple worth $2 million, both dying in 2002, can effectively pass their entire joint estate to devisees without incurring any tax liability, so long as they have planned appropriately to take advantage of the $1 million exemption equivalent amount on each death; the first spouse's exemption is "lost" if everything passes to the survivor and is only taxed at

his/her death. Credit shelter trusts, QTIP (qualified terminable interest property) trusts, and QDOTs (qualified domestic trusts) fare typically used in marital deduction planning. Estate tax repeal as adopted in 2001 will accelerate the increase in the exemption equivalent amount, but will retain federal estate taxes until 2010. Meanwhile, state estate tax systems, long relegated to near-irrelevance by the use of the federal credit for state estate taxes paid, will gradually increase in importance as individual states decide whether to abandon, maintain, or even increase their estate tax collections.

2. *Lifetime gifts.* Gifts completed during the decedent's lifetime can reduce the taxable estate on death. The fact that the federal tax system is unified—that is, gift and estate taxes are calculated on the basis of the total amount given during life and at death—reduces the effectiveness of lifetime gifts. Still, gifts of $11,000 per year or less ($10,000 plus an inflation factor that by 2002 had increased the amount to $11,000) avoid gift taxation altogether, so annual gifts can be structured to reduce the final estate size without incurring any current tax liability. A common method of making gifts is to transfer life insurance (or give cash to be used to pay life insurance premiums) to maximize the value of the property received by the beneficiary. Gifting techniques to make transfers without incurring tax frequently involve irrevocable life insurance trusts (ILITs) and so-called "Crummey" trusts (see Q 5:28). Under some circumstances, it may even be advisable to make gifts early and incur gift tax liability, if tax liability is certain to occur later on. The reason for this is that the amounts used to pay the gift tax will not be subject to the gift tax themselves, whereas the entire estate is taxed even though some must go to pay taxes. Phase-out and ultimate repeal of the federal estate and generation-skipping taxes will not necessarily affect the gift tax, which is also subject to a cap.

3. *Charitable giving.* Lifetime gifts and bequests (at death) to charitable organizations avoid taxation altogether. They do not usually increase family wealth; the estate tax saved is usually offset or exceeded by the "loss" of the gifted property. (One way of putting this to a client is that the client can

choose to leave something to charity or to have the IRS take it instead.) Some of the more complicated charitable instruments can at least theoretically actually reduce taxes while maintaining (or even possibly increasing) total estate size, but these should be viewed with some skepticism. If it looks too good to be true, it probably is. In addition to outright gifts or bequests to charity, charitable planning techniques include charitable remainder trusts (CRTs) and charitable lead trusts (CLTs). The financial value of these devices will decrease as the estate tax repeal is phased in, though income tax benefits will continue to be realizable using charitable planning.

4. *Irrevocable trusts.* Technically not a separate planning device at all, irrevocable trusts are usually used as a means of effecting one tax planning technique (lifetime giving) without giving up the ability to impose restrictions on the use of the gift by its recipients. An irrevocable trust can be designed to receive (or purchase) life insurance on the grantor's life, in which case it will often be referred to as an irrevocable life insurance trust. With the increase in federal exemption equivalent amounts and the ultimate elimination of federal estate taxes, irrevocable trusts will become less important as an estate planning tool. This is especially true because gift taxes will remain in effect, although the elimination of basis step-up may actually make some gifts easier to make during life.

5. *Valuation discounts.* Several of the more popular modern estate planning techniques are effected by discounting the value of assets. This can be accomplished by limiting the transferability or majority control of property, for example. Because of the relationship of capital gains taxes and estate taxes, such valuation discounts do not avoid taxes altogether: What is saved in estate taxes will later incur capital gains taxes, although the capital gains tax rates will be far less. Because of the wide difference in the maximum tax rates between those two systems, coupled with the desire to delay tax liability to later dates, valuation discounts can still significantly increase the total amount distributed to heirs. Some of the more common examples of valuation discount techniques include family limited partnerships (FLPs), limited liability companies (LLCs), and qualified personal residence trusts

(QPRTs). Valuation discounts often are accompanied by a gifting regimen: The value of the gift can be reduced, permitting larger portions of discounted assets to be transferred and, in turn, further increasing the valuation discount. If estate taxes continue to be phased out, and "carryover basis" is reinstated as scheduled for 2010 (that is, no more "step up" in basis at death for assets over a certain amount), valuation discounts will become unattractive in most circumstances.

Q 5:2 What tax considerations affect estate planning choices?

The estate and gift tax system was established by the federal government to prevent individuals from accumulating great wealth and passing it intact to succeeding generations. Avoidance of these taxes, or minimizing their impact, was the impetus behind the creation of most current estate planning techniques. Substantial gifts of real and personal property transferred during one's lifetime and at death are subject to federal taxes, but the vast majority of American taxpayers are not affected because federal law imposes estate tax only on those estates that exceed $1,000,000 (increasing incrementally to $3.5 million in 2009), and is scheduled to be completely eliminated in 2010 (see Table 5-1 in Q 5:7).

Until the tax law changes in 2001, at least thirty-five states followed suit, assessing no separate inheritance tax but instead, "picking up" the maximum amount the federal estate tax allowed as a "state death tax credit" (see Table 5-3 in Q 5:14). With the decline in revenues as a result of federal estate tax repeal, however, some states have altered their laws in response to the progressive repeal so that estates no longer subject to federal tax will be subject to state tax computed according to 2001 or pre-2001 law. In addition, many states still impose an inheritance tax where the recipient, not the decedent's estate, is technically liable for the tax. The result may be a shift from planning to reduce or eliminate federal estate taxes, to planning addressed primarily to state taxes.

During the period of transition until 2010, transfers of assets made during one's lifetime are subject to gift tax, and those made at death are subject to estate tax. The federal estate and gift tax systems share similar exclusions, exemptions, and deductions available to ease the tax burden. The most important of these are the unified credit exemption equivalent, which exempts combined gift and estate transfers up to $1,000,000 in 2002, [I.R.C. § 2010(c)] and the unlimited marital deduction, which allows assets to pass tax-free to the donor's or decedent's spouse. [I.R.C. §§ 2056, 2523] (Note, however, that the unlimited marital deduction is not available to a noncitizen spouse (see Q 5:62).) Until 2004, the federal estate and gift tax systems will have had lock-step identical exemptions, but thereafter the two will part company. (See Table 5-1.)

Tax avoidance inevitably generates new laws designed to close loopholes. The gift tax was first created because the wealthy began making *inter vivos* (lifetime) transfers to avoid death taxes. The "generation-skipping tax" (GST, see Q 5:102) and "kiddie tax" (by which the net unearned income of a child under age 14 at the end of the taxable year is generally taxed at the parent's marginal rate if it is greater than the child's rate) were established to thwart planners trying to beat the system by passing wealth directly to their grandchildren or assigning income-earning assets to their toddlers, respectively. The diversion of exemptions for gift and estate taxes will forestall an attempt by individuals (a) to take advantage of the phase-out that may, after all, be only temporary, and (b) to discourage transfers to family members with lower income tax brackets.

Income tax is a factor when trust assets or the decedent's probate estate earn income prior to distribution. Because the tax rate imposed on a trust can be significantly higher than that imposed on the trustor as an individual, the impact on the total income taxes to be paid should be carefully calculated before assets are transferred into a trust, particularly income-earning assets, such as pension plans, and particularly when there is no plan to distribute out income from the trust.

Q 5:3 What is the general relationship of estate planning to long-term care planning?

Although estate and inheritance tax considerations and long-term care concerns may be incorporated into the same client's estate plan, the direct connection will appear relatively infrequently, and sometimes, the planning involved may be directly contradictory. Still, a client with tax planning issues may also have a child, spouse, or other beneficiary with long-term care concerns, so an elder law attorney must be conversant with both tax and long-term care issues in order to adequately assess clients' needs (see chapters 14 through 18 for a discussion of long-term care).

Even though most clients concerned about paying for long-term care expenses need not also fear paying estate tax, they must nonetheless be advised of the importance of estate planning as part of the long-term care plan. It may be desirable, or even necessary, to disinherit a disabled spouse or child, for example, or to provide for a spouse's share to be held in a testamentary trust, in order to qualify for public assistance (see chapter 19 for a discussion of Medicaid trusts and chapter 17 for a discussion of special needs trusts).

Other taxes may be more important in planning for long-term care expenses, particularly if the gift is large and the possibility of requiring long-term care uncertain. These will include gift taxes, particularly in states which impose gift taxes on transfers far below federal thresholds; capital gains tax payable by transferees; loss of the capital gains tax exclusion on sale of a principal residence when the home is transferred; potential loss of property tax exemptions for the elderly (or gain of such exemptions by transfer to a disabled person); and income tax payable when retirement assets are cashed in.

Estate and Gift Tax Basics

Q 5:4 Where are the relevant tax statutes and regulations found?

The Internal Revenue Code of 1986 is a comprehensive code, covering income, estate and gift taxes, as well as administrative matters. Chapter 11B, Estate Tax [26 U.S.C. §§ 2001 et seq.], and chapter 12B, Gift Tax [26 U.S.C. §§ 2501 et seq.], are the principal sources of law on estate and gift taxes.

A large body of regulations interprets the federal tax code. Private letter rulings, tax court, and other court decisions add to the extraordinary abundance of law on tax and tax planning issues. Add innumerable commentaries and treatises, and the interpretation of the tax laws can be seen as a major national industry. It is important for the practitioner to remember that private letter rulings may not be cited or used as precedent by anyone except the private party that requested the ruling; the IRS is not bound by decisions of state courts interpreting state law except those of the highest state court; and the IRS is not bound by decisions of federal courts, except by decisions of federal appeals courts in the circuit with jurisdiction over the taxpayer.

There are many useful online sources for the tax code and other tax research materials, provided the practitioner is attentive in checking how current the available copies. Leaving aside the commercial sites (such as CCH) that may be helpful but expensive, the following are some useful free web sites:

- Internal Revenue Code (FINDLAW site): http://caselaw.lp.findlaw.com/casecode/uscodes/toc.html
- Code of Federal Regulations (Check Title 26 for the Treasury Regulations): http://www.access.gpo.gov/nara/cfr/cfrhtml
- IRS Forms (this site has changed its URL often, and you may have to return to the IRS main page): http://www.irs.ustreas.gov/formspubs/index.html; fill-in forms: http://www.irs.ustreas.gov/forms_pubs/fillin.html
- Revenue Rulings (and more): http://www.taxlinks.com/
- Letter Rulings (not indexed): http://www.irs.gov/news/efoia/determine.html
- "Chief Counsel Documents" including letter rulings, also "actions on decisions," etc. (this site may also change): http://www.irs.gov/taxpros/display/0,,i1 = 5&genericId = 16985,00.html

Q 5:5 What is the difference between an estate tax and an inheritance tax?

Two different types of taxes can be imposed on the death of a property owner. These "death taxes" can be "estate" taxes or "inheritance" taxes. An estate tax (the one applied by the federal government and most states), is paid by the estate as a result of the death of the original property owner. An inheritance tax (still imposed by only a handful of states, but common in European countries) is imposed on the recipient of a gift or inheritance, at rates that typically vary depending on the beneficiary's "class" or relationship to the decedent, with gifts to unrelated parties taxed the most heavily.

Q 5:6 What is the interplay between federal estate taxes and gift taxes?

Gift taxes are imposed on gifts made during the life of the transferor. However, "annual exclusion" gifts escape tax entirely, and are disregarded. The "annual exclusion" is available to $11,000 gifts per donor, per donee, in each year, provided the gift is of a "present interest" (see Q 5:19). The amount doubles if the donor's spouse agrees that both partners' annual exclusions may be used even if the gift is actually made by just one partner. Thus, a couple with five children and five unusually lovable sons- or daughters-in-law might give $220,000 per year, if they so chose, without any gift or estate tax consequences whatsoever.

Through 2004, the federal estate and gift tax structure unifies the two taxes. (See Table 5-1) Both taxes are graduated, so that larger gifts (and estates) incur a higher percentage tax. Because the federal estate tax and gift tax are "unified," the higher tax rate is based on the entire value of gifts and estate transferred during life and at death. At the same time, the federal estate and gift tax system exempts total combined transfers up to an "exemption equivalent amount," set at $1 million in the year 2002 and scheduled to increase incrementally thereafter. [I.R.C. § 2010(c)] In other words, a lifetime gift of $1 million will completely exhaust the estate and gift tax exemption amount for a decedent dying in 2003, and every dollar of the net estate remaining at death will be subject to the federal estate tax.

> **Example 5-1.** Mrs. Jones has an estate valued at $2 million. In 1999, she made a gift of $500,000 to her daughter, and in 2000 another gift of $250,000 each to her daughter and granddaughter. Mrs. Jones dies in 2002. The 1999 gift reduced her lifetime exemption equivalent amount by $490,000 (the first $10,000 of that gift bore no gift tax consequences—the annual exclusion then was $10,000 and had not yet increased to $11,000), leaving her with a total available credit exemption amount in that year of $160,000 ($650,000, the applicable exemption equivalent amount in 1999, minus the $490,000 used by the gift). Because she did not die in 1999, the remaining exemption equivalent amount in that year became irrelevant.

Mrs. Jones's 2000 gifts would have reduced her exemption equivalent amount by an additional $480,000 (because $10,000 of the gift to each recipient bore no tax consequences), except for the fact that in 2000 she had only $185,000 remaining of her exemption equivalent amount ($675,000—the 2000 equivalent amount —minus the $490,000 used by the 1999 gift). Consequently, she had to pay a gift tax on $295,000 of the gift (the $480,000 taxable gift minus the remaining $185,000 exemption equivalent amount).

In the year of her death, the exemption equivalent amount rose to $1 million. She used only $675,000 of that, so the next $325,000 of her estate will pass tax-free. The result: even though she paid gift taxes at the time of her 2000 gift, the increasing estate tax exemption equivalent amount operated to relieve her estate of some of the additional estate taxes in subsequent years. Of course, if her total estate had been just enough to incur gift taxes with her 2000 gifts and not enough to reach the exemption equivalent amount upon her death in 2002, she would have paid transfer taxes that she could have avoided by simply retaining her assets until death.

This interplay between federal estate and gift taxes is slated to end in 2004. In that year the estate tax exemption amount will rise to $1.5 million but the gift tax exemption amount will remain at $1 million. Thereafter the gift tax exemption amount is scheduled to remain at the same level even as the exemption amount increases for estate taxes and the estate tax is ultimately repealed. After the estate and gift taxes are "decoupled" but before repeal of the estate tax, use of the gift tax exemption amount will continue to reduce the remaining available estate tax exemption equivalent amount, but taxable gifts over $1,000,000 during the donor's lifetime will be subject to gift taxation even though there might not have been an estate tax if the donor held the same property until death.

Q 5:7 How does the unified estate and gift tax system work?

The Internal Revenue Code imposes a tax on gift transfers [I.R.C. § 2501] and estate transfers [I.R.C. § 2001], but allows U.S. citizens a substantial credit, or exemption, on all transfers under both categories. [I.R.C. §§ 2505, 2010, respectively] Gift tax is cumulative over the lifetime of the donor, that is, even if no tax is owed yet, it must be recalculated every time a taxable gift is made. At the death of the donor, any amount of the gift tax credit not used during the donor's lifetime can be applied to his or her estate tax liability. If gift transfers have used up the unified credit, no exemption is available for death transfers on the same individual's estate.

From 1987 through 1997 the unified credit was $192,800, which is the tax imposed on an estate valued at $600,000. In other words, $600,000 of one's estate would not be subject to estate or gift tax, thus constituting a tax savings of $192,800. The Taxpayer Relief Act of 1997 (TRA '97) increased the exemption amounts gradually, and were expected to increase the amount to $1 million in the year 2006. [Former I.R.C. § 2010(c)] The Economic Growth and Tax Relief Reconciliation Act of 2001 further modified the schedule for incremental increases in the exemption amount (and ultimate repeal of the estate tax). At the same time the maximum estate and gift tax rate decreases from the pre-2001 55 percent (including a 5 percent surcharge immediately repealed beginning in 2002) to a high of 45 percent in 2007 (with a 1 percent decrease each year in the top tax rate beginning in 2003). Under the 2001 Act, exemption equivalent amounts for the two taxes will increase (though not identically) and maximum tax rates decrease as shown in Table 5-1.

Table 5-1. Estate and Gift Tax Exemptions and Rates

Year	*Federal Estate Tax Exemption Equivalent*	*Maximum Rate*	*Gif Tax Exemption*	*GST Exemption*
2002	$1 million	50% (+ 5% surcharge)	$1 million	$1.1 million
2003	$1 million	49%	$1 million	$1.1 million
2004	$1.5 million	48%	$1 million	$1.5 million
2005	$1.5 million	47%	$1 million	$1.5 million
2006	$2 million	46%	$1 million	$2 million
2007	$2 million	45%	$1 million	$2 million
2008	$2 million	45%	$1 million	$2 million
2009	$3.5 million	45%	$1 million	$3.5 million
2010	Tax Repeal	0%	$1 million	Tax Repeal
2011	$1 million	50%	$1 million	$1.1 million

Until 2004 the tax burden is the same whether the decedent's property is transferred during his or her lifetime, after death, or both. In the meantime, gift tax is "tax-exclusive," meaning that the tax is imposed only on the amount actually transferred to the donee, and the amount used to pay the gift tax is not subject to tax. Estate tax is "tax-inclusive," because the tax is imposed on the value of the property transferred and on funds used to pay the tax. At least at face value, making a lifetime gift looks preferable, although it must be kept in mind that the donor and donee lose the value of the tax money for the period between the time of the gift and the time of the donor's death. The total amount of tax paid (assuming no significant diminution in the donor's estate size) should always be lower with substantial gifts, and so wealthy clients are well advised to make gifts even though the credit amount may be fully utilized and the tax paid. This good planning technique will largely evaporate after the decoupling of estate and gift taxes in 2004.

Further thoughts on planning in light of these tax changes may be found in Q 5:55.

Q 5:8 What is the "step-up" in basis, and what is "carryover basis"?

Capital gains tax is imposed on the difference between the proceeds of a sale or other disposition of an asset (other than a gift), and the owner's "basis" in the property. "Basis," in the hands of the original owner, is what he or she paid for the property.

Under existing law, when one person gives property to a second person, the second person "takes" the first person's "basis" in the property. That is carryover basis. If *A* buys Blackacre for $100, and gives it to *B* (at which time it is worth $200), when *B* sells it for $300, *B* pays capital gains tax on the difference between *B*'s sales price ($300) and *A*'s original basis ($100). Capital gains tax is due on $200.

Under existing law, when one person dies owning property, and as a result the property passes to a second person, the property's basis is "stepped up" to its value on the date of death. This is the "step-up" in basis. If *A* buys Blackacre for $100, and dies leaving the property to *B*, at which time it is worth $200, when *B* sells it for $300, *B* pays capital gains tax on the difference between *B*'s sales price ($300) and the date of death value ($200). Capital gains tax is due on

$100. Also under current law, if the property were worth $50 when *A* died, *B* would pay capital gains tax on the difference between $300 and $50—this is a step *down*, something not seen in many years, but now commonplace with the steep stock market declines following the year 2000.

The Economic Growth and Tax Relief Reconciliation Act of 2001 [H.R. 3, 107th Cong. (2001)] calls for the imposition of a modified carryover basis structure beginning in 2010 (after full repeal of the estate tax). Property received as a result of the death of the original owner will maintain the same income tax basis as it had in the original owner's estate (unless the fair market value on the date of the decedent's death is lower than the decedent's basis), resulting in the imposition of capital gains taxes upon sale by the recipient. This is the same rule that now applies to property received by gift.

This significant change in the income tax treatment of inheritances would be tempered by a substantial exemption. The recipient(s) of a decedent's property will be permitted to claim a basis "stepped-up" to the date of death values totaling $1.3 million, and surviving spouses will receive an additional $3 million of "stepped-up" basis. In other words, the appreciation in value (not the total value at death but the increase in value) during the decedent's life will remain untaxed up to as much as $4.3 million. Any increase in value over that exempt amount will be taxed to the recipients at sale.

Q 5:9 How will values be determined so that carryover basis exemptions can be determined?

Under the Economic Growth and Tax Relief Reconciliation Act of 2001 the carryover basis exemptions will be established by the decedent's personal representative based on fair market values as of the date of death. Final regulations for determining carryover basis in individual situations will need to be adopted before the effective date of the carryover basis regime. Unfortunately, there is no relief for taxpayers who did not receive the exemption and who cannot establish the original basis. Many practitioners feel that a "carryover basis" regime will be a nightmare of administrative complexity. In many cases, clients seem quite unable to track their own basis in property, and it is inconceivable that a family will be able to track basis for centuries as it is "carried over" from generation to generation.

Q 5:10 What assets are subject to estate and gift taxes?

For purposes of federal tax computation and payment, the "gross estate" includes all property, real or personal, tangible or intangible, under the control of the decedent immediately prior to death (or gift), including revocable living trusts, most life insurance, and innumerable other categories of assets. [I.R.C. § 2033] Most states follow the same approach to defining "estate" for tax purposes, although "inheritance tax" states may exclude certain types of property, such as life insurance, or the employer-provided portion of retirement benefits. The definition of "estate" for probate purposes has almost no relevance to estate or gift tax considerations.

Q 5:11 What is the interplay between estate and gift taxes, on the one hand, and federal income tax, on the other hand?

When an appreciated asset is sold, income tax is imposed on the capital gains thus recognized. Although the tax is usually lower than the tax on other income, it still figures prominently in asset (and estate) planning.

Until the scheduled repeal of the estate tax and imposition of a carryover basis system, at the time of death appreciated property owned by the decedent is given a new "stepped-up" basis for income tax calculation periods. In other words, because the asset is subject to estate taxes, the federal tax system exempts the increased value from exposure to the second (capital gains) tax. Assets subjected to the estate tax acquire the new income tax basis even though the estate might escape taxation altogether: A highly appreciated estate worth less than the exemption equivalent amount in the year of the decedent's death will avoid both estate and capital gains taxes (see also Q 5:8).

Q 5:12 How do the states' estate and gift tax systems figure into estate planning decisions?

Most states have estate and gift taxation systems modeled on the federal tax structure. Although a handful (about 15) impose an inheritance tax, and states are free to set their estate tax at whatever level they choose, until 2001 the trend was to track the federal exemption equivalent amount.

In fact, federal estate and gift tax includes a tax credit (not a deduction but rather a dollar-for-dollar reduction of federal tax liability generated by payment of state taxes) for state estate and gift taxes paid. The federal tax credit is limited by a formula set out in the federal Tax Code. As a result, if a state chooses to set its estate and gift tax in accordance with the federal credit formula, the state tax is effectively paid through the federal tax liability. [I.R.C. § 2011(b)] Thus, a state can choose to impose such a tax without increasing the tax liability of its decedents' estates, and most states have followed the federal invitation.

This federal credit system is being phased out under the Economic Growth and Tax Relief Reconciliation Act of 2001, which became effective in 2002. For 2002 the value of the state estate tax credit was reduced by 25 percent, and continues to shrink by 25 percent each year until complete repeal of the credit in 2005. Beginning in 2005, state estate taxes actually paid will be a deduction (but not a credit) against federal estate taxes. If states continue to tie their own estate tax to the amount of the federal credit, they will see their estate tax revenues shrink and disappear altogether in 2005.

States may respond to this change either by leaving their statutes in place (resulting in an automatic reduction and eventual elimination of tax), by changing their laws to leave the current rates unchanged (usually by revising the law so that the tax is computed based on the credit available in 2000 or 2001 and thereby effectively increasing the total estate tax liability), or by increasing their estate taxes in some other way in order to take advantage of the savings in taxes by estates. Individual states may respond differently, depending on local politics, budget considerations, and history of state transfer taxes. Most current state laws set the state estate tax at the federal credit amount, so state estate taxes will begin to disappear in 2005 unless states take some affirmative steps.

As of this date (2003), many states have already begun to "uncouple" their own estate taxes from the amount of the federal credit, and it is expected that others will follow suit. In most cases the option chosen is to tie the state's tax to the credit in effect in 2001, computed as follows:

Table 5-2. State Death Tax Credit

Adjusted Taxable Estate	*Maximum Tax Credit*
Not over $90,000	8/10 of 1% of the amount by which the adjusted taxable estate exceeds $40,000
Over $90,000 but not over $140,000	$400 plus 1.6% of the excess over $90,000
Over $140,000 but not over $240,000	$1,200 plus 2.4% of the excess over $140,000
Over $240,000 but not over $440,000	$3,600 plus 3.2% of the excess over $240,000
Over $440,000 but not over $640,000	$10,000 plus 4% of the excess over $440,000
Over $640,000 but not over $840,000	$18,000 plus 4.8% of the excess over $640,000
Over $840,000 but not over $1,040,000	$27,600 plus 5.6% of the excess over $840,000
Over $1,040,000 but not over $1,540,000	$38,800 plus 6.4% of the excess over $1,040,000
Over $1,540,000 but not over $2,040,000	$70,800 plus 7.2% of the excess over $1,540,000
Over $2,040,000 but not over $2,540,000	$106,800 plus 8% of the excess over $2,040,000
Over $2,540,000 but not over $3,040,000	$146,800 plus 8.8% of the excess over $2,540,000

Table 5-2. State Death Tax Credit (*cont'd*)

Adjusted Taxable Estate	*Maximum Tax Credit*
Over $3,040,000 but not over $3,540,000	$190,800 plus 9.6% of the excess over $3,040,000
Over $3,540,000 but not over $4,040,000	$238,800 plus 10.4% of the excess over $3,540,000
Over $4,040,000 but not over $5,040,000	$290,800 plus 11.2% of the excess over $4,040,000
Over $5,040,000 but not over $6,040,000	$402,800 plus 12% of the excess over $5,040,000
Over $6,040,000 but not over $7,040,000	$522,800 plus 12.8% of the excess over $6,040,000
Over $7,040,000 but not over $8,040,000	$650,800 plus 13.6% of the excess over $7,040,000
Over $8,040,000 but not over $9,040,000	$786,800 plus 14.4% of the excess over $8,040,000
Over $9,040,000 but not over $10,040,000	$930,800 plus 15.2% of the excess over $9,040,000
Over $10,040,000	$1,082,800 plus 16% of the excess over $10,040,000

Q 5:13 Which states impose an estate and gift tax based on the federal credit?

In 2001 every state imposed an estate and gift tax of at least the federal credit amount, and most relied solely on the credit amount, at least for estates taxed solely within the state. (Problems in calculation may arise when more than one state seeks to impose a tax on the same property.) Reduction in the state death tax credit, and increases in the federal unified credit exemption equivalent, meant massive loss of tax revenues to those states. The solution, for many states, was to "decouple" their statutes from federal law. As of January 2003, 17 states plus the District of Columbia are decoupled from the federal changes. The estate tax laws in six states plus DC were already written in such a way that the federal change does not affect them, and 11 others (Kansas, Maine, Maryland, Massachusetts, Minnesota, Nebraska, New Jersey, North Carolina, Rhode Island, Vermont, and Wisconsin) have "decoupled" as well. [See *www.cbpp.org/1-31-02sfp.htm* "States Can Retain Their Estate Taxes Even As the Federal Estate Tax is Phased Out"] This is a reversal of prior trends that favored repeal of any state estate taxes in excess of the federal credit amount: e.g., Maine and Delaware repealed their separate inheritance taxes in 1998 and 1999, respectively; New York eliminated its tax in excess of the credit amount beginning in 2000; and Connecticut had begun a repeal of its inheritance tax (temporarily halted while the state considers decoupling its estate tax). Fiscal needs are likely to dictate further reversals.

Q 5:14 Which states impose separate inheritance taxes?

As of 2002, 15 states still imposed their own, separately computed inheritance taxes (see Table 5-3). These generally vary in rate depending on the relationship of the decedent to the beneficiary. Only four, Connecticut, Louisiana, North Carolina, and Tennessee, imposed their own separate gift taxes. However, most of the inheritance tax schemes provide an unlimited marital deduction and many also exempt most or all of property passing to descendants or ancestors.

Table 5-3. States Imposing Inheritance Taxes and Non-Unified Gift Taxes

State	*Inheritance Tax Statute*	*Imposes Separate Gift Tax*
Connecticut	12-340 (due to exp.)	12-640
Indiana	6-4-1.2	
Iowa	450.1	
Kentucky	140.010	
Louisiana	RS 47:2401 (exp. 2004)	RS 47:1201

Table 5-3. States Imposing Inheritance Taxes and Non-Unified Gift Taxes (*cont'd*)

State	*Inheritance Tax Statute*	*Imposes Separate Gift Tax*
Maryland	Tax - Gen. 7-202	
Nebraska	77-2001	
New Hampshire	86:6	
New Jersey	54:34-1	
New York	221	
North Carolina		105-188
Ohio	5731.02	
Oklahoma	68 § 802	
Pennsylvania	72 § 01116	
South Dakota	10-40-2	
Tennessee	67-8-303	67-8-101

Q 5:15 Can states impose estate or inheritance taxes on nonresident decedents?

Every state has a mechanism for capturing estate or inheritance taxes on property located in the state, even where the owner-decedent is a nonresident of the state. Most states adopt one of two mechanisms for calculating the tax: Either the tax is levied on all property with an actual situs in the state (thereby avoiding taxation of resident decedents' out-of-state property) or the estate tax is computed as a fractional share of the total federal tax credit amount, based on the proportion of the taxable estate located in the taxing state. These two calculation methods can lead to different results; consequently, even though two or more states limit their estate tax to the federal credit amount, a decedent's estate can end up paying more state estate taxes than the applicable federal credit amount.

With each computation, the situs of a decedent's intangible personal property is usually deemed to be the state of the decedent's domicile, while tangible personal property and real property is deemed to have a situs in the actual state in which it is located. Personal effects, however, are usually considered to be located in the state of domicile, and if actually situated elsewhere, treated as if they are only "temporarily" outside the state of domicile. Problems can arise when valuable items are actually located out-of-state, such as jewelry.

Q 5:16 Who typically prepares estate, inheritance, and gift tax returns?

Some lawyers routinely prepare tax returns. Indeed, some tax practitioners insist that the only way truly to understand estate and gift tax planning issues is regularly to prepare the tax returns. They are uncommonly complicated, and require a great deal of specialized knowledge. Some choices made on an initial estate tax return are final, even if the return is later amended, so there is tremendous opportunity for unrecoverable mistakes if an attorney unfamiliar with the mechanics of estate tax calculation and payment prepares the returns.

By the same token, few accountants are familiar with estate and gift tax return preparation. Before retaining an accountant to prepare the returns, the attorney should determine whether he or she has any prior experience with their specialized preparation.

Most lawyers and accountants who prepare estate and gift tax returns rely on one of a handful of tax return preparation software packages. Although software properly formats the returns, makes calculations easily and reliably, and forces the user to prepare the appropriate supporting schedules, such software does not substitute for familiarity with the actual returns and the method of preparation. On the other hand, any lawyer or accountant who regularly prepares estate or gift tax returns should unquestionably invest in tax preparation software.

For states with their own inheritance tax systems, particularly those that require tax returns for estates far below the federal threshold, the attorney rather than an accountant usually prepares the inheritance tax returns. (For example, Connecticut is in the process of phasing out its inheritance tax returns, but still requires that they be filed even for estates where no tax is due and the estate assets are minimal.) Many software programs will not even include a component that permits preparation of the inheritance tax return.

Gift Tax

Q 5:17 What transfers are subject to the federal gift tax?

With some exceptions, property transferred for less than "an adequate and full consideration in money or money's worth" will be subject to gift tax [I.R.C. § 2512]; the tax applies to the amount by which the property value exceeds the value of the consideration. There are the obvious gift transfers of cash, cars, real estate, and jewelry; however, the Code also characterizes as gift transfers the forgiveness of loans and the transfer of ownership of a life insurance policy. [Rev. Rul. 77-299, 1977-2 C.B. 343]

Services provided are usually not characterized as gifts, nor is the refusal to accept a gift or bequest (as, for example, by a properly executed disclaimer; see chapter 7 for a discussion of disclaimers). There is no tax imposed on any gifts made to one's spouse, to a government unit, to a veterans' organization, or to any qualifying entity organized for religious, charitable, scientific, or educational purposes. (Note, however, that a gift to a foreign charitable organization may be exempt for gift tax purposes but not give rise to an income tax deduction, which requires a gift to a "domestic" charitable organization.)

Q 5:18 What is the annual gift tax exclusion?

Under Code Section 2503, taxpayers may make gifts of $10,000 annually to each of an unlimited number of persons, with no gift tax consequences. Beginning in 1999, under the Taxpayer Relief Act of 1997, the $10,000 gift exclusion is indexed annually for inflation, rounded to the nearest $1,000 increment. [I.R.C. § 2503(b)] In 2002, the number rose to $11,000.

The amount doubles if the donor files a federal gift tax return on which the donor's spouse agrees that *all* gifts made that year will be treated as having been made by both partners, so that both partners' annual exclusions may be used. [Treas. Reg. § 25.2513-1(b)] Thus, a couple with five children and five unusually lovable sons- or daughters-in-law might give $220,000 per year, if they so chose, without any gift or estate tax consequences whatsoever. [I.R.C. § 2513] It is important to remember that the election applies to all gifts, not only annual exclusion gifts. [Treas. Reg. § 25.2513-1(b)(5)] This can be an issue if both spouses wish to make a $22,000 gift to their child, but only one spouse wishes to make taxable gifts (in excess of the exclusion) to children of a first marriage.

Of course, if the gift is made from jointly-owned assets, or from non-separate property in a community property state, the gift will simply be treated as made one-half by each spouse, without the need for the election.

Q 5:19 What is the present interest requirement for annual exclusion gifts?

The $11,000 annual exclusion applies only to gifts of a so-called "present interest." [I.R.C. § 2503(b)(1)] A "present interest" means the right to immediate use and enjoyment of the property. A gift made in trust will usually not meet the present interest test. Exceptions: the gift of a present right to all the income or principal from a trust, or a percentage of trust income or principal, for a defined period of time, constitutes a present interest. [Treas. Reg. § 25.2503-3(b)] Thus, a "Crummey Trust" will typically allow the beneficiary the right to withdraw the amount of any gift to the trust for a "reasonable" period of time, in order that the gift will qualify as a present interest. Gifts in trust (or other gifts of interests while retaining an interest such as a life estate) can, however, present other problems (see Q 5:100).

Q 5:20 When does an individual have to file a gift tax return?

Any gift greater than $10,000 (indexed for inflation beginning in 1999; as of 2002, $11,000) made by a single donor to a single donee in any given year must be reported. Married couples can make gifts from jointly held or community property totaling $22,000 to a single recipient without having to file a return. In a non-community property state, if the gift were made from solely owned property, that spouse would have to file a return on which the non-giving spouse would consent to have the gift treated as made 50-50 by each spouse, but (s)he would not have to file a separate return as well. [Treas. Reg. § 25.2513-1(c)]

Although gifts in excess of the annual exclusion amount must be reported, no tax liability is incurred unless the donor exceeds the exemption equivalent amount in effect in the year of the gift. In other words, a donor who makes a $50,000 gift to a single donee in 1998 must file a return, but will not pay any federal tax. The donor will, however, have used $40,000 (the amount of the gift reduced by the annual exclusion amount) of his or her exemption equivalent, and will therefore have an estate tax liability if he or she dies in 2003 owning more than $960,000 (the 2003 $1,000,000 exemption equivalent amount minus the $40,000 used by the 1998 gift). If the same donor does not die in 1999, but does make an additional $1,000,000 gift to a single donee in that year, the donor will be liable for gift tax on $40,000 of that transfer.

If a state imposes its own gift tax regime, however, a gift that exceeds the annual exclusion amount for that state (usually tied to the federal exclusion) may require the payment of tax even if the donor has not exhausted the federal exemption equivalent. Thus, a Connecticut donor who gives $211,000 in 2003 will pay tax on the $200,000 above the exclusion, for a total of $7,500 in taxes.

Q 5:21 Are there any lifetime transfers that can be made with no gift tax consequences?

Yes. The federal estate and gift tax system allows certain *inter vivos* and testamentary transfers to be made with no tax consequences. For instance, an unlimited amount of wealth may be transferred to a spouse or to charity, and, as previously discussed, gifts of up to $10,000 each (indexed; currently $11,000) to an unlimited number of individuals may be made annually. [I.R.C. § 2503(b)]

In addition, the grantor can make unlimited payments to medical providers and educational institutions for health and tuition, respectively. [I.R.C. § 2503(e)] These gifts are not subject to the gift tax and do not use up any exclusions or deductions. For example, a grandparent may pay the college tuition of a grandchild without gift tax consequences. The payments must be made directly to the educational institution or medical provider. But the medical expense exclusion does not apply to amounts that are reimbursed by an insurance company. [Treas. Reg. § 25.2503-6(b)(3)]

Finally, investments in tuition savings accounts defined in Code Section 529 are not only treated as "present interest" gifts despite the intended beneficiary's lack of direct access to the funds, but the five years' worth of annual exclusion may be "bunched" into the first year. [I.R.C. § 529(c)(2)] Provided the donor survives the five years, the donor will have been able to exclude $50,000 (indexed, currently $55,000) made in the first year. This gives the account, which grows tax-free, an extra four years of growth on the funds. (See Q 5:38.)

Q 5:22 Who must file a federal gift tax return and pay the tax?

The donor is responsible for filing the tax return form and paying any tax due on lifetime gifts. [I.R.C. § 2502(d)] If the donor does not do so, the federal government has the authority to hold the donee personally liable. [I.R.C. § 6324(b)] No gifts have to be reported on a federal gift tax return if they fall under the annual exclusion or if a complete gift is made to charity. This applies only if the transfer is of the entire interest in property; charitable remainder trusts (see Q 5:77) and charitable lead trusts must be reported (see Q 5:83).

Q 5:23 When must the federal gift tax return be filed?

The federal gift tax return is IRS Form 709. It is due on April 15 of the year after the end of the calendar year in which the gift was made. [I.R.C. § 6075(b)(1)] Late filing subjects the taxpayer to both interest and penalties based on the amount of unpaid tax.

Gift Tax Planning

Q 5:24 What disadvantages are there to making substantial gifts during a lifetime?

One never knows what life holds in store: Will one live another 3 years or 30 years? What about chronic illness? Remarriage? Will the value of remaining assets increase or decrease? Will future acts of family members cause one to regret making gifts to them now? Will there be more descendants in the future, and will one of them have a medical emergency? Thoughtful planners should advise clients of all the ways the assets they are considering gifting now could come in handy down the road.

Q 5:25 What advantages are there to making substantial gifts during the donor's life?

Assuming the donor has determined that he or she can afford to (or simply wishes to) make gifts in excess of the annual exclusion amount, there are several estate tax benefits. Any gifts will not only reduce the estate by the amount of the gift, but also by the income that would have been generated by the gift for the rest of the donor's life. In addition, if the wealthy donor's income tax bracket is higher than that of the donee, there will be some net income tax savings from the transfer.

Most important, a large gift directly reduces the total estate and gift tax liability. This is true because the gift tax due on a large gift does not count as an additional gift. By contrast, the tax due on an estate remains part of the estate for tax calculation purposes. The effect of this difference in estate and gift tax calculations is that the total savings on taxable gifts made during life will equal at least the amount of the (estate) tax that would have been paid on the amount of (gift) tax actually paid.

This benefit calculation will change somewhat in 2004, when estate tax exclusion amounts begin to exceed gift tax exclusion amounts. The calculation should change even more radically in 2010 if the eventual repeal of federal estate taxes remains on the books. After that time, substantial gifts (in excess of the exemption amount) will incur a tax that could have been avoided altogether by holding the property until death. In the meantime, gift planning remains a viable and important part of general estate planning.

Q 5:26 What controls can the donor place on property while retaining its characterization as a gift?

To complete a gift under general property law principles, all that is required is donative intent coupled with actual delivery of the property; however, tax law treats gifts differently. Even though a gift is completed, and the donor has no legal power to recover the gift, it may be treated as part of the donor's estate for tax purposes if the transfer is conditional, or if the donor retains a reversionary interest. As a consequence, gift planning frequently becomes a process of balancing the need to make the gift complete against the donor-client's desire to avoid giving recipients unrestrained access to the gift property.

Even as lawyers consider planning techniques permitting the donor to restrict access to gift property, it is important to remember that the client should make the balancing decision. While the lawyer may be enamored of clever and creative gift planning devices, the client may be willing to give property outright to children or other family members. It is important to recognize the tendency to substitute one's own attitudes about the importance of restricting asset availability for the attitudes of the client. After explaining the alternatives, the lawyer must permit the client to balance the tax and control considerations, and make the final decision about whether to undertake more creative gift planning.

Q 5:27 What steps must be taken to obtain the $11,000 exclusion when making gifts to a trust?

To qualify for the annual exclusion, a gift must be of a present interest (see Q 5:19). A gift directly to a trust will therefore usually not qualify for the exclusion, unless the trust is fully revocable (or the gift subject to withdrawal) by the recipient.

It is important to understand that the exclusion availability is not the same as removing the asset from the grantor's taxable estate. It is possible to make a completed gift (and thereby remove the gifted amount from the grantor's estate) without qualifying for the gift tax exclusion (as, for example, in the case of a gift to an irrevocable trust for the sole benefit of the recipient). With some exceptions (QPRTs; see Q 5:101), the usual purpose of the gifting process is to both remove the asset from the grantor's estate and simultaneously qualify for the exclusion.

Q 5:28 What is a "Crummey" trust?

One of the most popular and pervasive of the gift planning techniques is the so-called "Crummey" trust, named after the case *Crummey v. Commissioner*. [397 F.2d 82 (9th Cir. 1968)] In order for a gift to be deemed completed by the Internal Revenue Service, the donee must receive a present interest in the gift—in other words, the donee must have an unrestricted right to the possession or use of the property transferred. This creates a problem when the grantor wants to delay distribution of a gift to a beneficiary, especially a minor beneficiary. Grantors can reap substantial tax benefits by giving $11,000 per year to a child, but making an immediate and outright gift is unwieldy and usually undesirable. Gifts subject to state laws following the Uniform Transfers to Minors Act must be released to the beneficiary when he or she reaches the age of 21 (see Q 5:31); gifts to "minor's trusts" must permit the beneficiary to withdraw the entire trust property within a reasonable time after reaching age 21. [I.R.C. § 2503(c)]

To address this problem, the grantor can establish an irrevocable trust with "Crummey" powers that gives to one or more of the beneficiaries the power to withdraw from the trust either all or a portion of the amount given to the trust. If this provision is included, the trust language can delay the distribution of the trust assets to the beneficiary to any age. However, if the person holding the Crummey power does not hold a significant interest in the trust, the power may be considered only a sham. Usually, the Crummey power holder will have the right to unqualified distribution at some future point, but this is not necessarily required. The point is that one must be able to show that the non-exercise of the power was not as the result of a pre-arranged scheme, but was actually in the power-holder's interest.

How does the Crummey power work? The beneficiary is given a short window (typically 30 days, but maybe even shorter) to withdraw the gift from the trust; if no withdrawal is made, that window closes and the gift becomes part of the irrevocable trust. For tax purposes, the donor has made a gift to the beneficiary, and the beneficiary (by allowing the power to lapse) has in turn made a gift to the ultimate trust beneficiaries. The second gift ordinarily has no gift tax consequences, because the recipient of most of that gift is the beneficiary himself or herself, but two separate gifts have been completed. To further prevent any gift tax liability on the second gift, the beneficiary can be given a special testamentary power of appointment (a power to name the trust's remainder beneficiaries in his or her own will, from among a group of candidates; see also Q 4:20); this will result in the second gift having no tax consequences at all.

It is important to recognize that a gift into a trust is still "completed" in the sense that the gifted property is removed from the estate of the donor. The failure to provide a Crummey power in a gift-recipient trust will simply cause the annual gift tax exclusion to be unavailable for that gift, and therefore result in reduction of the unified credit exemption amount for the donor (and the imposition of gift tax in a state that does not follow the same "unified" approach). If, on the other hand, the annual gift exclusion amount has already been utilized for that recipient in the year of gift into a trust for the same beneficiary, there is no need to add Crummey withdrawal powers to the gift. For that reason, as well as out of concern for future changes in the tax law governing Crummey-type transfers, some practitioners provide that the Crummey withdrawal terms appear in the gift deed or other transferring document itself, rather than in the text of the trust.

Why does the Crummey power work? First, because there is no statutory requirement that the beneficiary be notified of this power or of the time frame for its exercise, many practitioners feel that the power alone, without more, should be sufficient to withstand IRS objections. Second, even though the Internal Revenue Service insists that reasonable notice and a reasonable time frame be offered in order for the arrangement not be treated as a sham, the relatively short period of thirty days has been found acceptable to the IRS. (An advance waiver of notice of gifts made in future years has not passed IRS scrutiny, however.) Third, the grantor can tactfully suggest that gifts to the trust might be discontinued if the beneficiary insists on exercising the power. Particularly if the trust property consists of life insurance, so that future gifts are essential to preserving the death benefit, this is a persuasive argument. However, the donor must be careful not to set any actual conditions on the gifts, or the IRS will consider them incomplete transfers. Finally, the right to withdraw is generally noncumulative, so the beneficiary cannot withdraw an amount greater than what was contributed to the trust in any given year. The only exception would be when a "hanging power" is included. The "hanging" power states that the withdrawal right continues to the extent that the value of the amount subject to the right exceeds the greater of $5,000 or 5 percent of the value of the trust property. This is to prevent a gift by the holder of the power, which might otherwise be deemed to "own" the trust. As a practical matter, this means that it is preferable that each beneficiary's withdrawal right not exceed $5,000. If it does, the attorney must choose between a hanging power and a power of appointment retained by the beneficiary holding the power to avoid the deeming of any inadvertent gifts.

Q 5:29 What if the recipient exercises his or her right to withdraw gifts from a Crummey trust?

One concern in the use of Crummey powers is how to convey the existence of the withdrawal right to the beneficiary so that he or she receives sufficient notice but is not encouraged actually to make the withdrawal (in nearly all cases, the donor's purposes will be frustrated by a withdrawal—if that were not the case, an outright gift to the beneficiary would accomplish all the same goals). Usually the trustee provides the required Crummey notification; the donor may simultaneously let the beneficiary know that the present gift is intended to be one of many annual gifts into the trust, but that those plans could change if the withdrawal right is exercised.

Notice of the withdrawal right can be given to minor beneficiaries by notifying parents or guardians. Notice to competent adult beneficiaries must be given to the beneficiary, with sufficient time to allow the exercise of the power to withdraw the gift. The trustee is usually responsible for the preparation and delivery of the Crummey notice.

Q 5:30 What are "Christofani" powers?

Some tax practitioners have taken Crummey powers to the next level by giving withdrawal rights to several individuals who may not otherwise be beneficiaries of the trust. Assuming the withdrawal powers lapse unexercised, a larger gift can thus be made to the trust (and, ultimately, the beneficiary or beneficiaries) without exceeding the annual exclusion amount for any of the individual holders of the withdrawal powers. This technique is sometimes referred to as using "Christofani" powers after the Tax Court case of *Christofani v. Commissioner*. [97 T.C. 74 (1991)] Typically, several family members are given withdrawal rights as to $11,000 gifts for each, and upon lapse of the unexercised rights the combined gifts become part of the irrevocable trust for the primary intended beneficiary. Of course, if any individual actually exercises the withdrawal right, the donor's intention is frustrated, at least as to the amount of the withdrawn gift.

The Internal Revenue Service persists in its disapproval of Christofani-type powers, despite having a perfect record of losses in courts considering the validity of the gifting technique. The IRS has nonetheless served notice that it will continue to challenge such trusts where it determines that the particular arrangement is abusive, although it is not clear what specifics offend the IRS more in some cases than in others. [See IRS *Action on Decision*, 1996-010, 1996-29 I.R.B. 4]

A compromise technique may be used by giving some members a small interest in the trust, sufficient to satisfy the IRS concern that there has been a pre-arranged agreement not to withdraw, but small enough to satisfy the donor's wish to benefit primarily other parties. Thus, a trust intended to provide the benefit of insurance proceeds to one child with special needs might give smaller interests, perhaps 5 percent, to other children who could hold Crummey powers.

Q 5:31 How else might one make gifts to a minor?

Gifts to minors can be made directly to the child, although for obvious reasons this is not advisable if the gift exceeds several thousand dollars, or to their parents, who may or may not follow the donor's wish that the gift be held for the direct benefit of the child. If the minor is under the supervision of a court-appointed guardian/conservator, the court will monitor management of the gift. The money will be distributed as soon as the child reaches majority and the conservatorship terminates. In many states, a gift that exceeds a certain amount may require the appointment of a guardian, who will also be required to post a bond, file accountings, and meet other burdensome requirements.

Most states have adopted some form of the Uniform Transfers to Minors Act (UTMA) or its predecessor, the Uniform Gifts to Minors Act (UGMA). Instead of requiring a court-appointed conservator or guardian, the UTMA allows the gift assets to be managed by a custodian, who may be the donor, the child's parent or other adult, or a professional fiduciary. The bank account, real estate, or other asset is titled in the name of the custodian, who is designated by the title as custodian of the assets under the state's version of the UTMA. Transfers into UTMA accounts in amounts greater than $11,000 will be subject to gift tax or generation-skipping tax as if they were made directly to the minor. [Rev. Ruls. 56-86, 1956-1 C.B. 449; 59-357, 1959-2 C.B. 212]

As long as the assets are managed prudently, the custodian has the power to invest the money as he or she wishes for the benefit of the minor, without regard to the minor's other assets, including the resources or support obligations of the parents. Under the UTMA and most court-appointed conservatorships, the presence of the transferred assets does not release the parents from their support obligations, but if in the best interests of the child some assets are used to provide for his or her support, those transfers may be considered income to the parents and taxed accordingly. Some states forbid a parent acting as custodian to use the UTMA funds for the child's support or have found a parent liable for breach of fiduciary duty by so doing. [See, e.g., Hall v. Hall, (Conn. Super. Ct. April 11, 2002) (unreported decision)]

Although state versions of the UTMA may differ, some types of UTMA accounts may be continued in the account until the beneficiary reaches 21, even though the age of majority may be 18. UTMA usually does require the assets to be turned over to the child at the age of 21 (up to 25 in California), so some donors may prefer a more formal trust device to exercise greater control over the distribution.

Another option, similar to the Crummey trust, is the "minor's trust" under Code Section 2503(c). Instead of giving an annual notice, the trust simply provides that once the minor reaches age 21, (s)he either receives the funds entirely (similar to an UTMA account), or, more likely, has the right to withdraw all of the trust assets at age 21, for a specified, usually brief, period of time. In effect, there is a single massive Crummey power. For the client that prefers greater control, and deferral of distribution, the risk of a minor's trust is that at age 21 the child will have sufficient assertiveness to exercise the power, but not the judgment to deal with the assets prudently. On the other hand, the point can still be driven home that exercise of the power may have repercussions the child would not appreciate. Certainly this approach may be easier to cope with than the UTMA account.

What to do if the UTMA account has already been used, or a minor's trust requires distribution? There are two options donor parents may choose:

1. Practically speaking, possession is 9/10 of the law. That is, although the child may have the right to the funds, as a practical matter the parent may simply delay in affording the

child his or her rights, and the child is unlikely to force the issue. The same is true for the minor's trust.

2. The parent may "encourage" the child to fund a trust for the child's benefit with the parent as trustee. This will not insulate the funds from the child's future creditors, but will put a level of bureaucracy and control between the child and the money.

Q 5:32 What options are available to a donor who wishes to provide specifically for the education of a child, grandchild, or other individual?

Donors may make gifts for the benefit of individuals without using their $11,000 annual exemptions, permitting larger gifts (and therefore greater reductions of the donor's estate) in some circumstances. Tax-free gifts that do not utilize the annual exemption amount include:

1. Direct payment of educational expenses for the beneficiary;
2. Contributions to state prepaid tuition plans;
3. Education IRAs; and
4. Education gifts to "Section 529" plans.

Education IRAs or "Coverdell Accounts"

Q 5:33 What is an Education IRA?

An Education IRA (now known as a "Coverdell account") is not a retirement account at all; rather, it is a modest tax incentive program for future education costs. [I.R.C. § 530] Any person under age 18 may have an Education IRA established for his or her benefit. Contributions are not tax-deductible, but distributions (including earnings) may be tax-free to the extent that they are exceeded by the beneficiary's qualified educational expenses in the year(s) of withdrawal. [I.R.C. § 530(d)(2)(B)]

Q 5:34 Who may establish an Education IRA?

An Education IRA may be established for any individual under the age of 18. Contributions must be in cash, but may come from the beneficiary or any other person. The total amount of contributions in any one year may not, however, exceed $500. [I.R.C. § 530(c)] Any contributions to a qualified state tuition program on behalf of the beneficiary will preclude any Education IRA contributions.

Q 5:35 How are distributions from an Education IRA treated?

Distributions to the Education IRA beneficiary are taxed to the extent that they represent income earned on the original investment. This calculation is made by dividing (1) the total value of the Education IRA account at the time distributions are made by (2) the undistributed contributions, and applying the resulting fraction to the total distribution. [I.R.C. § 530(d)(1)] Distributions are not taxable to the extent that the beneficiary's qualified post-secondary education expenses exceed the total distribution. If those expenses do not exceed the distribution, the excess of the distribution over expenses will be taxable in proportion to the percentage representing income to the Education IRA. [I.R.C. § 530(d)(2)(B)] In addition, any taxable distribution may be subject to a 10 percent additional tax unless it is occasioned by the death or disability of the beneficiary, or because the beneficiary qualified for a scholarship excluded from gross income, or certain other limited circumstances are met. [I.R.C. § 529(d)(4)]

Q 5:36 What expenses qualify to reduce the taxability of Education IRA distributions?

Education IRA distributions are nontaxable to the extent that the beneficiary has qualified post-secondary education expenses in excess of the distributions. Qualified expenses include tuition, fees, books, supplies, equipment, and room and board (for students who are least half-time, and with some limits). [I.R.C. § 529(e)(3)] Expenses can also include contributions to a qualified state tuition program.

Q 5:37 When must an Education IRA be fully distributed?

Even if the beneficiary has not used the Education IRA for higher education, the entire balance must be distributed when the beneficiary reaches age 30 (or upon the death of the beneficiary). In the year of required distribution, the proportion of the account representing income will be taxed to the beneficiary. [I.R.C. § 530(d)(1)]

At any time before the beneficiary reaches age 30, the Education IRA can be rolled over into a new Education IRA for the benefit of the original beneficiary's child, grandchild, stepchild, sibling, step-sibling, parent, grandparent, step-parent, aunt or uncle, or any of several in-laws. [I.R.C. § 530(e)]

529 Plans

Q 5:38 What is a 529 plan and what are its advantages and disadvantages?

A Section 529 account works as follows: A contributor sets up the account in a state's 529 plan and names a beneficiary. Provided the contribution is no more than $11,000 (or even $55,000, in which case the gift is treated as if spread over five years, using five years' worth of annual exclusion), the gift is treated as a "present interest" and does not incur gift tax, even though the beneficiary does not have full access to the funds. No income tax is paid as the account funds grow or generate income. When the beneficiary needs the funds to finance higher education, the account owner authorizes their release. No tax is paid on distributions for tuition, room, board, and certain other expenses. The account owner can elect to name a new beneficiary for any remaining funds, or instead, can elect to have the funds revert, subject to a 10 percent penalty and payment of tax on deferred income. The funds are not included in the account owner's estate at death.

The disadvantage, from the donor's standpoint, is that the right to take back the funds (subject to penalty) might leave the funds vulnerable to claims against the donor. A few states have chosen to include creditor protection features in their 529 plans, but these are in the minority (as of 2002, only Ohio, Pennsylvania, Alaska, Colorado, Kentucky, Louisiana, Maine, Nebraska, Tennessee, Virginia and Wisconsin). And the Federal Bankruptcy statutes were amended to exclude from the bankrupt's estate contributions to 529 accounts made two years prior to filing. ($5,000 is protected if contributed between 1 and 2 years prior to filing.) However, no state appears to exclude 529 plan accounts from consideration as "available assets" for purposes of Medicaid eligibility. [For a discussion of this potential drawback, see L. Davis, "Keeping the Promise of Section 529 a

Reality," Elder Law e-Bulletin (April 30, 2002), available only online at *www.tn-elderlaw.com/telb/020430.html#e1*]

For a comprehensive and constantly updated survey of individual state plans and their benefits and drawbacks, see *www.savingforcollege.com*. The site author, Joseph Hurley, also sells a book that provides yet more details about different state plans.

Estate Tax

Q 5:39 What is the gross estate?

As with the definition of gross income for income tax purposes, the definition of "gross estate" for estate tax purposes is very broad. It includes all property, whether real or personal, tangible or intangible, "to the extent of the interest therein of the decedent at the time of his death." [I.R.C. § 2033]

Q 5:40 What assets are includible in the gross estate?

All assets in which the decedent had any ownership interest at the time of death are included in the gross estate, valued at the interest held by the decedent. The Internal Revenue Code not only makes the broad inclusive statement, but also specifically lists numerous types of assets includible as part of the gross estate, including many particular examples of property transferred by the decedent before death if certain powers were retained by the decedent:

- A life estate [I.R.C. § 2036]
- A reversionary interest (if that interest is of a value of at least 5 percent of the total value of the transferred property), if the beneficiary must survive the decedent in order to receive the property [I.R.C. § 2037]
- The power to "alter, amend, revoke, or terminate" the recipient's power to use and possess the property [I.R.C. § 2038]

In addition, the Code lists a number of specific property types includible in the gross estate:

1. Life insurance proceeds, if the decedent "possessed any of the incidents of ownership" at the time of death. [I.R.C. § 2042]

2. Property subject to a general power of appointment held by the decedent (even though the exercise of the power would require a lapse of time, so that the decedent could not actually have successfully exercised the power of appointment in the instant before death). [I.R.C. § 2041] (Whether a power of appointment is a "general" or "special" power is discussed in Q 4:20.)
3. The remaining value of any annuity from which the decedent retained the right to receive income during life. [I.R.C. § 2039]
4. Property jointly owned with another person is included, with the presumption being that the entire asset belonged to the decedent "except such part thereof as may be shown to have originally belonged to" the other joint owner. [I.R.C. § 2040] A different rule governs handling of property jointly owned by the decedent and his or her spouse; that property is included in the decedent's estate to the extent of half of the value at the date of death, provided that the spouses are the only joint tenants. [I.R.C. § 2040(b)] An exception to this exception may be used to advantage if the property were acquired by one spouse prior to 1977 (see Q 5:47).
5. Property subject to a surviving spouse's dower and curtesy rights. [I.R.C. § 2034]
6. Property transferred by the decedent for less than adequate consideration. [I.R.C. § 2043]
7. Property that would have been included pursuant to Code Sections 2036, 2037, 2038, or 2042 (including life insurance, property subject to a general power of appointment in the decedent, or property in which the decedent retained other powers) but in which the decedent either transferred his or her interest or relinquished the retained powers within three years of death (see Q 5:42). [I.R.C. § 2935]

Q 5:41 Is community property includible in the gross estate?

Property held in joint tenancy between spouses (with no other joint tenants) or in tenancy by the entireties will be taxable in the deceased spouse's estate only to the extent of the decedents one-half interest. This is true even though the property once belonged solely to the deceased spouse and was transferred into joint tenancy before death. Essentially, this permits such a transfer to be treated as a completed gift, because no gift tax consequence would have occurred at the time (gifts between spouses not being subjected to gift taxation).

The deemed 50-50 spousal share under current (post-1977) law also applies to community property, but for a different reason. While community property may, in some states, carry an automatic right of survivorship, each of the spouses already owns a one-half interest in the property. The Code tacitly recognizes this distinction when it includes property jointly held by the decedent and any other person [I.R.C. § 2040] by limiting its application to property held in joint tenancy or as tenancy by the entireties. Because community property is not specifically included here, it is not necessary to include an exception for community property in Code Section 2040(b).

Q 5:42 Is property transferred by a decedent during his or her life included in the gross estate?

Property transferred by the decedent during life is not ordinarily included in the gross estate for tax purposes; however, there are a number of circumstances in which such property (even though effectively transferred during life) will be included in the estate. Property that the decedent transferred during his or her life will be includible in the gross estate if at the time of death he or she retained the power to alter, amend, revoke, or terminate the property interest [I.R.C. § 2038(a)] or if the decedent retained the right to use or enjoy the property or receive income from it during his or her lifetime. [I.R.C. § 2036(c)] One common problem is property transferred to an irrevocable trust; even though the grantor (now decedent) did not retain any beneficial interest in the property, its full value will still be included in the gross estate if the decedent retained a reversionary interest in the trust. This can occur, for example, if a trust established for the donor's child provides that distribution will be made to the child's intestate heirs. Even though the child may have children, there is some prospect that the donor/parent will regain the property on the death of the child, and the full value of trust assets will therefore be included in the estate. [I.R.C. § 2037]

Q 5:43 Are gifts made within the three years preceding the donor's death brought back into the estate for tax purposes?

Gifts made within three years of the donor's death are generally not included in the donor's gross estate; however, certain gifts made within three years of the donor's death—even if made through an irrevocable trust vehicle—may be includible in the donor-decedent's estate. The three-year rule applies to life insurance if ownership was transferred to another person within three years of the death, gifts of life estate or income interests (such as irrevocable trusts in which the donor retained the right to receive income, or transfer of a life estate in a residence), and gifts that become complete at the donor's death under Code Section 2036. [I.R.C. § 2035(a)] Gift taxes actually paid on gifts made within three years of the decedent's death are also included in the gross estate for estate tax purposes. [I.R.C. § 2035(b)]

Q 5:44 What is a 5 & 5 Power and is anything included in the estate of a decedent who holds such a power?

Yes. Similar to a general power of appointment (property subject to such a power being included under Section 2041) is a right to take out, or withdraw, or appoint, property of a trust to such a degree that one is treated as the owner of the trust. Conversely, the IRS has decided that this power will be considered *de minimis*, and disregarded, when the power extends to property that does not include the greater of 5 percent of the trust property, or $5,000. This is known as a "5 & 5 power" and is commonly included in trusts to give the surviving spouse better access to trust funds than if he or she had to depend upon the judgment of the trustee. It is used as a limiting provision whenever a surviving spouse or beneficiary might otherwise be treated as the trust owner, such as a credit shelter trust. However, if the owner dies with such a power still exercisable, that 5 percent will still be included in his or her estate for tax purposes.

Q 5:45 How is property in the gross estate valued?

Any real or personal property in which the decedent had an interest—even a conditional or remote interest—may be included in the gross estate for estate tax purposes, and fair market value at date of death or, alternatively, six months after the date of death pursuant to Code Section 2032 (see Q 5:46), is the valuation standard usually applied. [I.R.C. § 2033] Life insurance policies on the decedent's life and in which the decedent held incidents of ownership are deemed to be worth the amount of proceeds payable (death benefit, often, but not always, the same as face value); policies in which the decedent held an interest but was not the insured are valued according to their "interpolated terminal reserve" value, close to their cash surrender value but not exactly; stocks and bonds are assigned a fair market value based upon the average of the highest and lowest selling prices on the date of death; real estate value is determined through appraisals; and the value of promissory notes is determined by adding unpaid principal and accrued interest.

Closely held corporations, limited partnerships, and other family business assets are also valued at their fair market value for estate and gift tax purposes. Because of the illiquidity and limited market for such assets, valuation can be a very difficult (and potentially controversial) process. It may be appropriate to reduce the value of such assets for factors such as lack of control: A 95 percent interest in a family business is not worth 95 percent of the fair market value of the entire business. Highly specialized appraisals may be required to set both the value of the underlying property and determine the appropriate valuation reduction. While formal appraisals may be required for the property or business interest, accountants or economists may be needed to set the valuation discount. This is a controversial area, and an attorney planning to claim a substantial discount should be prepared with a thorough appraisal justifying the discounted value through reference to legal precedents, and not a simple summary conclusion.

Some categories of property may be valued according to "special valuation rules." Notable among these are the rules applying to farm property, provided that it consists of real estate located in the United States, it passes to an ancestor, spouse, or descendant (or descendant's spouse), and it constitutes at least 50 percent of the decedent's estate. If those tests (and other, less significant requirements) are met, the property can be valued at its value for farming purposes, rather than the highest and best use of the property. [I.R.C. § 2032A]

One persistent valuation problem occurs in determining the value of closely held stock or family businesses. When no public market exists for valuing such assets, Revenue Ruling 59-60 [1959-1 C.B. 237] spells out the basic requirement that the appraisal of value must be based on the best available information and a reasonable effort to value the property. Selling prices for shares of similar companies (in product, focus, and structure) may be considered, as may the book value and/or earnings of the closely held stock. Valuing closely held businesses, the IRS recognizes, is not an exact science but requires a reasonable and informed approach by a professional appraiser.

Q 5:46 What is meant by the "alternate valuation date"?

Estate assets are normally valued at their fair market value on the date of death. The valuation can instead be made on the six-month anniversary of the date of death, but only if the total estate size and total tax liability are both reduced by the use of the alternate valuation date. In those cases where the alternate valuation date is to be used, assets that have been disposed of between the date of death and the alternate valuation date will be valued at the sale price (or fair market value on the date of distribution). [I.R.C. § 2032(a)(2)] The alternate valuation election must be made on the federal estate tax return, IRS Form 706. The election is irrevocable and must be made on a timely filed return or the first late return within one year of the due date. [I.R.C. § 2032(d)]

> **Example 5-2.** George, a single man, died September 1, 1999, with an estate valued at $1 million and consisting primarily of marketable securities. His will leaves his entire estate to his children in equal shares. On March 1, 2001, the remaining securities were worth $650,000 and another $200,000 of securities had been liquidated to pay claims against the estate. His executor may elect to use the alternate date of death valuation for the remaining securities, and value the liquidated securities at the $200,000 sales price, because both his estate size and the amount of tax due will be reduced by using the alternate valuation date.

If, on the other hand, George's estate had been valued at $600,000 on the date of his death and $450,000 (including the actual sales price of liquidated securities) on the alternate valuation date, the election would not be available. In the latter case, while George's estate would be reduced by use of the alternate valuation date his estate tax would remain $0 using either valuation date. Of course, using the alternate valuation date would not benefit the estate or heirs anyway, as the only practical effect would be to reduce the heirs' basis in the inherited property. Unfortunately, it is not possible to use the special valuate date to *increase* basis when the assets appreciate during the six months following date of death.

Q 5:47 What happens to a couple's tax basis in property after the death of one spouse?

"Basis" is a tax concept intended to permit calculation of the actual investment in property. Basis is the value assigned to an asset for the purpose of determining gain or loss on the sale or transfer of the asset. [*Black's Law Dictionary* 151 (6th Ed. 1990)] It usually signifies the value of the asset at the time the asset was first transferred to the current owner. Upon the sale of the asset, proceeds in excess of the basis amount constitute gain, and will ordinarily be taxed as capital gains. Upon the death of a property owner, the property assumes a new basis in the hands of its recipients. Generally (until the imposition of the modified carryover basis system beginning in 2011) where the property is part of the decedent's taxable estate, its new basis will be its fair market value as of the date of death (which of course may require that the property be appraised, even though no tax will be due). [I.R.C. § 1014] This is commonly referred to as stepped-up basis (see also Q 5:8).

The treatment of jointly owned property will vary depending on the type of joint ownership. Property owned by spouses as tenants in common, tenants by the entireties, or joint tenancy will obtain a step-up in basis as to the one-half interest held by the deceased owner. (The *Gallenstein* case holds that in this situation, the property is included in the decedent's estate to the actual extent contributed. [Gallenstein v. United States, 975 F.2d 286 (6th Cir. 1992); Patten v. United States, 116 F.3d 1029 (4th Cir. 1997)] This may permit a "step-up" in basis of more than 50 percent where the first spouse to die was the spouse who actually purchased the property. The IRS has finally acquiesced in this result and in Action on Decision 200016, reported that it will no longer litigate the issue.

Property belonging solely to the deceased spouse will acquire a full step-up in basis to the date-of-death value.

Property held as community property, even though each spouse retains a one-half ownership interest, will nonetheless acquire a full step-up in basis. For this reason, couples living in community property states (California, Nevada, Washington, Arizona, New Mexico, Texas, Idaho, and Wisconsin) may recognize significant income tax savings from electing to hold property as community property. Residents of other states may choose to hold property in one of the community property states to take advantage of the full step-up in basis. (Alaska, for example, expressly permits some trusts to employ another state's community property rules, even though Alaska is not itself a community property state.)

Under Code Section 2040, with the exception of property held jointly by spouses, the entire value of jointly held property is deemed includible unless evidence is produced indicating that the property was acquired by gift, bequest, devise, or inheritance, or, in the case of property held with rights of survivorship, if the survivor can prove that he or she furnished consideration. Tangible personal property, such as clothing and furniture, may be hard to value until the items are actually sold—remember that fair market value is based on what a willing buyer and willing seller would agree to in an arm's-length transaction, and there may be no such transactions available to gauge the fair market value. The personal representative may have to go to great lengths to establish the worth of annuities, life estates, and remainder and reversionary interests in property.

With the repeal of the federal estate tax in 2010, a modified system of carryover basis will be instituted. While most decedents' estates will enjoy a $1.3 million exemption from carryover basis liability (i.e., up to $1.3 million of the decedent's estate will acquire the new, presumably higher, basis at date-of-death values), the exemption for married couples is much higher. In addition to transferring $1.3 million without carryover basis liability, a married decedent will be able to transfer an additional $4 million to his or her spouse.

Q 5:48 What can be deducted from the gross estate?

After determination of the gross taxable estate, a number of deductions are permitted in order to calculate the taxable estate. Those deductions include:

1. Expenses, indebtedness, and income taxes owed by the decedent. Deductions are available for the costs of estate administration, funeral expenses of the decedent, claims against the decedent (e.g., creditor's claims in a probate proceeding), income taxes owed by the decedent (but not including taxes on income received after the decedent's death), and mortgages (to the extent that the unencumbered value of mortgaged property is included in the gross estate). [I.R.C. § 2053]
2. "[L]osses incurred during the settlement of estates arising from fires, storms, shipwrecks, or other casualties, or from theft" to the extent that such losses are not compensated by insurance. [I.R.C. § 2054]
3. Public, charitable, and religious bequests. [I.R.C. § 2055] (Note that charitable bequests to foreign organizations will be entitled to an estate tax deduction even though they would not have given the decedent an income tax deduction.)
4. Bequests to a surviving spouse, provided that the spouse is a citizen or the bequest is to a qualified domestic trust [I.R.C. § 2056A] and the bequest is not of an interest that is terminable automatically upon occurrence of an event (or the failure of an event to occur) or the passage of a specified period of time. [I.R.C. § 2056] For some QTIP interests, the executor may elect to treat the transfer as deductible notwithstanding the fact that it fails to meet the nonterminable interest test. [I.R.C. § 2056(b)(7)(B)]

Q 5:49 Are there any credits against the estate tax?

After the taxable estate has been determined (by subtracting deductions from the gross estate) and the tax due has been calculated, a handful of credits are available to be applied against that tax. Those credits include:

1. The unified credit available to every decedent's estate (to the extent that it has not been utilized as a credit on gift taxes due during life). Under the Economic Growth and Tax Relief Reconciliation Act of 2001 the 2002 credit is $1 million and will gradually increase to $3.5 million in 2009 before repeal of the estate tax.

2. The credit for state death taxes paid. The Code permits a credit on federal estate taxes for all state inheritance, estate, or death taxes paid by the estate or on property passing as a result of the death of the decedent. This credit is limited to a percentage of the estate, which increases as the estate grows larger. [I.R.C. § 2011] Under the Economic Growth and Tax Relief Reconciliation Act of 2001 the state death tax credit was reduced by 25 percent in 2002, and will continue to be reduced by 25 percent each year until it is eliminated altogether in 2005.
3. Gift taxes previously paid on property includible in the decedent's gross estate. [I.R.C. § 2012]
4. Estate taxes previously paid on the same property when received by the decedent from another decedent's estate. [I.R.C. § 2013] This credit is allowed only for property passing (and taxed) in the 10 years before the current decedent's death, and is reduced by 20 percent every two years (in other words, 100 percent for prior estate taxes is available for the first two years after the first decedent's death, but is reduced to 80 percent for the next two years and so on, until the credit is limited to 20 percent of the tax previously paid in the 9th and 10th years after the death of the first decedent).
5. Death taxes paid to a foreign country, to the extent that such taxes were imposed on property located in the foreign country but still included in the decedent's estate for U.S. tax purposes. [I.R.C. § 2014] (Tax treaties may provide an alternative method for applying a credit for foreign death taxes.)

Q 5:50 Who must prepare the federal estate tax return and pay the tax?

The personal representative named in the will of the deceased is responsible for preparation of the estate tax return and payment of the tax. [I.R.C. § 2002] If no personal representative has been appointed, any person "in actual or constructive possession of any property of the decedent" is responsible. [I.R.C. § 2203] If a trust was created by the decedent, either as a revocable *inter vivos* instrument or as part of the will, then the trustee is responsible for payment of the tax out of the trust assets.

Q 5:51 When must the federal estate tax return be filed?

The federal estate tax return form is Form 706. It is due nine months from the date of the decedent's death, on the same day of the month as the date of death. [Treas. Reg. § 20.6075-1] When the day of the month on which the decedent died does not exist in the month nine months later (for example, where the date of death was the 31st, and there is no 31st of the month nine months later), the return is due on the last day of the month. A single extension of six months can be granted by request to the IRS, but any tax due must be paid with the extension request. [Treas. Reg. § 20.6081-1] Late returns are subject to both penalties and interest, although both are dependent on the amount of unpaid tax. Although the general rule in tax matters is that the return is deemed filed on the date of mailing, given the immense potential for late filing penalties, estate tax returns should be filed by certified mail, return receipt requested, to be received by the due date. Returns must be filed in the office of the IRS division in which the decedent was domiciled at the time of death.

Q 5:52 How are estate taxes apportioned among probate assets, trust assets, and nonprobate assets?

The Internal Revenue Code does not regulate apportionment. Instead, it authorizes the federal government to collect from any number of sources to satisfy the tax obligation: the estate itself (whether the assets pass through probate or are held in trust), property held in joint tenancy with right of survivorship, property over which the decedent had a power of appointment, certain assets over which the spouse has a qualified terminable interest, retained life estates, proceeds of insurance on the life of the decedent (even if the policy has already paid), and anyone who received or holds property that was part of the taxable estate at the decedent's death. The federal government is not authorized to recover taxes from assets assigned to a charitable remainder trust. Except in the case of fraudulent transfers, or failure to make adequate disclosure of the interest subject to tax, the government is limited to a three-year period during which it can recover taxes. [I.R.C. § 6501]

Although the tax can be collected from almost any asset available to the decedent before death, the wishes of the decedent with regard to apportionment, as expressed in a will or trust instrument, control apportionment of taxes as between heirs and beneficiaries. In other words, the decedent's will can specify which recipient should be liable for estate taxes, or that every kind of recipient should be liable for that recipient's proportional share of taxes. Even though the IRS may collect the tax from, for example, the probate estate, the estate may then have a claim against recipients or holders of other assets for portions of the tax liability. Estate planners typically give both the personal representative of the probate estate (which typically consists of those assets not held in joint tenancy or trust) and the trustee(s) of *inter vivos* or testamentary trusts full powers to pay the tax, and allow for some flexibility between them. Clients usually do not want recipients of pay-on-death benefits to be liable for estate tax, so the planner should make every effort to ensure that there are sufficient liquid assets in the probate estate or trust to satisfy the obligation, for example, by assigning life insurance proceeds to the estate itself.

Some state laws provide default apportionment rules that permit the recovery of taxes from recipients of nonprobate or nontrust assets. Typically, those state rules direct proportional liability, at least as between the probate and trust estates; they may excuse pay-on-death beneficiaries from any share of tax liability. In states with such apportionment statutes, it is important to remember that the legislative scheme is a default approach, and to draft an appropriate apportionment provision after determining who the testator wishes to be responsible for estate taxes.

Overview of Estate Planning Techniques

Q 5:53 What common techniques are available to reduce or eliminate federal estate taxes?

The taxpayer can simply maintain the estate at or below the unified credit amount by gifting excess assets to individuals, through the $11,000 annual exclusion ($22,000 for couples if an election is made) or payment of educational and medical expenses, and gifting to charities, all with no tax consequence. To escape any tax fully the gift must be complete—that is, the donor cannot retain indicia of ownership or a reversionary interest. The donor does have the option of making the gift through an irrevocable trust, and thereby exercising some control over the method and timing of distribution of the gift assets. An elderly parent who spends down his or her estate through gifts to his or her children may hope that the children use part of that money to care for him or her in the future, but there cannot be any such legal commitment attached to the gift. Estate planners should carefully weigh the benefits of saving taxes against the security that a sizeable estate can provide an aging individual, especially in an age when individuals may live 20, 30, or 40 years after they stop earning income.

For larger estates (that is, when a structured use of exclusion gifts is insufficient to reduce the estate below taxable levels), several types of planning devices are available. Principal techniques in the estate planner's toolbox include marital deduction planning, charitable giving, and valuation reductions (see ensuing discussion).

Q 5:54 Which clients must be concerned about the tax aspects of estate planning?

Individuals and married couples whose accumulated wealth is approaching the exemption equivalent amount in any given year, and those who stand to benefit from *inter vivos* and death transfers of that wealth, have the most to gain from the tax avoidance aspects of estate planning. Many clients do not realize their estate (or their parents' estate) is large enough to trigger estate and gift tax consequences, and the estate planner must interview them thoroughly to determine all potential sources of wealth. A client with assets less than the unified credit amount may see his or her personal value skyrocket as a result of an inheritance or a bull market, or may not be aware of all the different kinds of assets that are counted when computing the value of the estate at death (e.g., the face value of life insurance policies).

Clients frequently undervalue their assets, for whatever reason. In evaluating the relevance of tax considerations, always assume that assets exceed stated values, that significant assets have been overlooked, and that growth will be greater (and expenditures less) than clients estimate. Consequently, any client with identified assets over $500,000 in value should be a candidate for at least rudimentary tax planning analysis.

Q 5:55 How can one plan for the possible repeal of the estate tax?

Rapid reduction, ultimate repeal, and possible subsequent restoration of the federal estate tax poses significant challenges to the estate planner. Among the challenges: the lack of federal regulations interpreting the new provisions, and the prevailing notion that estate tax repeal may not ever be fully implemented despite adoption of the Economic Growth and Tax Relief Reconciliation Act of 2001. Nonetheless, a few planning points are clear:

1. Smaller estates (less than the 2002 exemption amount of $1 million and those of healthy individuals slightly above that figure) can safely be planned without consideration of federal estate tax liability unless and until estate taxes are reimposed in the near future. State estate tax changes triggered by the federal action must be considered, and clients with property in (and ties to) more than one state may require more careful planning, especially in the near term.
2. Larger estates, especially for young and healthy individuals and couples, may benefit from disclaimer trusts which will permit the surviving spouse or heirs to elect whether estate tax planning is necessary after the death of the property holder. An alternative approach is a "Q-Tippable" trust (one that may qualify as a Q-TIP marital trust, but need not) that leaves it up to the executor to decide how much will be included in the estate of the first to die, and how much in the estate of the second.
3. Very large estates will, at least in the short term, continue to benefit from the same estate tax planning devices in widespread use for the past two decades, so long as (a) the client understands that the funds that are held in the bypass trust (and thus not entirely available to the survivor) will increase and may result in a "lopsided" arrangement; and (b) the formula clauses already in place will work in the current scheme.
4. Carryover basis will not seriously begin to affect estate planning choices for the next several years, allowing some time for regulations (and possible legislative adjustments) to

clarify the rules and permitting practitioners to develop appropriate strategies.

5. It appears ever more likely that some estate tax may be retained, and carryover basis not imposed, due to budgetary constraints—but this will remain to be seen.

Q 5:56 What assets are commonly overlooked or undervalued?

Most seniors who have lived in the same home for many years have no real notion of the value of the property. Local tax assessment systems usually systematically undervalue real estate, so clients are regularly misled about the value of the home. Rental and investment real estate may be less prone to undervaluation, but clients are still likely to undervalue any real estate that has been held for an extended period.

Clients frequently forget to mention some classes of assets. Notably, life insurance benefits are often missed in client interviews (most life insurance is owned by the client-insured, so the full value of the death benefit will be included in the client's estate). Younger clients may have life insurance provided by their employer, which often has a substantial face value; older clients may have old, fully-paid-up life insurance with cash surrender and face value higher than the client recalls.

Personal property sometimes has significant value, surprising clients. Antiques, collectibles, and family heirlooms may push a smaller estate into the taxable realm. More commonly, however, clients and family members have been led to overvalue personal property. Jewelry, coins, and stamps, in particular, may have been appraised "for insurance purposes" at several times their resale value, and clients will often have assumed those already inflated values have risen faster than inflation in the intervening years.

Q 5:57 What is the marital deduction?

Transfers to a spouse, either through gifts [I.R.C. § 2523] or after death [I.R.C. § 2056], are fully protected from any tax liability. There is no limit to the amount covered by the marital deduction, except for certain terminable interests as defined in Code Section 2056. In other words, simply being married can be the best estate tax planning technique.

Full use of the marital deduction will not eliminate all tax liability. If the decedent's estate was taxable, adding it to the estate of the surviving spouse simply ensures that the spouse's estate will be taxable in turn. Marital deduction planning attempts to balance competing desires: While most married clients wish to benefit the surviving spouse, they also will choose to take advantage of planning techniques that fully utilize both spouses' credit exemption equivalent.

Q 5:58 What is the charitable deduction?

To encourage gifts and bequests to charities, the Code allows a full deduction for all amounts contributed. The charity must take a form approved by the Code and must serve a religious, charitable, scientific, or educational purpose to qualify. [I.R.C. § 2055] Gifts to a government unit and to veterans' organizations are also fully deductible. Lobbying organizations are not eligible, nor are "charities" whose earnings benefit stockholders.

Q 5:59 Other than using the marital and charitable deductions and the unified exemption amount, what techniques are available to reduce federal estate taxes?

Valuation discounts can reduce the tax liability by the simple device of lowering the value of the client's assets. Ideally, the technique for lowering the value will be temporary, and the value can be restored to the pre-planning level some time after the client's death. More sophisticated planners may opt to use family limited partnerships, limited liability companies, or other business organizations to reduce the open-market value of the underlying assets. The client-donor can make the partnership the recipient of gifts pursuant to the annual exclusion (in other words, instead of writing $11,000 checks to four children, the client can place the $44,000 in the partnership and continue to exercise control over the funds and protect them from the children's creditors).

While insurance planning is not actually a means of reducing federal estate taxes, it may be useful to guarantee that the decedent's heirs will have sufficient liquid resources to pay the estate tax when it comes due. Insurance planning typically involves the transfer of an existing life insurance policy directly to the heirs or devisees, or to a trust for their benefit (utilizing "Crummey" powers effectively to remove the insurance from the grantor's estate). Alternatively, the grantor may choose to gift an amount sufficient to permit the heirs or devisees to pay annual premiums on a life insurance policy; those gifts might be made to a trust as a means of providing for continuity and control while still removing the premium amounts (and the policy itself) from the grantor's taxable estate.

Marital Deduction Planning

Q 5:60 What property interests qualify for the marital deduction?

As previously mentioned (see Q 5:57), the marital deduction is the unlimited estate and gift tax deduction for transfers made to a spouse either during life or at death. [I.R.C. § 2523] All assets that qualify for inclusion in the donor's or decedent's gross estate are potentially eligible for the marital deduction, including probate assets, joint tenancy, any property in which the surviving spouse has a general power of appointment, and, in some instances, transfers made within three years of death. Where a credit shelter trust (see Q 5:65) has been established or a devise made to someone other than the surviving spouse, the remainder of the estate distributed to the spouse will qualify for the deduction. The importance of the unlimited marital deduction continues under the phased-in elimination of the estate tax, at least until full elimination in 2010. Thereafter the much larger carryover basis exemption will continue to emphasize transfers to spouses.

Transfers that qualify for the marital deduction (at death, or even during lifetime) include:

- Outright gifts and bequests; payments of life insurance or annuity proceeds;
- Gifts in trusts in which (1) the spouse has the right to withdraw all of the assets, (2) all income is distributable to the spouse, and (3) no property may be distributed to any other party during the spouse's lifetime ("general power of appointment" trust) [IRC § 2056(b)(5)];

- Life insurance or annuity payments with power of appointment in surviving spouse [IRC § 2056(b)(6)]; and
- "Terminable interests" that qualify under 2056(b)(7).

Terminable interest property can qualify for the marital deduction (and therefore be "qualified terminable interest property" or a QTIP election) if it passes from the decedent, the surviving spouse has an income interest for life (and a right to demand that the property be made income-producing), no other person has the power to appoint any portion of the property away from the spouse, and a proper election has been made on the decedent's estate tax return. [I.R.C. § 2056(b)(7)(B)(i)] A "legal life estate" is also eligible for QTIP treatment. [I.R.C. § 2056(b)]

Q 5:61 What requirements must be met for a transfer to qualify for the estate tax marital deduction?

The following requirements must be met for the transfer to qualify for the estate tax marital deduction:

1. The decedent must be a U.S. citizen or resident at the time of death;
2. The property must pass to a surviving spouse who is a U.S. citizen (but see Q 5:62);
3. The interest in property must be included in the decedent's gross estate; and
4. The surviving spouse must not receive a nondeductible terminable interest in the property.

Q 5:62 Can a transfer qualify for the marital deduction if the surviving spouse is not a U.S. citizen?

Yes. If the surviving spouse is not a U.S. citizen the marital deduction is allowed if the property passes to the surviving spouse in a qualified domestic trust. [I.R.C. §§ 2056(b)(7)(B)(i), 2056(b)(7)(B)(ii)(II)]

Q 5:63 What is a qualified domestic trust?

The unlimited marital deduction is not available for gifts or bequests to noncitizen spouses. Consequently, where the spouse is not a citizen the exemption equivalent amount will be used for any transfer of the decedent's assets to the spouse. For larger estates, that may lead to tax liability even where the spouse is the primary beneficiary. The loss of marital deduction availability is not absolute. A qualified domestic trust is a QTIP trust (see Q 5:71) created by a grantor whose surviving spouse is not a U.S. citizen. Assets passing to a U.S. citizen ordinarily do not qualify for the marital deduction, but QTIP trust language adhering to Sections 2056 and 2056A of the Internal Revenue Code (clarified in the Taxpayer Relief Act of 1997) can make the assets of the trust eligible. Important: a will or trust may be "reformed" to provide for a QDOT within nine months of death and the marital deduction will be allowed; the alternative is for the surviving spouse to attain citizenship within the same nine months.

For the trust to qualify (and therefore be a qualified domestic trust), four criteria must be met:

1. At least one trustee must be a U.S. citizen or domestic corporation, and that trustee must consent before any distribution of principal can be made;
2. The executor of the decedent's estate must make a QDOT election on the estate tax return by its due date (including extensions);
3. Treasury regulations intended to ensure the collectibility of estate taxes imposed on the trust must be met; and
4. The surviving alien spouse must be entitled to all income from the trust (on at least an annual basis), as in any other marital deduction qualifying trust.

Q 5:64 If there is a disparity between the assets of the respective spouses, how can the estates be equalized in order to utilize the marital deduction?

One common problem is that the first spouse to die may not have sufficient assets to utilize fully the exemption equivalent amount. If there is a great disparity between the assets of the respective spouses (often the case in second marriages, where one or both spouses have substantial separate property), the richer spouse may wish to make gifts to the poorer spouse during his or her lifetime to permit full use of the exemption regardless of which spouse is the first to die. The wealthier spouse may even determine that the gift should be large enough to equalize the estates completely, in order to lower the marginal tax bracket for the wealthier spouse.

One method to equalize estates is through a gift of life insurance or through an irrevocable life insurance trust (see Q 5:87), whereby proceeds of the policy pass to the surviving spouse at death. The donor-decedent cannot retain any rights of ownership in the policy or the tax benefit is lost, so generally a gift is made of the policy itself, even if the donor continues to pay the premiums personally.

Another method of equalizing estates is for the wealthier spouse to establish an *inter vivos* QTIP trust. The QTIP trust is more frequently established after the wealthier spouse's death, but the rules and effect are essentially similar (see Q 5:71).

Q 5:65 What is a "credit shelter trust"?

The primary purpose of the classic credit shelter trust, also called an A/B trust or bypass trust, is to protect the unified credit exemption of both spouses. A (unified) credit shelter trust is a joint living trust created by both spouses who have sufficient assets to trigger estate tax consequences. It protects the unified credit exemption of both spouses, so that a maximum amount equal to double the current unified credit (which in the year 2000 stands at $1,000,000) can be protected. No estate tax is usually owed at the death of the first spouse because the unlimited marital deduction protects the transfer. But without a trust, the estate value exceeding the unified credit will be vulnerable to estate tax at the death of the second spouse. A properly constructed credit shelter trust protects the unified credit of the first spouse to die by placing certain restrictions on the surviving spouse's access to the assets that shield the assets from being taxed in the surviving spouse's estate.

A credit shelter trust may be a joint revocable trust created by the agreement of both spouses during their lifetimes. At the death of the first spouse, such a trust separates into two subtrusts: the decedent's trust (also sometimes referred to as the B trust, bypass trust, exemption trust, or credit shelter trust), which is irrevocable, and the survivor's trust (or A trust), which is revocable and whose assets may be distributed outright. At the first death, the assets of the deceased spouse held as part of the parent trust are segregated into the decedent's trust. The maximum amount so segregated will usually, but not always, be limited to the exemption equivalent amount, so that no estate tax is incurred on the first death.

The decedent's trust is usually maintained for the benefit of the surviving spouse, although he or she cannot be a remainder beneficiary of the subtrust. The survivor may collect all income from the decedent's trust. The decedent's trust may also pay for all expenses related to the survivor's health, education, maintenance, or support, such as mortgage payments, dentist bills, tuition toward a graduate degree, or clothing. The trust may even give the surviving spouse the right to demand an annual distribution of up to $5,000 or 5 percent of the trust principal, whichever is greater, without causing the decedent's trust to be treated as part of the surviving spouse's estate.

In other words, the surviving spouse—who often is the trustee of the decedent's trust as well—has broad access to the trust assets, but there is at least the possibility of some protection of those assets for remainder beneficiaries. As with any trust, the remainder beneficiaries may take the trustee to court if they have evidence of mismanagement or misapplication of trust benefits. This may not be a likely option when the trustee is a parent, and the grantors may want to take this into consideration when creating the revocable trust and appointing trustees.

Q 5:66 What is the importance of the health, education, maintenance, and support (HEMS) standard in a credit shelter trust?

The credit shelter trust is effective only if the language clearly protects the decedent's trust from unlimited access by the spouse. In the past planners commonly permitted the surviving spouse to have access to trust principal based on standards like "care and comfort," which the Internal Revenue Service deemed too broad to protect the assets properly. The HEMS (health, education, maintenance, and support) standard uses terminology provided expressly in the Code, and is now the preferred language. The Code excludes trust property when any right to distribute principal is subject to an ascertainable standard such as the "health, education, support, or maintenance of the decedent." [I.R.C. § 2041(b)(1)(A)] Other language may be sufficient to protect the credit exemption, but most practitioners will prefer the safe harbor of HEMS.

Q 5:67 What is the difference between a "fractional share" and "pecuniary" clause?

Trust or will language pertaining to the distribution of assets typically directs that the distribution be made in "pecuniary," or straight monetary amounts, or in "fractional shares," by which each beneficiary is assigned a percentage of the assets. For instance, the testator or grantor may provide for "My daughter Annie, $20,000," or "My daughter Annie, thirty percent (30%) of the residuary estate."

Q 5:68 How is fractional share and pecuniary share distribution used in marital deduction trust planning?

A deceased spouse's property may be divided into two shares, one of which will utilize the decedent's exemption equivalent amount. There are two different approaches to calculating the actual division. A pecuniary approach to the trust division commonly uses language such as:

> Trustee shall transfer to the Marital Share the smallest pecuniary amount of the trust estate that, if added to the total value for federal estate tax purposes of all other interests in property that pass or have passed from the Grantor to or in trust for the surviving Spouse, and, if includible in the Grantor's gross estate for federal estate tax purposes and qualified for the marital deduction, will entirely eliminate (or reduce to the maximum possible extent) any federal estate tax at the death of the Grantor after taking into account all deductions allowed to her estate otherwise than for this gift and all other factors pertinent to the computation of the federal estate tax in the Grantor's estate.

A fractional formula for funding the subtrusts might look something like:

> Trustee shall transfer to the Marital Share the smallest fractional share of the trust estate that, if added to the total value for federal estate tax purposes of all other interests in property that pass or have passed from the Grantor to or in trust for the surviving Spouse and if includible in Grantor's gross estate for federal estate tax purposes and qualified for the marital deduction, will entirely eliminate (or reduce to the maximum possible extent) any federal estate tax at Grantor's death after taking into account all deductions allowed to her estate otherwise than for

> this gift and all other factors pertinent to the computation of the federal estate tax in the Grantor's estate. [The fractional share formulae may then go on to define the numerator and denominator of the fraction.]

The difference between the two approaches is more than academic. Under a fractional share approach, the portion of the decedent's estate or trust that is eligible for the marital deduction (usually the entire amount) is totaled and the appropriate fraction calculated for each asset. Assuming each asset is divided proportionally, no income tax effect occurs, and the two resulting trusts (although the surviving spouse's share need not be in trust) will jointly own indivisible assets such as the home, other real property, and limited partnership interests. Upon the later sale of those assets, the proceeds (and any capital gains incurred since the division) will be allocated in the same proportions, with the increased value attributed to the bypass share escaping estate tax upon the death of the surviving spouse.

Under a pecuniary share approach, each asset can be considered for transfer to the two separate trusts. The trustee may well determine that appreciating assets should be held in the bypass share, for example, to avoid estate taxation on the appreciation upon the death of the surviving spouse. But, to the extent that assets have appreciated during the period of administration, the unequal allocation between the two trusts is treated as a taxable event and fiduciary income tax liability may be incurred as of the date of the transfer (of course, the income tax liability would be incurred anyway, but could be delayed until the actual sale by the use of a fractional formula).

In other words, there are two moments at which consideration must be given to the income tax effect of fractional or pecuniary share formulae. At the time the trust is established, the drafter must decide which formula is more likely to be favorable at the later death. At the time of actual division, the adviser (not necessarily an attorney) must consider the income tax effect of choosing particular assets to fund the divided shares.

Q 5:69 Which approach is preferable for most common usage?

Fractional shares may be preferable for clients because the proportional shares are easier to conceptualize. Pecuniary shares may provide better flexibility at the time of division, permitting the trustee to make some income tax choices and, if necessary, still retain a strict proportional division. Many practitioners employ a pecuniary formula with reference to an "aggregate value" or "fairly representative" concept, either of which is an attempt to minimize the possible adverse income tax consequences inherent in an unequal division months after the death of the grantor. Such language might include provisions like:

> Property allocated in kind shall be valued at its value as finally determined for federal estate tax purposes in Grantor's estate, provided that the pecuniary amount is satisfied in a manner that fairly reflects the net appreciation or depreciation (occurring between the date of death of the Grantor and the date of distribution) of all of the assets from which the pecuniary amount could be satisfied.

Other practitioners, using a fractional approach, also allow the personal representative to allocate different property to different shares without requiring a division of each asset. This is known as a fractional share with "pick and choose" funding.

Q 5:70 What is a terminable interest?

Property passing to the surviving spouse will not qualify for the marital deduction if the surviving spouse's interest in the property terminates upon the occurrence of an event or the passage of time. Such an arrangement is a "terminable interest," and results in the property being taxed in the first spouse's estate. In other words, if the deceased spouse leaves assets in a trust for the benefit of the surviving spouse, but provides that the trust will terminate and be distributed to the children if the surviving spouse remarries or dies, the trust assets will be taxed in the deceased spouse's estate. While this may be a desirable result in some cases, in other circumstances the deceased spouse may hope to limit the use of trust assets by the surviving spouse while delaying the estate taxation of those assets until the surviving spouse's death. The purpose of the terminable interest rule is to ensure that property that avoids estate tax upon the death of the decedent will be subject to tax upon the death of the surviving spouse.

Q 5:71 What is qualified terminable interest property?

Despite the general rule that terminable interests do not qualify for the marital deduction, some such interests do qualify. Property that meets the test for such qualification goes by the unromantic description of qualified terminable interest property or QTIP. QTIP interests are usually conveyed by trusts, whether testamentary or *inter vivos*. An *inter vivos* QTIP trust may be irrevocable at the time of establishment or a subtrust of a previously revocable trust that becomes irrevocable upon the death of the grantor. The QTIP election allows an interest in trust property to qualify for the marital deduction. A QTIP trust must provide that the surviving spouse is entitled to receive all of the income for life, and may compel the trustee to invest any unproductive trust assets productively; however, the trust need not give the surviving spouse the power to appoint the trust principal at death or during life, which leads to the most common scenario for the use of QTIP trusts.

In order to qualify for the marital deduction, the QTIP trust's provisions must state that all income from the property will be distributed to the surviving spouse during his or her lifetime, and that the trustee may not appoint the QTIP trust property to someone other than the spouse. [I.R.C. § 2056(b)(7)(B)]

As with the credit shelter trust, the trustee is allowed to distribute to the surviving spouse such principal of the QTIP trust corpus as is needed for the health, education, maintenance, and support of the survivor, or may use a broader standard since the property will be included in the survivor's estate in any event.

Q 5:72 What is a reverse QTIP election?

Because the estate tax exemption equivalent amount and the generation-skipping tax exclusion are different ($1,000,000 and $1,100,000, respectively, in 2002), a possibility exists that making a QTIP election will result in no estate tax on the first spouse's death but increased GST on the death of the second spouse. In such a case, the surviving spouse might make a "reverse" QTIP election, permitting the QTIP interest to escape estate taxation on the first death, but still utilize the first decedent's GST exemption in excess of the estate tax's exemption equivalent amount.

Q 5:73 How is the QTIP election handled?

QTIP interests will actually receive the marital deduction only if an election is made on the grantor-decedent's initial estate tax return (the failure to make a QTIP election cannot be rectified by filing an amended return). Because the surviving spouse is likely to be the person filing the estate tax return, he or she will frequently have discretion as to whether to treat an otherwise qualified interest as QTIP. The QTIP election is irrevocable. [I.R.C. § 2056(b)(7)(B)] The executor for the decedent spouse must elect to take the marital deduction (see Q 6:11).

The QTIP election must be made at the time of the filing of the estate tax return at the death of the first spouse, with a six-month extension possible. The post-mortem planner can elect or fail to elect a marital deduction with respect to a portion or all of the QTIP trust. If only a portion of the trust is covered under the election, then any appreciation or depreciation of the trust assets must be allocated pro rata, under Code Section 2056(b)(10). If a reverse QTIP election is made, it must cover all the property in the trust. Some planners prefer to provide in the trust the authority for the trustee to split the QTIP into two trusts, in case the survivor makes a partial election.

Q 5:74 When is a QTIP trust most likely to be useful?

When spouses have unequal assets, it may be difficult to ensure that the maximum exemption equivalent amount ($1,000,000 in year 2002) is utilized in each estate. If the wealthier spouse dies first, there may be plenty of assets fully to fund a credit shelter trust, but the wealthier spouse may be reluctant to give the surviving spouse control over the assets by leaving them outright. If the poorer spouse dies first, there may not be sufficient assets to fund the credit shelter trust at all, and the wealthier spouse may be reluctant to make a lifetime gift of assets large enough to ensure that the poorer spouse can fully utilize the exemption. QTIP trusts give the wealthier spouse a chance to reduce the total estate tax (by fully using the exemptions for both spouses) regardless of which spouse dies first, and without giving the poorer spouse control over the final disposition of the property. Consequently, QTIP trusts are especially useful in second marriage situations.

When the wealthier spouse dies first, he or she can fund a QTIP trust that will qualify for the marital deduction. The surviving spouse cannot encumber or distribute the principal, so the wealthy spouse can ensure that the property ultimately goes to his or her choice of beneficiaries. In addition, the total estate tax liability of the couple can be reduced by the consequent full use of the exemption equivalent.

To protect against the tax consequence of the poorer spouse dying first, the wealthy spouse may choose to fund a lifetime QTIP trust. Such a trust will be treated as part of the poorer spouse's estate upon his or her death, and still flow to the wealthy spouse's chosen beneficiaries.

In addition, unlike the credit shelter trust that places few restrictions on the surviving spouse (although they are important restrictions, and must be adhered to for the tax benefits to apply), the grantor can place additional restrictions on the assets through the use of QTIP trust language. For example, grantors who have children from a former marriage, or who do not want to risk their assets passing to the surviving spouse's new family if he or she remarries, could place additional restrictions on the assets by using a QTIP trust.

Q 5:75 Are there other exceptions to the terminable interest property rules?

Although the QTIP rules are the most important exception to the rule that terminable interests do not qualify for the marital deduction, there are several other exceptions provided in the Code. These include:

1. *Charitable remainder trusts* (see Q 5:77). If the spouse is the sole noncharitable beneficiary of a CRT, the spouse's interest will still qualify for the marital deduction. Consequently no tax will be due on the CRT's present value at the time of death of the first spouse to die; because the remainder interest goes to charity, it will also escape estate taxation.
2. *Life insurance and annuities.* The surviving spouse's right to receive all of the income from a life insurance or annuity contract will not cause the terminable interest to be taxed, so long as the surviving spouse has the power to appoint the

principal to his or her estate or himself or herself during life or by will.

3. *A general power of appointment trust.* If the surviving spouse is entitled to receive all the income of the trust during life, and the power to appoint the trust to himself or herself or his or her estate during life or at death (it is not sufficient for this purpose to give the spouse the power to appoint the trust principal only to his or her creditors), the trust principal will qualify for the marital deduction. It is important that no other person have the power to appoint trust principal: A discretionary power in the trustee to make distributions to the trustor's children, even if unexercised, will cause the trust to be taxed in the deceased spouse's estate.

Charitable Gift Planning

Q 5:76 How does charitable planning fit into estate planning?

Many clients will have some charitable intentions, and the estate and gift tax codes encourage charitable bequests and gifts. Charitable bequests will be deducted from the taxable estate in calculating final estate tax liability, so a client with a taxable estate may determine that a greater benefit is gained from leaving all, or a significant portion, of the taxable portion of the estate to charity. Put another way, clients often see that charitable bequests are partially matched by the federal and state government, by their decision to forgo tax collection from those bequests. A charitable bequest will, however, have no immediate income tax benefit to the client.

A charitable gift, on the other hand, not only reduces the size of the estate but also inures to the benefit of the donor by virtue of a current income tax deduction. Any charitable transfer that postpones the loss of the use of the funds for the grantor (as in a charitable bequest) while giving the grantor current favorable income tax treatment (as in a charitable gift) will obviously be of special interest to the charitably inclined client.

Q 5:77 What is a charitable remainder trust?

A charitable remainder trust is an irrevocable trust that holds and invests assets for the benefit of one or more noncharitable income beneficiaries and for one or more charitable remaindermen. The CRT allows an individual and a charity to share income and remainder interests, by setting up a gift to charity while retaining an interest for the spouse that will not be treated as a terminable interest. For the marital deduction to be available, the spouse must receive a qualified lead interest and must be the only income beneficiary other than the charities that are benefiting from the trust. The charitable remainder trust must be a unitrust, an annuity trust, or a pooled income trust [I.R.C. § 2055(e)], but if the marital deduction is sought the trust must be set up as a unitrust or an annuity trust.

Under the Taxpayer Relief Act of 1997, a trust cannot qualify as a charitable remainder annuity trust (CRAT) if the annuity for any year is greater than 50 percent of the initial fair market value of the trust assets, or as a charitable remainder unitrust (CRUT) if the annual distribution exceeds 50 percent (and if either of these do not meet the requirements, the trust income will be taxed to the beneficiaries or to the trust). [I.R.C. § 664(d)(2)(A)] TRA '97 also imposes a "10 percent test," requiring that the remainder interest of the charity be worth at least 10 percent of each transfer to the trust at the time of each transfer. [I.R.C. §§ 664(d)(1) and (2)] These restrictions mean that charitable remainder trusts may not be feasible for trustors under the age of 60, because the interest in transfers made by younger individuals may be too remote to meet the 10 percent test. The intent of these changes was to end perceived abuses of CRTs, which had been highly touted as investment havens, particularly to extremely high-net-worth individuals with recent run-ups in asset value (e.g., software industry multimillionaires and others with no particular charitable intentions).

Q 5:78 What is the difference between a charitable remainder unitrust and a charitable remainder annuity trust?

The income beneficiary of a charitable remainder unitrust is paid at a fixed percentage rate of the corpus of the trust, while the income beneficiary of a charitable remainder annuity trust is paid a fixed amount. With both trusts, income must be paid at least annually, and the income interest can be distributed during the life of the beneficiary or for a fixed number of years.

With a unitrust, the amount of the payment will vary as the trust value varies. In other words, the actual investment and earnings experience of the trust will benefit (or harm) both the income beneficiary and the charitable beneficiary; higher investment return will simultaneously increase the unitrust calculation in future years and increase the value of the trust corpus ultimately distributed to the charitable beneficiary. On the other hand, both beneficiaries will share negative investment experience as well, so the income beneficiary will be unable to rely on the future stream of income.

The grantor of an annuity trust must fix the amount of the annuity at the creation of the trust. Even if investment experience changes, the annuity amount will not vary. If investments underperform the annuity amount, the trust will slowly (or rapidly) diminish in value. Meanwhile, the income beneficiary will have a predictable and reliable stream of income.

Q 5:79 What is a pooled income fund?

Another choice for charitable gift planning is a pooled income fund. Like a charitable remainder trust, such a device will permit a present charitable deduction, avoidance of capital gains taxes, and an income stream for life; however, a pooled income fund is established by the charity itself and managed by trustees selected by the charity. This simplified version of a charitable remainder trust permits the donor to take advantage of the increased yield and safety available from pooling several donors' funds, while avoiding the cost of establishing a separate trust (and the problems associated with continuing management of such a trust). A pooled income fund will often produce a larger present charitable deduction as well. The donor completely loses control of investments by the pooled income fund and will not benefit from any nontaxable income earned by the pooled income fund; by contrast, the donor may choose to remain as trustee of a charitable remainder trust, and may invest some portion of the trust in assets that do not produce taxable income (and thereby reduce the donor's tax liability for future trust distributions).

Q 5:80 What relief is available if a charitable remainder trust fails to meet the 10 percent minimum remainder rule?

As previously noted, a charitable remainder trust must be structured so that the value of the charitable remainder interest is at least

10 percent of the value of a contribution at the time the contribution is made. If a trust fails to meet this requirement, two alternatives are available: The donor may declare the trust void *ab initio* or reform the trust to make it comply with the requirement. If reformation is the chosen solution, it must be initiated within 90 days of the due date (with extensions) of any estate tax return or, if no estate tax return is due, by the due date (with extensions) for the first income tax return for the trust. If the trust is declared void *ab initio,* no charitable deduction may be claimed and the income earned by the trust will be taxable to the donor.

Q 5:81 What are the tax benefits of charitable remainder trusts?

Charitable remainder trusts offer a number of planning opportunities, particularly for clients with highly appreciated assets and some charitable inclinations (although some projections can make charitable remainder trusts appear to be excellent investment choices quite aside from charitable intentions). A client might establish a CRT with such an asset, providing for personal income and income for his or her spouse for life or for a term of years, and upon the second death (or the expiration of the term of years) arrange for the balance to be distributed to one or more qualified charities. In some cases, the client might also choose to remain as trustee of the CRT for life, and even to retain the power to designate the final charitable beneficiary (or beneficiaries), so long as the trust terms require the client's choice of beneficiary to qualify as a charitable donee. By taking this action, a number of tax-based benefits accrue to the client:

1. The capital gain on the appreciated asset is effectively taxed to the charity and, because the charity pays no income tax, tax is avoided on the gain.
2. The client receives a stream of income that is either fixed (if the CRT is an annuity trust or CRAT) and reliable, or at least increased over the low rate of return the appreciated asset may have yielded (if the client selected the unitrust option, or CRUT).

3. The increased yield can be used to make annual exclusion gifts to the client's children or other beneficiaries, from which they might choose to purchase life insurance to replace the value of the asset given to the CRT, so that beneficiaries receive an amount equivalent to what they would have received if the CRT had not been established.
4. The value of the gifted asset is removed from the client's estate, reducing estate tax liability.
5. The client is entitled to a current income tax deduction, based on the actuarial present value of the future gift.

The value of CRTs will obviously vary significantly depending on the age of the client, the value of the asset, the amount of appreciation, the medical condition of the client and spouse, the cash needs of children and other family members, and the charitable inclination of the client. In an appropriate case, the CRT can be a powerfully useful estate planning vehicle.

It is important to remember that payments *from* the trust are taxed on a "WIFO" basis—"worst in, first out." This is more technically referred to as the "tier" system of taxation. Payments from the trust will be taxed to the beneficiary first, as ordinary income; then, to the extent the payment exceeds ordinary income for that year, as capital gains to the extent thereof; then as tax-exempt income to the extent thereof; and finally as return of principal. This means that a donor cannot hope to have the trust sell property and invest immediately in tax-exempt income so that the donor receives a tax-free stream of income. At the very least, the donor will have to pay the capital gains tax, but over time, rather than all at once as would have been the case were the trust not created.

Q 5:82 What are charitable annuities?

Although the concept and result of a charitable annuity resemble those of charitable remainder trusts, the mechanics are somewhat different. In a charitable annuity, the donor makes a current gift to a specified charity in return for an agreement to pay a fixed percentage rate of return on that gift for either the life of the donor (and others, if the donor chooses), or for a term of years. As with a charitable remainder trust, the gift can be of appreciated property, and the unpaid capital gains liability can be avoided.

Just as with a charitable remainder trust, actuarial tables are employed to calculate the present value of the charitable gift in a charitable annuity. As in a charitable remainder annuity trust, the future payments are predetermined and reliable.

The benefit of a charitable annuity is usually that the donor need not bother with the expense or trouble of establishing a charitable remainder trust. The drawbacks to this type of instrument are several: (1) not all charities offer charitable annuities; (2) those that do may not offer favorable rates of return; and (3) the donor to a charitable annuity loses all ability to control the investment or disposition of the underlying property, or the ultimate recipient of the charitable gift.

Q 5:83 What is a charitable lead trust?

The charitable lead trust, in which the charity's interest comes first pursuant to Code Section 2055(e)(2)(B), allows the grantor to receive an income tax deduction at the creation of the trust. To qualify for the deduction, the trust must be a charitable lead annuity trust or a charitable lead unitrust. The spouse (or other beneficiary) receives a remainder interest rather than a lead interest. In order to meet statutory requirements, the grantor must guarantee that the charity receive an annuity or unitrust interest. Typically, charitable lead trusts are used as a method of securing a present income tax deduction for the donor, while assuring availability of funds for children or grandchildren at some later date. (Note that only a charitable lead *unitrust* will permit allocation of a grantor's generation-skipping tax exemption to the trust property that upon termination will pay to grandchildren. [Treas. Reg. § 26.2642-3]) Otherwise, the value of a charitable lead trust is similar to the benefits outlined for a charitable remainder trust: The donor secures a current income tax charitable deduction and avoids the imposition of capital gains tax on appreciated property. In addition, the donor may be able to transfer future income rights to a beneficiary at less than the date-of-death value of those same rights (thereby reducing the total estate tax liability). The charitable lead trust is also particularly attractive to a charitably inclined donor with unusually high income in the year of the gift, because the property (and future income stream) can be returned to the donor in later years when, presumably, income (and income taxes) will be lower.

To qualify as a CLT for estate and gift tax purposes the trust must meet the following requirements:

1. An irrevocable trust valid under state law must be created;
2. The property or funds must be transferred to the irrevocable trust referred to in item 1;
3. A qualifying income interest in the form of a guaranteed annuity or charitable unitrust must exist;
4. The governing instrument must contain language that (a) prohibits the trust from engaging in actions under which Code Section 508(e) would cause a private foundation to be taxed for federal income tax purposes and (b) restricts the use of the income of the charitable component of the trust to exclusively charitable purposes.

[Treas. Reg. § 25.2522(c)-3(c)(2)(vi)]

Life Insurance as an Estate Planning Tool

Q 5:84 Can life insurance be used as an estate planning tool?

Planning an estate using insurance proceeds is sensible but often risky. Making a probate or trust estate the beneficiary of life insurance proceeds is desirable when the rest of the estate assets are not sufficiently liquid to take care of taxes and administrative expenses; however, if the insured retains any ownership rights in the policy, the entire policy proceeds will be included in the insured's estate and thus subject to estate tax. [I.R.C. § 2042] If the policy is gifted to another, the value of the policy will be subject to gift tax, and if the gift is made within three years of the insured's death, it will still be deemed includible in the insured's estate. [I.R.C. § 2035]

For most people, estate taxation of life insurance is not an issue because the value of their assets is far less than the $1,000,000 unified credit exemption (in 2002); neither the insured's estate nor the beneficiaries are required to pay taxes on the proceeds. For those who have substantial assets, adding a $100,000 life insurance policy can translate into quite a tax risk, because the initial taxable rate is usually 37 percent. In other words, it is easy to overlook the value of life insurance in calculating the likely estate tax liability while estate planning, particularly for younger clients who may have smaller estates but large life insurance policies.

Q 5:85 When are life insurance proceeds includible in the gross estate?

Life insurance proceeds are includible in the gross estate if:

1. The proceeds are payable to the insured's executor or receivable by or for the benefit of the decedent's estate; [I.R.C. § 2042(1)]
2. The decedent possessed at the time of death any incidents of ownership with respect to the policy that was exercisable alone or in conjunction with any other person; [I.R.C. § 2042(2)] or
3. The insured transferred ownership of the policy in which he or she had any incident of ownership within three years of his or her death. [I.R.C. § 2035(d)(2)]

Q 5:86 What can the insured do to avoid having the insurance proceeds includible in the insured's gross estate?

Where there is no existing insurance policy and a policy is being purchased, the policy should be owned by someone other than the insured and the insured should have no incident of ownership with respect to the policy. If there is an existing policy, the insured can avoid the risk of having the insurance proceeds includible in the insured's gross estate by forgoing any ownership rights, such as the power to name or change beneficiaries, borrow against the policy, cash in the policy, or assign it to another. As previously mentioned, if an existing policy is gifted to another, the value of the policy will be subject to gift tax, and, if the gift is made within three years of the insured's death, it will still be deemed includible in the insured's estate. [I.R.C. § 2035]

Transferring the policy to the spouse and making the spouse the beneficiary of life insurance also avoids this pitfall because an unlimited marital deduction applies to all gift and estate transfers to the spouse; however, the insured may want to exercise some control over how the insurance proceeds are managed, particularly if he or she has some concern about how effectively the surviving spouse handles money. Even if such an arrangement makes sense in an individual case, it will have the effect of increasing the spouse's estate and eventually exposing the proceeds to estate taxation. It may, however, be a useful tool for ensuring that the surviving spouse's estate is at or near the exemption equivalent amount, while also providing liquidity for the surviving spouse after the first spouse's death.

Making the children the beneficiaries of the life insurance is another popular choice that may reduce the transfer taxes payable on the death of the insured or the spouse, but this again raises concerns regarding the ability of the children to manage these proceeds, particularly if they are minors or are unskilled in managing large sums. Also, if a policy is transferred to the children as owners, the gift may not qualify for the annual exclusion because most policies require the consent of all policy-holders to exercise incidents of ownership and thus the gift may not qualify as a present interest. If the insured has such concerns, an irrevocable life insurance trust may be the best solution.

Q 5:87 What is an irrevocable life insurance trust?

An irrevocable life insurance trust, often known as an ILIT, is a trust created to hold and own life insurance policies in order to keep the policy proceeds out of the insured's estate and the estate of his or her spouse. Life insurance proceeds held in an ILIT, if properly transferred, will not be deemed includible in the insured's estate, and can be managed and distributed according to the wishes of the insured if the insured:

1. Has no ownership rights in the policy;
2. Is not a beneficiary of the policy; and
3. Is not the trustee.

The trust instrument and all transfers are irrevocable and cannot be amended. If the settlor transfers an existing insurance policy into the trust, this will be considered a gift transfer by the IRS, and if the insured dies within three years of making the transfer, the trust assets will be considered includible in the settlor's estate. [I.R.C. § 2042]

The insured can be the settlor of the trust (and thus can structure how the proceeds are to be managed and distributed), but should not be the trustee. The trustee of the trust should ideally be the original applicant and owner of the insurance (to avoid the inclusion of life insurance transferred within three years of the settlor's death). Because the trust is irrevocable, the settlor is completely removed from any economic benefit emanating from the life insurance policy.

ILITs are particularly popular among life insurance salespersons and stockbrokers. Many insurance companies, brokerage houses, and banks actively market life insurance products through ILITs, and the attorney who accepts referrals from any of these professionals should expect to see clients who are already convinced of the value of an ILIT. While life insurance may well be an appropriate estate planning tool in each such case, the attorney is well-advised to develop a clear understanding of the investment value of life insurance and help the client to reach a balanced appreciation of the alternatives (a Crummey trust without life insurance investments, or outright gifts to children, who might or might not choose life insurance as the best investment, for example) and relative merits of the available options.

Q 5:88 Can spouses make separate ILITs making each other or their children beneficiaries?

Some attorneys feel strongly that spouses cannot create separate ILITs making each other or even their children the beneficiaries of life insurance policies, for fear that the IRS will apply the "reciprocal trust doctrine" to include both trusts in the estate of one of the spouses, presumably the second to die who has been enjoying a life estate in the trust established by the first spouse to die. The *Grace* case, *U.S. v. Estate of Grace* [395 U.S. 316 (1969)], applied the "reciprocal trust doctrine" to include property in a trust established by the wife in the husband's estate. The Court stated, "application of the reciprocal trust doctrine requires only that the trusts be interrelated, and that the arrangement, to the extent of mutual value, leaves the settlors in approximately the same economic position as they would have been in had they created trusts naming themselves as life beneficiaries." [395 U.S. at 325] Therefore, some attorneys feel that it is too dangerous, and risks application of the reciprocal trust doctrine, when spouses make life insurance trusts of which the other is a beneficiary.

Other attorneys feel that the *Grace* case would not apply, and indeed, has never been applied to a life insurance trust situation in the Supreme Court or any circuit court. First, the spouses are not in the same economic position they would have been had they created trusts naming themselves as beneficiaries, since the policy does not pay out until the insured's death. To achieve the same result, the second to die would have had to fund the trust with a policy insuring the life of the other spouse. Second, even where there is such a concern, the reciprocal trust doctrine should not apply if the trust terms are not identical (for example, one spouse has a five-and-five withdrawal right and one does not) or if they are funded with significantly different levels of insurance

Both points of view agree that spouses can fund their trusts (or a joint trust established by both) with second-to-die life insurance policies, which are generally less expensive than standard policies and are especially effective when the marital deduction has deferred taxation of assets to the death of the second spouse.

Q 5:89 What are some of the problems with using life insurance trusts?

An ILIT (or a STDLIT—second-to-die life insurance trust) is not without its administrative costs and problems. In addition to the expense of establishing the trust, the arrangement requires (like all nongrantor irrevocable trusts, and unlike revocable grantor trusts) that a separate tax identification number be assigned to the trust at its creation. If the trust has any income over $100 (the standard deduction for trusts) the trustee must file annual returns. (During the grantor's lifetime the trust is a "grantor trust" and the trustee need only provide a statement to the grantor for inclusion in the grantor's tax return, while providing information about to whom the statement was delivered when filing the trust's own 1041 income tax return.) As discussed in Q 5:28, any life insurance trust will likely be designed as a "Crummey" trust, requiring annual notices to beneficiaries of their Crummey withdrawal rights—a requirement that clients tend to forget but are unwilling to pay their attorneys to remember.

There are additional problems, related to the very nature of life insurance. First, some clients may intend to access the cash value of the policy for future needs, and will be unpleasantly surprised to find that the cash value is no longer available, and they can no longer borrow against the policy, since trust assets may not be used for the client's own benefit. Second, the life insurance itself, not the trust, may cause anguish. Examples of problems: the agent sells a policy with an "increasing premium"—here the problem is obvious. Or the agent touts the policy as able to "pay for itself" in 5 years, 10 years, or 15 years, but uses overly optimistic forecasts of dividend performance. When the anniversary rolls around, the client finds that further premiums are still required, perhaps indefinitely. Or the agent sells a blended policy of term and whole life, expecting to buy additional paid-up whole life with any dividends and ultimately phase out the term component, and the client does not understand the complexity of the arrangement and is unhappy with the risk of paying premiums into infinity. The attorney must at all costs avoid being associated in the client's mind with an insurance agent who the client believes has over-promised or who is unwilling to respond clearly and in detail to the client's fears.

Q 5:90 Can the surviving spouse act as trustee of an irrevocable life insurance trust?

Yes, provided that the surviving spouse is not a grantor and has no administrative powers of appointment over the trust that would be considered a general power of appointment. Neither spouse should act as trustee of a jointly-funded second-to-die life insurance trust.

Q 5:91 How are the premiums paid during the life of the insured?

The trust may be funded or unfunded. A funded life insurance trust has both the insurance policy (or policies) and other assets that produce enough income to pay the premiums. Policy premiums in an unfounded trust are paid through gifts to the trust from the insured. These gift transfers are covered by the annual gift exclusion, which allows up to $11,000 per year to be transferred with no tax or reporting consequences. Planners usually advise against funded trusts, because the settlor may have to pay the gift tax upon the transfer of income-producing assets into the trust, and income tax on the trust's income. Furthermore, if community property rather than the separate property of the insured is used either to fund the trust or pay premiums, the IRS will consider the noninsured spouse a settlor of the trust and its tax advantages are lost. [Treas. Reg. § 20.2042-1(c)(5)] Sometimes, however, the insurance policy itself may generate income that is then the property of the trust, such as a dividend from a policy that does not permit dividends to be applied to reduce premium, or a stock dividend if an insurance company demutualizes.

Q 5:92 What is the difference between a "Crummey" trust and an irrevocable life insurance trust?

As discussed in Q 5:28, a "Crummey" power written into a trust enables the settlor of the trust to make annual gifts to the trust and still maintain some control over how the transferred assets are managed and distributed. As long as the beneficiary is allowed a brief window period each year (usually two to four weeks) during which he or she can withdraw the assets, the IRS will consider transfers into the trust to be completed present-interest gifts rather than a gift of a future interest and the $11,000 annual gift tax exclusion will apply.

One of the most common uses of Crummey provisions is in the purchase of life insurance. In order to prevent the value of life insurance from being counted as part of a decedent's estate, the decedent must not have been the owner of the policy within the three years prior to his or her death. This requirement can often be met by having other individuals (usually the children) purchase the policy, even if the purchase is made with funds given to the individuals each year. An irrevocable life insurance trust may, however, be more attractive, because it permits the grantor some assurance that the insurance will remain in force, and that the proceeds will be available to ensure liquidity of the estate after the grantor's death.

Some practitioners believe that a Crummey trust must have liquid funds available for the beneficiary during the withdrawal window. This would mean that the settlor of the trust must transfer enough money into the trust not only to cover the insurance policy premiums, but also to provide available funds for the beneficiary if he or she exercises the withdrawal right. There are additional problems if the sole asset of the trust is a single insurance policy and multiple beneficiaries are given Crummey powers in the trust: If one beneficiary wishes to exercise his or her right of withdrawal, the insurance company might demand that the beneficiaries agree to this before the policy can be invaded. However, other practitioners believe there is authority that a Crummey ILIT is effective even if the only asset that may be used to meet the beneficiaries' withdrawal rights is life insurance, even, the IRS has held, group term life insurance. The reasoning is that the Trustee can always borrow to meet the withdrawal obligation. Another, more conservative approach is to require that the contribution to the trust be made sufficiently in advance of the premium due date that for the period of time subject to the withdrawal power, the trust does in fact hold liquid assets. Once the period (for example, 30 days) has expired, the trustee can make the wise investment choice to pay the policy premium. Those who elect this approach are still uncomfortable with trusts funded only with group term life insurance, but there have been several IRS letter rulings approving such arrangements.

The settlor must take care that the language of the trust document allows for the withdrawal of an amount no greater than the annual exclusion amount, or the entire trust corpus may be deemed includible in the beneficiary's estate at his or her death. In addition, as discussed in Q 5:28, a trust that expects to hold insurance with high premiums, but have few beneficiaries to share the withdrawal rights over contributions, may need a "hanging power" to prevent beneficiaries from being deemed owners of the policy, and for some attorneys, this provision is boilerplate.

Q 5:93 Can the generation-skipping tax exemption language be incorporated into a life insurance trust?

Yes. Settlors who wish to name grandchildren or other "skip persons" as beneficiaries of their estates should consider generation-skipping insurance trusts. A great deal of money can be leveraged through such an insurance vehicle because for generation-skipping tax purposes, the premium constitutes the transfer, not the face value of the policy. Because up to $1 million in gift or death transfers is exempt if made to skip persons, both the settlor and the trust can benefit from that exemption. Transfers either of assets or of premium payments into the trust are exempt up to $1 million; thus the settlor can ensure the beneficiaries a substantial "return" on the premiums paid.

However, the final generation-skipping tax regulations have now made it clear that the "leveraging" made possible by an insurance trust funded by "annual exclusion" gifts used to pay premiums, will not work unless the "skip" generation, the grandchildren, each have separate shares of the trust as to which the exclusion gifts apply. It is no longer possible, therefore, to set up a trust that benefits children and grandchildren, fund it with gifts that qualify for the annual exclusion, have the trust continue for the lifetimes of children and grandchildren with benefits for both, and then pass GST tax-free to the grandchildren. Instead, the trust would have to be set up from the beginning with separate sub-trusts for each grandchild only. [Treas. Reg. § 26.2642-1(c)(3)]

Valuation Discounts as an Estate Planning Tool

Q 5:94 What are valuation discounts?

Where one individual controls all of the rights with regard to a given asset, it will be valued at its fair market value—what a willing buyer and willing seller would agree upon as a price to exchange the asset. Where the owner's ability to transfer or control the property has been reduced, the property's value to a willing buyer will be lower.

> **Example 5-3.** Kathleen owns The Widget Factory and all its machinery, receivables, and inventory. It has been valued at $1,000,000. Kathleen creates TWF, Inc., and transfers all of the assets to the new corporation in return for all of the shares of stock of TWF. Her resulting 1,000,000 shares are worth $1 each, and her investment retains its original total value. When Kathleen sells (or gives away) 1,000 shares of TWF, Inc., her remaining stock is no longer worth $1 each; even though she has disposed of only $1,000 worth of stock, an appraiser determines that her remaining stock is now worth only $650,000. Her principal asset has thereby been reduced in value, and on her death her estate will pay tax only on the lower value.

Q 5:95 How can discounting be utilized in estate planning?

Valuation discounting usually comes into play when assets of the donor-decedent are held in a family limited partnership, limited liability company, or other non-individual capacity. A share in such a partnership may be worth much less on the open market than its fractional value of the underlying assets would indicate, especially where the share is a minority share with only limited control over the total assets. Discounting can substantially reduce the tax liability, although it will almost always require the services of a professional appraiser.

For the client with nondiscounted assets and a desire to minimize estate taxes, establishment of an appropriate ownership vehicle may permit a substantial reduction in the assets' value. Although most of the early use of discounting occurred with family limited partnerships, the concept of a limited liability company (LLC) recently developed in many states has made the LLC the instrument of choice for most practitioners.

A family limited partnership (FLP) usually provides that the parents act as general partners, with other family members holding limited partnership interests. The structure of the FLP will permit the general partners to determine when and whether to distribute income, but problems may arise with any structure that permits distribution to be allocated on anything other than a non-pro rata basis, either because the parents will be deemed to have so much control that the FLP is includible in their estate, or because the possibility of never receiving a distribution will make the gift to children ineligible for the annual exclusion by failing the "present interest" test. (See Q 5:19) Because the limited partners have some rights with regard to the partnership's assets, even though limited, the value of the general partner's ownership interest is thus reduced, resulting in a lower value for estate tax purposes. Depending on the structure of the FLP (e.g., whether the limited partners share in current profits), the reduction in value may be more or less.

In general terms, the LLC combines the tax advantages of partnerships with the inherent advantages of corporations (primarily reductions in personal liability for LLC "members"), permitting the separation of ownership and voting rights, simplifying the reporting requirements, and minimizing the income tax effect, while still permitting the individuals to shield themselves from the prospect of personal liability for the LLC's actions. The valuation reduction for assets transferred to an LLC will be similar to those for an FLP's property, and for the same reasons of reduced control and marketability.

Typically, an LLC (or FLP) will be established by the owner of the assets to be included, and the assets transferred to the entity. Other family members will either purchase shares in the entity, or receive their shares as gifts (subject to the annual gift exclusion amount). Immediately upon the transfer of a small minority interest, the value of the entity's remaining shares will be substantially reduced. Over time, as more shares are transferred, the remaining value may become a minority interest, with even larger valuation discounts. If the entity is funded with real estate, it is important to consider whether the transfer of control from the original owner (as majority stakeholder) to the other parties, will be considered a transfer of a controlling interest subject to a special conveyance tax known in some states as the "controlling interest transfer tax."

In many cases, the death of the original owner will vest the remaining interests in the other owners (usually the decedent's children). The value of the remaining interests at the time of the decedent's death will be reduced as a result of the partial ownership, thereby substantially reducing the taxable estate. [Rev. Rul. 93-12, 1993-1 C.B. 202]

Q 5:96 Are there negative tax effects of using valuation discounts?

Upon the subsequent liquidation of the LLC/FLP and distribution of the proceeds, the recipients will recognize a substantial capital gain for income tax purposes, because they will "carry over" the original owner's basis. Nonetheless, the result is favorable: The capital gains tax may be incurred many years later, and will (at least under current tax law) be no more than 20 percent of the gain, while estate tax liability is incurred immediately upon the death of the original owner, and may be as high as 50 percent (reduced in 2003 to 49 percent) of the value of the assets. Of course, after the scheduled elimination of the federal estate tax and imposition of carryover basis rules in 2011, the calculus of valuation discounts will change radically.

Q 5:97 Are there any limitations on the types of property that might be subject to a valuation discount?

In numerous cases and memoranda the Internal Revenue Service has opposed valuation discounts for marketability and lack of control when the FLP was created less than a year prior to the death of the decedent. [See, e.g., Ltr. Ruls. 9719006, 9725002, 9723009, and 9730004] The IRS frowns on family partnerships that were clearly set up solely to shelter gifts to family members, there has to be at least the appearance of an operating business. "Deathbed planning" will at the very least bring a lengthy audit and challenge in the tax court. On the other hand, some partnerships funded solely with marketable securities have been able to withstand scrutiny.

Q 5:98 What is an estate tax freeze?

One common technique utilized to reduce estate taxes is to establish a business entity (corporation, FLP, or LLC) structured so that the future appreciation in value inures to the benefit of one class of shareholder or partner. If the owner of the property transfers (by gift or sale) those interests enjoying the future appreciation to family members, the value of the asset for estate tax purposes is "frozen" at its current value, resulting in a reduction in estate taxes, even though the current owner may retain the right to control and receive current income from the property (or business). In order to better control the use of "estate tax freezes," Congress in 1990 adopted Code Section 2701, which requires the use of special valuation rules for transfers of "applicable retained interests" to family members. An applicable retained interest includes any right to an extraordinary payment or distribution from an entity controlled by the family immediately prior to the transfer.

Q 5:99 What are the special valuation rules?

In valuing the transfer of future appreciation rights in an estate tax freeze, Code Section 2701 requires that the applicable retained interest first be valued, and then deducted from the total value of the entity held by all family members. Applicable retained interests are valued at zero unless one of several exceptions applies, so that the estate tax freeze method will only be effective (at least as to transfers among family members) if one of those exceptions is applicable. As a result, estate tax freeze valuation rules require that the retained interest be a "qualified payment right." That definition, in turn, requires that the payment right be a periodic preferred stock dividend (or equivalent payment in the case of a partnership), although variable payments based on fluctuating interest rates are permitted. [I.R.C. § 2701(c)(3)]

In addition, chapter 14 states that in valuing a share of a business entity, any "applicable restriction" will be disregarded. A typical "applicable restriction" would be restriction on transferability. However, chapter 14 also states that it will be disregarded except to the extent it applies by virtue of state law, rather than by the parties' agreement. This has meant that valuation discounts are still available in states in which transferability of partnership interests, or LLC shares, is statutorily restricted. Unsurprisingly, most states have amended their statutes to make these restrictions possible, in order to encourage businesses to form in that state. The practitioner expecting to obtain an appraisal that will show a "valuation discount" because of a transferability restriction must realize that the restriction will be disregarded to the extent that it is more restrictive than state law. In effect, the only relevant restriction will be the restriction imposed by state law, not by the agreement. More restrictive provisions should be included only if they are necessary to carry out the client's wishes, not to obtain a better "discount" or estate freeze.

Q 5:100 Do the special valuation rules apply to trusts?

Section 2702 of the Code applies the "special valuation" rules to trusts. Any transfer in which there are one or more term interests is considered a gift in trust. [Treas. Reg. § 25.2702-4] The most important thing to keep in mind here is that a gift of property with a retained life interest is subject to the special valuation rules. This means that the retained interest will be valued at zero unless certain exceptions are met. For example, the gift of $1,000,000 in trust, income to spouse or self for life, remainder at death to one's children, will be treated for gift tax purposes as a gift of $1,000,000, with no reduction for the retained interest—no discount for the fact that the possession of the interest is deferred. If the client does want to make such a gift, but does not want to pay gift tax on $1,000,000 (or use up the entire unified credit exemption equivalent), the attorney must include a special or limited power of appointment so that the gift to the remaindermen will be "incomplete."

Q 5:101 Are there exceptions to the special valuation rules for trusts?

There are some exceptions to these rules. First, rules are directed to transfers that create split interests. If the only interest the transferor possesses is the income interest, or the remainder interest, a transfer of that interest will not be subject to the special valuation rules. Second most popular as an exception is the "qualified personal residence trust." The requirements of the trust are set forth in Treasury Regulations Section 25.2702-5. The qualified personal residence trust, or QPRT, was designed to make it easier to transfer the family home. Essentially, the trust provides that for a term of years, the grantor retains the right to use the trust property as a residence; when the term expires, the trust property passes to the remaindermen; and if the trust terminates sooner (e.g., because the property is sold and thus ceases to be a residence), the trust property will be repaid to the grantor, either in its entirety, or as a qualified annuity interest. If these requirements are met (and the details set forth in the regulations), the value of the transferred interest (the remainder) will be determined applying a discount, as a remainder interest, using the federal Adjusted Federal Rate (AFR). The parties gamble that the property's value will grow faster than the AFR so that the growth is transferred tax-free to the remaindermen.

Since chapter 14 was adopted, the IRS has had the opportunity to issue numerous private letter rulings on QPRTs, covering every issue from whether or not 50 acres of farmland with a house in one corner qualifies as a "residence," to whether or not occasional renting out of the guest-house will cause the property to cease to qualify as a residence. Suffice to say that the practitioner desirous of establishing a QPRT would do well to research the details. This device is no longer popular, however, due to the steep drop in the AFR. With discounts determined using a rate less than 4 percent, the QPRT may have become more trouble than it is worth.

Another popular method (before the interest rates dropped) was the "GRAT." The GRAT is essentially a private annuity agreement between grantor (annuitant) and grantee (trust). The grantee trust agrees to pay the grantor an annuity determined based on federal rates. The difference between the property placed in trust, and the value of the annuity, is the value of the gift. GRATs can be arranged so as to "zero out" and be taxed as a gift of zero, gambling that the performance of the trust will exceed the AFR and/or that the grantor will die prematurely.

Generation-Skipping Tax Planning

Q 5:102 What is the "generation-skipping tax"?

The generation-skipping tax is a tax imposed under Code Section 2601 on any transfer of assets to a skip person (e.g., grandchildren or more distant issue), whether the transfer is a bequest or gift outright to a "direct skip" or is channeled through a taxable distribution or taxable termination. The intent of the generation-skipping tax is to prevent families from accumulating wealth by establishing multigenerational "dynasty trusts" in order to escape repeat taxation.

The GST is a flat tax, equal to the highest federal transfer tax rate in existence at the time of the transfer, 50 percent in 2002. Each transferor has a $1 million exemption, indexed for inflation, increasing to $1,100,000 for gifts made in the year 2002. The generation-skipping tax is imposed in addition to any gift tax or estate tax payable by the transferor and is based on the amount received by the transferee. [I.R.C. § 2623]

Q 5:103 What changes are planned for the generation-skipping tax in the future?

Individuals. As with the estate tax itself, the generation-skipping tax is slated for complete repeal in 2010. In the meantime, the Economic Growth and Tax Relief Reconciliation Act of 2001 schedules increases in the GST exemption amount in concert with the estate tax amount. Since the GST exemption will be slightly more than the $1 million estate tax exemption in 2002 and 2003, the two figures will not equalize until 2004. In that year the GST will be linked to the estate tax exemption, and the GST is scheduled to be eliminated in 2010 along with the estate tax.

Table 5-4. Changes in Generation-Skipping Tax Exemption Amounts and Rates Made By EGTRRA

Year	*Exemption*	*Maximum Rate*
2002	$ 1,100,000	50%
2003	$ 1,100,000 (plus inflation adjustment)	49%
2004	$ 1,500,000	48%
2005	$ 1,500,000	47%
2006	$ 2,000,000	46%
2007	$ 2,000,000	45%
2008	$ 2,000,000	45%
2009	$ 3,500,000	45%
2010	N/A repealed	Repealed

Business Owners. Current estate tax law allows some owners of family businesses to pass a larger amount to their heirs without incurring state taxes. Although it can be difficult to qualify for the favorable treatment, at least some small business owners can take advantage of the so-called QFOBI (Qualified Family Owned Business Interests) rules to pass a total of up to $1.35 million without estate tases. Special deductions end after 2003, however, and therefore are not discussed here.

Q 5:104 Who is a skip person?

The tax applies to transfers to "skip persons." Skip persons are individuals who are two or more generations below the transferor. Between unrelated parties, a "generation" means 12½ years. A trust can be a skip person if all interests in property held in trust are held by skip persons or there is no nonskip person holding an interest in the trust and no distributions can be made from the trust to nonskip persons. [I.R.C. §2613(a)]

Q 5:105 Are there any exceptions to the GST?

Yes. There are two important "exceptions."

There is a "predeceased ancestor" exception to the skip rule: a bequest from a grandparent to a grandchild whose parent is deceased will not be subject to the GST. [I.R.C. § 2651(e)] This also applies to great-nieces and great-nephews. Whether or not the ancestor is "predeceased" is determined 90 days after the transfer occurs. This makes it desirable to include in documents dealing with sums over the GST exemption that a person is deemed to have predeceased if (s)he does not survive 90 days after the testator's death. Very important: the timely disclaimer by a child is *not* treated as if the child had predeceased the testator. The child who disclaims $1.2 million so that it passes instead to a grandchild will have caused a direct skip of $1.2 million, resulting in a significant tax.

Secondly, trusts that were irrevocable when the GST tax was created, October 22, 1986, are "grandfathered" and distributions from or terminations of such trusts are *exempt* from the GST. However, if the trust is substantially reformed or amended, the exemption disappears. There are innumerable letter rulings in which beneficiaries sought IRS approval for changes to GST-grandfathered trusts that would not affect the exemption, usually when multiple beneficiaries wish to sever the trust into separate trusts. Usually it is inadvisable to exercise any power of appointment over a grandfathered trust, as well.

Q 5:106 What transfers will result in the imposition of the generation-skipping tax?

Three types of generation-skipping transfers can result in the imposition of the GST:

1. A direct skip;
2. A taxable termination; or
3. A taxable distribution.

[I.R.C. § 2611(a)]

Q 5:107 What is a direct skip?

A direct skip is a taxable gift during life or a transfer at death directly to a skip person. [I.R.C. § 2612(c)] For example, an outright gift from a grandparent to a grandchild in excess of the annual exclusion is a direct skip. If the property interest is transferred to a trust, the transfer is a direct skip if the trust is a skip person—that is, if all of the interests in the trust are held by skip persons. Note: A direct skip is subject to both the GST and the estate or gift tax. [I.R.C. § 2612(c)(1)]

The GST is imposed at the time of the transfer, and the taxable amount is the value of the property received by the transferee. [I.R.C. § 2623] The tax is payable by the transferor or the transferor's estate. If the transferor pays the GST, the amount of tax paid is treated as an additional gift for gift tax purposes. [I.R.C. § 2515] When a direct skip is made from a trust, the trustee is liable for the tax. [I.R.C. §§ 2603(a)(3), (2)]

Q 5:108 What is a taxable termination?

A taxable termination is a termination of an interest in trust property by reason of death, the passage of time, or the release of a power or otherwise, unless there is no chance a skip person will receive a distribution, or the interest in the property passes immediately upon termination to a nonskip person. [I.R.C. § 2612(a)(1)]

If a taxable termination occurs, the taxable amount is the value of the property to be transferred, minus any deductions for expenses, indebtedness, and taxes. [I.R.C. § 2622] For taxable terminations occurring at death, an alternate valuation election is permitted that enables the executor to value the trust property six months after death in accordance with Code Section 2066. The trustee of the trust pays the tax out of the assets being transferred. [I.R.C. § 2603(a)(2)]

Q 5:109 What is a taxable distribution?

A taxable distribution is any distribution from a trust (that is not a direct skip or a taxable termination) transferring income or principal to a skip person. [I.R.C. § 2612(b)] A transfer to a trust is a taxable distribution only if the recipient trust is a skip person. The taxable amount is the value of the property received by the transferee minus expenses incurred by the transferee in connection with the determination, collection, or refund of the generation-skipping tax. [I.R.C. § 2621] The tax is imposed at the time of the distribution and is payable by the transferee. [I.R.C. § 2603(a)(1)] If the trustee pays the GST from the trust assets, the tax paid constitutes an additional taxable distribution and the generation-skipping tax is also imposed on that amount. [I.R.C. § 2621(b)]

Q 5:110 When might it be advisable to incur the generation-skipping tax?

Notwithstanding the punitive nature of the generation-skipping tax, it may actually be advantageous to distant beneficiaries to incur the GST tax at the time of the grantor-decedent's death, if the result is to permit perpetuation of the family fortune for multiple generations. Of course, any "dynastic" plan must be mindful of the applicable rule against perpetuities of each state. The traditional "rule against perpetuities" states that to be valid, trust property must vest 21 years, plus the period of gestation, after the death of the last to die of all the beneficiaries named in the trust instrument. Some states have followed a "wait and see" approach whereby the validity is tested, not by what could happen, but by what actually does happen; others have adopted a set period of time within which any interest that vests will be valid, such as 90 years. Recently, states have rushed to establish themselves as jurisdictions receptive to "dynasty trusts" by extending the maximum period for the rule against perpetuities to a longer period of time, for example, in Alaska, 1,000 years.

Ordinarily, this type of planning will make economic sense only for very large estates that will continue in trust for as many generations as may be permitted by local application of the rule against perpetuities. Partly as a result of the tax-driven interest in dynasty trusts, the venerable rule against perpetuities has undergone a rapid change in many states over the past decade, or has been abolished altogether in a number of states. Other states have adopted so-called "opt out" rules, by which the trust document itself may elect not to have the rule against perpetuities apply. One approach or the other has effectively emasculated the rule in Alaska, Arizona, Delaware, Idaho, Illinois, Maine, Maryland, Ohio, and South Dakota. Several other states are considering elimination or restriction of the rule.

Q 5:111 How should an attorney draft to avoid the imposition of the generation-skipping transfer tax?

In this area as in many others, flexibility is the key. Some attorneys are inclined to assume the "worst" (or in another sense, the best) case: that the client will die with more assets than the GST exemption amount, or that the amount held in trust for a long period of time, such as the lifetime of the client's children, will ultimately exceed the GST exemption amount. Taken to its extreme, this can result in a client with relatively modest assets carrying home a 50-page trust document complete with GST-exempt and non-GST-exempt shares. Why? If the GST exemption is not "allocated," at the client's death, entirely to one share and not at all to the other share, a proportion of each distribution to a skip person will be subject to the GST. This is annoying, to say the least, and thorough drafters will wish to put everything in place to avoid such an eventuality entirely.

However, an alternative is simply to be sure that the Trustee has the power to divide any trust into two shares. If "worst" comes to worst and the client dies with over $1,000,000, the trustee can carve up the shares, allocate the exemption to the biggest shares, and try to make distributions to non-skip persons from the non-exempt shares. Of course, this may result in "wasted" GST exemption if the trusts to which the exemption is allocated wind up being consumed for the benefit of children rather than lasting to the next generation. But the attorney should remember that the ultimate goal of estate planning is to meet the client's dispositive wishes, not to take advantage of every tax strategy in the book in order to extend tax exemptions into perpetuity if possible.

This approach can also be used for the division between bypass and marital shares of a trust, but the disadvantage is that the entire trust property must be set up so as to qualify for QTIP treatment in order to give the trustee the option to make such a choice. With the trust-splitting for GST exemption purposes, there need not be any change to the trusts.

Q 5:112 What is an intentionally defective irrevocable trust?

When a living grantor has determined that it is appropriate to incur the GST during life, usually in order to transfer highly appreciating property to future generations before the value increases exponentially, it is possible to improve the tax effect of such a transfer even further. Because the rules for estate, gift, and generation-skipping tax treatment differ from those for income tax treatment of trusts, it is possible to retain a power in the grantor that has the effect of causing the future income of the trust to be taxed to the grantor even as the trust's assets are moved out of the grantor's estate for transfer tax purposes. In other words, assets with a value of up to the GST exemption amount can be transferred into a GST trust even as the grantor is treated as the owner for income tax purposes, and pays the income tax incurred by trust earnings for the rest of the grantor's life. This effectively increases the amount transferred to "skip" generations, because any outright gift to skip persons would result in the recipients' paying income taxes on subsequent earnings. The value of this type of planning will be limited to high-income assets (whether because of yield or recognition of capital gains) owned by extremely wealthy individuals so that they would prefer to bear the income tax themselves, thereby further reducing the taxable estate while concomitantly *benefiting* future generations.

> **Example 5-4.** Diane has an estate of $10,000,000. She establishes an intentionally defective (grantor) lifetime GST trust for her grandchildren, and transfers $1,000,000 in growth stock to the trust. During her life, she will pay tax on the trust's income (including any capital gains generated by sale and reinvestment); upon her death, the trust will have grown by the full amount of capital growth and accumulations without any reduction for tax paid, while Diane's estate will have been reduced not only by the initial gift but also by the income taxes paid on the trust's income.

Practice-Related Issues

Q 5:113 What practical problems and issues might an elder law attorney confront in the tax-planning portion of an elder law practice?

Because the area of "estate planning" encompasses so many different issues, the problems confronted on a daily basis can include tax avoidance, control over the distribution of assets, probate mechanics, and retirement benefits, plus myriad individual concerns brought to the planning process by clients. The remaining Q&As in this chapter use examples to help illustrate the variety and complexity of problems encountered in estate planning.

Q 5:114 How should the elder law attorney advise clients with over $1 million in assets who wish to leave everything ultimately to their only child?

A married couple consults an attorney about establishing tax-wise estate planning. The couple's assets consist of just under $1 million in total nonretirement assets, but the husband has a $500,000 rollover IRA. Absent tax restrictions, the couple would prefer to leave everything to one another and, upon the second death, to their only son. Knowing how little their son has set aside for his own retirement, they hope to allow him to use the IRA as his own retirement account, extending the tax deferral as far as possible into his life expectancy. What planning might the attorney undertake to meet this couple's goals?

The clients have several choices, and each choice can be constructed to meet two of their three goals. It will be impossible to meet all three.

In order to provide sufficient funds for the wife (assuming she survives the husband), the husband might choose to name her as beneficiary of his IRA. The couple could then establish credit shelter trusts for one another (whether by a joint revocable trust that divides into two trusts on the first death or by two separate trusts, each holding half the couple's assets). This approach maximizes the benefit for the surviving spouse (particularly assuming that the wife survives), and also permits a slight reduction in the minimum required distribution (because joint lives can be utilized). If, however, the wife dies before the husband and after his required beginning date, the IRA must pay out over his remaining life expectancy, which may be much shorter than the son's. If the husband dies first, the wife will either be forced to disclaim a portion of the IRA, or his credit shelter trust will be insufficiently funded; if the wife dies first, her credit shelter trust will always be underfunded. Although scheduled increases in the exemption equivalent amount may alleviate any estate tax problems, likely growth in both the IRA and nonretirement assets will increase the probability that the estate of the second spouse to die will bear at least some estate tax liability.

The husband could, instead, name the son as beneficiary of the IRA (but only with the wife's consent). This would permit easy funding of the credit shelter trust if the husband died first (a portion of his assets would still need to go into the trust, but there should be sufficient assets to fund it fully). If the wife died first, her credit shelter trust might be inadequately funded. On the plus side, the son would be able to use his life expectancy to slow the withdrawals from (and maximize the income tax benefit of) the IRA after the husband's death. Unfortunately, this approach completely misses the couple's primary planning goal by not giving the wife access to the IRA benefits if she survives her husband.

A third approach would be to name a credit shelter trust as beneficiary of the IRA. Of course, the precise rules governing the use of trusts as beneficiaries of retirement assets must be complied with, but this approach permits the minimization of estate tax (at least if the husband dies first) while keeping the IRA assets out of the wife's estate. The goal of extending the payout period is only minimally met: The IRA would have to make distributions based only on the wife's life expectancy after the husband's death. This approach may be an improvement over simply naming the wife as beneficiary (because it gets money out of her estate for estate tax purposes), but it has one significant drawback over that approach: All distributions of IRA "principal" (for accounting purposes) will be taxed as "income" to the trust at the highest marginal rate. This will reduce the security afforded to the wife by the IRA.

Q 5:115 How should the elder law attorney advise a conservator of a living parent's estate regarding the estate tax consequences of the parent's death?

An adult child has been appointed conservator of the assets of his mother, a widow, which total more than $1 million. He is concerned about estate tax consequences when she dies. What questions should the attorney ask, and what advice can he give?

Possibilities for tax planning do not necessarily end with the loss of the principal's capacity. Depending on state law, it may be possible for the conservator to secure authority to make gifts of his mother's assets or even to engage in more complicated tax planning approaches such as establishment of a family limited partnership or limited liability company.

Under most state statutes governing gifts or transfers by conservators, a key question will be whether the ward has previously engaged in gifting or other tax planning. A full history of gifts should be obtained from the conservator-client, along with any indications of his mother's feelings regarding taxes in general and estate taxes in particular. In addition, even an incapacitated ward may have some ability to understand and participate in tax planning decisions; every effort should be made to explain the value and importance of tax planning to the ward and secure her approval (even if it is limited by her ability to comprehend the nuances of the proposed plan) for presentation to the court. To that end, it may be advisable to secure independent counsel for the ward; if a court-appointed attorney was involved in the initial proceedings, he or she may be in a position to participate in the subsequent petition for approval of the tax plan.

Once information about the ward's history and wishes has been accumulated, a proposal might be made to the court for permission to make appropriate tax plans. In most cases, the obvious choice will be to request authority to make gifts from the ward's estate. That may require showing that there has been a history of gift-giving in the past, that the ward's welfare will not suffer as a result of the gifts, or that the ward's personal value system would support making gifts to reduce taxes paid by her heirs. If approval for a program of gift-giving is sought, it might make sense to request that the authority continue for future years, to permit the annual exclusion amount to be gifted to each of the ward's heirs or devisees on a repeating basis.

Q 5:116 What are some important estate planning considerations for a married couple with a large estate whose eventual beneficiaries may include their children and various charitable interests?

This question may be best answered with an example:

Example 5-5. Homer and Fern are 63 and 60. They have been married for 40 years and raised three children. They have a combined estate of over $5 million, which includes a significant amount of highly appreciated stock and investment real estate, both of which categories produce little income but great potential for growth. Their children are all successful professionals, and have children of their own. None of Homer and Fern's children will depend on an inheritance from their parents to make their own ways in life. Homer and Fern have long been interested in the arts and their local university; they are both actively working, and with their investment income they are in the highest income tax bracket.

Homer and Fern might want to consider a charitable remainder unitrust. They could transfer some portion (or all) of their appreciated stock and investment real estate to the trust, and the trust could immediately sell the property so transferred. The proceeds would not be subjected to capital gains taxes and could be invested in less risky holdings (with more modest growth) more suitable for Homer and Fern's future needs. The unitrust payment would be recalculated each year based on the current value of the trusts assets, so they could expect the payments to grow over time.

Importantly, Homer and Fern would have thereby converted non-income-producing property into a reliable annual yield of, say, an 8 percent return on their investment. Although their actual payout might go down over time (if market growth fails to keep up with the 8 percent payout requirement), it will never be eliminated entirely, so they will continue to enjoy a high level of security. Meanwhile, they will receive a current charitable income tax deduction of about 20 percent to 25 percent of their contribution (depending on the payout structure, their precise ages, and the then-current interest rate presumed by the IRS regulations). They may elect to make a series of contributions over a period of years, each one calculated to have maximum effect based on their taxable income for that year.

Because the remaining trust assets will pass to charities on the death of both Homer and Fern, there is no property to be included in their taxable estate. They may even retain the power to change the ultimate charitable beneficiary without compromising the integrity or effectiveness of the trust, so that the final distribution can reflect their wishes as of the latest possible opportunity.

The principal problem with this plan is that Homer and Fern's children will not receive any of the property given to the charitable remainder trust after Homer and Fern die. If this concerns them, Homer and Fern may choose to use a portion of their 8 percent income to purchase life insurance with a value approximating that of the gifted assets; such an arrangement, of course, would need to be accomplished through either an irrevocable life insurance trust or by gifts of the premium amounts to their children each year. But if they have been actively making gifts to their children as a means of reducing their estates, they will not be able to increase the amount of the gifts to cover the life insurance premiums without eating into their lifetime exemption equivalent amount.

A secondary problem may be that the trust return cannot keep up with the 8 percent requirement. Recent stock market downturns have caused interest rates to plummet, and the "adjusted federal rate," used to compute the tax deduction upon funding the trust, is as of this writing (February 2003) at a nearly all-time low of 3.8 percent. Homer and Fern may wish to wait until there is some recovery in the market before undertaking this plan.

Chapter 6

Post-Mortem Estate Planning

Qualified disclaimers and other post-mortem planning techniques have become more important in recent years. With more estates at taxable levels, and with retirement accounts and the value of real estate both rising rapidly in many estates, the circumstances when the estate was originally planned are often no longer operative at the time of death. This chapter is intended to provide an understanding of disclaimers and post-death elections and their use in post-mortem estate planning.

Overview

Q 6:1 Why is post-mortem tax planning important?

The circumstances in place at the time an estate is originally planned are often no longer operative at the time of death. Family members may also want to rearrange the benefits of inheritance after the death of one family member. For example, children may feel that their own estates are already large enough, and see disclaimers (see Qs 6:24–6:40) as a way of transferring significant assets to grandchildren without incurring any gift tax complications. Similarly, a surviving spouse may wish to use post-mortem planning to reduce his or her estate and shift assets to the next generation, especially where the surviving spouse is already wealthy. In fact, the use of disclaimers can even be planned during the planner's life. Many families with assets approaching the level of a taxable estate will purposely establish a "disclaimer trust," to be funded by the surviving spouse's use of disclaimers if (and only if) the estate turns out to be taxable at the time of the first spouse's death (see Q 6:35).

Post-Mortem Tax Reporting

Q 6:2 What tax liabilities will a decedent's estate incur?

The death of the decedent may require the personal representative, executor, trustee, or even heirs to deal with at least three different types of tax liability:

1. Estate (and possibly inheritance) tax;
2. Decedent's final income tax; and
3. Fiduciary income tax.

Usually, each type of tax will require both federal and state (and sometimes local) filings.

Q 6:3 Must the federal estate tax return be filed?

Although the federal estate tax equivalent credit will mean no estate tax liability in most estates, the question of potential estate tax liability must still be addressed after every death. The estate tax return—Form 706—must be filed if the value of the decedent's gross estate exceeds the amount of the unified credit. Even though no federal estate tax is due, it may be necessary (or advisable) to file a federal estate tax return (as, for example, when an otherwise taxable estate will utilize the marital exemption). State estate taxes may be imposed on estates that escape the federal estate tax exemption. Finally, many state revenue departments require an affirmative filing to demonstrate that no estate tax liability is due; a state form based on such filings may be required to permit the transfer of some types of property (especially real estate and sometimes securities).

Q 6:4 When must the estate tax return be filed by the decedent's estate?

The federal estate tax return (Form 706) is due nine months after the date of the decedent's death. [I.R.C. § 6075] While an extension can be granted for an additional six months [I.R.C. § 6081], the tax liability must ordinarily be paid within the nine-month period from the date of death. Exceptions to the rule requiring estate taxes to be paid within nine months can be made for certain small business interests of the decedent [I.R.C. § 6166] and in limited other circumstances. [See I.R.C. § 6163 for reversionary or remainder interests subject to estate tax liability, and I.R.C. § 6161 for the Internal Revenue Service (IRS) Secretary's authority to extend time for payment "for a reasonable time"]

Q 6:5 Who is responsible for calculating and paying taxes on a decedent's estate?

Ordinarily, the executor or personal representative of the decedent's estate is required to file the estate tax return [I.R.C. § 2002]; however, where no formal probate proceeding has been commenced, the definition of "executor" includes "any person in actual or constructive possession of any property of the decedent." [I.R.C. § 2023] In other words, a trustee, joint tenant, beneficiary, or other recipient may be required to file the estate tax return in the absence of an executor.

Q 6:6 What are the requirements for filing the decedent's final income tax return?

Unless the decedent died before receiving any income in his or her final calendar year, a federal (and state) final income tax return will usually be required. This may be true even though the decedent owed no income taxes, and must not be overlooked in concluding the decedent's estate. The decedent's final income tax return covers the period starting on the first day of the decedent's regular tax year and ending on the date of the decedent's death. [I.R.C. § 6012(b)]

The executor or personal representative of the decedent's estate must file Form 1040, 1040A, or 1040EZ. If a refund is being claimed, a Form 1310 (Statement of Person Claiming Refund Due to a Deceased Taxpayer) must be filed with the return unless the person filing the return is a surviving spouse filing a joint return with the decedent or is a court-appointed or certified personal representative.

The return is due on the same day it would have been due had the decedent not died. [I.R.C. § 6072(a); Treas. Reg. § 1.6072-1(b)] An automatic four-month extension is available by filing Form 4868 (Application for Automatic Extension of Time to File) by April 15 and paying the amount of tax the decedent is expected to owe. [Treas. Reg. § 1.6081-4] An additional extension, up to two months, *may* be granted upon showing a good reason for being unable to file by filing Form 2688.

Q 6:7 When must fiduciary income taxes be filed?

Estates and trusts are separate taxpaying entities. In fact, the executor or personal representative of the estate must obtain an employer identification number for the estate (Form SS-4); therefore, if the decedent's estate or a trust established by the decedent earns income before it is wound up and assets distributed, the fiduciary must file an income tax return and pay any necessary taxes for the probate estate and/or any trust. [I.R.C. § 641(b)] Usually the income reported on such returns is "passed through" to the beneficiaries, which causes the tax return to be an informational filing only; nonetheless, the return(s) must be prepared and the resulting tax liability information conveyed to beneficiaries. The beneficiary is generally taxed on distributions received from the estate or trust.

Q 6:8 When must the estate fiduciary tax return be filed?

The personal representative or executor of the decedent's estate must file an income tax return—Form 1041 (U.S. Income Tax Return for Estates and Trusts)—for any taxable period during which the estate's gross income is $600 or more or if any beneficiary is a nonresident alien. [I.R.C. § 6012(a)(3); Treas. Reg. § 1.6012-3(a)] The estate's taxable income is income that the estate receives during the period of administration or settlement. [Treas. Reg. § 1.641(b)-3(a)] The fiduciary must also file a separate Schedule K-1 for each beneficiary. This schedule must show the beneficiary's share of income, deductions, and credits.

The estate fiduciary tax return is due on the fifteenth day of the fourth month following the close of the tax year of the estate. The executor can choose either a calendar or fiscal year. The personal representative chooses the estate's accounting period when the first Form 1041 is filed. (Form SS-4, which is used to apply for an estate tax identification, requests a fiscal year, but it is not required to be completed, and can be changed.) Estates must pay estimated taxes in the same manner as individuals and use the same estimated tax payment. Form 1041-ES is used to pay estimated taxes. New estates for their first two years do not have to report and pay estimated taxes. [I.R.C. § 6654(1)]

Some planning opportunities exist in the choice of the estate's tax year. The estate may "pass through" to the beneficiaries any excess estate administration expenses not claimed on the estate tax return, but *only* on the final tax return. [I.R.C. § 642(h)(2) and Treas. Reg. § 1.642(h)-2] If it is likely that estate administration expenses will not be used on the estate tax return, and it is also likely that they will exceed income, it is advisable if possible to incur the expenses during what will probably be the estate's final tax year so that the beneficiaries can take advantage of the deductions distributed to them.

Q 6:9 What is income in respect of a decedent?

While not a tax return filed by the estate or a trustee, income in respect of a decedent (IRD) filings require some special mention. Income in respect of a decedent is any item of gross income that cannot properly be included on the decedent's final return, but to which the decedent had a right and which the decedent would have received if he or she had not died. [I.R.C. § 691(a)(1)] In those cases where the decedent's estate was taxable and included income items (such as individual retirement account or pension benefits payable directly to a beneficiary), the beneficiary's income tax will be affected by the amount of estate tax paid; that is, the beneficiary will be able to deduct a portion of the estate tax paid that was attributable to the IRD items. This does not require a special filing by the estate or trustee but is important to keep in mind in post-mortem planning. Most beneficiaries will be unaware of the concept of IRD and will not realize that they will have to make complicated tax calculations on income received from the decedent in the future in order to take advantage of the deduction.

Q 6:10 Is it possible to time distributions so that some beneficiaries will receive income in one tax year and others in a different tax year?

No. The "separate share" rule requires that beneficiaries' distributions be taxed as income not in proportion to what they actually receive but in proportion to their interests. For example, when the "credit shelter" share is 65 percent of the residue, and the marital share is 35 percent, and one would like to distribute to the marital trust only so that all could be distributed out to the spouse and taxed at her income tax rate rather than the higher trust rate, one cannot make a premature distribution to the marital trust only and accomplish this goal. Even if the distribution is 100 percent to the marital share, the taxable income portion of the distribution will be allocated between both shares. [Treas. Reg. § 1.663(c)-1(a) & 4(a)] This also means that it is not possible to make distribution early to charities (who will not pay tax on income) and distribute later to noncharitable beneficiaries who will have the benefit of the final year's deduction for administration expenses (to offset the taxable income).

Estate Tax Elections and Valuations

Q 6:11 How is the qualifying terminable interest property election handled?

The qualifying terminable interest property (QTIP) election allows an interest in trust property to qualify for the marital deduction (see Q 5:71). The QTIP election is irrevocable. [I.R.C. § 2056(b)] In order to qualify for the QTIP election, the surviving spouse must have an income interest in the trust for life, payable at least annually, and the income interest cannot be appointed to anyone other than the spouse. The QTIP election must be made at the time the estate tax return is filed at the death of the first spouse. An extension to make a QTIP election may be allowed at the discretion of the IRS if the taxpayer demonstrates that he or she acted reasonably and in good faith and granting the relief will not prejudice the government.

[Treas. Reg. § 301.9100-1(c)] The executor can make the QTIP election by listing the QTIP on Schedule M on the estate tax return and deducting its value. The current procedure requires the action on the part of the executor to elect out of the QTIP marital deduction.

The post-mortem planner can elect or fail to elect a marital deduction with respect to a portion or all of the QTIP trust. If only a portion of the trust is covered under the election, then any appreciation or depreciation of the trust assets must be allocated pro rata, under Internal Revenue Code Section 2056(b)(10).

Sometimes it may be beneficial to the entire community estate to choose not to make the QTIP election, even as to a trust that was expressly established to meet QTIP rules. When such a "reverse QTIP election" is made, it must cover all the property in the trust. Some planners prefer to provide in the trust the authority for the trustee to split the QTIP into two trusts, in case the survivor makes a partial election. Such a reverse election might, for example, be made to maximize the credit exemption equivalent amount in the first spouse's estate or intentionally to incur estate taxes on the first death in order to prevent later taxation at higher bracket rates. More commonly, the term "reverse QTIP election" is used to describe the election made when the executor of the first spouse to die elects to treat estate property for which the QTIP election has been made as if it had not been made, in order that the decedent's (GST) exemption can be allocated to that property. [Treas. Reg. § 26.2652-1(a)(3)] Otherwise, the surviving spouse would be treated as the transferor because the property will be includible in his or her estate by virtue of the QTIP election made by the first spouse to die. The easiest way to plan for this possibility (when it is not a certainty) is to be sure that the executor or trustee has the power to split any QTIP trust into shares, one of which can receive the reverse QTIP election, and one will not. This used to be standard practice when planning for couples with large estates, because the marital share was likely to exceed the amount of the GST exemption less the credit shelter amount. Soon the credit shelter amount will meet or exceed the GST exemption, and this technique may become an anachronism. Instead, the trustee will need to have the power to split the credit shelter trust into shares —but no QTIP issue will be involved.

If the fiduciary makes a QTIP election on an early federal income tax return, and the spouse subsequently disclaims the property, the disclaimer is deemed valid and the QTIP election is ignored. [Rev. Rul. 83-26, 1983-1 C.B. 234]

Q 6:12 Are there times when it makes sense to pay estate tax at the death of the first spouse?

Fiduciaries can administer the marital deduction and QTIP election either to equalize the tax burdens of both the decedent's and the survivor's trust, or defer the tax burden until the death of the second spouse. Equalization is possible through the use of the marital deduction when the spouse with the larger estate dies first; although taxes may therefore become due on the death of the first spouse, this may reduce the tax risk at the death of the survivor. The fiduciary should first determine the amount likely to be needed by the survivor for his or her remaining years; if the survivor is young, a deferral may make more sense. Then the choice between equalization and deferral should be based on a comparison of the income earnings likely on the deferred tax and the tax liability itself.

> **Example 6-1.** John dies in 2000 with an estate of $4,000,000. His surviving (and second) wife, Mary, has a $1,000,000 estate of her own. John's will names his oldest son as executor and establishes a trust for Mary's benefit that will be funded with the maximum exemption equivalent amount ($675,000 in the year of his death); the rest of his estate passes to a QTIP trust for Mary's benefit and, upon her death, to his children from his first marriage. Assuming a full QTIP election, no estate tax will be due on John's death. On Mary's death in 2006, the entire remaining QTIP trust balance will be subject to estate tax as part of her estate, which will cause taxation (assuming no growth or reduction in value of the trust or her estate) at a marginal rate of 55 percent. Instead, John's executor (his son) might choose not to elect QTIP treatment for the entire trust and (assuming he has authority to make a partial reverse QTIP election by dividing the trust into two separate trusts) instead incur and pay the tax on about $2,000,000 of the QTIP trust. By doing so, he causes an immediate estate tax liability, but at a marginal rate of 45 percent. Although the calculation is complicated (and requires guesses about future earnings and losses, expenditures by the surviving spouse, and an estimate of the likely date of death for the surviving spouse), it is safe to assume that the partial reverse QTIP election saves several hun-

dred thousands of dollars—albeit for John's children, and at the expense of Mary's income interest for the rest of her life.

Q 6:13 How can taking elective shares against a will benefit the surviving spouse?

State statutes often allow the surviving spouse to take an election that would allow the elective share to pass to him or her from the decedent under Code Section 2056 and thus qualify for the marital deduction. For instance, in some states the surviving spouse could elect to take his or her intestate share if it qualifies for the marital deduction, then make a gift of that share to the children. The post-mortem planner should examine the state laws closely to see which strategies are possible.

> **Example 6-2.** Mary died in 2000, leaving an estate of $4,000,000. She is survived by her husband John and their children. Her will provides for establishment of a bypass trust for the benefit of John, with the balance of the estate being transferred to a QTIP trust. Upon John's death, both trusts devolve to a combination of the couple's children, other individuals, and several named charities. John has substantial assets already and does not wish to accumulate additional income for the remainder of his life; he also wishes primarily to benefit the children. He might elect under state law to receive his intestate share rather than the benefits provided by Mary's will, and then to gift all or a portion of that share to the children. By doing so, he might use up his lifetime exemption amount but reduce the total tax paid by the combined estates and effectively alter the dispositive provisions of Mary's will.

Q 6:14 How might taking the elective shares not benefit the surviving spouse?

For purposes of eligibility for long-term care benefits under Medicaid, the spouse is usually required to elect to take the statutory or spousal share by virtue of the requirement that a Medicaid applicant try to access all available resources. Failure to make the election most likely will be treated as a disqualifying transfer, even if the spouse is incapable. However, making the election will not benefit the spouse but rather the Medicaid authority, which will cease providing benefits to the spouse who is now over assets. Of course, if the spouse has needs not covered by Medicaid and that can be met from the spousal share, making the election can be to the spouse's advantage.

Q 6:15 How can the alternate valuation date election be used to save taxes?

An estate's assets are valued based on their fair market value of the assets. The fiduciary can, however, be inventive in his or her approach to valuation. First, for estate tax purposes the estate assets can be valued as of the date of death or as of six months after the decedent's death. [I.R.C. § 2032] If the latter is selected, then assets sold or distributed during that six months can be valued as of the date of sale or distribution of the property. The alternative valuation methods can be elected only if by doing so the value of the estate is decreased, under Code Section 2032, and the election must be made on the federal estate tax return, IRS Form 706. The election is irrevocable and must be made on a timely filed return or the first late return within one year of the due date. [I.R.C. §2032(d)] If the election is made, all property in the trust must be valued the same way.

> **Example 6-3.** Mary's estate consists of real estate and various stock holdings. Since her death four months ago, market forces have resulted in a substantial reduction in the value of her largest single stock holding; if by the alternate valuation date (two months from today), the stock has not recovered its value, the estate tax savings on that stock could be substantial. Unfortunately, both the real estate and the remaining stock have increased in value beyond the substantial loss, and the total estate value has increased. Mary's executor might elect to sell the real estate and the appreciating stocks before the alternate valuation date, and thereby gamble that the poorly performing stock will not recover. Complicating the calculation, of course, is the dilemma of capital gains incurred by the estate; by sale of the appreciating assets, capital gains tax costs will be passed along to the devisees.

Q 6:16 How does the valuation date election affect the income tax basis?

Under Code Section 1014, the valuation of estate property serves as the income tax basis of the property. The fiduciary of a small estate may elect the date of death valuation method in order to get a higher valuation of the property and thus a higher stepped-up basis for the beneficiaries to whom the property is to be transferred. This may even be preferable in large estates where the spouse is the sole beneficiary and the marital deduction can offset any estate tax liability. Unfortunately, the requirement that the alternative valuation date be used only when it will reduce *estate* taxes means that when the estate is not "taxable" in any event (whether or not Form 706 is required), the executor cannot choose to elect to report *higher* values occurring six months after death in an attempt to increase the "stepped-up" basis.

Q 6:17 How does the lack of marketability discount and minority interest discount affect valuation of estate assets?

Substantial valuation discounts (often as high as 35 percent or even 45 percent) may reduce the estate (and/or gift) tax liability when assets are difficult to value or market. This discount can be effected for partnership and limited liability corporation (LLC) interests, corporate stock, real estate, and mortgages. The management of a closely held corporation holding estate assets may consist of family members, which may also affect the desirability of the corporate stock. Although the value of a closely held business may be uncertain, IRS rules require the valuation to be made by reference to similar but publicly traded corporate interests. [I.R.C. § 2031(b)]

Minority interests get an even greater discount because there are fewer buyers interested in holding anything but a controlling interest. This is particularly true in the case of minority interests in family or closely held businesses, as it exacerbates the already difficult task of valuation. Even a majority interest will usually be subject to some valuation discount if there are other, minority interest holders who must be contended with.

When planning for valuation discounts, careful drafting and qualified appraisals are important. The IRS frequently takes an adversary position with regard to discounts for assets that would otherwise be easily divided (such as passive investment holdings in an LLC or limited partnership), and careful documentation of the validity of the claimed reduction in value is critical (see Qs 5:95–5:97).

Q 6:18 How can the special use valuation be used to save taxes?

Under Code Section 2032A, the executor may elect for estate tax purposes to value qualified real property according to the use under which it is qualified, rather than using fair market value. The property must have been acquired by a qualified heir from the decedent and used for a "qualified use" by the decedent or the decedent's family at the time of the decedent's death. The fiduciary must go by the "highest and best use" of the property. The special use valuation rules apply only to real property located in the United States and used for farming purposes or in a closely held business.

The special use valuation must be elected on a timely filed estate tax return (Form 706) or on the first return filed after the due date if no timely return was filed. [I.R.C. § 2032A(d)(1)] It must be signed, and the election is irrevocable. The IRS can recapture the lost taxes if within 10 years the property is no longer being used for farming closely held business purposes or is transferred to someone other than a family member or qualified heir. [I.R.C. § 2032A(c)]

Q 6:19 What elections can the executor make to defer payment of the estate tax?

While the estate tax is generally due nine months after the decedent's death, the executor may make the following elections:

1. *Code Section 6161.* To defer paying estate taxes for 12 months from the date the tax is due. The IRS may extend the time for payment of the estate tax for up to 10 years. The executor must show reasonable cause for the extension, and the election must be approved by the IRS. Form 4768 is used to request the extension and must include a written statement explaining why it is impossible or impractical to pay the estate tax on time.
2. *Code Section 6166.* To pay the part of the estate tax bill in up to 10 annual installments and defer paying estate taxes if a substantial portion of the estate consists of interests in closely

held businesses or farm property. The interest rate on the first $1,010,000 (adjusted for inflation in multiples of $10,000) in value of the closely held business is 2 percent, and the remainder of the federal estate tax bears interest at the prevailing interest rate. For this election to apply, the decedent's closely held business must equal at least 35 percent of the gross estate. This election allows a small business to keep operating after the owner dies. The election is made by attaching a Notice of Election to the estate tax return on IRS Form 706.

3. *Code Section 6163.* To postpone paying the estate tax attributable to reversions or remainder interests that are includible in the decedent's gross estate. Payment of the applicable amount of the estate tax can be deferred until six months after the reversion or remainder interest is in the hands of the decedent's estate or heirs. The IRS has the discretion to defer the payment for up to three years if it determines that there is reasonable cause for the additional extension. The executor should note on IRS Form 706 that a Code Section 6163 election was made.

Income Tax Elections

Q 6:20 What is the election to treat a revocable trust as part of the probate estate?

The executor of an estate can make an irrevocable election to treat revocable trusts as part of the deceased person's probate estate for income tax purposes. [I.R.C. § 645(a)] Unless the election is made, the trust is treated as a separate taxpayer (and must have a tax identification number different from that of the decedent's Social Security number). The election must be made by the due date, including extensions, of the first income tax return. The election, which is irrevocable, is in effect for two years from the date of the decedent's death if no estate tax return is filed, or, if an estate tax return is required, until six months after the estate tax is due. [I.R.C. § 645(b)(2)] To qualify for the election, the trust must be a qualified revocable trust. A trust is a qualified revocable trust if the decedent retained a power of the trust such as the power to affect beneficial enjoyment of the income for a period commencing after the occurrence of some stated event. [I.R.C. § 676]

Q 6:21 How can the revocable trust election be used to save taxes?

By electing to have a revocable trust included in the probate estate for income tax purposes, the trustee and personal representative may realize significant tax savings. This is not the case for the majority of trusts, of course, because trusts are usually distributed quickly and little income is earned during their administration.

The tax savings can be accomplished in several ways:

1. Trusts as separate entities must adopt calendar years, while probate estates can choose a noncalendar tax year. The Taxpayer Relief Act of 1997 has made it possible for fiduciaries to elect to include the trust in the probate estate and choose a noncalendar tax year [I.R.C. § 645], which can be particularly advantageous when, for instance, a significant amount of income is expected within a limited period of time.
2. Estates are permitted a charitable deduction for amounts permanently set aside for charitable purposes, while post-death revocable trusts are allowed a charitable deduction only for amounts paid to charity.
3. With the passage of the Taxpayer Relief Act of 1997, trusts created after August 5 of that year no longer have to follow the "throwback rule." Under the law as it existed before the 1997 Act, beneficiaries whose trust bequests earned income during one year but were not distributed until the following year were required to file amended income tax returns for the years in which they earned income. The throwback rule did not apply to income distributions from probate estates. Code Section 645 (adopted as part of the Taxpayer Relief Act) permits the executor and trustee jointly to elect to treat the trust as part of the estate for income taxation purposes, effectively eliminating the throwback rule when the election is made.
4. Whereas a probate estate can realize a loss when funding a pecuniary bequest with depreciated property, a trust cannot take a similar loss deduction, under Code Sections 267(a),

267(b)(5), 267(6). (The trust administrator can still recognize a loss by selling property to an unrelated party.) Both probate estates and trusts realize gain on appreciated property used to fund a pecuniary bequest.

5. Under Code Section 642(b), a probate estate can take a $600 personal exemption, while trusts are entitled only to a $300 personal exemption, if all the assets are to be distributed immediately, or a $100 personal exemption if the trust will be in existence long enough to draw income.
6. A trust administrator may wish to take advantage of certain probate estate rules regarding passive losses on real estate rentals. Whereas either trusts or probate estates can deduct up to $25,000 per year in such losses, estates have the advantage of being able to extend this over a two-year period. [I.R.C. §§ 469(g), 469(i)(4)] The post-mortem planner can take advantage of this extension by electing to bring the trust into the probate estate, but should first investigate whether this benefit will outweigh the disadvantage of having the rental property pass through probate.

Deduction of Administrative Expenses

Q 6:22 Does the post-mortem planner have any flexibility with regard to administration expenses of the estate?

The fiduciary and his or her advisers will have numerous expenses, both deductible and nondeductible, incurred as a result of administration of the estate. Nondeductible expenses (for estate or income tax purposes) include federal income taxes and those expenses not allowable under Code Section 2035(a). Expenses deductible for income tax but not estate tax purposes include foreign, state, and city income taxes, as well as property taxes and other obligations accruing after the decedent's death. Expenses deductible for estate tax purposes but not income tax purposes include funeral expenses, certain claims against the estate, and federal gift and income taxes.

Some expenses can be deducted as either estate or income tax items, and here the fiduciary's creativity comes into play. These items include:

- Medical expenses paid within one year of the decedent's death;
- Casualty and theft losses;
- Fees and commissions of the attorney, fiduciary, and accountant;
- Court costs for probate;
- Expenses of administering an estate;
- Interest on deferred estate taxes; and
- Broker's commissions and closing costs if property was sold to pay estate taxes.

The fiduciary should select the expenses to characterize as income or estate tax deductions (or both, for certain expenses) by comparing the marginal estate tax bracket with the marginal income tax bracket of the estate and of the beneficiaries of distributions from the estate. Often the decision means shifting the tax burden from one class of beneficiaries to another, and the fiduciary must weigh the consequences.

Where a choice is allowed, the fiduciary should characterize expenses as income tax deductions in estates where estate tax is not an issue (e.g., insolvent estates or those whose transfers would be protected by the marital deduction).

Q 6:23 If deductions are made on the estate's income tax return, must the estate tax deduction be waived?

Double deductions are generally prohibited. Deductions may be taken on the estate's income tax return if the executor waives the right to take the deduction for estate tax purposes. [I.R.C. § 642(g)] A waiver of the estate deduction is filed with the IRS for the district in which the return was filed. The waiver may be filed at any time before the expiration of the statutory period of limitations applicable to the taxpayer for which the deduction is sought. Prior to filing the waiver, the executor can tentatively claim the deductions against the estate tax because the deductions may not be allowed by the IRS; the estate can preserve the opportunity to take the deductions against the income tax. Once the waiver is filed, the option to use the deduction against the estate tax return is lost.

Disclaimers

Q 6:24 What is a disclaimer?

A disclaimer is a refusal by a person (the disclaimant) to accept a gift or bequest of property. The disclaimant is treated as having died immediately prior to the event that caused his or her interest to be passed to him or her. Once the disclaimer is completed, the disclaimed property will pass as if the disclaimant predeceased the decedent. Disclaimers are an important estate planning tool because they can save wealth transfer taxes. They provide an alternative estate plan to fall back on and an opportunity to correct any drafting errors or omissions in the original estate plan.

Q 6:25 What are the requirements for a qualified disclaimer ?

Federal and state law may differ on the formalities of a disclaimer. To be a qualified disclaimer under Code Section 2518(a) (that is, to be a disclaimer that will treat the disclaimant as having predeceased for federal estate and gift tax purposes, not only for purposes of determining the ultimate recipient of the property) the following requirements must be met:

1. The disclaimant must submit a writing that states an unequivocal, irrevocable, unqualified refusal to accept the property that is signed by the beneficiary or the beneficiary's legal representative [I.R.C. § 2518(b)(1)];
2. The disclaimer must be delivered to the transferor (if a decedent, the personal representative) or the entity holding title to the property no later than nine months after the later of (a) the date of the transfer itself or (b) the day on which the disclaimant turns 21 [I.R.C. § 2518(b)(2)];
3. The disclaimant cannot accept or benefit, expressly or implicitly, from any portion of the interest, then change his or her mind [Treas. Reg. § 25.2518-2(d)(1)];
4. The interest in the property must pass without any direction on the part of the disclaimant to the decedent's spouse or to a person other than the disclaimant [I.R.C. § 2518(b)(4)]; and
5. The disclaimer must be valid under state law.

If the beneficiary has any control over distribution of the disclaimed property, for instance through special powers of appointment granted in a will (but not if the power is pursuant to an ascertainable standard), the disclaimer does not qualify; the beneficiary must relinquish the power of appointment in order to benefit from the disclaimer.

State disclaimer rules may differ slightly, but for tax purposes the federal rules are critical. A disclaimer relying on state rules will not qualify for federal estate tax purposes unless it meets federal requirements.

Q 6:26 What is the legal effect of a disclaimer?

A qualified disclaimer does not result in estate or gift tax liability for the disclaimant, and disclaimed property cannot be reached by the disclaimant's creditors. In other words, the disclaimed property is treated as having passed directly from the donor to the recipient, and not through the control or estate of the disclaimant. An exception is tax liability. It has been held that a person cannot disclaim property when subject to a repayment obligation for back taxes. [Drye v. United States, 528 U.S. 49 (1999)]

Moreover, the requirement that the disclaimer be valid under state law may impair its effectiveness for creditor avoidance, because many states (such as Massachusetts) state that a purported disclaimer by a person who is insolvent will be ineffective. In other states, state courts have reached the same conclusion when the person is a current or former recipient of Medicaid benefits. [See, e.g., Department of Income Maintenance v. Watts, 211 Conn. 323 (1989)] This means that even if one might be willing to disclaim and accept the negative Medicaid consequences, the disclaimer is impossible to accomplish. Thus creditor avoidance may not be available unless the creditor in question is a potential or future creditor.

Q 6:27 Are partial disclaimers allowed?

Yes. A partial disclaimer is allowed if the interests in the property are severable and an individual portion of an interest is disclaimed. [Treas. Reg. § 25.2518-3(a)(1)(i)] Severable property is property that can be divided and that retains a complete and independent existence after the division.

Example 6-4. Mary's estate consists of her home, a farm totaling 1,000 acres, a bank account of $100,000, and a diversified stock portfolio worth a total of $400,000. Her will leaves her entire estate to her daughter, Diane. In the event that Diane predeceases Mary, the will provides that the estate passes equally to Diane's three children. Diane has a taxable estate herself, and does not want to add to her estate tax burden; she further wishes to assist her children, who are all recent college graduates and beginning careers and families. Diane might choose to disclaim all her interest in any one or more of the items she is to inherit from Mary. She might also choose to disclaim a specific portion of the farm property, electing to receive the remaining acreage. With regard to the stock portfolio, she might elect to disclaim any interest in named stock holdings, or a specified number of shares of some holdings, or a fractional interest to be applied across the entire portfolio. With regard to the bank account, Diane might choose to disclaim the entire account, a fraction of the account, or a specified dollar amount. Her disclaimer of any asset or portion of any asset will result in that asset (or portion) passing to her children as if she had predeceased her mother.

In addition to pecuniary or fractional bequests, the beneficiary may disclaim a general power of appointment, with or without a retained income interest; an undivided interest in a trust or community property interests; or a joint and survivor annuity attached to a qualified retirement plan. Even joint tenancy property can be disclaimed, at least to the extent of the right of survivorship (the surviving joint tenant already owned an undivided fractional interest, and that interest is not subject to disclaimer). Partial disclaimers are tricky; for instance, a trust beneficiary cannot choose the assets he or she wishes to disclaim.

Q 6:28 How can disclaimers benefit the surviving spouse?

At the death of the first spouse, the surviving spouse may find that a transfer of all the available assets to him or her would impose a significant estate tax risk. By estimating what he or she will need for his or her remaining years and disclaiming the rest at the time of the division of assets of the trust, the surviving spouse can ensure that the maximum available amount will go to the remainder beneficiaries instead of the IRS, without incurring a gift tax liability. Code

Section 2518 provides the legal authority for any beneficiary to disclaim gift, estate, and generation-skipping transfers, so that those transfers will be treated as though they were never made to the beneficiary. Under Code Section 2518(c)(3), if the entire interest is disclaimed, state law is bypassed.

Q 6:29 Can the surviving spouse benefit from property he or she has disclaimed?

The general rule is that a disclaimant cannot receive any benefit from the property after disclaimer. [Treas. Reg. § 25.2518-2(d)(1)] The disclaimer must be absolute and unconditional, but a surviving spouse enjoys an exemption from this general rule. Under Treasury Regulations Section 25.2518-2(e)(2), disclaimed property can pass to a trust for the benefit of the surviving spouse even if he or she is the disclaimant; however, the spouse cannot disclaim an interest that passes into a trust that gives the spouse the power to direct to whom the interest will go. A common strategy is to transfer the disclaimed property to a bypass, or decedent's, trust which in most cases provides substantial benefits to the surviving spouse (including income and a discretionary amount of principal for health, education, maintenance, and support of the survivor and dependents); however, the spouse will also have to disclaim any power of appointment she has over the trust.

> **Example 6-5.** John's will leaves his entire estate to his wife, Mary. If Mary predeceases John, the will provides for distribution to the couple's children. If, however, Mary survives John but disclaims any interest in his estate, the disclaimed property passes instead to a bypass trust (sometimes referred to as a credit shelter or decedent's trust) for Mary's benefit; she is entitled to receive all the income from the trust, and the trustee is permitted to invade principal for her benefit if necessary to provide for her health, education, maintenance, and support. Upon Mary's death, the trust divides equally among the couple's children. Even though the general rule prohibits a disclaimant from receiving any benefit from the property after disclaimer, John's "disclaimer trust" will effectively remove the disclaimed property from Mary's taxable estate. This provides flexibility for Mary to decide whether the bypass trust should be funded based on financial and personal circumstances immediately after John's death.

Q 6:30 Can a party enter into an agreement to execute a disclaimer?

No. The requirement that the disclaimant derive no benefit from the disclaimed property also means that the disclaimant cannot receive any consideration for making the disclaimer. In cases in which it was clear that the other estate beneficiaries had given some consideration to the disclaimants, courts have held that the disclaimer was not qualified. On the other hand, where the disclaimant was promised something, but not by an enforceable agreement, courts have upheld the validity of the disclaimer. This distinction may be critical when one is faced with persuading a probate court that a person subject to a guardianship or conservatorship should disclaim a future contingent interest in an estate. For example, one wishes to explain that the family will instead fund (*inter vivos* or by will) a special needs trust for the beneficiary that will put the beneficiary in the same or a better position if he or she disclaims, but this smacks of consideration. There are also other situations in which a will contest or other claim might be well solved with a disclaimer, but the concern will again be the appearance of consideration.

Q 6:31 Other than tax savings, what reasons might a beneficiary have to disclaim property?

A spouse or any beneficiary may decide to disclaim property because he or she wants to ensure that another beneficiary will receive the property. The same generous spirit may motivate a beneficiary to disclaim property if by doing so the trust is terminated and distributions are accelerated. If the will is being contested, the beneficiary may decide that the costs of defending ownership of the property outweigh the value of the property itself. Disclaimers can also be used to cure defective tax clauses in wills or trusts, avoid the establishment of a generation-skipping trust, redeem stock, and avoid creditors (but state law should be reviewed to determine the consequences of this action).

Q 6:32 How do disclaimers affect those who are receiving (or might receive) government entitlement benefits?

Although disclaimers are generally treated as if the disclaimant had no actual or constructive control over the property, an important exception to that application arises in the context of eligibility for long-term care assistance through the federal Medicaid program. Because the program is based on financial eligibility determinations, Medicaid is permitted to require its recipients to exercise every right they may possess to receive property. Consequently, even if a disclaimer is valid under state law and completely effective for both tax and creditor protection purposes, in most states it will nonetheless be treated as a disqualifying transfer under Medicaid rules. (Some states will not accept a disclaimer as valid if the disclaimant is receiving benefits or is "insolvent.") The calculation of the disqualifying period in the event of a transfer is discussed in chapter 14.

A disclaimer is worth considering, however, even taking into account the resulting ineligibility. This may be the case especially when the beneficiary is either not yet receiving benefits or may not receive needs-based benefits for some time. An example might be a beneficiary with special needs who is receiving Social Security disability and Medicare benefits (neither of which impose penalties for transfers) and is either currently insured (under a parent's coverage or under a supplemental insurance plan) or living in the community. The requirement that states impose periods of ineligibility as the result of transfers applies to long-term care Medicaid benefits and does not always apply to medical assistance received in the community. Alternatively, it may be financially preferable to disclaim and have the recipient (a sibling or parent) use some of the disclaimed funds to pay insurance for the disclaimant over any ineligibility period.

Another situation that suggests a disclaimer as a possibility is the disclaimer of a *contingent interest*, the right to receive a benefit as a remainderman. Not infrequently an ancestor will die leaving property for life to a disabled beneficiary's parent, on that parent's death, to the parent's issue outright. While state law may permit disclaimer of such an interest at any time up to nine months after the parent's death, federal law seems to require disclaimer within nine months of knowledge of the interest, in this case, most likely within nine months of the date of the ancestor's death (unless the disabled beneficiary truly has no notice of the interest whatsoever). Although the planning is being done well in advance, the ancestor's death may be the best time for the disabled beneficiary to disclaim, and the likelihood is that the disclaimer will thus occur long before the expiration of any look-back period. The only risk here is that the state will begin the imposition of the penalty at the time of the parent's death, rather than the time of the disclaimer, and for this it will be necessary to check the experience of local attorneys.

If the disclaimant is under a conservatorship or guardianship, it will be necessary to obtain court permission. If the person is receiving benefits or likely to receive them and the disclaimer is clearly for the purpose of eligibility, this may be difficult to obtain. If the receipt of needs-based benefits is hypothetical or far in the future, it may be possible to convince the court that the disclaimer is in the individual's best interest, particularly in conjunction with a parent's estate plan to leave a greater sum in a third-party special needs trust for the disclaimant. Of course, this may be tricky to balance with the requirement, for a federally qualified disclaimer, that there be no "quid pro quo" or consideration for the disclaimer.

Q 6:33 When must jointly held property be disclaimed?

The time when the beneficiary's interest in property is considered to have been transferred is usually clear, for example, at the date of the death of the first or second spouse to die, or when the beneficiary reaches a certain age. It is not clear when the nine-month period begins in the case of jointly held property—at the creation of the joint interest or at the death of a joint tenant. The general rule is that interests in joint tenancies that are unilaterally severable must be disclaimed within nine months of the death of the first joint tenant to die. [IRS Action on Decision CC-1990-06 (Feb. 7, 1990); Kennedy v. Comm'r, 804 F.2d 1332 (7th Cir. 1986); Dancy v. Comm'r, 872 F.2d 84 (4th Cir. 1989)] These interests include an irrevocable trust agreement with a remainder interest; a joint account with vested rights; jointly held real property; jointly owned notes, cash management accounts arranged through a broker; and bonds. Interests in jointly held property that is not unilaterally severable must be disclaimed within nine months after the creation of the interest. Such interests include revocable trusts, joint bank accounts and money market accounts, and joint brokerage accounts.

Under Code Section 2040 as interpreted in *Gallenstein v. United States* [975 F.2d 286 (6th Cir. 1992)], 100 percent of the value of real property owned jointly by spouses can be treated as held in the estate of the deceased spouse who actually furnished the consideration, so that the surviving tenant can receive a stepped-up basis for the property at the decedent's death (see Q 5:47).

Q 6:34 Can the nine-month period for a qualified disclaimer be extended?

Extensions are allowed by the IRS for closely held business and business interests up to five years [I.R.C. § 6166]; for payment of tax on reversionary or remainder property interests up to six months after the precedent interest terminates [I.R.C. § 6163(a)]; and for any reasonable cause up to 12 months. [I.R.C. § 6161(a)(2)] Under the Taxpayer Relief Act of 1997, a qualified family-owned business interest may make an election for special tax treatment, but the interest must comprise more than 50 percent of the individual's estate. [I.R.C. § 6166A] The government may request a bond for the period of the extension, pursuant to Code Section 6165, for up to double the amount of tax owed.

Q 6:35 What is a "disclaimer trust"?

Because of the exception permitting a surviving spouse to enjoy a benefit from disclaimed property so long as it passes to a bypass trust (otherwise referred to as a credit shelter trust), disclaimer trusts are commonly established before death to provide maximum flexibility for the surviving spouse after death. As described in Q 6:29, the disclaiming spouse can be a beneficiary of such a trust. With current uncertainty about the continued imposition of estate taxes and the possibility of a return to carry-over basis, disclaimer trusts may become a planning tool of choice, especially during the transition period before full repeal of federal estate taxes.

> **Example 6-6.** Martin leaves everything to his wife Lucy, but provides that if Lucy predeceases him his property will go into a credit shelter trust for her benefit. While this may seem absurd—why have a trust for her benefit if she is already deceased?—the effect permits the use of disclaimers after his death, based on the value of the estate at that time. If, after Martin's death, Lucy

decides that there are no estate tax issues, she will simply accept the bequest. If, on the other hand, she determines that their combined estates have grown to the point that a credit shelter trust is appropriate, she can disclaim some or all of his property, and it will then flow into the credit shelter trust. Because a spouse can benefit from disclaimed property, this permits the decision about credit shelter trust planning to wait until after the first spouse's death.

The ideal trust or will language allows for flexible post-mortem estate planning, giving the surviving spouse the option of either receiving the entire estate or the maximum amount available without incurring estate tax. Disclaimer language should be expressly included that would allow for the passing of disclaimed property to a bypass trust; without such express language, state law may preclude the spouse from benefiting from disclaimed property. In the preceding example, Martin's trust or will might provide that if Lucy disclaimed, the disclaimed property would pass to the bypass trust, but if she predeceased, the property would instead pass to issue directly.

Again, the surviving spouse cannot have the power to control the direction of the transferred property, and any special powers of appointment over assets held in the bypass trust must be limited by an ascertainable standard (e.g., withdrawals of principal for health, education, maintenance, and support) or will have to be disclaimed as well. If the trust would only be funded by a disclaimer, the drafting attorney should either limit the exercise of the powers as noted, or exclude them entirely.

Q 6:36 Can a fiduciary disclaim property as well?

Under Treasury Regulations Section 25.2518-1(b), personal representatives of the estates of deceased beneficiaries can disclaim all or part of a bequest, but the post-mortem planner should first determine whether state laws permit disclaimers by personal representatives of marital deduction bequests. The state court may require a showing that no devisees or creditors would be negatively affected by such a disclaimer.

Q 6:37 If property passes to a grandchild as a result of a disclaimer, will the GST apply?

Yes. Even though a disclaimer valid under state law means that the disclaimant is treated as having predeceased the transferor, the GST statutes and regulations do not allow the "pre-deceased ancestor" exception to apply to interests that pass because the ancestor disclaims rather than actually being deceased. [Treas. Reg. § 26.2612-1(a)(2)(i)]

Q 6:38 What happens if the disclaimer is valid under state law but does not qualify under federal law?

If a disclaimer qualifies as valid under state law but not under federal law, the transfer will be treated as a gift by the disclaiming party to the party who receives it as a result of the disclaimer. [See, e.g., U.S. v. Irvine, 511 U.S. 224 (1994)] This may or may not be important depending upon the tax consequences. If the disclaimant is unlikely to have a taxable estate (for example, if the disclaimant is disabled and likely to require government benefits), and there will be no gift tax consequences, this may be unimportant. An interesting problem may result when the state gift tax "piggybacks" on federal taxable gifts but the disclaimer is still valid under state law. Presumably state gift tax would apply notwithstanding.

Q 6:39 When might a disclaimer be used to extend the distribution period for retirement benefits?

Suppose Martin, the husband in Example 6-6 (Q 6:35), had designated the bypass trust as his primary beneficiary of his qualified employee retirement plan account, and his wife Lucy had consented to the designation. Under federal law, she had a right under ERISA to the death benefit on the retirement plan. If the trustee were to disclaim the retirement benefit, by law she might be the beneficiary of the plan account and could roll over the account into an IRA, in this case the trust provided for Lucy for life and upon her death, to Martin's "issue." Whether or not the trustee may disclaim will then depend upon state law. In some states, the living representatives of Martin's "issue," e.g., his children, could decide whether to approve the disclaimer and/or disclaim their own interests in the trust. In others, the court would have to appoint a guardian *ad litem* for unborn or unascertained heirs, and the guardian *ad litem* might be harder to persuade that the disclaimer was in those heirs' best interests. After all, Lucy would then be free to designate anyone she chose as the beneficiary of her rollover IRA.

Q 6:40 What are some practical problems that arise with disclaimers?

The concept of a disclaimer seems simple enough. The party disclaiming signs a document that complies with state and federal law and gives a copy to the appropriate person, usually the fiduciary. Complications can arise, however, where the property is actually in custody of a third party, such as a life insurance company, a retirement account custodian, or a trustee located in another state. These may require that the disclaimer be recognizable as complying with the law of the state in which the property is being held. For a retirement account, this could mean the law that applies in the custodian's state. In addition, most corporate fiduciaries that receive disclaimers will demand that the disclaiming document also agree to indemnify and hold harmless the fiduciary for its decision to distribute in accordance with the result of the disclaime. Failure to include such a provision might result in the rejection of the disclaimer, which will complicate explanation on the Form 706 about the disclaimer having been timely made.

Other problems may relate to execution. Some corporate fiduciaries may require that the disclaimer be "acknowledged" by a notary. This is a simple matter in the United States, but overseas a notary's fee may be hundreds of dollars (equivalent to an hour or more of an attorney's time in the U.S.) or the signatory may need to seek the assistance of a U.S. consul. There may also be questions about whether the form of acknowledgment must comply with state law or the law of the jurisdiction in which the acknowledgment is being made.

Other problems include the need to appoint an appropriate fiduciary (guardian, etc.) to make a disclaimer on behalf of a minor or person subject to a disability or by unborn and unascertained heirs, as discussed in Q 6:39. In short, the potential problems with disclaimers may reduce one's desire to plan for their use as the solution to changing tax laws.

Post-Mortem Retirement Account Planning

Q 6:41 What steps should be taken post-mortem in order for the best tax result with respect to retirement benefits?

Under the old regulations, there was not much one could do when the owner of an IRA had "tainted" the entire designation by including a pecuniary share for a charity, estate, or other entity considered to have no life expectancy. The account would be considered to have no designated beneficiary. Under the new rules, effective for those dying on or after January 1, 2002, the problem is less catastrophic in the first instance (see Qs 3:75–3:76) but may be cured in any event provided such beneficiaries' shares are distributed by September 30 of the year following the year of death. It is as of that date that the plan fiduciary must be able to determine who are the beneficiaries of the account. Provided the problematic interests have been paid out, they no longer affect the ability of the other beneficiaries to defer distributions over their life expectancies.

This does not work to "save" the designation of an estate that might better have designated the surviving spouse. Even if the executor disclaims the interests of beneficiaries under the will, and the spouse would be sole heir under the state's laws of intestacy, this will probably not be enough to make the spouse a beneficiary entitled to take a spousal rollover. However, even this is not clear, a few private letter rulings have seemed to permit such a result if the spouse was also the sole executor.

Post-Mortem Reformations and Other Fixes

Q 6:42 Can something be done *post-mortem* to fix a charitable gift or trust if it does not qualify for the tax deduction?

Yes. A charitable interest that is less than the transferor's entire interest in property (such as an interest in a "split interest" trust or other partial interest) will not qualify for the federal estate tax charitable deduction under Code Section 2055(a) unless it is either a qualified annuity or unitrust interest under Code Section 664. [I.R.C. § 2055(e)(2)] Many documents written prior to 1969, when this rule was adopted, instead left such interests as "to my wife for life, on her death, to charity." This would no longer qualify under 2055(e)(2) and would therefore be ineligibile for the charitable deduction under 2055(a). Fortunately, the Code permits an executor or trustee to commence a reformation proceeding within 90 days following the due date of the 706 Code Section 2055(e)(3)(C). There are, however, many detailed requirements for such proceedings; these include the rule that the interest under the reformed instrument not differ from the interest under the actual instrument by more than 5 percent [I.R.C. § 2055(e)(3)(b)(i)] and the further rule that the reformation be "effective," which means that the disclaimer pass muster under state law. Since any change to a charitable disposition is likely to involve notice to the Attorney General of the state, and state law will vary as to the basis on which a will or trust may be reformed, it is by no means a foregone conclusion that every misdrafted charitable instrument can be reformed so as to save the charitable deduction.

Q 6:43 Can something be done *post-mortem* to save the marital deduction when the surviving spouse is not a U.S. citizen?

Yes. Although the marital deduction is not available unless the interest passes to (or for the benefit of) a spouse who is a U.S. citizen, or to a qualified domestic trust described in Code Section 2056A, the Code also permits post-mortem solutions. One solution is for the surviving spouse (if a U.S. resident) to be naturalized within nine months of the decedent's death. [I.R.C. § 2056(d)(4)] On the other hand, this may be difficult to accomplish, since it requires action on the part of the Immigration and Naturalization Services (INS), not only the spouse. Another solution may be to reform a trust or will to provide for the spouse's share to pass to a QDOT rather than outright. This must be accomplished by transfer to a QDOT "(ii) if a judicial proceeding is commenced on or before the due date (determined with regard to extensions) for filing such return to change such trust into a trust which is a qualified domestic trust, as of the time when the changes pursuant to such proceeding are made." [I.R.C. § 2056(d)(5)] There are no restrictions on such reformations as to surviving spouses as there are with respect to charitable trust reformations, but certainly the additional burden and expense of this result is something to be avoided if at all possible.

Q 6:44 How can the value of real estate be reduced for tax purposes after the owner's death?

In addition to seeking appraisals that factor in a marketability and lack of control discount, the personal representative may actually do something affirmative to reduce the taxable value of real estate in a decedent's estate. Under Code Section 2031(c), the value of real property in a decedent's estate may be decreased by up to 40 percent (up to $500,000) if the property is subject to a qualified "conservation easement," provided one has been granted prior to filing the estate tax return. In other words, like the post-mortem QDOT (Q 6:43), an estate can have a post-mortem conservation easement. [I.R.C. § 2031(c)(9)]

Q 6:45 What is a qualified conservation easement?

A qualified conservation easement is a conservation easement (restricting development) imposed on land owned by the decedent or family for three or more years continuously prior to the decedent's death, and is located within 25 miles of a metropolitan area, national park, or designated wilderness area (with some exceptions) or within 10 miles of an "Urban National Forest." To qualify, the executor must make an election on the 706 that the easement will qualify. A conservation easement is described further in Code Section 170(h) (with some modifications under Section 2031(c)) but generally will limit the use of the property "in perpetuity" to certain "conservation purposes" and will grant enforcement of this covenant to a charitable organization. Some rights may, however, be retained, including the right to maintain a residence on the property, but no right to commercial recreational activity other than *de minimis*. "Conservation purposes" are further defined as:

i. The preservation of land areas for outdoor recreation by, or the education of, the general public;
ii. The protection of a relatively natural habitat of fish, wildlife, or plants, or similar ecosystem; or
iii. The preservation of open space (including farmland and forest land) where such preservation is
    I. for the scenic enjoyment of the general public, or

II. Pursuant to a clearly delineated Federal, State, or local governmental conservation policy, and will yield a significant public benefit.

[Section 170(h)(4)(A), modified by Section 2031(c)(8)(B) (to delete 170(h)(4)(A)(iv) relating to historically significant buildings)]

A difficulty has been that state law rarely gives an executor the right to grant such an easement, which by definition destroys certain property rights for no direct consideration accruing to the estate. In "title" states such as Connecticut, in which title to real property passes automatically at death, arguably this can be solved by having the devisees sign any deed along with the executor. (The devisee will not be entitled to an income tax deduction as a result, however. One deduction precludes the other.) Presumably, an easement could always be granted by a release and indemnification agreement signed by the beneficiaries. A complication may arise if a beneficiary is a trust, but in those states that have adopted virtual representation (Q 7:56), this too may be solved. The biggest problem will arise when the recipients of the real estate to be burdened by the easement are not identical with the recipients of the residue who will pay the taxes.

Practice-Related Issues

Q 6:46 When is disclaimer planning utilized in actual practice?

Post-mortem planning, particularly the use of disclaimers, is usually encountered when planning before death was inadequate; however, post-mortem planning can be anticipated and even encouraged by the decedent. Two typical scenarios illustrate the use of disclaimers in practice:

1. *Curing a defective plan*. Steven's wife Wynette has just died. She had property worth over $1 million, and Steven himself is worth over $2 million. The couple had two children, both attending high school. Although they had meant to come in for more elaborate trust planning, they had not gotten around to it. Wynette's will, drafted when the couple was first starting out in their now-successful business, leaves everything to Steven and, if he is deceased, to a trust for the benefit

of their two children, to be distributed to them when they are 21. Her assets consist of her interest in the business, a stock portfolio (in joint tenancy with Steven), a small retirement account, and her half of the family home. Steven wants to know what he can do to minimize estate taxes.

Of course, if Steven does not disclaim any property there will be no estate tax as a result of Wynette's death; however, Steven will now be worth over $3 million. If he dies within the next few years his estate will pay a substantial estate tax. He might choose to disclaim some of Wynette's property in order to reduce the ultimate tax liability.

Selecting which assets to disclaim will involve consideration of a number of factors. If Wynette's interest in the family business is held by a trustee for the benefit of Steven's children, it might cause some difficulties in the future if he decides to sell out, expand, or change the business's direction. On the other hand, if Steve owns only a portion of the business it will be valued at a lower amount on his later death, and he will have not only helped fund Wynette's credit shelter trust but reduced the tax on his own estate at the same time. Depending on the business organization (stock, Subchapter S, partnership, LLC), there may be other advantages or problems with disclaiming the business interest.

The joint tenancy stock portfolio can also be disclaimed, although there is some concern that Steven might have accepted the benefits of Wynette's interest in the portfolio prior to contacting the lawyer. Depending on the state and the broker, the mechanics of disclaiming joint tenancy property may be more or less problematic. From a tax standpoint, the stock account may be the most attractive candidate for disclaimer. It is easily divisible, and the administration of the trust will not likely adversely affect Steven's use or administration of his own assets.

Wynette's half interest in the home could be disclaimed, despite the fact that Steven has resided there continuously since her death (as a joint tenant or tenant in common, he has the right to possession—he has not received any "benefit" from the use of her interest). The mechanics of disclaiming may once again be problematic depending on state law and title insurance practices. If any of these three assets (business, stock, or home) is disclaimed, a probate proceeding will almost assuredly be required, increasing the cost of the disclaimer decision.

Steven can easily disclaim his rights to receive Wynette's retirement account; however, doing so will result in immediate income taxation of the benefits, and the account may then flow to the children outside the trust (depending on the beneficiary designation on the account).

In balancing all these considerations, Steven will have to consider whether the size of his estate is sufficient to provide him adequate security, whether the ability to make gifts and other tax planning choices during the rest of his life will sufficiently protect his estate from taxes, whether the trust established for his children is adequately protective of their interests, and the mechanical and tax considerations involved in each kind of proposed disclaimer.

2. *The rapidly growing estate during a period of uncertainty about the estate tax.* Harvey and Sandra are in their mid-40s, both professionals, and have two children. Their estate now is valued at approximately $600,000 (including retirement benefits), plus some life insurance. They anticipate that their combined earning potential is increasing, but that expenses of college and launching their children will consume most of their income for the next few years. They understand that the exemption equivalent amount is scheduled to increase sharply in the next few years, and the estate tax may be completely repealed before either is likely to die. Both are in good health.

   Harvey and Sandra are not particularly good candidates for credit shelter trusts. Although their combined estate is nearly at the taxable level, that level will likely increase faster than their net worth at least for the next 5 to 10 years. In fact, there is a considerable likelihood that the federal estate tax will have been completely repealed before the death of either spouse. In a post-estate tax world, the state estate tax may have become an important planning issue, or may have also been repealed. They are relatively young, and it is not too likely that both will die within the 5-to-10-year period during which their estate plan will remain fixed, and during which the future of the estate tax will become clearer.

If they should have a slight increase in their estate in the near future and then die in rapid succession, the estate tax consequence could be serious. Similarly, if their children do not go to college, or accept scholarships, or if Harvey and Sandra do not get around to revising their estate plans for a decade or more, they may be seriously adversely affected by estate taxes.

On the other hand again, a credit shelter trust could be unnecessarily restrictive in their current situation. If Harvey were to die this year, Sandra might chafe under the restrictions imposed by dividing the estate into two shares and placing one in an irrevocable trust for the rest of her life, which is likely to be fairly long. The same reaction might be expected of Harvey if Sandra were to die in the near future.

A disclaimer trust might be exactly what this couple needs. By placing all their assets into a joint trust, or funding two separate trusts, or transferring assets into a tenancy in common, coupled with a bequest to each other and an alternate bequest to a credit shelter trust, they can proceed secure in the knowledge that the survivor can assess the circumstances at the time of the first death and make an appropriate election to either receive the deceased spouse's property outright or partially or fully fund a credit shelter trust for estate tax minimization.

Part III

Fiduciary Administration

Chapter 7

Probate and Trust Administration

Upon the death of someone close, one of the first questions faced by the survivor (or survivors) is whether it will be necessary to probate the estate of the decedent. The circumstances requiring probate proceedings can be confusing, as can the probate process itself. This chapter will address the necessity for probate proceedings, administration of the probate estate, the duties and responsibilities of the personal representative, the principles of estate distribution, the rights of the surviving spouse, and the closing of the estate. It will also briefly discuss the administration of trusts upon the death of the settlor (or settlors) and how the administration rules differ for trusts and probate estates. More detailed discussion of the tax planning involved may be found in other chapters.

Overview

Q 7:1 What is the probate process?

Probate is the system of court proceedings by which a will is validated and its terms carried out (or, if there is no will, the heirs are determined), and a personal representative is appointed. The personal representative must give proper notice to creditors and beneficiaries, collect and inventory the assets of the decedent, pay the debts of the estate (including taxes) in accordance with priorities set by statute, pay expenses, and make distributions to beneficiaries.

Q 7:2 What is the Uniform Probate Code and what has been its effect on probate?

Until a few decades ago, laws governing the management and transfer of assets at death varied significantly from state to state, and many states still had vestiges of old English common law. Probate costs increased disproportionately when decedents' estates included property in several different states. The laws also varied greatly from state to state with regard to the guardianship of minors and incapacitated individuals and the protection of their assets. A joint effort between the Probate Section of the American Bar Association and the National Conference of Commissioners on Uniform State Laws produced a Model Probate Code that was revised and ultimately approved in 1969, and was subsequently revised periodically with a thorough rewrite in 1991.

The Uniform Probate Code (UPC) includes a comprehensive approach to intestate succession, wills, trusts, probate, guardianship and conservatorship, nonprobate transfers and fiduciary relationships in general, and is an attempt to make those proceedings more consistent from state to state. More fundamentally, the UPC has promoted a less formal and more independent structure for the probate process, rather than requiring direct court supervision for every aspect of administration. In UPC states, the personal representative of an estate is usually given broad latitude to liquidate probate assets, pay debts, negotiate claims, and even make distributions without prior court approval; in fact, accountings and inventories can be avoided altogether in most cases. Unless a beneficiary or creditor objects to the administration of an estate, the UPC approach is to assume that the personal representative is acting appropriately.

While only 18 states have adopted the Uniform Probate Code in its near-entirety (and many of these still adhere to the original 1969 version), portions of the Code have been adopted by approximately 20 other states. Even some states that have not expressly adopted the probate administration provisions of the UPC have either changed their procedures to conform to some of the UPC concepts and principles, or already used a less formal approach and chose not to make the further changes required by the UPC.

Table 7-1. Uniform Probate Code States*

Alaska	Michigan	North Dakota
Arizona	Minnesota	Pennsylvania
Colorado	Montana	South Carolina
Hawaii	Nebraska	South Dakota
Idaho	New Jersey	Utah
Maine	New Mexico	Wisconsin

* Proposed for adoption in 2003–2004 legislative session: Massachusetts

Q 7:3 What is the difference between the probate estate and the taxable estate?

The probate estate includes all property owned by a decedent that is subject to probate process (Q 7:4). The taxable estate includes all property owned by the decedent, including those assets that bypass probate, such as life insurance in which the decedent had an interest, IRAs, trust assets, and property held in joint tenancy. It is possible for a decedent's taxable estate to be worth many millions, with no assets (or very few) subject to probate proceedings.

Q 7:4 What property is subject to the probate process?

Generally, only property in the sole name of the decedent at the time of death is subjected to the probate process. This includes the decedent's interest in property held as a "tenant in common," because the decedent retained the right to dispose of the interest. Property held in trust or "joint tenancy," in tenancy by the entireties or community property with right of survivorship, accounts bearing "Payable on Death" (POD), "In Trust For" (ITF) or "Transfer on

Death" (TOD) designations, and assets passing "by contract," through the designation of beneficiaries will usually not be subjected to probate unless (1) the beneficiary named was the decedent's own estate, or (2) the named beneficiary (or joint tenant) has predeceased the decedent, is deemed to predecease because of a disclaimer, or has been disinherited by operation of law (see chapter 4).

Q 7:5 Why is probate so expensive?

The common public perception of the probate process is that it is extraordinarily expensive. Clients will frequently have encountered published reports that suggest that the typical probate proceeding will cost 10 percent, 12 percent, or more of the estate's value. This is seldom the case; probate costs are much more likely to be from 1 percent to 2 percent in some states to as much as 5 percent in others. Even well informed clients might reasonably question why the probate process should be even as expensive as it actually is, never mind as expensive as its reputation would suggest.

There are two answers to questions about the cost of probate. On the one hand, there are often procedural and statutory reasons for probate expense. On the other hand, there are philosophical and historical reasons for the development of a system as costly as the probate system.

In the first category are the fees charged for probate administration. In a shrinking number of states, those fees might be set by statute. More commonly, the statute may provide for a maximum fee, or a presumptively reasonable fee. In practice, regardless of how they are described, statutory fee schedules in fact tend to become minimum fee schedules. The states that still employ statutory fee schedules typically provide for a fee of about 3 percent (the actual number may vary depending on the size of the estate) for the attorney for the executor; most states with statutory fee schedules provide a similar fee for the executor as well.

Q 7:6 What is the more modern (UPC) approach to costs?

The more modern approach (and the one embraced by the Uniform Probate Code) is to require only that attorney fees and executor fees or commissions be "reasonable." Reasonableness may be judged by the concepts of the Model Rules of Professional Conduct proposed by the American Bar Association. The reasonableness of both attorney's and executor's fees should be evaluated based on the amount of time actually expended on the proceeding, the amount of time a reasonably efficient professional would have spent, the lawyer's (and executor's) hourly rate and the hourly rates of others similarly experienced in the community, the complexity of the proceeding, the nature and value of any unusual benefit obtained by the representation, and even the lost opportunity to take on other clients or matters. Reasonable fees necessarily are gauged against an hourly billing structure, although courts are increasingly willing to allow for transactional billing, value billing, and other approaches to minimizing the importance of the hourly fee. The very nature of reasonable bills makes it impossible to generalize about the range of fees, but in states employing a reasonable fee standard the cost of probate proceedings is likely to be about 1 percent to 2 percent of the estate size in most cases.

In addition to fees charged by the attorney, the probate process imposes filing fees, fees for certified copies, publication costs, and other related charges; however, in most states these fees will not materially affect the total cost of the probate process. In states requiring more formal administration, additional accounting fees, increased use of professional fiduciaries (and the fees imposed by that systemic choice), and related costs will increase the expense to the estate, though none nearly so much as the attorney's and executor's fees.

Q 7:7 How can the expensive probate system be justified philosophically?

Although cynics might insist that the probate process was invented and perpetuated for the benefit of the legal community, the original goals of probate were twofold: to ensure that transfer taxes were collected, and to protect heirs and devisees from malicious and incompetent estate administrators. Thus, over many centuries, probate developed into a system tightly controlled by trusted agents of the state—probate judges. By the middle of this century, every transaction in the typical probate required notice to all interested parties and specific prior approval of the probate judge.

As the cost of such "protection" became prohibitive, alternatives to probate became more popular. Simultaneously, the probate administration itself was made more inexpensive and responsive to public perception of the tradeoff in value between cost and protection. With widespread use of living trusts and other probate alternatives, and easing of probate procedures in most states, the pendulum has swung quite far in the other direction. Even as the populace rushes to embrace living trusts, for example, stories about abuses of the uncontrolled discretion given to trustees have become commonplace, and some states have begun to move toward tighter regulation of trusts and trustees. In Florida, for example, homestead property placed in a living trust will have to be submitted to the probate process upon the death of the trustor/owner, the legislature having been persuaded that important protections are lost when trusts are used. In most states, trust administration promises to be the new wave of legal growth for the next generation of elder law attorneys.

When Are Probate Proceedings Required?

Q 7:8 When are probate proceedings required?

A probate proceeding is usually required whenever the property of a decedent is not distributed to beneficiaries through other means. In other words, probate proceedings will be required as to any property in the name of the decedent, without beneficiaries, joint tenants, or other successors designated in the title or ownership documents itself. Court intervention is usually unnecessary for ordinary transfers of pay-on-death benefits such as life insurance and IRAs (provided that beneficiary designations or policy terms properly designate a beneficiary), and for assets held in trust or joint tenancy with right of survivorship; however, even the most carefully planned estates may have some assets that cannot be transferred into nonprobate assets, such as tangible personal property, or that were not transferred because of oversight or some other reason.

Q 7:9 Must even small estates be subjected to the probate process?

Most states (but not including Alabama, Georgia, Iowa, Maryland, Oklahoma, Pennsylvania, and Vermont) have procedures allowing small estates to be distributed without court intervention, usually by providing a simple affidavit to the holder of property owned by the decedent. A handful of states (Georgia, Kentucky, Ohio) permit the court to dispense with probate administration if the estate is valued at less than a low threshold amount. Still other states, including many of those with affidavit procedures, permit slightly larger estates to be transferred by some sort of summary administration (see Q 4:38). If an estate's value is less than the cutoff amount set by statute, and if the beneficiaries are in general agreement about the distribution of assets, there is no need to file probate. Tangible personal property may be distributed at the discretion of the personal representative named in the will, or by agreement of the beneficiaries if there is no will. Transfer of property that is titled, such as real estate, automobiles, or mobile homes, may require the filing in court of an affidavit by a beneficiary stating that he or she is the proper successor to the property.

Probate may well be necessary even with small estates if there is a dispute concerning the validity of the will or the distribution of assets, because interested parties will have the right to object to the proceeding. Creditors have the right to initiate probate to compel payment of the debts, or formally to confirm the insolvency of the estate. Even if all property has been distributed by means of a funded living trust, disinherited heirs who feel the trust was invalid because of undue influence or some other reason may petition for probate and the appointment of an administrator who can then bring a legal challenge to the trust.

Q 7:10 What property is subject to probate in community property states?

Under community property laws, each spouse has the power to bequeath only his or her one-half share of the marital estate and his or her separate property. The survivor keeps his or her one-half share (that is, it is not transferred to him or her) and dower and curtesy interests do not apply. The decedent's share, to the extent that it has not been assigned to bypass vehicles such as living trusts or POD designations, will be subject to probate. Because at the death of one spouse the marital community is terminated, and because the debts of the decedent are presumed to be the debts of both spouses (the community), the entire community property may be subject to probate administration until all obligations are satisfied. Community property may be used to satisfy community debts, but only the deceased spouse's half of community property may be used to satisfy separate debts (and then usually only after separate property has been exhausted) (see Q 7:28).

Q 7:11 What is an "ancillary" probate, and when is it required?

Probate proceedings are generally conducted in the state in which the decedent was domiciled at his or her death. The domiciliary jurisdiction (that is, the state in which the primary probate proceeding is commenced—usually the state of the decedent's death and/or the decedent's residence prior to death) has no authority to administer assets located in other states, thus separate ancillary proceedings must be initiated in those states in which properties of the decedent are located. Ancillary administration is usually required only for real estate, because the domiciliary probate state has the ability to direct the management and distribution of personal property even if the depository (bank, brokerage house, stock issuer, etc.) is located in another state. This process has been streamlined in states that have adopted the Uniform Probate Code. It is the responsibility of the personal representative to determine not only the location of all the decedent's property, but the applicable state laws if the property is sited out of state.

Q 7:12 How can the probate process be avoided?

When planning for the distribution of property to be made after death, an individual who wishes to avoid probate has numerous vehicles through which he or she can direct assets to beneficiaries. Assets transferred to revocable and irrevocable trusts set up before the decedent's death will usually bypass probate, as will life insurance proceeds, IRAs, deferred compensation and other pay-on-death accounts, and assets held in joint tenancy (see chapter 4). At least one state permits the functional equivalent of a TOD/POD titling for real estate. Beginning in 2001, Arizona recognizes a "beneficiary deed" designation, revocable by the property owner during life, which effectively avoids the probate process. [Ariz. Rev. Stat. § 33-405(G)].

After the decedent's death, probate avoidance will be possible only if there are no assets to be transferred (or if the small estates procedures are available in individual cases). In other words, probate avoidance should be planned before death.

Q 7:13 What are the advantages and disadvantages of probate?

Although probate proceedings are not as burdensome as some estate planners suggest (and most clients believe), they have certain drawbacks. Because they are a matter of public record, outsiders can gain access to the will and (in many states) information about assets and beneficiaries, including addresses. The court must appoint the personal representative, and a public hearing with attendant notice may be required to determine heirs, or to establish the validity of a will. Creditors must also be given notice, and must be given time to make claims against the estate (usually four to six months). Although the inventory itself does not have to be filed in court in every state, in some states it does, and otherwise it must be made available to the beneficiaries and delivered to those requesting it, with proof of delivery filed. All this requires a significant amount of paperwork, which executors unrepresented by counsel may find confusing and time-consuming (and represented executors may find expensive).

For the same reasons probate may, however, be seen as a safer alternative by the individual planning his or her estate, particularly if dissension among the beneficiaries is anticipated. Under probate, all beneficiaries and creditors are guaranteed notice and the court oversees the inventory and accounting process. Beneficiaries (and disinherited heirs) are entitled to notice of the proceedings in probate, and an opportunity to produce more recent documents. There is no such guarantee with the administration of trusts; although statutes protect both, it is more difficult as a practical and legal matter to meet the evidentiary and procedural requirements for trust litigation.

In some cases, there may even be a financial reason for filing a probate proceeding. Particularly in the case of deceased professionals, it may be advantageous to utilize the probate process to cut off the potential claims of creditors. Because professional liability is always possible, probate proceedings may give heirs and devisees useful protection from unknown (and unascertainable) claimants.

Personal Representative

Q 7:14 What is the difference between a personal representative, an executor, and an administrator?

Historically, the title of the person entrusted with the administration of a decedent's estate depended both on the nature of the estate and the nature of the administrator. An "executor" was a male named as such by the will, with the female equivalent being an "executrix." An "administrator" or "administratrix" was the male or female person, respectively, appointed to handle the estate of a person who left no will. An "administrator CTA" or "administrator cum testamentum annexum" (with will attached) would be the person appointed to handle the estate of a person who did leave a will, but who did not name that person as executor.

The approach taken by the Uniform Probate Code [§ 1-201(36)] (and adopted here, partly for ease of reference and partly for consistency) is to refer to all of those fiduciaries by the generic term "personal representative." Where the context requires, or clarity is improved, the term "executor" or "administrator" may be added or substituted.

Q 7:15 How is a personal representative chosen?

Although a personal representative or executor may be nominated by the decedent's will, the actual appointment of the fiduciary is a court process. Most state statutes permit the court to bypass the nominee in the will for good cause—if, for example, the nominated personal representative has failed to act and the estate has suffered from that failure, or if the nominee has an irreconcilable conflict. Usually there will be a priority list of candidates for the position of personal representative, led by the decedent's nominee and followed by spouse, children, parents, other heirs, creditors, state agencies, or other interested persons.

Probate proceedings are usually initiated by a request for the court to consider the validity of any offered will and appoint a personal representative. Although the court can determine the validity of a will without appointing a personal representative, no person (or corporate entity) will be empowered to begin administration of the estate until the court appoints the personal representative.

Q 7:16 Can a nonresident be personal representative of an estate?

A few states require that the executor or administrator of an estate be a resident of the state in which the proceedings are initiated. Some states treat executors (of wills) and administrators (of intestate estates) differently, permitting the former to be nonresidents but not the latter. Those states permitting nonresident fiduciaries sometimes require the fiduciary to designate a resident of the state as agent for acceptance of service of process. States requiring executors or administrators to be residents include Alabama (as to administrators), Florida (except for certain relatives), Indiana (unless serving jointly with a resident), Kentucky (except for relatives), Nevada (as to administrators), New York (unless serving jointly with a resident), Ohio (as to administrators), Rhode Island (as to administrators), and Wyoming (as to administrators, and unless serving jointly with a resident).

Q 7:17 What are the powers and duties of a personal representative?

In order to handle probate affairs with the utmost efficiency, personal representatives are given broad powers in most states with regard to dealings with third persons. The powers conferred in most wills correspond with the powers given in general durable powers of attorney and trust documents (see chapter 10 for a discussion of durable powers of attorney). The personal representative is restricted, by statute and common law, only by his or her fiduciary duties to the estate and to the beneficiaries and creditors of the estate.

Some states still require all probate proceedings to be closely supervised by the courts. In those states, the personal representative's powers may be limited to only those specifically conveyed by the order appointing him or her. The sale of property, distribution of assets to heirs or devisees, payment of creditors' claims and costs of administration, and even valuation of estate assets may all require prior court approval, often after notice and after all interested persons have been accorded an opportunity to object to such actions. Even in these states, however, the testator usually may confer these powers by will so that court approval is not required. The power to convey real estate would be typical.

In more modern probate systems, the powers of a personal representative may include the ability to lease or sell realty; to enter into, honor, or refuse contracts; to convert nonliquid into liquid assets; to take possession of property; to make repairs; to vote securities; to borrow money; to sue on behalf of the estate and to defend the estate against claims, and to enter into settlements.

The personal representative has a duty to give notice to creditors and beneficiaries; to collect and inventory the assets of the estate; to file necessary tax returns and pay the resultant taxes; and to distribute the estate assets in accordance with the will or, if there is no will, according to the terms of intestate succession.

Q 7:18 Is the personal representative compensated by the estate?

The personal representative is entitled to a fee for services rendered to the estate, as well as reimbursement for costs expended in the discharge of his or her duties as personal representative. In some states a presumptively reasonable fee is established by statute, usually as a declining percentage of the estate value. A growing number of states have adopted the Uniform Probate Code's provision that a "reasonable" fee is chargeable against the estate, or have already used such a standard.

Q 7:19 How is the reasonableness of a personal representative's fee determined?

In those states that have adopted a "reasonable fee" standard it may be difficult to determine what constitutes a reasonable fee. Some guidance can be had by reference to lawyers' ethical rules on reasonable attorney's fees. Rule 1.5(a) of the American Bar Association's Model Rules of Professional Conduct sets out the elements to consider when assessing the reasonableness of an attorney's fee, and most of those elements are equally applicable in determining a reasonable fee for a personal representative. Those elements, with modest adjustments made to accommodate their use in probate estates, include:

1. The time and labor required, the novelty and difficulty of the question involved, and the skill requisite to perform the service properly;

2. The likelihood that acceptance of the particular employment will preclude other employment by the personal representative;
3. The fee customarily charged in the locality for similar serv ices;
4. The size of the estate and any especially favorable results obtained in the course of the estate's administration;
5. The time limitations, if any, imposed by the need to complete the estate quickly;
6. The experience, reputation, and ability of the personal representative; and
7. The use, where appropriate, of a percentage fee calculation.

Conversely, the following formulation, specifically directed towards fiduciaries, and usually to be tailored when addressing an attorney's fee, has long been the rule in Connecticut:

> "[R]easonable" means what is fair in view of the size of the estate, the responsibilities involved, the character of the work required, the special problems and difficulties met in doing the work, the results achieved, the knowledge, skill and judgment required of and used by the executors, the manner and promptitude in which the estate has been settled and the time and service required, and any other circumstances which may appear in the case and are relevant and material to this determination.

[Hayward v. Plant, 98 Conn 374, 384–385 (1923)]

Issues have arisen recently regarding the deductibility for income tax purposes of an investment manager's fee when the personal representative chooses to delegate the duty of managing funds as is permitted by such statutes as the Uniform Prudent Investor Act. Notwithstanding that the fiduciary would have been compensated for his or her own time in fulfilling the duty to manage and invest assets, and that the fiduciary's fee would have been fully deductible, the IRS has recently succeeded in arguing that the broker or other manager's fee should only be deductible as a "miscellaneous" expense, that is, to the extent it exceeds 2 percent of adjusted gross income. [Mellon Bank, 265 F.3d 1275 (Fed. Cir. 2001). *Compare* O'Neill, 994 F.2d 302 (6th Cir. 1993), *rev'g*, 98 TC 227 (1992), nonacq. 1994-1 CB 1, taking the opposite position] It is conceivable that proper bookkeeping methods may address this problem, such as by the fiduciary charging the time through as part of the fiduciary's own fee, and being directly responsible for paying the manager or broker's fee out of the compensation received.

Q 7:20 Will the personal representative be required to post bond, or give any other surety for performance of his or her duties?

Most states have provisions for setting surety bonds to guarantee the faithful performance of the duties of personal representative or executor. If bond is posted, any action against the personal representative (for breach of fiduciary duty or for negligence) will give rise to a claim against the bond. Bond requirements can usually be waived, either in the decedent's will (where waiver of bond is commonplace) or by court order (although in some states it may require consent of all heirs or devisees). The cost of the bond premium, when bond is required, is a charge against the estate. Bond is often set, or required to be set, based upon a combination of (1) the estate assets and (2) one year's income. Because in most states the "letters testamentary" or "probate appointment" or "probate certificate" will not be issued until the bond has been posted (by filing the bond contract with the court), the bond requirement may be problematic where the fiduciary has a history of problems with debt, and can result in frustration and delay.

Q 7:21 What is the extent of the personal representative's personal liability?

The personal representative owes the usual fiduciary duties to the estate (and to heirs, devisees, and creditors), including the duty to account, the duty not to commingle assets, the duty of fidelity, and the duty to utilize any special skills. In the event that any of those duties are breached, or the personal representative behaves negligently in performance of those duties, the personal representative may be surcharged for any resulting loss. Although a surety bond (if posted) may satisfy the claims against the personal representative, the bonding agent will usually have a right of subrogation (or will have received assignment of the claims). In other words, the personal representative's potential liability is substantial and requires good-faith efforts to discharge the duties of the office to the best of the individual's ability.

Principles of Estate Distribution

Q 7:22 What controls the distribution of the decedent's assets?

The distribution of a decedent's estate will be controlled either by the terms of the decedent's will or (if there is no valid will, or if a portion of the decedent's estate is not disposed of by the will) by the rules of intestate succession; however, even if there is a will, the probate process may include protections for some classes of beneficiaries, particularly spouses and minor children.

A number of the principles governing estate distribution may be default rules, provided only in the event the decedent's will is silent on a particular point. Thus, for example, a given state statute may provide that a bequest to a child presumptively passes *per stirpes,* or by "right of representation." In that case, if the child predeceases the parent the child's issue will take the deceased child's share. This is known as an "anti-lapse" statute. The same state might provide that bequests to unrelated individuals do not flow by right of representation (that is, they lapse if the devisee predeceases the testator) unless expressly provided for in the will. Another state might provide that all bequests presumably lapse, or that all bequests presumably pass by right of representation. Regardless of which state the decedent lived (or died) in, the decedent's will might provide for any of the distribution choices, and the default rule of each state would be unimportant. A statement that property passes "to my son if he survives me" imposes a survival requirement that should trump the "anti-lapse" statute.

Q 7:23 What are "testacy" and "intestacy?"

When the decedent has properly executed a will, he or she is said to have died "testate." Conversely, the decedent who has not left a valid will has died "intestate." The difference may be small, because every state provides for an order of "intestate succession" that will govern the distribution of the decedent's estate in the absence of a valid will. Further, one may die "testate" even if under the probate laws there is no need for probate.

Q 7:24 What is "intestate succession?"

The default rule governing the distribution of a decedent's estate in the absence of a will is called "intestate succession." In most states, the decedent's will can completely rewrite the intestate succession rules, although some rights may be retained (despite the terms of any will) by spouses, minor children, and even, in some cases, adult children. Typically, intestate succession rules direct that the estate be distributed first (or largely) to any surviving spouse. If no spouse survives, the intestate estate may be distributed among the decedent's children (or, in the case of deceased children, to the deceased child's issue); usually distributions are "by representation."

The Uniform Probate Code (and most states) directs the distribution of assets in an intestate estate in the following order: first to a surviving spouse; next to the decedent's descendants; if there are no descendants, to the decedent's parents; if the parents do not survive, then to the parents' descendants; if there are no descendants of the parents, then to the grandparents or to the grandparents' descendants.

Q 7:25 What is the difference between an heir and a devisee?

An "heir" is one of the individuals who would take the decedent's estate by principles of intestate succession in the absence of a valid will. A "devisee" is anyone who is named in the decedent's will, whether their devise will ultimately be satisfied or not. Frequently, heirs and devisees are the same individuals, although the proportions or specific property they would take under the will and by intestate succession may be different. While an heir may be completely disinherited by the decedent's will, he or she may retain some rights to notice and perhaps even accountings from the estate's personal representative. At the very least, the heir will be entitled to notice of the application for probate of a will, giving the heir a chance to challenge admission of the document on the grounds of invalid execution, undue influence, etc. This may be a primary reason to avoid probate: deliberate disinheritance of unpleasant heirs. Although the disinherited heir can still challenge an estate's disposition by bringing a court action, this is typically more difficult than simply bringing one's claim to the probate court in the context of an existing proceeding to probate a will.

Q 7:26 What rights does a surviving spouse have in a decedent's estate?

While a decedent may have attempted to disinherit a spouse (or to reduce the share of the decedent's estate left to the spouse), most states place a limit on the ability to do so. Some states set aside a portion of the decedent's estate for a homestead and/or family allowance, but most states provide for a mechanism to "elect against the will." Typically, the spouse is entitled to choose the method of calculating his or her share of the estate—either by accepting the amount provided for in the decedent's will or by electing instead to receive a portion of the estate set by statute. In most of the states providing for election against the will, the surviving spouse will be entitled to one-third of the decedent's estate; a common variation is to guarantee the surviving spouse a life interest in one-third of the property, or a life interest in some or all of the real estate.

States with no provision for election against the will include Arizona, California, Georgia, Nevada, New Mexico, Texas, Washington, and Wisconsin (as to property acquired after Wisconsin became a community property state). Of these states, all but Georgia are community property states.

Q 7:27 What right does a surviving spouse have in community property states?

A handful of states have adopted the French and Spanish concept of "community property" to deal with the property acquired by married couples during the marriage. The community property states are Arizona, California, Idaho, Louisiana, Nevada, New Mexico, Texas, Washington, and Wisconsin. In addition, Alaska permits property held in Alaskan trusts to be treated as community property. Under community property laws, each spouse has the power to bequeath only his or her one-half share of the marital estate and his or her separate property. The survivor already owns a one-half share (that is, it is not transferred from the deceased spouse's estate), and dower and curtesy interests (see Q 7:29) do not apply. The essential characteristic of community property is often seen as a substitute for the elective share approach, because the surviving spouse is the presumptive owner of half of all property acquired during the marriage.

In community property states, all income and assets obtained during the marriage are considered community property except those acquired through gift, inheritance, or devise. There is a presumption that all property in either spouse's name is community property, although the presumption can be overcome by showing that the property was brought into the marriage, or received as a gift or inheritance. Spouses can agree to hold assets in a form other than community property, although it may be difficult to prove the couple's intentions after the death of one spouse. Typically, a written agreement will be used to "convert" community property to separate property.

Q 7:28 Can a surviving spouse disclaim community property?

While the surviving spouse in a community property state may disclaim the deceased spouse's share of property which he or she would have received, the surviving spouse already owns his or her own interest in community property and therefore cannot disclaim it. If the survivor wished for some reason not to retain the community property interest, he or she would have had to commute it to separate property of the decedent spouse before the decedent's death. Disclaimers in general are discussed at length in chapter 6.

Q 7:29 What are "dower," "curtesy," and "election against the will?"

At common law a widow was entitled to receive a minimum distribution from her deceased husband's estate (dower), and a widower was entitled to a similar allowance (curtesy). Most states have abandoned the concepts of dower and curtesy, and have employed the "election against the will" strategy (or community property) instead. Those states retaining an explicit dower and/or curtesy provision include Arkansas, Massachusetts, New Jersey, New York (as to dower only, and then only as to couples married before 1930), Ohio (dower only), and Virginia (as to interests "vested" before 1991).

The right of election entitles the surviving spouse to take a statutory share rather than be governed by the terms of the will. Typically, elective-share law entitles the surviving spouse to one-third of the decedent's estate. Whereas community property states promulgate the "partnership" theory of marriage, that is, a spouse is deemed to have contributed equally to the marriage even if a higher proportion of the assets were in the decedent's name, elective-share statutes relegate the spouse to a lower status. In effect, spouses may end up with more assets through divorce proceedings, which typically entail an equitable division of assets, than through right of election. Moreover, in some states it is still possible to entirely disinherit a surviving spouse simply by taking the necessary steps to avoid probate. For example, in Connecticut the elective share is a life interest in one-third of the decedent's *probate* estate, with no rights whatsoever to other assets, and without the share taking into account other assets including those held in revocable living trusts.

The Uniform Probate Code has redesigned the right of election to better reflect the more modern "partnership theory" of marriage, by using a schedule correlating years of marriage with entitlement to assets. Although proceedings for elective share claims vary from state to state, the UPC suggests that the election must be made by filing the petition in court and delivering it to the personal representative within nine months after the date of the decedent's death, or within six months after initiation of probate proceedings, whichever limitation expires later.

State statutes often allow the surviving spouse to elect to have the statutory share pass to him or her from the decedent under Internal Revenue Code (I.R.C. or Code) Section 2056 and thus to qualify for the marital deduction.

Q 7:30 What other protective rights may be available to the surviving spouse?

The omitted spouse and/or dependent children may be given a right under state law to make claims against the probate estate for homestead, exempt property, and family allowance benefits, which compensate them respectively for the loss of home, personal property, and income from the estate. Usually (but not always) these rights are not separately available in the states that recognize a right to elect against the will (or receive an elective share). Where both are available, a paltry elective share may be augmented by such a claim for a family allowance, and the result may even be essential for income tax purposes when the estate has been named beneficiary of a retirement plan. State statutes usually set fairly low limits for this compensation, but may provide for judicial discretion to increase the allowances in individual cases.

In addition, ERISA provides substantial protection for spouses as to retirement benefits in qualified employee benefit plans. The employee may not name a beneficiary other than the spouse without the spouse's consent. [I.R.C. § 401(a)(11)(A)(ii)] (See Q 3:58.) Unfortunately and paradoxically, the U.S. Supreme Court has also held that such a designation (of one's spouse) is not revocable under a state statute attempting to revoke beneficiary designations in the event of divorce. [Egelhoff v. Egelhoff, 532 U.S. 141 (2001)] This could inadvertently result in the disinheritance of an actual surviving spouse in favor of a former spouse. Note that a properly drafted qualified domestic relations order (QDRO) may be effective to change the beneficiary even if the decedent had not gone the further step of making the appropriate change. [Metropolitan Life Ins. Co. v. Bigelow, 283 F.3d 436 (2d Cir. 2002)]

Finally, without regard to probate, a surviving spouse will have statutory rights to the decedent's Social Security benefit (for decedent retirees or disabled individuals if the spouse is also retired, disabled, or caring for a minor child) (see chapter 15).

Q 7:31 What protections exist for the minor children of a decedent?

In addition to election against the will by surviving spouses some states provide for "forced heirship" or similar rights for minor (and/or dependent) children. In some of those states, the child or children are entitled to a lump-sum or periodic allowance, while others provide for a share of the decedent's estate (as much as one-fourth of the estate, in some states) to be directed to the child or children. Sometimes those rights are dependent on the child's surviving parent not being married to the decedent at the time of death; in other words, the rights of children in some states will be assumed to be protected by the surviving parent.

Q 7:32 What happens when an heir or beneficiary has died before the decedent?

An heir or beneficiary may die before the decedent, or may be treated as having died before the decedent. The latter can happen in any of several circumstances, including when the heir or beneficiary disclaims any interest, when the heir or beneficiary fails to survive for a certain period of time (set either by the will or by state statute), or when the heir or beneficiary is responsible for the death of the decedent (as defined by the state's "slayer statute" or equivalent law; see Q 7:33). When the heir or beneficiary predeceases or is treated as predeceasing the decedent, the applicable state law or the provisions of any will may direct that the interest:

1. Lapses (e.g., returns to the estate to be divided among remaining distributees or to be distributed to the residuary devisee);
2. Is distributed to a named substitute beneficiary or beneficiaries; or
3. Is distributed to the heir's (or beneficiary's) issue, usually by right of representation or *per stirpes*.

Q 7:33 What happens when an heir or beneficiary murders the decedent?

At common law a person criminally responsible for the death of another could not inherit from that person's estate; the killer is usually treated as if he or she predeceased the victim. That common-sense provision has been incorportated into the law in every state, although the precise approach varies somewhat. In a community property state, for example, the fact that the victim and killer were married will not cause the killer to lose his or her interest in community property, though it will prevent inheritance of any of the victim/spouse's community interest. Similarly, the fact that the killer's heirs benefit from the slaying will not necessarily prevent them from inheriting. [In re Estates of Covert, 97 N.Y.2d 68 (2001)] Finally, some states may only disinherit the killer in the event of a criminal conviction; a failed conviction, even if followed by a successful suit for wrongful death, will not cause disinheritance.

Q 7:34 What is meant by "right of representation"?

At common law, "right of representation" referred to a distributive scheme under which the deceased beneficiary's share would be distributed to his or her children in equal shares, with any deceased child's share to be further divided among his or her children in equal shares.

Example 7-1. Martha died leaving an estate of $150,000. Martha had three children, a son Sam (who predeceased her) and daughters Diane and Deborah. Sam had two children, Diane has four children, and Deborah three children. Under the right of representation, Sam's children will split his share equally (i.e., they will receive $25,000 each). Diane and Deborah each inherit $50,000, and their children get nothing.

Example 7-2. With the same family relationships described in Example 7-1, Diane also predeceased Martha. Sam's two children will still receive $25,000 each (i.e., one-sixth of the estate). Deborah will receive one-third, as before. The remaining third will be divided equally among Diane's children, so that they will each receive $12,500 (i.e., one-twelfth of the estate).

The calculation becomes more convoluted if all representatives of a given generation have died. "Right of representation" requires that the shares be calculated at the first generation with surviving members.

Example 7-3. In the preceding example, all three of Martha's children have predeceased her. Her nine grandchildren will share the estate equally, without regard for how many of the grandchildren have common parents.

At common law and expressly in most states, right of representation is synonymous with *per stirpes* distribution (see Q 7:35). Inexplicably, the latest revision of the Uniform Probate Code redefines the phrase "right of representation" to be synonymous instead with *per capita* distribution (see Q 7:36). In order to prevent a reversal of a client's intentions when he or she moves into states having adopted the latest version of the Uniform Probate Code, it is probably preferable to utilize the terms *per stirpes* and *per capita* even though they may be less understandable to clients.

Q 7:35 What is *per stirpes* distribution?

Per stirpes (Latin: "by roots" or "by stocks") refers to a distributive scheme under which the deceased beneficiary's share would be distributed to his or her children in equal shares, with any deceased child's share to be further divided among his or her children in equal shares. It is synonymous with the "right of representation" concept described above (see Q 7:34) before the changes introduced by the UPC. It is to be distinguished from the other common (though less common) distributive scheme, *per capita* distribution.

Q 7:36 What is *per capita* distribution?

Per capita (Latin: "by head") distribution describes a mechanism whereby each member of the surviving family shares equally in the estate. *Per capita* distribution tends to "reward" grandchildren from larger families, while *per stirpes* distribution "rewards" grandchildren from smaller families.

The difference between *per capita* and *per stirpes* is best illustrated with an example. Assume that a child, and two grandchildren who are the children of a predeceased child of the testator survive the testator. If the will were to provide that the issue take *per stirpes*, then the surviving child would take one half, and each of the grandchildren would take one quarter (i.e., divide the total by the number of "stems" or "stocks," and thus the grandchildren split the share that would have gone to their parent if he or she had survived). If, on the other hand, the will were to provide that the issue take *per capita*, then each of the surviving children and the two grandchildren would take one third (i.e., divide the total by the number of heads).

Q 7:37 What happens in the case of simultaneous death?

If the testator (or decedent dying intestate) and one of his or her beneficiaries die in a common accident, the result could be legal confusion, increased administration costs, and double taxation. If one person dies before another (even if only by minutes), and he or she leaves property to the second to die, administration could be required in both estates, and estate tax and income tax liability could be increased.

To deal with this problem most states have adopted some sort of simultaneous death provision. Under that approach, unless the decedent's will provides otherwise every devisee must survive the decedent by at least a specified short period, frequently five days. That, for example, is the approach of the UPC, which provides for a 120-hour (five-day) default survivorship requirement in Section

2-702. The portion of the UPC dealing with simultaneous death has also been promulgated as the Uniform Simultaneous Death Act, and has been adopted in at least five non-UPC jurisdictions (District of Columbia, Kansas, Kentucky, Ohio, and Virginia). States that have not adopted this rule may provide that the property of each passes as if the devisee had predeceased the testator. [See, e.g., Conn. Gen. Stat. § 45a-440 ("When the title to property or the devolution thereof depends upon priority of death and there is no sufficient evidence that the persons have died otherwise than simultaneously, the property of each person shall be disposed of as if he had survived, except as provided otherwise in this section.")]

Most states also permit the testator to set a different survivorship period by will; 30- or 90-day survivorship is a common requirement. The marital deduction is not imperiled by a survivorship requirement of six months [Treas. Reg. § 20.2056(b)-1(d)(i)]; the GST allocation will not be lost (and on the contrary, may be saved) by requiring a child to survive 90 days in order to take (meaning that a child who does not survive 90 days is deemed to have predeceased the testator so that the child's share usually passes to the child's issue, the testator's grandchildren). [Treas. Reg. § 26.2612-1 (a)(2)(i)]

Federal estate tax rules accomplish a similar result, with even more liberal rules. The second decedent's estate receives a credit for estate taxes paid on property inherited by that decedent within the 10 years prior to the second decedent's death (or, for that matter, for up to 2 years after the recipient/decedent's death). Although the credit does extend for the entire 10-year period, it is reduced by 20 percent for each 2-year period the second decedent survives the first decedent. [I.R.C. § 2013]

Q 7:38 What if the property devised to a given person no longer exists?

A decedent may have made a specific devise of a given piece of property (real or personal) to one or more individuals, yet not own that property at the time of death. For example, a devise of "my family home at [address] to my daughter Mary" may cause problems if the family home has been sold, given to Mary (or, more complicated yet, to another family member), condemned, or destroyed before the decedent's death.

Rules of "ademption" direct the treatment of property no longer owned at the time of death, or transmuted into other property. Generally, those rules reflect a logical approach; if the testator disposed of the property through some voluntary act (sale, for example, or gift—whether to the originally intended recipient or to another), he or she is presumed to have understood that the transfer effectively revoked the will provision; if, on the other hand, the conversion was involuntary, as by condemnation or merger, the converted property will ordinarily be subject to the specific devise. If, for example, the decedent conveys "all my stock in XYZ Company" to child A, and two years later XYZ Company is bought out by ABC Inc., the resulting ABC Inc. stock will usually pass to A. This may be more difficult to compute if (as too often happens) the decedent already owned some stock in ABC Inc. before the merger, and had dividend reinvestments purchasing new stock after the merger. Usually, however, this problem is one of calculation rather than construction. Where the involuntarily converted property is no longer identifiable, the devise will usually fail. For example, if the specifically devised real property is condemned, the condemnation award paid, and the proceeds placed into the decedent's general operating account, two years later it may be impossible to segregate those condemnation proceeds, and the specific devise will fail.

A special rule applies where the specifically devised property has been sold but a note secured by an interest in the property remains. In most states, the remaining indebtedness will be subject to the specific devise. In other words, if the decedent's will leaves "my family home at [address] to my daughter Mary," and the decedent subsequently sold the home for $100,000 (including $10,000 down and the balance on an interest-bearing note), Mary will be entitled to the note and security. She will not be entitled to receive the $10,000, nor the original amount of the note; her specific distribution will be limited to the remaining value of the note.

The Probate Process

Q 7:39 Does the probate process vary by state?

Although the actual pleadings and procedures will vary tremendously by state, the basic outlines of the probate process will usually be similar. Some states may provide for several different approaches to probate proceedings, depending on the size (or nature) of the estate or the choice of the personal representative. With the adoption of the Uniform Probate Code (and similar approaches in some non-UPC states), the concept of "informal" and "formal" probate further divides the probate process, even within a given state.

Q 7:40 How is a probate proceeding initiated?

Usually an application to initiate probate is filed by the personal representative named in the will, or, in the case of an intestate estate, the person who has priority to be named personal representative and is willing to take on the responsibility. The application requests formal appointment of the personal representative and acceptance of the original will. If there is no will, a hearing is set at which the court makes a determination of the legal heirs of the estate and appoints the personal representative.

Sometimes probate is initiated by a creditor with a claim against the estate, or by a potential beneficiary. For example, if the value of the probate estate assets falls below the mandatory amount in a certain jurisdiction, and if there is no dispute, the personal representative may not wish to incur the expense of initiating probate, and in fact is not obligated to do so even if there are claims against the estate. The representative can still fulfill his or her fiduciary duties to the estate and to the beneficiaries (including payment of debts), but without court involvement. Creditors who are uncomfortable with this can initiate probate themselves, thereby confirming the existence of their claims and their payment prior to the closing of the estate. Similarly, an heir or beneficiary under the will who fears that the estate has been improperly depleted may initiate probate in order that the fiduciary can pursue any claims.

Q 7:41 Is a death certificate required to initiate a probate proceeding?

In some states, yes, or at least, if not technically required, it will be required as a matter of custom and procedure by the particular court. In other states, a death certificate may provide useful information, but is not normally required to initiate a probate proceeding—the sworn statement of the applicant for personal representative is usually sufficient. In fact, mechanisms exist for establishing the death of a person who can be assumed to be dead because of long absence; some courts may then be able to direct issuance of a death certificate.

Q 7:42 What is required to establish the death of a missing person?

In most states, unexplained absence without contact for a period of either five or seven years will be grounds for a probate proceeding, in the course of which death will be judicially established. For most purposes, the date of death is set at the date of the court order, not the date of the initial disappearance. In addition to any other notice requirements, establishment of death of an absent or disappeared person will usually require publishing a notice of the proceedings in local newspapers as well as in newspapers in the locale in which the missing person was last known to live; notice mailed to last known addresses; and reasonable efforts to locate the missing person (often including police reports, private investigations, Social Security requests, and other such search efforts). State laws may also provide for unwinding probate proceedings when a missing (and presumed dead) person reappears after the initiation of the proceedings.

Q 7:43 What notice must be given of a pending probate proceeding?

Depending on the nature of the proceeding, all interested parties, including known and as-yet-unidentified creditors, beneficiaries named in the will, and all family members who could conceivably be deemed heirs of the decedent should be given notice. For instance, creditors do not necessarily need to be notified of a hearing set to determine intestate succession and appointment of the personal representative, but they should be given notice immediately upon initiation of the estate and appointment of the personal representative. Adequate notice must be given of the hearing date and the nature of the proceedings, and generally those entitled to notice must receive it no less than two weeks prior to the proceeding.

Most states will have specific notice requirements that must be closely followed. Typically, notice must also be published one or more times in a newspaper of general circulation in the community where the proceedings have been initiated; at least in theory, this gives unknown heirs an opportunity to appear and make their claims.

Q 7:44 How is a will determined to be valid?

If the original will is available, if the signatures are self-proving (in other words, meeting the appropriate witness and notary requirements), and if there is otherwise no challenge to the validity of the will (see chapter 8), it will usually be accepted by the court. Some states may expressly require testimony or affidavits of witnesses to the will's execution; even in the absence of any requirement to produce witnesses, they should be located to prepare for the possibility that someone might challenge the validity of the will.

Q 7:45 What if a holographic will is presented?

Some states still accept holographic, or handwritten, wills that are otherwise insufficiently witnessed and/or notarized if the handwriting can be confirmed to be that of the decedent. In some states only the "material provisions" must be in the decedent's handwriting. With the advent of pre-printed do-it-yourself will kits, many documents may fail to meet the requirements of holographic wills (see Q 4:32).

Q 7:46 What is a "self-proving" will?

Some states permit the use of "self-proving" affidavits at the time a will is executed. Although the will may require only two witnesses (and no notarization), an appropriately worded affidavit sworn to before a notary (usually in language specifically set out in the state's statute) will make both the testator's signature and those of the witnesses "self-proving." This relieves the proponent of the will from later having to introduce the affidavits of the witnesses as to the circumstances of the will signing. In most states permitting self-proving wills, compliance with the requirements of the statute creates a conclusive presumption that the will was executed with due formalities. In some states, even if the affidavit is not completed at the time of the execution, it may be signed later by the witnesses (see Q 4:26).

Q 7:47 What if the decedent's will is missing?

Most states have a mechanism for "proving" a missing will, but usually start with a strong presumption that a missing will indicates that the decedent revoked the will during life. This presumption can sometimes be overcome by evidence that the original will was not in the possession of the decedent, or that the original was seen after the decedent's death. It may be possible in such circumstances to admit a copy of the missing will, or even to prove the contents of a missing will by testimony of witnesses who saw the will or discussed its contents with the decedent.

Q 7:48 Can a foreign will be admitted to probate?

"Foreign" can mean a will executed in another state or a will executed in a foreign country. In the former case, every state will accept a will validly executed in another state. In the latter case, the treatment of a foreign will may vary widely, particularly in the ability to establish the validity of the foreign will. To a considerable extent this problem will depend on how difficult it is to establish the minimum execution requirements in the foreign country. If the will meets the minimum execution requirements in the state in which probate is sought it will be admissible without regard to whether it satisfies the requirements in the foreign jurisdiction. However, the United States is a signatory to the Convention of October 26, 1973, Providing a Uniform Law on the Form of an International Will, and state courts should at least admit a will executed in accordance with the provision of that agreement.

Q 7:49 When is "ancillary" probate necessary?

When a decedent owned property (particularly real property) in a state other than the state of domicile (or other than the state in which probate proceedings have been initiated), it will usually be necessary to institute separate probate proceedings to arrange for the administration of the property in both states. The proceedings in the primary state (usually the domiciliary state) will be the more important proceedings. Most states have a mechanism for more summary proceedings when the primary/domiciliary probate is another state. The secondary proceedings are referred to as "ancillary" probate proceedings, and will usually be limited in several important ways:

1. The personal representative appointed in the domiciliary state will be automatically entitled to appointment as ancillary personal representative (subject, however, to the state's residency requirements for personal representatives).
2. No will contests or other challenges to the authority or effect of the domiciliary state proceedings will be permitted.
3. No formal accounting requirements will be imposed on the ancillary proceedings, on the theory that the accounting will be completed in the domiciliary state.

Not all states have simplified proceedings for ancillary probates. Mississippi and Missouri have no provisions for ancillary proceedings; every other state (and the District of Columbia) provides at least some special accommodation to foreign personal representatives.

Q 7:50 Must notice of the probate proceeding be given to creditors of the decedent?

Some proceedings are not relevant to the interests of the creditors, such as admission of a will or appointment of a personal representative; however, upon appointment the personal representative usually must notify all known creditors of the initiation of probate, and notice must also be published to inform those creditors not identified by the personal representative. As soon as notice is published and/or mailed to creditors, they have a designated amount of time—usually four to six months—to make claims against the estate. If claims are not presented within the allowed time period, creditors may be barred from pursuing recovery.

If a creditor is not given proper notice, the creditor may be able to pursue beneficiaries directly even after the estate has settled, to the extent of the property received (although state law will differ depending on the nature of the property). Fortunately, most states have a separate provision for an ultimate time limitation on actions by creditors. Typically, creditors are foreclosed from bringing an action to enforce a debt more than two (sometimes one or three) years after the death of the decedent, even if no probate proceeding has been commenced or if the personal representative has failed to provide notice to creditors.

Q 7:51 How long does the probate process typically take?

The time accorded to creditors to make claims against the estate may constitute the lengthiest part of the probate. If determination and collection of assets is straightforward, there is no real estate to be sold, and estate tax returns are not required, it is conceivable that probate can be closed within five or six months of initiation. Sale of real estate, squabbles among the beneficiaries, the location of assets in other states (necessitating ancillary probate), estate and income tax liability, and other impediments can significantly delay the proceedings by many months or years.

Estate Administration

Q 7:52 What steps must be taken to administer the estate?

After appointment of a personal representative and determination of the validity of the will, a number of steps must be taken actually to administer the decedent's estate. Before distributions can be made, the decedent's assets must be collected and valued, any claims against the estate must be satisfied, and appropriate tax returns prepared and filed, and usually, an accounting prepared and filed with the court. In making distributions of estate assets, and in order to establish the value of the estate for tax purposes, the personal representative will ordinarily need to employ professional appraisers to value real property and valuable personal property (such as art work or antique furniture). Appraisers often handle estate sales as well, and the personal representative may lack the expertise to value and market the assets properly. The sale of real property within the probate context is similar to any home sale—the personal representative may try to cut costs by selling the real property without a real estate agent, but must then be available to advertise and show the home to prospective buyers, and handle closing procedures personally.

Q 7:53 What costs should a client expect to incur in a probate proceeding?

Although in most jurisdictions it may be possible for a nonlawyer to handle all probate requirements, the process is often arcane and counterintuitive and the time expended in figuring out how to process a probate estate will usually overwhelm a lay person. The client should expect to retain a lawyer and an accountant to take care of the legal and tax reporting requirements, in addition to the usual filing and other court fees. If there is real estate to be sold, then realtors and title companies will also demand payment.

Q 7:54 What is a probate accounting?

Precise accounting rules vary tremendously by state, but the general rule is that the personal representative or executor must account to the estate's beneficiaries and, at least in traditional probate proceedings, to the court. Accounting requirements are usually fairly formalized. Standards developed by the Committee on National Fiduciary Accounting Standards in collaboration with the National Center for State Courts are widely recognized across the country, but each local jurisdiction may have special rules and requirements for probate accounting.

In states that have adopted the Uniform Probate Code, or that have followed a similar approach to probate administration, the requirement of an accounting may be waivable, or may even be in the discretion of the personal representative or executor. From an estate planning perspective, the importance of this sort of state approach is that the probate administration may be less expensive and less onerous than under prior law and rules, and probate itself will be less necessary to avoid.

It is important to remember that an estate required to file federal estate and income tax returns should already have organized the data that will be needed for the probate accounting. With widespread use of tax preparation software, many courts are increasingly willing to accept accountings generated by the same software packages, or, at the very least, to accept the concept of attached schedules containing the assembled date.

Q 7:55 What is a "mutual distribution agreement"?

A mutual distribution agreement is in effect a settlement among the fiduciary and beneficiaries, or possibly the fiduciary, beneficiaries, and claimants (including attorneys or others with charges against the estate relating to administration) respecting the distribution of the estate. The most frequent use may be a rearrangement by the beneficiaries of the dispositive scheme set forth in the will. In some cases, an agreement will also resolve the claims that the disputing parties' attorneys may have against the estate for payment of fees, or the fiduciary's fee as well. In some states, the agreement alone is sufficient, and the distribution may proceed "by agreement." Other states with a more active probate process will require that the court approve the agreement to be sure that unfair advantage has not been taken of any signatory and that all parties are properly represented. In states that do not permit "virtual representation," a court-appointed guardian *ad litem* may have to sign the agreement on behalf of unborn and unascertained heirs when property will otherwise pass in trust to "issue" or terminate at a future date when specified beneficiaries may no longer be living or in existence.

Q 7:56 What is "virtual representation"?

"Virtual representation" is a policy of allowing parties to "represent" others with similar interests by signing agreements, receiving notice, and the like. For example, one statute provides:

> Sec. 4. In connection with trust matters, unless otherwise represented, a minor, incapacitated or unborn individual, or a person whose identity or location is unknown and not reasonably ascertainable, may be represented by and bound by another person having a substantially identical interest with respect to the particular question or dispute, but only to the extent there is no conflict of interest between the representative and the person being represented.

[Connecticut Public Act No. 01-69 (eff. October 1, 2001)]

Arizona Revised Statutes Section 14-3951 provides:

> 14-3951. Effect of approval of agreements involving trusts, inalienable interests, or interests of third persons
>
> A compromise of any controversy as to admission to probate of any instrument offered for formal probate as the will of a decedent, the construction, validity or effect of any probated will, the rights or interests in the estate of the decedent, of any successor, or the administration of the estate, if approved in a formal proceeding in the court for that purpose, is binding on all the parties thereto including those unborn, unascertained or who could not be located. An approved compromise is binding

> even though it may affect a trust or an inalienable interest. A compromise does not impair the rights of creditors or of taxing authorities who are not parties to it.

These statutes may apply to trust matters only (as in the Connecticut instance), or also to estates. This approach is included in Article 3 of the Uniform Trust Code (2000) and in the Uniform Probate Code. Without such a statute or policy, it may be difficult to resolve matters by agreement even if statutes permit.

Q 7:57 How are attorney's fees determined in probate?

Attorney's fees, like personal representative's fees (discussed above, see Q 7:19) are sometimes set by statute, or a maximum or presumptively permissible rate of payment may be set by statute. In those states with permissible fee schedules, the permissible fee in practice usually becomes the presumptive fee. Most statutory fee schedules are based on a percentage of the estate, and while they vary tremendously they will often approximate 3 percent of the estate value. Some states provide a sliding fee schedule, so that larger estates will pay a smaller percentage in fees (but, of course, a larger total fee).

In more modern jurisdictions (and particularly those adopting the Uniform Probate Code), statutory fee schedules have been done away with in favor of a "reasonable" fee. Rather than set a percentage fee, those states require the attorney for the personal representative (and the personal representative himself or herself) to maintain records indicating the amount of time spent, the complexity of the tasks undertaken, the ability to delegate individual tasks to more efficient and/or less expensive subordinates, and other related factors; while the fee is not set in advance, the court will consider the reasonableness of the fee at the request of any interested person.

States without statutory fee schedules (that is, those requiring fees to be "reasonable") include Arizona, Colorado, Connecticut, Idaho, Kansas, Maine, Massachusetts, Michigan, Minnesota, Mississippi, Nebraska, New Hampshire, North Dakota, Pennsylvania, Rhode Island, Tennessee, Utah, Vermont, Washington, West Virginia, and the District of Columbia.

Q 7:58 What happens when the attorney is both the fiduciary and the estate attorney?

When the attorney is the fiduciary, and the attorney (or attorney's firm) is also the estate attorney, total fees may theoretically be reduced (because the attorney will not be able to charge a standard hourly rate for fiduciary business that is not "legal services") or increase (because the attorney will charge for tasks that a family fiduciary might do for nothing). Some state statutes prohibit "double-dipping" and require an allocation of time to fiduciary duties or legal services and then assessing a "reasonable fee" standard for each. Others that follow statutory fee schedules for the fiduciary may also allow the attorney to charge the customary rate for specifically legal services. Still others may require a reduced rate or percentage when one party serves both as fiduciary and as attorney. When engaging an attorney to provide not only legal and tax-preparation services, but also to handle the other details of administration, it is important to ascertain that the attorney has sufficient support staff to handle these details at a reduced rate or as part of overhead.

Q 7:59 What kind of engagement agreement should an attorney have with an estate fiduciary?

Leaving aside those states where the fees are statutorily determined, the issue of an engagement letter can be very difficult for attorneys who handle probate matters. Subject always to the possibility that the court may apply the "reasonableness" test to reduce a fee, an attorney will require, as a practical matter, a way to pay the bills. Some options may include:

- Straight percentage rate (subject to court approval —and the attorney will want to keep time records to justify the resulting figure)
- Flat fee, particularly for simple estates
- Hourly rate; provided, however, that if there is no surviving spouse to pay the final bills, the charges may have to be either subject to a cap, or "topped off" at a particular stage in the proceedings to address estimated future expenses that must be taken as deductions on tax returns and used to prepare filings

- Hourly rate, but using a "premium" hourly fee for complex estates or certain tasks

The timing of reaching such an agreement is also difficult. Rules of professional conduct may require (or should require) that the agreement be reduced to writing within a reasonable time after the engagement has begun. Prudence dictates that the details of the agreement be reached and recorded before the attorney has invested too much time in the enterprise. However, any arrangement involving an estimate will be difficult to reach at an early stage in the proceedings. Even if the simplest approach, hourly fees, is agreed to, what should be done when preparing tax returns and accountings? If these are only estimates, and the estimates later vary wildly from the reality, there may be need for new accountings or amended tax returns to avoid over- or under-deducting fees.

Moreover, depending on the volume of probate business, certain billing practices may make it impossible to represent those with modest estates. The percentage approach can be too small to compensate for the numerous complications that can arise in any estate, no matter how small. The hourly rate may work better with those estates in the short term, but it may still be necessary to "write off" or underbill if one wishes the surviving widow to continue to retain the attorney's services. The percentage approach is offensive to the careful consumer, but in some sense may be the best way to ensure that all clients receive services in proportion to their ability to pay. Perhaps the other way is the "premium" hourly approach for preparation of estate tax returns or post-mortem planning.

There are also issues about the timing of fee payments. In some practices it is customary to present a bill only at the conclusion, with filing of an accounting. In others, bills are presented at stages such as inventory and tax return preparation with the final payment made only after the accounting is presented and approved by the court. Still others, trying to meet their own payment obligations, present and ask payment on monthly bills, risking the possibility that the court may deny the fee and require a refund, or even fine the attorney for payment prior to court approval.

There are no easy answers to this conundrum and every attorney must make his or her own judgment.

Q 7:60 What income tax returns must be filed after the death of a decedent?

The personal representative is responsible for filing a final income tax return (federal and state) for the decedent. The decedent's final federal income tax return (Form 1041 or equivalent) is due on April 15 of the year following the decedent's death. [I.R.C. § 691] The income tax return must be filed by the personal representative or executor; the only exception provided by the IRS is that if no personal representative has been appointed a joint return can be filed by the surviving spouse. [I.R.C. § 6013]

The estate (or trust) may also be liable for a fiduciary income tax return (federal Form 1040) if income was earned during the period of administration. The personal representative can elect to file the fiduciary income tax return on April 15 following the year of death, or on the fifteenth day of the fourth month after the one-year anniversary of the decedent's death. [I.R.C. §§ 641, 6072] Subsequent fiduciary income tax returns will be due each year on the same date, so long as the estate earned taxable income during the preceding year.

The fiduciary must also be aware that the surviving spouse and beneficiaries will also have their own income tax returns to file, and that the timing of the estate's reporting may significantly impact their lives. Anyone who prepares fiduciary income tax returns is aware that after February 1 it is open season on the telephone line for beneficiaries demanding their K-1s in order that they may prepare their own income tax returns. If an estate beneficiary is also the beneficiary on an IRD item such as retirement account, he or she may suddenly have substantial income and a higher tax bracket such that deductible expenses of the final year of administration would be particularly welcome.

Q 7:61 What other tax returns must be filed for a decedent?

If the decedent left an estate worth more than the amount of the unified credit for that year (set at $1,000,000 for 2002–2003, rising to $1,500,000 in 2004; see Q 5:7 and Table 5-1), taking into consideration lifetime gifts that would have eaten up some or all of the unified credit, then a Form 706 estate tax return is required. [I.R.C. § 2001 et seq.] There is significant variation among the states with regard to estate taxation, and it is the personal representative's responsibility to become familiar with state requirements (or hire someone well-versed in this area). The Form 706 estate tax return is due nine months after the date of the decedent's death, and must be filed by the personal representative or, if there is no personal representative, the individual or officer with information about the decedent's taxable estate (e.g., the trustee, surviving spouse, surviving joint tenant, or beneficiary). [I.R.C. § 2203] While a six-month extension can be granted, the tax must still be paid within the original nine-month period.

In addition, a gift tax return (Form 709) is due by April 15 following the year in which any taxable gift was made. [I.R.C. § 6075] In the event of a gift in the last year of the decedent's life, a gift tax return may also be required.

Claims Against the Estate

Q 7:62 How does the personal representative determine the validity of creditors' claims against the estate?

Claims against the estate are presumed valid; the personal representative usually has the burden to disallow them, and must do so within a prescribed period of time. Failure formally to disallow the claim may operate to approve the claim in full. The personal representative must investigate the claim, and, if there is doubt, either notify the creditor that the claim was disallowed or bring the matter to court. The personal representative may also have a duty to try to settle with the creditor if the amount of the debt is in dispute.

It is usually wise to wait a reasonable amount of time before obtaining "final" claim figures from medical providers, to be sure that all insurance carriers, including Medicare, have made payments and reduced the claim to what will truly become payable.

One claim may be very difficult for the personal representative to evaluate: the claim of a state for reimbursement of public or medical assistance payment. Suffice to say that the fiduciary should not simply roll over when presented with a state claim. The state frequently makes "mistakes" in its own favor.

Another problem claim may be the I.R.S. claim for back taxes. If the decedent failed to file an income tax return, the I.R.S. may present a substantial claim that will vanish once the return is actually prepared. For example, a non-filer may sell a residence. The proceeds are reported on the 1099 and generate a claim for taxes based on the total sales proceeds. If the property was the principal residence, or sold at a loss, the claim for taxes vanishes. However, the decedent's right to a refund will also vanish unless the unfiled income tax return is filed within three years of its original due date.

Q 7:63 When is it safe for the personal representative to pay creditors' claims that seem to be valid?

While statutes, or even the terms of obligation, may require payment by a specified time, it is still hazardous for a representative to pay a claim unless absolutely certain there will be sufficient funds in the estate to pay expenses and all creditors. Even preferred creditors may not be paid unless it is certain that there will be sufficient resources to pay them in their entirety. Moreover, the prudent attorney will recall that expenses of administration (including attorneys' fees) usually take precedence over all claims, and attend to that obligation first. It may not even be safe to pay funeral expenses; in some instances, the state's claim for reimbursement of certain assistance benefits may take precedence over all but the expense of a "pauper's" funeral (see also Q 7:65).

Q 7:64 Do different claims have different priorities?

Some claims will be preferred over others. The priority of payments will be determined by state law, usually, state statute. Typically, costs of administration have the highest priority, and are paid first. Funeral expenses and the expenses of the last illness may follow in priority order. Secured claims come next. General, unsecured claims (and the unsecured portion of secured claims) will usually have the lowest priority.

Although not a claim against the estate, statutory family allowances and the election, dower, or curtesy rights of surviving spouses may be considered "expenses of administration" or otherwise be entitled to payment before even priority claims, or may be given priority over other expenses. In effect, this can provide a way to get funds to the surviving family rather than the creditors. Secured creditors do not actually receive priority status, but usually are permitted to exercise their security interests even though the effect may be to remove assets from the estate and thereby defeat even family allowances and priority claims.

Q 7:65 What happens if there are insufficient assets in an estate to pay all of the creditor's claims?

As in bankruptcy, once expenses of administration and other preferred items are paid first, the secured claims will be satisfied first, either through payment or by turning over the secured property. Although generally mortgages are not (and should not be) paid off by the probate estate (this will be determined by statute), the personal representative has an obligation to keep up the payments of these and other debts until the obligations are satisfied and/or the assets are distributed to beneficiaries who will then assume the debt obligations. Unsecured debts may be settled on a *pro rata* basis or through agreement with the creditors. When assets are insufficient to satisfy all categories of debts, the higher-priority debts will be satisfied completely before any payments can be made to lower-priority creditors. Distributions to beneficiaries are precluded when the estate has outstanding debts.

Estate Distribution and Closing

Q 7:66 When should beneficiaries expect distributions from a decedent's estate?

Only after administration of the estate has been completed is it time to distribute the remaining estate assets to the persons named in the decedent's will (or to heirs, in the case of intestacy). Although state law may permit earlier distributions, the personal representative will usually wait until administration is completed, to protect against the possibility of unknown creditors' claims or challenges to the will or determination of heirs, and unforeseen expenses (including attorneys' fees).

If the estate is clearly solvent, those given specific devises in the will may receive them early in the proceedings; however, the personal representative may be personally liable if he or she makes distributions to beneficiaries before all claims against the estate have been satisfied. For this reason there will ordinarily be no distributions until just before the final closing of the estate. If an early distribution is in order, the personal representative should get permission from the court at a hearing, notice of which should be given to all beneficiaries and unpaid creditors. A family agreement may be in order if some of the beneficiaries are willing to risk their inheritances to satisfy the hardship needs of other beneficiaries.

In most states (particularly those that have streamlined probate proceedings in recent decades), a probate proceeding might typically be concluded in six months or less, at least if no federal estate tax returns are required. Many states provide for even more summary proceedings where the estate is small, especially where the estate is insufficient to satisfy all creditor claims, administrative costs, and family entitlements; in some cases, it may actually be possible to open and close a small probate proceeding simultaneously.

Q 7:67 Are there emergency circumstances that permit earlier distribution of the estate?

When a spouse and/or dependent children have been omitted from a will, and thus do not have the benefit of the decedent's home, property, or income, the personal representative may get permission from the court to make partial distributions. (In that situation, the family may also make support claims that can often be paid as court-approved administration expenses rather than as either claims, or distributions to beneficiaries.) As long as all beneficiaries receive notice and the distribution of assets would not encroach on creditors' claims, the court is usually willing to entertain motions for partial emergency distributions. The personal representative may be personally liable for claims against the estate if distributions made to beneficiaries exhaust assets that should otherwise have been available to creditors.

It is also commonplace to permit family members to take distributions of tangible personal property prior to the conclusions of administration, particularly when the real estate must be emptied in order to be sold.

Q 7:68 What happens if there are insufficient assets to make all of the distributions described in the decedent's will?

This frequently occurs when pecuniary, rather than fractional, bequests are made in the will. For instance, the will might state, "$10,000 to each of my six children, $20,000 to the Humane Society, and the residue of my estate to my sister." If the decedent leaves a net estate of $30,000, the sister will take nothing, which may not have been the decedent's intent. Drafters of wills should take special care to avoid this kind of outcome.

Claims and administrative expenses are ordinarily paid out of the residue of the estate. If the residue is insufficient to satisfy claims, then other classes of distributions will ordinarily "abate" (be eliminated) in a specified order. Usually, residuary devises abate first, then pecuniary devises, then specific devises. Within each class, devises abate proportionally, or in some cases, real estate has a preferred status and is not abated until bequests of personalty have been consumed.

> **Example 7-4.** John's will provides for distribution as follows: (1) his home goes to his daughter Julia, (2) his car goes to his son Rudy, (3) $20,000 goes to his son Edward, (4) $10,000 goes to his daughter Rafaela, and (5) the residue of the estate goes to his daughter Cindy.
>
> If (after payment of claims and administrative expenses) the estate consists of the home, car, and $30,000, no residue remains to distribute to daughter Cindy. If the remaining estate consists of the home, car, and $15,000, Edward and Rafaela will receive $10,000 and $5,000, respectively, and the home and car will be distributed as directed. If, on the other hand, there are insufficient assets to pay claims and administrative expenses without sale of the home and/or car, Julia and Rudy will receive the remaining amounts in proportion to the values of the home and car. In some cases, the car must be sold before there is any requirement that the home be sold.

The personal representative may wish to have the beneficiaries enter into a family agreement to come up with an alternative plan. In most states, a family agreement executed in accordance with statutes will bind the personal representative. It will require approval, of course, of not only heirs but also devisees; if any heir or devisee is a minor or a distribution is in trust, it may be impossible to secure the necessary approvals (see Qs 7:55–7:56).

Q 7:69 What is the process for closing a probate proceeding?

Procedures vary depending on state law. The personal representative must file with the court or present to all beneficiaries a final accounting of the probate estate assets, listing all assets and costs and a proposal for distribution. Assuming that the specific devises and all debts have been honored, in some states only the residuary beneficiaries (or, in the case of intestate estates, all beneficiaries) must be given notice; in others, all parties originally entitled to notice in the estate will customarily be given notice by the court. Once the court has approved the final accounting and proposal for distribution, the estate may be distributed and the estate closed. Some states require a final "affidavit" explaining any transactions that have occurred subsequent to the accounting and affirming that distribution has been made and claims paid according to the accounting as approved.

Under the Uniform Probate Code, the personal representative may opt to file a verified statement with the court confirming that all statutory requirements have been met and proper notice given to the relevant parties. This avoids some of the procedural hassles attached to formal closing, but such "informal" closing may substantially extend the period of time during which the personal representative may be sued or surcharged.

Trust Administration

Q 7:70 How do the rules governing trusts differ from probate rules?

Although trust administration is not directly controlled by the same statutes and procedures governing probate administration, the general rules are similar. Both the trustee and the personal representative are fiduciaries, so the duties of faithful performance and impartiality among beneficiaries, the proscription against self-dealing, and the application of the prudent investor rule (to name some of the more frequently encountered fiduciary rules) will apply in the trust setting as well as the probate context. In most states, trust administration is assigned to the probate court, so the procedural rules will usually be similar.

At the same time, there are a number of important differences in trust and estate administration. Chief among these is the reason an increasing number of individuals have turned to the living trust as a probate avoidance mechanism: While the probate process is necessarily court-supervised (even in those states adopting relatively relaxed probate rules and requirements), the administration of trusts comes before the court only upon the specific request of an interested party. That is both the great strength and the major weakness of trust administration: Without unexpected complications, the total cost, time, and difficulty involved in administering a trust should be dramatically lower than that required for a comparable probate estate; however, a lack of court supervision also means less oversight of the fiduciary's behavior, and an increase in the risk of undetected and/or unrecoverable losses to the trust's beneficiaries.

Q 7:71 What rules control trustees administering the trust estate?

The common law of trust administration is one of the best-developed areas of the law. Most of the general principles governing trust administration are relatively well-settled, and an abundance of case law exists to guide the trustee and his or her counsel. The Restatement of Trusts [1959 2d ed., except for the Prudent Investor Rule sections—primarily §§ 227–229, which have been published as the partial 1990 3d ed.] extensively details the existing law and, in the case of the prudent investor rule, aspirations for the developing law. The Uniform Trust Code (formerly the Uniform Trust Act) currently being prepared by the National Conference of Commissioners on Uniform State Laws generally codifies the pre-existing common-law principles governing trust administration in its Chapter 8, although it makes many other significant changes. [NCCUSL, Uniform Trust Code, §§ 801–817] The Uniform Trust Code has only been adopted in four states thus far (Kansas, Nebraska, New Mexico, and Wyoming). Of course, individual states may have more or less developed case law or statutory requirements relating to trust administration.

Q 7:72 How do default distribution rules apply to trusts?

As has been previously discussed, probate statutes usually provide for default rules of interpretation, so that *per stirpes* or *per capita* distribution is presumed, or distributions do not lapse as a result of the death of a devisee who is a family member, for example. Those default rules do not usually apply to trusts, with the result that the distribution must be provided for in the trust document. Without well-developed default rules, a failure to specify distribution provisions may result in unanticipated distributions or even the failure (or partial failure) of the trust itself.

Q 7:73 Must a trust be established by a writing?

At common law a trust could be established without any written memorandum, and so an oral trust may be enforceable absent any statute requiring a writing. [Restatement (Second) of Trusts § 39] The same principle is codified in the Uniform Trust Code. [NCCUSL, Uniform Trust Code, 2000 draft, § 401] Trusts involving real estate may, by individual state interpretations of the statute of frauds, require a written and signed transfer of the property into trust executed according to requirements for the conveyance of real estate in that jurisdiction. [Restatement (Second) of Trusts § 40]

Q 7:74 How may a trust be amended or revoked?

The law of wills usually provides that revocation can be accomplished by destruction of the original will [See U.P.C. § 2-507], and that a missing will gives rise to a presumption of revocation. [See U.P.C. § 3-415]. Trusts are usually revoked in accordance with the terms of the trust itself, and destruction of the original trust document will ordinarily not be sufficient to revoke the trust. Consequently, a missing trust does not give rise to a presumption of revocation. [Restatement (Second) of Trusts § 330] At common law, a trust was presumed to be irrevocable unless the settlor expressly reserved the right to revoke or amend the trust, although the accidental failure to include a power to revoke might not preclude revocation if it could be shown that the omission was a mistake. [Restatement (Second) of Trusts §§ 330, 332] Some states have abandoned the common-law rule, and presume trusts to be revocable unless a contrary intention is expressed in the trust instrument;

that approach is adopted in the Uniform Trust Code as currently proposed. [NCCUSL, Uniform Trust Code, 2000 draft, § 602(a)]

Assuming that the trust is revocable and amendable, the validity of an amendment or revocation will be tested by the terms of the trust instrument. The trust may, for example, require that any revocation or amendment be delivered to the trustee before it becomes effective. Such a requirement will usually be strictly enforced.

Q 7:75 Will a trust protect the settlor against creditors' claims?

Normally a trust established for the benefit of the settlor utilizing the settlor's own assets cannot be shielded from the claims of the settlor's creditors. This general principle may not apply to trusts established in some foreign jurisdictions, which have for decades encouraged the use of so-called "asset protection" trusts to shield settlors from at least those creditors not known or reasonably ascertainable at the time of establishment of the trust (although the foreign asset protection trust may actually shield the settlor from those claims as well, transfer of assets into a trust to defeat known creditors will be a criminal act under most states' fraudulent transfer rules).

In recent years a small number of states have adopted creditor protection schemes that mirror the off-shore asset protection trust. Notable among those states is Alaska, which has aggressively moved into the sale of trusts to out-of-state residents by not only protecting trust assets from creditors' claims, but also eliminating the Rule Against Perpetuities and permitting limited use of community property to secure stepped-up basis in assets held in trust. [1997 Alaska Laws ch. 6, adopted April 2, 1997] Other states with relatively aggressive asset-protection provisions include Delaware [The "Qualified Dispositions in Trust Act" is codified at 12 Del. Code § 3570 et seq.], Rhode Island [Rhode Island largely copied the Delaware QDTA at R.I. Gen. Laws § 18-9.2-1 et seq.], and Nevada [Nev. Rev. Stat. § 166.010 et seq.].

However, there is a significant difference between the duties of a trustee and the duties of a personal representative, and that may act to shield the settlor's beneficiaries from the settlor's creditors following the settlor's death. The personal representative has a duty to pay creditors' claims, whereas the trustee may only have an affirmative duty to the trust beneficiaries. If the trust instrument does not require payment of debts, the trustee may be able to make trust distributions to beneficiaries without fear of personal liability to a creditor who remains unpaid. Indeed, the creditor will have to invoke its own court proceeding, typically in a less flexible proceeding, and reduce the claim to a court judgment, in order to get the trustee to pay. If at that time the trust is itself judgment proof, the creditor will then have to pursue the claim against the beneficiary. Depending on the beneficiary's liquidity, this may be more trouble than it is worth to the creditor or its collection agent. All this may make it at the very least easier to settle claims against the settlor following death and maximize what passes to the beneficiaries.

Practice-Related Issues

Q 7:76 What kinds of probate-related issues typically arise in an elder law practice?

1. *No original will.* A client whose father recently died brings in all the paperwork she believes is relevant to the estate, including a photocopy of his will. When you ask where the original is, she admits that she has looked all through his house and cannot find it. The other siblings also have copies, but no original is available. Should the attorney file testate or intestate?

   The law correctly presumes that the absence of an original will indicates revocation; thus, intestate proceedings are the likely alternative. Because most wills replicate the intestate succession laws anyway—with the estate passing to the spouse, or, if the spouse is deceased, to the children in equal proportions—it may not make much difference whether the original will can be found or not. There may, however, be situations when the attorney may want to take a different approach: The will may have unequal distributions or make specific bequests of property, or the circumstances of the loss or destruction of the original will may be known—for instance, if a caretaker for a demented testator saw him tear it up. If nothing else, the will may have appointed the siblings as executors and excused the requirement of bond, and it is at least worth trying to avoid that expense for the family and have the will admitted. In such circumstances, the attorney may want to set a formal hearing, and as with most probate matters, try to have all interested parties sign waivers of any objection. In the worst case scenario, if the will cannot be admitted, an alternative will be to suggest a mutual distribution agreement (see Q 7:55) replicating the dispositive scheme in the questioned will.

2. *Outdated will.* The adult child of a decedent retains an attorney to initiate probate proceedings on his father's estate. The original will, which the decedent had conscientiously kept in a safe deposit box since it was executed in 1980, bequeaths the testator's 1978 Ford Thunderbird to his nephew Bill, 20 shares of his Esso stock to neighbors who helped care for his ailing wife, and his home to his children in equal shares. Predictably, the Ford is long gone (but there's a brand new Cadillac in the decedent's garage), the Esso stock has been replaced by Microsoft stock (with the decedent's estate named as pay-on-death beneficiary), and the house was titled in joint tenancy with his caretaker daughter a year before his death. Can any of these be honored?

   Attorneys probably learn more about proper drafting of wills from doing probate than from any CLE program. Obviously the testator intended that persons other than his children would benefit from his estate, but none of these bequests can be honored. The bequest of the car is too specific, and the decedent—perhaps forgetting what he had put in his original will—made modifications to the objects of the other bequests so that they bypassed the will entirely. The attorney may suggest to the personal representative that a family agreement be reached so that the terms of the will can still be honored, but the refusal of even one beneficiary to sign the agreement means none of the devisees will benefit.

3. *Ascertaining the personal representative, intestate estate.* The son of a decedent calls an attorney and asks what he needs to do to be named personal representative of his mother's estate. She did not leave a will, and she has a rather sizeable estate. The unsuspecting attorney meets with the son and has him sign all the paperwork necessary for filing for informal probate proceedings. However, when he goes to file, he learns that another child of the decedent has beaten him to it.

He calls his client, and learns that there are four children, none of whom get along and all of whom want to be the personal representative of the estate. His client does not have any money of his own. After some discussion, the attorney gets the uncomfortable feeling that none of the children, including his own client, can be fully trusted with the estate property (or will pay for the time he has already spent). What should he do?

The attorney may hate to relinquish the chance to represent the personal representative of a large estate, but many prefer that to the alternative in this case—a prolonged, messy family dispute, which will only get worse as the final distribution date approaches. If he decides to represent the client at the formal intestacy hearing, he may spend many hours in preparation only to have another sibling appointed personal representative (and the estate will not pay his fees, of course). If the attorney is successful at the hearing, he may wish to draw up a private agreement/special power of attorney with his client so that he has the authority to hold and manage the estate property and co-sign on all transactions.

If he decides to withdraw, the attorney can rely on ABA Model Rule 1.16, which states that a lawyer may withdraw if withdrawal can be accomplished without material adverse effect on the client's interests, or if "(1) the client persists in a course of action involving the lawyer's services that the lawyer reasonably believes is criminal or fraudulent, (2) the client has used the lawyer's services to perpetrate a crime or fraud, (3) a client insists upon pursuing an objective that the lawyer considers repugnant or imprudent, (4) the client fails substantially to fulfill an obligation to the lawyer regarding the lawyer's services and has been given reasonable warning that the lawyer will withdraw unless the obligation is fulfilled, (5) the representation will result in an unreasonable financial burden on the lawyer or has been rendered unreasonably difficult by the client, or (6) other good cause for withdrawal exists." The attorney is expected to give his client reasonable notice of withdrawal, allowing time for the client to find other counsel, and turning over all necessary paperwork.

Chapter 8

Will and Trust Contests

Disgruntled heirs or devisees may contest the validity of a testator's will. Elder law attorneys may represent the contestants or may have represented the decedent and prepared the contested will. In either event it is important to understand how will contests proceed, how likely they are to succeed, and how to minimize the likelihood of will contests while conducting estate planning. In addition, it is becoming increasingly common for contests to be filed by disgruntled trust beneficiaries; what once would have been a will contest may now manifest itself as a trust contest because of the testamentary effect of the living trust. This chapter discusses the bases and procedures for contesting a will or a trust and possible challengers of wills and trusts.

Wills: Validity and Challenges

Q 8:1 On what bases are wills typically contested?

In most states, the only available challenges to the validity of a will are that the testator:

1. Failed to carry out the formalities, including execution of the will and, in the case of testamentary trusts, failed to obey the rule against perpetuities;
2. Lacked sufficient mental capacity to make a will;
3. Was under duress or undue influence;
4. Was mistaken in the execution of the will; or
5. Intentionally or accidentally revoked the instrument.

Q 8:2 How frequent are will contests?

Will contests actually reaching litigation are extremely rare. Wills commonly reflect intestate succession laws anyway: for example, the estate passes to the spouse, or, if the spouse has predeceased the decedent, to the children in equal or substantially equal proportions (see Q 7:24). Most probate estates are small, with tangible personal property comprising the bulk of the estate (meaning the estates may not even be subject to probate). Because case law indicates that the courts usually rule in favor of validation of the will, attorneys frequently prefer to negotiate a family agreement rather than bring litigation. On the other hand, because litigation is expensive and it is unlikely that the party bringing the suit will ever have to compensate the estate for its costs, will contestants may be able to extract a settlement from the estate to buy their cooperation, and the number of times this occurs cannot be documented.

Q 8:3 What is required to establish due execution of a will?

To help guard against challenges based on the mental state of the testator and undue influence, all states have set minimum requirements for will execution. While oral ("nuncupative") wills may be valid in some states for limited amounts of property, the general rule is that the will must be signed; state statutes vary as to whether the testator can sign by proxy and how many witnesses are required. (See chapter 4 for a detailed discussion of wills executions.) Some states require that the will be signed in the actual presence of the witnesses; others allow the testator to sign the will in private and then acknowledge the signing to the attesting witnesses. While the precise rules vary by state, they are almost all based on the English common-law statute of wills, which required three witnesses (now reduced to two in all states but Vermont) to be present at the time of the testator's signing, and the testator to be present when the witnesses signed. Although usually the witnesses are not required to be disinterested parties, there are sound practical reasons to utilize only disinterested witnesses; in the event of a later contest, the honesty of a witness who benefits from his or her own testimony is subject to an obvious challenge. (In most states, a witness who is named in the will may not take the legacy the will contains.)

The exception to statute of wills principles is the holographic will, which is not witnessed but is signed by the testator and is entirely in the testator's handwriting. A minority of states permit holographic wills, though some will recognize a holographic will that was valid in the place and at the time it was executed (see Q 4:32).

Q 8:4 What is required to establish due execution of an amendment of a will?

Usually the will may be amended only by a codicil signed with the same formality as is the will itself. A codicil is an amendment to a will, changing only some of the provisions of the original document. Notes in the margins and corrections in the text could be interpreted as a revocation of the instrument rather than an amendment, and even clearly worded marginal notes will not satisfy the formalities of a will or codicil. Arguably, in states permitting holographic wills, marginal notes signed by the testator may have been "duly executed."

Q 8:5 What is a "self-proving" will?

Many states permit a will to be "self-proving." This usually means that the signatures of the testator and witnesses have been acknowledged and/or notarized; most state statutes provide a formula recital that must be sworn to by the testator and witnesses (see Q 4:26). A self-proving will usually cannot be challenged on the basis of failure to comply with execution requirements: Typically, self-proving wills are conclusively presumed to have been properly executed; however, this may not prevent a challenge on the basis of mistake (the testator may still have been operating under a misapprehension of the contents of the will) or on the basis of lack of testamentary capacity or undue influence.

Q 8:6 What is a "mistake" in the context of a will contest?

Occasionally the evidence may show that the testator did not actually know that the document he or she signed was a will, or was mistaken about the contents of the will. Although those facts may also be the basis of a showing of undue influence (particularly if the individual responsible for the testator's mistaken understanding is also a primary beneficiary of the will), the notion of "mistake" is a separate basis for challenging the validity of the document. In order to prevail on this theory, the challenger must be able to show that the testator truly was unaware of the nature or contents of the document.

Q 8:7 What is required for the testator to revoke his or her will?

In most states, a will must be revoked with certain formalities. It is usually insufficient to indicate an intent to revoke the will, even in writing. A direction to another person to destroy a will, if the actual destruction is not in the testator's presence, will usually not amount to a revocation of the will even if the evidence indicates that the testator wanted to revoke the will and actually directed its destruction. In most states, revocation of a will requires that the testator either (1) actually destroy or mutilate the physical document, or (2) publish a new will that either expressly or implicitly revokes the old document. In the language of the Uniform Probate Code (UPC), a will can be revoked by committing a "revocatory act" upon the actual document; partial obliteration, tearing, crossing out, burning, or other acts may all qualify as revocatory acts. [U.P.C. § 2-507] Obviously, the most effective and efficient method of revoking a will is to prepare a new will that expressly revokes the prior will.

Q 8:8 When a will is revoked without a new will being prepared, how is the testator's estate distributed?

Revocation of a will may result in either intestacy or a finding that a prior will has been "revived" by the revocation ("the doctrine of relative revocation"). The Uniform Probate Code provides that the previous will is revived if the circumstances of the revocation of the subsequent will, or declarations from the testator personally, indicate that the testator intended the earlier will to be revived. [U.P.C. § 2-509] Otherwise, revocation of a subsequent will does not act to revive the earlier will provisions; instead, the decedent who revokes his or her most recent will without preparing a new one dies intestate.

Q 8:9 What happens when the testator's will cannot be found?

A missing will usually gives rise to a presumption that the testator destroyed the original with the intent to revoke it; however, the presumption is not absolute, and the proponent of a missing will may be able to establish that the will was still in existence at the time of the testator's death, or that the original will was not in the testator's possession (and therefore could not have been destroyed by the testator personally), or that the testator was incapacitated at the time the will was destroyed. In such cases, a copy of the will may be admitted to probate; in unusual cases, it may even be possible to "prove" the contents of a missing will by testimony from witnesses who saw the document and remember its contents.

Q 8:10 What is testamentary capacity?

In order to make a valid will, an individual must meet minimum levels of mental competence. The test for capacity to make a will varies slightly by state, but is usually based on traditional common-law principles. As formulated in most states, the standard of testamentary capacity requires the testator to be able to do the following three things:

1. Understand the nature and extent of his or her assets;
2. Identify the "natural objects" of his or her bounty; and
3. Understand the nature of a will and express an intention to provide for the distribution of his or her estate.

(See also Q 4:22.)

Q 8:11 How does testamentary capacity compare to other standards of competence?

The level of competence required to undertake different acts will vary by the nature of the act. Competence to enter into a contract ("contractual capacity") usually requires the contractor to be able to understand the nature and effect of the contract. The level of competence necessary to overcome a guardianship petition may be even lower. Typically, all that is required to defeat a guardianship petition is the ability to make and communicate responsible decisions concerning personal matters. The level of competence necessary to sign a health care directive, or to revoke one, may be even lower. Testamentary capacity is usually viewed as among the lowest of these standards. Even a person who is unable to enter into a contract, or who has a guardian appointed, may be able to execute a valid will.

Q 8:12 What is the difference between lack of capacity and undue influence?

The second most common challenge to a will (after lack of testamentary capacity) is that someone—usually the beneficiary of the will—unduly influenced the testator to sign the document. The concept of undue influence is distinct from lack of testamentary capacity, although an individual with marginal capacity is more likely to be susceptible to undue influence. While it is difficult to imagine a fully competent individual succumbing to undue influence, it happens.

Q 8:13 How can a will contestant show undue influence?

It is in the nature of undue influence that it is usually exerted in secret, and must be shown by inference. Some states have articulated a list of factors tending to indicate undue influence and case law will state that the burden "shifts" to one side or the other depending on certain of the factors. The trier of fact may find undue influence without evidence of any of these factors, or may not find undue influence even if all these factors are evident. Generally speaking, if more indicators can be shown to exist, the likelihood of a successful challenge increases.

The typical indicators of undue influence include:

- Fraudulent representations made by the person alleged to have influenced the testator;
- Hasty execution of the will;
- Concealment of the fact a new will was executed;
- Active involvement in procuring drafting and execution of the will by the person benefiting from the will;

- Lack of consistency between the challenged will and prior estate plans;
- Unusual or unnatural will provisions, given the testator's circumstances, attitudes, and family situation;
- Susceptibility of the testator to influence by another; and
- The existence of a "confidential relationship" between the testator and the alleged influencer.

[For an excellent review of the law of undue influence, see Turkat, "Psychological Aspects of Undue Influence," *Probate & Property* (a publication of the Real Property, Probate and Trust Law Section of the American Bar Association) Jan./Feb. 2003 (Vol. 17, No. 1)]

Q 8:14 What is a confidential relationship and how does it relate to the presumption of undue influence?

Many states have adopted a presumption of undue influence in some circumstances. If the testator and the alleged influencer were in a "confidential relationship," and the will results in a benefit to the alleged influencer, the burden of persuasion (if not the burden of proof) may shift to the beneficiary to show that there was no undue influence.

"Confidential relationship" is not a clearly defined concept. It is something more than a family relationship: A family member will not necessarily have a confidential relationship. An agent who actually manages the testator's finances almost certainly has a confidential relationship. Any fiduciary relationship involving personal intimacy, entrustment of power, and disclosure of secrets will give rise to a confidential relationship.

Where a confidential relationship has been shown between the testator and a beneficiary of the will, the other elements of undue influence need not be shown. The confidential relationship gives rise to a presumption of undue influence, which requires the will's proponent to go forward with evidence rebutting that presumption. In some states, the change may be described as a shift of the burden of proof to the will proponent; in others, it may simply be a shift of the burden of going forward with evidence of lack of undue influence.

Example 8-1. An elderly widower needs assistance with personal hygiene and housekeeping, and his family hires a woman to come to the house every day to run errands and otherwise provide assistance. As the months go by, the widower becomes increasingly fond of and dependent upon the caretaker, including giving her authority to sign his checks. He eventually rewrites his will, leaving everything to the caretaker. The family challenges, producing evidence and testimony that the caretaker was manipulative and controlling of the widower, who because of his ailments and age was particularly vulnerable to this kind of influence; the burden of proof shifts to the caretaker, who produces evidence and witnesses supporting her argument that she provided loving care to the widower, something the family never did, and he was fully competent when he wrote the new will.

Q 8:15 Does the involvement of the beneficiary in the preparation of a will always invalidate the will?

In most states, involvement of the beneficiary in the preparation of a will is one of the indicators of undue influence. Nonetheless, a beneficiary may be legally capable of serving as a witness or event drafter of a will, and the active involvement of a beneficiary in securing or preparing the will does not automatically invalidate the document. As a matter of practice, beneficiaries should not be utilized as witnesses or permitted to be involved in the preparation of documents except in the most unusual of circumstances.

Q 8:16 May a lawyer who drafts a will include a provision benefitting himself or herself?

As a threshold matter, of course, the draftsperson of any testamentary instrument that benefits the drafter is subject to allegations of undue influence. This is true whether the drafter is a lawyer or not. Lawyers face an additional impediment in the form of ethical proscriptions against some kinds of behavior.

The Model Rules of Professional Conduct, which have been adopted in a majority of states, expressly deal with this concern. Model Rule 1.8(c) provides that, "A lawyer shall not prepare an instrument giving the lawyer or a person related to the lawyer as parent, child, sibling, or spouse any substantial gift from a client, including a testamentary gift, except where the client is related to the donee." The Rule does not define "related to," and there is no provision limiting the bequests that can be made to the lawyer/relative. Clearly, however, the non-relative lawyer is prohibited from preparing a will naming the lawyer or a close family member as a beneficiary. A lawyer may be disbarred for preparing a will for a long-time client, in which the lawyer was the sole beneficiary. [See, e.g., Committee on Professional Ethics v. Randall, 285 N.W.2d 161 (Iowa 1979), *cert. denied*, 446 U.S. 946 (1980)]

Pending changes to the ABA Model Rules of Professional Conduct (though not yet adopted) may change the ethical rules slightly in connection with this issue. The proposed new version of Rule 1.8(c) maintains the same basic structure, but defines "related to" to include "a spouse, child, grandchild, parent, grandparent or other relative or individual with whom the lawyer or the client maintains a close, familial relationship." Comments [6] and [7] to the proposed new rule clarify the proscription:

> [6] A lawyer may accept a gift from a client, if the transaction meets general standards of fairness. For example, a simple gift such as a present given at a holiday or as a token of appreciation is permitted. If a client offers the lawyer a more substantial gift, paragraph (c) does not prohibit the lawyer from accepting it, although such a gift may be voidable by the client under the doctrine of undue influence, which treats client gifts as presumptively fraudulent. In any event, due to concerns about overreaching and imposition on clients, a lawyer may not suggest that a substantial gift be made to the lawyer or for the lawyer's benefit, except where the lawyer is related to the client as set forth in paragraph (c).
>
> [7] If effectuation of a substantial gift requires preparing a legal instrument such as a will or conveyance, the client should have the detached advice that another lawyer can provide. The sole exception to this Rule is where the client is a relative of the donee.

Some lawyers also feel that it is improper to draft a will that appoints the lawyer as personal representative because of the financial benefit to the lawyer as a result. This is not, however, the majority rule, although the situation should be handled with discretion and consulting with a different lawyer can be recommended.

Q 8:17 Who has the burden of proof in will contest proceedings?

The proponent of a will has the burden of establishing that the testator duly executed it. Once that has been established, because most states presume that a competent testator who was not under duress validly executed a will, the contestant has the burden of proof in challenging the validity of the will. Except for the shift of burden described previously in cases of undue influence based on a confidential relationship (see Q 8:14), the burden remains on the objectors to prove the invalidity of the will. Usually the standard of proof required is a simple preponderance of the evidence, although undue influence may have to be shown by clear and convincing evidence.

Q 8:18 Who may contest the validity of a will?

Only those parties who can lay some claim to real or personal property passing testate or intestate from a decedent's estate have legal standing to challenge a will. The challenging parties thus typically include devisees or assignees named in earlier wills but not in the contested will, intestate successors, and omitted spouses and children. The state may contest a will if there are no heirs, because the property would escheat (pass) to the state under intestate succession. As with other civil actions, the challenging party who can evidence injury or potential injury by the actions or omissions giving rise to the claim, injury that is greater than that suffered by the general population, meets the minimal requirements for legal standing to sue.

Pay-on-death benefits, such as proceeds from life insurance policies, are distributed according to their contractual terms and generally bypass the terms of the will and probate itself; however, contracts whose terms would be breached by the terms of the will can be the basis of will contests. These scenarios typically involve creditors and persons who claim to have been contractually or equitably adopted by the decedent. Heirs who acted in reliance on a promise of the decedent to be named as beneficiaries in the will, but were nevertheless omitted, have also contested wills, often with some success. Secured and unsecured creditors may file a claim against the estate, but ordinarily would not have standing to challenge a will itself unless the claim is somehow linked to an expectancy of a beneficiary under the will or an heir under intestate succession.

Q 8:19 What is an *in terrorem* provision, and is it an effective protection against will contests?

A will may include language that purports to disinherit any person who challenges the validity of the will itself. Such a provision is often referred to as an *in terrorem* clause. Of course, if the testator was incompetent to execute a will in the first place he or she was also incompetent to disinherit an heir or prior devisee. Given the strong presumption in favor of the validity of testamentary documents, and the law's desire to effect the wishes of the decedent, the general trend is to permit such provisions to be effective.

Because of concern about the possibility that legitimate heirs who contest invalid documents could be disinherited, many states permit contests despite the language of *in terrorem* provisions. In some states, the contestants must first establish that there is a reasonable basis for the contest before initiating it. In some other states the reasonableness of the challenge is determined after the fact when the challenge fails.

As a strategic and drafting matter, an *in terrorem* provision should always be accompanied by a significant bequest to the otherwise disinherited individual. Outright disinheritance creates no disincentive to trigger the *in terrorem* clause. It is only when the disgruntled heir has something to lose by a challenge that the provision has any effectiveness.

Q 8:20 What is the process for contesting the validity of wills?

Although a handful of states permit a court proceeding to determine the validity of a will before the death of the testator, the common rule is that a will contest must be filed in response to the probate (or proposed probate) of a decedent's will (see chapter 7 for a discussion of probate). Procedures for filing a will contest will vary by state, not only as to the process but even as to the terms. For example, a will contest may be referred to as a "caveat" in some jurisdictions.

Q 8:21 Is a jury trial available?

About two-thirds of American jurisdictions allow will contests to be tried before a jury. Even in those jurisdictions permitting jury trials, the jury may be an advisory jury only.

Q 8:22 Who pays for a will contest?

Ordinarily the costs of a will contest are borne by the contestants, whether successful or unsuccessful. In the case of a challenge to a will where a personal representative or executor has already been appointed, the estate may bear the cost of even an unsuccessful defense of the will by the personal representative, provided that the personal representative has acted reasonably. In the case of a successful will contest by one of several beneficiaries the costs of litigation may in some circumstances be charged to the estate on the theory that the successful challenger(s) acted for the common good of the true beneficiaries of the estate.

Q 8:23 How is the judgment in a will contest different from judgments in standard civil cases?

There is usually only one decision to be made: Whether or not the will (or any portions of it) is valid. The outcome determines whether or not probate will proceed as a testate or intestate matter. Thus there are no direct money damages, and a judgment cannot quiet title to real estate.

Q 8:24 What evidence is admissible and useful for establishing the validity of a will?

Because courts are most interested in the mental status of the testator at the time of execution of the document and in the formalities themselves, the witnesses to the execution of the will are of great importance. Even when the witnesses have no clear recollection of the circumstances of the signing of a particular will, they can at least testify that their signatures are genuine and that they would not have gone along with the proceeding if they had any suspicions about the circumstances. Attorneys should be consistent in the way they conduct will executions in their offices, so that they can later testify with assurance that standard procedures were followed when the will was executed. Some offices keep a written record of the witnesses, the attorney, who was present, and other relevant data, retained in the same file in which the will (or its copy) is kept.

Q 8:25 What evidence might a will contestant produce to demonstrate the invalidity of the will?

The instrument itself may provide the evidence of an insufficiency in the formalities: It may not have been signed, or the testator may have amended the original by hand at a later date. The witnesses to the execution may serve as witnesses for either party in a will contest, although they are of course more likely to testify that the will was properly executed. Family members or even handwriting experts may be summoned to examine and challenge the validity of (or confirm) the testator's signature. Such proof is particularly important in the case of a holographic will. If the challenge is based on the decedent's capacity to sign, then his or her treating physicians or other medical experts may be called to testify, although such testimony may not carry great weight unless it can be linked to the moment of signing.

Trust Challenges

Q 8:26 How are trust challenges different from will contests?

A typical revocable living trust will have the same dispositive effect as a will. In other words, the trust may seem to be a testamentary instrument; in fact, a lay trustor who wishes to change the trust's terms likely will think and say "I want to change my will." Even though the trust may provide for distribution of assets on the death of the trustor, it is not a will, and is not (usually) subject to the same requirements of formality and capacity as a will.

A trust is usually categorized as a contractual arrangement between the trustor and the trustee (who may be the same person or persons). Consequently, the level of capacity required to create a trust, and the formalities necessary for the establishment to be effective, are usually those of contracts. (The Uniform Trust Code, however, requires the same level of capacity—testamentary—which is intuitively more appropriate when a trust is being used as a will substitute. [UTC § 601]) Generally speaking, the level of capacity to enter into a contract will be greater than that required to execute a will, although the comparison is difficult; contractual capacity is usually described as the ability to understand the purpose and effect of the proposed contract. Although the required level of capacity may be higher, it can be argued that the much more vague definition of capacity actually makes trust challenges more difficult than will contests.

The differing formality requirements between wills and trusts also make the process of challenging a trust more difficult. While every state has clear and precise requirements for execution of a will (usually two witnesses, and frequently the two witnesses must actually witness the testator's signature as well as one another's signatures), trust formalities may be simple or even unprovided for by statute. It may be that a trustor's signature, without witnesses or notarization, is sufficient to make a trust effective. Furthermore, the signature on the trust instrument itself may not be the only (or even the most) important signature; much more importance might attach to the signature on a deed, a stock transfer document, or a letter of instructions transferring each asset into the name of the trust. In other words, the challenger may be faced with a series of signatures and a paucity of witnesses to the principal's capacity, understanding, or intent.

Most lawyers agree that it is much more difficult to challenge a trust's dispositive provisions than to challenge a will making the same disposition. This is partially because of the differing standards of capacity and formalities required for effective execution, but also in large part because of the procedural differences involved.

Q 8:27 What are the procedural differences between will contests and trust challenges?

Will contests usually take place in the context of a probate proceeding. In fact, the proponent of the will is obligated to file the original with the appropriate court, give notice to the persons named in the will and those persons affected by the terms of the will (e.g., heirs at law, or those who were named in prior, revoked, wills), and prove the validity of the offered will. The burden lies with the proponent of the will, and the process requires affirmative steps accompanied by notice and a formal opportunity for objectors to be heard.

By contrast, trust procedures are much less formal. Assuming the decedent's assets have been transferred into the trust during life, there is usually no requirement for any court proceeding to complete the distribution directed by the terms of the trust. There may be no duty to report (or account) to interested persons, and those who would have received property but for the existence of the trust (e.g., heirs at law) may not be entitled to any notice of the existence, value, distribution, or administration of the trust. No court proceeding is usually required, and so contestants have no formal opportunity to complain of the trustor's capacity, the valuation or administration of the assets, or their proposed ultimate distribution.

While the proponent of a will has the burden of going forward and the burden of proving the validity of the will, the contestant in a trust challenge carries both burdens. Not only must the contestant in a trust challenge carry the burden of going forward, he or she must actually initiate the legal proceedings, and must do so without (usually) sufficient information or evidence to know exactly what challenge to make.

For all of those procedural reasons, trust challenges are usually much more difficult for the objecting party than will contests. In fact, despite the arguably higher level of capacity required to execute a trust, the difficulty in challenging trusts is one of the strongest selling points in the current national trend favoring living trusts as estate planning tools in preference to wills.

Q 8:28 Do trust grantors need a higher level of understanding than testators of wills?

Evidence of diminished mental capacity may go farther to invalidate a trust than a will; a person who can articulate the nature and objects of his or her bounty may not be able to articulate, or even grasp, the trustor-trustee relationship or restricted distribution of assets. A minimally competent testator who is able to verbalize a wish that, for instance, "I don't want any of my kids to get the money until they're 30," likely will be held to have sufficient understanding to effect the trust's terms. While the level of capacity required to execute a trust may be higher than that required to execute a will, in practice only those testators/trustors who clearly do not understand the effect of their actions are likely to have those actions successfully challenged.

Q 8:29 Is reformation of a trust allowed?

Reformation of trusts is allowed under the Restatement of Trusts and the common law of most states, and courts are usually willing to allow reformation if there is some evidence of the original intent of the trustor. Extrinsic or parol evidence may be admissible if it sheds light on the intent of the trustor. An increasing number of courts are adopting the doctrine of "probable intent" in order to construct an instrument that may be contrary to the express language of the document, and will bring in parol evidence to assist them with this construction. Some construction is necessary anyway when there is ambiguous language addressing substantive issues. Trusts may also be reformed on the basis of "scrivener's error," a situation most attorneys would really rather avoid.

When the reformation of a trust creates a tax advantage, it may be subject to challenge by the Internal Revenue Service. Generally speaking, the IRS will not be bound by the agreements of trust (or will) beneficiaries in interpreting the documents, and may effectively require relitigation (in the tax court or other tax forum) to determine whether the beneficiaries could have obtained the same result in a contested proceeding. Even if the court rules in favor of the reformation, and the IRS does not oppose that conclusion, it still may not be bound by the court's decision unless it is the decision of the highest state court. [Commissioner v. Estate of Bosch, 387 U.S. 456 (1967)] This can be a real problem for parties seeking certainty when reforming a trust.

Q 8:30 Who has standing to contest trusts?

As with wills, anyone who has an interest in the property managed by or passing under the trust can challenge the trust, including omitted heirs, fiduciaries appointed under earlier documents, and creditors challenging spendthrift provisions. The issue in trust contests is not usually a question of standing, but rather a question of whether the challenger has been given sufficient information to mount a successful and timely challenge.

Q 8:31 How has the current public interest in revocable living trusts changed the nature of will and trust contests?

Much of the current impetus behind estate planning with revocable living trusts is generated by a public dissatisfaction with the probate process and a desire to avoid probate. While probate is expensive, time-consuming, invasive, and bureaucratic, it was not invented overnight by lawyers hoping to make money from the death of testators. The probate process was developed to increase the likelihood that the distribution of assets will be fair, honest, and in accordance with the decedent's real wishes. Probate has a poor reputation, largely based on the belief of many individuals that their own personal situations do not merit the kind of protection and scrutiny afforded by the probate process. Many will be wrong—their families will in fact cheat, steal, exaggerate (or minimize), and otherwise take advantage of one another. As probate-avoidance trusts become more popular, incidences of trust abuse will become more common. Trust administration can be taken before a court by anyone contesting the actions of the trustee or challenging the claims of a beneficiary, but many challenges will be made after the damage has already been accomplished and no protection remains available for the injured beneficiary.

Already some states have begun to impose probate-like proceedings on trust administration in order to protect beneficiaries and other claimants. Florida, for example, has extended its homestead provisions to property placed in trust, requiring a separate, probate-like proceeding to confirm transfers of at least some real property despite the probate-avoidance intentions of the trustor. [Fla. Stat. Ann. § 732.4015] Trust challenges have become administratively easier in recent years with the proliferation of trusts among the middle class, and practitioners should expect that trend to both continue and escalate in coming years. Eventually, probate-like protections will almost certainly be created for many living trusts, and to a large extent, this will be required in the Uniform Trust Code in those states that adopt it.

Practice-Related Issues

Q 8:32 What are some of the real-world problems that give rise to will contests or trust challenges?

In practice, will contests and trust challenges are uncommon and seldom successful. When contests do arise, they often fall within a narrow range of typical fact situations.

1. *A will based on separate writings.* The attorney is representing a personal representative and notice has been given to devisees and creditors. The will states that all tangible personal property shall pass to the residuary of the estate unless a separate writing states otherwise. The personal representative did not find a separate writing attached to the will; however, the woman who had been the paid caretaker of the decedent during her last months produces a paper, unquestionably written by the decedent but not signed or dated, that states that her diamond necklace shall go to the caretaker. The family thinks highly of the caretaker, but the diamond necklace is a family heirloom. What should the attorney advise?

   The easy answer is that the family can probably ignore the separate writing with impunity, because the caretaker will have an extremely difficult time proving that the decedent was lucid and not under duress at the time of the separate writing. She will have trouble finding an attorney to represent her in this matter, and may lack the funds to take it to court. The personal representative should talk this over with all beneficiaries and family members. They may agree that it was the decedent's wish that the caretaker benefit from the estate, and may wish to offer a cash gift in lieu of the necklace.

   It should be pointed out here that many states would simply invalidate the entire provision, saying that there could be no "incorporation by reference" into the will of the terms of extraneous documents, and that the missing document was no more than precatory.

2. *Unrecognizable handwriting.* The attorney represents a personal representative and is administering a will that leaves $1,000 to a son, who loses that amount if he challenges the

will, and everything else to the only other child, a daughter, who also happens to be the personal representative. The estate is fairly sizeable, and the son has found an attorney who has agreed to represent him in contesting the will. The basis of the challenge is that the signature on the will is shaky and illegible, and doesn't look anything like Mom's usual handwriting. The daughter points out that her mother had suffered a stroke prior to the execution of the will, but insists that she was lucid at the time of the signing because the daughter was standing right there and can testify that the mother knew what she was signing.

This appears to be a fairly strong will contest. The issues are clear: Was the mother lucid when she signed the will? Was she under the undue influence of the daughter? Was she even the one who signed the will? The attorney should work quickly to retrieve hospital records and locate the witnesses to the will, and perhaps even hire a handwriting expert to detect similarities between the will's signature and the mother's known handwriting. The attorney should closely question his client to try to determine why the son would have been essentially omitted from the will, and to see if there was indeed some coercion, even if the daughter thought it was in her mother's best interests. In a situation as messy as this, the attorney may counsel the daughter to settle rather than get into an expensive and time-consuming will contest.

Chapter 9

Guardianship and Protective Proceedings

Guardianship and conservatorship are among the most state-specific (some might even say idiosyncratic) areas of practice encompassed by elder law. Although the Uniform Probate Code and the Uniform Guardianship and Protective Proceedings Act have brought some consistency to state statutes, even those states adopting the "uniform" acts have tended to modify them extensively. This area of elder law practice varies widely by state, and the entire body of guardianship and conservatorship law is usually contained in state statutes even though common law on guardianship and conservatorship developed early. This chapter discusses guardianship and conservatorship proceedings including when a guardian or conservator can be appointed, who can petition for guardianship or conservatorship, the rights of the ward, the appointment process, powers and duties of the guardian or conservator, the role of the guardian in health care decision-making, conflicts of interest, and termination of the guardianship or conservatorship.

Overview

Q 9:1 What is the origin of guardianship of the person and guardianship of the estate?

Guardianship of the person and estate (or guardianship and conservatorship, as the distinction is made in more modern statutes) have a long common law pedigree. Originally, there were two different systems for providing for those unable to make their own decisions—one system for idiots and another for lunatics. Although the terms are no longer common, the duality continues. The distinction was once mostly functional—idiots (today we would use the much kinder term "developmentally disabled") were usually born without capacity, and could not be expected to improve. Their assets were taken by the king, and the king undertook a responsibility to care for them. Lunatics (today we would categorize them as mentally ill), on the other hand, had become incompetent but might return to competence. The king also took control of their assets, but had a duty to manage and use those funds for the benefit of the ward, mindful of the possibility that the ward might one day be restored to competence and require the return of his or her property. [See Louise Harmon, "Falling Off the Vine: Legal Fictions and the Doctrine of Substituted Judgment," 100 Yale L.J. 1, 20 (1990)]

Although those two categories from early common law development remain, a third important category has arisen that has become the focus of most modern guardianship and conservatorship law. The demented adult shares characteristics with both of the other two categories. As with the mentally ill, the disability may be of recent development. But as with the developmentally disabled, the condition is unlikely to improve. In fact, the early law governing decision-making for demented adults actually developed in a different context, that of civil commitment proceedings. Many states followed the lead of California in establishing three kinds of mentally ill patients who could be involuntarily committed: (1) those dangerous to themselves, (2) those dangerous to others, and (3) the "gravely disabled." This third category, although based in the nineteenth century management of tertiary syphilitics, established the format for dealing with at least the health care and placement problems of managing demented patients.

Regardless of the categorization or historical development in individual states, one thread consistently runs through the law of guardianship and conservatorship. Most states explicitly require that the primary interest of the state in such proceedings is the "best interests" of the ward. This focus has led in most states to two centuries of strong paternalism in dealing with the mentally and physically disabled—from suspension of ordinary due process and procedural rights to lack of mechanisms for consideration of the marginally competent ward's wishes, or the prior expressed wishes of the ward who has since lost competence.

More modern guardianship and conservatorship law attempts, however, to ameliorate those historical trends. Due process protections are increasingly provided to the subjects of guardianship and conservatorship proceedings, ranging from simple notice requirements to appointment of counsel to represent the proposed ward's wishes. Even after appointment of a guardian and/or conservator, the courts are increasingly turning to a "substituted judgment" approach to decision making by those surrogates, in which the once-expressed wishes of the now-incompetent ward are given strong preference in current decision-making.

Much of the recent trend in improving guardianship and conservatorship law can be traced to a single event. In 1987, the Associated Press (AP) undertook a nationwide investigation of local guardianship and conservatorship practices. In a weeks-long series of articles, abuses and failures of the existing system were revealed in individual stories. At the same time, virtually every state AP group prepared a thorough analysis of that state's practices to focus the public's attention on failures within each state. The result was an unprecedented public interest in guardianship and conservatorship, and a strong shift toward more modern laws in many of the states. Almost two decades later the effects of that news project can still be seen in the developing law of substituted judgment.

Q 9:2 What is a "guardian of the person?"

A guardian of the person is an individual or agency appointed by the appropriate court to make health care, housing, and other life decisions for a mentally incapacitated person. The guardian of the person generally does not have authority to manage substantial assets of the ward. Guardianship of this type is typically sought when:

1. An incapacitated minor reaches the age of majority;
2. The elderly parents of an incapacitated individual are no longer able to care for their child; or
3. A previously healthy person becomes mentally incapacitated because of injury, alcoholism, or drug use, or the onset of mental illness or dementia.

The very term "guardian" usually suggests guardianship of the person, although the same terminology is not used in every state. In California, for example, guardians are appointed for minors only; conservatorships apply to management of both personal and financial affairs of adults and married minors. [Cal. Prob. Code §§ 1500, 1800.3, and 1801] In Louisiana, the guardian is known as a curator. [La. Civ. Code art. 389.1, and 422] Connecticut uses the same terminology as California but in addition to guardians for minors, guardians are also appointed for mentally retarded persons.

Q 9:3 What is a "guardian of the estate" or "conservator of the estate"?

The conservator, or guardian of the estate, is appointed by the court to manage the assets of a person determined to be in need of protection. Some evidence is usually required that the assets would otherwise be "wasted," or improperly spent, by the ward. A disorderly payment history such as an occasionally missed utility bill is probably not enough. Such evidence must be something substantial; examples include, for instance, the vulnerable elder, absolutely convinced that he is about to win, whose entire monthly Social Security check is spent on sweepstakes entries and "Special Gifts Just for You" orders; the absent-minded widow with $1,000 credit on her account with one utility while simultaneously receiving final shut-off notices for nonpayment on another, or the confused elder who falls for the high pressure door-to-door salesman every month when he comes to remind her that it is time to reseal her driveway again. The guardian of the estate and the guardian of the person are often the same individual, but the court may scrutinize more closely the appropriateness of the petitioner when there are substantial assets at stake. A court-appointed conservator is usually, but not always, given the full authority to make all financial decisions for the protected person, including decisions regarding the purchase and sale of real estate and investment of estate assets.

For purposes of this chapter, unless the context indicates otherwise the Uniform Probate Code distinction is used: "guardianship" of the person, "conservatorship" of the estate.

A general durable or springing power of attorney executed by a competent individual provides the designated agent with nearly the same degree of authority as that of a conservator (see chapter 10); however, because of the potential for abuse the cautious planner may decide against signing such a power of attorney, opting instead to compel family members to go through the more burdensome process of court appointment so that there is proper notice to all interested parties, bonding of the estate assets, and monitoring of the conservatorship by the court.

Q 9:4 What is the Uniform Guardianship and Protective Proceedings Act?

The Uniform Guardianship and Protective Proceedings Act (UGA) of 1982 has been adopted in whole or in part in Alaska, Arizona, Colorado, the District of Columbia, Hawaii, Maine, Michigan, Montana, Nebraska, New Mexico, North Dakota, South Carolina, and Utah. In general, its provisions are also included in the Uniform Probate Code, of which at least one version has been adopted in whole or in part by Alaska, Arizona, Arkansas, Colorado, Florida, Hawaii, Idaho, Maine, Michigan, Minnesota, Montana, Nebraska, New Mexico, North Dakota, South Dakota, and Utah.

A new version of the UGA was finalized in 1997. The drafters sought input from a task force that included, among others, the ABA Commissions on Legal Problems of the Elderly and Mental and Physical Disability Law, as well as a variety of other groups interested in guardianship, such as AARP and the National Senior Citizens Law Center.

In describing the new Act, the Commission on Uniform Laws states:

> The 1982 Act, with its emphasis on limited guardianship and conservatorship, was groundbreaking in its support of autonomy. This revised Act builds on this and the revisions occurring in the states, by providing that guardianship and conservatorship should be viewed as a last resort, that limited guardianships or conservatorships should be used whenever possible, and that the guardian or conservator should always consult with the ward or protected person, to the extent feasible, when making decisions.

Q 9:5 What was "Wingspan"?

The "Wingspan National Guardianship Conference" took place on November 30 and December 1, 2001, at Stetson University College of Law in Florida. Sponsors included the National Academy of Elder Law Attorneys and the Borchard Center on Law and Aging. Participants included attorneys, judges, and others experts. Some of the conference recommendations are discussed in chapter 2 (see Q 2:7), and the recommendations as a whole may be found online at the NAELA website or at *http://www.law.stetson.edu/lawrev/abstracts/PDF/31-3Recommendations.pdf.* [Wingspan—The Second National Guardianship Conference, Recommendations, 31 Stetson Law Rev. 595, 596 (2002) ("Wingspan")] The one topic subject to the greatest amount of debate before adoption was the meaning of zealous advocacy as used in the role of counsel. The ultimate resolution of the conference was that a proposed ward should always be represented by an attorney, who should not act as guardian *ad litem* (reporting on the ward's best interests) but instead "zealously advocate the course of actions chosen by the client." [Wingspan No. 28–29]. Another important recommendation was the need for increased use of public guardianships. [Wingspan No. 44]

Q 9:6 What is a "public" guardian or conservator?

A number of states have established government agencies to act as guardian and/or conservator of incapacitated adults and minors. In some states the role is given to county agents; in others, statewide offices fulfill that capacity. Some states have established only one or the other (to manage only the funds, or only the medical and placement decisions, of incapacitated persons), while other states have combined the functions into a single office, or established two separate offices. Some states have created public guardianship or conservatorship programs only for larger cities or counties, or as a local option. In some states and localities, the guardianship/conservatorship functions are taken on by state adult protective services (or similar social service agencies), or are handled strictly by volunteers. In yet other states, probate courts can appoint any person to serve as guardian or conservator of persons without ability to pay, with a (usually) meager fee from a state or court fund. Most states have established some form of public guardianship for veterans; many of those programs date from World War II. In short, the approach to public guardianship and conservatorship varies tremendously from state to state.

Q 9:7 What is a "ward"?

Although the term is not universally used in the same fashion, the subject of a guardianship or conservatorship proceeding is usually referred to as a "ward." This term may be used expressly in state statutes (and may have a limited meaning as a result), or may be borrowed from common parlance.

Q 9:8 What is a "ward of the state"?

In a sense, every ward is a "ward of the state." Because guardianship and conservatorship law is primarily controlled by statutes, and the continuing management of guardians' and conservators' actions is directed by the court (which is, after all, one of the branches of the government, or state), every ward can be said to be a ward of the state. More precisely, a "ward of the state" is usually someone who has either been physically placed in the custody of a state institution (a state mental hospital, for example), or a person whose guardian or conservator is a state agent (a public guardian, for example, or a guardian whose fee is paid by the state).

Q 9:9 What is the difference between "incompetent" and "incapacitated?"

Because the term "incompetent" has such an elaborate history of interpretation (most of it imprecise at best), and because it had been so thoroughly co-opted by the medical field, the Uniform Probate Code introduced the term "incapacity" to describe the inability to make or communicate responsible decisions as a result of mental illness or disorder. [U.P.C. § 1-201(7)] Even states that have not adopted the Uniform Probate Code may have changed their terminology so as to use the term "incapacity" rather than "incompetence." Increasingly, the legal system is prepared to concede the use of "incompetent" to the medical community, except that it remains firmly embedded in the context of the ability to make a will or enter into a contract.

The latest trend is even to move away from "incapacity" as the term of art. The Wingspan Conference recommends that "[f]unctional and multi-disciplinary assessment be used in determining diminished capacity. The terms 'incapacity,' 'incapacitated,' and 'incompetent' should be rejected and in place, the term 'diminished capacity' should be used." [Wingspan No. 2]

Q 9:10 What is the legal meaning of "incapacity"?

The definition of "incapacity" varies from state to state. The Uniform Probate Code defines an incapacitated person as "any person impaired by reason of mental illness, mental deficiency, physical illness or disability, chronic use of drugs, chronic intoxication or other cause (except minority) to the extent that the person lacks sufficient understanding or capacity to make or communicate informed decisions regarding his person." [U.P.C. § 5-103 (7)] Similar definitions have been adopted in most states. In older statutes, one of the "reasons" given was often "advanced age." Even where "age" is no longer a justification in and of itself for a guardianship, practitioners may well find that a judge is all too ready to agree that a person over the age of 90 (for example) suffering from any more than insignificant physical or, especially, mental limitations should have a guardian, especially if the petition is presented by someone demonstrably concerned about the person's best interests.

Q 9:11 What is an "adult protective service"?

Adult protective services is a program that offers identifiable and specialized social services to resolve problems of abuse, exploitation, or neglect of an incapacitated or vulnerable adult. It is frequently a state agency designed to receive and investigate incidents of abuse, neglect, or exploitation of incapacitated or vulnerable adults and offer social services in accordance with an individual's needs and willingness to accept such services.

To address abuse and victimization of many kinds, state statutes may obligate certain types of licensed professionals to report suspected abuse. These statutes, known as "required reporter" statutes, may also provide limited immunity for reports of abuse by other persons as well. (This is recommended by Wingspan, No. 61.) The public is generally more familiar with the statutes that require reporting of child abuse than those requiring reports of "elder abuse." Such statutes may include a mandate that the state's attorney or other official pursue a report, and/or that adult protective services investigate.

A child may confide in a practitioner about his or her parent that "I am afraid that (s)he will burn the house down, but I don't know what to do." One solution may be to call adult protective services to investigate; protective services may then itself petition for a guardianship, acting as the "heavy," and the concerned child is then able to act in a more effective supportive role.

Q 9:12 What is a "guardian *ad litem*?"

A guardian *ad litem*, who in most states may be an attorney, is a special guardian appointed by the court to represent the interests of a minor or an incapacitated person in a particular legal matter. The use of guardians *ad litem* is common in divorce and child custody proceedings, in personal injury actions (where the action is sometimes brought by a "next friend" for a minor plaintiff), and in guardianship and conservatorship proceedings. The guardian *ad litem* answers to the court, not to the ward, and is not expected to act as the ward's advocate, but rather to act in the ward's best interests even when this may be in conflict with the wishes of the ward. A difficult question for an attorney appointed to represent the respondent (proposed ward) in a guardianship proceeding may be whether and when to request the court to appoint a separate guardian *ad litem*. This question arises when the attorney feels compelled to represent zealously the respondent's own wishes but feels strongly that those wishes are not in the respondent's best interests. The Model Rules would seem to permit an attorney to make such a request when convinced that the respondent is incapable; the difficulty is that in a guardianship proceeding, that claim is already being made by a third party and the respondent is in need of a truly single-minded advocate. In practice, rightly or wrongly, an attorney who feels thus conflicted will probably argue less forcefully as to the respondent's competence and spend more effort on limiting the extent of the protective action, validating the respondent's preference as to a proposed guardian, etc. (see chapter 2 for more discussions of these ethical dilemmas).

Although the use of guardians *ad litem* is still widespread in some jurisdictions, the modern trend is to assign guardians *ad litem* to nonparties who may be affected by the litigation. For example, appointment of a guardian *ad litem* for unborn and unascertained heirs and beneficiaries may be necessary in order to reach a mutual distribution agreement or obtain consent to a disclaimer by a trustee. Full guardianship or conservatorship (as may be appropriate under local law and practice) is usually required when an incapacitated person is a party in the action, for instance in a divorce matter.

Q 9:13 Are guardianship and conservatorship always necessary?

Guardianship and conservatorship will usually not be required in situations where the incapacitated person had signed powers of attorney when he or she was still competent (see chapter 10). If a spouse becomes incapacitated, the competent spouse may be able to manage the community assets unless or until a large transaction, such as purchase or sale of a house, necessitates the signatures of both spouses. If there is no general durable power of attorney and the incapacitated person has substantial assets (not held in trust or some other protective device), then conservatorship is advisable to protect those assets. Financial institutions, brokers, real estate agents, mortgage companies, etc. will not allow substitute decision-making without a general durable power of attorney (sometimes not even then, as discussed in chapter 10) or court-approved conservatorship.

Court involvement may not be necessary for incapacitated persons who have minimal assets and whose day-to-day needs are being met satisfactorily. The Social Security Administration, the Veterans Administration, and most private pensions recognize a less formal system for appointing surrogates to manage funds (such appointees are called "representative payees" by the Social Security Administration). For example, for the incapacitated individual with no income other than retirement and Social Security benefits, the representative payee system may suffice without any need for recourse to the courts.

Health care practitioners, residential facilities, and educational institutions will usually accept spouses, parents, or other family members as substitute decision makers for routine situations. In fact, a growing number of states (including at least Alabama, Arizona, Arkansas, Colorado, Connecticut, Delaware, the District of Columbia, Florida, Hawaii, Illinois, Indiana, Iowa, Kentucky, Louisiana, Maine, Maryland, Montana, Nevada, New Mexico, North Carolina, Ohio, Oregon, South Carolina, Texas, Utah, Virginia, West Virginia, and Wyoming) have given family members or others specific authority to make medical decisions for incapacitated persons; however, cautious family members may want to have guardianship in place in the event a crisis arises.

Recent interest in cases implementing the decision in *Olmstead v. Zimring* [527 U.S. 581 (1999)], requiring consideration of the "least restrictive alternative," have also now found their way into views on conservatorship. Early statutes often declared that once a court had found "incapacity," the appointment of a guardian was mandatory. More recent statutes will require the court to consider whether the appointment is necessary considering all other surrogates and arrangements that are in place to protect the proposed ward. In a recent case, *In re Guardianship and Conservatorship of Amelia Hartwig* [11 Neb. App. 526; 656 N.W.2d 268 (Neb. App. 2003)], the Court explicitly states that a guardian may be appointed only when there is a "clear and convincing" need for one, and that the durable power of attorney then in effect was the "least restrictive alternative" that was preferable. The Wingspan Conference recommends that "[s]tatutes require that guardianship petitions include a review of alternatives and a statement as to why none are appropriate" [Wingspan No. 20] and that "[m]ulti-disciplinary diversion programs be developed with collaboration among financial institutions, law enforcement, and adult protective services as an early intervention process to avoid the need for guardianship." [Wingspan No. 23]

Selection or Appointment of a Guardian or Conservator

Q 9:14 Who can petition for appointment of a guardian or conservator?

In most states, any "interested person" can bring the petition for appointment of a guardian and/or conservator before the court. Although the tendency has been to interpret the concept of "interested person" quite broadly, it is clear that the petitioner must have some real connection to the subject of the proceeding, and will not have standing merely because of a generalized concern for the well-being of similarly situated persons. For example, a right-to-life activist will probably not be held to have standing to bring a petition for the purpose of compelling continued administration of food and fluids, absent some actual connection to the ward in the individual case. An "interested person" also is not always going to be a family member. A long-time friend probably would have standing to bring a petition in most states. Adult Protective Services may also be able to bring the petition.

Q 9:15 Can an attorney petition for appointment of a guardian for a client?

Yes. ABA Model Rule 1.14 regarding clients under a disability suggests that an attorney may be required to file a petition for the appointment of a guardian or take other protective action with respect to a client, but only when the attorney reasonably believes that the client cannot adequately act in his or her own interests (see also Q 9:12).

Q 9:16 When can a guardian or conservator be appointed for an adult?

A petition may be filed for guardianship or conservatorship anytime, as long as the incapacitated person has reached the age of majority (18 or 21, depending on state law). Because the petition in essence requests that the court take substantial rights away from the person deemed incapacitated, a hearing is required and notice of the hearing and the petition must be given to the proposed ward, family members, and other interested parties. This process may take several weeks or longer. Notice may be waived and a temporary guardianship or conservatorship ordered by the court only if the petitioner can prove an emergency exists, for instance if the incapacitated person is refusing lifesaving surgery or is being victimized by unscrupulous individuals; however, temporary appointment of a guardian or conservator is effective for only a limited time and the petitioner must still meet all notice, hearing, and evidentiary requirements for the permanent appointment.

Q 9:17 When can a guardian or conservator be appointed for a minor child?

The loss of one or both parents may trigger the need for appointment of a guardian or conservator of a minor child. Even if the parent names a guardian or conservator for the child in his or her will, the designated guardian or conservator must still go through court proceedings to obtain such an appointment. Grandparents or other relatives may be willing to assume guardianship of a child if the parent is temporarily unable to care for the child, or if there is a residency requirement for a preferred school that the parent cannot meet. If a child is the direct recipient of substantial assets through inheritance, pay-on-death benefits, or personal injury awards, and no other provision has been made, a conservator may need to be appointed to manage the child's assets. Most states have adopted some form of the Uniform Transfers to Minors Act [see prefatory note, Uniform Transfers to Minors Act, U.L.A. Master Edition Vol. 8 B at 498], which allows persons who have been designated in wills or trusts as custodians for bequests made to minors, to manage those assets without court intervention (but statutory requirements, which vary from state to state, must be followed). Although parents may presumptively be chosen as a conservator for a minor's assets, a third party may be appointed if it becomes clear that the parents are inappropriate, incapable of posting bond, or otherwise disqualified to serve.

Q 9:18 What constitutional rights does the ward have in a guardianship or conservatorship proceeding?

Appointment of a guardian or conservator imposes limitations on the ward's freedoms. A guardian may be given the authority to place the ward in a hospital, to authorize the administration of sedating drugs, and to consent to the withdrawal of even life-sustaining medical treatment. Consequently, courts have consistently held that the guardianship and conservatorship process must satisfy the ward's rights to due process under the U.S. Constitution. [See State ex rel. Shamblin v. Collier, 445 S.E.2d 736, 191 W. Va. 349 (W. Va. 1994)] In order to meet this test, the ward must have a right to counsel (and may be entitled to the appointment of an attorney in every case, or at least in any case in which the request for counsel is made), a right to confront and cross-examine witnesses, and to compel the appearance (by subpoena or otherwise) of witnesses in his or her defense. The handful of courts addressing the constitutional dimensions of the ward's rights usually have held that the standard of proof must be by clear and convincing evidence—more than the "preponderance of the evidence" standard usually used in civil actions, but something less than the "beyond a reasonable doubt" standard employed in criminal matters. [See State ex rel. Shamblin v. Collier, 445 S.E.2d 736, 191 W. Va. 349 (W. Va. 1994); see also In re Conservatorship of Edelman, 448 N.W.2d 542 (Minn. Ct. App. 1989); In re Forward, 86 A.D.2d 850 (N.Y. App. Div. 1982)]

Q 9:19 Can more than one individual serve as guardian or conservator?

Co-guardianship and co-conservatorship is very common, and may be an ideal solution in certain situations. For instance, a family member who lives some distance from the ward may wish to share guardianship responsibilities with a close friend or neighbor of the ward, in order for the friend to have the legal authority to deal with an emergency situation, while the family member can stay fully involved. Co-conservatorship sometimes (not always) works when there are two family members who want control over the assets, and neither trusts the other to manage them alone.

The only drawback with co-guardianship and co-conservatorship is that some institutions may require signatures from both individuals, and this may cause logistical problems. The petitioners may wish to consult institutions in their area (banks, nursing homes, etc.) to determine whether having co-fiduciaries would be feasible. It is not clear whether one conservator or guardian can delegate to the other or to a third party (while remaining separately responsible).

Q 9:20 Who can serve as guardian or conservator?

State law will specify who can qualify to serve as guardian and/or conservator, and what priorities apply to the consideration of competing candidates. Some states require either guardians or conservators or both to reside in the state; some other states impose additional obligations of bond or surety on out-of-state fiduciaries. As a practical matter, the difficulty of qualifying for a surety bond may often preclude family members from serving as conservator or guardian of the estate, though some courts and jurisdictions misguidedly waive bond for close family members who serve as fiduciaries.

In at least two states (Arizona and Florida) a non-relative professional fiduciary (that is, one who receives a fee) is required to qualify under state registration or licensing provisions. This is also the recommendation of the Wingspan conference. [Wingspan No. 45–46] In other states, a court will be so hard-pressed to find an appropriate fiduciary that it will turn to attorneys, social workers and others who have registered as willing to serve in such capacity for a modest court-established fee (for those unable to pay) or at usual rates (subject to court approval), for those with means.

Most states also establish a priority list of guardians and conservators, though the court usually has full discretion to ignore the priority list or skip over higher priority candidates if it finds that the best interests of the ward require it to do so. Typically, the ward's own nominee will occupy the highest priority position, followed by any fiduciary appointed in another jurisdiction, and then family members in a logical order (e.g., spouse, child/children, parents, siblings, etc.).

Q 9:21 Must the guardian or conservator live in the same state as the ward?

Once again, state rules differ. In many states, the fiduciary must either be a resident of the same state as the ward, or must at least designate a state resident who will serve as agent for the service of process. There may be logistical problems with serving as guardian or conservator of a person residing in another state, but there are fewer legal barriers today than in previous decades. Most states (with the exception of Illinois, Oklahoma, and Virginia) will allow a nonresident individual to act as conservator for both minors and adults. Arkansas will appoint a nonresident conservator for a minor, but not for an adult. [ACTEC Studies, Oct. 1998, The American College of Trust and Estate Counsel, Study 3: Rights of Nonresident Individuals to Act as Fiduciaries in Various States]

Practically speaking, it may be perfectly acceptable to have an out-of-state guardian or conservator of the estate, but counterproductive to have a guardian or conservator of the person who lives out of state. The job of guardian or conservator of the person may require frequent personal visits, review of medications, discussions with physicians, emergency medical decisions, arrangements for transportation, and attending to personal needs. Unless it is clear that the guardian or conservator of the person is able to appropriately delegate these duties, it may not be possible for someone at a distance to fulfill these duties.

Q 9:22 Can an individual select his or her own guardian or conservator?

Fully competent individuals can sign powers of attorney designating health care and financial agents to manage their affairs when they are no longer able to do so. If the powers of attorney prove to be insufficient for some reason, and guardianship/conservatorship proceedings are necessary, powers of attorney may be presented as evidence of the proposed ward's preferences. Wingspan recommends that "[s]tatutes give preference to the person nominated in the advance directive, power of attorney, or other writing in appointing the guardian." [Wingspan No. 18] Some states specifically authorize a person to make an advance selection of conservator "for future incapacity," using formalities similar to those used for power of attorney or other health care directive. If there are no such documents, the proposed ward will have the opportunity to communicate his or her preferences with his or her lawyer, guardian *ad litem*, or other persons appointed by the court. If the ward is able to attend the hearing, the judge will usually make every effort to elicit testimony from the ward.

Most state statutes (and particularly more modern ones) give at least some priority to the person nominated as guardian or conservator by the proposed ward. Usually, that priority exists even if the nomination is made when the ward is already incapacitated. To help ensure that the individual's choice of surrogate is honored wherever possible, elder law attorneys should consider adding language to powers of attorney nominating an appropriate person (usually the agent named in the power of attorney) as guardian or conservator in the event a later appointment is made and, in those states that specifically provide a form for advance designation, should consider routinely suggesting that clients may wish to do so. Clients should be advised that the most likely scenario in which a guardian or conservator is to be appointed for someone who has executed appropriate powers of attorney is where the agent has misbehaved in some fashion. In such cases, the court hearing the request for appointment of a fiduciary is unlikely to honor the client's earlier nomination.

In *Conservatorship of Ramirez* [90 Cal. App. 4th 390 (2001)] the ward had named her son as fiduciary in her living trust and durable power of attorney. The ward's daughter, however, sought appointment of an independent, professional fiduciary. The court permitted the son to serve as conservator. The court reasoned that there was no evidence that the son had done anything but take excellent care of his mother, the ward possessed at least sufficient capacity to nominate the son as conservator, and her wishes were consistent with those in her living trust and durable powers of attorney.

Q 9:23 Why would an individual want to nominate a guardian or conservator?

Nominating a guardian or conservator in an estate planning document such as a living trust or power of attorney is a way to preselect, influence, or even compel the court's choice of candidate should the individual become incapacitated and in need of a guardian or conservator.

Q 9:24 What if an individual consents to the appointment of a guardian or conservator?

The court almost always seeks the consent of the ward, although it is not dispositive. Determination of incapacity is difficult enough for the ward; selection of a fiduciary whom the ward dislikes adds insult to injury, and the court will try to avoid any situation where the ward will not wish to cooperate with the appointee. If the ward consents to the guardianship/conservatorship, and if the petitioner has presented sufficient evidence and there are no objections from other parties, the court will usually grant the appointment.

In addition, some states specifically provide for a "voluntary" conservatorship appointment. That approach requires that the proposed ward himself (or herself) sign the petition requesting appointment and specifying the preferred appointee. If appointed, the conservator or guardian has all of the powers of one appointed in an "involuntary" proceeding (discussed below). For this reason, there are procedural steps to ensure that the petition is truly "voluntary." In Connecticut, the petitioner must be physically present at the time of the hearing, and the judge will travel to the petitioner's bedside if need be. The judge then advises the petitioner that a guardianship or conservatorship will severely limit his or her rights.

The voluntary conservatorship is generally intended to be less intimidating and demeaning to the ward. The ward is advised that the conservatorship is revocable: the ward may revoke the conservatorship within 30 days by notice to the court. (Practically speaking, such notice is a signal to interested parties that they may wish to institute a petition for an involuntary proceeding.) There is no finding of incapacity, which may be extremely important to the proposed ward.

However, in practice, the procedure may be more disruptive than the traditional "involuntary" proceeding. The very procedural requirement that is intended to make the procedure less upsetting may make it worse: the required attendance of the proposed ward at the hearing. Whereas in an involuntary proceeding the proposed ward may not wish to attend and need not do so provided he or she is represented by an attorney, in the voluntary proceeding the proposed ward is also the petitioner and must be present. The simple act of appearing in front of a judge (even a judge who comes to your bedside) may be more disruptive to a mentally impaired individual than any court decree of incapacity when all concerned are doing their best to minimize the impact of the proceeding and appointment on the ward's mental state.

The Appointment Process

Q 9:25 How does the appointment process usually proceed?

The person or agency willing to assume guardianship or conservatorship responsibilities must file a petition in court, usually in the jurisdiction where the proposed ward resides, and set a date for a hearing at which the petition will be heard. Guardianship and conservatorship issues can and should be combined in a single court proceeding. The petition must state reasons why guardianship and/or conservatorship are necessary, and why the petitioner is the appropriate person to assume these duties. Additional evidence, in the form of written reports or testimony from qualified health practitioners, caseworkers, and family members, should be submitted before or during the hearing to support the petition. Timely notice of the hearing must be given to the proposed ward, family members, and other interested parties so that they have sufficient opportunity to object to the guardianship or to the petitioner himself.

In recent years courts and the general populace have become increasingly enlightened about the rights of the mentally disabled. Abuses of those rights, particularly among the elderly, are on the rise. As a result, what used to be a rubber-stamp procedure is now set up in many jurisdictions as an adversarial process. The court will generally appoint an attorney, guardian *ad litem*, or other disinterested person to represent the interests of the proposed ward, and other personnel may be appointed to investigate the matter and make recommendations to the court. Most courts will require that the appointees address the functional abilities of the proposed ward; it usually is (and always should be) insufficient for a medical evaluator to make the conclusory statement that the ward "is incompetent and requires a guardian." Most courts will expect to see some explanation of how appointment of a guardian will improve the ward's quality of life or treatment.

Notice requirements will vary by jurisdiction, but absent an emergency the petitioning process should be expected to take three to four weeks. If state law, local practice or congested court calendars necessitate a longer period, individual experience may vary tremendously. Most states do have a mechanism for appointment of a temporary guardian or conservator in the case of an emergency, although courts may be disinclined to view the convenience or inconvenience of the parties as an emergency requiring special treatment and the suspension of the proposed ward's constitutional due process rights.

Q 9:26 Who pays for the costs of guardianship or conservatorship proceedings?

Theoretically, all court costs and attorney's fees to obtain guardianship and conservatorship are paid out of the ward's estate. In other words, the ward pays for the filing fees, service of process, fees charged by all court-appointed personnel, the fees of his or her own attorney, and those of the petitioner's attorney. Often, however, the petitioner will not have access to the ward's assets until letters of guardianship or conservatorship are issued. The petitioner may thus have to pay these costs and fees in advance (and if the petition is rejected by the court, may not be reimbursed for those costs or fees).

If the ward does not have sufficient assets, the court may assume the costs of those persons appointed to represent the ward's interests and to investigate the matter, and may even waive the costs of filing and service of process, if the ward and the petitioner are impoverished. The court will usually not pay the fees of the petitioner's attorney; therefore, the petitioner without other resources may have to seek the help of an attorney who is willing to offer services *pro bono* or at a reduced rate. Some states may use a court fund to pay fees (albeit minimal) to a court-appointed attorney for the ward who has registered as willing to accept such cases.

The costs of obtaining guardianship and conservatorship are usually given priority over all other creditors of a ward's conservatorship or probate estate (similar to the priority status of administrative costs in bankruptcy).

Q 9:27 How might the appointment process differ if the proposed ward objects to the guardianship or conservatorship?

The wishes of the ward should always be taken seriously by everyone involved in the proceeding, including the judge, regardless of the degree of incapacity suffered by the ward. If the ward objects to the determination of incapacity or the selection of the guardian or conservator, and unless there is dispositive evidence that the ward does not have the capacity to understand the proceedings, the judge may decide to reschedule the hearing and require additional evidence from both parties. The proposed ward will be given the time and opportunity to hire an attorney, if one is not already appointed, and to present evidence demonstrating that there is no incapacity and/or that the petitioner is not a suitable appointee.

If the petitioner presents sufficient evidence that honoring the ward's wishes would not be in the ward's best interests, or if the judge is otherwise convinced that the ward is not making a valid objection, the appointment may be made regardless of the ward's testimony; however, the fact that a ward can communicate an objection is often enough to convince a judge that the ward has the capacity to make the objection, and as a result the appointment may be limited or the petition rejected outright.

Q 9:28 Who, other than the proposed ward, might object to the guardianship or conservatorship proceeding?

As with initial petitions, any interested person may object to the appointment of a guardian or conservator (or simply intervene in the proceedings) in most states. Few guardianship or conservatorship proceedings are contested by either the proposed ward or any other interested person; experience suggests that the most likely contest is raised by a family member who feels that the "wrong" person is seeking appointment. Contested proceedings may involve two (or three, or more) different positions taken by various parties, and can and do often resemble custody proceedings, with the twist that the children are usually battling over custody of a parent.

Q 9:29 Does the proposed ward have the right to a jury trial?

State statutes may specifically provide for a jury right in guardianship and conservatorship proceedings. Although the history is unclear, it is likely that in the absence of statutory authority there will be no right to a jury trial. In states that have provided such a right, the jury may be advisory only. Whatever the status of the law in individual states, jury trials in guardianship and conservatorship proceedings are exceedingly rare.

Q 9:30 Does the proposed ward have the right to be represented by an attorney?

Yes. Everyone has the right to be represented by an attorney in any court proceeding; however, not every jurisdiction guarantees that an attorney will be appointed to represent the proposed ward, and if the incapacitated person does not have the capacity to find an attorney or the financial resources to pay for one, his or her rights may not be fully protected. The court may instead be able to provide some representation in the form of guardians *ad litem* or investigators.

Q 9:31 Does the proposed ward have the right to hire his or her own attorney to substitute for appointed counsel?

The proposed ward in a guardianship or protective proceeding may have a Constitutional right to counsel of his or her own choice. A problem may arise if either the court-appointed attorney or the court itself raises questions about the proposed ward's capacity to enter into a retainer agreement with counsel. Although the proposed ward is presumed to be competent to enter into the lawyer-client relationship, the presumption could be overcome by sufficient evidence of fact of the ward's incapacity. This can lead to a conundrum: The only way to adduce evidence of that incapacity would be to conduct a preliminary proceeding, at which the proposed ward would be entitled to be represented by counsel of his or her own choice. This is the dilemma that led the court in *Holmes v. Burchette* [766 So. 2d 387 (Fla. App. 2000)] to determine that the presumption of capacity should be applied, and that the proposed ward should be permitted to retain his or her own attorney over objections of the court-appointed attorney and the trial court's summary determination of incapacity.

Q 9:32 Can the attorney filing the guardianship or conservatorship petition also act as the proposed ward's attorney?

The petitioner's attorney cannot act as the ward's attorney in most jurisdictions, because there is a clear conflict of interest between the petitioner, who wants to override the wishes of the proposed ward by proving incapacity, and the ward, who either has full capacity (and thus does not need guardianship) or may lack the capacity to object to the proceedings and to his or her representation. Even if acting with the best of intentions, the petitioner's attorney by definition cannot advocate for the ward to the same degree as he or she does for the petitioner.

Q 9:33 May the ward waive any conflict of interest, so that his or her attorney may also represent other parties in the guardianship proceeding?

A ward's capacity to understand the purpose and effect of a waiver of his or her lawyer's conflict of interest is problematic at best. Because the court must be concerned with the ward's best interests, a waiver may not be effective and the ward's attorney may not then represent other family members or parties to the proceedings. [Guardian and Protective Placement of Lillian P, 238 Wis. 2d 446 (2000)] The recommendations of the Wingspan Conference (see Q 9:5) and the commentary on the revisions to the ABA Model Rules (Q 9:14) forbid an attorney for a proposed ward from representing the proposed fiduciary, although the attorney for the ward may file the petition for appointment of a guardian/conservator in some limited circumstances.

Q 9:34 Who should be called as witnesses in a guardianship or conservatorship proceeding?

Determination of mental incapacity is a serious matter: It legalizes actions that in any other context would be considered intrusive violations of a person's most basic freedoms and constitutional rights. To make such a determination, the court (and usually, the statute) will require much more than the petitioner's testimony. A medical doctor, psychologist, or other qualified professional to measure mental status and diagnose the underlying causes of the mental incapacity must examine the proposed ward. The current treatment regimen, including medications, and recommended level of care are also useful information for the court. The petitioner may wish to add testimony from family members, caretakers, caseworkers, and others who live or work with the proposed ward.

The petitioner who does not anticipate any opposition to his or her appointment may be able to meet the evidentiary requirements by filing documentation supporting the petition, such as written medical or psychiatric assessments and affidavits from case managers or caretakers. With sufficient documentation and advance preparation, it may not be necessary to have witnesses at the actual hearing (other than the petitioner, and the ward if possible).

Powers and Duties

Q 9:35 What are "letters" of guardianship or conservatorship?

Letters of appointment constitute notice to third parties that the appointee has been given authority by the court to manage the ward's affairs, and the letters will include any restrictions placed on the fiduciary's powers by the court. The order signed by the judge at a hearing on a petition for guardianship or conservatorship cannot by itself convey this authority. The clerk of the court will issue letters of appointment only when the petitioner/appointee has supplied all documentation needed to satisfy procedural requirements, such as evidence of the purchase of a surety bond. Some jurisdictions may require a sworn statement from the appointee attesting that there is nothing in his or her background that would affect his or her ability to carry out his or her duties, such as a criminal conviction, ownership interest in a nursing home, or removal from previous fiduciary positions.

The appointee ordinarily purchases certified copies of the letters of guardianship/conservatorship from the clerk of the court, and should always keep at least one certified copy in his or her possession. Other states do not use the term "letters" but issue a "probate certificate" or "fiduciary certificate" to the guardian or conservator. This serves the same function as letters of guardianship.

Q 9:36 Must a conservator of the estate post a bond?

A surety bond insuring the full value of the estate may be required by the courts, to protect the assets of the ward from theft or negligence on the part of the conservator or any other individual who has access to those assets. Although state statutes may presumptively require a bond, it will often be waived (if statutorily permitted), especially for family members, or if not permitted, may be reduced to "minimum" bond. Attorneys representing the conservator frequently argue for a lower bond, viewing the bond as an unnecessary cost or a nuisance. A better approach would be to advocate for a full bond in nearly every case. For a relatively low cost—roughly $100 for every $20,000 in assets, and a smaller percentage on larger estates—a surety bond protects the ward, the appointee, and the appointee's attorney; thus, many attorneys routinely advise their clients to post bond even when it is not required by the court.

The value of the estate for bonding purposes may include not only the assets, such as cash, real estate, stocks, or bonds, but also the annual income of the ward. The petitioner can reduce the bond amount by requesting the court to place certain restrictions on the conservatorship, such as on the sale or lease of a home.

Q 9:37 What is the guardian's liability for theft or negligence?

Sanctions for theft of a ward's assets or negligence by the guardian could include facing removal as guardian by the court, defending against a petition for surcharge to recover any resulting loss to the ward's estate, and possibly criminal prosecution depending on the seriousness of the crime.

Q 9:38 What is the difference between limited and "plenary" guardianship and conservatorship?

The guardian or conservator may be granted "plenary," or broad-based, powers by the court. Other than adhering to the applicable statutory requirements and code of ethics required of fiduciaries, these appointees are authorized to make whatever decisions are necessary to carry out their duties.

At times, however, such unrestricted powers are considered too intrusive. The ward may be capable of handling most activities of daily living, but forgets to take lifesaving medications. The ward may be able to manage a small checking account and pay monthly bills, but in the past has given large sums of money to unscrupulous individuals. The court will make every effort to allow the ward to maintain control over as much of his or her life as is feasible, and thus may place restrictions on the powers of the guardian or conservator, resulting in a "limited" guardianship or conservatorship. The court may also restrict the powers of a conservator over large transactions, such as the sale or lease of real estate, requiring that court permission be sought first.

Q 9:39 What powers and duties does a guardian (of the person) ordinarily have?

The guardian given plenary powers by the court has full responsibility for the care and comfort of the ward. The guardian decides whether the ward can live at home or requires institutional care, and arranges for medical care and gives consent for medical treatment. Whether or not the guardian is the actual caretaker, he or she must make sure that the ward is properly housed, fed, educated, entertained, and supervised. The guardian may hire aides to care for the ward—a necessity when the guardian lives out of state—but is still fully responsible for the ward's care. If the ward does not have assets substantial enough to warrant a conservatorship, the guardian should arrange to become payee of Social Security or other income and manage the ward's financial affairs. The guardian may also initiate lawsuits on behalf of the ward, and dissolve debts incurred by the incapacitated person prior to the appointment of a fiduciary.

In most jurisdictions the guardian must file an annual report to the court detailing the ward's care, housing, and health status. The guardian must verify in each report that the ward still lacks the mental capacity to manage his or her own activities of daily living, and must show that all fiduciary obligations have been met. Any change in address of either the ward or the appointee should be reported immediately.

Q 9:40 What powers and duties does a conservator (of the estate) ordinarily have?

The conservator of the ward's estate is responsible for making all financial decisions with regard to the ward's assets, including prudent investment of the estate assets, management of bank accounts and other liquid assets, maintenance of the ward's home, and preparation of tax returns. If the ward has an ownership interest in a business, the conservator may be required to participate in the operation or management of that business. If the ward has dependents, the conservator will usually be responsible for their financial support.

Upon appointment, the conservator must establish and maintain fiduciary accounts for the ward's money, then make a complete inventory of the ward's assets and file the inventory with the court. Periodic accountings must also be filed, detailing all transactions made on behalf of the ward.

The guardian's powers and duties are often compared to the relationship between a parent and an unemancipated minor child. The obvious irony is that the guardian may be the biological child, but the legal "parent." One exception to the applicability of the parent/child analogy: a guardian is not liable for the cost of care for the ward, but is only responsible for making suitable arrangements for that care, considering the ward's assets, the availability of services, and the needs (and wishes) of the ward.

Q 9:41 What resources are available for guardians and conservators in fulfilling their responsibilities?

Wingspan recommends that lawyers turn to the National Guardianship Association Standards of Practice [National Guardianship Association, "Standards of Practice," reprinted in 31 Stetson L. Rev. 941, 996–1026 (2002)] and "A Model Code of Ethics for Guardians" [Michael D. Casasanto, Mitchell Simian & Judith Roman, (Natl. Guardianship Assn. 1991). A copy of this work in PDF format is available through the National Guardianship Association's Web site at http://www.guardianship.org/ngamembership/modelcode], in absence of mandatory minimum standards. [Wingspan No. 65] A conservator or guardian whose ward suffers from mental impairment, whether lifelong (such as schizophrenia), the result of a dementing illness, or a temporary symptom of illness or treatment (such as dementia resulting from an infection) should have at least a passing acquaintance with the symptoms and treatments of these conditions. A valuable resource on psychotropic medication is the website of the National Alliance for the Mentally Ill; the local Alzheimers Association chapters or other on-line resources may also provide valuable information. When the ward's placement or care plans are at issue, the lawyer serving as conservator may also wish to consult other professionals not yet in place, such as care managers and social workers, both private and those available through a state agency on aging.

Q 9:42 What is the conservator's liability with respect to handling the ward's assets?

There are severe legal repercussions if the conservator commingles the ward's assets with those of other individuals, including him or herself. A conservator who commingles assets might be unable to obtain court approval for his or her annual accounting, or might face more stringent sanctions such as a petition for surcharge against him or her personally or his or her bond to recover any loss to the ward's estate, or even have to defend against an action for breach of fiduciary duty.

The conservator is also held to the usual standards of a fiduciary with respect to the ward's estate, including prohibitions on self-dealing such as sales of property to him or herself (without court approval) and the like. In addition, the conservator is charged with the duty to "manage" the ward's assets and prevent waste of assets. Some jurisdictions will simply require the conservator to preserve the ward's assets in their existing state; others will require a more active role, including the duty to act as a prudent investor.

In some states, the conservator has been held to have a specific statutory duty to "pay the ward's debts." Although determined not to be a separate duty to creditors, as is the case with the personal representative of a decedent's estate, the duty may give creditors a derivative right to sue on the conservator's bond (which may then result in a suit against the conservator by the bond issuer). [The Jewish Home for the Elderly of Fairfield Cty., Inc. v. Cantore, 257 Conn. 531 (2001)] In the *Cantore* case, the plaintiff nursing home successfully sued the conservator for negligence in mishandling the ward's Medicaid application combined with dissipation of the ward's assets on other expenditures during the application process. Conservators for wards who may require Medicaid in the reasonably foreseeable future should either be familiar and experienced with the Medicaid application process or seek professional guidance.

In addition, elder law attorneys are interested to determine whether a conservator of the estate of a disabled person under age 65 will be in breach of duty to manage assets if failing to request funding of an OBRA '93 Supplemental Needs Trust. [See Department of Social Services v. Saunders, Conservatrix, 247 Conn. 686 (1999)] In the *Saunders* case, the Connecticut Supreme Court held that it "might" have been a breach of duty had the conservator failed to make such application, given the obvious benefit to the ward (a younger person residing in a nursing home, already on Medicaid). [Id. at 709] For further discussion of OBRA '93 Trusts, see chapter 14.

Q 9:43 What should a conservator do when the ward wishes to have control over a portion of his assets, such as having some check-writing ability?

Conservators have generally taken two approaches when a ward wishes to have some direct involvement with bills and expenditures and is not entirely incapacitated. The conservator may either state that this is not permitted but perhaps make a small cash allowance available to the ward or, on some occasions, actually permit the ward to handle a portion of the estate on his or her own through a smaller bank account or large "allowance."

It is one author's opinion that the trusting conservator acts at his or her peril. Allowing the ward to handle funds, without court approval, in any more than a tightly controlled arrangement, is an invitation to be charged with breach of duty. If the ward were able to handle funds, he or she would not have had a conservator appointed.

There are assorted practical solutions to this dilemma. In some instances the conservator may wish to obtain specific court authorization for any arrangement that gives an allowance or otherwise re-entrusts any of the ward's funds to the ward's control. This might include requesting a limitation on the conservator's duties to specifically allow the ward to retain access to a specific checking account. The conservator can then control the flow of funds into that account and obtain records of expenditures.

In this modern age, it may also be possible to make arrangements through on-line account management. The conserved individual might have, rather than checks (which might bounce, resulting in liability), a debit card tied to an account with very limited funds. This would permit the ward to have access to small amounts of cash when desired with the maximum ability on the part of the conservator to cut off the flow at any moment. In addition, the debit card might be given a VISA or MasterCard imprint if the ward felt demoralized by existing without a credit card. Again, because of the card's funding limit, presumably this would restrict the ability of the ward to waste assets and simultaneously would provide the conservator with an itemized record of expenditures. Although the ward might make one large and prohibited expenditure, if the conservator is vigilant, it would be the last. This approach would be particularly helpful to minimize the demoralizing impact of a determination of incapacity for an aging ward not subject to financial imprudence or undue influence.

Q 9:44 Can a conservator or guardian secure insurance coverage for potential liability?

Insurance for fiduciary activities is available. Professionals who serve as fiduciaries should, however, review their own errors and omissions (malpractice) coverage and not simply assume that if appointed as a fiduciary, they are insured. This is not always the case. Bonding protects the ward's estate, but does not protect the fiduciary in the event of a suit for reimbursement by the bonding company. Wingspan recommends that "lawyers who serve as guardians should have professional liability insurance that covers fiduciary activities." [Wingspan No. 60]

Q 9:45 What limitations should be considered on a guardian's or conservator's authority?

Guardians and conservators are encouraged to allow the ward to make as many decisions as possible concerning his or her care, comfort, and finances. The court will usually make every effort to restrict the fiduciary if plenary powers would be too burdensome, and these restrictions will be reflected in the letters of appointment.

Certain rights are considered so inviolable that guardians may be precluded from substitute decision-making, at least without approval from the court. Incapacitated people fall in love and sometimes wish to marry. The guardian may support the idea of marriage and be willing to provide whatever assistance is necessary, but guardians generally do not have the power to prohibit a ward from marrying. A petition to the court and appointment or reappointment of counsel for the ward may be necessary. The guardian should not be allowed to vote for the ward, but may be able to assist the ward at the voting booth. Wingspan recommends that the guardian not have the power to consent to civil commitment, electric shock treatment, or dissolution of marriage without obtaining specific judicial authority.

When it comes to executing substituted judgment regarding estate planning matters, guardians or conservators are usually limited in their ability to make substantive changes. The old rule was clear. *In Sanford v. Hayes* [19 Conn. 591 (1849)], the court held: "The parties [the conservator and a contracting party] attempted to settle her estate, before she was dead. This they could not do." The court's concern was dilution of the Statute of Wills, and courts still share this concern. [In re Falucco, 2002 Pa. Super. 3, 791 A.2d 1177 (2002)] Exceptions may arguably be made where the change is in the *ward's* best interests rather than the interests of third parties. In one recent case a guardian/conservator was denied authority to amend the ward's living trust because the guardian/conservator failed to produce clear and convincing evidence that the proposed amendment was in the ward's best interests. [Guardianship and Conservatorship of Garcia, 631 N.W.2d 464 (Neb. 2001)] By contrast, when it comes to funding an OBRA '93 Trust, courts have held that the authority arises from the fact that the trust's establishment is in the ward's interest. [Department of Social Services v. Saunders, Conservatrix, 247 Conn. 686, 709 (1999)]

For that matter, the ward may still be capable of making his or her estate plan. Many incapacitated persons are capable of making a will; as long as a person knows what his or her assets are and to whom he or she wishes to bequeath them, the standard of competency for a will is met. The guardian or conservator who suspects that the will might be challenged may wish to better document the execution. Some attorneys bring in a mental health professional and videotape the proceeding, including an interview of the incapacitated person by the mental health professional about his or her wishes prior to the signing. Statutes regarding the rights of wards vary widely from state to state and should be scrutinized by petitioners or their attorneys.

Q 9:46 Can a conservator make gifts of the ward's property and/or engage in estate planning?

The power to make gifts to third parties from the ward's property, or to engage in any kind of estate planning, will usually be set out in the state statute, and in the absence of authority, may be difficult to exercise. See, for example, *Marcus' Appeal from Probate* [199 Conn. 524 (1986)]. The "best interest" standard would usually preclude such actions, except perhaps with respect to the establishment of an OBRA '93 Trust or the gift to a caretaker.

Applying "substituted judgment," however (see Q 9:48), gifts and estate planning (such as funding a trust with provisions for disposition on death) may well be possible, even in the absence of statutory authorization. See, for example, *In Re Trott* [118 N.J. Super 436, 440, 288 A.2d 303, 306 (1972)] in which the court authorized gifts anticipating the will of the 86 year-old incompetent ward, declaring broadly that such authority "inheres in a court of chancery by virtue of its position as protector and general guardian of all persons under disability," and that the guardian should act as a reasonable and prudent man absent evidence of settled contrary intent of the incompetent. Also, in *In Re Morris* [111 N.H. 287, 281 A.2d 156 (N.H. 1971)], authorizing gifts to minimize death taxes, the court observed: "the modern trend, both in England and in the United States has been to permit guardians to make gifts from the estate of an incompetent which are consistent with sound and prudent estate planning and which are in no way inconsistent with the needs of the incompetent." Lastly, in *Strange v. Powers* [358 Mass. 126, 260 N.E.2d 704 (Mass. 1970)], the court authored gifts to "charities, relatives and friends as would be likely recipients of donations from the [formerly competent] ward."

Given the possibilities for abuse, and the need to ensure no detriment to the ward, it is highly unlikely, however, that any gift or estate planning done by the conservator would pass muster if done without prior court approval. Even with court approval, however, it is questionable when and whether "Medicaid planning" by gift or transfer may be authorized. Some states are on record describing such planning as prudent and presumptively appropriate [In re Shah, 694 N.Y.S.2d 82, 86–87 (App. Div. 199), *aff'd,* 733 N.E.2d 1093 (2000)], while others have taken the contrary position. [In the Matter of Mildred Keri, 356 N.J. Super. 170, 811 A.2d 942 (N.J. App. Div. 2002)] While it may be possible to make a gift to a spouse, and it may also be possible to make a gift to children provided enough is retained to cover not only a "penalty period" but an entire look-back period, other gifts are considerably more dubious.

Q 9:47 What factors should a guardian or conservator consider in making decisions for the ward?

Because the guardian or conservator is acting on behalf of the ward, every effort should be made to involve the ward in as many decisions as possible. Those who are only partially incapacitated, or who have moments of lucidity, may be able to provide valuable guidance to the fiduciary. The guardian should make every effort to ensure some continuity of the more pleasant aspects of the ward's life, including visits from friends and neighbors, inclusion in family events, and participation in favorite activities and hobbies. The conservator must adhere to strict fiduciary standards with regard to investment of the ward's assets, but should try to manage them as he or she believes the ward would have managed them if still competent.

Q 9:48 What is the difference between the "best interest" and "substituted judgment" standards for surrogate decision making?

Guardians and conservators may assume that they should always act in the best interests of the ward, and at first glance this may seem a wise course of action. Under the "best interest" standard the fiduciary is required to act in the best interest of the ward even if the action is contrary to what the ward would have done if competent. In some states the guardian or conservator is statutorily required to act according to the "best interests" standard.

Many jurisdictions take the view, however, that this is a patronizing approach that does not take into account the personal preferences of the individual, and thus require that fiduciaries adhere as much as possible to the doctrine of substituted judgment. Under the "substituted judgment" standard the fiduciary acts as he or she believes the ward would have acted were the ward competent to act on his or her own behalf (i.e., in accordance with what the fiduciary believes are the ward's preferences). [See Rasmussen by Mitchell v. Fleming, 154 Ariz. 200 (Ct. App. 1986)] Most people do not act in their own best interests all the time, but enjoy the freedom of choice. An occasional trip to the casino may not be in the "best interests" of the ward, but it may give the ward a rare opportunity to cut loose and have some fun. A ward may be able to afford to live in the best assisted living facility in town, but may prefer to live with friends in a run-down hotel. (Even where the "best interests" standard applies, it can be argued that it is in the best interests of the ward for the ward to be happy.) Even applying this standard, however, the appointee must use care not to endanger the health or waste the assets of the ward in acting under the substituted judgment standard.

When the stakes are high, courts have sometimes applied an objective, "reasonable person" substituted judgment with respect to those whose incapacity is life-long so that no wishes have ever been expressed. [Strunk v. Strunk, 445 S.W.2d 145, 148 (Ky. 1969) (authorizing consent to removal of low-I.Q. incompetent's kidney to save brother's life)] The court may also apply this "objective" substituted judgment when there is no evidence regarding what the incapable person actually would have wanted. The court's decision in *Matter of Mildred Keri* [356 N.J. Super. 170, 811 A.2d 942 (N.J. App. Div. 2002)] includes a useful discussion of these approaches. An alternative approach is for the conservator to consider whether the ward's preferred course of action would be *against* his or her best interests and otherwise to seek to accommodate the ward's actual or objectively presumed wishes. [See, e.g., In re Trott, 118 N.J. Super 436, 440, 288 A.2d 303, 306 (1972)]

Health Care Decisions

Q 9:49 How should the guardian deal with doctors and medical staff?

The guardian has the power to consent to medical care. Implicit in the power to consent (and explicit in some state statutes) is the power to withhold consent for medical treatment. The guardian should not routinely approve proposed medical treatments; one of the most important duties of the guardian is to become familiar with the ward's medical condition, to understand proposed treatments and the alternatives, and to be inquisitive about risks, the likelihood of success, and the probable outcome if no treatment is pursued. When the medical staff has not made a convincing case for treatment, or is unable (or seems unwilling) to answer thoughtful questions, the guardian should not hesitate to insist on and arrange a second medical opinion.

Q 9:50 What is the responsibility of the guardian when the ward has been admitted to a long-term care facility?

Although the ward's daily needs may be taken care of in an adult care home or nursing home, the guardian's duties are not reduced by that fact. Monitoring the continuing care of the ward, discussing medical questions with doctors, nurses, and nurse practitioners, and reviewing medications and treatment regimens can be even more important when the ward is institutionalized. Active institutional abuse may be rare, but it is probably more common than most people expect. Even if uncommon, it is the guardian's duty to protect against the possibility of abuse.

Problems are much more likely to arise from inadequate staffing, facility inattention, polypharmacy, and the inappropriate use of restraints. The guardian's duty is to become familiar with these concerns, and to be diligent in monitoring the ward's care. Most advocates for the institutionalized elderly insist that the most effective method of maximizing the quality of care is to have active and concerned visitors on a regular basis.

There are any number of ways to become actively involved in the care of an institutionalized ward. The guardian can check out alternative facilities, request second opinions from other medical personnel, or hire professional care managers or nursing supervisors. The guardian should be available to discuss care issues with residential staff, and to suggest "drug holidays," reduced restraints, and adaptive techniques to maximize the independence of the ward.

Q 9:51 What is the relationship between a health care proxy or living will and a guardian's powers?

A health care power of attorney, signed while the principal was still competent, usually eliminates the need for a guardianship proceeding should the principal become incapacitated because the document authorizes an agent to perform in the same decision-making capacity as a court-appointed guardian without having to go through a court proceeding; however, guardianship proceedings offer the added protection of notice and hearing requirements and accountability to the court.

A guardian of the person should in most instances follow the expressed wishes of his or her ward in medical care decisions as in other matters. When the ward has previously made a clear expression of desire to have health care decisions made by an attorney in fact, the guardian should ordinarily honor that preference (as well as the health care preferences themselves). [In re Maria Isabel Duran, 2001 Pa. Super. 52 (2001)]

Q 9:52 May a guardian of the person authorize or direct the withholding of life-sustaining medical treatment?

State statutes may be unclear about whether the guardian has the authority to make this decision. If the ward signed a health care power of attorney and living will during his or her competency, the treating physicians may accept this as sufficient authorization under certain circumstances (see chapter 17). If there is some concern on the part of the doctors, family members, or any other interested parties that there is insufficient evidence of the wishes of the ward, then the guardian may wish to seek permission for termination of life-sustaining treatment from the court. The court may require appointment or reappointment of counsel for the ward so that all constitutional protections are met.

In some jurisdictions, the question for the guardian (or the judge, if the matter is submitted to the court) is whether there is clear and convincing evidence of the ward's prior expressed wishes regarding continued treatment. In most states the guardian and the court will be concerned first about those expressed wishes and then, if there is no clear prior expression of intent, about the "best interest" of the ward-with the realization that "best interest" can sometimes be served by termination of treatment. This may be particularly true when the burden of the treatment is substantial (e.g., it is painful or invasive) or the possibility of recovery is slight.

Recent cases reflect a trend toward permitting guardians to make the decision to withhold or withdraw life-sustaining treatment. [But see Conservatorship of Wendland, 26 Cal. 4th 519, 28 P.3d 151 (2001)]

Q 9:53 May a guardian of the person authorize or direct the forced medication of the ward?

The forced medication issue is one that has been a subject of news reporting for some time, particularly after notorious cases of crimes committed by patients discharged from mental institutions subject to a medication plan, but who failed to take their medication and committed crimes while delusional as a result of their psychoses. The guardian of a ward with mental illness may be confronted with difficult ethical dilemmas. If approached to give consent, and fearing the worst if consent is denied, should the guardian give consent, even if unsure as to the legal status of the consent? Or seek court approval that may be denied? Many anti-psychotic medicines have terrible side effects, and the ward who ceases to self-medicate should be an object of pity and understanding, rather than state-sponsored oppression. On the other hand, what of the risk to the public? Ideally, a conservator or other surrogate should try to resolve these issues with the ward at a time when the ward's judgment is not impaired and give the ward a chance to express his or her "better" judgment. These guardians could then adhere to these wishes in good conscience and present a better argument to the appropriate tribunal should that be necessary.

In Washington v. Harper [494 U.S. 210 (1990)], the U.S. Supreme Court established that individuals (in this case, a prison inmate) have a constitutional right to due process (although not necessarily judicial) before they can be forced to take psychotropic medication. Guardians who are lawyers should, of all people, wish to ensure that the ward receives due process to ensure that the need for forced medication is clearly established.

Fortunately, many states have specific statutory requirements for forced medication orders. In New York, a judicial finding is required as a matter of state constitutional law for a person who is "decisionally competent." [Rivers v. Katz, 495 N.E.2d 337 (N.Y. 1987)] The Massachusetts Supreme Court has held that to forcibly medicate an individual who has an appointed guardian, a judicial finding is required where the court must itself apply "substituted judgment," using six factors: the patient's expressed preferences regarding treatment, the patient's religious convictions, the impact of the decision on the patient's family, the probability of adverse side effects, and the prognosis for the patient with and without treatment. [Guardianship of Roe, 411 Mass. 666 (1992)] Short of forced medication, "assisted outpatient treatment laws" such as "Kendra's Law" in New York (Mental Health Laws 9.60) may authorize a period of "evaluation" (72 hours) without a prior judicial determination. A source of reference for all states' laws on mental illness is at the legal resources page of the Treatment Advocacy Website, *http://www.psychlaws.org*.

Proposals involving forced medication and/or required assisted outpatient treatment will no doubt continue to occupy the news and the mental health community. The attorney serving as (or advising) a guardian is unlikely to keep pace with these developments but should be aware of the seriousness of the legal issues involved.

Q 9:54 May a guardian of the person commit the ward to a mental institution and/or force the ward to enter a skilled nursing facility against the ward's will?

A difficult problem may arise when the ward's "behavior" is such that an independent living arrangement is no longer appropriate. State law may or may not address whether the guardian can call police or other authorities to forcibly remove a ward from his or her residence to be placed, even on a temporary basis, in a skilled nursing facility or mental institution, on account of dementia or other symptoms of mental illness. (Many laws authorize a physician or a police officer to involuntarily commit a person for a limited time before commitment proceedings are held, or longer if none are requested.) Civil fines and penalties may be imposed on someone who "falsely" causes an involuntary commitment, and the possibility of liability for damages for defamation, false imprisonment, assault and battery, or mere negligence should be a cause for concern. Involvement or approval of such a "forced removal" action without first-hand knowledge of the relevant facts could well be considered negligent, depending on the circumstances. Before undertaking such an action, the guardian should be sure to verify the facts, consult the appropriate authorities, and review the relevant state statute.

Some assisted living facilities may develop an end-run around the commitment statutes by forcibly removing residents on the claim that the residents are a danger to themselves or others. Once in a hospital, the resident may be forcibly sedated on an "emergency" basis by a physician, probably because the means of medicating the person will fall short of "forced medication," and he or she will be sedated to the point of being unable to assert objections to discharge to a skilled nursing facility or the Alzheimers' wing of the assisted living facility. A conservator, to whom this approach has been suggested, whether or not the strategy is technically legal under the state's laws, must consider the dreadful emotional impact on the ward that can result from such an action, quite apart from the liability issues. Should the guardian's cooperation prove unwarranted, the ward's wrath and shame is likely to pursue the guardian indefinitely.

Finally, any state policy encouraging or authorizing such measures may also run afoul of the Americans with Disabilities Act. In the landmark case *Olmstead v. Zimring* [527 U.S. 581 (1999)], the U.S. Supreme Court held:

> [U]nder Title II of the ADA, States are required to place persons with mental disabilities in community settings rather than in institutions when the State's treatment professionals have determined that community placement is appropriate, the transfer from institutional care to a less restrictive setting is not opposed by the affected individual, and the placement can be reasonably accommodated, taking into account the resources available to the State and the needs of others with mental disabilities. [Id. at 561-62]

The Court went on to state: "Unjustified isolation, we hold, is properly regarded as discrimination based on disability." [Id. at 556]

Conflicts, Renewals, and Terminations

Q 9:55 What if the guardian's or conservator's interests conflict with those of the ward?

When the ward's interests and those of the guardian or conservator conflict, the ward's interests must be paramount. This is true for two reasons: (1) the guardian/conservator owes a duty to the ward, and the reverse is not true, and (2) the ward is incapable of protecting himself or herself, and may even be unable to determine when protection is required. If the conflict is unresolvable, the guardian/conservator should step aside, and the fiduciary's lawyer may have a duty to encourage, facilitate, or even force that decision.

There are a number of circumstances in which the interests of the guardian/conservator and those of the ward could conflict. Following are two common examples:

1. The ward is facing years, perhaps decades, of expensive institutional care, and the guardian is the primary heir. If care is continued, the guardian's inheritance will be dramatically reduced.
2. The conservator is collecting a fee for managing the ward's estate. Assets are shrinking steadily. The ward now requires placement in a more protective environment, and the two final choices differ in cost by hundreds of dollars a month. If the more expensive (but more pleasant) facility is chosen, the money will likely run out in a few months, and the conservator's fee will terminate.

Q 9:56 What is the duty (to the ward or the court) of the attorney for a guardian or conservator if the fiduciary client misbehaves?

The attorney who knows (or has a reasonable basis to believe) the client has misbehaved in some way has a duty to the ward and the court system to take steps to protect the ward and prevent further misbehavior. An obvious conflict between the lawyer and the fiduciary/client exists, and it may be exacerbated by the source of the lawyer's information; if it was divulged to the lawyer in the course of a confidential communication, the lawyer may have a duty to disclose the information and a simultaneous duty to maintain the confidence.

In such a situation, the lawyer's obligation to the ward and system must ultimately prevail. As with conflicts between the fiduciary and the ward, the fiduciary's one-way duty to the ward and the ward's position of helplessness militate in favor of disclosure, or at least sufficient disclosure to permit the court, or the appropriate state agency, or the attorney appointed by the court, to end the abuse or exploitation. The appointment of a guardian *ad litem* might be desirable depending on the facts of the situation, the jurisdiction, and the attorney's level of discomfort.

Q 9:57 How often is a guardianship or conservatorship reviewed?

Most state statutes provide for an annual review of guardianships, and an annual accounting for the administration of a conservatorship. In order to permit the court actually to review the actions of the guardian, the guardian may be required to file a report detailing the ward's location, condition, medical treatment and contacts with the guardian. The conservator will probably be required to file a detailed accounting on court-sanctioned forms, and may be subject to audit or more detailed investigation based on the contents of the accounting.

Q 9:58 Must a guardianship or conservatorship be renewed periodically?

Unless specifically time-limited, a guardianship or conservatorship usually continues until terminated by the court. One common exception to this principle: A guardian's power to place her ward in a mental health treatment facility, or to consent to the administration of psychotropic drugs or other psychiatric treatment, may automatically lapse in one year under many state statutes.

Q 9:59 When can a guardianship or conservatorship be terminated?

Once again, state statutes vary widely, and should be consulted to determine who has standing to bring an action to terminate the guardianship or conservatorship, who has the burden of proof (and by what standard), and what findings are required before termination. As a due process matter, the ward probably has the right to initiate an action to terminate the guardianship or conservatorship by simply alleging that the continuing appointment of a fiduciary is not necessary, or is not in the best interests of the ward. Other interested persons (spouses, siblings, perhaps even neighbors and friends) will typically have standing to bring an action to terminate, as well.

Q 9:60 What is the appropriate test in a proceeding to remove a guardian?

Removal of a guardian or conservator ordinarily requires a showing of misfeasance, malfeasance, or nonfeasance on the part of the fiduciary. It is not enough that another proposed guardian or conservator could perform more effectively, or has higher priority, after the appointment has been concluded. The test for the court in a proceeding to remove a guardian or conservator is first to determine whether the existing guardian or conservator has performed badly such that removal is warranted. [Matter of Geldert, 621 N.W.2d 285 (Minn. App. 2001)]

Q 9:61 How is dissolution of a guardianship/conservatorship initiated?

In most states termination of a guardianship or conservatorship can be initiated by petition of the guardian/conservator, the ward, any interested person, or the court on its own motion. Although the burden of proof may rest with the guardian/conservator to show the continuing need for the appointment, there may be a presumption of that continuing need, which requires the contestant to produce some evidence before termination or dissolution can be obtained. On the other hand, a statute authorizing "voluntary" conservatorships will provide that dissolution of the conservatorship is effective within a set period of time after the court has been so notified, on a "no fault" basis. Parties can then seek an involuntary conservatorship if desired.

Q 9:62 What if the guardian or conservator can no longer serve?

Circumstances often arise when appointees are no longer willing or able to carry out their fiduciary responsibilities: they get older, they get tired of the responsibility, they move out of state, or the court removes them because of improper acts. Sometimes a family member is willing to assume guardianship responsibilities from a public agency; sometimes the opposite occurs. Whoever is willing to assume fiduciary responsibilities must essentially start from scratch, by petitioning the court for successor guardianship or conservatorship. Unless sufficient evidence of the ward's incapacity is already on file, the court may require the successor petitioner to have the ward reassessed by a medical doctor or psychologist. The petitioner must submit evidence that he or she is appropriate to assume these responsibilities; in other words, he or she must jump through the same hoops as the original petitioner.

Practice-Related Issues

Q 9:63 What are some of the practical problems that arise in the guardianship and conservatorship arena?

A guardianship and conservatorship practice can be as diverse as the whole range of human experience. The elder law attorney with a substantial practice in guardianship and conservatorship may appear before tribunals and agencies as diverse as the Federal Elections Commission (marginally competent wards frequently are caught up in political developments, and may spontaneously send large donations to favored candidates) and state adult protective services. Some common themes do tend to repeat themselves in guardianship and conservatorship law, however. The practice-related problems discussed below include: (1) representing an uncommunicative fiduciary, (2) determining whether guardianship or conservatorship are needed, (3) justifying immediate withdrawal after representing a client in a guardianship or conservatorship proceeding.

1. *The uncommunicative fiduciary.* Some months ago the attorney represented a client in her petition for guardianship and conservatorship of her mother. At the time, there was no objection from the only other sibling, a brother. He now calls the attorney and complains that his sister has moved his mother into a nursing home, but will not tell him where she is, and that he has no idea what the daughter has done with the contents of the apartment his mother used to occupy. Should the attorney continue to communicate with the brother? If the brother's complaints turn out to have some validity, can the attorney continue to represent the daughter?

   As long as the attorney communicates early in the conversation that her client is the sister, and determines that the brother is not represented by separate counsel, she may continue to gather information. A subsequent conversation with the daughter may reveal that there are in fact some excellent reasons for the daughter's actions—the brother may have been abusing or otherwise upsetting the mother, and the daughter may have felt it was in her mother's best interests to keep the brother away from both his mother and the personal property. If in fact the daughter is acting arbitrarily, the attorney may be faced with a practice dilemma. There is no conflict, of course, and she may continue to represent the daughter if she believes that she can help resolve the problem. Such family disputes can, however, be time-consuming and expensive, and the attorney must advise the daughter that her fees related to the dispute probably could not be charged against the conservatorship estate. If the guardian refuses to come to terms with her brother or refuses to pay the attorney's fees out of her own pocket, the attorney may withdraw.

2. *The need for guardianship and conservatorship.* The attorney has been appointed by the court to represent the interests of a proposed ward in a petition for guardianship and conservatorship. She visits her client at his home, which is littered with uneaten food and dog feces. The client appears to be malnourished and his teeth are rotting, and he appears to be oblivious to his surroundings. However, as soon as the attorney identifies herself, the client explodes, "I know what this is about! My kids are trying to run my life again! There's nothing wrong with me and I'll be happy to go to that hearing next month and tell the judge myself!" The attorney is now confronted with the classic "substituted judgment versus best interest" dilemma. What should she do?

   At issue is the client's mental capacity, not the dirty house or even the evidence of poor personal care. Guardianship and conservatorship involve severe restrictions on the ward's freedoms and constitutional rights, and the requirements for setting those restrictions are just as severe. If after a prolonged discussion with the ward the attorney believes he is competent, she should review the other evidence in the case. The report of the physician should be scrutinized, and if it does not include damaging mental status test results the attorney has a sound basis for an objection.

   However, if the client is having only occasional lucid moments, the attorney's role becomes less clear. Those adhering to the "best interest" approach would point out that objecting to the petition would lead to an expensive trial that the ward would surely lose. Zealous advocates would argue that attorneys should have faith in the justice system—that if the client objects, he should have the proper forum for his objection and all the attendant benefits of due process. The attorney in this scenario may wish to alert the petitioner's attorney to the objection well before the hearing, to give the petitioner the opportunity to beef up the evidence of incapacity.

3. *Immediate withdrawal following the hearing.* An attorney has represented a pleasant but none-too-bright client in his petition for guardianship and conservatorship of his aged mother. There are considerable assets in the estate, and the attorney helps the client set up a fiduciary account and advises him to keep track of all records. The attorney fears that the client, although honest, will not do a competent job of managing the records and check register and that the annual accounting will be a nightmare. Is he justified in withdrawing from representation as soon as the hearing is over and the letters of appointment issued?

   Attorneys routinely and with impunity withdraw from representation immediately after the hearing. The withdrawing attorney in this case would, however, be doing his client a disservice if he does not advise the client, in writing, of the client's obligations with regard to the annual accounting. The client should be encouraged to hire a bookkeeper or paralegal soon after the hearing to assist him with the books, and the attorney should provide forms and sample accountings for guidance. The attorney should advise the client about the kinds of issues he might face as guardian, including placement or health care decisions, and any reporting requirements or other obligations, such as an annual report to update the court about the ward's circumstances.

Chapter 10

Powers of Attorney

The power of attorney enables a designated individual to take over the affairs of another person in the event of incapacity or absence. It is really an agency agreement by which the person who signs (the "principal") grants powers and authority to a designee (the "agent" or "attorney-in-fact"). The durable power of attorney, which allows a competent adult to appoint individuals to manage his or her own affairs even after he or she becomes disabled, ill, or otherwise unable to manage his or her own affairs, has become a key element in long-term care and estate planning. This chapter discusses the different kinds of powers of attorneys, the duties and powers of the attorney-in-fact, and termination and revocation of the power of attorney.

Overview

Q 10:1 What is the history of the power of attorney?

Agency law is an old and well-settled legal discipline, with roots deep in the common law of England. Because of its lengthy pedigree, most mid-twentieth century observers would probably have found it difficult to imagine a significant new development in powers of attorney. Then, beginning in the late 1960s, a revolution in the law of agency was unleashed. Under traditional agency law, the agent's powers were limited to those possessed by the principal. With the principal's incapacity, the agent, too, was unable to act. The concept of a "durable" power of attorney—one that would survive the incapacity of the principal—may have seemed at first to be a logical outgrowth of the staid history of agency law. As it developed, however, it completely reworked the legal community's (and, later, the lay public's) view of powers of attorney. Instead of uncommon and fairly esoteric commercial instruments, powers of attorney suddenly became mainstream planning devices, with the concomitant pluses and minuses that tend to accompany such uses.

Contemporaneous with the development of durable powers of attorney as a planning tool, the general public was bombarded with messages about the evils of probate and the importance of avoiding court involvement in personal affairs at death. While most states responded by simplifying the process of probating an estate at death, the allied procedures for managing the affairs of a living incapacitated adult, guardianship and conservatorship, have remained stubbornly resistant to simplification. In fact, as abuses mount, most states have moved toward more restrictive and tightly controlled guardianship and conservatorship proceedings. This has created fertile ground for the further expansion of powers of attorney, both by creative lawyers and by eager clients.

One of the most dramatic of those expansive powers has been the use of powers of attorney to grant health care decision-making authority to a selected and trusted agent. The invention of durable powers of attorney, and the climate for expanded utilization of those powers, coincided nicely with the dramatic advances in medical technology—advances that are widely seen as part miracle, part terrifying personal burden. Lawyers and clients alike seized on the new concept of durable powers of attorney to create a whole new legal concept—the health care power of attorney.

Even as the use of durable powers of attorney has expanded, so too has the abuse of the popular instruments. It has become more important to ensure that clients understand not only the good reasons for giving a power of attorney to a trusted agent, but also the dangers inherent in that authority, and the importance of safeguards and fallback positions. In less than three decades of development, the law of durable powers of attorney has become one of the central issues in mainstream middle-class long-term care and estate planning.

Q 10:2 What is a power of attorney?

A power of attorney is a written instrument in which the principal authorizes another to act in the principal's place as the principal's agent. As a result, the agent has the "power to affect legal relationships between the principal and third parties." [Restatement (Second) Agency § 12] In other words, the attorney-in-fact has the power to obligate the principal and to act as the principal would act. The power of attorney can be extremely limited, giving the designee, or agent, the authority to make a single decision on behalf of the principal or to act in a single situation, or it can be so broadly written that the agent can do virtually anything the principal could do at any time. A power of attorney is effective only until the moment of the principal's death.

Q 10:3 What is the difference between a general and a limited power of attorney?

A general power of attorney is intended to give broad powers to the agent to make decisions on behalf of the principal, while a limited or "special" power of attorney is designed to restrict the agent's powers to, for example, make health care decisions during the incapacity of the principal or real estate transaction powers during the principal's absence. A classic (and common) example of the limited power of attorney is naming an agent on a single bank account, which enables the agent to draw checks on and make withdrawals from the account for the account-owner's benefit (usually to pay bills and take care of the principal's needs during his or her incapacity). Another might be the document granting a closing attorney the power to sign the deed when the grantor is out of the country.

Q 10:4 Are different levels of competency required for executing different powers of attorney?

Only a "competent" individual can execute a power of attorney (or, for that matter, any other document with legal effect). "Competence" is usually defined, in classically circular fashion, as the ability to understand the purpose and effect of the document being signed, to understand the underlying powers being conveyed, although the principal may not need sufficient competence actually to complete the tasks he or she is delegating by executing the power of attorney. [See Golleher v. Horton, 148 Ariz. 537, 540, 715 P.2d 1225, 1228 (Ct. App. 1978)] In similarly circular fashion the Restatement (Second) of Agency observes that the level of capacity need not be "contractual," but rather, "consensual," in that the principal must have capacity to consent to the delegation. [Restatement (Second) Agency § 20, Comment b]

Since a general durable power of attorney instructs third parties to recognize the agent's authority to deal without restriction with the principal's affairs, the general durable power of attorney and limited financial powers of attorney are very powerful documents. Accordingly, most states that impose statutory requirements demand at least one witness and/or a notary to be present at the signing of the document, as evidence that the principal was competent and not under duress at the time of signing. (In other states, this sort of requirement exists only de facto, because third parties will refuse to recognize the document without such formalities, or exists only for the conveyance of real estate.) Health care powers of attorney are sometimes held to a less strict standard—not because the document is any less important, but because even a partially incapacitated person may be able to understand the implications of designating a family member or close friend as the health care decision maker. Even these documents, however, often require witnesses.

Q 10:5 Can a power of attorney avoid the necessity of conservatorship (or guardianship of the estate)?

Powers of attorney are usually executed for the express purpose of avoiding court proceedings. A health care power of attorney can anticipate and preclude the need for guardianship of the person, and a general durable or springing power of attorney is usually sufficient authority for third parties so that conservatorship of the estate is not necessary. In many cases, the mere existence of a valid power of attorney will be found to be the less-restrictive alternative, obviating the need for a guardianship or conservatorship. The power of attorney may also give rise to a presumption that the agent has priority for appointment as guardian or conservator, even if the court decides to appoint a fiduciary in the face of the power of attorney. The principal should be advised beforehand of the drawbacks and benefits of each: While a power of attorney is convenient and allows the principal to choose the agent, guardianship and conservatorship proceedings ensure notice to all interested parties and at least some degree of monitoring by the court.

Q 10:6 Can a power of attorney ever survive the death of the principal?

No American jurisdiction recognizes powers of attorney after the death of the principal, although a few provisions purport to give agents authority to consent to autopsy or burial arrangements. Generally speaking, even durable powers of attorney end as soon as the agent has received information indicating that the principal is deceased.

Q 10:7 What happens if an agent acts *after* the death of a principal (with or without knowledge of the death)?

A power of attorney, even though durable, ends when the agent becomes aware of the death of the principal. Actions taken by the agent after the principal's death, but before the agent learned of the death, are valid and effective. Actions attempted by the agent after learning of the principal's death are void, although the affected parties may choose to ignore that fact, or subsequently validate the agent's actions. Theoretically, at least, an agent's actions taken after learning of the principal's death could subject the agent to not only civil liability, but also criminal sanctions, because the agent has no authority to take any such actions.

Durable Power of Attorney

Q 10:8 What is a durable power of attorney?

A "durable" power of attorney is one that survives (or comes into existence upon) the disability of the principal. Although "durable" suggests that the power of attorney continues indefinitely, even a durable power of attorney ends with the principal's death (or, rather, with the agent's knowledge of the principal's death).

Q 10:9 What distinguishes a durable power of attorney from a nondurable power?

At common law, all powers of attorney ceased upon the death or disability of the principal (except for those circumstances where the agent was unaware of the principal's death or disability). Legislatures traditionally avoided giving greater powers to agents both because of centuries of legal tradition and because the potential for abuse was so great, but eventually American jurisdictions began to acknowledge the need for an alternative to court proceedings. Pursuant to the widespread enactment in the 1970s of the Uniform Probate Code (UPC) and the Uniform Durable Power of Attorney Act, all states now have statutes that allow competent adults to appoint individuals of their own choosing to manage their affairs even after they become disabled, ill, or otherwise unable to manage their own affairs.

All durable powers of attorney must contain language stating that the powers given shall not be affected by (i.e., they shall "endure" through) the subsequent disability of the principal. In addition, a state may include other requirements. For example, North Carolina law provides that in order for the agent to continue to have authority after the disability of the principal, the durable power of attorney must be recorded. [NCGA 32A-9]

Q 10:10 Which is preferable, a durable power of attorney or a regular, nondurable power of attorney?

The decision to make a power of attorney durable depends on the principal's wishes and the circumstances under which the power is given. A nondurable power of attorney may be perfectly sufficient to permit the agent to complete a single transaction, such as the purchase of a parcel of real estate; in the event of the principal's incapacity it may even be undesirable to permit the transaction to be completed. A nondurable power of attorney does not, however, help in managing the affairs of the principal when assistance is most needed—after disability. If the principal's intention is to establish a mechanism for handling business (or health care decisions) in spite of incapacity, a nondurable power of attorney will obviously be inadequate.

By the same token, the principal who has given a nondurable power of attorney can rest easily in the knowledge that he or she will always be able to monitor the agent's actions. If the power of attorney is durable, there is real danger that the agent will take advantage of the principal at the very moment when the principal is most vulnerable. Because of the difficulty in setting up any sort of monitoring mechanism, durable powers of attorney are extraordinarily dangerous devices, and should be considered carefully by any client before execution.

Q 10:11 How is a power of attorney made durable?

The Uniform Durable Power of Attorney Act and the Uniform Probate Code use similar approaches: A power of attorney is made durable by the inclusion of language like "this power of attorney is not affected by subsequent disability or incapacity of the principal or lapse of time." [U.P.C. § 5-501] Most states do not require specific language to make a power of attorney durable, but a document denominated "durable power of attorney" may not in fact be durable unless it contains express language establishing the durability. A power of attorney may be made durable by language similar to that provided in the statutory provisions. Each of the following formulations would suffice to make a power of attorney durable under the Uniform Probate Code:

- "This power of attorney shall not be affected by the disability of the principal."
- "This power of attorney shall become effective upon the disability of the principal."
- "This power of attorney shall be immediately effective, and shall continue in full force and effect even in the event that the principal shall later become disabled or incapacitated."

Q 10:12 Are any dangers inherent in using a durable power of attorney?

Absolutely. As the use of durable powers of attorney has grown more widespread, reports of abuses by agents have grown dramatically in recent years. The very nature of the durability provision makes the instruments dangerous: Just when the principal is most vulnerable, the agent has unfettered access to assets. If the principal is incapacitated, the agent's access to those assets is usually also unmonitored.

Most clients cannot imagine that the person (often a family member) they have chosen as agent could possibly misuse the principal's assets. In fact, adult protective services workers, public guardians, police, and prosecutors uniformly agree: family members are absolutely the most likely individuals to abuse the authority given under a power of attorney. Clients need to understand clearly that the choice of whether to execute a durable power of attorney is really about balancing the risks. On one hand, there is the risk that the agent will misbehave, or fail to perform his or her duties. On the other hand, there is the risk that failure to make plans will compel family members to resort to the cumbersome, expensive, invasive, and debilitating guardianship and conservatorship alternative. No one approach will work in every case, and it is essential that the client be informed about the choices.

Q 10:13 What is a "springing" durable power of attorney?

At common law, powers of attorney always became effective immediately upon execution. The principal may not wish to grant any powers as long as he or she is competent. In most states, the principal may choose instead to execute a "springing" durable power of attorney instrument, which becomes effective only upon his or her incapacity. Typically, state law provides that a durable power of attorney can be made to "spring" into existence by the inclusion of language as simple as "this power of attorney shall become effective upon the disability of the principal." In other states, however, the power can only "spring" if it is triggered by a specified event, and an affidavit has been signed that the triggering event has occurred.

While in theory this is a common-sense alternative, the logistics of proving incapacity can be burdensome and time-consuming, and must be carefully handled by the drafter. The language must adequately protect the principal and his or her wish to have the power of attorney become effective when necessary, but must not cause the determination of incapacity to be so problematical that the convenience of having the power of attorney is lost.

Q 10:14 What is a "surviving" durable power of attorney?

When a durable power of attorney uses the formulation "this power of attorney shall survive the disability of the principal" (or similar language), it is often described as a "surviving" power. In other words, such a power of attorney has vitality and effect at the time of execution, and continues to be effective (survives) even after the principal's incapacity.

Q 10:15 Which is better in most cases, a "springing" power of attorney or a "surviving" power of attorney?

Once again, the answer will depend on many factors. Principal among these factors, of course, is the client's wish; common local practice and the routine acceptance of durable powers of attorney may also play a part in the choice.

For the client who is uncomfortable with establishing a currently effective (surviving) power of attorney, several points should be made. First, if the client is in any way reluctant to entrust the power to his or her chosen agent during capacity, the client should seriously reconsider whether the agent should be given such broad powers after the principal is unable to monitor the agent's behavior. Second, to the extent that the purpose of a durable power of attorney is to avoid the necessity of any formal declaration or finding of incapacity, a springing power of attorney will defeat that purpose. Third, the client should be reminded that establishment of a power of attorney does not limit the principal's authority; the agent is an additional person able to handle the principal's personal and financial affairs, and does not usurp the principal's own authority over those same affairs. Finally, the administration of a "springing" power of attorney may be more problematic: Banks and other third parties may be more reluctant to accept the authority of an agent under a springing power of attorney, and may require periodic demonstrations of the principal's continued incapacity.

All of those considerations notwithstanding, many clients will simply be uncomfortable with giving current authority to the agent. In such a case, the client's peace of mind should not be overburdened, and some sort of mechanism must be utilized to prevent current use of the power of attorney.

Some states (notably Florida, via Fla. Stat. Ann. § 709.08(1)) do not expressly permit the creation of a "springing" power of attorney. In the absence of statutory authority, it is probably inadvisable to utilize such powers.

Q 10:16 What is the difference between a durable power of attorney and a guardianship or conservatorship?

Although some states permit a competent individual to petition for appointment of his or her own guardian (or conservator), the general rule is that a guardian or conservator can be appointed only upon the incapacity (or incompetence) of the ward. A power of attorney, on the other hand, can only be executed by a competent principal. In other words, the central difference between powers of attorney, on the one hand, and guardianship and conservatorship, on the other, is that the former is a volitional act by a competent individual, and the latter are (usually) involuntary proceedings brought against an incompetent individual.

Beyond that difference, there is the immense gap in how these two kinds of proceedings are supervised. Whereas guardians and conservators usually are required to account annually (or more often) to the supervising court, may be required to post a surety bond, and may be removed for any reason by the court, agents operating under a power of attorney usually account to no one other than the principal, even after the incapacity of the principal. Although a judge may be empowered to remove an agent, or suspend an agent's authority, few agents ever find themselves in court answering for any of the actions undertaken on behalf of the principal.

A guardian or conservator is subject to the obligation under state law to act in the "best interest" of the ward, whereas the duty of an agent has a duty of "obedience" to the principal. [Restatement (Second) of Agency § 377] For an agency relationship created by a durable power of attorney, the scope of the attorney-in-fact's powers and authorities will be strictly limited to those in the instrument unless otherwise provided by statute. Moreover, the duties of an agent under durable power of attorney are considerably more limited, and depend in part upon the degree to which the agent appears to have accepted responsibilities.

A durable power of attorney is usually the preferred tool when convenience and cost-effectiveness are important and when the principal fully trusts the attorney-in-fact. Married couples are generally good candidates for powers of attorney, as are widowed parents who have a single trustworthy child. If the principal cannot name a trustworthy individual, keeping in mind that many otherwise dependable individuals might be sorely tempted by having total access to the principal's accounts, he or she may be willing to let the courts take over if he or she becomes incapacitated.

Q 10:17 What is the difference between a durable power of attorney and a living trust?

A durable power of attorney is a very inexpensive and (usually) easy-to-prepare document that allows the attorney-in-fact to make decisions for the principal during the principal's incapacity; however, even with gifting provisions it is not a vehicle designed for the ultimate distribution of the principal's estate to others. Because it terminates at the death of the principal, unless a will has been prepared the principal's wishes will not be honored past his or her death. A living trust, although more complicated and expensive to prepare, allows an agent much greater flexibility with regard to distributions before and after death. (See chapter 4 for a discussion of trusts.) For instance, a trust encourages distributions to beneficiaries in need of health, education, or support assistance, and of course dictates how the assets are to be managed and for whose benefit. The principal's wishes can be carried out through a trust vehicle for many decades after his or her death.

Even when a living trust has been executed, a power of attorney is probably advisable. Some actions are not delegable to a trustee (signing tax returns, for example, or the power to transfer assets into the trust's name), and so at least a limited power of attorney covering those items may be necessary. Of course, the same individual can serve as trustee of the living trust and agent under the power of attorney.

The living trust is also a contract whereby the trustee who signs accepts certain responsibilities towards the grantor and the beneficiaries, which may include the full scope of duties under the applicable prudent investor law. The durable power of attorney, however, is a gratuitous grant of power and authority that does not impose any obligation until the agent has agreed to act. That is, the parent who names someone as agent cannot assume that the same someone will actually be there and take action when needed; if, however, someone agrees to act as trustee, and signs the trust agreement accordingly, obligations are imposed that remain in place until the trustee resigns.

Q 10:18 Should an attorney agree to hold a durable power of attorney in escrow for the client?

One problem that frequently arises with durable powers of attorney is how to safeguard the document, make it available when it is needed, and yet simultaneously prevent its use before the principal has become incapacitated. One way of dealing with this dilemma is to use a so-called "springing" power of attorney—the agent's authority will not be effective until he or she can establish the incapacity of the principal (see Q 10:13). This approach does not address the possibility that a disgruntled family member might locate and destroy the original document (if, for example, he or she believes that it names the wrong agent), or that an overzealous agent might seek to establish incapacity before the principal would have wished. In some jurisdictions (e.g., Florida), the springing power of attorney may not even be an option. To resolve these problems, some elder law attorneys choose to hold the original documents (in escrow, as it were) for the client, and agree in advance to determine themselves when the power of attorney should be released to the agent.

Any agreement to "escrow" a power of attorney (or, for that matter, any other original documents) should be clearly spelled out, in writing, and specifically agreed to by the client. Such an agreement might provide, for example, that the attorney will release the original power of attorney to the agent only if the agent's request is accompanied by a statement from the principal's physician, or only after the attorney has separately met with the principal (his or her client) to assess the principal's condition and needs. Any agreement to escrow original documents places additional responsibilities on the attorney: He or she must maintain regular contact with the client/principal, and be prepared to take whatever steps are necessary to discharge the responsibility undertaken by the escrow contract (home visits, multi-disciplinary evaluations, etc.). The possibility of personal liability against the attorney/escrow agent is both unsettled and unsettling.

The principal may have concerns about giving copies of a durable power of attorney to the agent or other family members, or even keeping a copy at home, in case someone is tempted to use it with third parties to rifle the principal's assets; however, the attorney may not be in a position to learn of the principal's illness or incapacity until long past the time the document would have become useful, and may himself or herself become ill or die. A principal who is concerned about the safety of such a document in the hands of the agent should probably not have a power of attorney naming that agent in the first place—the foundation of such a document is complete trust in the agent, and if there is no such trust, then the principal may prefer to let the courts decide who should manage the assets during times of incapacity.

This is not to say that an attorney should not retain custody of one signed copy of the power of attorney. Attorneys who have good storage facilities and file retrieval systems in place can provide a valuable service by remaining the source of last resource when the original cannot be located and the bank will not accept a photocopy (no matter what the document, or the statute, may say). Retaining an original can also be a way to retain contact with the client, who will be sure to contact the attorney when any change is required. Attorneys who follow this approach should make clear to the client that a duplicate original has been retained and that if the client does wish to revoke the document, (s)he should be sure to contact the attorney to retrieve the document.

If the attorney retains a photocopy, but not an original, it may be possible to deal with the balking bank problem by attaching to, or inscribing the photocopy with a statement under oath (before a notary who affixes a seal) that the copy is a true copy of the original. Check state law to determine whether a notary can certify a "true copy" or not; if not, the notary must take the oath of a third party.

What the bottom-level official at the bank is looking for is the raised seal.

Health Care Power of Attorney

Q 10:19 What is a "health care power of attorney"?

Powers of attorney at common law terminated with the disability of the principal, so their use was limited to commercial transactions. With the advent of durable powers of attorney in the last three decades, the classical conception of powers of attorney has shifted. Concurrent with the development of durable powers of attorney, the science of medicine developed to the point where the lives of at least some permanently unconscious individuals could be maintained for extended periods of time. Eventually, lawyers and health care advocates began to recognize the utility of durable powers of attorney for health care decision-making.

Every state and the District of Columbia recognize some form of health care power of attorney. Although the concept has been modeled on the commercial durable power of attorney, the specific state statute authorizing a health care power of attorney may refer to the instruments as an "advance directive" (the generic term for health care powers of attorney, "living wills" and, in some states, "do not resuscitate" orders), a "health care proxy," or another similar term. Some states may have a different term for the document that grants authority regarding end-of-life decisions than is used for more routine health care decisions. Regardless of the state's choice of terminology, the documents have the same effect as any other durable power of attorney, except that the purpose is to provide for medical and personal, rather than commercial or financial, decision-making. (See chapter 17 for a discussion of health care decision-making.)

Q 10:20 Can the health care power of attorney be combined with a general financial power of attorney?

Although most states may permit health care powers to be incorporated into a general durable power of attorney, some attorneys prefer to separate the two kinds of documents. Clients may want to separate the duties, with one person handling financial matters and another making medical decisions. Privacy principles also militate in favor of separate documents; while most clients will want to maintain the privacy of their financial powers of attorney, multiple copies of a health care power of attorney can and should be distributed to family members, health care providers, religious advisers, and friends. On the other hand, if the client intends to distribute both documents, and both documents will name the same agents (for example: the spouse; the trusted only child), a single form may be used unless state law provides otherwise.

Attorney-in-Fact

Designation and Qualifications

Q 10:21 What is the proper title for a person who has been given a power of attorney?

The person designated to act for the principal (the signer of the power of attorney) is properly referred to as the agent or attorney-in-fact. The agent is universally and incorrectly described by most laypersons as "the power-of-attorney" (see also Q 10:26). In other words, in common parlance the distinction between the document and the holder of the power is often lost.

Q 10:22 What qualifications are required of an attorney-in-fact?

In most states, any competent adult can be named as attorney-in-fact. Although there may be no formal requirements for being an agent, the principal should establish appropriate minimum qualifications (depending on the nature and type of decisions that will need to be made, the number of persons affected by the agent's decisions, and the imminent or distant likelihood of need for the agent to act). Ideally, any agent should:

1. Be conversant with the types of investments, income, and assets held by the principal;
2. Be familiar with the principal and his or her family background, preferences, and any special needs of either the principal or those reliant on him or her;

3. Have a sufficiently professional background, and a long enough (and strong enough) tie to the principal, to ensure availability when called upon to act;
4. If possible, have some prior experience with managing the affairs of another individual;
5. Have ready access to social service, financial and investment, health care, and other professionals, and be willing to utilize those experts in determining the best course of action for the principal's benefit.

In practice, however, the principal may well select an agent who is a close family member but otherwise meets none of these qualifications, and indeed the principal may have no other available choices. In that situation the agent really must possess two qualifications: (1) honest dedication to the principal and a good-faith commitment to fulfilling the principal's wishes; and (2) the wisdom to know where to go for help—with an attorney being a good start, and the principal's attorney usually a reasonable choice for advice, even though potential conflicts may limit that advice to a referral to a separate practitioner.

Q 10:23 Can or should a trustee also be an attorney-in-fact?

When an estate plan includes both a trust and a durable power of attorney for financial matters, the trustee and agent may be the same person. In fact, the duties of an agent and a trustee are often similar, and there may be some problems of overlapping powers and responsibilities if the same person does not fill both offices. In some cases, there may be good reason to name a nontrustee as agent. Corporate trustees, for example, usually will decline to act as agent under a power of attorney; it may be necessary to name an individual as agent to transfer assets into the trust, to execute tax returns, and to complete other ministerial (but essential) acts. It may also be appropriate in some circumstances to name a separate agent precisely to provide an appropriate person to oversee the actions of the trustee; an agent might, for example, be authorized to compel an accounting from the trustee and/or to bring a court action for accounting by or instruction of the trustee.

Q 10:24 How many attorneys-in-fact should a power of attorney name?

The answer to this question may depend upon whether under state law it is possible or customary to name multiple attorneys to serve in succession. Just as it is usually preferable to include a successor personal representative if the first-named cannot serve, it is usually prudent to consider what will happen if the preferred attorney-in-fact cannot serve.

If a state does not clearly authorize successors (see Q 10:25), it may be appropriate (or even necessary) to appoint multiple agents each with the power to act independently of the other. The principal can always acknowledge in a separate writing that while all are given equal powers to act, it is the principal's preference and intention that they act sequentially. This instruction will be binding upon the agents who are aware of it, but will not restrain the freedom of third parties to rely upon the orders of any of the agents. That is, the third party will not feel any need to investigate the agent's authority, which is the entire purpose of a durable power of attorney. The principal may also handle this by only giving a copy to the "preferred" agent but letting the family know others may be able to act if necessary. Of course, this may only work in a relatively harmonious (or obedient) family unit.

Certainly it is easier for a single individual to be able to make decisions quickly and without hindrance, and with a single agent obviously only one signature will be required on legal documents, checks, etc. Sometimes, however, the principal may prefer to name two persons so that a system of checks and balances is established, or to avoid showing preference for one family member over another. (Of course, there is an argument that if the principal does not trust one agent alone to handle the job, but prefers to appoint two so that each can monitor the other, then perhaps a power of attorney is not appropriate at all.

Unless the power of attorney expressly permits the multiple agents to act independently of one another, most third parties will require the signatures of every agent before permitting a given transaction, which is cumbersome if even one agent lives out of state. Therefore, in order to delineate clearly the powers of each agent when multiple agents are named, the language appointing agents should be formulated as either: "I hereby appoint X and Y as my attorneys-in-fact, with the express authority to act independently of one another" or "I hereby appoint X and Y as my attorneys-in-fact, with the requirement that they act together in all instances." With more than two agents, the drafter might choose to provide that a majority of the agents could act without the consent (or over the objections) of the remaining agent(s).

Q 10:25 Can the principal provide for a successor attorney-in-fact?

If state law permits, not only can a successor attorney-in-fact be named, but it is almost always a desirable step for the principal to take. Of course, the naming of an alternate or successor complicates things somewhat—it now becomes necessary to describe the circumstances under which the successor will succeed to the authority of the attorney-in-fact. The successor might be empowered to act only upon the death of the primary agent, or upon death or disappearance, or death, disappearance, or disability (which itself needs definition). It may be sufficient to authorize the successor agent to execute an affidavit setting forth the inability of the primary agent to act (or the unavailability of the primary agent):

> I hereby appoint X to serve as my agent. I also appoint Y to serve as alternate agent hereunder but without authority to exercise any of the powers set forth as follows except that if my agent shall be unable or unwilling to serve or to continue to serve as such agent, then my alternate agent shall be fully authorized to serve hereunder and shall have all of the powers granted originally to my agent. My alternate agent may execute and attach hereto an affidavit to the effect that my agent is unwilling or unable to serve or to continue to serve. Such affidavit shall be conclusive evidence insofar as third parties are concerned of the facts set forth, and any person acting in reliance upon such affidavit shall incur no liability because of such reliance.

This does, however, to some extent recreate the problems inherent in any springing power of attorney (see Q 10:13). For this reason, naming alternates, rather than successors, is sometimes simpler and equally effective, unless clashes are likely to occur.

State law or the document may also authorize the agent to delegate powers—in effect allowing the agent to name a substitute to act in his or her place. If no successor or alternate attorney-in-fact is named, upon the death or incapacity of the agent the power of attorney ceases to be useful. This is also true if all named successors die or themselves become incapacitated. Agency law does not authorize an attorney-in-fact to name his or her successor, unless the power of attorney itself authorizes such an arrangement. Consequently, it is important to gauge the need for multiple attorneys-in-fact, and to name an appropriate number of successors or alternates based on the age and medical condition of the principal and of each of the named agents.

Q 10:26 How should an attorney-in-fact sign documents on the principal's behalf?

The attorney-in-fact may sign his or her own name and add some evidence of the authority to do so, such as "Jane Doe, POA," or "Jane Doe, as agent for Mary Roe under POA dated...." Alternatively, the principal may sign as "Mary Roe, by her agent Jane Doe" or "Mary Roe, by Jane Doe DPOA." While it is usually permissible for the agent simply to sign the principal's name, without disclosing the existence of the agency relationship, clearly indicating the status as agent or attorney-in-fact is preferable in most cases.

Duties and Powers

Q 10:27 What duties and liabilities does an attorney-in-fact have?

The attorney-in-fact has the duties of an agent. The core duty of an agent is loyalty to the principal. "An agent owes a duty of 'utmost loyalty' and fidelity to a principal." [Gussin v. Shockey, 933 F.3d 1001 (4th Cir. 1991), *citing* King v. Bankerd, 492 A.2d 608, 613 (Md. 1985)] Although the instrument may empower the agent to do just about anything with the principal's assets, the agent's actions and decisions must be solely for the benefit of the principal absent express instruction to the contrary.

The agent's duties are to be determined in the first instance by the terms of the instrument. [Restatement (Second) Agency § 376] It is in the absence of such direction that the duties to act in the principal's interests will control. [Restatement (Second) Agency, Ch. 13] Therefore, the principal may specifically empower the attorney-in-fact to take any steps that do not violate law or public policy. Thus, a power of attorney might specifically authorize gifts in the agent's discretion or (more safely) in accordance with the principal's prior pattern of giving.

In one situation, the agent designated may have no duties. According to the Restatement, if the instrument is really a unilateral contract in which the agent makes no promises, even if the principal has promised to compensate the agent for the agent's actions, the agent would not be liable for failing to act. [Restatement (Second) Agency § 377]

In another situation, where the client names a family member who will serve without compensation, the duties may be quite minimal. The Restatement proposes as the duties of the "gratuitous agent" loyal service; the duty to account; the duty to be obedient to reasonable orders of the principal; and a duty of care factoring in the fact that the services are being performed gratuitously. [Restatement (Second) of Agency § 378, Comment d] However, the agent may also decide to stop acting as agent, and provided that there has been no detrimental reliance by the principal, the agent should not be liable.

Finally, even if the agent has a duty to act with "care" in performing services, the standard of care of the gratuitous agent is limited to that that would "customarily" be imposed on a similar gratuitous agent. [Restatement (Second) of Agency § 379(2)] The agent who has told the principal of the agent's lack of skill does not violate duties to the principal in management of the principal's property if the agent exercises as much skill as the agent in fact possesses. [Restatement (Second) of Agency § 376, Comment d]

By contrast, the professional employed to manage the principal's investments as an agent are subject to the full requirements of "prudent investing" by fiduciaries.

Q 10:28 Does the attorney-in-fact have any duties or liabilities to third parties?

Unlike a personal representative, an attorney-in-fact does not owe a duty to third parties or creditors of the principal. Depending on the circumstances, the agent may have a duty to pay the principal's bills, however. Although the law is not settled in this area, the Restatement (Second) of Agency suggests that affirmative duties of this nature may arise from (1) the terms of the instrument if the agent named has in fact "accepted" the agency, especially for compensation, and/or (2) if the agent creates a situation where one would rely upon the agency, e.g., the principal names an agent and believes that the agent is paying the bills, and the agent does not tell the principal that the agent has decided not to accept the agency. [Restatement (Second) of Agency § 378] Whether or not the agent might be liable to a third party would depend on either a third-party beneficiary theory, or the principal having assigned its claims to the third party (such as the state Medicaid agency).

The courts so far have appeared reluctant to impose upon the agent the same liability that would have been imposed upon the principal. In one case, a nursing home with a judgment against a resident brought proceedings against the resident's attorneys in fact, alleging that they had a fiduciary duty to account to the principal and that the creditor could assert the right to such accounting. The creditor then deemed the accounting inadequate and argued that the agent had the burden of proving the accuracy of their accounting and the validity of expenditures. The Indiana appellate court affirmed the trial court's denial, holding that the burden of proof of showing the breach of fiduciary duty lay with the creditor. [WW Extended Care, Inc. v. Swinkunas, 764 N.E.2d 787 (Ind. App. 2002)]

Q 10:29 What rules apply to the attorney-in-fact's management of the principal's assets?

The extent of the attorney-in-fact's duties, as discussed above, vary depending upon the gratuitous or compensatory nature of the relationship, and the level of skill that the agent has held out himself or herself to possess (see Q 10:27).

Assuming that the attorney-in-fact is a professional or otherwise would have investment skills, and is being compensated to "manage" the principal's assets, the attorney-in-fact has a duty to apply appropriate principles to the investment and management of the principal's funds. The "prudent person" rule applies to all fiduciaries, and requires that the attorney-in-fact manage and invest the principal's assets as a prudent person would when dealing with the assets of another. In some jurisdictions, the prudent person rule has been replaced or supplemented with the "prudent investor" rule; the principal difference to the fiduciary is that the latter rule evaluates the total investment portfolio and approach, rather than encouraging after-the-fact judgment of individual investments. Under the Restatement formulation, however, the duty of a prudent investor arises *only* if the agent has agreed to "manage" the funds; if the agent has only agreed to "invest," the agent may not be liable for simply preserving the status quo. [Restatement (Second) of Agency § 425]

In the more common situation, however, it must be remembered that the power of attorney creates an agency relationship, not a trust. Instead the agent has a more passive duty, the duty not to intentionally cause harm to the principal or to contravene the principal's instructions as set forth in the instrument. Once the agent has gratuitously undertaken to manage the principal's assets, presumably the duty of care would apply—like other Good Samaritans, the gratuitous agent may still be liable for making matters worse.

In order to prevent unintended liability being imposed on the principal's near and dear serving as the client's attorney-in-fact, the client may wish to include in the document an express liability waiver, for example:

> I hereby exonerate my attorney(s)-in-fact from liability arising from actions taken in good faith and decisions not to act made in good faith pursuant to the authority granted by this instrument.

Either way, however, the agent must assume that even though the power of attorney is not likely to come under the scrutiny of the courts, any challenge to the exercise of his or her powers may trigger close scrutiny. Appropriately conservative investment strategies, careful recordkeeping, and reliance on professional advice and recommendations are essential. In particular, recordkeeping should be able to show clearly that no improprieties have been committed by the agent; inability to explain where the funds have gone may be interpreted as misappropriation.

Q 10:30 How should a durable power of attorney be drafted?

There are two basic approaches to the preparation of a durable power of attorney.

The first is to locate the statutorily approved form for the client's residence, and either use it "as is," or add additional language, subject to any requirements the statute may specify regarding such additions. This approach often has the virtue of brevity, as "statutory form" durable powers of attorney typically include a list of itemized powers that incorporate by reference vast sections of statutory detail. It is also probably the most practical provided the principal is virtually certain to remain in the same state and will not be dealing extensively with out-of-state institutions or real estate. (Even if there are out-of-state intangible assets, this approach may work although it can be advisable to provide a photocopy of the relevant state statute by way of explanation.) Some states may either require that the state form, and no other, be accepted, or require institutions to accept the state form, but not others.

There are drawbacks, however. The true breadth of the itemized powers may be lost on the client, despite the usual language at the top that "THESE POWERS ARE BROAD AND SWEEPING," because the client simply treats the document as a form to be signed and forgotten. The agent is unlikely to have a copy of the statute handy and the lawyer may not wish to provide the fifty-odd pages of statute required to interpret the form. The form may also be unintelligible to an out-of-state institution. Finally, and importantly, the form may be inadequate to convey real estate located in another state.

What is the alternative? Many attorneys use what is known as a "manuscripted," or longhand, durable power of attorney document. This document follows whatever execution requirements the state may impose but rather than using a concise statutory reference, will describe the agent's powers in detail. Even with a manuscripted document, however, as with all legal drafting, there are generally two extremes between which the attorney must either choose, or compromise. The most common is perhaps the "kitchen sink" approach, which can come close to duplicating the lengthy statutory descriptions, with further additions where the statute is inadequate. This may be the "safest" approach to getting the institution to accept the agent's power, and will also be safest in addressing the various particular tax, Medicaid planning, and other issues. Unfortunately, it may result in a 20-page document for a client that expected something "simpler" than a guardianship. The other approach is the "K.I.S.S." approach, intended so that a fairly unsophisticated client will be comfortable actually reading the document and having a reasonable grasp of the principal's rights and agent's powers. This might result in a one-, two-, or three-page document, with all the practical benefits of brevity, but may require more effort on the part of the agent (and the client's attorney) when third parties refuse to honor the document.

Finally, most attorneys will agree that where there is a reasonable likelihood of the agent conveying real estate, it is critical to ensure that the form used will satisfy the applicable title insurance companies. This may mean preparing a separate statutory form for that particular purpose.

Q 10:31 What powers does an attorney-in-fact usually have?

A typical general durable power of attorney allows the agent to handle all financial matters for the principal, including bank accounts, investments, purchase or sale of real estate, and initiation and settlement of lawsuits. A handful of actions have been held to be so personal as not to be delegable to an agent: The agent does not have the power to make, amend, or revoke a will for the principal, consent to marriage, or vote on behalf of the principal.

A special or limited power of attorney, on the other hand, may authorize the agent to undertake only those actions specifically listed in the power of attorney. A limited power of attorney might, for example, authorize the agent to vote the principal's shares in a corporate restructuring, or to conclude the purchase of a piece of real estate.

Because of perceived and actual abuses, some state legislatures have acted to restrict the ability of the agent to make gifts to himself or herself or others, to compensate himself or herself for services rendered, or to take some other steps without the prior express consent of the principal. Those restrictions might require a specific section of the power of attorney, signed or initialed by the principal (and, sometimes, the witnesses and/or notary public) before the agent may exercise those powers. [Ariz. Rev. Stat. § 14-5506(B)] In the District of Columbia, the agent has no power to convey the principal's residence unless special language is included at the beginning of the document. [D.C. Code § 45-601] Because powers of attorney drafted in one state may be utilized in another state, the elder law attorney should consider whether it is appropriate to include such initialization provisions.

Q 10:32 Can an agent be given authority to manage retirement accounts, insurance, and similar assets?

The possibility for abuse in naming (or changing) beneficiaries should be obvious, as should the danger of permitting someone other than the principal to manage the interrelated estate tax, income tax, inheritance, and control issues. If the agent decides, for example, that the principal's child (maybe the agent's sibling) is a spendthrift, should the agent be empowered to direct that child's insurance or retirement account proceeds into a spendthrift trust, or maybe even effectively to disinherit the spendthrift child?

While most commentators agree that an agent cannot be given the power to change the principal's will, those same commentators usually agree that the agent can be empowered to change beneficiary designations and even trust beneficiaries. As a practical matter, such powers need to be set out expressly in the document, as they are unlikely to be presumed by the retirement account administrator, trustee, or life insurer.

In addition to the power to change beneficiaries, it might be appropriate in some cases to give an agent the power to establish or add to a retirement account, to change the method or calculation of distributions, or to roll over the principal's account into an IRA or other retirement plan. Remember that many of these powers will require consent from the principal's spouse, if he or she is still living. Even if the principal does not own separate retirement benefits, it may become necessary to administer rollover benefits if, for example, the principal's spouse seeks dissolution of marriage and the principal acquires retirement benefits through the dissolution proceedings.

Q 10:33 What are some examples of language conveying a durable power of attorney to manage retirement accounts, insurance, and similar assets?

Inclusion of retirement planning and trust modification powers in a power of attorney should be carefully considered. Where appropriate, language like the following might be utilized:

1. *Durable Power of Attorney: Retirement Planning.* My agent is specifically authorized to establish one or more individual retirement accounts, Roth IRAs, or other appropriate retirement plans or accounts in my name and for my benefit.

   My agent shall also have the following powers with regard to any pension, profit sharing or stock bonus plan, individual retirement account, Section 403(b) annuity or account, or any other retirement plan or arrangement in which I am a participant or of which I am a beneficiary:

   a. To make contributions (including "rollover" contributions) or cause contributions to be made to such plan with my funds or otherwise on my behalf.

   b. To receive and endorse checks or other distributions to me from such retirement plan, or to arrange for the direct deposit of such distributions into an account in my name, in the name of my agent for my benefit, or in the name of any trust of which I may be an income beneficiary.

   c. To elect a form of payment of benefits from such plan, to withdraw benefits from such plan, and to make, exercise, waive, or consent to any and all elections and/or options I may have available regarding the contributions to, investments or administration of, distribution from, or form of benefits payable by, such plan.

   d. To designate one or more beneficiaries or contingent beneficiaries for any benefits payable under such plan on account of my death, and to change any prior designation of beneficiary made by me or by my agent, provided, however, that my agent shall have no power to designate my agent directly or indirectly as a beneficiary or contingent beneficiary to receive a greater share or proportion of any such benefits than my agent would have otherwise received unless such change is consented to by all other beneficiaries who would have received the benefits but for the proposed change, with the beneficiaries to be determined as of the time of the proposed change. This limitation shall not apply to any designation of my agent as beneficiary in a fiduciary capacity, with no beneficial interest.

2. *Durable Power of Attorney: Life Insurance Beneficiary Designations.* My agent shall also have the express power to designate one or more beneficiaries or contingent beneficiaries, outright or in trust, on any contract of life insurance or other instrument that might include a benefit to be paid upon my death, and to change any prior designation of beneficiary or recipient previously made by me or by my agent. My agent shall have no power to designate my agent as beneficiary or contingent beneficiary to receive a greater share or proportion of such benefits than my agent would have otherwise received unless such change is consented to by all other beneficiaries who would have received benefits but for the proposed change, with the beneficiaries to be determined as of the time of the proposed change. This limitation shall not apply to any designation of my agent as beneficiary in a fiduciary capacity, with no beneficial interest.
3. *Durable Power of Attorney: Trust Amendments.* My agent shall also have the express power to amend, or join or concur in amendments to, any trust I may have established to the same extent I could if competent. In exercising this power, my agent may not make or join in any amendment that would increase the share or proportion of the benefit my agent would receive from such trust, unless the proposed amendment is consented to by all other persons then eligible to receive benefits outright or in trust from such trust. This limitation shall not apply to any designation of my agent as beneficiary in a fiduciary capacity, with no beneficial interest.

Note. The final portion of each set of provisions is intended to ensure that the respective retirement plan, life insurance benefit, or trust corpus not be included in the agent's own estate in the event he or she predeceases the principal. In an appropriate case, where estate taxes are not a concern and the client is aware of the risks, those provisions may be deleted.

Q 10:34 What other specific powers should be included in a power of attorney?

While the variety of possibilities may seem endless, most general durable powers of attorney include express provisions referring to specific powers. Although the power of attorney may be general, third parties will occasionally refuse to permit the agent to act without express language granting the specific authority in question. As previously discussed, even a broadly worded general power of attorney may not permit some actions (gifting, beneficiary designation changes, etc.) without express provisions. In addition to those previously suggested, the most commonly included powers in a financial power of attorney include:

1. *Safe deposit box opening and drilling.* "My agent shall have the power to have access to any safe deposit box rented by me or by me with others (including authority to have it drilled), to remove the contents therefrom and to terminate the lease."
2. *Real estate sales.* Be aware that some title insurance companies may require the specific legal description of the property, and perhaps even the name of the buyer, to be included in the document, making a prospective power of attorney impossible to create. Also be aware that local law may require that the power of attorney be acknowledged (in addition to being notarized), or otherwise to include the execution requirements applied to deeds generally. With those limitations, language might include: "My agent shall have the power to manage, sell, convey, and mortgage realty, to foreclose mortgages and to take title to property, and to execute, acknowledge, and deliver deeds of real property, mortgages, releases, satisfactions, and other instruments relating to realty."
3. *Tax return signing.* Federal income tax rules require that the specific form and years in question must be included in the text of the power of attorney, making it especially difficult to grant a general power to sign tax returns prospectively. Language might include: "My agent shall have the power to make, verify, and sign income and gift tax returns for the years 1990 through and including 2025, and to represent me in all income and gift tax matters before any office of the Internal Revenue Service or any office of the state revenue department, within the limitations of the applicable Revenue Rulings and Procedures." Some feel it is sufficient to grant the agent authority to execute IRS Form 2848 on behalf of the principal. This is the IRS official "Power of Attorney form" that must be completed with the forms and years in question.

4. *Agent compensation arrangements, or at least reimbursement for costs incurred.* Some states do not view the power to pay the agent as a power "for the benefit of" the principal, and therefore require that it be separately included: "My agent shall have the power to pay reasonable fees and reimburse costs to my agent to compensate my agent for the time spent in performing the duties of agent, taking into consideration the actual time spent, the types of issues my agent is required to address, the training or education of my agent, and the income and opportunities my agent must forgo in order to discharge these duties." However, the principal and agent should know that accepting compensation may subject the agent to a higher standard of care than acting on a volunteer basis (see Q 10:27).

5. *Payment of home or assisted living care costs, even though institutional care might be less expensive.* In order to encourage the agent to keep the principal at home, and to provide a shield against any challenge to the prudence of paying high home-care costs, a separate provision might include: "My agent is expressly authorized to provide adequate funds for payment of my health care, social, and companionship needs as determined by the person named as agent in any power of attorney for health care I have executed."

6. *Arranging for care of pets, even though the principal may be unable to return home and it would be less expensive to have the animals put to sleep.* For example: "My agent is expressly authorized to provide adequate funds for the care and feeding of my pets as in my agent's discretion is appropriate for my pets' happiness and welfare, even if this means paying a caretaker to occupy my residence in order to care for my pets, paying to board them, or paying a friend or relative of mine to house and care for them. If I am unable to care for my pets myself and it is virtually certain that I am unlikely to be able to care for them in the future, my agent has the power to continue such arrangements or to find good homes for my pets, but shall not—unless there is no other practical alternative—have my pets euthanized."

Q 10:35 Can an attorney-in-fact make gifts on behalf of the principal?

The power to make gifts is especially dangerous, and often controversial. Precisely because there is usually little oversight of the agency relationship created by a power of attorney, the power to make gifts is easily abused.

At the same time, there are often very good reasons for the principal to make gifts (and, after incapacity, for the agent to be able to make gifts). Those may be tax-based (aggressive gift giving is often the best protection against estate tax liability, and charitable gifts may reduce income taxes while fulfilling the principal's other goals), related to long-term care concerns (it may be prudent to make gifts so that the principal's assets are not entirely consumed by long-term care expenses, rather than on the principal's spouse or other intended beneficiaries, before Medicaid eligibility becomes available), or simply born of the principal's desire to continue a long-standing pattern of gift-giving, including regular charitable gifts.

Other than the emotional satisfaction of knowing that gifts will be made, there is usually no direct benefit to the principal from the making of a gift. Even though estate tax may be reduced, or expensive long-term care costs shifted to government programs, the beneficiaries of those savings will necessarily be the heirs and the recipients of the gifts, not the principal. Consequently, there is a substantial body of law limiting the power to make gifts on behalf of the principal.

Notably, federal tax law presumes that a gift made by an agent is not a completed gift (and therefore the property is not removed from the principal's taxable estate) unless there is specific gift-giving authority in the power of attorney or state law expressly permits gifting. [Estate of Casey v. Comm'r, 948 F.2d 895 (4th Cir. 1991)] If state law imposes any restrictions (for example, requiring that gifting powers be separately subscribed), the power of attorney must comply with those requirements in order for the gift to be completed. Although most states have not explicitly adopted the same rule for gifts made for reasons other than estate tax minimization, the likely result of challenges would be the same holding. At the very least, it will be presumed that no power to make gifts is included, and the burden of any alternative reading of the document will be placed squarely on the agent. In other words, if the principal intends to give the agent the power to make gifts on behalf of the principal, the power of attorney should expressly grant that power and it may be preferable for the principal to initial such powers separately on the document.

Q 10:36 Can the attorney-in-fact take acts that effectuate a gift at the express direction of the principal, even if there is no gift-giving power in the durable power of attorney itself?

Not infrequently, the elder law attorney will meet with an attorney-in-fact who has made gifts on behalf of the principal, but the durable power of attorney does not include the gifting provision. The agent will either pull out a signed letter from the principal asking that the gift be made, or stating that the gift is being made, or will have witnesses that the principal specifically requested the gift to be made.

How will this stand up in court? Not clear. Section 416 of the Restatement (Second) of Agency states that ratification by the principal relieves the agent of liability, and validates the original act. However, the Federal Circuit has interpreted California law to say that once the attorney-in-fact has been appointed pursuant to the durable power of attorney, ordinary principles of agency cannot apply to actions performed by the agent supposedly at the principal's direction. The court concluded that this would subvert the protective rules relating to powers of attorney. It held that a power that does not include a gifting provision affirmatively reflects the intention of the parties to deny the agent the power to make gifts. [Estate of Swanson v. U.S., 13 Fed. Appx. 979 (Fed. Cir. 2001)] (The principal nodded her head when the attorney-in-fact asked if she wanted the checks to be signed.) In another case, however, a court held that the agent was simply an "amanuensis" when she signed a deed conveying the principal's residence to herself at the direction of and in the presence of the principal. Still other cases would permit evidence of the principal's conduct to determine whether the principal had "ratified" the actions of the attorney-in-fact.

Confronted with a situation like this, if convinced there has been no abuse of power, the elder law attorney should be sure to document the circumstances under which the gifts were made. (Sometimes one cannot "re-do" the gift because timing is important—the gift needed to be made when it actually was made.) The principal can further ratify the gifts in writing and by executing a new durable power of attorney.

Q 10:37 What should a gift-giving power include?

As with all estate planning issues, the primary concern is to determine the actual wishes of the client; however, a gift-giving power might typically be limited in any of several ways:

1. The power to make gifts might be limited to the annual exclusion amount (currently $11,000 per donee per year). If this approach is to be used, consider wording the gift-giving authority in such a way as to permit larger gifts as the exclusion amount increases. Such a power might be effected by, for example, including the following language: "I specifically authorize my agent to make gifts to or among my issue and the spouses of my issue in an annual amount not to exceed the applicable federal gift tax exclusion amount in each year such gifts are made." It might be advisable in individual circumstances to either compel equal gifts among all issue (or all issue at the same level of descent), or to require that resulting gifts to the agent himself or herself be consented to by another person, preferably not one of those entitled to consideration for gifts (in order to avoid any concerns about either self-dealing or inclusion of a power of appointment in the agent's estate).
2. If the intent is to permit the agent to make gifts in order to qualify the principal for Medicaid coverage of long-term care costs, the gift-giving power should expressly permit unlimited gifts, or gifts in the pure discretion of the agent. Because of the tremendous opportunity for abuse, this type of unlimited authority should not be used routinely, and really requires separate discussion with clients before signing. To effect this authority, the power of attorney might include language like: "I authorize my agent to make gifts in an unlimited amount to or among my issue in such proportions as my agent determines appropriate, including specifically the power to gift all or substantially all of my assets if my agent determines such transfer would be in my best interests

to allow me to qualify for future government benefits or otherwise." Some attorneys assist clients in providing a more detailed letter to supplement the power of attorney and explaining thoroughly the client's wishes in the event that long-term care is required—not because they fear abuse, but in order to protect the agent from liability for carrying out the principal's wishes.

Q 10:38 Should gift-giving powers be included in every durable power of attorney?

No—with one possible exception.

The gift-giving power is obviously riskier than any other power included in most financial powers of attorney. Particularly where the power of attorney includes an unlimited power to make gifts, including gifts to the agent and his or her family, the effect can be a literal license to steal.

Even where the agent is completely trustworthy, and can be absolutely relied upon to exercise the gift-giving power only in accordance with the wishes and plans of the principal, there are good reasons to limit the authority or exclude it altogether. If, for example, the agent has an unrestricted power to make gifts and dies before the principal does, the argument is occasionally made that the agent died holding a general power of appointment over the principal's estate. Theoretically, this could lead to the result that the principal's entire estate must be included in the deceased agent's estate for purposes of calculating estate tax liability. This would be true even though the agent never exercised the power to make gifts, or exercised it only in accordance with the prior, limited gifting patterns of the principal.

The concern about inclusion of the principal's estate in the deceased agent's estate for tax purposes may be an entirely theoretical concern. No reported cases invoke such a doctrine, and there is certainly no widespread effort by the IRS to force such a result. Still, the possibility of that result should alarm any agent who happens to have a taxable estate, if the principal's estate is also significant.

The possible exception is the power to make gifts to the principal's spouse. For many practical purposes, in non-community property states it is vital to be able to move assets from one spouse to the other, and in community property states, it may be vital to convert community property to separate property. The best solution is to have an alternate attorney-in-fact (for example, the durable power of attorney names spouse and one or more children) and give the spouse-gift-giving power to the children, and the power to make gifts to children, to the spouse. Even if the only attorney-in-fact is the spouse, it is still advisable to include ample power to make gifts to that spouse, unless (1) one really is concerned about the tax implications for a federally taxable estate, or (2) there is mistrust between spouses—in which case the spouse should not be named an agent at all!

Q 10:39 Can an attorney-in-fact create a will, trust, or other "testamentary substitute" for the principal?

The agent cannot create a will, which specifically requires execution by the testator. However, it may be possible for the attorney-in-fact to establish a trust and then to transfer the principal's assets to the trust. Whether or not this is permitted may depend upon (1) the authorizing language contained in the instrument, (2) state law, and (3) whether the trust is a cost-saving device, or actually alters the principal's overall estate plan. One court has held that a power of attorney with express provisions permitting establishment of a trust but no provisions authorizing any change of beneficiary can permit the agent to establish a trust naming the principal as sole beneficiary, and that a trust providing for ultimate distribution to the same persons who would receive under the principal's existing estate plan (or under intestate succession in the absence of any estate plan) would probably be acceptable. [Schubert v. Reynolds, 95 Cal. App. 4th 100, 115 Cal. Rptr. 2d 285 (2002)]

Q 10:40 May an attorney-in-fact in turn hire agents to perform the duties delegated by the power of attorney?

The Restatement (Second) of Agency has long held that, absent specific authority in a power of attorney, the agent may not delegate authority to a subagent. It is probably more accurate to say that the agent may employ experts and even agents, but will usually remain liable for the actions of those he or she so employs. [Restatement (Second) of Agency § 406]

Like other fiduciaries governed by the prudent investor rule, an attorney-in-fact may actually be bound to delegate investment decisions to suitable employees, because a prudent investor would use only qualified persons to conduct certain activities. To resolve such potential conflicts, the power of attorney might contain language addressing various scenarios under which hiring additional agents would be appropriate. Such a provision might, for example, include language like: "My attorney-in-fact is specifically authorized to select, employ, and pay from my funds attorneys, accountants, investment advisers, and such other agents as my attorney-in-fact shall determine may be necessary or appropriate to permit the orderly management of my affairs." It may even be appropriate to provide specifically that other agents selected by the agent are answerable directly to the principal; the effect of such a provision would be to relieve the agent from liability for the acts of agents so selected. Of course, some statutory durable powers of attorney may expressly authorize delegation.

Usually the attorney-in-fact will not be given the power to choose a successor attorney-in-fact; exceptions may include a situation where the principal anticipates a lengthy incapacity and has no person available to name as successor attorney-in-fact.

Q 10:41 Who is the client when the attorney-in-fact engages the elder law attorney?

It is important to make clear whether the individual person named as attorney-in-fact is being represented (unlikely, unless the fiduciary has been accused of wrongdoing of some kind) or whether, as is more likely the case, the principal is the true client. If the elder law attorney has prepared the durable power of attorney for the principal's signature, clearly the principal is the client, and the elder law attorney and attorney-in-fact work together to serve the principal's interests. If the principal's interests diverge from those of the attorney-in-fact, it is the attorney's duty to serve the principal. The difficulty is that this divergence is not clear. If the principal authorized gifts to the agent, but the elder law attorney does not really know the scope of gifts intended, should the elder law attorney advise the agent how to proceed so that the gifts will not be challenged? This difficult topic is further addressed in chapter 2.

Refusal to Honor Power of Attorney

Q 10:42 Why do third parties refuse to honor powers of attorney?

There are several reasons a power of attorney may be rejected. First, all powers of attorney are revocable as long as the principal is alive and has capacity. But tearing up the original power of attorney may not serve as sufficient revocation, because copies may have the same effect as originals. The third party may demand additional proof of the principal's incapacity, such as letters from doctors. Sometimes banks or other institutions insist that powers of attorney be executed only on their own forms, a policy that has become a specific target for state statutes supporting the powers of agents, because it creates a commercially unreasonable requirement for incapacitated principals and their agents. Some third parties reasonably refuse to honor a document that does not contain language addressing the transaction at hand; for instance, if the power of attorney authorizes banking activities but not the sale, purchase, or lease of real estate, a real estate agent or mortgage company will be unlikely to honor it. Some third parties are simply reluctant to implement policies and controls sufficient to protect against the abusive use of powers of attorney, and decline to accept the power of attorney rather than run any risk of later action by a disgruntled principal. Finally, some third parties (such as bank tellers) are simply ignorant of the law in this area and will reject a power of attorney on the basis that it is "stale," too old, or does not have an embossed seal, even if state law does not include requirements to that effect.

Q 10:43 What can an attorney-in-fact do when a third party refuses to honor the power of attorney?

Banks, title companies, and other third parties may arbitrarily decide that a general durable power of attorney is not sufficient authority, and either insist on execution of their own powers of attorney (which will of course no longer be possible once the principal is incapacitated) or refuse to accept the document altogether. This usually forces the agent to initiate conservatorship proceedings, which completely defeats one of the primary purposes of having a power of attorney in the first place. Because there is usually no way the principal can anticipate this kind of disaster, at least one state [cf.

Fla. Stat. Ann. § 709.08(11)] has enacted laws compelling third parties to honor powers of attorney and allowing agents to sue if damages result from the actions or inaction of the third parties.

In the absence of state law compelling compliance with the power of attorney, the elder law attorney may still have a number of options:

1. Negotiation with bank officials, brokerages houses, and other commercial enterprises often leads to a positive resolution, particularly as the attorney (or agent) works up the institution's chain of command. This can be bolstered by reassuring language in the document indemnifying and holding harmless the financial institution that acts in good faith reliance upon the document, such as: "Third parties, including financial institutions, shall be held harmless and indemnified by me and my estate with respect to any loss to me, my estate, my heirs, successors, and assigns, arising from such institutions' good-faith reliance upon this instrument."
2. Threatening litigation may be effective, even in states without clear authority for such actions. (Some powers of attorney expressly authorize such litigation, and it is reported that highlighting such a provision can be very effective.)
3. Securing the signature (however incompetent) of the principal on a new, approved form of power of attorney may work (to the objection that this is fraudulent, the obvious answer is that the power of attorney already exists, and the signature on an additional form is a legal non-event).
4. Providing affidavits of treating physicians, the power of attorney's scrivener, or even the agent himself or herself (to the effect that the power of attorney remains valid) may satisfy the institution (particularly after the discussion has become a war of wills, and the institutional bureaucrat needs something to count as a victory in the legal tug-of-war).
5. Finally, consider simply moving the account to a more compliant institution; many times, the resistance is to complete closure of the account, or to sale of a particular asset, but not to management of the entire account. In more than one instance, a brokerage house that adamantly refused to permit sale of securities within an account on the basis of a power of attorney has blithely permitted the transfer of the entire

account to another brokerage house on the basis of that same agent's signature.

Termination and Revocation of Power of Attorney

Q 10:44 When does a durable power of attorney end?

All powers of attorney terminate at the death of the principal; nondurable powers of attorney terminate at the incapacity of the principal. A principal can revoke the powers at any time.

Q 10:45 How can the principal revoke a power of attorney?

State statutes may be explicit, or silent, on the revocation of a power of attorney. Certainly the power of attorney can be revoked by destroying all originals. This is not always easy to do, and a formal revocation, executed with the same formalities of the original, is advisable. If the original or a copy of the power of attorney has been given to the agent, it is probably necessary to deliver notice of the revocation to the agent; however, this may not suffice, especially when copies of the power of attorney are still in circulation or the document has been recorded. The principal should make every effort to collect all copies of the document (a good argument for allowing only the agent to have a copy). If the original power of attorney has been recorded, the revocation should also be recorded; if the principal is concerned about misuse of the power of attorney, it may be advisable to record the revocation even if the original power has not been recorded. If there is still some doubt about whether the revocation is complete, the principal may publish notice of the revocation for the benefit of third parties. Keeping a copy of the defaced original is also a good idea. The principal who creates a new document naming a new agent may wish to include in the new document express revocation of the old; conversely, the principal who creates a new document naming an additional principal may wish to clarify that the old is not being revoked.

Q 10:46 Can an incompetent principal revoke a durable power of attorney?

An incompetent individual can revoke the power of attorney, but the revocation can be proven to be invalid by the agent (of course if the principal destroys the only copy of the document, the argument may be moot). Rather than raising the incapacity issue in litigation, the attorney-in-fact may instead choose to petition for guardianship and conservatorship, an arena specifically designed for determining incapacity and appointment of an agent (see chapter 10 for a discussion of guardianship). Alternatively, the attorney-in-fact may simply seek to utilize the power of attorney, armed with appropriate evidence (an affidavit from the principal's attending physician, for example) of the ineffectiveness of the revocation in the event that any third party challenges the validity or currency of the power of attorney.

Paradoxically, these problems can be more pronounced when dealing with a health care power of attorney. Despite the fact that the agent may be dealing with the principal's health care providers, and that those same providers are clearly aware of the principal's incapacity, they may be less willing to accept instructions from the agent in the face of the incompetent principal's revocation. This may be because the level of capacity required to make health care decisions is generally conceded to be lower than that required for financial decisions, or because of the inherent conservatism of medical professionals when dealing with legal issues, or a mixture of both. In any event, the health care agent may find that the only remaining avenue after revocation by an incompetent principal is to pursue guardianship of the person, despite the intention of the principal to avoid such proceedings by the initial execution of the health care power of attorney.

Q 10:47 How can the principal challenge the actions of an attorney-in-fact?

If the attorney-in-fact has acted in good faith pursuant to a document that, to his or her knowledge, had not been revoked, there is little the principal can do to undo the attorney-in-fact's actions. And, of course, third parties are never held liable for relying in good faith on a power of attorney. If the attorney-in-fact or the third party had prior knowledge of the revocation of the document, both can be sued for fraud. As with any litigation, the principal must prove that notice was provided to the agent and/or third party of the revocation, and that the principal was damaged by their actions. Because the power of attorney, unlike a trust, does not usually dictate how assets are to be managed, the principal must prove to the court not just that the agent's actions were not in accordance with the wishes of the principal, but that the actions taken were not in the principal's best interests, and that he or she was damaged as a result.

Q 10:48 How can an *incompetent* principal challenge the actions of an attorney-in-fact?

Theoretically, the properly worded power of attorney should preclude any challenge from an incompetent principal—the whole idea of the durable power of attorney is management of the principal's assets with minimal court interference. The reality is that a truly incompetent individual would be unable to formulate an objection or handle the logistics of retaining an attorney. Conceivably an individual who is only partially or sporadically incapacitated could convince an attorney and, ultimately, the court that the actions of the attorney-in-fact are not proper. It is even more likely that an outsider, such as a caretaker or family member, would become aware of improper actions on the part of the attorney-in-fact and notify the authorities. Emergency proceedings to have a guardian or guardian *ad litem* appointed to represent the incapacitated principal in a lawsuit against the attorney-in-fact would then be in order. Once a guardian *ad litem,* a conservator, or a guardian of the estate has been appointed, that person will have the power to compel an accounting and bring an action against the agent in the same fashion that the principal would be able to do but for his or her incapacity.

Practice-Related Issues

Q 10:49 What problems might an elder law attorney encounter in dealing with powers of attorney?

In addition to obvious drafting considerations, problems frequently arise in the administration of powers of attorney. These may involve misbehavior by the agent, interpretation of poorly worded or ambiguous powers of attorney, tax considerations, and even the possibility of abuse, neglect, or exploitation by the agent (and the resultant duty, in some jurisdictions, of the attorney to report that abuse, neglect, or exploitation).

1. *The questionable fiduciary.* The attorney is called by a son who has been named agent in his father's power of attorney. The father, a widower, has become demented and can no longer live independently. He has a nice house, and the son decides to move into the father's house with his family so that they can take care of him. He believes that it's only fair that in return the title to the house should be turned over to him (it turns out that he needs security for a bank loan), and he wants the attorney to help him with the transfer. The attorney asks if there are other siblings, and the son replies, "Just my sister, but she lives in another state and hasn't done anything at all to help my dad. I've done it all." Are there circumstances that would justify the transfer of the house? What precautions should the attorney take for herself and on behalf of her client?

   There are a number of red flags here, but no direct evidence yet of abuse or coercion. Some investigation is necessary. First, the power of attorney may not have express gifting language; thus, in some states the transfer of title could constitute criminal behavior on the part of the son. If that is not an issue, then the son's plan may not be all bad: The family members can help the father with his activities of daily living and provide social diversions. The attorney should advise the son that transfer of the title to the house to the son might jeopardize the father's eligibility for long-term care Medicaid benefits, but if it appears the father will remain healthy for the three-year look-back period, then the transfer may in fact reflect the father's pre-dementia wish that his children get the house after he dies, not the state. The wild card is, of course, the daughter. It would be inadvisable to initiate any part of this plan without getting the go-ahead from the daughter, and the son may have to compromise by putting title in both their names.

2. *Third-party resistance.* Six months ago an ailing client retained an attorney to draw up a general durable power of attorney. He is now very ill and unable to communicate, so

his daughter has begun to get his affairs in order. Because her father was adamant that he never use public assistance, the daughter wants to sell his house to pay his nursing home bills rather than resort to Medicaid benefits. The attorney for the potential buyers refuses to honor the general durable power of attorney, insisting that the father himself sign. The realtor sides with the buyer's attorney, stating that although the power of attorney gives broad powers, it doesn't specifically address the sale of real estate. The daughter argues that her father would have no idea what he was signing, and she doubts that she could get him to collect his thoughts enough to even hold a pen. Does she have any recourse?

If neither side will budge, the only alternative may be to have the daughter appointed conservator of her father's estate, then get court approval for the sale of the house. The father's attorney may break the deadlock by advising the other parties that obtaining conservatorship will delay the process by about a month, and that the daughter will almost certainly succeed in her petition. Some agents have also been successful in taking third parties to court for not honoring a general durable power of attorney; the attorney should check the state statutes and case law to determine whether this is an option (if so, this would constitute good leverage to break the deadlock).

3. *The demented principal.* The attorney gets a call from a long-time client for whom she drew up a general durable power of attorney. She knows that the client has been living with the agent, his son, for several months because he had been unable to bathe or feed himself. The client now wishes to amend his power of attorney to name his daughter as agent, and explains that his daughter-in-law finds the caretaking tiresome and he fears being put in a nursing home. Should the attorney honor this wish? What investigation should she undertake, and what facts would be helpful? Is there an ethical problem with calling the son or daughter?

Here again is the "best interests versus substituted judgment" argument. Some attorneys would not hesitate to redo the power of attorney, and in fact there is probably sufficient evidence of the occasional lucid moment so that the family members would have trouble challenging the document; however, there is no guarantee that this would help—in fact, the daughter may be unable to care for her father. The attorney should probably get her client's permission to talk to all family members and see if the problems can be worked out in some other manner. And, of course, the son as agent can designate his sister as caretaker.

Part IV

Paying for Medical and Long-Term Care

Chapter 11

Long-Term Care Options

The aging of the American population has become a matter of much public discussion in recent years. As the "baby boomer" generation begins to turn 50, the prospect of medical and long-term care for a rapidly increasing segment of the population becomes even more important, both on a public policy level and as it affects more and more individual families. Aging need not be (and is not) automatically associated with high medical costs, debilitating conditions, and the need for protective housing. In fact, recent studies indicate that the American population is aging comparatively well—that the incidence of nursing home placement and debilitating medical treatments may actually decrease as longevity grows over the next few decades. The sheer size of the aging population does make the availability of medical and long-term care critically important for many individuals and families. This chapter discusses the continuum of care and the long-term care options available including home care, congregate living, assisted living, adult care facilities, continuing care retirement communities, nursing homes, and hospice care.

Overview

Q 11:1 What are some settings in which medical care might be provided?

The aging of the population, the popular perception of breakdown of the nuclear family, longer lifespans, increased government benefits, and the relative prosperity of many senior citizens have brought about profound changes in the long-term care marketplace in the past 20 years. Although most people still have a visceral fear of ending up in a nursing home, there have never been more choices available for everyone from the healthy or frail elderly to the chronically ill. Nursing home stays can be quite short or extended, but the average nursing home stay is a little less than one year. According to Census Bureau statistics, the need for assistance increases dramatically with age: Although only about 8 percent of non-institutionalized individuals aged 65 to 69 suffer from limitations in the ability to care for themselves, 28 percent of those over age 85 require assistance. [Census Bureau: "Selected Characteristics of Civilian Noninstitutionalized Persons 65 and Over"—see *http://www.census.gov/hhes/www/disable/census/tables/tab2us.html*]. The 2000 Census shows that 41 percent of the population 65 and over have a disability of some kind. [Census Bureau: "Table DP-2. Profile of Selected Social Characteristics: 2000"—see *http://censtats.census.gov/data/US/01000.pdf*] Similarly, while 1 percent of those aged 65 to 74 lived in nursing homes in 1990, nearly one-quarter of those aged 85 or older did. [Census Bureau: "Sixty-Five Plus in the United States" Statistical Brief, 1995] While diagnosis and projections of dementia (one of the most frequent causes of need for assistance) have proven to be particularly difficult, medical research indicates that between one-third and one-half of all those aged 85 or older suffer from some form of dementia. [Cf. Skoog, et al., "A Population-Based Study of Dementia in 85-Year-Olds," N. Engl. J. Med. 328(3):153–158 (Jan. 21, 1993)]

Increasingly sophisticated home health care services allow many individuals to continue to live at home and, if they choose, to die at home. Hospitals now focus their care on short-term, acute illnesses, and injuries, and discharge patients as quickly as possible to rehabilitation facilities, nursing homes, assisted living facilities, board and care homes, or, if possible, the patients' own residences. As Alzheimer's disease and other dementias claim an increasing number of victims, in part because of increased longevity, day care and respite care programs provide relief for exhausted family caretakers. Many nursing homes now have locked Alzheimer's units.

Of course much medical care is still provided in hospitals. Government pressure to reduce the cost of medical care, coupled with individual preferences, have driven much medical care out of those hospitals and into rehabilitation facilities and outpatient care. The former may look like a hybrid between a traditional hospital and a nursing home; the latter may require one or a few short visits to a hospital-based or community clinic, but rely heavily on family care and support during the recovery process.

Q 11:2 What is the "continuum of care" concept?

With the aging of our population, concern has increasingly focused on providing the appropriate level of care for each stage in a senior's life. In an ideal arrangement, simple assistance in the home should progress from increased at-home care, to day programs outside the home, to assisted living in a dedicated facility, to nursing services, and (if the individual ultimately requires such care) to a skilled nursing facility (SNF). Of course, some individuals may move to a higher level of care temporarily, and then return to a previous setting as medical or social problems are resolved. In some communities, this "continuum of care" may be provided by a single facility with various levels of care under one roof. In practice, of course, the seamless continuum of care is more often theory than fact.

Q 11:3 What is meant by "aging in place?"

Most seniors strongly prefer to spend the rest of their lives in the one place where they are comfortable, where they have fond memories, and where their families and friends can most easily find them —at home. To the extent possible, plans for future care needs should facilitate the provision of care at home. Plans should help assure this kind of "aging in place" despite the possibility of future loss of cognition—in other words, even though the senior may not later be able to appreciate fully the benefits of home care. This not only helps ensure that the senior's future needs are met in accordance with current wishes and desires, but it also provides current peace of mind to the older client with anxieties about future institutionalization.

Q 11:4 What choices are available for long-term care?

Those who can afford to pay for their own long-term care have almost unlimited choices, including total care in the home. Those dependent on Medicaid benefits are limited to facilities that meet Medicare and Medicaid requirements, and may not be allowed to live at home if it is not cost-effective for the provider. Medicaid will not pay for mere custodial care—the applicant must have mental or physical conditions that require medical care—but room and board are covered if the applicant is medically eligible (see chapter 14 for a discussion of Medicaid). In most communities, those needing long-term care and their families can choose among a number of long-term care facilities, including nursing homes, board and care homes, and assisted living facilities. Case management services can be especially useful in helping families choose the best care for the money, and monitoring that care after the patient has moved into the facility.

The government's participation varies tremendously by the type of care. Government money is particularly important in the nursing home industry, and in recent years government support for home care services has grown substantially. Among the choices for long-term placement are (ranging, roughly, from less to more restrictive):

1. *Home care.* Home care encompasses a wide variety of services and levels of care. Home care is provided by both nonprofit agencies and for-profit franchises. Some seniors can be cared for at home by one caretaker who visits a few times a week, or every day. Others may require live-in assistance, perhaps from family members (or a combination of family and paid caregivers). At the other extreme, home care can duplicate the highest level of care provided by skilled nursing facilities (or even hospital care), but usually at a tremendous cost. While home care is the stated preference of

most seniors, the practical realities of providing medical care at home may make it prohibitively expensive, particularly if the resident requires round-the-clock nursing care. The cost of that level of care will probably be four or five times the cost of comparable nursing home care. The cost of occasional home visits, housework, and assistance with meal preparation (a typical combination for the largely independent senior) may be a fraction of any of the other care alternatives.

2. *Continuing care retirement communities (CCRCs).* CCRCs have now been around for some time. They usually combine several levels of care in a single campus or facility. In theory, a resident can move into an "independent living" apartment with the knowledge that, if he or she should fail, assisted living and even nursing home placement will be available (or at least nearby) without having to move to another facility. CCRCs frequently require a substantial down-payment, which may or may not be refundable when the resident moves out of the complex or dies. Many CCRCs are marketed as luxury complexes, and so (while costs may vary tremendously) they tend to be extremely expensive care alternatives in the short run while the resident is able to manage independently. If, however, the contract requires a large down payment or "loan," and also guarantees lifetime skilled nursing care at no extra charge, and the resident later requires the care, the gamble can pay off. The contract and payment provisions also tend to be quite complex, often requiring legal assistance and advice in negotiation before entering the facility, and making it very difficult to shop around.

3. *Board and care facilities.* More commonly referred to today as adult care homes or residential care homes, these facilities usually provide room and board for four or five to twenty or more elderly residents. While private rooms are usually available, most adult care home residents will share a room with at least one other resident. All meals and social activities are provided at the home, which frequently will be owned and run by a resident manager or an owner who lives nearby and spends most days working at the home. Most elderly residents find adult care homes to be quieter, more homelike, and more pleasant than nursing homes, although adult care homes usually are unable to deal with serious medical

conditions. As a result, incontinence, the need for breathing assistance or tube feedings, or any other serious medical condition will probably result in the transfer of the resident to a nursing home. The costs of adult care homes also vary widely, but may typically be between half and two-thirds of the cost of a nursing home in the same locale. A related class of facility is a residential care facility that may be as large as a nursing home (and to many residents, indistinguishable from such a facility). However, because it is not a skilled nursing facility it will not accept Medicaid payments. Instead, the state supplemental security income payment may be tailored to meet the facility cost for those that qualify.

4. *Congregate living.* Large apartment-like complexes may house many elderly residents who have access to a common dining room and activities but also have individual apartments with kitchens (and perhaps with spare bedrooms). Although there may be nursing staff on site, the primary focus of congregate living facilities is to provide a comfortable, supportive apartment setting where residents may, but need not, participate in services. Typically, congregate living arrangements provide two meals a day (perhaps a single meal on Sunday), programs, excursions, and social events. The residents may be expected to provide their own third meal. Independence is encouraged, but limited support is available when needed. Congregate living costs may vary from as little as the cost of a nice apartment complex in the area to as much as a nursing facility.

5. *Assisted living facilities.* Assisted living facilities provide an apartment-like setting, accompanied by on-staff nursing assistants and oversight. Meals are usually provided in a central dining facility, and staff regularly check on residents every day. Group activities may help maintain mobility, orientation, and socialization. Costs for assisted living facilities vary widely, though they will generally be less expensive than comparable nursing facilities. Much of the higher cost of some such facilities comes from additional amenities: better food, private apartments, nicer common areas, and more activities, for example. Many facilities "unbundle" their charges so that those with more needs pay an additional fee on top of the standard fee. Others include partial endowment

or large "entrance fee" requirements and then try to keep the monthly charges lower.

6. *Skilled nursing facilities.* With prices ranging from $2,500 per month to $9,000 (or more) depending on geography and level of care, nursing homes are today the most familiar long-term care settings. Although they are now commonplace, the phenomenon is largely a recent development; nursing homes have their organizational roots in the "poor houses" and old-age homes of earlier centuries. Modern nursing homes are based on a strong medical model of care: Even though the primary problem of the resident may be social (no place to live, or no family to help provide care), the care provided will be medical, and will be at the hands of nurses, nurses' aides, therapists, and other medical professionals.
7. *Hospice care.* Although the hospice movement is relatively new (the first hospice organization in this country was established in Branford, Connecticut, in 1974), it has grown quickly. One of the key reasons for that growth has been the increasing coverage for hospice benefits through the federal Medicare program. The Medicare hospice benefit was first provided in 1990 and in the 10 years since then, expenditures quintupled, at a time when total Medicare expenditures increased by about 60 percent. Hospice care is based on the premise that death is itself a natural event, and that care for a participating terminally ill patient should focus on comfort, reassurance, and support rather than curative measures. Hospice care can be provided in a separate facility or in the home; in fact, hospice care at home (or in whatever facility the patient is in at the time of initiation of hospice services) has become the norm in most communities.

Q 11:5 Who can help assess an individual's long-term care options?

Although American society has increasingly treated aging as a medical condition requiring diagnosis, treatment, and nursing care, other professionals in many cases may better assess long-term care options. Geriatric care managers, a profession unknown a decade ago, have become pivotal in arranging placement and monitoring care in many communities. The National Association of Professional

Geriatric Care Managers [1604 N. Country Club Road, Tucson, AZ, 85716-3102, (520) 881-8008, *http://www.caremanager.org/*] can provide additional information about local members and suggestions for the productive use of geriatric care managers. Nurses, social workers, psychologists, care home administrators, and other professionals also can provide useful direction and advice in determining whether placement is necessary and appropriate, and in choosing the right placement setting.

Local agencies that provide home care and other assistance may also provide placement services. The first place to start is the local area agency on aging, which may not only assess individuals for eligibility in home care or other programs, but may also provide placement assistance.

Q 11:6 What are ADLs?

ADL is an acronym for "activities of daily living." The ADL is the key diagnostic tool in assessing long-term care needs. ADLs are usually listed as six: eating, toileting, transferring (from bed to chair), bathing, dressing, and continence. (Some programs may use eight "critical need areas" instead: eating, meal preparation, medication management, dressing, transferring (i.e., moving from a bed to a chair) and ambulating (in some fashion—walking, using a wheelchair or walker, etc.), toileting and bathing.) Frequently, "assistance with two or more ADLs," or "a cognitive impairment that requires supervision because of health or safety risks," may be required before benefits will be payable for home care. The term may also be used by Medicaid agencies administering home care or assisted living benefits under waiver plans or state plans. Frequently, nursing home placement may be recommended for someone who needs assistance with three or more ADLs (see also Q 12:23 regarding ADLs and Medicaid eligibility).

Q 11:7 Who regulates the quality and availability of long-term care outside skilled nursing facilities?

To the extent that Medicaid and Medicare are involved in the patient's care outside of a skilled nursing facility environment—for instance, Medicaid-covered home health services—that care is overseen by the state Medicaid agency in accordance with federal regulations. Medicare and Medicaid facilities have reporting and assessment requirements, and their residents are guaranteed certain rights under federal law (see chapters 13 and 14 for a discussion of Medicare and Medicaid); however, because Medicaid and Medicare only cover the medically eligible, the rest of the long-term care population is especially vulnerable to overcharging, poor care, and abuse. Those who have no family and limited income are completely at the mercy of their caretakers, usually at unlicensed board and care homes. State licensing requirements provide some oversight, although they vary greatly from state to state, but it is estimated that the number of unlicensed homes is at least equal to that of licensed facilities. Predictably, the value of licensing requirements correlates with the level of state enforcement and the ability (and willingness) to impose monetary penalties; if enforcement is weak, these requirements can be illusory.

Home Care

Q 11:8 What is usually included in home care?

Home care can include a broad range of services. Home care is frequently provided for individuals who suffer from loss of sight, loss of hearing, and dementia. The working caretaker may hire an untrained companion to stay at home with the patient during the day and fix lunch. Home health aides may be brought in for elderly persons living alone, to provide companionship, light housekeeping, meal preparation, and assistance with activities of daily living such as bathing and dressing. Licensed practice nurses can assist with the preparation and administration of medications, dressing changes, and blood draws. Registered nurses, social workers, and of course physicians may make periodic visits to assess the patient's care and medications. For the few patients who can afford it, full-time nursing care and hospice care can also be provided in the home. Families often rely on case management services to oversee the hiring, monitoring, and discharge of paid caretakers and other services. The Older Americans Act of 1965 generated a number of community programs that offer home health, housekeeping, counseling, and legal services, and information on these programs can be obtained from area agencies on aging.

Q 11:9 How should a care plan be developed for an individual receiving home care?

Every home care recipient should have a formal care plan developed by the home care organization or care manager—for example, as a condition of payment, Medicare requires the establishment and periodic review of a plan of care by the attending physician. [42 C.F.R. § 424.22] The patient (and the patient's guardian or family, where the patient is incapacitated) has a right to participate in the development of the plan, and the right to be informed of the details of (and any changes in) the plan. [42 C.F.R. § 484.10] The plan should include a functional analysis of the patient's need or limitations, an indication of the results the treatment will seek, and a specific plan of approach to meet those expected results. Ordinarily the care plan will be prepared by the home health agency and reviewed by the physician, but patient and family involvement in the development of the plan can be instrumental to understanding the treatment course and evaluating the agency's performance.

An important detail, often overlooked, is to ensure that all proper tax and labor laws are obeyed with respect to private aides and caregivers. If the patient is receiving daily care from an individual not otherwise employed by an agency (employed by, not contracting with), the individual more than likely will be considered the patient's "employee." This is the "Nanny tax" problem but at a more senior level. Recently, an estate was found liable for unemployment benefits when the elderly patient had received services from a caregiver for years, who then filed for unemployment compensation benefits. The estate was liable even though the caretaker understood that she was an independent contractor and had agreed to pay all taxes, estimated taxes, and self-employment taxes. [Estate of Dulaney v. Mississippi Employment Security Commission, 805 So. 2d 643 (Miss. App. 2002)] Moreover, if the caregiver fails to pay self-employment tax, the IRS may take an interest and charge the patient with the amount, as being unpaid Social Security contributions by an employer and unpaid withholding on behalf of the employee, not to mention any income tax that should have been withheld. Unfortunately, some home health agencies claim that the aide is an "independent contractor" and that they (the home health agency) will take care of all the paperwork. This may be well and good when the client is paying the agency, but some agencies make such a claim and then ask that the aide be paid directly. If the aide is being paid directly, the aide will likely be found to be an employee.

Realistically, although attorneys must advise their clients to comply with the laws in this area, it is likely that families will continue to be noncompliant, and even continue to pay some aides "under the table" to get the aide they want at the price they want to pay. All the attorney can do is to advise of the risks, to both employer and employee, of such conduct. If it is the worker who insists on being paid "on the side," you can offer to persuade the worker of the long-term drawbacks.

Q 11:10 What sources of payment exist for home care services?

Often home care services are provided by volunteers—family, neighbors, church members, etc. Spouse caretakers are the least likely to turn to others for help, and often become prisoners in their own homes, caring for disabled spouses to the point of endangering their own health. Home companions may be affordable, but once the patient begins to require more services, such as bathing, limited nursing care, and wheelchair transfers, the expense of bringing in trained help may be too great for the patient to bear, and transfer to a facility may be necessary.

Improvements in long-term care insurance coverage have made home care a more viable option for those who were or are able to procure such coverage. Most insurance companies will or are required to provide home care coverage when the insured requires assistance with two or more ADLs (see Q 11:6). Moreover, while the insurance home care benefit was previously pegged at only a percentage of the skilled nursing facility benefit (e.g., 50 percent), many policies now provide a 100 percent benefit. The long-term care industry has come to realize that the promise of coverage to keep the insured at home is its biggest selling feature.

Reverse mortgages may be another available resource in the effort to defray the costs of home care. For this reason, if a client wants to "age in place" at home above all other available options, it may be important *not* to transfer the home to a child, at least not without consideration, because a reverse mortgage is only available if all persons "on the deed" are 62 or older.

Some state Medicaid agencies will pay for limited home health care, especially if it is cheaper than nursing home care, but will usually not pay for more than one caretaker shift per day, because it is far more cost-effective to provide such services in a centralized nursing facility. More and more states have applied for Section 1115 Waivers (see chapter 14) for approval to make home care benefits available up to the amount that the state would pay a skilled nursing facility; some states also have their own home care programs, and the combination can be very effective, especially when supplemented by family assistance. Medicare may also pay for home health services, and provided certain medical requirements are met, may pay indefinitely for the custodial care that is required as well (see Q 11:12). Volunteer organizations, often tied to churches, can also play an important supporting role. It is vital for clients and their families to understand the many options there may be to provide home care. Where the programs are available, clients and their families should never have the impression that skilled nursing facility care is an inevitable outcome of aging.

Q 11:11 What programs may benefit caregivers of those elders at home?

Caregivers may find some measure of relief from The Family Caregiver Initiative of the Older Americans Act, The Family and Medical Leave Act, and any state caregiver respite programs. In addition, the Alzheimer's associations or similar groups may have a private program to pay for "respite" for caregivers.

The Family Caregiver Initiative, establishing the National Family Caregiver Support Program administered by the Agency on Aging, is intended to provide help to those caring for individuals who require assistance with two or more ADLs, or who have a "cognitive impairment that requires supervision because of health or safety risks." There are two major components of the program: Respite Services and Supplemental Services. Respite Services can provide services such as adult day care, home health aide support, homemaker, companion, skilled nursing visits, and/or short-term stays in a nursing or assisted living facility. Supplemental Services can include payment for one-time, health-related items or services such as durable medical equipment, medically necessary items, minor home modifications, transportation, seasonal clothing, or emergency items or services. The program is not means-tested, but local programs may ask for a contribution or co-pay. The program is administered locally by a state's local agency on aging office, which should be contacted for more information.

The Family and Medical Leave Act of 1993 (FMLA) does not provide any additional government resources to help care for homebound elders, but it does mandate some relief for family caregivers. Under the FMLA, an employer is required to permit up to 12 weeks per year of unpaid leave for employees who must provide care for parents, spouses, or children as a result of serious health conditions. [29 U.S.C. § 2612(a)(1)(C)] The affected employee must be permitted to return to his or her prior position after the leave is completed. [29 U.S.C. § 2614(a)]

Q 11:12 When will Medicare pay for home care services?

Home health care is covered under both Medicare Part A and Medicare Part B (see chapter 13 for a more complete discussion of Medicare coverage). Medicare covers home health visits by a Medicare-participating agency without co-payments when the services are medically and reasonably necessary and when the patient:

1. Is homebound;
2. Requires intermittent skilled nursing care or therapy; and
3. Is under a physician's care.

[42 U.S.C. §§ 1395f (a)(2)(C), 1395x(m)]

Coverage under Medicare Part A requires a prior three-day hospital stay or skilled nursing facility stay. [42 U.S.C. § 1395x] The home health services must be initiated within 14 days of discharge. Coverage is limited to 100 visits per spell of illness. [42 U.S.C. § 1395d] However, coverage is available under Medicare Part B for all services not covered under Part A. This includes coverage for those individuals who do not meet the prior institutional requirement or have received more than 100 visits. Moreover, the prior institutionalization requirement and 100-day limitation do not apply to individuals who are enrolled only in Part A or only in Part B.

Q 11:13 What has been the recent trend for home care services?

Accommodating living at home has been improved on two fronts: physical aids and community-based services. Developers targeting retirees build homes that are small and easy to manage, with safety bars in bathrooms, wheelchair accessibility, and emergency alert systems. State agencies working with community groups provide meals on wheels, transportation, recreational activities, respite care, companion care, and housekeeping services on a sliding pay scale.

At the same time, government funding for home care services has increased (although the growth in home care has been deliberately slowed in the past few years). This is true largely because of changes in Medicare reimbursement practices; despite more recent attempts to curtail the growth of home care services, the availability and affordability of services have substantially increased over the past decade.

Q 11:14 What role can the elder law attorney play in ensuring quality care?

Patients and family members are often unable to evaluate the quality of home care they receive. This may be a result of unfamiliarity with the services and options, or because of medical, financial, and emotional crises, or a combination of factors. The elder law attorney who is familiar with services provided to other clients, federal standards and state regulations can provide a valuable resource to help judge the quality of those services. Perhaps more importantly, the elder law attorney may be able to determine when it is necessary or beneficial to involve the services of a geriatric case manager, or directly to request internal review of the home health agency's plan for treatment.

Q 11:15 What is adult day care?

Some programs provide care for seniors from one to eight hours each day, usually at a separate facility or as an adjunct to a nursing home, assisted living, or other facility. An adult day care program may be certified by Medicare or Medicaid, and will ordinarily provide nursing supervision, meals, and activities intended not only to provide care for but also to engage participants. Assistance with activities of daily living should also be provided in an adult day care program. Such a program may help the participant maintain a higher level of functioning by regular interaction and engagement with others, while simultaneously providing respite for home caregivers.

Q 11:16 What is respite care?

Sometimes family caregivers will become exhausted and unable to continue providing care. This increases the risk that the patient may be permanently institutionalized, and so short-term institutionalization may at least provide temporary relief for the caregiver. Inpatient respite care is therefore a useful tool to help maintain the patient's placement at home over the long term. Respite care in an institution is expressly permitted under the Medicare hospice benefit, but may be provided only on an occasional basis and then for no more than five days at a time. [42 C.F.R. § 418.204]

Continuing Care Retirement Communities

Q 11:17 What is a continuing care retirement community?

Continuing care retirement communities are a recent trend in retirement living, and have become controversial because of the contractual arrangements they require. CCRCs provide a continuum of care in one complex. As the individual's needs change, he or she moves to a facility that provides more care. An individual can, for example, start in an independent living facility and move to assisted living and then into a nursing home if necessary.

Before deciding on a CCRC, healthy seniors must first try to predict their futures: Will they enjoy continued health and mercifully quick death, or will they succumb to dementia or chronic illness and need skilled nursing care for many years? Those who fear the latter can contract with a CCRC which typically requires a large admission fee or purchase of real property such as a cooperative, plus monthly payments in return for lifetime accommodations and nursing home care if needed. When the resident dies, some or all of the admission fee remains with the community regardless of whether the resident needed nursing care. The advantage is that nursing home costs are at least theoretically fixed at an affordable rate; the disadvantage is that the resident may turn over a significant portion of his or her estate to a facility without ever having used the services. Critics warn that once the admission fee is paid, the facility has little incentive to maintain high-quality assisted living and nursing services. Because the financial stability of the community is based on actuarial expectations, a greater-than-average number of residents needing nursing care could endanger the assets of all the residents. The unhappy resident may not be able to leave the facility without losing equity in the cooperative and, of course, the admission fee.

CCRCs usually accept Medicare and Medicaid payments (and may be required by state regulations to accept such payments); however, because government benefits are available only for skilled nursing care, most CCRC residents will receive few benefits from Medicare or Medicaid. Because of the substantial financial commitments required by most CCRCs and the potential exposure to additional financial risk, they tend to cater to wealthier seniors.

Most CCRCs are nonprofit facilities. Because church-sponsored groups providing lifetime care for members with no family spurred the initial growth of the industry, the industry continues to be dominated by religious organizations.

Q 11:18 How are financial arrangements at CCRCs usually structured?

CCRCs usually charge an initial fee for admission to the facility. That fee is sometimes completely nonrefundable. In other facilities, the fee may become partially or completely nonrefundable over time —for example, the admission contract may provide that the maximum available refund will be reduced by a fixed percentage each month. Most facilities offer some type of refund, although the amount of the refund will vary widely. Some facilities offer the new member a choice of refundability provisions, with the entry fee increasing as the resident retains more refund rights.

In addition to the entry fee the CCRC will charge a monthly fee. This fee may include health care coverage, or may vary depending on the level of care required by the resident.

Q 11:19 Are CCRC life-care contracts enforceable?

As with any contract claim, residents must show a breach of the contract and ensuing damages for a valid action against the facility. Arguments that the contract is unconscionable, voidable for lack of consideration, or lacking mutuality have generally not succeeded. Most life-care contracts have a probationary period, during which time the resident can leave and obtain a full refund of money and property minus the cost of care. If the resident dies during the probationary period, the estate can collect. State insurance law will regulate life-care contracts, and the National Association of Insurance Commissioners has drafted stringent requirements for liquid reserves for CCRCs.

Q 11:20 What types of CCRC contracts are commonly available?

There are three types of CCRC contracts:

1. *Extensive contract.* In this arrangement the CCRC agrees to provide housing, residential services and amenities, and health-related services. If, for example, the CCRC includes a full skilled nursing facility the contract may provide that nursing home care is included, either in the basic contract price or with a small increase in payment.
2. *Modified contract.* In a modified contract, the CCRC agrees to provide housing and residential services and amenities. In addition, health care will be covered, but with a limitation on the amount of health care provided. For example, the CCRC contract may provide that the resident will receive 30 (or 60, or 90) days of nursing care without paying any additional fees; after that period has been exhausted, the resident would pay the regular daily rate for nursing care. That rate may be discounted for CCRC residents, but may also be the facility's standard daily rate.
3. *Fee-for-service contract.* In a "fee-for-service" arrangement, the resident receives no extra health care benefits as part of the monthly fee. That fee covers only housing and residential services and amenities; any health or nursing costs are paid by the resident separately.

Q 11:21 Who regulates CCRCs?

The only federal regulation of CCRCs occurs when Medicare or Medicaid provides reimbursement for nursing or home health services provided by the CCRC. Because the lifetime CCRC contract resembles an insurance arrangement, most states regulate the industry through state insurance commissioners. In addition, the state may regulate the operation of the nursing or other health care facility that is part of the CCRC. Although CCRCs are located across the country, nearly half are concentrated in five states: Pennsylvania, California, Florida, Illinois, and Ohio. [American Association of Homes and Services for the Aging (AAHSA), Continuing Care Retirement Communities (1999)]

Many CCRCs are members of the AAHSA, which provides consumer information and suggestions. [AAHSA, 901 E St. NW, Suite 500, Washington, DC 20004-2011, (202) 783-2242, *http://www.aahsa.org*] A national accreditation organization, Continuing Care Accreditation Commission (CCAC), shares office space with and is sponsored by AAHSA and also provides some assistance and oversight, albeit voluntary. [CCAC, 901 E. St. NW, Suite 500, Washington, DC 20004, (202) 783-7286, *www.ccaconline.org*]

Q 11:22 What should the elder law attorney consider in reviewing a CCRC contract?

A CCRC contract can be daunting, not only for the client-resident but also for the elder law practitioner. Among the myriad of concerns raised by consideration of a CCRC contract are the following:

1. *Fees.* What is the entry fee and monthly fee, and how are they calculated? Are they based on actuarial assumptions, or designed to ensure that the CCRC is able to sustain itself? Is any portion of the entry fee refundable, and under what conditions? Is some portion of the entry fee tax deductible as a medical expense? What are the due dates and penalties for monthly fees? Is there a provision limiting the amount of future increases on monthly fees?
2. *Facility and services.* Does the agreement clearly specify which unit the resident will occupy, and under what circumstances the resident may choose to change locations? Is the resident's unit easily accessible, both now and if the resident loses mobility? Are meals, housekeeping, recreational activities, transportation services, and guest provisions clearly delineated?
3. *Health and nursing services.* Does the agreement provide for the availability and cost of home health care and possible

future nursing care? Will the CCRC's onsite nursing facility be able to handle the care of the resident for any likely future medical condition? Are there limitations for preexisting conditions? Who will determine what level of care the resident requires, and what appeal rights will the resident have if forced to move to a higher level of care? What will happen to the resident's unit if there is a temporary placement in the assisted living or skilled nursing facilities? What provisions are made for the relocation of the resident's spouse in the event the resident is institutionalized?

4. *Future care.* Because most CCRCs carefully guard their tax-exempt status, they probably have some internal provisions for the continuing care of residents after financial resources are exhausted. Does the contract make any reference to such a policy? If not, what are the terms of the CCRC's policy, and what has been its practice to date?

5. *Residence councils and governance.* What provisions are made for self-determination for the CCRC's residents? Is there a council or advisory group established for residents to voice their concerns and desires for change or improvement? Are residents' rights spelled out in a policy manual or handbook, and if so who has the power to change those provisions and under what circumstances?

6. *Financial stability.* One of the most pressing problems for CCRCs has been financial failures in the industry. What arrangements has the CCRC made for a fund to cover future expenses, especially medical care? Is any such fund based on a calculation of the present value of future expenses, including assumptions about resident mortality and morbidity? What organization sponsors the CCRC, and is its financial backing sufficient to help ensure success? Has the CCRC operated for a period of time already? Are the CCRC's finances currently sound?

7. *Quality of care.* Is the CCRC accredited by the Continuing Care Accreditation Commission? How does the nursing facility rate in reviews of such institutions? (Check, among other sources, the Health Care Financing Administration's "Nursing Home Compare" page at *http://www.medicare.gov/NHCompare/home.asp.*)

Q 11:23 What is a naturally occurring retirement community?

An alternative to CCRCs is the NORC, or naturally occurring retirement community. The developer offers homes for purchase with adjacent nursing home and hospital facilities. Others contract for services with nearby health care providers. This type of development relies on the residents having an affinity for similar services, and amounts to planned aging-in-place. That means, of course, that the resident retains personal autonomy and the comfort of staying at or near his or her home. Unless the NORC includes a wide variety of housing and health care options, the result may be that residents remain in settings where care becomes inadequate as their needs increase.

Congregate Living and Adult Care

Q 11:24 What is congregate living?

Congregate living (also referred to as independent living) usually refers to residential environments for healthy but frail elders, who generally function at a higher level than those needing assisted living care. These individuals do not need skilled nursing care, aside from a periodic meds check, and they can usually perform most activities of daily living; however, they do not have the energy or mental capacity to prepare adequate meals, do housework, or drive vehicles. Congregate living is not suited for individuals who have dementia. Congregate residents usually live in their own small apartments or casitas equipped with kitchenettes, and go to central dining rooms for most of their meals. Congregate living facilities do not provide health care, are not covered by long-term care insurance or Medicare or Medicaid. Payment is on a private-pay basis.

Q 11:25 How does congregate living differ from assisted living?

The main difference between independent living facilities and assisted living facilities is the availability of medical care. While an assisted living facility will be classified as "congregate living," not all congregate arrangements are as complete as assisted living. Generally assisted living facilities are required to have nurses on duty 24 hours a day while other congregate living facilities may have a nurse on duty for only several hours a day, five days per week. A key difference between assisted living and other congregate arrangements is that the latter will not supervise medications, although they may provide some prompting and may also assist with other activities of daily living.

Q 11:26 What is an adult care facility?

Until recently, adult care facilities were the primary alternative to nursing homes. Generally both adult care and nursing home environments were provided at the same location, with similar physical plants: large, hospital-like structures with semi-private rooms and central dining areas. When residents of the adult care facilities became too ill to function, they were moved to the nursing home portion. Now adult care facilities can include congregate housing, board and care housing, or any such facility geared to residents who are high-functioning but too frail or poor to live independently. An adult care facility may have only one or a few elements of the continuum of care; if the entire continuum is provided, the adult care facility may qualify as a continuing care retirement community.

Assisted Living

Q 11:27 What is assisted living?

Assisted living facilities are geared to individuals who are not yet medically needy enough to merit skilled nursing facility care, but still need assistance with their activities of daily living and some lower-level nursing assistance, such as oversight of medications and injections. Assisted living combines housing, support services, and health care. Some assisted living facilities offer progressive levels of care. Staff is available 24 hours a day and access to health and medical services is available. Assisted living facilities are generally more upscale, more modern, and more expensive than board and care homes, but residents still incur only 60 percent to 80 percent of the cost of nursing home care. Assisted living gives the residents much greater autonomy and privacy than they would have at a nursing facility, but still provides the social contacts, assistance with the activities of daily living, emergency systems, and monitoring that would not be available to these individuals at home. Residents generally need to be healthy enough to take all their meals in a central dining room. Transportation, daily exercise programs, arts and crafts classes, entertainment, transportation, housekeeping services, laundry, and other amenities are provided. Residents are not medically needy enough to qualify for Medicare or Medicaid assistance, and are generally affluent.

Q 11:28 What sources of payment exist for assisted living?

Generally, assisted living is paid for on a private-pay basis. The expenses of assisted living facility residents may be deductible as health-related expenditures for income tax purposes. Long-term care insurance may pay for some of the expense (depending on policy terms) if the facility qualifies as an institution and the policyholder needs some assistance with activities of daily living. Some states offer a Medicaid benefit through Medicaid waivers or state-funded programs. While most assisted living residents are affluent, if they run out of funds while in an assisted living facility they will be transferred to a nursing home covered by Medicaid.

A major problem in paying for assisted living is the "medical" charge that may be added to the base charge, often at the discretion of the assisted living facility. That is, the resident is "assessed" periodically for the kinds of assistance needed. If the facility believes the resident requires further assistance, they may increase the "level" of care provided and add another $200, $500 or $1,000 per month to the bill. It can be very difficult to determine ahead of time what the true cost of the facility is likely to be. As a result, some individuals who really cannot support the cost of the higher levels of care may nonetheless take up residence, only to see their monthly bill double.

One very important new development in ways to pay for assisted living is the growing trend for long-term care insurance to include assisted living costs (sometimes, the entire unbundled fee) as a long-term care expense provided the individual meets the ADL requirement, usually two out of six. Those with older policies should investigate whether they can "upgrade" to these new standards.

The cost of assisted living must be a key consideration for planners who advise the elderly to transfer homes to children, even with a retained life use. It is the sales proceeds from the home that typically finances the older person's admission to an assisted living or continuing care facility. When the older person's name is not on the deed, or upon sale a substantial portion of sales proceeds will pass to the remainderperson on the deed with retained life use, this opportunity may be lost.

Q 11:29 How much should a resident of an assisted living facility deduct as an itemized medical expense for income tax purposes?

An important feature for many elderly individuals is the ability to deduct the high cost of care from income for tax purposes. While deductibility is obvious for such expenses as nursing homes, it is less clear for the costs of an assisted living facility when the resident may initially require only a modest amount of assistance and is really moving as a form of insurance against increasing needs.

IRS Notice 97-31 explains that "qualified long-term care services" are deductible, defined as: "Necessary diagnostic, preventative, therapeutic, curing, treating, mitigating, and rehabilitative services, and maintenance or personal care services that are required by a chronically ill individual and provided pursuant to a plan of care prescribed by a licensed health care practitioner," defined as someone who cannot, without substantial assistance from another individual, perform at least two out of six ADLs (eating, toileting, transferring, bathing, dressing, and continence), *or* requires substantial supervision to protect from threats to health and safety due to severe cognitive impairment.

While there is no bright-line test, a common wisdom is that (1) residents who live in the assisted living facility independently and require no assistance cannot deduct; (2) those who receive some assistance, but that is not the primary reason for residing in the facility (e.g., a spouse), can deduct only the medical care portion, and should ask the facility to provide a percentage figure unless those charges are tabulated separately; and (3) those whose primary reason for staying in assisted living can deduct 100 percent. [Treas. Reg. § 1.213-1(e)(1)(v)(a)]

Q 11:30 How should one choose an assisted living facility?

A key issue for anyone considering moving to an assisted living facility will be the cost, both the "daily rate" and the hidden expenses: extra charges for medical expenses; extra charges for supplies the facility encourages the resident to purchase through the facility; $35 per trip for escort to a doctor's appointment or elsewhere. Especially if the client will be spending down principal to meet the monthly costs, and hoping to live longer than the money, financial planning is a must. For cost calculation, one approach is to demand to see the "evaluation" form the facility uses, not for the preliminary intake needs assessment, but for follow-up, and "check off" what you think the resident might need, then ask for a quote at that price. Needless to say, it is absolutely essential to review the entire assisted living contract before making the decision. You can read a sample assisted living contract provided online by the American Association of Homes and Services for the Aging at *http://www.aahsa.org/public/residentcontract.doc* (in MS Word); disregard the request for a login.

A good summary of these and other issues, a checklist, and a cost-calculator may be found in an article published by Consumer Reports, "Is Assisted Living the Right Choice?" [Consumer Reports Jan. 2001, p. 26] Other resources are the industry-sponsored National Center for Assisted Living, *http://www.ncal.org*, which offers a consumer guide and list of questions to ask, and the Consumer Consortium on Assisted Living, *http://www.ccal.org*.

Q 11:31 What rights does an assisted living resident have to prevent eviction?

Recently, there have been numerous reported cases of residents being "dumped" by facilities who believe they require further care than the facility provides, or summarily asked to leave. It is often unclear whether standard residential landlord-tenant protections apply to the facility, but at the same time, the discharge provisions of the Nursing Home Bill of Rights do not. A few states do require an administrative hearing process (e.g., Ohio Rev. Code Ann. § 3721.16(C); Okla Admin. Code § 310:680-17-3; Or. Rev. Stat. § 443.739(18); Vt. Code R. § 13 162 004-22 (§ V, § 5.3.a(2); Wis. Admin. Code HFS § 83.20(2)9 d)(1)). Massachusetts, Minnesota, and New York explicitly apply standard landlord-tenant protections (see Mass. Laws Ann. ch. 19D, § 9(a)(§ 8); Minn. § 144D.06, and Chapter 504d; N.Y. Soc. Serv. Law § 461-h), and this trend may increase as assisted living residents grow in numbers. Others either state that a resident may file a complaint, give the right to an informal conference, or say nothing.

Where law is silent, the attorney may have to make analogies to landlord-tenant law. Some states exempt from landlord-tenant protections arrangements in which the housing element is merely a component of treatment or training. In that case, thanks to the Fair Housing Act and Americans with Disabilities Act, the facility could find itself in a catch-22: if the housing is incidental to the treatment, on what basis is the person being asked to leave? Thus, Step Two in the eviction defense process is to charge a violation of the FHA and/or ADA. [42 U.S.C. § 3601 (Fair Housing Act); 42 U.S.C. § 12101 (ADA) (would apply to non-housing functions of the facility, such as meeting rooms, meal sites, adult day care, long-term care wings)] Assuming the resident can obtain sufficient means of assistance (e.g., family members who pay for additional aides or supervision), on what basis may the person be told to leave? Does the contractual agreement that the facility in its sole discretion (perhaps after only an informal conference) may reach that decision, overrule the resident's rights under federal law?

Because of these many problems, the ABA House of Delegates in August 2001 adopted a resolution supporting "uniform and comprehensive state and territorial standards, regulation, and oversight of facilities and programs, commonly referred to as assisted living."

Two resources that survey these issues are: "Consumer Issues in Assisted Living," by Eric Carlson of the National Senior Citizens Law Center (partially derived from the residential care facilities chapter of *Long-Term Care* Advocacy (Matthew Bender) by Carlson; and the National Academy of Elder Law Attorneys' "White Paper on Assisted Living," prepared by the NAELA Public Policy Committee Long-Term Care Subcommittee, 2001.

Skilled Nursing Facilities and Nursing Homes

Q 11:32 What is a skilled nursing facility?

A skilled nursing facility is defined in the federal regulations as an institution that provides skilled nursing care and rehabilitation services for the injured, sick, or physically disabled (not the mentally incapacitated, although emergency psychiatric assessments are covered). [42 U.S.C. § 1395i-3] SNFs include hospitals, nursing homes, and rehabilitation hospitals. Medicare usually covers costs. Patients are admitted at the recommendation of a physician and are under a doctor's care during their stay. Medicare coverage is available for up to 100 days per benefit period if the patient has had a qualifying three-day hospital stay and requires daily skilled care. [42 U.S.C. § 1395d] The first 20 days are paid in full and the patient must meet a copayment obligation for days 21 through 100. Medicare does not reimburse for custodial nursing home care.

Each SNF must have a physician serving as medical director, and 24-hour licensed nursing care must be provided (including the presence of a registered nurse during at least one shift per day, seven days per week). Nutritional, rehabilitation, pharmaceutical, lab, dental, and social services must be provided by the SNF, along with an activities program for all residents. A written health care plan is required for each patient. The SNF's goal is to attain the "the highest practicable mental, physical and psychosocial well-being of each resident" for its population. [42 U.S.C. § 1396r(b)(2)]

One essential resource for the practitioner with frequent need to access information about nursing homes is the National Citizens Coalition for Nursing Home Reform or "NCCNHR" ("nick-ner"); *http://www.nccnhr.org*. It is essential to purchase their book "Nursing Homes—Getting Good Care There." NCCNHR also publishes numerous helpful checklists and similar materials.

Q 11:33 When is nursing home care necessary?

Many elderly people have a horror of being "put in a nursing home" by uncaring children, where they will be expected to live out their days wandering the hallways and weaving baskets. Although everyone would prefer that elderly citizens live out their days in their own homes, surrounded by familiar objects and loved ones, the reality is that chronically ill and demented individuals are almost impossible to care for at home with any degree of safety. In fact, nursing homes can provide cost-effective care and close monitoring of these individuals in a secure environment. They can also provide a centralized location for a variety of services that would not be possible at home; for instance, in addition to doctors, nurses, and aides, the nursing home staff may include dietitians, pharmacists, social workers, and rehabilitation specialists.

The loss of privacy and independence may be offset by increased social activity, better nutrition, and respite for exhausted family caretakers; however, the nursing home industry has been plagued by poor management, inadequate staffing, and scandalous care of an inherently vulnerable population.

A frequently cited 1991 study in the New England Journal of Medicine projects that 43 percent of those age 65 and over will spend some time in a nursing home. At age 75, the risk is 50 percent; at age 90, 75 percent. Other studies generally confirm these figures. The same study shows an average stay of 1½–3 years, with 21 percent staying over 5 years. At least one state, Connecticut, reports that its residents' average length of stay is 2½ years, but this may be less than elsewhere because Connecticut has several state and federally funded home care assistance programs, for which the average time on the program is 3 years. Source: The Connecticut Partnership for Long-Term Care and the Connecticut Department of Social Services (data for 1988–1998).

Q 11:34 Who pays for nursing home care?

Depending on geography and the level of care needed, nursing home residency can cost between $2,500 and $9,000 or more per month. Few patients can afford to foot the total bill for more than a few months, so Medicaid benefits often make up the difference. An increasing number of individuals purchase long-term care insurance, which is expensive if purchased at 70 or older, but can generally enable residents to choose a high-quality nursing facility.

Q 11:35 How are Medicare and Medicaid benefits apportioned?

Medicare Part A benefits pay for skilled nursing facility care for medical, nursing, and rehabilitation services (see chapter 13 for a discussion of Medicare). Once the patient has been hospitalized for three successive days (not counting the day of discharge), a total of 100 days of SNF care is covered by Medicare; the first 20 days are totally covered, while the remaining 80 days requires a co-pay of $105 per day (amount for 2003) from the patient. [42 C.F.R. § 409.85] SNF services include room and board, nursing care, therapy, and drugs.

Medicaid benefits vary by state, but they are generally need-based and require that the patient be impoverished and pay almost all of his or her income for his or her share of the cost of care (see chapter 14 for a discussion of Medicaid). Medicaid pays for both skilled nursing and long-term care costs, and because federal law requires that a nursing facility provide services that would attain or maintain the highest practicable physical and mental well-being of the resident, the nursing home cannot deny services such as therapy or psychiatric assessments as not being covered by Medicaid.

Other than copayments, deductibles, and mandated contributions to the cost of care, Medicare and Medicaid patients cannot be charged for any medically related services, social activities, or personal hygiene items. The patient must foot the bill for telephone and television use, cosmetic items, clothing, and books. Under Medicaid, patients are allowed anywhere from $20 or so to as high as $75 (some states use fixed amounts, which may or may not change each year, others tie the figure to the maximum SSI benefit) per month, which may be applied toward such personal use. Nursing homes are forbidden from requiring waivers of Medicare or Medicaid benefits from patients. [42 C.F.R. § 483.12(d)(1)] And finally, Medicaid patients must be informed if their assets grow to a point where their need-based benefits may be threatened. [42 U.S.C. § 1396r(c)(6)(B)]

Q 11:36 Can nursing homes require third parties to pay the bill?

No. Nursing homes are prohibited under federal law from requiring a third party—for instance, an adult child—to assume responsibility for nursing home costs as a condition of admission. [42 U.S.C. § 1396r(c)(5)(A); 42 C.F.R. § 483.12(d)(2)] Although it is settled law that one person is not responsible for the debts of another, nursing homes often manage to lure third parties into signing contracts that ensure payments. Deposits are prohibited when care is covered under Medicare, and Medicaid patients cannot be required to produce more than two months of care in advance. There are no restrictions on deposits for private pay patients or those covered under other forms of insurance unless state law provides otherwise.

There is some question, however, whether a nursing home, as a creditor, has standing to bring suit against a resident's fiduciary—conservator, guardian, attorney-in-fact, trustee of a revocable trust—for supposed "negligence" that results in a denial of Medicaid benefits and accordingly, causes a loss to the nursing facility. In a Connecticut case, the state supreme court recently allowed a nursing home to claim on a conservator's bond for failures in handling the patient's finances, so that the funds were neither paid for care, nor dealt with in a timely fashion to ensure quick Medicaid eligibility. [The Jewish Home for the Elderly of Fairfield Cty., Inc. v. Cantore, 257 Conn. 531 (2001)]

With increasing frequency, nursing homes have tried to blend into contracts side agreements with third parties, such as the agreement by an attorney-in-fact to spend the principal's money only on nursing home care, or a similar promise by the "responsible party" who admits to having custody of the patient's funds. Most practitioners feel that these agreements would be unenforceable for the reasons discussed in the first paragraph, but at the same time, the expense and unpleasantness of litigation may cause such third parties to settle when the nursing home makes its claim, rather than fight. The best course is to advise that *no one* other than the resident sign any document, or if necessary, sign as "attorney-in-fact" (if that is in fact the case) to avoid any personal liability.

Q 11:37 What should the lawyer for a patient or patient's family look for in an admission contract?

The agreement to be signed by the patient or responsible party at the time of admission should clearly state the costs of care, services covered by those costs (including meals and social activities), legal responsibilities of the patient, the patient's rights under federal and state laws, and grievance procedures. The agreement should *not* name a third party as a responsible party, should *not* require a deposit for Medicare patients or more than two months' advance payment for Medicaid patients, and should *not* require a "donation" to the facility.

Patients and their families should also be wary of any waivers of liability, particularly contractual provisions that release a nursing home from responsibility if the patient is injured after restraints are removed. Experts suggest that such provisions are against public policy and may violate state consumer protection statutes. If a patient challenges the admission contract and is not admitted as a result, the state long-term care ombudsman should be notified.

Other contract provisions to watch for include any requirement that the resident have or sign an advance medical directive or consent to particular medical procedures, any restriction on visiting hours or contact by family members, and any requirement that the resident's income be automatically turned over to the facility. For more suggestions on nursing home contract provisions, consider the AARP Web site at *http://www.aarp.org/confacts/health/nhcontract.html.*

Sadly, many contracts do not live up to the requirements. Then the family must choose:

- reject the nursing home out of hand, despite the fact that the care and facilities are the best available;
- annotate the document to delete offensive positions and hope this will be a sufficient defense should problems arise (unilateral modifications, one hopes, may at worst nullify the contract entirely);
- sign, but only in a capacity as agent; or
- sign what and how the nursing home wants, and hope that all such provisions are against public policy or preempted, and therefore unenforceable.

Q 11:38 What laws protect the rights of nursing home patients?

A large body of federal and state law protects nursing home patients, including civil rights and consumer protection regulations. Tort remedies have always been available to nursing home resident plaintiffs, but until recently did not bring in significant damages because the plaintiffs were usually elderly, nonworking, and in poor health before the tortuous occurrence. Outrage at nursing home conditions has now encouraged juries to return much larger awards based on quality, rather than quantity, of life, at least in those states where "tort reform" does not limit non-economic damages or punitive damages.

The strongest protection for the rights of nursing home patients is the federal Nursing Home Reform Act (NHRA), which was enacted in 1987 as part of the Omnibus Budget Reconciliation Act. [42 U.S.C. §§ 1395i-3 (skilled nursing facilities) and 1396r (nursing facilities), et seq. (42 C.F.R. § 483)] In addition to requiring nursing homes to screen and frequently assess their patients and employees, NHRA has imposed a patient's bill of rights to assure quality of life. All nursing facilities that accept Medicare and Medicaid payments "must" provide services geared to attaining and maintaining "the highest practicable mental, physical and psychosocial well-being of each resident in accordance with a written plan of care." [42 U.S.C. § 1396r(b)(2)] In addition, some states have a parallel "nursing home bill of rights" patterned on federal law.

Q 11:39 What is the office of the long-term care ombudsman?

Each state is required to establish and operate an Office of the State Long Term Care Ombudsman, pursuant to the federal Older Americans Act (OAA). [42 U.S.C. § 3058] Local ombudsmen throughout the state are authorized to work on behalf of residents to resolve complaints. Ombudsmen have the authority and the responsibility to investigate any activities that could threaten the health, safety, or welfare of residents of nursing homes and other long-term care facilities. They are allowed to represent residents before other government agencies and are expected to help develop advocacy groups.

Q 11:40 What are the repercussions to nursing homes for violations of federal and state regulations?

States are required to survey nursing homes to make sure they comply with federal regulations, and may have additional and more stringent regulations of their own. [42 U.S.C. § 1396r(d)(4)] No facility can operate without state licensure; thus, facilities that do not meet state requirements may lose their license, and those that do not meet federal regulations may lose their Medicare and Medicaid reimbursement (which may constitute up to half of the nursing home's income). Deficiencies are made public and may even be published in local newspapers; the Centers for Medicare and Medicaid site, *http://www.medicare.gov*, includes various "comparison" pages and makes available these same state surveys on the internet. States are also required to provide intermediate sanctions, such as denying federal funds, prohibiting the facilities from taking on new patients, and appointing a receiver to ensure the correction of deficiencies. [42 U.S.C. § 1395i-3(h)(2)(B)]

Q 11:41 What are the rights of nursing home residents?

The Residents' Bill of Rights provided by the Nursing Home Reform Act includes the following specific rights protecting nursing home residents:

1. *Free choice.* The patient's right to participate actively in his or her care, including choosing a physician and establishing a care plan.
2. *Notice of rights.* The right to obtain full information from the health care provider regarding medical status, residents' rights, grievance procedures, costs of care, and available Medicare and Medicaid benefits.
3. *Privacy and confidentiality.* The right to privacy during medical treatment and during communications with family and friends; the right to confidentiality of medical and other personal records; and the right to authorize access to medical records to family, health care practitioners, and advocacy groups.
4. *Participation.* The right to decline to participate in social activities; the right to have family visitors at any time and nonfamily visitors during reasonable visiting hours.
5. *Transfer and discharge.* The right not to be transferred without sufficient notice, and then only if the patient's medical needs are no longer being met, the patient can no longer pay, or the patient is disruptive or dangerous.
6. *Transaction review.* The right to review all transactions made on behalf of the patient, and to keep independent checking and interest-bearing accounts.
7. *Freedom from restraints.* The right to be free from abuse and, unless authorized by a physician, from restraints.

8. *Accommodation of needs.* The right to reside and receive services with reasonable accommodation of individual needs and preferences and to receive notice before the room or roommate of a resident is changed.
9. *Grievances.* The right to voice grievances regarding treatment or care without discrimination or reprisal for voicing such grievance and the right to prompt resolution of any grievances by the facility.
10. *Examination of survey results.* The right to examine the results of the most recent facility survey with respect to the facility and any plan of correction in effect for the facility.

[42 U.S.C. § 1395r(c)]

Each resident must be informed at the time of admission, both orally and in writing, of the resident's rights. The facility must make a written statement of the rights available to each resident upon reasonable request. [42 U.S.C. § 1395r(c)(1)(B)]

Q 11:42 How often are nursing homes required to assess their patients' medical, rehabilitation, and social needs?

The statute says that nursing homes are required to assess needs "regularly," which means every 12 months. The Nursing Home Reform Act mandated an assessment system that was put into place in 1990. [42 U.S.C. § 1395r(b)(3)] All Medicare- and Medicaid-certified facilities must measure the functional, medical, and mental status of patients upon admission and regularly during residence at the facility. The assessment must describe the resident's capability to perform the daily life functions as well as any significant impairment in functional capacity. Promptly upon admission (but no later than 14 days after admission), patients must be assessed using a "minimum data set" (MDS) for behavior, decubitus sores, depression, incontinence, need for restraints, vision, hearing, nutrition, activities of daily living, hydration, and general mental status. Each patient must be assessed every three months after admission using "resident assessment protocols" (RAPs), as well as after hospitalizations or other transfers. [42 U.S.C. § 1395r(b)(3)(C)] The plan must be updated every 12 months.

Q 11:43 Are nursing homes required to provide a plan of care for each resident?

A comprehensive care plan must be prepared by an interdisciplinary team within seven days after the completion of the assessment. [42 C.F.R. § 483.20(k)(2)(i)] The plan of care must describe the medical, nursing, and psychological needs of the resident and must describe how the resident's needs will be met. [42 U.S.C. § 1395r-3(b)(2)] The plan is prepared by the resident's attending physician and a registered professional nurse with responsibility for the patient. Where practicable, the plan should be prepared with the participation of the resident and the resident's family or legal representative. The plan of care must be updated every 12 months. [42 U.S.C. § 1395r(b)(3)(C)]

Q 11:44 What are the staffing requirements for nursing homes?

Nursing home staff are regulated. Licensed nursing staff must be on duty 24 hours per day, a registered nurse must be on site at least 8 hours a day, and all patients must be seen by a physician or, in some states, an alternative professional such as a nurse practitioner or physician's assistant. [42 U.S.C. § 1395r(b)(4)(C)(i)] Nursing homes with more than 120 patients must have at least one full-time social worker on staff. [42 C.F.R. § 483.15(g)] Staff must be checked against a state registry listing persons convicted of abuse or theft (see Q 11:45). Minimum requirements are also set by the NHRA for training and in-service education.

Unfortunately, no federal national minimum patient/staff ratio has been established by law or regulation. The absence of such a requirement has been criticized, and is the subject of continuing legislative discussions. See, for example, the Department of Health and Human Services' 2000 study which suggests that a reasonable minimum staff ratio might be one full-time nurse's aide for every four residents, and about one RN/LPN for every eight residents. The federal study also determined that about half of nursing homes studied fell below those minimum standards. The DHHS/HCFA report is available online at *http://cms.hhs.gov/medicaid/reports/rp700hmp.asp*. Phase II of the study, published in 2002, presents "thresholds" below which there are more likely to be quality of care deficits but above which there may be little improvement, coming to essentially the same conclusions, and concluding that few U.S.

nursing homes meet this level. [Report to Congress: Appropriateness of Minimum Nurse Staffing Ratios In Nursing Homes Phase II Final Report, Ch. 3, online in Adobe Acrobat separate chapters, *http://cms.hhs.gov/medicaid/reports/rp1201home.asp*]

Q 11:45 Do states prohibit nursing homes and other elder care facilities from hiring staff applicants with criminal backgrounds?

At least 39 states require background checks for long-term care workers. Nearly all of these state statutes cover nursing home employees. The state laws vary. At least 30 states' statutes cover home health care workers. Some include direct care employees in residential care homes, assisted living, and other settings. A few of the state statutes even cover volunteers. A chart of the states from the Department of Health and Human Services is available online as part of a State of Connecticut Office of Legislative Research Report Number 2002-R-0574 for which the link runs on for about a paragraph, but which you can search for using the search function at *www.cga.state.ct.us*, using the number shown as the "title" and the database as "OLR Reports."

Q 11:46 Under what circumstances can a nursing home resident be physically or pharmacologically restrained?

A nursing home resident has the right to be free from any physical restraints imposed, or any psychoactive drugs administered for purposes of discipline or convenience, unless they are required to treat the patient's medical symptoms. [42 U.S.C. §§ 1395r(c)(1)(A)(ii), 1395r(c)(1)(D)] Psychoactive drugs are defined as those used to control mood, mental status, or behavior. Patients are also protected from the use of unnecessary drugs and antipsychotic drugs, the latter being allowed only if the patient has specific psychiatric conditions and demonstrates violent behavior or is in great distress. Antipsychotics are not to be used for relatively benign behaviors such as pacing, anxiety, uncooperativeness, or impaired memory. State laws also provide protections. A compilation of state laws relating in general to mental illness, which generally cover "forced medication" issues, may be found online at the Treatment Advocacy Center website, www.psychlaws.org.

Q 11:47 Under what circumstances may a nursing home discharge a resident?

As stated in the patients' bill of rights, transfers are allowed under federal law only if:

1. The patient's physician confirms that his or her needs cannot be adequately met at the facility;
2. The patient no longer needs nursing home care;
3. The patient presents a danger to the health and safety of others;
4. After reasonable notice the patient fails to pay or arrange for the payment of costs; or
5. The facility closes.

[42 U.S.C. § 1395r(c)(2)(A); 42 C.F.R. § 483.12(a)(2)]

If a patient is determined to be mentally retarded or mentally ill (not including dementia) within 30 months of admission to a nursing home facility, the state must arrange for his or her transfer to a more appropriate facility. Those who have lived at the facility for more than 30 months have the option of remaining there or moving to another facility. [42 U.S.C. § 1396r(e)(7)(C)] The patient has the right to challenge the diagnosis of mental retardation or mental illness at a properly noticed hearing prior to the transfer.

Q 11:48 What notice must be provided by a nursing home before discharging a resident?

The nursing home patient must be given at least 30 days' notice prior to transfer or discharge unless an emergency situation exists or if the patient can be upgraded immediately to a less restricted environment. The notice must include the reasons for the transfer, the patient's rights with regard to appeals, and the name, address, and telephone number of the local long-term care ombudsman or similar advocate. [42 U.S.C. § 1396r(c)(1)(B)]

Nursing homes are no longer allowed to refuse to readmit a Medicaid patient who has been transferred for hospital care. If the patient's bed is filled during his or her absence, another must be made available when he is ready for discharge from the hospital. [42 U.S.C. § 1396r(c)(2)(D); 42 C.F.R. § 483.12(b)(3)] Some nursing homes set a "limited bed" policy, whereby only a certain number of beds are available for Medicaid patients. A federal court has held that such a practice violates Medicaid and civil rights laws. [Linton v. Commissioner of Health and Environment, 65 F.3d 508 (6th Cir. 1995), upholding the district court determination in Linton v. Carney, 779 F. Supp. 925 (M.D. Tenn. 1990)]

Q 11:49 What remedies does a nursing home resident have for the facility's improper attempt to discharge the resident?

Initially, of course, the resident's attorney (or other representative) should make clear to the facility that it is in violation of the relevant laws, that this must of course be a mistake, but that if the mistake is not immediately remedied, the facility (and the administrator) will be held accountable. It may even be useful to provide family with copies of the patient's bill of rights for this purpose. If this is not effective, after suggesting to the nursing home administrator to inform the facility's insurance carrier, the patient should immediately notify the local long-term care ombudsman, who should investigate the matter and take the necessary action to protect the patient. If this does not happen, however, the attorney may have to consider other injunctive action. At this point the attorney may want to contact the National Senior Citizens Law Center or other nonprofit organization for assistance.

Q 11:50 How does a rehabilitation hospital differ from a regular hospital?

Rehabilitation hospitals are staffed and equipped to deal with patients who no longer need the acute care services provided by a regular hospital, but who are not yet ready to be discharged to a long-term care facility. Usually the patients need physical or speech therapy, retraining in activities of daily living, or strength-building exercises. The usual stay is one to four weeks. Rehabilitation hospital care will usually be covered by Medicare; however, "restoration capacity" is required for care at such facilities. (Coverage may still be available if no appropriate skilled nursing facility can be located; see chapter 13).

Hospice Care

Q 11:51 What is hospice care?

Hospice care is intended to provide relief from pain, palliative care, and assistance with the dying process, without attempting to provide curative treatment to terminally ill patients. Since hospice programs first began to appear in this country in the mid-1970s, the programs have become widely accepted by the public and have experienced phenomenal growth. Although hospice programs were initially institutional in nature, recent trends have favored hospice services provided in the patient's home, in adult care homes, or in whatever setting the patient may already be in.

Q 11:52 What are the requirements for admittance to a hospice?

Hospice services by definition are provided to terminally ill patients. No national regulation requires all hospice programs to screen patients for terminal condition, although Medicare rules restrict hospice benefits to those diagnosed with a terminal illness and given less than six months to live. [42 C.F.R. § 418.22] The Medicare limitation has established the *de facto* standard for hospice admittance.

Q 11:53 What sources of payment exist for hospice care?

Hospice benefits are provided under both the Medicare and Medicaid programs. Many private insurance policies also cover hospice care. In 1996, according to U.S. Census figures, over two-thirds of those who were enrolled in hospice programs were over age 65. The Medicare program's excellent hospice benefit is a key reason for the growth of the hospice industry. For more on Medicare's hospice benefit, see chapter 13.

Practice-Related Issues

Q 11:54 What typical problems might an elder law attorney encounter regarding the choice of care facilities?

In assisting with the selection of a care facility, an elder law attorney typically might have to deal with issues relating to: (1) the need to use drugs to control a patient's behavior, (2) the appropriateness of a board and care facility versus an assisted living facility, (3) life-care contracts, (4) local community services available, or (5) conflicts between caregivers.

1. *Behavior-controlling drugs.* The daughter of a couple in their 80s who live independently consults an attorney about obtaining temporary guardianship of her father. The father is still capable of performing all of his ADLs (although he relies completely on his wife for cooking, cleaning, and other household duties), but he has become increasingly angry and abusive toward both his wife and daughter. The daughter suspects that he has early dementia, but he adamantly refuses to see a doctor. The daughter is now worried for her mother's safety, and wants to obtain temporary guardianship so that she can move her father to a secure facility. Her attorney arranges for the father to be assessed in the home by a geriatrician, then files the petition; however, the attorney appointed to represent the father objects to the guardianship at the hearing. She states that there is no reason to remove the father from the home, because his erratic behavior can be controlled with drugs. What is the petitioner's attorney's next step?

   This is a situation where the patient might be much better off in a nursing home, rather than at home with his wife. The petitioner's attorney should consult with the father's geriatrician or a mental health expert to determine the type and dosage of drugs that would be needed to guarantee the mother's safety in the home. The physician may be willing to testify that the father would be better supervised in a health care facility and would need fewer medications, so he would likely be able to perform his ADLs much longer than if he stayed at home in a drugged state. A patient who has loss of vision or hearing may be in even greater danger of losing his overall level of functioning if he is heavily medicated.

2. *Board and care home versus assisted living facility.* The attorney has been following the progress of her client, a 75-year-old woman who suffered a stroke and, following recovery at a rehabilitation hospital, has been discharged to a board and care home located a few blocks away from the client's oldest son. The stroke affected the client's ability to

speak and walk, but there is no doubt that she still has full mental capacity. As the weeks go by, the client makes remarkable progress, but appears to be increasingly depressed. The son suspects nothing, because his mother is always cheerful when he visits, and he is pleased that he has been able to keep her close to home in a home-like environment. Should the attorney talk to the son about scheduling his mother for an appointment to deal with the depression?

Although it is tempting to work with family members in dealing with an elderly client's problems, the attorney's first duty is to her client. Her client's mind is intact, and there is no reason why the attorney can't discuss her concerns with the client. There may be situational, rather than physiological, reasons for the depression—perhaps there is an aide at the home who has been unpleasant to the patient, or perhaps the client is a smoker and is unhappy about having to forgo the habit (and in fact there may be good arguments why she should be allowed to resume). Often in these scenarios the patients are simply bored. Board and care homes are excellent for frail and demented patients, but cannot offer the social services that an assisted living program could. If this is the case, the attorney should suggest a three-way meeting with the client and her son to discuss a transfer to a higher-level facility, or perhaps enrollment in an adult day care program.

3. *Review of life-care contracts.* A couple in their 70s meets with an attorney after visiting several continuing care facilities in the area. They like one in particular, but are horrified at the admission fee of $200,000 for both of them. They own a home worth $100,000, which they plan to sell, and they have another $200,000 in liquid assets. The CCRC's monthly fee almost exactly equals the couple's combined income. They are in good health now, but their siblings have succumbed to cancer and Alzheimer's disease. What should the attorney advise?

   The couple should investigate the developer—is this a nationwide chain, and if so how are the other facilities doing? If there is a history of bankruptcy, the couple should reconsider, as the loss of the admission fee might decimate their life savings without a guarantee of housing or services. The contract should also specify the exact kind of living unit provided, any health or financial conditions of a resident that would jeopardize resident status, all refund policies (including when the resident dies), the resident's prorated share of income tax and medical deductions; and what happens if the resident needs nursing care but there are no beds available at the CCRC at that time.

4. *Community services.* An attorney has a thriving elder law practice, but has little spare time to figure out what is out there in the community. Clients occasionally ask her about local board and care homes, and about community services for the homebound, and she usually refers them to the local council on aging. Is there a way she can find out more without using up all of her free time?

   Most communities have an information and referral services that maintain lists of all residential care homes in the area, and the local council on aging is usually a wealth of information about the quality of some of these homes and services. It is unrealistic for the attorney to try to offer too much assistance in this area, especially because the quality of care in any given facility may deteriorate (or improve) quickly as a result of changes in management. The attorney may wish to meet periodically with a case management service representative, who could provide information about community services. As for local adult care residences, this is the kind of project that is perfect for law students, college students, or even high school students who are interested in the elderly. The attorney may wish to contact professors who run school clinical programs and suggest that students locate and visit the various facilities, then rate them according to checklists. The list could be updated each year and distributed to all local attorneys. The students should be reminded that board and care facilities should not be unfairly compared to Medicaid facilities, because their available income is significantly less.

5. *Conflicts among caregivers.* The niece of an Alzheimer's patient consults an attorney about the care of her aunt. The niece is concerned because her aunt is in a locked Alzheimer's unit in a well-regarded nursing home, but does not seem to be getting much one-on-one care. She often sleeps in other patients' beds, and on several occasions the

niece has found her wandering the halls without any clothing on. The niece would like to have her aunt moved back home (to a house now shared by the niece) and receive 24-hour care at home. The aunt's care is currently paid for through a trust managed by a corporate trustee, and there are more than sufficient assets to pay for the aunt's care to the end of her days. The niece acknowledges that her mother, who is the remainder beneficiary of the trust, is against the idea of so much money being spent for her sister's care at home: "She's doing fine at the nursing home, leave her be!"

First, the attorney needs to determine who the client is. Does the niece have standing to compel the transfer of her aunt out of the nursing home? Is the aunt competent to voice any thoughts of her own on the matter? Does the trustee take a position on this? Are there case managers or social workers familiar with this matter who might recommend against transferring the aunt, because it might only disorient her more? If the attorney is satisfied that the move in fact would be for the aunt's benefit, he might suggest to the niece that she petition for guardianship of her aunt (after making sure there would be no objection from the trustee or the sister). This way the niece would have the primary responsibility for determining the aunt's needs and the authority to make the transfer, if she decides such a move would be beneficial. The attorney might suggest that the niece bring the aunt to the house for a couple of brief visits, to see if she remembers her surroundings and is comforted or alarmed by them.

Chapter 12

Paying Privately for Long-Term Care: Long-Term Care Insurance

Nearly half of all formal long-term care costs are paid for by private wealth—the savings and income of the patients or their families. Informal care arrangements also abound, from spouses caring for one another to children and grandchildren who quit outside employment and stay at home to care for ill elders. Although the value (and the lost-opportunity costs) of such informal care arrangements is not well documented, it is clear that considerably less than half of long-term care is provided in institutions or other formal arrangements.

With costs averaging between $30,000 and $100,000 or more per year (depending on the area of the country and the level of care required), long-term care costs can easily bankrupt most families. Protecting against the cost of long-term care can take the form of planning for government (usually Medicaid) benefits, accumulation of substantial wealth, or advance purchase of long-term care insurance to cover the risk. This chapter discusses purchasing long-term care insurance; costs; policy provisions including the benefit period, elimination period, inflation protection, preexisting condition coverage, and guaranteed renewability; deductibility of long-term care insurance premiums; and taxation of long-term care insurance benefits.

Overview

Q 12:1 Who actually pays for long-term care?

Payments for nursing home and home care costs can come from several sources. In the past two decades, about half of nursing home costs have been paid by the federal-state Medicaid program. Another small, but significant portion (10.3 percent in 2000, up from about 3 percent 10 years earlier) is paid by the federal Medicare program. Veteran's benefits pay for a small portion, as do other government programs—other than Medicaid and Medicare, government payments amount to barely 2 percent of the total cost of nursing home care. Charities and service organizations pay another small fraction —although their share has ranged as high as 7.5 percent in the past decade, for 2000 it was 4.3 percent.

Private insurance in 2000 paid 8.1 percent of the total cost of nursing home care nationwide. That figure includes both long-term care insurance and the small portion of long-term care costs paid by Medicare supplemental insurance policies. The 8.1 percent figure represents a seven-fold increase over two decades, and an almost 50 percent increase over the preceding decade.

The current balance (27 percent in 2000 of the entire cost of nursing home care) is paid by private savings and income. That figure has steadily decreased since the inception of Medicare and Medicaid; in 1980, for example, 40 percent of nursing home expenses was paid by private wealth. These statistics are from the Centers for Medicare and Medicaid Services' (formerly Health Care Financing Administration's) Office of the Actuary, National Health Statistics Group. At the time of publication, 2000 statistics were the most current available. Statistical updates can be reviewed at the CMS/HCFA Web site, *http://cms.hhs.gov/researchers/pubs/datacompendium/*.

Q 12:2 How much does nursing home care cost the country?

In 2000, total national nursing home costs amounted to $92.2 billion. That figure represented an increase of $2.9 billion over the previous year, and an increase of nearly $49.5 billion over the 1990 figure. By comparison, hospital care cost Americans $412.1 billion, physician's services cost $286.4 billion, and drugs and other nondurable medical supplies cost $121.9 billion in 1998. Incidentally, "other personal care" (including, but not limited to, a portion of the cost of home care) cost about $32 billion in 1998; that figure does not include the informal care arrangements and lost opportunity involved in family caregiving. [Health Care Financing Administration's Office of the Actuary, National Health Statistics Group]

Q 12:3 How much does nursing home care cost individuals?

Individual nursing home costs vary tremendously by state, and sometimes by city within a given state. Generally, urban nursing homes cost substantially more than their rural counterparts. "Extra" care costs can inflate costs in individual circumstances even further, and make it much more difficult to predict the real cost of nursing care in any given case. In the more rural parts of smaller states, the cost of nursing home care may be as low as $2,000 to $2,500 per month. In urban New York, the base cost may range above $9,000 per month. In most areas of the country, nursing home residents should expect to pay between $3,500 and $4,500 per month for the lowest level of nursing home care, and more for higher levels of care. In 1998, the average actual nursing home cost per day was about $130, or $4,000 per month (source: Kiplinger's Retirement Report, February 1999), and a MetLife Mature Market Institute study in 2001 found an average of $153. For a state-by-state listing based on Kiplingers, see Table 12-1. The Federal Long-Term Care Insurance Program has a web-based calculator to help determine the actual cost of nursing home and home care in a particular locale at *http://www.ltcfeds.com*.

Table 12-1. Nursing Home Costs by State (1999)

State	*Average/Day*	*Average/Mo.*
Alabama	$103	$3,090
Alaska	$143	$4,290

Table 12-1. Nursing Home Costs by State (1999) (*cont'd*)

State	*Average/Day*	*Average/Mo.*
Arizona	$137	$4,110
Arkansas	$118	$3,540
California	$158	$4,740
Colorado	$117	$3,510
Connecticut	$202	$6,060
D.C.	$184	$5,520
Delaware	$129	$3,870
Florida	$120	$3,600
Georgia	$102	$3,060
Hawaii	$127	$3,810
Idaho	$136	$4,080
Illinois	$133	$3,990
Indiana	$141	$4,230
Iowa	$101	$3,030
Kansas	$110	$3,300
Kentucky	$127	$3,810
Louisiana	$90	$2,700
Maine	$175	$5,250
Maryland	$151	$4,530
Massachusetts	$201	$6,030
Michigan	$127	$3,810
Minnesota	$133	$3,990
Mississippi	$100	$3,000
Missouri	$105	$3,150
Montana	$100	$3,000
Nebraska	$142	$4,260
Nevada	$130	$3,900
New Hampshire	$109	$3,270
New Jersey	$192	$5,760
New Mexico	$144	$4,320
New York	$178	$5,340
North Carolina	$126	$3,780

Table 12-1. Nursing Home Costs by State (1999) (*cont'd*)

State	*Average/Day*	*Average/Mo.*
North Dakota	$100	$3,000
Ohio	$151	$4,530
Oklahoma	$92	$2,760
Oregon	$142	$4,260
Pennsylvania	$149	$4,470
Rhode Island	$155	$4,650
South Carolina	$118	$3,540
South Dakota	$100	$3,000
Tennessee	$126	$3,780
Texas	$130	$3,900
Utah	$115	$3,450
Vermont	$100	$3,000
Virginia	$115	$3,450
Washington	$177	$5,310
West Virginia	$125	$3,750
Wisconsin	$166	$4,980
Wyoming	$100	$3,000
Average	$132	$3,972

Source: Kiplinger's Retirement Report (1999)

Generally, rates for nursing homes increased by 6.5% annually from 1995 to 1999, three times the national Consumer Price Index, and it is expected that similar increases have occurred since 1999. (Estimates provided by the analysis of Department of Health and Human Services—CDC Health data for 1991 provided by *www. ElderWeb.com*, an award-winning site published by accountant Karen Stevenson Brown).

Q 12:4 How much can round-the-clock home care cost individuals?

Although "long-term care" popularly is associated only with nursing home care, more and more individuals are recognizing the possibility of receiving long-term care services at home. Medicaid waiver programs, and state programs as well, are providing Medicaid coverage for some level of home care, but not enough to provide 24-hour care. At $10 per hour for unskilled aides, and $25 per hour or more for professional nursing care, prolonged home care needs can run to an expense far in excess of nursing home costs even in states with high nursing home rates. An individual could spend $150,000 to $200,000 per year on intensive home care. At the same time, more and more people are looking for ways to fund home care as an alternative to the disagreeable alternative of nursing home care.

Q 12:5 Is long-term care covered under Medicare?

Medicare does not provide long-term care in the general sense of the term. Medicare Part A covers inpatient hospital services, rehabilitation services, certain types of home health care and hospice services, and of course any of these may involve many months of care (see chapter 13 for a discussion of Medicare). "Long-term care" usually refers to intermediate or skilled nursing care provided at skilled nursing facilities (SNFs), assisted living facilities, Alzheimer's units, board and care homes, or in the home. Long-term care programs are designed for those who lack the physical or mental ability to perform some or all of the activities of daily living (ADLs), such as bathing, dressing, and feeding oneself.

Medicare coverage for nursing home care is available for up to 100 days, provided that the following requirements are met:

1. The patient has been hospitalized for at least three consecutive days before being admitted to the nursing home. [42 C.F.R. § 409.30(a)]
2. The patient must be admitted to the nursing home and receive the needed care within 30 days of discharge from the hospital. If it is not medically appropriate for the patient to be admitted to the nursing home within 30 days of discharge from the hospital, the patient can be admitted at the time it would be medically appropriate to begin an active course of treatment. [42 C.F.R. § 409.30(b)]
3. The patient must require skilled nursing or rehabilitation on a daily basis that can be provided only in a skilled nursing facility. [42 C.F.R. § 409.31(b)]

4. The physician has certified that the patient needs the skilled nursing facility. [42 C.F.R. § 409.31(a)]
5. The condition treated and the daily services provided must be for a condition for which the patient was receiving care in a hospital or that arose while the patient was receiving care in the nursing home for a condition that was treated in the hospital. [42 C.F.R. § 409.31(b)]

(For more detailed discussion of the Medicare long-term care benefit, see chapter 13)

However, Medicare coverage for home care (not including custodial care) can continue indefinitely. Conceivably, an individual could receive ongoing Medicare home care services and privately contract for all additional custodial care services at a lower rate.

Medicare coverage for home care (which has no durational limit) is available if the following conditions are met:

1. The beneficiary must be homebound, confined to his or her home (or to an institution that is not a nursing home, a hospital, or a skilled nursing facility). [42 U.S.C. § 1395n(a)(2)(A)]
2. The beneficiary's doctor must have established a care plan (for example, a podiatrist may establish a care plan for services within the podiatrist's authority) and periodically review the plan. [42 U.S.C. § 1395n(a)(2)(B)]
3. The beneficiary must need intermittent skilled nursing care, physical or speech therapy, or occupational therapy (see Q 13:35). While occupational therapy will qualify the beneficiary for continued home health services, it may not serve as the basis for initial qualification. [42 C.F.R. § 409.42(b)] Part-time or intermittent services are skilled nursing and home health aide services furnished any number of days per week so long as they are furnished less than eight hours each day and 28 or fewer hours each week combined, or, subject to review on a case-by-case basis, up to 35 hours per week combined.
4. The home health care services are provided by, or under, arrangement with a Medicare-certified home health care agency. [42 U.S.C. § 1395f(a)(2)(C)]

(See further discussion at Q 13:33)

This can be a significant benefit, *provided* the skilled nursing care is only required on an intermittent basis.

Q 12:6 Is long-term care covered under Medicaid?

Medicaid benefits are available for the long-term care needs of individuals who are medically eligible (i.e., requiring at least intermediate-level care in a facility), and who do not have sufficient income or savings to pay for their own care (see chapter 14 for a discussion of Medicaid). Home care under Medicaid is becoming more available, but even then, Medicaid will not cover home care costs that exceed what the Medicaid agency would have to pay a skilled nursing facility, even in those states that offer a Medicaid home health care benefit. In other words, even where home care is available, Medicaid will not pay for home care 24/7.

Q 12:7 Is long-term care covered under federal veteran's benefits?

Nursing home care and some home health benefits are provided through the Department of Veterans Affairs, but usually such services are limited to veterans who are deemed 50 percent or more disabled. Until recently, services were also limited because of the shortage of bed space at VA facilities. There has been a movement to provide all veterans with long-term care benefits, using other non-VA facilities in the community (see chapter 16 for a discussion of veteran's benefits).

Q 12:8 What role does long-term care insurance play in financing care?

Although long-term care insurance has historically paid an almost insignificant portion of total long-term care costs, that small share is growing. Despite limited market penetration, in individual cases the availability of long-term care insurance can and does provide financial security and promote autonomy and independence. Recent government initiatives have further emphasized the utility of long-term care insurance, at least for some seniors (and younger persons concerned about the future cost of care). Three additional facts will inexorably lead to a greater role for long-term care: (1) individuals recognize that long-term care insurance may be essential to preserve the option of staying at home; (2) insurers are recognizing that assisted living is cheaper than nursing home care and adding an assisted living facility benefit; and (3) employers are starting to include long-term care insurance in the stable of options presented to employees. In other words, the idea of long-term care insurance is no longer for the anxious few, but is becoming the norm. In a recent survey by the Connecticut insurance department, 96 percent of respondents said that coverage for home and community-based services was very important in their decision to purchase long-term care insurance. [*Executive Summary of the Connecticut Partnership For Long-Term Care Evaluation, 2003 (http://www.opm.state.ct.us/pdpd4/ltc/researcher/evalrept.htm)*]

Q 12:9 What trends are developing in long-term care insurance?

Prospective long-term care insurance buyers will benefit from several recent trends in the industry. Many of the early problems with policy terms and practices have diminished in the face of increasing regulation and strong industry competition. "Post-claim underwriting" (in which insurers decided that coverage should not have been extended only after a claim is made, and refund premiums but refuse coverage) has all but disappeared from the industry. Sale of inadequate levels of coverage, while not unheard of, seems to be less common.

But problems in the industry still abound. Buyers are still older and at more risk of claims than is desirable (this self-selection of policy purchases significantly increases the cost of coverage and reduces the risk-sharing inherent in the concept of insurance). Individual agents (and some insurance companies) still prey on customer's fears and anxieties, rather than helping them to make reasonable decisions about the quality of public (Medicaid) care and the difficulty of qualifying for government assistance. Denial and the failure to seek independent advice still lead to inappropriate long-term care insurance purchases.

The long-term care insurance industry, and the products offered by that industry, have significantly improved in recent years. This may lead to a significant paradox in many cases: The client who responsibly purchased long-term care insurance years ago is likely today to hold a less-desirable policy than if he or she made the purchase more recently. One important piece of advice for clients with older long-term care insurance policies might be to review the policy and seek independent advice about the quality and convertibility of the policy. Some carriers are now routinely giving insured's the option to "upgrade" by adding additional benefits with an increased premium. A particularly attractive new coverage item is payment for assisted living expenses—including room and board—provided the insured has met the tests for the disabling condition, usually two or sometimes three ADL deficiencies, or severe cognitive impairment.

Purchase of Long-Term Care Insurance

Q 12:10 Which clients should purchase long-term care insurance?

Generally, there are at least two kinds of clients who should consider purchasing long-term care insurance:

1. Those with assets well in excess of Medicaid eligibility minimums, but insufficient to provide their preferred mode of long-term care (including home care) solely from their income (or, if the client is willing to experience diminution of principal, from their income and assets amortized over a period of time at least as long as their life expectancy), and
2. Those clients who are completely risk-averse, and who wish to leave the maximum possible amount to their heirs or devisees regardless of the current cost.

Although probable costs of long-term care vary tremendously by region of the country, the first group can safely be described as the middle class. Most individuals with lower levels of assets (and income) are likely to find it difficult to afford long-term care insurance; however, if a person with a smaller estate strongly feels that the quality of Medicaid-subsidized care might be inferior to that of privately paid care, he or she might choose to purchase long-term care insurance to minimize the likelihood of ever requiring government assistance with such care. Conversely, wealthier individuals will find that they can afford to pay for long-term care from income.

In a recent survey by the Connecticut Partnership for Long-Term Care, nearly one-half (43 percent) of respondents who had purchased long-term care insurance reported assets over $350,000, while 20 percent indicated their assets were less than $100,000. Thirty-seven percent fell into the $100,000–$350,000 range. (In Connecticut, a three-year nursing home stay would cost approximately $250,000 in 2002.) Clearly, those with something to lose by waiting until Medicaid would be available to pay for care purchased most long-term care insurance.

Q 12:11 At what age should a client consider long-term care insurance?

When the first edition of this book was published, the average age of new long-term care insurance purchasers was about 70. This may well have diminished in the intervening five years. The survey by the Connecticut Partnership for Long-Term Care for 2000-2001 shows an average age of 61 years for those purchasing policies, with 66 percent under the age of 65. The study notes that the percentage of respondents under the age of 65 has been steadily increasing over the past few years from 54 percent in the 1996 data, to 61 percent in the 1998/99 data, and then to the current 66 percent. As in the past, the majority of respondents (56 percent) were female. Three-quarters (77 percent) were married and 76 percent lived with their spouse, showing that in a state like Connecticut, with relatively poor protection of the "community spouse," preventing spousal impoverishment is probably another motivating factor. [The entire study is online at *http://www.opm.state.ct.us/pdpd4/ltc/researcher/Research-Rept.pdf*]

Age at the time of purchase is one of the most important factors in determining the price of long-term care insurance, so potential purchasers should consider buying at a younger age to save costs. Of course, one of the reasons policies are less expensive for younger purchasers is the likelihood that a younger insurance buyer will allow the policy to lapse before claims are made. Younger buyers should consider the likelihood that the policy might be allowed to lapse in deciding whether to wait before the initial purchase of long-term care insurance.

Most commentators agree that the best age for purchase of long-term care insurance is somewhere in the mid-50s for most people.

Younger prospective buyers might still consider buying a policy in particular circumstances (family history of illness or strong risk aversion, for example). Older buyers should not continue to delay purchasing just because the optimum age has passed; costs continue to escalate quickly in the mid-60s and later. Many policies are simply unavailable to prospective buyers after age 80.

Q 12:12 How much long-term care insurance should a client consider?

Most long-term care insurance policies are sold in increments of $10/day or $50/day benefits. In 1995, average cost per day was about $100–$110. [Centers for Disease Control, Department of Health and Human Services, Health, United States, 1999, with Health and Aging Chartbook; available online at *http://www.cdc.gov/nchs/data/hus/hus99.pdf*] However, by 1998, the average actual nursing home cost per day was about $130 (source: Kiplinger's Retirement Report, February, 1999); with some states nearer $200 per day. Even these numbers have been exceeded since the 1998 figures. In order to pay for the actual costs of long-term care, many clients will consider purchasing daily coverage at or above the daily nursing home cost in their state, to make sure full coverage is provided, and will also purchase the cost-of-living inflation protection offered, which will significantly increase the price of insurance.

There are two competing considerations on the appropriate level of coverage.

First, because most insurance buyers will probably prefer to stay at home as long as possible, long-term care insurance that also provides a home-care benefit is usually desirable. Typically, home-care benefits are provided at either 50 percent or 100 percent of the maximum nursing home benefit, so (depending on the policy terms) a $100/day benefit may provide only $50/day for in-home care. Home care is usually substantially more expensive than nursing home care, so a $100/day benefit may prove inadequate to permit the purchaser to remain at home. In fact, an inadequate home-care benefit may result in strong financial incentives for the institutionalization of the insurance buyer. Fortunately, the trend is towards a 100 percent home care benefit.

Second, a competing argument can be made for a lower level of benefits in at least some cases. If the buyer's intention is to prevent any substantial diminution of assets, reliably available income should also be considered in determining the amount of benefits. In other words, Social Security and retirement benefits can reduce the necessary level of benefits in many cases. The buyer may wish to purchase insurance that will not so much cover the entire cost of care, but "bridge the gap" between available income (and disposable principal) and the anticipated cost.

Care should be taken to avoid purchasing inadequate long-term care benefits. Particularly in states with an income cap for qualification for Medicaid benefits, it is entirely possible to purchase a level of long-term care insurance that fails to provide adequate care but disqualifies the purchaser for government assistance. Even if the income-cap problems can be resolved, the purchase of inadequate long-term care insurance coverage will only reduce the level of government benefit assistance, without improving the quality of care or preventing the pauperization of the insurance buyer.

Q 12:13 What is the "asset protection" feature available in some states?

Prior to 1993, a few states had experimented with offering long-term care insurance that provided an "asset protection" feature. This meant that the insured could apply for and receive Medicaid while retaining assets equivalent to what the policy had paid out. These states were California, Connecticut, New York, Indiana, Illinois, and Washington. In Connecticut, this type of insurance is the "partnership" program.

When OBRA '93 was enacted, with its enhanced requirements for states to seek recovery and tighten eligibility rules, this asset protection feature was grandfathered. Moreover, the states that had offered asset protection long-term care insurance prior to 1993 were permitted to continue to authorize it. OBRA '93 includes an express exemption from repayments and liens for assets retained that are equivalent to the benefits paid out under such policies. [42 U.S.C. § 1396p(b)(i)(C)(ii)]

In those states, the choice should be to purchase the highest possible daily benefit, even if the total period of coverage is shorter.

This is because the sooner the benefits pay out, the sooner the asset protection is provided. If the daily benefit is too low, the person might be forced to seek Medicaid (and spend assets that might otherwise be protected) before the policy had paid out to its limit.

Because such policies anticipate that the purchaser may ultimately require Medicaid, often they do not offer lifetime coverage, but a term of years. These policies are also tightly regulated to require clear descriptions, a cost of living rider, and other consumer protections, that while desirable, historically had driven up the cost of the policy as compared to non-partnership policies. However, in recent years the price gap has narrowed. The other distinguishing feature may be a case management benefit.

Q 12:14 What should a client expect to pay for long-term care insurance?

Costs for long-term care insurance vary tremendously. The most important determinants of price for most policies include:

1. *Age at policy inception.* A 45-year-old is likely to pay about half the premium of a 60-year-old for comparable coverage, and the premium cost is likely to double again by age 70.
2. *Daily benefit.* It should be obvious that a $100/day benefit will cost more than a $50/day benefit. It will not, however, cost twice as much.
3. *Elimination period, inflation provision, and benefit period.* All of these contribute to the cost of the policy, although none of them will be have as large an effect as the other factors.

Given the high degree of variability in policy terms and the different pricing structures of insurance companies, generalization is both difficult and dangerous. A recent comparison presented by the Connecticut Partnership for Long-Term Care provides an example, however:

Average Annual Premiums Across Partnership Policies

Nursing Facility and Home Care ($200 per day benefit)

Coverage	*Purchase Age*

Average Annual Premiums Across Partnership Policies (*cont'd*)

Approximate Amount	*Minimum Duration*	*45*	*55*	*65*	*75*
$73,000	1-Year	$700	$1,000	$1,700	$3,600
$146,000	2-Years	$1,000	$1,400	$2,400	$5,200
$219,000	3-Years	$1,200	$1,700	$3,100	$6,800
Unlimited	Unlimited	$2,100	$2,900	$5,300	$12,400

Q 12:15 Why are long-term care policies expensive?

A number of explanations have been advanced for the high cost of long-term care insurance. The industry is relatively young (and therefore does not have an extensive history of claims experience). Despite general insurance concepts of spreading the risk across a broad base of buyers, long-term care insurance is disproportionately sold to older individuals. Insurance companies must factor into their rates the possibility that physically debilitating illnesses will be successfully treated, leaving healthy, long-lived policy holders who are unable to care for themselves because of advancing mental disabilities. All of these factors contribute to long-term care insurance remaining relatively expensive. Over time, at least some of these factors may fade into unimportance, particularly in the face of increased marketplace competition. In fact recent years have seen a gradual reduction in the relative cost of long-term care insurance, with a significant increase in the quality of policies and the benefits offered. Increased competition and the government's push to get seniors to buy long-term care policies may also be having an effect. This trend should be expected to continue.

Long-Term Insurance Policy Provisions

Q 12:16 What types of long-term care policies are available?

The most popular policies are designed to contribute toward the health care needs of an individual for a period of three or four years; this is a direct response to the Medicaid three-year lookback period for gifting. This allows an insured individual going into long-term care to transfer part or all of his or her assets to beneficiaries if desired, and still receive health care during the lookback period.

Example 12-1. A widow with $300,000 in funds and $2,000 per month income becomes too feeble to live independently. She makes the decision to transfer to an intermediate care facility, and her long-term care insurance kicks in. Her insurance and income are sufficient to pay for all her needs. The widow transfers $250,000 immediately to her children. That gift disqualifies her from receiving Medicaid benefits for three years; once the three years are up, and if her remaining $50,000 has been spent down, she can qualify for Medicaid assistance.

Although this "half-a-loaf" approach works without long-term care insurance, having the insurance allows for more assets to be transferred (see chapter 14 for a discussion of Medicaid).

Those considering long-term care insurance should also consider the following factors provided by Ploniaszek and Firman, *Long-term Care Insurance: A Professional's Guide to Selecting Policies* (2d ed. 1993): the amount of the daily benefit compared with actual rates in the community, automatic inflation protection, renewability of the policy (although most policies will only offer reduced premium rates, not fix them permanently), home care services provided, and coverage of adult day care and respite care. The policy should provide a minimum of four days of care per week.

Of course, asset transfers may only be a secondary consideration in many cases. The individual who seeks long-term care coverage to ensure the ability to stay at home would be unlikely to make asset transfers in light of the relatively inferior home care benefits provided by Medicaid. Such an individual would be most interested in purchasing enough to bridge the gap between income and expense over their remaining lifetime, and in that case the cost of living rider (often an expensive feature) is essential.

Q 12:17 What policy terms should a client consider when buying long-term care insurance?

There are a number of fairly standard policy provisions that should be considered when purchasing long-term care insurance. These include:

- Daily benefit rate
- Elimination period
- Benefit period

- Eligibility to receive benefits
- Inflation protection
- Pre-existing condition provisions
- Home health coverage (including "informal" care)
- Nonforfeiture

The National Association of Insurance Commissioners publishes a guide to help evaluate and compare policies, on the Federal Long-Term Care Insurance Program website, *http://www.ltcfeds.com*.

Q 12:18 What is the daily benefit rate?

Most policies provide care in $10/day increments; long-term care currently average $153 or more per day, and a steady increase in rates should be anticipated (long-term care costs increase at a much greater rate than can be accounted for by ordinary inflation).

Q 12:19 What is meant by an elimination period?

Other than the daily benefit rate, the two principal limitations on long-term care insurance policies (and two of the most important determinants of price) are the elimination period and the benefit period. Usually, the elimination period is stated in terms of days of institutionalization (or disability) required before the benefit begins, rather than the dollar cost the policy holder must incur before coverage begins (commonly referred to as a deductible). In most policies, the buyer may select from a handful of elimination periods—typically 0 days (immediate coverage) to 100 days. In some policies, the elimination period is a single lifetime figure, while in others it must be met for each institutionalization.

Q 12:20 Which elimination period should a long-term care insurance buyer select?

Depending on the other financial resources of the policyholder, the purpose behind buying the insurance, and the cost of coverage, the long-term care insurance buyer may prefer a shorter or longer elimination period. For most buyers, an elimination period of 30 to 60 days will provide real protection without dramatically increasing the cost of coverage.

Q 12:21 What is the benefit period?

The final major determinant of policy cost is the length of coverage, or "benefit period." Plans can be purchased to cover nursing home placements of two, three, or five years. For a significantly higher cost, a long-term care insurance plan may be designed to cover the policyholder's entire nursing home stay, regardless of length. In a few plans (particularly those marketed in connection with single-premium life insurance policies), the limitation may be a total dollar figure rather than a period of time; after benefits of, say, $1,000,000 have been paid, the policy will end.

Q 12:22 What benefit period should a long-term care insurance buyer select?

Once again, the answer will depend on the purposes for which the policy was purchased. There are, however, three typical approaches to determining the appropriate benefit period:

1. *Playing the averages.* The average length of institutionalization is about one year. Most seniors will never enter a nursing home at all. Given those two risk factors, a policy covering two years of institutionalization should cover most people. Of course, the purpose of insurance is to spread the risk of loss; this strategy shifts the risk of loss somewhat, but does not cover the possibility that the buyer will fall outside the "typical" range of experience.
2. *Planning for Medicaid coverage.* As explained previously, under current federal rules, eligibility for Medicaid coverage can be obtained after waiting 36 months from the date of substantial transfers of assets. Some individuals might purchase long-term care insurance for the purpose of covering that 36-month period of ineligibility, intending to transfer all assets immediately upon institutionalization. Of course, this strategy assumes that eligibility rules will remain static, that the patient will retain the capacity to make transfers upon institutionalization, and that the transfers will actually be made immediately (rather than deciding to wait for a period of months to see how things work out). To hedge against all those potential problems, an alternate approach might be to purchase a four-year or five-year policy.

3. *Full coverage.* Rather than trying to predict either of the preceding scenarios, a long-term care insurance buyer might choose to insure fully against the risk of loss. This would require purchasing a lifetime policy. Of course, the cost of such a policy will be significantly higher than for a policy with a limited benefit period, and the risk of requiring such coverage is slight (although, if it is required, the benefit is tremendous).

Q 12:23 How is eligibility to receive benefits determined under the policy?

Most long-term care services are correlated with the individual's ability to perform six "activities of daily living," or ADLs, specifically: eating, toileting, transferring, bathing, dressing, and continence. Insurance policies are generally triggered by the insured's inability to perform at least two ADLs without assistance (e.g., a demented individual may be able to perform all the ADLs, but only with regular direction from a companion or health care worker). This is referred to as the ADL trigger. [I.R.C. § 7702B(c)(2)] Under the cognitive impairment trigger, an individual who is physically able but who has a cognitive impairment is treated the same as an individual who is unable to perform without substantial assistance. [IRS Notice 97-31(1); 1997-14 I.R.B. 16]

Q 12:24 How does inflation protection work, and should it be part of a long-term care insurance policy?

Inflation protection provides increased daily benefits over time. Given a long history of steady increases in the cost of long-term care, it is likely that future costs will continue to increase. In fact, long-term care costs have historically risen faster than other medical costs, and medical costs (in turn) have risen faster than general increases in the cost of living—some estimate twice as fast as the consumer price index. Although the past few years have seen a slowing (and even a reversal) of this trend, it is certainly predictable that long-term care costs will continue to rise steadily.

In that environment of increasing costs, a given daily benefit rate (selected at the time of policy purchase based on then-current assumptions) will become inadequate over time. Inflation protection can provide automatic increases in the daily benefit rate, usually at the same premium rate as the original policy. This, of course, means two kinds of increases in the policy cost: The base rate will be higher at the policy's inception, and the annual premium costs will increase as the amount of coverage increases. Although this additional coverage will substantially increase the cost of long-term care insurance coverage, it is advisable to consider adding inflation protection, particularly if the buyer is relatively young, and expects to maintain the policy over a period of years.

Some policies provide an intermediate choice: optional additional coverage that can be purchased at set policy intervals. For example, the policy might permit the insured to add an additional $10/day of coverage every three years at the same premium rate; the policyholder can then assess the circumstances (personal wealth and income, inflation in nursing home costs, general health, and premium costs) at the time of each scheduled increase. Of course, this relies on the insured's ability to assess the situation and make an appropriate choice in the unknown future.

Q 12:25 Are preexisting conditions covered under long-term care policies?

The National Association of Insurance Commissioners (NAIC) in 1986 established a model act and regulations for consumers that offer various protections, including prohibitions against exclusions for pre-existing conditions. Although most states have adopted some form of the act, they vary widely with regard to specific requirements and enforcement. Obviously the long-term care insurer would be much more likely to accept applicants with pre-existing conditions that would indicate a quick death, such as heart attacks, rather than automatic long-term care triggers such as Alzheimer's disease or congestive heart disease.

Q 12:26 What is guaranteed renewability?

Although the NAIC rules (and some, but not all, states) require renewability and forbid cancellation of long-term care policies, most insurers do not guarantee that premium rates will be fixed or offer reduced premiums past a period of about seven years. The insurer may give itself the option to cancel upon expiration of the term of insurance, or may have the option to cancel for reasons other than the poor health of the insured.

Q 12:27 What home health coverage benefit should a long-term care insurance policy include?

Although home health care coverage was uncommon in the first generation of long-term care insurance policies, such coverage has now become almost standard. In most currently offered policies, the home health benefit is pegged at a maximum of the daily benefit rate; in other words, the insured's $100/day benefit can be used in the nursing home or in home care. This provides a much more comfortable choice for most policy buyers, because remaining in the home is a nearly universal preference among seniors (and, for that matter, among their juniors). Remember, however, that the cost of home care is likely to be higher than nursing home costs—a policy that is adequate to provide nursing home care may fail to provide enough benefits to cover extensive home care. Furthermore, most policies do not permit payments to family caregivers (unless, in some policies, they have been certified by the appropriate state agency as licensed caretakers) or other unlicensed caregivers; those that do may charge premiums nearly twice as high. This significantly limits the utility of home health coverage for many individuals, who will anticipate receiving most of their long-term care at home from family caretakers.

An important factor with a home care benefit may be the method of reimbursement applied. In general, the usual approach is to require that the insured submit claims for reimbursement. As with any health insurance, the home health agency may say that it will handle this and will bill directly, but if that does not take place, and the insured (or spouse) has dementia or similar problems, there can be a real risk of losing benefits. Ideally, the policy should not require submission of claims within a short period of time. Policies that permit payments to family usually simply pay the daily benefit once the criteria are met rather than requiring submission of claims, which is probably why the premium cost can be so high.

Q 12:28 Will a policy include coverage for assisted living expenses?

Increasingly, coverage for assisted living expenses—including room and board—may be available once the same ADL trigger as is required for home care benefits has been met. At that point, even room and board expenses may be covered, within policy limits.

Q 12:29 What is nonforfeiture?

Some policies provide for a "paid-up" benefit to accrue over time. In such policies, failure to pay the premiums will not cause the policy to lapse altogether. A policy with a nonforfeiture provision will continue to provide some coverage (with the initial daily benefit rate diminishing over time, in most cases) despite nonpayment of the premium. This is especially important for those with deteriorating mental status who may not be able to keep track of their bills. In order to qualify for preferential income tax treatment, a long-term care insurance policy must provide either reduced paid-up insurance benefits, extended term insurance, or a shortened benefit period. [I.R.C. § 7702B(g)(4)(B)]

In addition to nonforfeiture of coverage, some policies now provide for a partial refund if the insured dies without ever having used the policy. However, the increased premium may not be worth it, and the money would be better spent on a small life insurance policy.

Q 12:30 How should someone select a policy?

Long-term care insurance is now so widely sold that the first step in buying good insurance—an honest and reliable agent—is easier to find. In those states offering "partnership" policies (see Q 12:13), the agent's certification to sell partnership policies may be some indication of competence.

Long Term Care Partners, LLC, the company administering the Federal Long Term Care Insurance Program sponsored by the U.S. Office of Personnel Management, offers a checklist, "Top Ten Considerations for Purchasing Long Term Care Insurance," available on the web at *http://www.ltcfeds.com/*.

Tax Issues

Q 12:31 Are long-term care insurance premiums deductible?

Federal tax law finally recognized concerns about the taxability of long-term care insurance benefits and the deductibility of premiums beginning in 1997. Under the Health Insurance Portability and Accounting Act of 1996 (HIPAA), long-term care insurance premiums for qualified long-term care policies are deductible as a medical expense. [I.R.C. § 213(d)(1)(D)] The amount of the premium that is deductible is indexed for inflation and is dependent on the insured's age:

Age by End of Year	*Deduction Limit on Premium (Tax Year 2002)*
40 or under	$ 240
41–50	$ 450
51–60	$ 900
61–70	$2,390
71 or older	$2,990

It is important to remember that the medical expense deduction is subject to the 7.5 percent adjusted gross income floor; medical expenses cannot be deducted unless they exceed 7.5 percent of adjusted gross income.

Q 12:32 What is a qualified long-term care insurance contract?

For tax purposes, a qualified long-term care insurance contract meets the following requirements:

1. The only insurance protection provided under the contract is for qualified long-term care services;
2. The contract does not pay or reimburse expenses that are reimbursable under Medicare or would be reimbursable but for the application of a deductible;
3. The contract must be guaranteed renewable;
4. The policy must not provide for a cash surrender value or other money that can be paid, assigned, or pledged as collateral for a loan, or borrowed;
5. Refunds of premiums, and all policyholder dividends must be applied to reduce future premiums or to increase future benefits;
6. The contract must contain the consumer protection provisions of Code Section 7702B(g) [I.R.C. § 7702B(b)], which include provisions regarding nonforfeiture and disclosure as well as certain requirements of the NAIC Long-Term Care

Insurance Model Act and Regulations covering guaranteed renewability, prohibitions on limitations and exclusions, extension of benefits, continuation or conversion of coverage, discontinuance and replacement of policies, unintentional lapse, prohibitions against post-claim underwriting, minimum standards, inflation protection, and prohibitions against preexisting conditions and prior hospitalizations. [I.R.C. § 7702B(g)]

Q 12:33 Are long-term care insurance benefits taxable?

Under HIPAA, if an individual plan is "qualified" (for tax purposes) (see Q 12:32), benefits received under the plan will not be taxable income. [I.R.C. § 7702B(a)(2)] Benefits received that pay or reimburse qualified long-term care expenses under a qualified long-term care policy are tax-free up to $210 per day or $76,650 annually. [I.R.C. § 7702B(a)] Qualified long-term care services includes necessary diagnostic, preventive, therapeutic, curing, treating, mitigating, and rehabilitative services, and maintenance or personal care services. The services must be for a chronically ill individual and provided pursuant to a plan of care prescribed by a licensed health care practitioner. [I.R.C. § 7702B(c)(1)] A chronically ill individual is any individual who has been certified by a licensed health care practitioner as:

1. Being unable to perform at least two activities of daily living (eating, toileting, transferring, bathing, dressing, and continence) for at least 90 days because of loss of functional capacity (ADL trigger); or
2. Requiring substantial supervision to protect the individual from threats to health or safety because of severe cognizant impairment (cognizant impairment trigger). [I.R.C. § 7703B(c)(2)]

A policy will not be a qualified long-term care policy if there is a "medical necessity" trigger for benefit payments.

Q 12:34 Are there state tax incentives for the purchase of long-term care insurance?

Nearly half of the states offer some state income tax incentive for the purchase of long-term care insurance. The incentives range from income tax credits (in Colorado, a 25 percent credit up to $150 for taxpayers earning less than $50,000) to a straightforward deduction from premiums paid (Kentucky and Alabama). For state-by-state details, see *http://www.neamb.com/insurance/ltctax.html.*

Q 12:35 Are payments received under a nonqualified long-term care insurance plan taxable?

Although the tax law specifically exempts benefits received from qualified plans, an argument can be made that there is no real difference for nonqualified plans. Although the plan's benefits may constitute income, the long-term care costs incurred by the policy holder (which must be incurred in order to qualify to receive benefits) should be deductible medical expenses, leaving no more than 7.5 percent of the benefit effectively taxable. Even that small tax effect should be further reduced (and perhaps eliminated) if there is little other income, or if there are medical expenses (or other deductions) not covered by the policy benefits.

A contrary argument relies on the fact that the federal income tax deduction for medical costs is available only for *unreimbursed* costs. In other words, a nonqualified plan's benefits will constitute income, and the medical costs paid by that plan may not be deductible. This could be disastrous, especially because the medical costs may be substantial, and the taxpayer's ability to pay income taxes limited by the very same medical or social condition giving rise to the benefit payments.

This question has not yet been resolved. If IRS regulations treat nonqualified plan benefits as income and do not allow offsetting medical expense deductions, nonqualified plans will be strongly disfavored. If, on the other hand, final IRS treatment permits the medical deduction (or treats the plan benefits as nonincome), the principal difference between a qualified and a nonqualified plan will be the deductibility of premiums. Given the 7.5 percent limitation on medical expense deductions, that difference will be completely unimportant to the vast majority of taxpayers.

Practice-Related Issues

Q 12:36 How might an elder law attorney counsel a client regarding long-term care insurance?

1. *Determining the need for insurance coverage.* Mr. and Mrs. Summers (aged 68 and 64, respectively) are concerned about paying for nursing home care in the event either should need to be institutionalized at some future time. Both are in good health today, but Mrs. Summers' mother recently passed away after a long nursing home stay and they watched her assets being consumed by the cost of care. The Summers' own their home, two automobiles, household effects and bank and brokerage account assets of about $400,000. Their annual income from Social Security, pensions, and investments totals about $50,000. They wonder whether they should make gifts to qualify for Medicaid, establish an irrevocable trust, or simply ignore the potential cost of long-term care.

   While long-term care insurance is not for every client, consideration of the appropriateness of purchasing insurance should be undertaken in almost every case. Mr. and Mrs. Summers may indeed be excellent candidates for such insurance. They are relatively young, currently healthy, and have significant assets and income to protect. Because their assets and income are significant, either of them will have a difficult time qualifying for Medicaid eligibility for long-term care subsidies. Because their assets are limited, however, they will also have difficulty paying privately for any needed nursing home care without seriously depleting their assets.

   In many, perhaps most, states Mr. and Mrs. Summers' income would be sufficient to pay the costs of nursing home care. Even so, the non-institutionalized spouse would have difficulty making ends meet in the community without spending down the couple's assets. In general terms, long-term care insurance is a product for the middle class, and Mr. and Mrs. Summers are solidly in that category by most standards. If their assets were twice what they actually have, they might be comfortable self-insuring, since the cost of nursing home care would probably be less than their annual income.

If their assets were significantly lower they would be able to qualify for Medicaid easily, and insurance would not be such a compelling option.

Because they are young, Mr. and Mrs. Summers should have an easier time qualifying for long-term care insurance, and the premiums should be markedly lower. Precisely because of their age they are even better candidates for insurance, since any institutionalization in the near future could drain the community spouse's assets for an extended period of time.

Mr. and Mrs. Summers should be advised to look into the availability and cost of long-term care insurance. Assuming that they do not have any medical conditions that make insurance unavailable or expensive, they will be excellent candidates for purchase of a policy.

2. *Evaluating the insurance policy.* Mrs. Rigby is considering purchasing long-term care insurance, and asks for assistance in reviewing the policy terms and prices.

   Most elder law attorneys are poorly equipped to evaluate the pricing of insurance policies, but it may still be possible to help Mrs. Rigby decide on the best course of action. It will be essential to collect information about Mrs. Rigby's financial situation and her reasons for seeking insurance, and to review the policy itself. The financial evaluation will be necessary in order to give advice about the utility of any long-term care insurance policy, and the latter will assist Mrs. Rigby to avoid dangerous limitations in the particular policy.

   In addition to a lawyer's evaluation of the policy, Mrs. Rigby would probably benefit from a second analysis by an insurance salesperson or consultant. When an elder law attorney evaluates an individual long-term care insurance policy, he or she might look for:

   Tax qualification. If Mrs. Rigby's plan is not tax qualified, she will not be able to deduct the premiums for federal income tax purposes. This is not likely to be a major issue, since the income tax deduction is limited to the amount by which total medical expenses exceed 7.5 percent of her adjusted gross income; few individuals will receive any income tax benefit from deductibility of the insurance premiums. The other benefit to tax qualification is more important; if the plan is qualified, any payments made to nursing homes will not be treated as income. Even if later nursing home payments are deductible (and they may not be, under one analysis of federal tax laws), the deduction will be limited by the same 7.5 percent threshold requirement, so at least some of the insurance benefits would likely be taxable.

Daily benefit levels. In order to economize Mrs. Rigby might make the mistake of purchasing too little insurance. This can result in making her ineligible for future Medicaid eligibility, or in simply reducing the amount of Medicaid coverage she might qualify for.

Definition of ADLs. How does the plan define activities of daily living, and how many of those ADLs must Mrs. Rigby need assistance with before qualifying for benefits?

Home care, assisted living, and other non-nursing home settings. Does the plan provide benefits for in-home care, or for care in other settings outside nursing homes? Most plans either provide such benefits up to the full daily benefit rate for nursing home care or, in some cases, up to one-half the daily benefit rate. If home care is important to Mrs. Rigby, the plan should cover the full daily benefit rate—especially since the cost of home care can easily exceed nursing home costs.

Inflation protection. What mechanism does the plan provide for future increases in nursing home costs? Can Mrs. Rigby purchase additional insurance at the then-current rates in the future? Such "guaranteed insurability" may be an effective inflation protection, though increased costs in the future can be considerable. If the plan provides for automatic cost-of-living increases, that coverage will likely be expensive.

Waiver of premium. Will the policy premiums be waived during any period of institutionalization? How about periods when Mrs. Rigby receives home health care services?

Benefit periods. Mrs. Rigby might want to purchase lifetime insurance coverage, though such policies can be quite expensive. Alternatively, she might prefer to purchase coverage for, say, a four-year period, anticipating that her children will help her transfer all her assets upon institutionalization and that she will then qualify for Medicaid once the policy benefit period has run. Of course, any such plan must include an appropriate trust or power of attorney to permit the gifting, in case Mrs. Rigby is not then able to direct the handling of her own finances.

Respite care, payments to family caregivers, payments for ambulance transport and durable medical equipment, and other miscellaneous provisions. In Mrs. Rigby's case, any or all of these provisions may be important. She should understand what benefits are available from this and competing plans.

Chapter 13

Medicare Benefits

The Medicare program provides most of the medical care for Americans over the age of 65. As a consequence, eligibility for benefits and the administration of the program are a central concern for most elderly clients. Although few elder law attorneys regularly practice in the Medicare arena, a passing familiarity with program benefits and limitations is critical to providing adequate legal advice to elders confronting medical problems or the prospect of future medical needs.

Although the extent of Medicare coverage varies, it generally covers hospitalization, home care, durable medical equipment, hospice, and doctor's visits. Some of those benefits are optional, requiring the senior to sign up and pay an extra premium. Recent changes in the structure of the program have made it more critical to understand the extent and limitations of coverage. This chapter discusses eligibility and enrollment requirements; benefits available under Part A, Part B, and Medicare+Choice; Medicare HMOs; and Medigap Insurance.

The first stop for answers about Medicare coverage may be not only the Centers for Medicare and Medicaid Services website, *http://www.medicare.gov*, but also sites maintained by the nonprofit Center for Medicare Advocacy, *http://www.medicareadvocacy.org*, and the Medicare Rights Center in New York, *http://www.medicarerightscenter.org.*

In recent years the Medicare program has been the subject of nearly continuous attention on the part of

Congress, the White House, the press, and public and private interest groups. Proposals for Medicare "reform," plans for the addition of some form of prescription drug coverage, and expressed concerns about the future security of the Medicare program have been proposed, debated and, as to a few small matters, adopted. Current specifics of Medicare eligibility, coverage, and administration are subject to change on very short (or no) notice.

Overview

Q 13:1 What is the purpose of the Medicare program?

Medicare is a federal insurance program that was established to provide medical care for the elderly and the disabled. The Medicare laws are found at 42 United States Code (USC) Sections 1395 through 1395xx and the regulations are found at 42 Code of Federal Regulations (CFR) Parts 405 through 489. Medicare is divided into three parts: Part A, Part B, and Part C.

Q 13:2 Who operates Medicare?

Medicare is an exclusively federal program, unlike Medicaid, which is operated as a federal-state partnership. While the actual administration of Medicare may be assigned to intermediaries (insurance companies that contract with the government to operate the program in individual states), the policies and regulations are established by the Health Care Financing Administration (HFCA). These intermediaries, including fiscal intermediaries for Part A skilled nursing facilities (SNFs), home health and hospice cases, peer review organizations for hospital cases, and carriers for Part B cases, review claims and, except in hospital cases, make payments.

Q 13:3 Who does Medicare benefit?

Medicare is available to the elderly, the disabled, and those with permanent kidney failure requiring kidney dialysis or kidney transplant. [42 U.S.C. § 1395c] Medicare benefits are tied to Social Security eligibility. For the elderly, this means someone age 65 or over who either has, or has a dependent relationship with someone else who has, entitlement to Social Security benefits (i.e., a former wage-earner). For the disabled, this means someone who has been entitled to receive Social Security disability benefits, either on his or her own account (as a former wage-earner) or because of a dependent relationship with another wage-earner who was a spouse or parent either disabled, deceased, or retired. Details on these relationships are discussed in chapter 15.

Q 13:4 Can a retired person under age 65 qualify for Medicare?

Even though Social Security beneficiaries are permitted to retire as early as age 62 (with a reduced benefit), Medicare is not available to retirees until age 65. As a result, the availability of alternative medical insurance coverage is frequently a critical element of any decision to retire before age 65. Conversely, a person age 65 who continues to work (either because he or she is younger than the presumptive retirement age for Social Security, which is scheduled to increase to 67 over time, or simply chooses not to retire) will qualify for Medicare while still employed.

Q 13:5 What is Medicare Part A?

Medicare Part A provides coverage for hospitalization, skilled nursing facility placement, home health care, and hospice care. [42 U.S.C. § 1395d] Over the next few years, the home health care benefit of Part A is scheduled to be transferred to Part B. Medicare Part A is funded by payroll deduction taxes.

Q 13:6 What is Medicare Part B?

Medicare Part B primarily provides coverage for physician's services. It also covers diagnostic tests, medical equipment, ambulance services, outpatient physical and speech therapy, certain home care, prostheses, and prescription drugs. [41 U.S.C. § 1395k(a)] Part B is optional. Unlike Part A, Part B requires the payment of a premium for all beneficiaries. Low-income beneficiaries may qualify for government payment of this premium under the QMB and SLIMB programs (see Q 13:14).

Q 13:7 What benefits are excluded from Medicare Parts A and B?

Medicare provides coverage for services that are medically "reasonable and necessary for the diagnosis or treatment of illness or injury or to improve the functioning of a malformed body member." [42 U.S.C. § 1395y(a)(1)(A)] The care received must be skilled. Although most seniors receive substantially all of their medical care through the Medicare program, there are major items not covered by Medicare. For most seniors, the most notable exclusions from Part A coverage are prescription medications and long-term custodial care. Although Congress attempted to add a more extended long-term care benefit in the 1987 Medicare Catastrophic Coverage Act, the overwhelming negative reaction from seniors (who would have been charged a separate tax to pay for the benefit) led to the repeal of the benefit in the next legislative session. Prescription coverage is the announced goal of both Congress and the Administration, but further attempts to add a prescription benefit to Medicare as it is now known have so far failed.

Other uncovered medical care includes eyeglasses, dental care, and annual preventive checkups, although Medicare beneficiaries who elect to receive care through an HMO may have some of these benefits provided, perhaps with a copayment requirement.

Q 13:8 What is Medicare Part C?

The Balanced Budget Act of 1997 (BBA '97) added Medicare + Choice. Although the Medicare + Choice program is sometimes referred to as "Part C," it is really a collection of alternative means of financing or receiving individual Medicare coverage. Medicare + Choice does not provide additional benefits or coverage, although it may make Medicare more financially attractive for some beneficiaries or may permit providers to provide additional benefits as an inducement to attract participants. [41 U.S.C. § 1395d] Part C also has a slightly different system for processing grievances and appeals.

Eligibility and Enrollment

Q 13:9 Who is eligible for Medicare?

Medicare is available to the elderly, the disabled, and those with permanent kidney failure requiring kidney dialysis or kidney transplant. [42 U.S.C. § 1395c]

For purposes of Medicare eligibility, "elderly" is defined as someone age 65 or older. Whether one is entitled to receive Social Security or Railroad Retirement benefits will affect whether or not the benefit is provided with no additional charge.

For purposes of Medicare eligibility, "disabled" means a person who has received Social Security disability insurance benefits for 24 months. [42 U.S.C. § 1395c] (The 24-month period begins on the date the person is determined to be eligible; for example, someone awarded a lump sum in October to cover benefits for which he or she was eligible starting in April can start the 24-month clock running in April, not October.)

Q 13:10 What qualifies a disabled person to receive Part A coverage?

For purposes of Medicare coverage, disability is defined as eligibility to receive Social Security disability insurance for a 24-month period. In other words, any person who receives SSDI will qualify for Medicare after two years of receiving benefits. [42 U.S.C. § 1395c] Note that benefits actually have to have been paid for two years; a disabled person who does not apply for and actually receive benefits will not qualify for Medicare coverage. Persons with end-stage renal disease qualify for Medicare three months after beginning renal dialysis. [42 U.S.C. § 1395c]

A person may be disabled but not receiving Social Security disability insurance. Those who receive SSI are not entitled to Medicare by virtue of their SSI eligibility (though of course a SSI recipient may also receive Social Security disability insurance benefits if he or she qualifies). A typical example will be an individual disabled from mental illness that began when he or she was young, or from a catastrophic injury (e.g., an automobile accident). Such persons may not have earned enough "quarters of coverage" to be entitled to Social Security benefits on their own account, and were not disabled early enough (before age 22) to be entitled to benefits on the account of a retired or deceased parent (see chapter 15).

Q 13:11 In general, is any payment required for Medicare coverage?

For the elderly, Medicare Part A benefits are available at no charge for those persons age 65 and older who are *entitled* to receive Social Security or Railroad Retirement benefits [42 U.S.C. § 426] (see Q 13:12). A Social Security retirement beneficiary under the age of 65 (e.g., a retiree who took early retirement at age 62) will not qualify for Medicare. By the same token, a 65-year-old who could choose to accept Social Security retirement will qualify for Medicare even though he or she chooses to delay retirement to a later age. Those not receiving Social Security but who have reached age 65 may "buy in" by paying a premium (see Q 13:12).

For the disabled person who is eligible for Medicare, Medicare Part A benefits are also available at no charge.

Medicare Part B coverage is *available*(subject to payment of a premium) for any person who receives Medicare Part A. In addition, any person over age 65 who does not qualify for Part A coverage can nonetheless purchase Part B coverage. [42 C.F.R. § 407.10]

Q 13:12 When must an elderly Medicare beneficiary pay a premium for Part A coverage?

Any person over age 65 who receives either Social Security retirement or Railroad Retirement benefits, or who is eligible to receive either kind of benefit, will automatically qualify for Medicare Part A without a premium.

The vast majority of seniors do receive Social Security, so this means that few will have to pay any Medicare Part A premium. Those who have 30 "quarters of coverage" (QCs) under Social Security rules (but not the 40 quarters required for retirement eligibility) may elect to purchase Medicare Part A at the 2003 rate of $174 per month. For those age 65 but with less than 30 quarters of coverage, Medicare Part A can be purchased at the 2003 rate for $316 per month. Because coverage is not automatic, seniors who do not qualify for Social Security Retirement or Railroad Retirement may elect not to purchase coverage immediately upon qualifying; for those who delay buying into the Medicare plan, the premiums will ordinarily increase to $192.50 per month (for those with 30 QCs) or $350.90 per month (for those with less than 30 QCs) (reflecting a total increase of 10 percent in each category—unlike Part B premium increases, Part A increases are capped at a maximum of 10 percent total). This increase in premiums will be waived for a late enrollee who has been covered by an employer-provided medical program since reaching age 65.

A typical non-recipient of Social Security would be an elderly woman who never worked, who is unmarried (or married to a similarly situated person), and who was not married to someone else who worked in a marriage that either lasted ten years or ended in the worker's death. Quite often a wealthy person who has simply clipped coupons or lived off a trust fund her whole life, will decide to buy-in to Medicare at age 65.

Q 13:13 Must an elderly Medicare beneficiary pay a premium for Part B coverage?

Yes. Unlike Part A, Part B requires the payment of a premium for all beneficiaries. In 2003, that premium is $58 per month and is ordinarily paid by automatic deduction from Social Security benefits. For those beneficiaries who elect not to enroll in Part B at age 65, premiums are increased (unless they have been covered by an employer-provided health benefit for the interim period). Part B premiums are presently fixed at 25 percent of the actual cost of the program to the federal government; in other words, Part B coverage is exceptionally inexpensive to the recipients. Accordingly, there are few (if any) Part B eligible beneficiaries who would be well advised to forego the coverage.

Q 13:14 What if an individual cannot afford to pay the premium?

If a Medicare Part A recipient's income is limited and financial resources (such as bank accounts, stocks, and bonds) are not more than $4,000 (for an individual) or $6,000 (for a couple), the Medicare beneficiary may qualify for assistance as a Qualified Medicare Beneficiary (QMB) or Specified Low Income Medicare Beneficiary (SLMB). The QMB plan pays the Medicare Part B monthly premium, all deductibles and coinsurance. The 2002 monthly income limits were at least $922 for an individual and $1,361 for a couple (higher in some states). The SLMB plan pays the Medicare monthly Part B premium for qualified Medicare beneficiaries. The 2002 monthly income limits for the SLMB program were at least $1,069.80 for an individual and $1,560 for a couple (higher in some states). [See *http://www.medicare.gov*] Income limits are set every April.

Q 13:15 When does an individual have to enroll in Medicare?

Individuals who are under age 65 and are receiving Social Security or Railroad Retirement benefits are automatically enrolled in Medicare Part A and Part B. [42 U.S.C. § 1395p(f)] Disabled individuals are automatically enrolled at the beginning of the 25th month of their disability.

Individuals who are not receiving Social Security or Railroad Retirement benefits three months before they turn age 65 and individuals requiring regular dialysis or kidney transplant must apply for Medicare. The initial seven-month enrollment period begins in the third month before the person turns age 65. [42 U.S.C. § 1395i-2(a)] The individual can contact any Social Security Administration office to enroll. An individual who does not enroll during the seven-month initial enrollment period must wait until the general enrollment period (which is held January 1 to March 31 of each year) to enroll. Part B coverage begins the following July.

Q 13:16 Is there a penalty for late enrollment?

Yes. Part A premiums (if a premium is required) go up 10 percent if an individual waits 12 or more months to enroll. [42 U.S.C. § 1395i-2(c)(6)] Part B premiums go up 10 percent for each 12 months that the individual could have enrolled but did not (unless the individual had equivalent employer coverage). The additional premium cost remains for the life of the beneficiary. [42 U.S.C. § 1395r(b)]

Q 13:17 What is the special enrollment period under Part B?

The special enrollment period is for persons (1) age 65 and over who are covered by an employer's large group health insurance plan based on their own or their spouse's employment, or (2) disabled individuals who are covered by a large group health insurance based on their own current employment or the current employment of a spouse or close family member. These individuals over age 65 may enroll in Medicare Part B, without penalty, either:

1. Any time while they are covered by the group plan; or
2. During the eight-month enrollment period that begins the month
   a. Employment ends, or
   b. The person is no longer covered under the plan,

   whichever is sooner.

[42 U.S.C. § 1395p(i)(3)(A), (B); 42 C.F.R. § 406.24]

There is also a six-month special enrollment period for disabled individuals whose group health plan coverage is involuntarily terminated. This six-month enrollment period begins on the first day of the month in which the benefits are terminated. [42 U.S.C. § 1395p(i)]

Q 13:18 How can an individual cancel enrollment in a Medicare+Choice Plan?

The Balance Budget Act of 1997 included "lock-in" rules that would have limited Medicare + Choice beneficiaries to disenrollment only once, from January 1 through March 31 of each year, beginning in 2002. [42 U.S.C. § 1395w-21(e)(2)] However, these new "lock-in" rules were delayed by the enactment of Pub. L. No. 107-108. Until 2005, beneficiaries can still enroll and disenroll whenever they want. Beneficiaries must call the plan they wish to leave and ask for a disenrollment form; or call 1-800-MEDICARE (1-800-633-4227) to request that disenrollment be processed over the phone; or call the Social Security Administration (or visit the Social Security office) to file a disenrollment request. In most cases disenrollment is concluded the month after a request if it was filed before the 10th day of the month. If the request was made after the 10th of the month, disenrollment will be on the first day of the second calendar month after the request was made. If the beneficiary joins another managed care plan he or she will be automatically disenrolled from the old plan when the new plan enrollment becomes effective. [See *http://www.medicare.gov/*]

Part A Benefits

Q 13:19 What benefits are included in Medicare Part A?

Medicare Part A provides coverage for four types of medical care:

1. Inpatient hospitalization;
2. Home health care;
3. Skilled nursing facility care; and
4. Hospice care.

Most of these benefits are subject to deductibles or copayment requirements (see Q 13:20). Each of these coverage areas has requirements that must be met before care is covered.

Q 13:20 What are the copayments and deductibles under Medicare Part A?

Medicare has many copayment requirements for care and deductibles from covered care. The deductibles and copayments (all are 2003 numbers and will change each year unless indicated) include:

1. *Part A hospitalization.* During the first 60 days of care, the patient will pay the first $840 of care. For days 61 through 90 (the last day of the basic hospitalization benefit), the patient will pay $210 per day.
2. *Part A lifetime reserve days.* After 90 days of hospitalization, the patient will begin to use the 60 lifetime reserve days. Each lifetime reserve day will require a $420 copayment. The combination of these two hospitalization benefits mean that a Medicare beneficiary who spends 150 days in the hospital in 2003 will be liable for a total of at least $32,340.

3. *Part A skilled nursing facility.* The first 20 days of covered SNF care will not require any copayment or deductible, but the next 80 days (until the patient uses the total maximum of 100 days) will require a $105 daily copayment. The total cost to the beneficiary for 100 days of SNF placement (assuming Medicare covers the entire period, which is uncommon) will therefore be $8,400.
4. *Part A hospice benefits.* Although hospice-related prescription drugs are covered, there will be a $5 or 5 percent copayment per prescription.

Inpatient Hospital Care

Q 13:21 What eligibility requirements must be met to qualify for hospital benefits under Medicare Part A?

To qualify for inpatient hospital benefits the following requirements must be met:

1. Hospitalization must be based on a doctor's prescription for treatment of an injury or illness;
2. The patient requires care that can only be provided in hospital;
3. The facility must be a hospital and must participate in Medicare; and
4. The hospital's peer review organization, the utilization review committee, and the fiscal intermediary must not disapprove the hospital stay.

[42 U.S.C. § 1395f]

Q 13:22 Is continued Medicare coverage available for care in a hospital when no nursing home bed is available?

Yes. There is a "no appropriate facility" exception to the requirement that hospital coverage be provided only if the care is such that it can only be provided in a hospital. Even if the patient only requires services that could be provided in a skilled nursing facility, "extended coverage" (the nursing home benefit) will be made available while the patient is still in the hospital, if the patient requires skilled care but no appropriate skilled nursing facility placement is available. [42 U.S.C. § 1395x(v)(1)(G)(i); 42 C.F.R. § 424.13(b)]

The two criteria for extended care coverage in a hospital are (1) need for skilled care (which may include skilled assessment and observation), and (2) lack of a nursing home placement that is not the fault of the patient. For example, if the patient requires the use of a ventilator, and no nursing facility placements for "vent beds" are available, the hospital coverage should continue.

The key is the requirement of a skilled level of care, not where the care was provided. [Monmouth Medical Center v. Harris, 646 F.2d 74, 80 (3d Cir. 1981)] If, on the other hand, the patient requires purely custodial care, Medicare coverage under this exception will not be provided, even if a discharge to the home would be medically contraindicated [Gonzalez v. Secretary of HHS, 644 F. Supp. 1086 (E.D.N.Y. 1986) (unsanitary and unsafe home)], or there is no mechanism at home to provide the needed custodial care [Friedman v. Secretary of HHS, 819 F.2d 42 (2d Cir. 1987)].

Once the need for skilled care is clear, the burden is on the provider to show that placement is available and was refused. [Hurley v. Bowen, 857 F.2d 907 (2d Cir. 1988); Friedman v. Secretary of HHS, 819 F.2d 42, 44 (2d Cir. 1987)] The primary burden of locating an appropriate SNF bed is on the discharge planner [42 C.F.R. § 482.43], who must prepare a discharge plan at the physician's request [42 U.S.C. § 1395x(ee)(2)(G)]. While the SNF must be in the "area," there is no clear definition of this term. The CMS Hospital Manual requirements for utilization review committees state that "as a general rule, a community or local geographic area should not be defined in such a way as to require a patient to be taken away from his family and transported over great distances." [CMS Hospital Manual § 290.3.C (Rev. 394); see also CMS Hospital Manual § 275.C, requiring certifying physicians to meet the same standards imposed on utilization review committees including 290.3] "Geographic area" is defined for similar purposes in CMS Hospital Manual Section 275.C as locations within 50 miles unless shown to be "inaccessible" to patients. (The Hospital Manual is online at *http://cms.hhs.gov/manuals/10_hospital/ho00.asp*.)

If, however, placement is available but the family refuses on the grounds that the facility is out of town (even though not far away), or that another facility is preferred, there will be no coverage. [Melson

v. Secretary of Health and Human Services, 702 F. Supp. 997 (W.D.N.Y. 1988); Lerum v. Heckler, 774 F.2d 210 (7th Cir. 1985)] (Note that the regulation referred to in case law, 42 CFR Section 405.1627(b) is no longer in effect, apparently having been removed following the switch to a DRG payment system for hospitals.)

Q 13:23 What hospital coverage is provided under Medicare Part A?

Once the preceding requirements are met (see Q 13:21), Medicare Part A covers up to 90 days of hospitalization for a single benefit period (usually a single hospitalization or a series of hospitalizations for the same illness). [42 U.S.C. § 1395d] In addition, the beneficiary has a total of 60 "lifetime reserve" days, which, as the name indicates, can be used only once in the lifetime of the beneficiary. [42 C.F.R. § 409.61(a)(2)] If a patient does not want to use the lifetime reserve days the hospital must be notified in writing either upon admission or at any time within 90 days after discharge. [42 C.F.R. § 409.65(d)] A patient who uses reserve days may request approval from the hospital to have them restored.

During the first 60 days of care, the patient will pay a $840 deductible. For days 61 through 90 (the last day of the basic hospitalization benefit), the patient will pay $210 per day. For Part A lifetime reserve days, after 90 days of hospitalization the patient will begin to use the 60 lifetime reserve days. Each lifetime reserve day will require a $420 copayment. The combination of these two hospitalization benefits mean that a Medicare beneficiary who spends 150 days in the hospital will be liable for a total of $32,340.

There is a special limit on inpatient psychiatric care under Medicare: a lifetime maximum of 190 days. [42 U.S.C. § 1395d(c); 42 C.F.R. §§ 409.62 et seq.] Psychiatric coverage is limited to "active treatment" for a psychiatric condition with services provided under an individualized treatment or diagnostic plan, reasonably expected to improve the patient's condition or for the purpose of diagnosis, and supervised and evaluated by a physician. Coverage may be denied if the beneficiary could be safely and effectively treated on an outpatient basis or a lesser care institution, such as a skilled nursing facility.

Q 13:24 What is meant by "spell of illness?"

Most Medicare benefits are limited in duration, with the most common benefit period being the "spell of illness." The phrase is similarly defined in the context of hospitalization, skilled nursing care, and home health care. In each type of coverage, a spell of illness begins with the first day of hospitalization (or placement in a SNF, or receipt of home health care, as is appropriate for each definition) and continues until 60 days after release of the patient from that level of care. [42 U.S.C. § 1395w-4; Eisman v. Mathews, 428 F. Supp. 877 (D.C. Md. 1977)] In other words, readmission to the same level of care within 60 days of discharge will lead to treatment as a continuing "spell of illness." Conversely, readmission more than 60 days after discharge (even if for treatment of the same condition) will be treated as a new admission, with new copayments and time limitations. [See Mayburg v. Secretary of HHS, 740 F.2d 100 (1st Cir. 1984); Levi v. Heckler, 736 F.2 848 (2d Cir. 1984)]

Q 13:25 What hospital services are covered by Part A?

The following hospital services are covered under Medicare Part A:

- Room and board in a semi-private room. Medicare will pay for a private room only if the patient requires isolation or semi-private rooms are not available. [42 C.F.R. § 409.11(a)]
- Nursing and related services ordinarily furnished by the hospital for the care and treatment of inpatients.
- Services of medical or surgical interns or residents provided through an approved teaching program.
- Medical social services.
- Operating and recovery room costs.
- Drugs, medical supplies, equipment, and appliances provided in the hospital.
- Diagnostic and therapeutic services including psychologists, physical therapy, occupational therapy, rehabilitative care, respiratory therapy, and speech pathology.
- Radiology services.
- Laboratory tests.

- Blood after the first three units of whole blood or units of packed red cells that a patient receives during a calendar year as an inpatient or as an outpatient under Medicare Part B. The patient can replace the blood rather than paying for it. Medicare pays the blood processing charge beginning with the first pint. [The first three pints of blood are excluded from coverage: 42 U.S.C. § 1395e(a)(2)]

[42 U.S.C. § 1395x(b)]

Skilled Nursing Facility Care

Q 13:26 What is a skilled nursing facility (SNF)?

A skilled nursing facility is a facility (or part of a facility) that is primarily engaged in providing (1) skilled nursing care and related services for patients who require medical or nursing care, or (2) services provided for the rehabilitation of injured, disabled, or sick persons, and not primarily for the care and treatment of mental diseases. [42 U.S.C. § 1395i-3(a)] The SNF must have a written transfer agreement with one or more participating hospitals providing for the transfer of patients between the hospital and the facility and for the interchange of medical and other information. [42 U.S.C. § 1395i-3(a)] The facility must also be licensed under state or local law and must meet the health and safety requirements prescribed by the Secretary of the Department of Health and Human Services (HHS). Skilled nursing facilities are required to provide nursing services at all times and must employ at least one full-time registered nurse. [42 U.S.C. § 1395i-3(b)(4)(C)] In addition, the medical care of every patient must be under the supervision of a physician and a physician must be available to provide medical care in case of an emergency. [42 U.S.C. § 1395i-3(b)(6)]

Q 13:27 What eligibility requirements must be met to qualify for skilled nursing facility benefits under Medicare Part A?

Skilled nursing facility care is available for up to 100 days, provided that the following requirements are met:

1. The patient has been hospitalized for at least three consecutive days before being admitted to the SNF [42 C.F.R. §

409.30(a)] Where the number of days is a problem, hospital records should be carefully examined to determine if the patient was physically in the hospital for three days, even if the formal admission occurred later in the stay. [Jenkel v. Shalala, 845 F. Supp. 69 (D. Conn. 1994) (where hospital provided emergency room treatment prior to "formal" admission the following day, the date on which treatment began is the beginning date of the hospitalization for determining qualification for skilled nursing facility coverage)]

2. The patient must be admitted to the SNF and receive the needed care within 30 days of discharge from the hospital. If it is not medically appropriate for the patient to be admitted to the SNF within 30 days of discharge from the hospital, the patient can be admitted at the time it would be medically appropriate to begin an active course of treatment. [42 C.F.R. § 409.30(b)]
3. The patient must require skilled nursing care or rehabilitation on a daily basis that can be provided only in a SNF. [42 C.F.R. § 409.31(b)]
4. The physician has certified that the patient needs a SNF. [42 C.F.R. § 409.31(a)]
5. The condition treated and the daily services provided must be for a condition for which the patient was receiving care in a hospital or that arose while the patient was receiving care in the SNF for a condition that was treated in the hospital. [42 C.F.R. § 409.31(b)]

Q 13:28 What are the limitations on the skilled nursing care benefit through Medicare?

In order to qualify for the skilled nursing care benefit, the patient must (1) require "skilled services" on a daily basis," of a kind that as a practical matter can only be provided in a skilled nursing facility, and (2) have been admitted to a Medicare-certified skilled nursing facility within 30 days of a three-day admission to a hospital. (Problems can arise when coverage is denied on the basis that it is only necessary to treat a pre-existing condition unrelated to the hospital stay.)

Services are "skilled" when they "require the skills of or must be performed under the supervision of technical or professional personnel," either because of the services' inherent complexity [42 C.F.R. § 409.32(a)], or because of risks posed by the claimant's special medical complications [42 C.F.R. § 409.32(b)], unstable condition [42 C.F.R. § 409.33(a)(2)], or overall condition [42 C.F.R. § 409.33(a)(1)]. "Skilled nursing services" expressly include "management and evaluation of a patient's care plan, observation and assessment of the patient's changing condition, and patient education services." [42 C.F.R. §§ 409.33(a)(1)–(3))] (In 1998, Medicare issued regulations deleting the quoted description of services included as "skilled nursing services" described above. However, these changes were rescinded in 1999. [64 Fed. Reg. 41,670 (July 30, 1999)])

"Daily basis" means skilled nursing care seven days a week or therapy five days per week. (Short lapses, such as those caused by another condition that requires a halt to therapy, should not justify a denial.)

Q 13:29 Does Medicare coverage for therapy cease if the patient has "plateaued"?

Services of a therapist are considered and billed as "skilled services." It is common for patients and their families to hear that rehabilitation will be discontinued because the patient has "plateaued," has made as much rehabilitative progress as possible. Without therapy, the care provided in the nursing home may not be "skilled care," and therefore, Medicare coverage will end.

However, the nursing home benefit for "skilled services" does not in and of itself require that the patient have "restoration potential." Federal regulations plainly state that "restoration potential of a patient is not the deciding factor in determining whether skilled services are needed. Even if full recovery or medical improvement is not possible, a patient may need skilled services to prevent further deterioration or preserve current capabilities." [42 C.F.R. § 409.32(c); see also 42 U.S.C. § 1395y(a) (services must be "reasonable and necessary for the diagnosis or treatment of illness or injury *or* to improve the functioning of a malformed body member")] Indeed, even the Medicare Intermediary Manual chapter on *nursing home* services states:

> The repetitive services required to maintain function sometimes involve the use of complex and sophisticated therapy procedures and, consequently, the judgment and skill of a physical therapist might be required for the safe and effective rendition of such services. (See § 3132.1.B.) The specialized knowledge and judgment of a qualified physical therapist may be required to establish a maintenance program intended to prevent or minimize deterioration caused by a medical condition, if the program is to be safely carried out and the treatment aims of the physician achieved. Establishing such a program is a skilled service.

[Medicare Intermediary Manual § 3132.3.A.1.e] Similarly, the Manual gives as an example at § 3132.1.B:

> **Example.** Even where a patient's full or partial recovery is not possible, a skilled service still could be needed to prevent deterioration or to maintain current capabilities. A cancer patient, for instance, whose prognosis is terminal may require skilled services at various stages of his illness in connection with periodic "tapping" to relieve fluid accumulation and nursing assessment and intervention to alleviate pain or prevent deterioration. The fact that there is no potential for such a patient's recovery does not alter the character of the services and skills required for their performance.

Unfortunately, many other portions of the Medicare Intermediary Manual apply a circular reasoning that leads inexorably back to the termination of Medicare coverage for therapy once "restoration potential" has been maximized. Medicare reasons that in most cases, "maintenance therapy" need not be performed by *skilled* personnel. Once the person has reached his or her maximum "restoration potential" the only apparent alternative purpose for therapy is "maintenance." Therefore, by definition the need for a skilled therapist is no longer "reasonable and necessary." For example, the same section states as a criteria for Medicare coverage for therapy: "The services must be provided with the expectation, based on the assessment made by the physician of the patient's restoration potential, that the condition of the patient will improve materially in a reasonable and generally predictable period of time, *or the services must be necessary for the establishment of a safe and effective maintenance program.*" The examples then go on to give a clear indication that the only purposes for which a skilled therapist might provide services are (1) restorative therapy or (2) maintenance therapy with the ultimate objective of establishing a maintenance program that will not require skilled care. Many providers are more familiar with this guidance than with the presumably overriding provisions of the CFR.

In short, practically speaking Medicare coverage for therapy will probably be terminated (or notice of non-coverage given) whenever the person no longer has "restoration potential." There is still grounds for appeal, however, if it can be shown that the services of *skilled* personnel were required to maintain condition or prevent deterioration, such as the example shown. What is important is not the patient's potential, but the level of skill required. If the patient's physician agrees that *skilled* personnel are essential to the patient's care, Medicare ought to cover the therapy. The patient in the nursing home may demand that the claim be submitted to Medicare and then appeal, continuing therapy all the while. However, the patient will risk having to pay for care out-of-pocket if the claim is eventually denied. This is a judgment call for the family, and it may well be that in most cases the family will succumb to fear of financial exposure. The point is, however, that provided the physician will support the claim and provide detailed explanations to back up the support, the appeal should ultimately be successful (see also Q 13:83).

Interestingly, the Intermediary Manual provisions governing the mental health benefit do recognize the need for maintenance and the prevention of deterioration. Moreover, they also make clear that "restoration" means any improvement whatsoever, rather than restoration to the original functioning level. [Medicare Intermediary Manual § 3112.7]

Of course, the care must also be "reasonable." The fact that a skilled therapist might be more persuasive, gentle, and less clumsy, so that the patient is more motivated with that individual, would not make it reasonable for Medicare to pay that therapist.

Q 13:30 What services in a skilled nursing facility are covered by Part A?

Part A covers extended care services for an inpatient of a skilled nursing facility, including the following services:

- Nursing care provided by or under the supervision of a registered nurse
- Bed and board in a semi-private room

- Physical, occupational, or speech therapy
- Medical social services
- Drugs, biologicals, supplies, appliances, and equipment
- Services furnished by a hospital with which the SNF has a transfer agreement
- Other services necessary to the health of the patient that are generally provided by a SNF, or by others under arrangements with a SNF

[42 C.F.R. § 409.20]

Q 13:31 What is the scope of coverage for skilled nursing facility care provided under Medicare Part A?

Skilled nursing facility care is available for up to 100 days per spell of illness if the preceding requirements are met. [42 U.S.C. § 1395d(a)(2)] The first 20 days are paid in full: No copayment or deductible is required. The patient must pay a copayment for days 21 through 100, and Medicare pays the balance. The 2003 copayment, for example, is $105 per day. The total cost to the beneficiary for 100 days of SNF placement in year 2003 (assuming Medicare covers the entire period, which is uncommon) will therefore be $8,400. After the 100th day the patient must pay the entire cost.

If Part A payments are exhausted, or expenses are not reimbursable under Part A, the expenses may be reimbursable under Part B if there are medical and other health services and the patient is entitled to Part B benefits.

Q 13:32 Who determines whether skilled nursing facility care is covered?

The skilled nursing facility itself initially determines eligibility for Medicare coverage for its patients; however, if the facility makes a determination of ineligibility, the beneficiary has a right to request submission to the intermediary. [42 C.F.R. § 424.36; Centers for Medicare and Medicaid Services Intermediary Manual § 3630.1] The beneficiary also has the right to appeal an adverse determination. [42 C.F.R. § 405.704(b)]

One important practical consideration arises from the structure of the eligibility determination process. Because the SNF makes the determination itself, beneficiaries may expect more generous treatment from an entity with a vested interest in approving Medicare coverage. In fact, however, the SNF has an incentive to deny eligibility in any close case, because post-determination reviews may cause the facility to lose the authority to make its own determinations, and thereby cause the facility to lose substantial revenue streams.

Home Health Care Services

Q 13:33 When is a Medicare beneficiary entitled to home health care services?

Home health care services are fully covered under Medicare Part A and Medicare Part B when the services are medically reasonable and necessary, and when the following criteria are met:

1. The beneficiary must be homebound, confined to his or her home (or to an institution that is not a nursing home, a hospital, or a skilled nursing facility). [42 U.S.C. § 1395n(a)(2)(A)]
2. The beneficiary's doctor must have established a care plan (e.g., a podiatrist may establish a care plan for services within the podiatrist's authority) and periodically review the plan. [42 U.S.C. § 1395n(a)(2)(B)]
3. The beneficiary must need intermittent skilled nursing care, physical or speech therapy, or occupational therapy (see Q 13:35). While occupational therapy will qualify the beneficiary for continued home health services, it may not serve as the basis for initial qualification. [42 C.F.R. § 409.42(b)] Part-time or intermittent services are skilled nursing and home health aide services furnished any number of days per week so long as they are furnished less than eight hours each day and 28 or fewer hours each week combined, or, subject to review on a case-by-case basis, up to 35 hours per week combined.
4. The home health care services are provided by, or under, arrangement with a Medicare-certified home health care agency. [42 U.S.C. § 1395f(a)(2)(C)]

In addition to the preceding requirements, if the coverage is being provided under Medicare Part A, the beneficiary must have been hospitalized for at least three consecutive days and the home health services must be provided within 14 days of discharge. Discharge from a skilled nursing facility carries similar requirements. [42 U.S.C. § 1395x]

Q 13:34 For purposes of Medicare home health services coverage, what does homebound mean?

Although a Medicare beneficiary must be "homebound" before qualifying for home health care visits, the beneficiary need not be completely confined to the home. Medicare considers the beneficiary homebound if leaving the home requires considerable effort or is medically contraindicated. If the beneficiary is unable to leave home without the assistance of another person (or the use of a supportive device like a cane, crutches, walker, or wheelchair), he or she may qualify as homebound. Similarly, if the person has dementia and would be a danger to himself or herself or others if leaving home, so that leaving is medically contraindicated, the person is homebound. Homebound status should not be affected by infrequent and short-term absences, such as visits to the doctor, to church, get a haircut, etc. A Centers for Medicare and Medicaid Services Transmittal states that absences for other "unique or infrequent" events, such as weddings, funerals, and the like, will not affect homebound status. Medicare Home Health Agency Manual, Transmittal 302 (26 July 2002). The physician is required to certify to the patient's homebound status.

Q 13:35 What does "skilled care" mean for the Medicare home health benefit?

Eligibility for the Medicare home health benefit requires a need for skilled rehabilitation therapy *or* skilled nursing care at home. These terms are defined to mean those services "which require the skills of technical or professional personnel such as registered nurses, licensed practical nurses, physical therapists, and occupational therapists." [42 C.F.R. § 409.44] Speech, physical, or occupational therapy qualify. For nursing care to be skilled, it must be "so inherently complex that it can be safely and effectively performed only by, or under the supervision of, professional or technical personnel."

It is important to note that as with other Medicare skilled nursing care benefits, care and therapy are "needed" not only if they are needed to improve the patient's condition, but if they are needed to maintain the patient's condition and prevent deterioration. [42 C.F.R. § 409.44(c)(2)(iii)] The regulations state clearly: "Even if full recovery or medical improvement is not possible, a patient may need skilled services to prevent further deterioration or preserve current capabilities." The elder law attorney should advise clients to be vigilant for a claim that the patient has "stabilized" or "plateaued" and that care will be discontinued. Often, a home health agency may stop submissions to Medicare having concluded that the person has "plateaued" and Medicare will be discontinued. At this stage, physician contact is vital. The decision must be made by the physician, and a call to the physician, followed by a call from the physician to the home health agency, may result in a quick reinstatement (see Qs 13:29 and Q 13:39).

Q 13:36 What coverage is provided for home health care?

Once the preceding requirements are met (see Qs 13:33, 13:34), Medicare beneficiaries are entitled to receive Medicare home health care for as long as they meet the coverage criteria. [42 U.S.C. § 1395f(a)(20)(c); 42 C.F.R. §§ 409. 31 et seq.] There is no coinsurance or deductible for the home health care benefit. The benefit provides for home health services such as assistance with ADLs together with intermittent skilled nursing services.

Q 13:37 What is the home health spell of illness benefit period?

The "home health spell of illness" benefit period is a period of consecutive days that:

1. Begin with the first day (not included in a previous home health spell of illness)
    a. On which the individual is furnished post-institutional home health services, and
    b. That occurs in a month for which the individual is entitled to benefits under Part A; and

2. End with the close of the first period of 60 consecutive days thereafter on each of which the individual is neither an inpatient of a hospital, nor an inpatient of a SNF, or a rural primary care hospital, nor provided home health services.

[42 U.S.C. § 1395w-4]

In other words, the concept of "spell of illness" for home health care benefits is similar to the related concepts for hospitalization and skilled nursing care.

The practical effect on the recipient, however, may be minimal.

Q 13:38 What are home health services?

Home health services include:

- Part-time or intermittent nursing care provided by or under the supervision of a registered professional nurse (including: observation and assessment of a patient's changing condition; management of the overall plan of care; and nursing education, such as teaching the patient or family how to care for a wound)
- Physical, occupational, or speech therapy
- Medical social services under the direction of a physician
- Part-time or intermittent services of a home health aide
- Medical supplies and durable medical equipment while under such a plan

[42 U.S.C. § 1395x(m)]

Home health services may not include household services (such as cleaning, cooking, laundry, etc.). However, associated light housekeeping is possible if provided by a home health aide. [42 C.F.R. § 409.45]

Q 13:39 Who determines whether home care services are covered?

The nursing or home health agency providing services submits the claim to the Medicare intermediary, which then approves or denies coverage. If the agency believes coverage will be denied (and therefore plans to deny, stop, or reduce services) it must provide an advance written notice, known as a Home Health Advance Beneficiary Notice or HHABN. As a result of a nationwide class action lawsuit, specific requirements for HHABNs became effective on March 1, 2001. Unfortunately, home health agencies will often simply inform the beneficiary that he or she no longer qualifies and the bill will not be submitted, for example, because the beneficiary has "plateaued" or "isn't improving," based on a mistaken belief that "restoration potential" is required (see Q 13:29). The physician should be contacted and asked to determine whether the particular services are still required. If they are, the physician (or other caregivers) should instruct the agency to resubmit and demand a written notice of termination. The agency must submit to Medicare if the patient requests (although the patient is then liable for the charge if Medicare denies). [See Centers for Medicare and Medicaid Services Medicare Intermediary Manual Transmittal 1821, § 3638.30 (available online at *http://cms.hhs.gov/manuals/pm_trans/R1821A3.pdf*)] Litigation is pending as to whether a pre-termination hearing is also required. [See Healey v. Thompson, 186 F. Supp. 2d 105 (D. Conn. 2001), decision pending (2d Cir.)]

Hospice Care

Q 13:40 What is hospice care?

Hospice care, a relatively recent development in American health care, focuses on palliative rather than curative treatment. It is a style of medical care provided to the terminally ill and consists of active pain management, counseling, respite care, and concern for the entire family (including caregivers). Pain management may include dosages that could lead to addiction or even to suppression of the ability to breathe and other autonomic functions; hospice philosophy first addresses comfort of the patient before addressing those concerns.

Q 13:41 What are the eligibility requirements for hospice care?

One of the most extensive benefits provided through Medicare is the hospice benefit. In order to qualify for benefits, the patient must be eligible for Part A benefits and must have been certified as terminally ill. For this purpose, "terminally ill" means that the patient's physician has determined that the patient's life expectancy is less than six months.

In addition, the patient must affirmatively elect hospice, must choose the particular hospice program (to the exclusion of other hospice programs), the hospice organization must participate in Medicare, and the patient must decide to forgo curative treatment for the terminal condition.

The hospice benefit regulations may be found at 42 CFR Part 418.

Q 13:42 When must the patient be certified as terminally ill?

The patient must be certified as terminally ill at the beginning of the first 90-day period by both the individual's physician and the medical director of a hospice program. Generally, the patient must be certified within two days after hospice care is initiated. If oral certification is provided within two days, the written certification may be provided within eight days after care is initiated. The patient must be recertified for subsequent periods by either the medical director or a physician member of the interdisciplinary hospice group. [42 C.F.R. § 418.22]

Q 13:43 When the patient elects hospice care, what other Medicare coverage is waived?

In order to secure Medicare coverage of hospice care, the beneficiary must file a statement electing that coverage and acknowledging that he or she waives:

1. Benefits from any other hospice program; and
2. Any Medicare coverage for illnesses treated by the hospice program other than those provided through hospice.

[42 C.F.R.§ 418.24]

This election effectively restricts the beneficiary to palliative treatment only, because the hospice program will not provide curative treatment. In practice, hospice organizations are careful to explain the effect of the election in detail. Patients who change their minds about hospice care can rescind the election and return to regular Medicare coverage at any time. The revocation of the hospice election may even include an effective date earlier than the date of the election. [42 C.F.R. § 418.28]

Q 13:44 What is the hospice benefit available through Medicare?

Hospice benefits are comparatively generous, and include:

- Nursing care
- Physician services
- Short-term inpatient care for pain control and symptom management
- Counseling (including grief counseling for family members)
- Physical, occupational, and speech therapy
- Medical social services
- Home health aides
- Homemaker services
- Medical supplies, equipment appliance, and biologicals including hospice-related prescriptions

[42 C.F.R. § 418.202]

Although hospice-related prescription drugs are covered, there is a $5 or 5 percent copayment. There is also coinsurance for respite care equal to 5 percent of the payment made by CMS for a respite care day. The patient's coinsurance liability for respite care may not exceed the inpatient hospital deductible applicable for the year in which the hospice coinsurance period began. [42 C.F.R. § 418.400]

Q 13:45 What is the maximum length of Medicare hospice coverage?

Hospice benefits are initially established at up to 90 days. If the patient is still living at the end of that 90-day period, it can be extended for another 90-day hospice period. If the patient is still alive at the end of 180 days, the hospice benefit can be extended for successive 60-day periods thereafter. [42 U.S.C. § 1395d(a)(4)] Realistically, if the patient survives the first two 90-day periods of terminal illness, it may be difficult to secure additional hospice coverage.

The hospice election is revocable. However, if the patient revokes the election of hospice care during the beneficiary period, any days left in the period are lost. The remaining periods are available.

Part B Benefits

Q 13:46 What benefits are included in Medicare Part B?

Part B primarily provides coverage for physician's services. Specific services covered include:

- Doctor's visits
- Outpatient and partial hospitalization services
- Ambulatory surgical services
- Diagnostic tests
- Ambulance services
- Durable medical equipment
- Home health services
- Prosthetic devices
- Braces, trusses, artificial limbs, and eyes
- X-ray, radium, and radioactive isotope therapy
- Prosthetic devices and orthotics
- Physical, occupational, and speech therapy
- Blood, blood components, and the cost of blood processing and administration
- Blood clotting factors
- Comprehensive outpatient rehabilitation services

[42 U.S.C. §§ 1395k, 1395x(s); 42 C.F.R. §§ 410.20–410.73]

Q 13:47 What medical supplies and equipment does Medicare Part B cover?

Medicare Part B helps pay for durable medical equipment such as oxygen equipment, wheelchairs, and other medically necessary equipment prescribed by a physician for use in the beneficiary's home. (A skilled nursing facility is not considered a "home." This can be a problem when these supplies are needed in a SNF, which is expected to provide them as part of the rate, but may insist that these are non-covered extras.) Medicare coverage is available for, among other items, arm, leg, back, and neck braces; medical supplies such as ostomy pouches, surgical dressings, splints, and casts; breast prostheses following a mastectomy; and one pair of eyeglasses with an intraocular lens after cataract surgery. Medicare pays for different kinds of durable medical equipment in different ways. Some equipment must be rented; other equipment must be purchased. [See *http://www.medicare.gov/*] Medicare will not pay for equipment that is NOT primarily and customarily used only for medical purposes, such as air conditioning, and will not pay for equipment used primarily for convenience, such as stair lifts. Medicare will also not pay for equipment that is mainly for use outside the home.

The Centers for Medicare and Medicaid Services contracts with four companies, known as Durable Medical Equipment regional Carriers, to process claims for durable medical equipment in their respective regions. Medicare will require a prescription from a physician and, usually, a "certificate of medical necessity."

As with other goods and services, a patient has a right to demand that the provider submit a request to Medicare for payment under Part B, even if the provider is virtually certain that the claim will be denied. However, the patient will be liable for the charge, provided the patient has been given proper notice of that initial determination, as demonstrated by the patient having signed an "ABN" or "advance billing notice." If the provider submits, but the patient has not signed the ABN, the provider may have to pick up the cost. [See, e.g., Centers for Medicare and Medicaid Services Program Memorandum Intermediaries/Carriers Transmittal AB-02-114, § 1.1.D. (July 31, 2002)]

Q 13:48 What preventative care is available through Medicare?

Although the Medicare program has historically limited the preventative care provided as part of its benefits, the recent trend has been to increase the availability of preventative care. In addition to an increased emphasis on Medicare HMOs (which usually include preventative care as part of the philosophical approach to care by the HMO), Congress has added coverage for a number of specific screening and preventative care procedures, including:

1. Mammography (for female patients over age 40), beginning January 1, 1998 [42 U.S.C. §§ 1395l, 1395m];
2. Annual pap smears and pelvic exams (for women at high risk or of childbearing age—other women are covered for pap

smears and pelvic exams every three years), since January 1, 1998 [42 U.S.C. §§ 1395l, 1395x]; and

3. Prostate cancer screening (for male patients over age 50), since January 1, 2000) [42 U.S.C. §§ 1395x, 1395y].

Q 13:49 What services are not covered under Medicare Part B?

Not all outpatient medical care is covered under the Medicare Part B program. [Specific exclusions from coverage are listed at 42 U.S.C. § 1396y(a)] Principal exceptions to the otherwise broad coverage include:

1. Prescription medications (although some limited coverage may be provided for beneficiaries enrolled in Medicare HMOs), other than medication that must be administered by a physician;
2. Dental care (except for dental surgery);
3. Eyeglasses, contact lenses, and eye examinations (unless they are related to eye surgery, such as cataract surgery);
4. Hearing aids or the examinations necessary to fit the hearing aids;
5. Routine physical examinations and immunizations (except, again, that the beneficiary may elect a Medicare HMO that provides such care);
6. Routine podiatric care or orthopedic shoes or supportive devices;
7. Personal comfort items (e.g., television or telephone in the beneficiary's hospital room); and
8. Custodial care.

In recent years there have been myriad proposals for adding a prescription drug benefit to Medicare. These have ranged from a discount card (somewhat redundant, as many such cards are currently available) to a plan similar to those offered by many states' P.A.C.E. programs (see chapter 11), involving annual fees and a copayment, with a cap on annual coverage and/or an additional 100 percent coverage after a further deductible is met. So far, Congress has not adopted any prescription drug benefit.

Q 13:50 What are the copayments and deductibles under Medicare Part B?

Medicare has many copayment requirements for care and deductibles from covered care. The structure of Medicare's reimbursement formulae can be thoroughly confusing to clients. In addition, many (but not all) of the numbers are indexed for inflation and the annual changes add to the confusion.

Part B requires that the beneficiary pay the first $100 of covered services each year. [42 U.S.C. § 1395l(b)] This deductible is waived when the patient is under continuous treatment that spans the new year.

More importantly, Part B usually pays for only 80 percent of covered services, requiring the patient to pay the remaining 20 percent. Furthermore, Medicare's 80 percent share is calculated based on the "reasonable charges" for those services. [42 U.S.C. § 1395l(a)(1)] This means that the beneficiary's share of medical costs is almost always greater than 20 percent, because the "reasonable charges" are nearly universally lower than the actual costs of services.

Even physicians who do not participate in Medicare are constrained by a "limiting charge" when dealing with Medicare beneficiaries. (They are relieved from the limitation only if they make a written commitment that they will not provide services to any Medicare beneficiaries for two years [42 C.F.R. §§ 405.410 et seq.].) Although such doctors are permitted to charge more than the "reasonable charges" for their services, they may not charge more than 115 percent of those reasonable charges. [42 U.S.C. § 1395w-4(g); Garelick v. Sullivan, 987 F.2d 913 (2d Cir. 1993), *cert. denied*, 510 U.S. 821] This combination of provisions can hopelessly complicate the calculation of the amount a Medicare beneficiary must pay toward doctor bills. A few examples may help to clarify the methodology:

> **Example 13-1.** Doctor A charges $100 for a procedure and Medicare allows $100 for that service. Doctor A's patients must pay the $20 not paid by Medicare and Medicare will pay $80.

> **Example 13-2.** Doctor B charges $110 for the same procedure and Medicare still allows $100. Doctor B's patients must pay $30 and Medicare will pay $80.

Example 13-3. Doctor C charges $120 for the same procedure. Doctor C's patients must pay $35, Medicare will pay $80, and Doctor C must "write off" $5. (Doctor C's charges may not exceed $115, so the patient need not pay the additional $5.)

Q 13:51 What does it mean that a physician "takes Medicare assignment"?

Although Medicare payments can be made to the patient, they are usually made directly to the physician or the provider under the assignment method of payment.

Under the assignment method of payment the physician or provider agrees to accept the Medicare-approved charge as full payment for the services provided. Medicare pays 80 percent of the allowable charges and either the patient or Medicare Supplemental Insurance (Medigap) pays the remaining 20 percent. In some states, low-income Medicare recipients are entitled to Medicare assignment from participating physicians.

Q 13:52 Is there a limit on the amount that a physician who does not accept assignment can charge?

Yes. If a physician does not accept assignment, the patient must pay the physician's charge above the Medicare-approved charge; however, the amount a physician may bill is limited by federal law. A physician who has not officially "opted out" of Medicare for two years, but does not accept assignment, generally cannot charge a total of more than 115 percent of the Medicare-approved rate. [42 C.F.R. § 414.48] The approved charge for the physician's services appears on the patient's explanation of Medicare benefits. The explanation of Medicare benefits is the written notice that is sent to the patient after the claim is processed.

Medicare+Choice Program

Q 13:53 What is the Medicare+Choice program?

The Medicare + Choice program, also referred to as Medicare Part C, is a collection of alternative means of financing or receiving individual Medicare coverage (see Q 13:8). Foremost among these is the use of an HMO to manage benefits, and more is often heard about "Medicare HMOs" than "Medicare + Choice." Medicare + Choice does not provide additional benefits or coverage, although it may make Medicare more attractive for some beneficiaries or may provide additional benefits as an inducement to attract participants. [42 U.S.C. § 1395w-21; 42 C.F.R. § 422.101] The Medicare + Choice plan must provide the same services available under Parts A and B and must pass on any cost savings to the beneficiaries. Part C is also sometimes used to describe proposed additional benefits, such as prescription drug coverage or long-term nursing care, that have not yet been adopted. [41 U.S.C. § 1395d] If supplemental benefits are offered under a Medicare + Choice plan, a separate premium is permitted, but the premium cannot vary among individuals within the plan and must not exceed certain actuarial and community ratings requirements. [42 U.S.C. § 1395-22; 42 C.F.R. § 422.102]

Q 13:54 What are the Medicare+Choice options?

As part of its continuing review of Medicare, Congress in 1997 created several new options for individual Medicare beneficiaries. It is important to realize that the Medicare + Choice program only permits private providers and insurance companies to offer alternative plans; the federal government does not directly provide any of the alternative plans. Consequently, the actual availability of Medicare + Choice benefits will depend on the decisions of local providers to offer alternative plans. Medicare + Choice was scheduled to begin offering those alternatives to Medicare beneficiaries in November 1999; few plans were in place by that time, and most beneficiaries found that no additional options were available. Medicare + Choice plans, depending on local availability, may include:

1. *Health maintenance organizations.* Actually, beneficiaries were permitted to select HMO providers for Medicare even before Medicare + Choice was established. In some areas, HMOs are already providing care for a third or more of Medicare beneficiaries. In other areas, the penetration of HMOs is slight. Furthermore, in some areas where HMOs once had a strong presence, there has been almost a mass exodus, with HMOs leaving the region entirely and participants scrambling to obtain (or re-obtain) Medigap insurance (see Qs 13:64–13:68).

2. *Provider-sponsored organizations (PSOs).* Local hospitals, clinics, or other health care providers may elect to establish qualified Medicare provider organizations. PSOs may resemble HMOs, but will be operated by existing health care providers.

3. *Preferred provider organizations (PPOs).* Insurance plans that permit beneficiaries to select their own health care providers, but that provide lower deductibles and copayments for health care received from an approved list of providers. By contracting with those preferred providers, the plan is expected to reduce costs. In August, 2002, the Department of Health and Human Services announced that 23 states would be offering PPO options as part of Medicare + Choice, starting January 1, 2003. The states are Alabama, Arizona, California, Florida, Illinois, Indiana, Kansas, Kentucky, Louisiana, Maryland, Missouri, North Carolina, Nevada, New Jersey, New York, Ohio, Oregon, Pennsylvania, Rhode Island, Tennessee, Virginia, West Virginia, and Washington.

4. *HMO/POS—The point of service option.* Essentially, this permits HMOs to operate captive clinics or other providers.

5. *Provider fee for service (PFFS) option.* Allows beneficiaries to select certain private providers. For those providers who agree to accept the plan's payment terms and conditions, this option does not place the providers at risk, nor vary payment rates based upon utilization. The provider is reimbursed at a rate determined by the plan on a fee-for-service basis. Medicare makes capitated payments to the private pay fee-for-service plan as it would to an HMO or PSO.

6. *Religious fraternal benefit society plan.* A "religious fraternal benefit society" may offer a Medicare + Choice plan to members of its church, or to members of a group of affiliated churches. [42 C.F.R. § 422.57] This type of Medicare + Choice plan is not really a separate category, because the plan must fall under one of the other categories of Medicare + Choice.

7. *Medical savings accounts (MSAs).* When a beneficiary elects this option, Medicare pays for a two-part approach to covering medical costs. First, the beneficiary selects (and Medicare pays for) a high-deductible traditional insurance policy. The unused dollar amount of the beneficiary's benefit is then

deposited into a savings account, which can be used for medical care until the high deductible is met. If the beneficiary does not use the medical savings account, it ultimately passes to heirs.

Q 13:55 How can a Medicare beneficiary evaluate the new options available through Medicare+Choice?

Medicare + Choice plans have still not yet become widely available and most Medicare beneficiaries will have difficulty evaluating the options. The variety of options and the similar-sounding acronyms make the choices more confusing. Area Agencies on Aging typically offer Medicare counseling services and may even offer informative seminars for seniors. National Medicare advocacy agencies have prepared and distribute explanatory literature, most of which is available on the Internet. Providers themselves may offer plan explanations, but beneficiaries should realize that they are promotional efforts. Unfortunately, there are few additional sources of information for Medicare recipients considering making a change.

Q 13:56 Who is eligible to enroll in Medicare+Choice?

Any Medicare beneficiary who does not have end-stage renal disease at the time of enrollment is permitted to enroll in a Medicare + Choice program, provided only that the program serves the beneficiary's geographic area and the beneficiary agrees to abide by the requirements of the chosen program. [42 C.F.R. § 422.50] Enrollment in the Medicare + Choice plan is accomplished simply by completing the enrollment form.

Q 13:57 When may the Medicare+Choice election be made?

Enrollment in Medicare + Choice must take place in one of these available enrollment periods:

1. In the first six months after the beneficiary becomes eligible for Medicare enrollment [42 C.F.R. § 422.62(a)(4)(ii)];
2. In the period from three months before Medicare eligibility until the last day of the month before eligibility (the "initial coverage election period") [42 C.F.R. § 422.62(a)(1)];
3. During November of each year (the "annual election period") [42 C.F.R. § 422.62(a)(2)]; or

4. During the first three months of each year (except that only one election can be made during each annual period) [42 C.F.R. § 422.62(a)(5)].

Q 13:58 When does a Medicare managed care plan's coverage begin for a new participant?

If the participant signs up during the November "open enrollment" period, coverage in the new managed care plan will ordinarily begin the following January 1; coverage will begin when the participant is notified that he or she has been accepted into the new plan, which will usually be the first of the month following the month after application.

Q 13:59 What if you move out of a Medicare+Choice plan's service area?

If the particular Medicare + Choice plan provides coverage in the new area, no change in Medicare benefits is required (though the plan itself will require updated address information and may require a change of primary care physician). If the same plan is not available in the new area, the participant must either disenroll (and thereby return to regular Medicare coverage) or enroll in a new plan offered in the new geographic area. Because of the geographic limitations on individual plans, Medicare managed care plans are usually less attractive to Medicare beneficiaries who travel extensively or move frequently.

Q 13:60 Can an individual's enrollment in a Medicare+Choice plan be terminated?

The Medicare beneficiary may choose to disenroll from a Medicare + Choice program at any time by simply filing the disenrollment election form with the program. Unless the beneficiary is eligible to elect another Medicare + Choice program and has actually made an election, disenrollment will return the beneficiary to regular Medicare coverage.

The Medicare + Choice program is permitted to terminate the beneficiary involuntarily only in one of three situations:

1. Failure to make timely premium payments;

2. Disruptive behavior by the beneficiary; or
3. Termination of the Medicare + Choice program for all beneficiaries in the geographic area.

In the last of these situations, the beneficiary is given a special enrollment period to choose another Medicare + Choice plan. If the beneficiary does not make a selection, or if the termination is for nonpayment or disruptive behavior, the beneficiary is returned to regular Medicare coverage. [42 U.S.C. § 1395w-21]

Q 13:61 How long are Medicare managed care plans and private fee-for-service plans required to stay in Medicare?

Medicare + Choice plans are required to continue to operate for a full calendar year. If a plan decides to terminate coverage (or eliminate a particular geographic area), it is required to notify all affected plan participants. Participants are then required to select a replacement plan or return to regular Medicare coverage.

Q 13:62 What premiums does an enrollee in Medicare+Choice have to pay?

Premiums for Medicare + Choice programs must be annually filed with and approved by the federal Department of Health and Human Services. Premiums must be uniform among beneficiaries enrolled in the Medicare + Choice program, and may not exceed set maximum amounts. [42 C.F.R. §§ 422.300–422.308] In addition to premiums specific to the Medicare + Choice plan, participants must also continue to pay the Medicare Part B premium required of all Part B enrollees.

Q 13:63 Can (or should) Medicare+Choice participants maintain their existing Medigap insurance coverage?

For most Medicare + Choice participants Medigap coverage will be duplicative, and the insured will consequently receive little benefit from the Medigap policy. Medigap insureds are permitted, however, to retain their policies, and they may choose to do so for at least a period of time after enrollment in a Medicare + Choice plan. In the event that a Medicare managed care plan terminates coverage in a participant's area, for example, Medigap carriers are required to permit the participant to re-enroll in a Medigap plan, but the costs may be significantly higher than if the original policy had continued.

Q 13:64 What is a Medicare HMO?

For several years, Medicare has permitted health maintenance organizations to provide Medicare services. Under the Medicare HMO arrangement, beneficiaries who choose to join the plan will receive all services from the HMO, and Medicare pays 95 percent of the average cost (to Medicare) of patients in that community. This may mean that the HMO receives a capitated rate of $400 to $500 per month for most areas of the country, and must provide all covered services for its Medicare beneficiaries. In addition, the HMO may (but is not required to) elect to provide additional benefits; frequently, HMOs provide limited eyeglass and eye examination coverage, transportation, periodic checkups, and sometimes even a limited prescription drug benefit. The federal government's decision to fix the capitation rate at 95 percent has come under considerable fire. Originally calculated to encourage managed care cost savings, the 5 percent discount has been criticized as instead encouraging HMOs to seek out only relatively healthy Medicare beneficiaries, and systematically to encourage plan participants to transfer back into "traditional" Medicare once they become ill. Medicare HMO operators insist that they do not do this, and point to surveys indicating that their members consistently rate their care as excellent.

Q 13:65 Who may enroll in a Medicare HMO?

As with the other Medicare + Choice plans, Medicare HMOs must accept any Medicare beneficiary who lives in the HMO's geographic service area, agrees to the HMO's regulations, and does not have end-stage renal disease. [42 C.F.R. § 422.50] Medicare HMOs may terminate the beneficiary from coverage only for nontimely payment of any premiums due, disruptive behavior, or termination of the HMO benefit for all beneficiaries living in the geographic area. [42 U.S.C. § 1395w-21]

Q 13:66 What benefits should a Medicare beneficiary expect to receive from joining an HMO?

Medicare HMOs may provide additional benefits such as transportation, preventive care, or a limited prescription drug benefit. These additional benefits are gradually being eliminated, and as a result, enrollment is declining. However, Medicare HMOs will usually be considerably less expensive than Medigap policies (see Q 13:69); even though there may be a per-visit copayment required, the total cost for copayments will likely be less than annual deductibles and copayments under a traditional Medicare program. Most importantly, perhaps, the Medicare HMO will save substantial paperwork and eliminate confusing (and often distressing) "explanation of benefit" forms: The nature of an HMO eliminates separate financial forms for each visit. The Medicare HMO patient simply pays the per-visit copayment, receives care, and completes the contact. Because the HMO is paid on a capitated basis (i.e., a fixed rate for each plan participant rather than a per-visit or per-service fee), there is no necessity to follow up with an explanation of benefits.

Q 13:67 What are the risks and drawbacks to joining a Medicare HMO?

While Medicare HMO enrollment may carry substantial benefits, the HMO participant will likely encounter a number of problems as well. Most importantly, HMO participants will usually have a limited selection of physicians and may have a difficult time securing access to specialists. The denial of the "right to choose your own doctor" has been decried by the media and consumer groups. Appointment delays may be greater for HMO participants, and there is at least a widespread perception that necessary care is more quickly denied in managed care systems generally.

A major problem for Medicare HMOs in recent years has been the frequency with which HMOs have "dropped out" or decided to cease offering benefits in a particular region. Some regions have almost no HMO options available. As a result, HMO beneficiaries must scramble to replace their coverage. In order to provide some relief, the beneficiary will have a three-month "special enrollment period" in which to obtain an "unrated" Medigap plan (the three months following the HMO's notice of termination and ending with the effective date of the termination). The special enrollment period only applies if the HMO terminates coverage, not if the beneficiary is simply dissatisfied and chooses to leave. Also, if a beneficiary enrolled in a Medicare HMO at age 65 and leaves the area for another region in which there is effectively no HMO coverage, he or she will be entitled to purchase an unrated Medigap plan.

Finally, Medicare HMOs, like other HMOs generally, have endured public relations setbacks following lawsuits alleging improper denial of treatment. The public perception is that "profits, not people" have been the source of coverage decision-making. Whether or not this is grounded in reality, the perception is such that an HMO beneficiary denied coverage is very likely to want to challenge the HMO's decision.

Q 13:68 What rights does a Medicare beneficiary have when he or she has enrolled in an HMO?

Just as with general Medicare, a Medicare HMO participant has rights to appeal coverage and other determinations. Those appeal rights may, however, be limited in the HMO. Despite an early court ruling extending identical appeal rights to HMO beneficiaries, subsequent decisions and legislation have shifted control of the appeal process back to the HMO itself. [Grijalva v. Shalala, 152 F.3d 1115 (9th Cir. 1998), *vacated and remanded*, 526 U.S. 1096 (1999), *injunction dismissed on remand as moot*, 185 F.3d 1075 (9th Cir. 1999)]

Q 13:69 What is a Medicare SELECT Policy?

Medicare SELECT policies are special Medigap policies that use preferred provider organizations or health maintenance organizations to lower the premium cost for the Medigap policy. A beneficiary who chooses a Medicare SELECT policy will receive the same Medigap benefits at a lower cost provided that he or she utilizes the plan's doctors and facilities. The beneficiary is also permitted to use outside providers, but then receives only standard Medicare benefits. [58 Fed. Reg. 35,017 (June 30, 1993)]

Medigap Insurance

Q 13:70 What is a Medigap insurance policy?

Although Medicare coverage is quite extensive, there are a number of items not covered by Medicare. Uncovered items include prescription drugs, substantial deductibles, and copayments. In order to provide coverage for those items and others, the insurance industry has extensively marketed so-called Medicare supplemental insurance products. [42 U.S.C. § 1395ss] More commonly, Medicare supplement policies are referred to as "Medigap" policies. With the exception of certain additional benefits such as a limited prescription benefit, in general Medigap simply covers the portion of Medicare-covered items not paid by Medicare. In other words, in most cases if Medicare would not pay, neither will Medigap.

Shortly after the institution of Medicare in the mid-1960s, the supplemental insurance industry was rife with abuses (including over-billing, sale of duplicate policies, sale of special-purpose policies with extremely limited coverage, and similar practices). In response, Congress adopted a uniform set of Medigap policy terms: All Medigap policies must offer one of ten pre-defined sets of benefits identified as standardized Plans A through J. In theory, at least, the plans must now offer competitive pricing, security of the insurance company, claims experience, and other, more easily quantified, variables, and avoid confusing and misleading plan provisions. State insurance department websites may offer a quick price-comparison of policies by plan number.

Q 13:71 What benefits are provided in every Medigap policy?

Every Medigap policy must include certain core benefits:

1. The deductible for hospitalization days 61 through 90;
2. The deductible for the "lifetime reserve" hospitalization days 91 through 150;
3. An additional 365 lifetime reserve days with no deductible;
4. The first three pints of blood not covered by Medicare; and
5. The Part B coinsurance (e.g., the 20 percent of allowable charges for outpatient services).

Those benefits are contained in the simplest of the Medigap plans, Plan A. Each succeeding plan builds on those benefits. Plans B and C provide additional benefits that are included in every succeeding plan. Plans D through J mix and match a collection of additional benefits. The standardized Medigap plans are as set out in Table 13-1:

Table 13-1. Standardized Medigap Plans

Plan	*Includes All Provisions of Plan*	*Additional Features*
A	Basic provisions only	
B	Plan A	—Coverage for the hospitalization deductible for the first 60 days
C	Plan B	—Daily deductible for SNF days 21-100 —Emergency care in a foreign country —$100 annual deductible
D	Plan C (but not the $100 deductible coverage)	—At-home recovery care up to $1,600 per year
E	Plan C (but not the $100 deductible coverage)	—Preventive examinations, flu shots, etc., up to $120 per year
F	Plan C	—"Balance billing" benefits for the portion of out-patient visits not covered under Part B

(Plan F is also available in a "high-deductible" version, under which benefits are not paid until the beneficiary has incurred a total of $1,530 (year 2000 figure)—this deductible does not apply to the foreign emergency care benefit.)

G	Plan D (but not the $100	—"Balance billing"

Table 13-1. Standardized Medigap Plans (*cont'd*)

Plan	*Includes All Provisions of Plan*	*Additional Features*
	deductible coverage)	benefits, but only at 80% of the non-covered charges
H	Plan C	—50% of prescription drugs after $250 deductible and with an annual limit of $1,250
I	Plan F (but not the $100 deductible coverage)	—50% of prescription drugs after $250 deductible and with an annual limit of $1,250
J	Plan F	—At-home recovery care up to $1,600 per year —50% of prescription drugs after $250 deductible and with an annual limit of $3,000 —Preventive examinations, flu shots, etc., up to $120 per year

(Like Plan F, Plan J is also available in a "high-deductible" version, under which benefits are not paid until the beneficiary has incurred a total of $1,530 (year 2000 figure)—this deductible does not apply to foreign emergency care or prescription drug benefits.)

[42 U.S.C. § 1395ss]

The site *www.medicare.gov* now offers detailed Medigap plan information through a "Medicare Personal Plan Finder'; another useful resources is the Center for Medicare Advocacy website.

Q 13:72 What factors should an individual consider when choosing a Medigap policy?

Of course the Medicare beneficiary considering a Medigap policy should be concerned about the cost of premiums (typically ranging from a few hundred dollars per year for Plan A to $200 per month for Plan J, the most expensive and extensive coverage). The stability and claims handling of the insurance company should also be considered.

The Medicare beneficiary might wonder whether the Medigap policy is necessary at all. Nearly all Medicare recipients should plan on purchasing Medigap insurance, as the shortcomings of Medicare coverage are substantial. The purchase of a Medigap policy does not, however, substitute for long-term care insurance. The Medigap policy will only cover the unpaid portion of Medicare-allowed long-term care, and Medicare imposes serious limitations on the availability of care in skilled nursing facilities.

Q 13:73 When should one purchase a Medigap policy?

It is usually of prime importance to purchase a Medigap policy during the initial enrollment period, during the first six months after a retiree enrolls in Medicare Part B (usually upon attaining age 65; the common exception is the working person over age 65, who will not purchase Part B until no longer receiving employee coverage; COBRA coverage may be insufficient to delay the initial enrollment period). This is because Medigap insurers may not refuse coverage on any of the policies based on the health of the beneficiary; in other words, the policies must be offered on an "unrated" basis. Thereafter, policies are underwritten, that is, eligibility may vary based on health.

This "window" does not open for the person receiving Social Security disability insurance until he or she reaches age 65. Prior to that time, he or she is limited to Medicare HMO coverage (if available), or Plans A through C.

> **Example 13-4.** John receives SSDI on his 50th birthday (with no retroactivity). He can receive Medicare and purchase a Plan C Medigap policy when he is age 52. Once he turns age 65, however, he will have a six-month window within which to purchase Plans D through J if he so desires.

In addition, "open enrollment," on an unrated basis, is available to:

1. Medicare + Choice participants who lose coverage because the plan was terminated, or because the participant moved out of the coverage area or terminated the Medicare + Choice plan for cause.
2. Beneficiaries who were covered by regular Medicare supplemented by a Medigap policy, then changed to a Medicare + Choice program but changed back within 12 months and apply for the Medigap policy within 63 days.
3. Medigap policyholders who are terminated from their prior Medigap plan for one of several reasons.

Although these beneficiaries do have a right to enroll in a new Medigap program, they may in some cases be limited to Plans A, B, C, or F, or to the same plan type they held previously. [42 U.S.C. § 1395ss]

Once the plan is selected, Medigap insurers may set policy premiums on the basis of "age rating." An age-rated premium will increase as the beneficiary ages; while premium costs will likely be lower in early years, they will increase substantially over time. If the insurer does not use an age-rating method (instead charging the same premium for all beneficiaries regardless of age), initial costs may be higher but the beneficiary may save costs over time.

Medicare Appeals Process

Q 13:74 What are the appeal rights for Medicare beneficiaries?

Appeal processes and rights differ depending on the particular decision, denial, or benefit under attack. Different appeals provisions apply to each of the following:

1. Appeals of determination of eligibility for Part A or Part B, or election of Medicare + Choice (Part C);
2. Appeals of payment denial for Part A benefits;
3. Appeals of payment denial for Part B benefits (including appeals from managed care plan benefit determinations); and

4. Appeals of service denials or charges for Medicare + Choice (Part C) benefits.

In addition, any appeal raising questions about whether particular types of services or items are covered by Medicare is further limited. Such appeals may not be entertained by an administrative law judge (ALJ), may not be based on alleged failure to publish the appropriate notice in the Federal Register, and may not be granted on the basis of an inadequate administrative record. [42 U.S.C. § 1395ff(b)(2)]

New appeals procedures were enacted as part of the Beneficiaries Improvement and Protection Act of 2000 (BIPA). [Pub. L. No. 106-554 (2000)]. These were to take effect October 1, 2002. [67 Fed. Reg. 62,478 (Oct. 7, 2002)] While some have been implemented, others have not.

In general, there has been a high success rate for appeals to an administrative law judge. As of this writing, the Bush Administration has presented proposals that would limit access to hearings before administrative law judges. Instead, "binding arbitration" or other mechanisms would be used. At the same time, the Centers for Medicare and Medicaid Services is proposing to move Medicare appeals from the purview of Social Security Administration administrative law judges, to judges within the Centers. A further proposal would be promulgation of a new rule requiring administrative law judges to "give deference" to policies adopted by Medicare and its contractors, which review and pay claims for the government, leaving the burden on beneficiaries to show why such policies should be disregarded. These controversial proposals are as yet not in place.

In short, the information in this chapter may no longer be current, and the elder law attorney is well-advised to review internet resources such as the Center for Medicare Advocacy website in order to remain current.

Q 13:75 In general, how does a beneficiary appeal a denial of eligibility?

A denial of eligibility for Medicare Part A, Part B, or Part C (Medicare + Choice) coverage is an "initial determination" and subject to appeal. [42 U.S.C. § 1395ff] That process includes these steps:

1. A request for reconsideration, filed within 120 days of receipt of the intermediary's decision (formerly 60 days, changed by BIPA) at the local Social Security office (or the Centers for Medicare and Medicaid Services, Railroad Retirement, or, more often, the fiscal intermediary rendering the original decision);
2. A request for an administrative hearing, filed within 60 days of the denial of the request for reconsideration;
3. An appeal to the Departmental Appeals Board at the Department of Health and Human Services within 60 days of an adverse decision at the administrative hearing; and
4. A federal court action, filed within 60 days of the denial of the final administrative appeal.

Q 13:76 What is the appeal process for denial of Part A benefits?

Part A benefits can be denied by the provider issuing a notice of noncoverage. Alternatively (or if requested by the patient), coverage for Part A benefits for hospital care is made initially by a peer review organization, and secondarily, or for all other Part A claims, by a "fiscal intermediary." All other Part A claims are handled by fiscal intermediaries. After the provider submits a bill to the fiscal intermediary that administers the Medicare program in the geographic area, the fiscal intermediary must issue a formal determination, which is then subject to further appeal. Special rules govern appeals of further inpatient coverage at a hospital (see Q 13:77).

Because of court action, hospitals and skilled nursing facilities are required to provide particular information and procedures when Medicare benefits are denied:

1. Denial notices must include information about the beneficiary's right to demand that the hospital or SNF bill Medicare for the questioned service.
2. On request of the beneficiary, the provider must submit the bill to the fiscal intermediary (so-called "demand billing").
3. No bill may be submitted to the beneficiary until the Medicare intermediary has ruled on the demand bill.

[Sarrassat v. Sullivan, 1989 WL 208444 (N.D. Cal. May 17, 1989) (settlement order)]

Q 13:77 What are the special rules for denials of continued hospital inpatient coverage?

Patients receiving inpatient care with a hospital have a special right to request immediate review by a peer review organization (now being referred to for managed care beneficiaries as a "QIO" or "quality improvement organization") of the initial denial by the provider of further inpatient care coverage. The request must be made by noon of the first working day following notice of the initial decision, and the PRO or QIO must respond by close of business on the following working day. Until the PRO or QIO has issued its decision the provider may not charge the patient, but will continue to bill Medicare; similarly, the HMO may not terminate coverage. [See, e.g., 42 C.F.R. § 422.622 (HMOs)]

For inpatient coverage in a hospital, there are two other important issues: (1) the right to continued hospital coverage if no "appropriate skilled nursing facility" is available elsewhere and (2) disputes with the hospital about the appropriateness of the facility the hospital chooses (see Q 13:22).

Q 13:78 What are the procedures for appealing a denial of Part A benefits by the fiscal intermediary?

Appeal of a denial of Part A benefits by the fiscal intermediary follows more or less the same procedure as Social Security appeals (see Q 13:74), with several exceptions. No administrative hearing is available unless the amount in question is at least $100 [42 U.S.C. § 1395ff(b)(2)], and no appeal may be made to federal court unless the amount in question is at least $1,000 for skilled nursing facility, home health and hospice appeals, and at least $2,000 for hospital appeals. Both limits are doubled for appeals of a determination by a peer review organization. [42 U.S.C. § 1320c-4]

Q 13:79 What appeal rights exist for Part B benefit determinations?

Determinations of Part B benefits are made by the Part B "carrier" (usually Blue Shield or an insurance company). Appeals of those determinations are made exclusively through the carrier and not to Social Security, CMS, or the courts. The appeal process consists of as many as four steps:

1. A request for review can be filed up to 120 days after the initial determination being challenged. The review may be requested in writing at the SSA or CMS office, or directly with the carrier. (This may be extended for 60 days if the beneficiary requires additional time to gather documents.) If the carrier does not respond within 60 days, the beneficiary may request a hearing. Otherwise, the beneficiary has the right to provide written documentation but does not have a right to a hearing. The carrier must explain its decision in writing. [42 C.F.R. § 405.810]
2. If the amount in controversy is at least $100, a written request for a hearing may be filed with the carrier or Social Security up to 120 days after denial of the review (with an extra 60 days if required in order to assemble medical information). The hearing will be conducted by a hearing officer employed by the carrier; the hearing officer must be impartial. [42 C.F.R. §§ 405.815 et seq.]
3. If the amount in controversy is over $100, an appeal may follow to an administrative law judge. If the claim is less than those limits, the carrier's hearing officer's decision is final. ALJ appeals must be requested within 60 days of the final carrier decision. [42 C.F.R. § 405.815]
4. To appeal the decision of the administrative law judge to a federal court, the amount in question must be $1,000 or more.

Q 13:80 How do appeal rights differ for managed care beneficiaries?

Managed care program participants do not have fiscal intermediaries or carriers to appeal to, and so CMS has adapted the appeal procedures for HMO and other managed care plans. The principal provisions of those procedures include:

1. A requirement that the HMO respond to a request for redetermination within 60 days unless there is good cause for further delay, and that the HMO respond to a request for determination on an expedited basis in 72 hours if you claim that your health could be seriously harmed by waiting for a decision about a service.

2. If the decision on redetermination is not fully favorable to the beneficiary, the decision must be submitted to CMS for review.
3. For immediate appeal of denial of inpatient hospital coverage, the HMO participant has a right to request an immediate review by a quality improvement organization ("QIO") (formerly referred to as a peer review organization; see 42 CFR Part 475). As with Medicare Part A, the request must be made by noon of the business day following the initial decision, and the QIO must respond within 24 hours. Also as with Medicare Part A, the hospital may not bill the patient until final resolution of the QIO review.
4. Sanctions may be imposed on the HMO for failure to follow the regulations.

[42 C.F.R. Part 417]

Q 13:81 What appeal rights are available for Medicare+Choice (Part C) determinations?

In addition to the special appeal rights relating to continued inpatient care coverage, Medicare + Choice beneficiaries may request reconsideration of other denials of benefits and the program must complete its reconsideration within 60 days. If the denial is based on a lack of medical necessity, the review must be by a physician other than the physician making the initial determination, and the second physician must have an appropriate level of expertise in the involved medical area. The Department of Health and Human Services is required to enter into a contract with a separate (outside) agency to conduct administrative reviews, and appeals of those reviews may be made to the Secretary of HHS if the amount in controversy is at least $100. [42 C.F.R. Part 422 Subpart M (42 C.F.R. §§ 422.619 et seq.)]

Q 13:82 What is "expedited review"?

Medicare + Choice beneficiaries have an additional right to request an "expedited" (within 72 hours) decision when asking for reconsideration. If the response is unfavorable, the beneficiary can still pursue review applying the traditional claims periods.

Q 13:83 What general principles should be applied when evaluating a possible Medicare appeal?

In deciding whether a Medicare appeal makes sense, the practitioner will of course consider whether there is a legal basis for the appeal, carefully applying the regulations and being conscious that they are frequently misapplied by providers and intermediaries. Assuming a good claim, however, the usual anxiety about cost should be offset by the high success rate for appeals that results from the following general principles the administrative judge will apply:

1. As with other Social Security Act cases, Medicare law views the patient's treating physician as the person best able to determine what care the patient needs. The rule that has been adopted by one circuit court, the Second Circuit Court of Appeals, is that "dual certification" as to the need for treatment, by the treating physician and the utilization review committee (a/k/a peer review organization) can only be challenged by CMS if there is "substantial evidence" to the contrary. [State of New York o/b/o Bodnar v. Secretary of Health and Human Services, 903 F.2d 122 (2d Cir. 1990); Schisler v. Heckler, 787 F.2d 76, 81 (2d Cir. 1986)] "The opinion of a non-examining doctor by itself cannot constitute the contrary substantial evidence required to override the treating physician's diagnosis." [Hidalgo v. Bowen, 822 F.2d 294, 296–297 (2d Cir. 1987) (SSI eligibility); see also, e.g., State of New York o/b/o Holland v. Secretary of Health and Human Services, 927 F.2d 57 (2d Cir. 1991); State of New York o/b/o Stein v. Secretary of Health and Human Services, 924 F.2d 431 (2d Cir. 1991); Friedman v. Secretary of HHS, 819 F.2d 42 (2d Cir. 1987)]
2. Whenever there is some doubt as to whether coverage should be extended, the patient should always get the benefit of the doubt. The courts have consistently ruled that the coverage standards set by Congress are to be liberally construed and broadly applied to ensure that the elderly and disabled receive the health care services they need. [See, e.g., Rosenberg v. Richardson, 538 F. 2d 487, 490 (2d Cir. 1976); Herbst v. Finch, 473 F. 2d 771, 775 (2d Cir. 1972); Haberman v. Finch, 473 F. 2d 664, 666 (2d Cir. 1969)] The Courts have also stated that the policy underlying the Act requires a liberal

interpretation, and that any doubts should be resolved in favor of coverage. [See, e.g., Herbst v. Finch, 473 F. 2d 771, 775 (2d Cir. 1972)] Exclusions from coverage should be narrowly construed lest they inadvertently encompass the qualifications for benefits. [Coe v. Secretary of HEW, 502 F. 2d 1337, 1340 (4th Cir. 1974)]

3. Administrative Law Judges are not affected by political shifts and pressures. They look exclusively to the law and the regulations in deciding cases. Assuming that Social Security Administration administrative law judges continue to handle appeals, high success rates are likely.

Practice-Related Issues

Q 13:84 Can an attorney charge a fee for assisting with a Medicare appeal?

Representation of Social Security claimants is hampered by strict fee limits, usually the lesser of 25 percent of the fee recovered or $4,000, although exceptions apply. [42 U.S.C. §§ 1395ii, 406(a); 20 C.F.R. §§ 404.1720 et seq.] The same applies to Medicare appeals heard by a Social Security Administration administrative law judge, but there are two important avenues for attorney compensation that may encourage attorneys to assist with Medicare claims. First, the fee limits do not apply to "consequential" damages recovered as a result of a successful appeal. In a Medicare case, these will include the coverage provided by the Medigap insurance policy, which may be substantial. Second, payment of attorneys' fees from the federal government is possible if the case is appealed and won in a U.S. district court. The Equal Access to Justice Act (EAJA) [28 U.S.C. § 2412(d)(1)(A)], provides for fees to be paid by the government when the beneficiary prevails and the government's position is not substantially justified. Although technically the fee is set at $75 per hour, many courts have applied a CPI cost-of-living index to raise the hourly rate well over $100 per hour.

Where the appeal is important, but the practitioner either lacks expertise or cannot afford to assist, the client should be encouraged to contact the Center for Medicare Advocacy, at *www.medicare*

advocacy.org or other Medicare rights organizations, particularly if a class action seems likely.

Q 13:85 What kinds of Medicare problems might an elder law attorney encounter?

Following are situations an attorney might typically encounter in an elder law practice: (1) conflicting information about the availability of Medicare coverage, (2) questions about the sufficiency of Medicare long-term care benefits, and (3) determining whether Medigap coverage or a Medicare HMO is more appropriate for an elderly client.

1. *Transfer of Medicare patient.* Mrs. Jones' daughter complains of the treatment her mother has received since her hospitalization for a fractured hip. First, she says, the hospital insisted on discharging Mrs. Jones to a nursing home before her condition was stabilized, telling her that Mrs. Jones would qualify for 100 days of Medicare coverage in the nursing home. Today (10 days after she was placed at the facility) the nursing home has informed her that her mother no longer qualifies for Medicare coverage and that she will have to begin paying $100 per day as a private patient or move out of the SNF. She wants to know what she can do about the treatment her mother has received.

   Medicare's 100-day SNF benefit is not limited to patients who will "improve," but is available whenever they can benefit from skilled therapy—which includes services to "prevent further deterioration or preserve current capabilities." Apparently the therapist has decided that Mrs. Jones is not "improving," and has overlooked this basis for continuing therapy. One immediate step the daughter can take is to ask the physician to renew the request for therapy.

   The nursing home's determination can only be guessed at, however, because no formal notice has been provided and Mrs. Jones' daughter may not have complete or accurate information. The first step should be to demand a written determination of Mrs. Jones' eligibility for Medicare coverage. Because facilities frequently do not provide written notices, the mere request may buy some time for Mrs. Jones, even if only another day of coverage. Once written notice has been received (and reviewed for compliance with the statutory requirements), the denial of coverage can be appealed: Nursing notes, family information, and second medical opinions could be sought to buttress the argument that Mrs. Jones continues to improve or will deteriorate if therapy is not continued. Even if the appeal is unsuccessful Mrs. Jones will probably have gained another day or two of Medicare coverage while the reconsideration is completed.

An important practical problem at this juncture may be the difficulties for Mrs. Jones' daughter to obtain medical records. The law restricts access to medical records to the patient and certain designated individuals. If Mrs. Jones' daughter is not authorized by an advance directive or durable power of attorney to obtain the records, she may have to be appointed conservator or guardian in order to get the facility to release the records. Moreover, even with appropriate authorization, release of the records may take time, often 30 days or more.

Meanwhile, Mrs. Jones' daughter may want to look into suitable placement in an adult care facility or other appropriate institution. Costs should be lower and Mrs. Jones may be able to get by with the lower level of care. Alternatively, Mrs. Jones' assets could be used for continued private care at the SNF, or she may qualify for Medicaid long-term care coverage.

2. *Advising clients on long-term care needs and alternatives.* A married couple consults the attorney about the possibility that one or both might require expensive medical care in the future. Both are in their mid-60s, and they understand that they have both hospitalization and long-term care benefits available through Medicare. They wonder if they need to do anything else.

   Although Medicare's hospitalization benefit is significant, the long-term care benefit is woefully inadequate. If this couple has any assets to protect, or any desire to remain out of the welfare-oriented Medicaid program, they should seriously consider long-term care insurance. Such insurance is likely to be both available and reasonably priced at their current (relatively young) age, but will become increasingly expensive if they wait to secure their initial coverage.

In addition, they almost certainly will want to look into purchasing a Medigap policy if they have not already done so. If either is within six months of his or her 65th birthday, or if the first Medicare Part B application has been made within the last six months, the Medigap insurer must accept that spouse regardless of medical condition. They need good advice to help select from the various plan options, competing policies from different insurers, and to decide whether to choose an age-rated premium structure.

3. *Advising about Medicare + Choice.* A client wonders whether to switch from traditional Medicare (plus the Medigap policy he or she currently holds, which costs nearly $200 per month) to a Medicare HMO.

   The client should expect several benefits from a switch, including simplicity (no more forms to understand, file, and monitor), better coverage for preventive care, and additional benefits. The HMO might, for example, offer a partial prescription program, or a program that resembles the client's prior Medigap policy but with much lower premium costs. In addition, the cost of the coverage will likely be reduced, especially in light of the expensive Medigap policy held by the client.

   On the other hand, several cautions must be voiced. Recently there has been outcry by HMO patients complaining of pressures brought to bear by the HMOs to reduce benefits, by forcing patients to accept discharge or by providing insufficient care. After the initial enthusiasm for Medicare HMOs in some areas (and particularly in rural areas), many plans have left the field; if the Medicare beneficiary gives up Medigap coverage and stays on the Medicare HMO for more than 12 months, it may be expensive to secure replacement Medigap coverage if he or she later decides voluntarily to leave the HMO. The likely use of the other benefits offered by the HMO, such as transportation (it may be a critical issue, or it may be relatively unimportant) and prescription drug coverage (although it sounds good, it may be a limited benefit) should be evaluated realistically. The client should consider that such benefits have been reduced or eliminated in many Medicare HMOs after enrolling new patients. Perhaps most importantly, the client must recognize that he or she will forgo the freedom to choose his or her own physician if he or she joins the HMO plan and accepts its list of primary care physicians.

Chapter 14

Medicaid Benefits

The federal-state partnership program known as Medicaid pays for about half of all long-term care costs in America. While seniors receive most of their general medical care through the similarly named (but quite different) Medicare program, Medicaid is a critical part of the safety net for seniors who confront the possibility of long-term nursing care.

Because Medicaid eligibility is based on both medical and financial need, qualifying for the program's benefits can be difficult. In fact, the rules and regulations governing Medicaid eligibility are bewilderingly complicated, and far beyond the ability of most seniors to navigate unaided. Medicaid eligibility planning is a core element of many elder law practices. This chapter discusses Medicaid eligibility requirements including income and resource eligibility, the minimum monthly maintenance needs allowance, the community spouse resource allowance, spending down assets, the look-back period for the transfer of assets, asset transfer strategies, Medicaid trusts, and estate recovery.

Overview

Q 14:1 What is the Medicaid Program?

Medicaid is a federal-state partnership program, begun in 1965, to provide medical care to the elderly, blind, and disabled poor. Medicaid benefits include acute medical care, outpatient treatment, medications, and long-term skilled nursing care. Increasingly, state programs are also incorporating long-term custodial care in adult care homes, assisted living facilities, and other venues outside the traditional nursing home setting.

Because most elderly citizens are covered by Medicare for inpatient and outpatient care, the Medicaid program's importance for the elderly lies primarily in the two benefits it provides that are not covered by Medicare: medications and long-term care. Unlike Medicare, which is approached as an insurance program, Medicaid is designed as a welfare program with eligibility based on financial need, so that not all elderly, blind, or disabled citizens qualify for Medicaid benefits.

Q 14:2 Where is Medicaid law found?

Federal law establishes the Medicaid program and dictates what provisions must be included in state Medicaid programs. Most of the federal statutes are found at 42 United States Code (USC) Sections 1396 et seq. The Supplemental Security Income (SSI) program eligibility rules, on which Medicaid eligibility rules are based, are found at 42 USC Section 1382. Some key provisions:

- 42 USC Section 1382b (Assets; part of SSI law)
- 42 USC Section 1396 (Nursing homes)
- 42 USC Section 1396p (Liens and transfers)
- 42 USC Section 1396k (Assignment of rights)

- 42 USC Section 1396r (MCCA, including spousal impoverishment rules for income and assets)

Important sections of the Code of Federal Regulations:

- 42 CFR Part 431 (Fair hearings)
- 42 CFR Part 435 (Medicaid eligibility)
- 42 CFR Part 483 (Nursing home requirements)

The Centers for Medicare and Medicaid interpretations of this law can be found in the "State Medicaid Manual," which is available online and for download at *http://www.cmms.gov/manuals/pub45/pub_45.asp*. This manual, intended to provide a source of interpretive guidance to state Medicaid agencies, can be very helpful, particularly sections 3257 through 3259, also known as "Transmittal 64," which address the transfer and trust provisions of the Omnibus Budget Reduction Act of 1993 (OBRA '93). (These provisions can also be viewed online at *http://www.sharinglaw.net/elder/Transmittal64.htm*.) However, not all states, particularly 209(b) states, agree with the CMS interpretations, and at best these can only provide general guidance and perhaps a useful reference in a lawsuit.

Finally, of great importance in "SSI states" (see Q 14:19) is the Social Security Administration Program Operations Manual System, or POMS. Formerly available only at Social Security Administration offices or, later on, by purchased computer disk, the POMS is now easily available and searchable online at *http://policy.ssa.gov/poms.nsf/poms?OpenView*.

As a practical, day-to-day matter, most essential for an elder law practice is an understanding of the particular state's own Medicaid program as the state itself interprets it. While the state medical assistance plan can be found on the Centers for Medicare and Medicaid website at *http://www.cms.gov/medicaid/stateplans*, the true working of the state program can only be understood through review of state regulations. The beginning elder law practitioner can expect to spend months if not years in becoming familiar with these provisions. In this area above all others it can be important to find a local mentor to provide quick answers and guidance, or to participate in a discussion group.

Q 14:3 Who operates the Medicaid program?

Medicaid is a federal-state cooperative program. Funding for Medicaid benefits comes from both federal and state governments (and, in at least some states, from local government as well). Eligibility and administration of each state's program are handled by the state government, subject to the oversight of the federal Centers for Medicare and Medicaid Services (CMS) (formerly the Health Care Financing Administration, or HCFA; references to "Transmittals" may be given as HCFA Transmittals if the agency was named HCFA at the time). Each state is required to adopt a plan for the administration of Medicaid benefits; the plan must comply with federal minimum requirements. Each state:

1. Establishes its own eligibility standards;
2. Determines the type, amount, duration, and scope of services;
3. Sets the rate of payment for services; and
4. Administers its own program.

To the confusion of consumers, several states have adopted plans that rename Medicaid. Consequently, for example, California residents may erroneously believe that "MediCal" is fundamentally different from Medicaid. Similarly, Tennessee recipients may be more familiar with "TennCare" and Arizona residents with "AHCCCS" (pronounced "access," and standing for the Arizona Health Care Cost Containment System).

Q 14:4 What agencies administer the Medicaid program on the state level?

Each state designates an agency to administer the Medicaid program. In most states, the same agency establishes eligibility rules, administers eligibility determinations, and directs the provision of services. The state agency is often the "Department of Health and Human Services," "Department of Social Services," or some variant; in some states, the state agency includes "Medicaid" in its name.

Q 14:5 What is the difference between Medicaid and Medicare?

Medicaid is a medical welfare benefit. Consequently, participants must be able to show that they qualify for the program financially (as well as meeting other eligibility criteria). Once established, financial eligibility for Medicaid benefits must be reviewed periodically (normally on an annual review cycle). Unlike Medicare, Medicaid generally does not require copayments or deductibles. [42 U.S.C. § 1396o] Medicaid coverage is also broader, for the most part. Coverage for long-term care is not limited to a number of days, as it is for Medicare, but is provided indefinitely. Medicaid also provides full coverage for drugs, medical supplies, vision correction, dental surgery, and other items not covered by Medicare.

Medicare, on the other hand, is a medical insurance program provided for the blind, disabled, and aged, with *no* financial eligibility requirements whatsoever. Medicare eligibility is automatically extended to those over age 65 who are eligible to receive Social Security retirement benefits (even though the beneficiary may elect to defer retirement and the right to receive benefits), as well as to those who have received Social Security Disability Insurance (SSDI) benefits for at least 24 months. Even though a Social Security beneficiary may choose to retire earlier than age 65 (and accept a reduced benefit), he or she will not qualify for Medicare coverage until age 65. (See chapter 13 for a detailed discussion of Medicare.) Unlike Medicaid, Medicare does not provide coverage for "custodial" care or other long-term care benefits for an indefinite period. Instead, Medicare provides only a limited benefit for skilled nursing care for a limited period of time. [42 U.S.C. § 1395d]

Q 14:6 What is the difference between long-term care and general medical care under Medicaid?

Medicaid eligibility may cover acute (inpatient) care, regular doctor and clinic visits (outpatient), long-term nursing care, mental health services, and care and treatment of the developmentally disabled. While an elder law practitioner may occasionally have to deal with the mental health and developmental disability care systems, the most important distinction is usually between general Medicaid coverage and Medicaid subsidies of long-term care.

Long-term care may be provided in a wide variety of settings. (See chapter 11 for a discussion of long-term care options.) Patients may require institutionalization in a nursing home, or may be able to stay in an adult care facility (such as a boarding home, adult foster home, or adult care home), a congregate living arrangement (such as assisted living, supportive living, or communal apartments), or even at home. Medicaid coverage may provide assistance in any of these settings.

In the vast majority of Medicaid cases in most jurisdictions, however, care is still provided in a nursing home setting. Most of the rules of eligibility and care are predicated on nursing home placement, and the eligibility workers, social workers, and medical providers in the state's Medicaid program will usually be focused on institutional placement. It is important to remember (and to remind clients) that home-based and community-based alternatives are available, and to explore appropriate placements even in the Medicaid long-term care arena. Increasingly, Medicaid agencies are recognizing that it may be possible to cut state costs by better arrangements for providing care at home or in an assisted living environment, and in some cases are being forced to do so in order to comply with the "least restrictive alternative" requirement of the *Olmstead* decision. [Olmstead v. Zimring, 527 U.S. 581 (1999)]

Q 14:7 What care is covered by Medicaid's long-term care benefit?

Federal law requires the states to provide certain minimum benefits. [42 U.S.C. §§ 1396a(a)(10)(A), 1396d(1)(a)] The states can, however, provide additional coverage. While eligibility and the scope of coverage are determined by the states, subject to federal parameters, nursing home care for individuals over age 21 is a mandatory Medicaid benefit. States may extend long-term coverage to other individuals (see Qs 14:17, 14:18).

Long-term care may include nursing home care, assisted living, or even in-home care. The Medicaid program focuses most of its benefits on nursing home care, although some limited benefits may be available (depending on state programs and federal limitations) in non-nursing home settings. Although the federal Medicaid program has resisted attempts by some states to move benefits into home care and assisted living, considerable movement in that direction has occurred in recent years.

Q 14:8 Are there any gaps in Medicaid coverage for seniors?

Yes, and these are growing as budget cutting fervor increases. A survey by the Kaiser Family Foundation, "State Budgets Under Stress: How are States Planning to Reduce the Growth in Medicaid Costs?," reports that 41 states have plans to reduce Medicaid spending, including through benefit reduction. Major drawbacks to Medicaid include:

- In general, Medicaid beneficiaries may be required to transfer out of a private room unless medically contraindicated.
- In many states, a skilled nursing facility that participates in the Medicaid program and has met a specific quota of beds occupied by Medicaid recipients is permitted to pass over Medicaid-eligible applicants in favor of private pay applicants.
- Regular Medicaid now largely requires the use of managed care plans; 58 percent of Medicaid recipients now receive managed care and are limited in choices. Moreover, even for those not in managed care, many physicians may not participate in the Medicaid program.
- Certain other "options" not required to be included in state medical assistance plans are either being eliminated. A major problem is dental coverage. Idaho and Missouri are two states that have dropped dental care from its Medicaid program for beneficiaries over age 21, except for emergencies (such as potentially life-threatening infections.) Instead of providing dentures, nursing homes will simply grind the food. Adequate eye care, hearing care, and access to speech technology are also weak in many areas. For example, Missouri has stopped providing glasses to adult Medicaid beneficiaries. There may be reductions in other areas as well. In Arkansas, physical therapy is not provided to those over age 18.
- Even if dental care is included in the Medicaid plan, few dentists may participate. Nursing homes required to provide dental care may be unable to find Medicaid-participating dentists willing to make "house calls" to the nursing home or otherwise accept Medicaid for a private visit by the patient.
- Many states now use a formulary to determine what drugs are appropriate for Medicaid patients. As many of the newer anti-

dementia drugs, with less side-effects, can be very expensive, these may not necessarily be available to Medicaid recipients.

Q 14:9 What is a Medicaid "Waiver"?

States may apply to the Centers for Medicare and Medicaid for a "waiver" from the requirements of certain provisions of the Medicaid program. In some instances these waivers have permitted states to expand benefits under Medicaid and close some of the aforementioned "gaps." In other instances, the reverse is true.

While there are various waiver provisions in the Social Security Act, including the waiver authorizing home and community-based services, under 42 USC Section 1396n, the provision with the broadest possibilities is Section 1115 (42 USC Section 1315). This section permits waivers from Medicaid rules in order to carry out "demonstration projects" or "experimental, pilot, or demonstration project(s) which, in the judgment of the Secretary, (are) likely to assist in promoting the objectives of (the Medicaid statute)"; in other words, to act as a laboratory. The provision was really intended to provide a means by which states might expand coverage if they could show that a change would be cost-effective; the Center for Medicare and Medicaid website states that "the authority provides flexibility, under the Secretary's discretion, for the provision of services which are not otherwise matchable, allows for the expansion of eligibility for those who would otherwise not be eligible for the Medicaid program." Most waiver programs follow this approach, and can be reviewed on the Centers for Medicare and Medicaid website at *http://www.cms.gov/medicaid/waivers/*. More recently, however, states have been seeking waivers to the spousal protection or other eligibility rules. In July, 2002, Connecticut's Department of Social Services filed a request for a waiver that would:

1. Delay the "start date" of the transfer penalty period to the date on which the applicant is "otherwise eligible" for Medicaid; and
2. Lengthen the look-back period for transfers of real estate from three years to five years.

As of this writing, President George W. Bush has proposed doing away with Medicaid requirements altogether and instead making block-grants to states. Needless to say, this would eliminate even the need for a state to justify its changes in coverage or policies.

Because of the possibility that such waiver requests might seriously undercut the present Medicaid system in every state, the National Academy of Elder Law Attorneys has spent considerable time seeking to defeat Connecticut's Section 1115 waiver proposal.

The elder law practitioner must be aware of which programs in his or her state operate under "waiver" authority, because the standard Medicaid rules set forth in this chapter may not apply.

Q 14:10 What is a "PACE" program?

"PACE" stands for "Program of All Inclusive Care for the Elderly." It is authorized under 42 U.S.C. §§ 1395eee and 1396 u-4 and is regulated under 42 CFR Part 460. Its intent was to permit states to provide a managed care approach to Medicare and Medicaid that would offer social and health services on a pre-paid, capitated basis and would be designed to meet the following objectives:

(1) Enhance the quality of life and autonomy for frail, older adults.

(2) Maximize dignity of, and respect for, older adults.

(3) Enable frail, older adults to live in the community as long as medically and socially feasible.

(4) Preserve and support the older adult's family unit."

In practice, many states have sought Section 1115 waivers to provide PACE-type benefits on a more limited basis—typically, to offer prescription assistance programs, in which participants that do not yet qualify for Medicaid (which covers prescriptions anyway) pay a flat annual fee and a per-prescription charge. At least two states, Connecticut and New York, have such programs. These programs, while technically falling within the Medicaid statutory scheme, have their own income and asset eligibility rules that are generally far more liberal than Medicaid.

More recently, the federal government has offered "Pharmacy Plus" options to state to construct programs similar to these PACE waiver prescription assistance programs. Such programs were approved in 2002 for Wisconsin, Maryland, South Carolina, Florida, Michigan, Illinois, and Wisconsin.

Q 14:11 Can anything be done when the state agency does not follow the federal rules for Medicaid?

As with other benefits programs, those denied benefits are entitled to an administrative hearing, which can then be appealed. [42 C.F.R. §§ 431.220 et seq.] In addition, the community spouse may request a hearing to argue the amount of his or her CSRA allocation. This takes time. For major systemic problems, federal court is often the answer. Practitioners may become frustrated when state agencies fail to issue regulations they are required to issue, apply standards that seem to violate the federal rules, or suddenly cut benefits without justification. Elder law attorneys have been forced to take a more active role in challenging these attempts in court. The consensus seems to be that action in federal court is the most likely to succeed; the trouble for clients is that such actions cannot award retroactive relief against a state. Nonetheless, injunctive relief may be available, and practices may be changed prospectively. Recently, the First Circuit Court of Appeals put its imprimatur on the proposition that a suit under 42 USC Section 1983 (for which attorneys' fees may be awarded) was available to compel compliance with Medicaid rules. [Rosie D. ex rel. John D. v. Swift, 310 F.3d 230 (1st Cir. 2002); another such case is Westside Mothers v. Haveman, 289 F.3d 852 (6th Cir. 2002)] In some instances, state court has provided injunctive relief, compelling the award of benefits. [Blue v. Bonta, 121 Cal. Rptr.2d 483 (Cal. App. 2002) (stairway lifts were covered as durable medical equipment)]

Q 14:12 What is the new program that provides Medicaid to the working disabled?

As part of the Ticket to Work and Work Incentives Improvement Act of 1999, the federal government authorized states to establish plans that would allow those disabled individuals who had been receiving Medicaid to continue to receive Medicaid once they returned to work. This is accomplished by substantially raising the earned income and asset limits for such individuals. For example, Connecticut's program of "Medicaid for the Working Disabled" has an annual earned income limit of $75,000 and asset limit of $10,000, but with significant premium cost-sharing when income exceeds 200 percent of the federal poverty level.

Q 14:13 How does one apply for Medicaid?

Applications for Medicaid coverage are made to the appropriate state agency, and follow that state's procedures. It is vital for the elder law practitioner to become familiar with his or her state's own special procedures and policies; generalizations can be fatal. Generally, however, the applicant will be required to show (or have someone demonstrate on his or her behalf) citizenship and residence status, together with all of the financial information necessary to determine eligibility. In practice this means that the applicant or designee must produce a birth certificate, marriage license, spouse's death certificate, naturalization papers, military service records, utility bills, voter registration, and innumerable other documents before even getting to the financial information. Financial information may include current bank statements plus several years' worth of statements and check registers; copies of insurance policies including statements of value; copies of funeral contracts; real estate deeds; etc. Locating financial information can be difficult, particularly if statements have been lost or the applicant formerly lived in another state. The entire process is usually daunting, particularly for the applicant (who is, remember, a candidate for nursing home assistance). The elderly spouse or distant children of the applicant may be only marginally better equipped to provide the details and follow-up required by the Medicaid agency.

Medicaid coverage can be retroactive to any or all of the three months prior to application, assuming that financial eligibility criteria were met at that time. [42 C.F.R. § 435.914] Although a decision regarding Medicaid eligibility must be made within 45 days of an application for the aged, applications are rarely processed this quickly. [42 C.F.R. § 435.911]

Timing can be very important. In some states, if the applicant meets the income and resource criteria by the last day of the month, Medicaid eligibility will be available for the entire month. This requires a rush to the agency office on the last day of the month to get the application in on time. This also means that assuming the applicant has in fact been financially eligible for not only that month, but the three prior months as well, and the nursing home is clamoring for payment, it may be critical to get the application in by the end of month #4 in order that all four months, the application month and the prior three, be covered by Medicaid. If a family member has inadvisably agreed to pay for care, it will be a better use of time to get the application timely filed than to argue in court later about whether that agreement can stand.

Q 14:14 Once Medicaid long-term care eligibility is established, does Medicaid pay for all the costs of long-term care?

While Medicaid pays for all of the costs of care (unlike Medicare, which does not cover medications and some other items), the patient is required to contribute some portion of that cost, sometimes referred to as "applied income" or the patient's "share of cost." For an unmarried patient, in fact, that contribution will be fixed at nearly all of the patient's income. Medicaid allows the patient to pay Medicare premiums from income (and in some states, Medigap premiums as well), and to retain a small "personal needs allowance" (the maximum amount of which varies from state to state, but which is usually less than $100), but requires that the balance be paid to the nursing home. Medicaid then pays the balance of the care costs that are not otherwise covered by Medicare —although Medicare is usually a "secondary payor," it pays before Medicaid benefits. A number of states fix the personal needs allowance at 15 percent of the maximum SSI benefit (in other words, $82.80 in 2003), while other states utilize a flat (and usually lower) amount—sometimes as low as $30 per month (the minimum level permitted by federal regulations). [42 C.F.R. § 435.725(c)(1)(i)] The personal needs allowance will be all that the resident retains to meet charges such as haircuts, telephone, and television. If the resident retains his or her home, the personal needs allowance will also be the only money available to pay upkeep, taxes, and utilities—unless the home is rented out, in which case any net rental income will be counted as income to the nursing home resident. More importantly, the personal needs allowance and the remaining small amount of resources will be all the resident retains in order to fill the "gaps" in Medicaid such as dental care, eyeglasses, decent hearing aids, and the like.

General Eligibility Requirements

Q 14:15 Who is covered by Medicaid?

Medicaid generally covers persons 65 and older, disabled persons, and blind persons whose income and available resources do not exceed a certain amount as set by federal law. [42 U.S.C. § 1396] All Medicaid programs (other than those in so-called "209(b) states," which apply similar but not identical criteria) must cover individuals receiving SSI (Supplemental Security Income) or AFDC (Aid to Families With Dependent Children). This group of individuals is referred to as the "mandatory categorically needy." In addition, the states also have the option of providing Medicaid coverage for other "categorically needy" groups (see Q 14:17) and the medically needy (see Q 14:18).

Q 14:16 When are non-citizens eligible for Medicaid?

Full Medicaid coverage is available only to citizens and to "qualified aliens." Other aliens, who are not "qualified," are only eligible for emergency services. [Personal Responsibility and Work Opportunity Reconciliation Act of 1996; Pub. L. No. 104-193] However, some states have elected to provide comparable benefits to residents who do not meet the test for a "qualified alien," based in some cases on state constitutional law concerning equal treatment of residents. [See, e.g. Aliessa v. Novello, 712 N.Y.S.2d 96, (N.Y.A.D. 1 Dept. 2000) (denial of benefits to lawful immigrants violates the New York State Constitution)]

A U.S. citizen is:

- any person born in one of the 50 states, the District of Columbia, Puerto Rico, Guam, Virgin Islands, Northern Mariana Islands, American Samoa, Swain's Islands;
- any person born outside the United States but to a U.S. citizen (shown by an INS Certificate of Citizenship); or
- a person born outside the United States who has been approved by INS as a naturalized citizen.

A "qualified alien" (eligible for full Medicaid) is a

- "lawful permanent resident" ("resident alien," who holds a "green card"), admitted *prior to August 1, 1996*;

- lawful permanent resident admitted August 1, 1996 or subsequently, but only *once a five-year ineligibility period has expired*;
- lawful permanent resident admitted August 1, 1996 or subsequently who: (a) is a honorably discharged veteran or on active duty in the military with a spouse and dependent child under age 21; or (b) was originally admitted by INS to the United States under a political designation but who has adjusted to lawful permanent resident status within five years; or (c) is an American Indian born in Canada to whom the provisions of section 289 of the INA apply, or who is a member of an Indian tribe as defined in section 4(e) of the Indian Self-Determination and Education Assistance Act; or
- an alien admitted under a "political designation" (as follows) but only for seven years *unless* the person is also an honorably discharged veteran, or on active duty in the military with a spouse or dependent child under age 21:
  - A refugee admitted under section 207 of the Immigration and Nationality Act (INA),
  - A person who sought political asylum and was admitted under section 208 of the INA,
  - A refugee whose deportation is withheld under section 243(h) of the INA,
  - An alien paroled under section 212(d)(5) of the INA for at least one year,
  - An alien granted conditional entry under section 203(a)(7) of the INA in effect prior to April 1, 1980, or
  - An alien granted status as a Cuban/Haitian entrant as defined in section 501(e) of the Refugee Education Assistance Act of 1980.
  - An Amerasian immigrant admitted pursuant to Section 584 of the Foreign Operations, Export Financing, and Related Programs Appropriations Act, 1988.

Possibly of greater relevance are the "deeming" rules relating to SSI (and by extension, to Medicaid in SSI states except where they are trumped by MCCA). When an alien is admitted in part due to a sponsorship, the sponsor's income and resources (and those of the sponsor's living-with spouse) are considered when determining an alien's SSI eligibility and payment amount, with certain exceptions. [Social Security Act §§ 1614(f)(3), 1621; 20 C.F.R. §§ 416.1160(a)(3), (d), 416.1166a; POMS § SI 01320.900] If one member of a couple sponsored the other, and they then separate, the sponsoring citizen's assets and income are then deemed to the alien spouse, unless of course MCCA applies because one is institutionalized.

Q 14:17 Who are the optionally categorically needy?

States have the option of providing Medicaid coverage to the "optionally categorically needy." Optional categorically needy groups include:

1. Infants up to age one and pregnant women not covered under the mandatory rules whose family income is below 185 percent of the federal poverty level (a different percentage may be set by each state);
2. Optional targeted low income children;
3. Certain aged, blind, or disabled adults who have incomes above those requiring mandatory coverage, but below the federal poverty level;
4. Children under age 21 who meet income and resources requirements for AFDC, but who otherwise are not eligible for AFDC;
5. Institutionalized individuals with income and resources below specified limits; persons who would be eligible if institutionalized but are receiving care under home and community-based service waivers;
6. Recipients of state supplementary payments; and
7. Tuberculosis (TB)-infected persons who would be financially eligible for Medicaid at the SSI level (only for TB-related ambulatory services and TB drugs).

[42 U.S.C. § 1396a(10); 42 C.F.R. § 435.2210-231]

These groups share characteristics of the mandatory groups, but the eligibility criteria are more liberally defined.

Q 14:18 Who are the medically needy?

As previously discussed, Medicaid regulations require that all states provide a certain level of services to the "mandatory categorically needy" (i.e., those individuals whose income and assets meet eligibility requirements). The states also have the option to have a medically needy program that allows them to extend Medicaid eligibility to additional qualified persons who may have too much income and resources to qualify under the mandatory or optional categorically needy groups. [42 U.S.C. § 1396a(a)(10)(A)(ii)] The medically needy are those individuals who do not qualify as categorically needy because their income and resources are too high, but whose income and resources are insufficient to meet the costs of necessary medical care. [42 U.S.C. § 1396a(f)] The income and asset requirements may be recalculated when an individual is deemed medically needy or whose medical bills are consistently high enough to merit special treatment.

Not all states recognize the medically needy category; those that do typically allow medical expenses and/or remedial care expenses to be deducted from the individual's income and/or assets so that the latter fall below the maximum limit allowed. This allows them to "spend down" to Medicaid eligibility, thereby reducing it to a level below the maximum allowed by that state's Medicaid plan. Different procedures will apply in different states. For example, the individual may have to "spend down" on medical expenses the difference between income and the categorically needy limits aggregated over a period of months, rather than on a monthly basis.

Q 14:19 What is an "SSI state"?

Individual states are permitted the option of automatically qualifying SSI recipients for Medicaid eligibility or, with some limitations, applying the eligibility rules they used for their state-run medical assistance programs before Medicaid was adopted. States which automatically qualify SSI recipients for Medicaid are referred to as "SSI states." [42 U.S.C. § 1396a(a)(10)(A); 42 C.F.R. § 435.120] In SSI states, SSI income and resource rules are used to determine Medicaid eligibility. In addition, the SSI definitions of aged, blind, and disabled apply. Although actual eligibility rules are set by state law or regulations, SSI states may not use a financial methodology "more restrictive" than the methodology established under the SSI program. [42 U.S.C. § 1396a(a)(10)(C)(i)]

Q 14:20 What is a "209(b) state"?

States that had assistance programs for the medically needy prior to the implementation of Medicaid were permitted to retain their preexisting financial standards for eligibility. [42 U.S.C. § 1396a(f)] States electing to retain their own eligibility rules as they existed prior to January 1, 1972, are referred to as "209(b)" states, after the section of the Medicaid law permitting the (then) more-restrictive methodology. [Pub. L. No. 92-603 § 209(b)] These states may impose stricter Medicaid eligibility requirements than the SSI requirements. They also may use more restrictive definitions of the blind and disabled, and may have stricter income and resource rules. [42 U.S.C. § 1396a(f)] Because the 209(b) states are permitted to use more restrictive eligibility requirements they are required to extend coverage to the "medically needy" (see Q 14:18). The 209(b) states are Connecticut, Hawaii, Illinois, Indiana, Minnesota, Missouri, Nebraska, New Hampshire, North Dakota, Ohio, Oklahoma, Utah, and Virginia.

Interestingly, it is not always true that 209(b) states are more restrictive in their eligibility rules. This is because they may not impose Medicaid eligibility requirements stricter than those in effect prior to January 1, 1972. Because of changes in the federal eligibility standards, coupled with the liberalization of some 209(b) state rules, it may occasionally develop that the 209(b) "restrictive" rule is actually more generous than the rule applicable to SSI states.

Q 14:21 Are the eligibility rules for married couples the same as those for single individuals?

No. The Medicare Catastrophic Care Act of 1988 (MCCA—usually pronounced "Mecca") not only enacted a prescription drug benefit later repealed by Congress, but also included the important provisions of 42 USC Section 1396r-5, intended to prevent "spousal impoverishment" (see also Q 14:47). Stories of the elderly living on pet food because all funds were being used for the spouse in the nursing home led to a series of "spousal protections." These protections apply only to "MCCA couples," that is, couples in which only one spouse is an "institutionalized spouse" and the other is a "community spouse" (see Qs 14:22, 14:23). Primary protections for the community spouse are as follows: (1) the community spouse is entitled to a "minimum monthly needs allowance" that can be met from the income or other resources of either member of the couple before contributing to costs of the institutionalized spouse's care; (2) the community spouse is entitled to a minimum Community Spouse Resource Allowance, or if the couple's assets exceed that amount, one-half of the total up to a maximum unless greater need is shown; (3) the community spouse is entitled to keep all his or her own income (although if support is sought, it may be obtained only up to 25 percent of the excess of income over the minimum monthly needs allowance); and (4) there is no recovery from the estate (or lien upon the home) until the spouse is no longer living. Conversely, these protections are offset by the "spousal unity" approach to a couple's assets: the assets of either count towards eligibility and the transfer by either spouse count also towards ineligibility that results from transfers. MCCA is therefore a double-edged sword. In some instances it may even be "better," depending upon the family goals, for one spouse *not* to qualify as a community spouse, where the cure of MCCA is worse than the disease. Another wrinkle: in most states, you are a "spouse," or not, with no halfway measures: no special exceptions from MCCA for estranged or separate couples; no special protections for unmarried couples, no matter how long the duration of their relationship. Needless to say, MCCA is of no use whatsoever for gay couples; even a registered "domestic partner" will not qualify as a spouse under federal law.

Q 14:22 What is meant by "institutionalized spouse"?

For Medicaid purposes the institutionalized spouse is a spouse who is likely to be in a medical institution (e.g., hospital, nursing home, etc.) for at least 30 consecutive days and is married to a spouse who is not an institutionalized spouse. [42 U.S.C. § 1396r-5(h)] For Medicaid waiver home care programs, the person receiving benefits is treated as an institutionalized spouse. Note that if both are receiving such benefits (or both in an institution) neither is the community spouse. The good side of this is that the one with fewer assets may qualify for benefits while the other keeps all the assets. If both are in an institution for 30 days, but one expects to return home after 90 days, there may be some valuable planning opportunities.

Q 14:23 What is a "community spouse"?

For Medicaid purposes, the community spouse is the at-home spouse of an institutionalized spouse. [42 U.S.C. § 1396r-5(h)] That is, the community spouse is the spouse of an institutionalized spouse who is not also institutionalized.

Q 14:24 What basic eligibility rules must be met before Medicaid will subsidize long-term care costs?

State eligibility rules vary slightly (within basic parameters set by federal law), but eligibility for benefits will require that applicants meet five tests:

1. *Citizenship.* A Medicaid long-term care recipient must be a U.S. citizen or a "qualified alien" (a permanent resident, an asylee, a refugee, a person paroled into the United States for at least a year, a person whose deportation is withheld for certain reasons, or a person granted conditional entry).
2. *Residence.* The applicant must be a resident of the state where application is being made. Residency requirements are usually fairly simple to meet: Physical presence in the state coupled with no current intent to move out of the state is a common test of residence.
3. *Medical need.* Before qualifying for long-term care assistance, the applicant must need long-term care. To test this eligibility criterion, states have adopted their own methodology. Typically, the applicant is scored on a test measuring functional disabilities; the applicant who is unable to complete at least several "activities of daily living" or "ADLs" without assistance will usually qualify. Greater medical need (such as intubation, persistent decubiti, or other active medical procedures often administered to nursing home residents) will almost surely qualify the applicant under this test.
4. *Resources.* The first of two financial requirements, resource eligibility, generally requires that the applicant have available resources worth less than $2,000 for a single applicant (in SSI states, less in three other states; see Q 14:33). The rules for married couples, and the exceptions and special rules applicable to both married and single applicants, are different in

order to avoid "spousal impoverishment" (see Qs 14:21, 14:33–14:45).

5. *Income.* Nearly half of the states (including Alabama, Alaska, Arizona, Arkansas, Colorado, Delaware, Florida, Idaho, Iowa, Louisiana, Oklahoma, Mississippi, Nevada, New Mexico, Oregon, South Carolina, South Dakota, Texas, and Wyoming) employ an "income cap" to determine eligibility. The income cap rules are more fully discussed in Q 14:28. Other states are called "medically needy" states, where income eligibility is met by the inability to pay the actual cost of private care from available income (see Qs 14:25–14:30).

Income Eligibility

Q 14:25 What income is counted in determining income eligibility?

Under Medicaid rules in SSI states and many 209(b) states, just as with Supplemental Security Income rules, income is defined broadly to mean any cash or in-kind benefit that could conceivably enable the recipient to obtain food, clothing, or shelter. [42 C.F.R. § 435.601] Income can be earned or unearned. Income amounts are calculated on a monthly basis. In SSI states, earned income deemed to be countable (or available) includes wages, commissions, and bonuses, whether paid in cash or "in kind" (i.e., payment in the form of food, shelter, clothing, or other kinds of barter, in return for services rendered). Even income earned at sheltered workshops is includible for Medicaid purposes. Usually, however, earned income has a slightly preferred status over unearned income; while it still "counts," a portion ($65/month or so) may be "disregarded" for computational purposes. Some 209(b) states may disregard some or all in-kind earned income as counted income, but cash is universally considered to be income. Of course, nursing home patients are unlikely to have earned income, so this "category of income" concern is not so important for most elder law attorneys.

All other receipts are categorized as "unearned income," including gifts from any source, interest on investments, alimony, insurance proceeds, Social Security, workers' compensation, unemployment benefits, annuity, and pension income. While all income must be disclosed, only "countable income"—in SSI states income not excluded by SSI rules and regulations—will be considered in the eligibility determination. Not counted are medical care, food stamps, other types of need-based assistance, or income received by other members of the family that is not otherwise "deemed" available to the individual. [See 42 U.S.C. § 1382a, 20 C.F.R. § 416.1103] Remember, however, that § 209(b) states may set different (more or less restrictive) income requirements. In at least some states, unearned income received in-kind has often remained uncounted, either tacitly or explicitly. In addition, some states may have an exception for payments received pursuant to a reverse annuity mortgage, depending on state policy. Such payments are in effect restoration of principal to the homeowner.

Q 14:26 What is "deeming"?

"Deeming" means that income and/or assets of one person are treated as if they were the income and/or assets of another who is applying for or receiving government benefits. Under SSI rules (and Medicaid), assets/income of a parent are deemed to a child, those of one spouse to another, and those of an alien's "sponsor" to the alien. The individual may therefore be "over income" despite having no income. MCCA rules "deem" to the applicant spouse the assets, but not the income, of the community spouse. Deeming can be relevant to the elderly but not usually in the long-term care context, except perhaps for elderly aliens. In the context of disabled children, a waiver known as the "Medicaid Deeming Waiver," formerly known as "Katy Beckett," does not deem parental assets and income to the severely disabled child, recognizing that the result would be to wipe out family finances.

Q 14:27 What is the "name on the check rule"?

Medicaid follows the "name on the check" rule in determining income eligibility. Under the name on the check rule, the income is assigned to the person who is named on the instrument. Most commonly, income eligibility is an issue when one spouse is facing institutionalization and the other spouse is able to remain at home. This is because under MCCA (see Q 14:18), a community spouse's income is not deemed to be available to the institutionalized spouse (although the institutionalized spouse may have certain support rights against the community spouse). A married applicant's income eligibility is usually determined by applying the name on the check rule. Under this approach, income actually received by the applicant-spouse is counted in determining eligibility, but income received by the non-applicant spouse is not counted. Income received in both names (such as investment or interest income on jointly owned assets) is divided equally between the spouses. [42 U.S.C. § 1396r-5(b)(1)] If the instrument specifies a specific division of income attributable to each spouse, then that income is attributed to each spouse in proportion to their respective share. Under the "name on the check" methodology, in an income-cap state (see Q 14:28), one spouse may qualify for Medicaid assistance, even though the other spouse, who may in fact have a substantial income, does not qualify; and in both income-cap and medically needy states, if the community spouse has substantial income, he or she may get to keep it entirely.

Q 14:28 What is an "income cap"?

Some states that provide optional Medicaid coverage to institutionalized individuals impose a cap on income for eligibility purposes. Individuals who meet the other eligibility requirements but whose income exceeds the cap will not be eligible for Medicaid. The "income cap" states currently include Alabama, Alaska, Arizona, Arkansas, Colorado, Delaware, Florida, Idaho, Iowa, Louisiana, Oklahoma, Mississippi, Nevada, New Mexico, Oregon, South Carolina, South Dakota, Texas, and Wyoming. The actual income cap varies from state to state. Most states fix income eligibility at 300 percent of the maximum federal benefit rate—the then-current Supplemental Security Income benefit for an individual. [42 U.S.C. § 1396a(a)(10)(A)] Thus, when SSI is capped at $552 (the year 2003 figure), most income cap states will limit Medicaid long-term care benefits to individuals with less than three times that amount, or $1,656 per month of income.

One state, Delaware, calculates the maximum income amount differently. In Delaware, a long-term care Medicaid applicant may have income no greater than 250 percent of the maximum SSI amount plus a $20 "disregard." In other words, the year 2003 maximum income in Delaware is $1,400.

Technically, Arizona, Arkansas, Florida, Iowa, Louisiana, Oklahoma, Oregon, and Texas are not income cap states; however, the income cap rules effectively govern those states, because they either do not cover the aged in their "medically needy" programs (Texas) or they do not permit the use of nursing home expenses in calculating the "spend down" for their "medically needy" programs (the other listed states). In other words, although these states offer coverage to those persons who are unable to "afford" their medical care, they do not permit the use of nursing home costs in calculating their ability to pay for that care, even though those same nursing home costs are the principal reason the applicant requires Medicaid assistance. In addition, Connecticut's Medicaid-funded program for home care subsidization (as distinguished from its wholly state-funded program), which operates by virtue of a waiver from the federal government (see Q 14:9), operates under an income cap, even though its general nursing care (institutional) program is not governed by an income cap.

Q 14:29 How does an income cap apply to married couples?

Most commonly, income eligibility is an issue when one spouse is facing institutionalization and the other spouse (the "community spouse") is able to remain at home or in some other noninstitutional setting. A married applicant's income eligibility is usually determined by applying the "name on the check" rule (see Q 14:27). Under this methodology, one spouse may qualify for Medicaid assistance, although the other spouse does not.

In the handful of income cap states that are also community property states (Arizona, Idaho, Louisiana, Nevada, New Mexico, and Texas), the rules may be less clear. In some (New Mexico), the total income of the couple (regardless of the name on the check) is combined; if the total income is less than twice the single-person income eligibility level, either spouse qualifies under the income rules. In at least Texas, community property rules affirmatively do not apply; each spouse must qualify under his or her own income eligibility determinations. In Arizona, either approach is permissible; thus, a married applicant may qualify under the "name on the check" rule or by having total community income less than twice the eligibility limit.

Q 14:30 What can be done to secure Medicaid eligibility for patients whose income exceeds the income cap even though they do not have sufficient income to pay for long-term care?

As a result of changes in federal law implemented in the Omnibus Budget and Reconciliation Act of 1993 (OBRA '93), every income cap state is required to recognize the validity of an assignment of income to an irrevocable trust that meets the requirements of 42 USC Section 1396p(d)(4)(B). The effect of the assignment to a qualified trust is to have the income not counted as available to the applicant for eligibility purposes, although the income remains countable for purposes of calculating the amount the applicant must pay toward the cost of his or her care. These trusts are sometimes called qualified income assignment trusts or qualified income trusts, but are more frequently referred to as "Miller" trusts in honor of the Colorado case that first officially recognized the technique. [Miller v. Ibarra, 746 F. Supp. (D. Colo. 1990)] Miller trusts permit most Medicaid applicants to qualify even in income cap states. (See Q 14:91 for a discussion of Miller trusts.)

In some of the income cap states, state Medicaid agencies have adopted the view that the assignment of income to the "Miller" trust amounts to a monthly uncompensated transfer. Under this analysis the effective maximum income that can be assigned to the "Miller" trust will be equal to the "average cost of care in the community," which varies by state (and sometimes by county or region). In those states, the effective "income cap" becomes the average cost of care.

Where a pension is involved, one available choice for married couples may be to secure a qualified domestic relations order (QDRO) to divide pension income between spouses. In most states a property division can be obtained in a separation (as opposed to a divorce) proceeding. In either case, a QDRO effectively divides pension income between spouses, and may in some cases reduce the income of the institutionalized spouse to below the income cap level.

Resource Eligibility

Q 14:31 What is the difference between a "resource" and an "asset"?

"Resource" usually covers what is thought of as an "asset" as distinguished from "income." However, USC Section 1396p applies the "transfer of assets" rule to cover transfers of both resources and income. Therefore, the Code uses assets as the more comprehensive term. The Social Security Program Operations Manual System or "POMS," in making the distinction for SSI purposes, states: "Resources are cash and any other personal property, as well as any real property, that an individual (or spouse, if any): owns; has the right, authority, or power to convert to cash (if not already cash); and is not legally restricted from using for his/her support and maintenance." The POMS goes on to say that "an individual who has an ownership interest in property but is not legally able to transfer that interest to anyone else does not have a resource." [POMS § SI 01110.100.B.1, B.3]

Popularly, however, what the Code terms as a "resource" is what we would think of as an "available asset," and in non-SSI states it may be more understandable to distinguish between an "available asset" and an "unavailable asset" rather than "resource" and "asset that is not a resource" despite the language of the Act.

Q 14:32 Do all states apply resource eligibility rules in the same fashion?

No. Because the structure of the Medicaid program relies on state administration and interpretation of federal mandates and regulations, there is substantial variance in state rules governing Medicaid eligibility. This is at least partially by design—the federal government was initially sensitive to concerns about overregulation of what had traditionally been the state's province of medical care for the needy. The result is a patchwork of rules, which shifts not only from state to state but also among regions within some states, and over time. Attention must be paid to the precise state and local rules, whether statutory, regulatory, interpretative, or simply common practice.

Q 14:33 What is the resource limit for Medicaid eligibility?

In most states, in order to be eligible for Medicaid the total value of a Medicaid applicant's resources (assets) other than income at the time of application and throughout the time he or she is receiving benefits cannot exceed $2,000 for an individual and $3,000 for a married couple when they both apply for benefits. [42 U.S.C. § 1382(a)(3)(B)] The resources of both the institutionalized spouse and the community spouse are considered available to the institutionalized spouse. [42 U.S.C. § 1396r-5(c)(1)(B)] The maximum resource limit for a single person is lower in Connecticut ($1,600), Indiana, and Ohio (both set at $1,500), all of which are 209(b) states (see Q 14:20).

Q 14:34 Is income also considered a resource?

No. Something will not be considered both as income and as a "resource." The usual rule is that property received is income in the month of receipt and a resource or asset the following month. This may give the recipient time to spend or otherwise dispose of the property. Certain exceptions are discussed in chapter 17.

Q 14:35 How are inheritances and other unexpected sums treated for income eligibility purposes?

Because income is not a resource, under SSI rules, the individual can spend or otherwise consume unexpected large amounts (or transfer, if in the community and not receiving benefits from a program that applies transfer penalties to any transfer). Possible exceptions: some medically needy states apply a "lump-sum income rule" for unusual amounts of income, so that disposing of the property received will still not work (unless the beneficiary first leaves the Medicaid program prior to receipt). That is, the "lump-sum" is recharacterized as if it had been spread out over a period of months.

Example 14-1. John is in a medically needy state. The categorically needy income limit ("CNIL") is hypothetically $500. He receives $750 per month in Social Security Disability, of which the state will hypothetically "disregard" $150 based on his living situation. That leaves $600, leaving him over income by $100 per month. The state will multiply $100 by six months to reach a "spend down" amount of $600. Once he has spent (or incurred debt for) $600 on qualified expenses (such as his very expensive prescription medicine), he will then be covered by Medicaid for any further medical expenditures during the balance of the six months. However, one December an aunt dies and he receives a check for $3,000. Technically, that $3,000 will be added to his spend down amount. (i.e., instead of receiving $600 ($750 - $150) multiplied by 6 months, or $3,600 as compared with the limit of $3,000, he will now be considered to have received $6,600 for the same period, giving him an enhanced spend down of $3,600. In effect he will have to spend the ENTIRE inheritance on medical expenses before Medicaid will pay $1. Even if he gives or gambles the money away, or spends it on rent, he would not get the Medicaid until he has spent the $3,600. Of course, if he keeps the money he will be "over-asset" the month after. The only solution may be to have him send a letter declining Medicaid coverage in December before he cashes (or better yet, receives) the check, spend it, and then reapply in January. This is a sufficiently drastic administrative hurdle that the agency may agree to simply ignore the check entirely.

Q 14:36 How are the resource eligibility rules applied to married couples?

The resources of both spouses, whether owned separately or jointly, are scrutinized when one is applying for Medicaid benefits. If neither spouse is institutionalized, then the assets of both are considered available to both; however, when one spouse is ready to enter a facility and apply for Medicaid benefits, an assessment of the couple's assets (sometimes referred to as a "snapshot") is taken. It is important to understand that the "snapshot" may not actually be calculated until months, or years, after the date of first eligibility for admission to the nursing home, but that the ultimate calculation of available resources will be made as of that date. Treatment of the couple's assets after the snapshot is taken differs from state to state. The "snapshot" may or may not be important, depending upon the amount of the couple's assets and the state. In those states which permit a community spouse to retain one-half of the couple's combined assets, subject to certain maximums and minimums, and the one-half is probably between the maximum and minimum, it is important to determine what the total assets are in order to determine the one-half that may be retained.

Q 14:37 How does Medicaid treat property belonging to the community spouse?

At the time of application all the assets of both spouses, without regard to whose name is on the title, will be considered for eligibility determination. As discussed in Q 14:61, transfers of ownership will be allowed to alter the shares of assets owned by each spouse.

Once the institutionalized spouse is receiving benefits, and presumably excess marital assets have been spent down, the community spouse's assets will not be re-examined until he or she personally applies for benefits. Because it is always allowable for the institutionalized spouse (after he or she has begun receiving benefits) to transfer property to the community spouse, even exempt property, if transferred to the community spouse, can be protected from a Medicaid lien against the costs of care for the institutionalized spouse.

Q 14:38 What are "available resources"?

Resources are cash or other liquid assets, or any real or personal property that could be converted to cash and used for support and maintenance. Resources are considered available when a person has the right to liquidate real or personal property. Assets include such obvious resources as real estate, bank accounts, and stocks. Applicants are often dismayed, however, when they learn that life insurance policies, promissory notes, revocable trust assets, certain annuities, and investments that carry penalties for early withdrawal are all included as available resources (in other words, they can be sold or converted to cash, even if doing so would be disadvantageous to the applicant). Also considered resources are inheritances, legal claims, and the like. Failure to "cooperate" in seeking access to these resources (such as the waiver of one's right to an inheritance, refusal to accept an injury settlement, and refusal to take legal action to obtain such entitlements as child support or spousal maintenance) may be treated as disqualifying transfer, in some states, or in others, may result in the resources being "deemed" to be available.

Certain resources are also exempt, chief among these being the home provided that the spouse, child under age 21, or disabled child is residing in the home (see Q 14:29).

Available resources are valued at their equity value, which is generally the market value less any encumbrances. [20 C.F.R. § 416.1216(c)(2)]

In many states, resources are determined as of the first day of each month. However, newly received resources are generally treated as "income" in the month of receipt and not counted as resources until the following month, following the approach of the SSI program. For example, the inheritance check that arrives in July will not put the individual "over asset" until August. Depending on the size of the check, it might be spent in July on needed but non-countable goods or services, thereby eliminating the problem, at least in non-income-cap states.

Q 14:39 How are jointly owned accounts treated for asset eligibility purposes?

There is a presumption that all bank accounts and similar assets owned jointly belong entirely to the applicant. This might be thought of as the "name on the account rule"—if the applicant's name is on the account, the asset belongs to the applicant, because the applicant would have the right to withdraw all of the funds on deposit. The other joint owner can, however, rebut that presumption, for example, by documenting his or her deposits to the account. This can be a real problem for those who are not careful recordkeepers.

Brokerage accounts in two names typically cannot be disposed of without both parties' signatures. If the other owner refuses to cooperate, the assets should be treated as inaccessible unless there is a way to sever the account. The same concern pertains to jointly held real estate (see Q 14:45).

Because assets owned by either spouse are counted for eligibility purposes this rule is not especially relevant for spouses where one is an applicant. It can be problematic, however, when both owners (e.g., siblings) are applicants. The entire value of the asset may be deemed available to each of the owners unless the Medicaid agency can be induced to apply a rule of reason.

Q 14:40 Can the joint owner of property simply transfer it away from the Medicaid applicant's control?

Medicaid agencies will generally treat any jointly held property as the property of the applicant until proved otherwise; thus, any transfers would be in danger of being deemed gifts or even fraudulent transfers. A joint owner of a home cannot usually by himself or herself transfer full title of the home to a third party, of course, but a jointly held bank account is vulnerable to such transfers and is thus subject to special scrutiny under Medicaid regulations. Normally any joint tenant or tenant in common of a bank account has the power to withdraw all funds, but under Medicaid rules any transfer out of the account will be deemed to have been made by the applicant-recipient and may affect his or her eligibility.

Q 14:41 How are retirement accounts treated in asset eligibility determinations?

If the applicant is eligible to receive payments from a retirement pension plan or annuity, in some states he or she must apply for those payments in order to be considered eligible for Medicaid benefits. Those payments will then be deemed income and may affect his or her eligibility. If the applicant is not entitled to receive payments but has the power to liquidate all or a portion of the retirement funds, those funds may be considered an available resource to the extent that the applicant has the power to remove them.

Considerable variation exists among states in their approaches to the qualified retirement plan benefits of the community spouse. While federal SSI law (on which state Medicaid law must be based) seems to exempt the community spouse's IRA and other qualified plan assets, many states treat those assets as available, or treat them as exempt only if the community spouse has begun to draw on the benefits. It may be necessary in some cases to annuitize IRA and other qualified plan assets in order to secure Medicaid coverage for either the plan owner or the owner's spouse.

Q 14:42 What assets are noncountable exempt resources?

The following assets may not be counted as "available resources" under federal rules:

1. *The applicant's home,* provided either that he or she "intends to return home" or his or her spouse continues to reside there. The proceeds from the sale of the home continue to be exempt for three months after the sale, to permit the applicant to purchase a replacement home. [Social Security Administration Program Operations Manual System § SI 01130.110] The home is exempt regardless of value, and the exclusion includes "the land that appertains thereto." In most states, the exclusion includes adjacent property regardless of property tax designations, so that the home and, say, an adjacent vacant lot or adjacent residence, may be exempt. An important variation among states is the "intent to return home" standard. Federal SSI rules apply a subjective intent standard set forth in 20 CFR Section 416.1212(c), which is controlling in "SSI" states where the state must apply rules that are "no more restrictive" than the income and resource standards of the SSI program. [42 U.S.C. § 1396a(r)(2)(A)(i)] [Anna W. v. Bane, 863 F. Supp. 125 (W.D.N.Y. 1993)] By contrast, 209(b) states may be able to apply a "reasonableness" test with a requirement that the individual have a reasonable (physician-approved) expectation of returning home in six months or less. [See, e.g., Connecticut Department of Social Services Uniform Policy Manual § 7510.15 *(http://www.sharinglaw.net/elder/liens.pdf)].*

2. *A vehicle.* If there is a "community spouse," one car of any value is exempt. [42 U.S.C. § 1396r-5(c)(5)(B)] If there is no "community spouse," the maximum exempt value of the vehicle is limited to $4,500, unless the vehicle is used for employment or medical treatment, it is a specially modified vehicle, or circumstances of terrain or distance require the retention of a vehicle.

3. *The entire value of household goods, furniture, furnishings, and personal effects,* unless there are items of unusual value. If there is a "community spouse," these items are exempt whatever their value. [42 U.S.C. § 1396r-5(c)(5)(B)] If there is no community spouse, federal rules set the maximum excluded value at $2,000, but the actual method of determination of higher value varies widely by state. In any event, medical equipment and wedding and engagement rings are exempt regardless of value. As a practical matter, many states

have opted to simply ignore such items except in very unusual cases, recognizing the difficulty (and probably low price) of most personal items sold in what would likely be a tag sale.

4. *Property used in the applicant's or spouse's trade or business, and necessary for support.*
5. *Tools of the applicant's or spouse's trade.*
6. *Life insurance policies* with up to $1,500 face value. If the total face value of life insurance policies exceeds $1,500, the cash surrender value will be counted as an available resource. If the total face value does not exceed $1,500, the entire cash surrender value will be exempt—even if it exceeds $1,500, as is often the case with "whole life" policies purchased in childhood for elders now in their 70s or 80s. Term life insurance, though it may trigger the requirement to calculate value (if the face amount exceeds $1,500), will not be an available resource because by definition it has no cash value; some states therefore simply exempt it altogether. The existence of life insurance may make the next two categories of exemptions—burial plots and prepaid funeral arrangements —unavailable to the applicant.
7. *Burial plots* for the applicant and family, plus prepaid costs of burial (as distinguished from funeral) expenses: casket, headstone, and costs associated with opening, closing, and lining the grave are permitted. (Note that some states apply a more restrictive interpretation and apply this exemption *only* to the plot itself (e.g., Connecticut).) Furthermore, "irrevocable prepaid burial arrangements" are excluded; funding of these may be restricted by state consumer protection laws and may be required to be held by licensed funeral directors.
8. *Up to $1,500 in "revocable" funeral arrangements*, including an account designated as for funeral arrangements. Such an account may accumulate interest without exceeding the eligibility limits. If life insurance policies have been excluded from assets as having a face value of less than $1,500, this exemption is not available in addition to such excluded policies. This will also be offset by any irrevocable prepaid burial arrangement.

[42 U.S.C. §§ 1382b(a)(1)–1382b(a)(3)]

In addition to those comparatively common excluded assets, a number of additional exemptions with less-frequent applicability include:

1. Resources of a blind or disabled person that are necessary to achieve a plan of self-support;
2. Some stock held by Alaskan natives and allotted land held by enrolled members of Indian tribes;
3. Retroactive Social Security and SSI benefits, for up to six months after receipt;
4. Payments received from the Agent Orange litigation settlement;
5. Some funds received from state crime victims' funds, for up to nine months from receipt;
6. State or local government relocation assistance funds, for up to nine months from receipt;
7. Federal or state disaster relief funds and the income on those funds;
8. Earned income tax credit receipts, for one month from receipt;
9. SSI received on behalf of a minor and deposited into a separate dedicated account in some circumstances; and
10. Segregated proceeds of a reverse annuity mortgage.

[42 U.S.C. §§ 1382b(a)(4)–1382b(a)(12)]

Q 14:43 Is an applicant's home considered an available resource?

Generally an applicant's home, even if it is located out of state, is deemed exempt as long as the applicant, his or her spouse, and/or a dependent child lives there. If an applicant has multiple homes, only one will be excluded. The primary place of residence may be determined by looking at indicia such as where the applicant votes, where he or she receives income payments, or where he or she spends the majority of time.

An unmarried applicant-recipient living in a long-term care facility risks losing the home if he or she does not affirmatively declare on the application his or her intent to return home even if the possibility of returning home is remote. The applicant should also obtain a letter from a doctor confirming the possibility that the applicant may eventually return home. In what is probably a violation of Medicaid regulations, some states have compelled the sale of homes of single applicants after they have spent six months in a long-term care facility by asserting that "intent" should be determined based on an objectively reasonable, rather than subjective, standard. These actions have been successfully challenged when there is no express statement from the applicant that he or she does not intend to return home. [Anna W. v. Bane, 863 F. Supp. 125 (W.D.N.Y. 1993)]

In some (but not all) states, homes whose legal titles have been transferred to a revocable trust may be deemed an available resource, because the Medicaid exemption applies only when the individual owns the property in his or her own name. The applicant may then have to transfer legal title back to himself or herself to regain the exemption. Attorneys should keep this in mind when advising their clients on the advantages and disadvantages of living trusts, particularly when the trustors' residence is their primary asset. There are circumstances when a house can be left in a revocable trust, for example, when the value of the house does not exceed the amount the community spouse is allowed to keep ($90,660 in 2003) and the couple chooses to use liquid assets for spend-down purposes (see Q 14:54). Some practitioners report that on some occasions, where there are assets low enough that one-half is below $90,660, it makes sense to put the house in the trust so that the "snapshot" will include more assets for the community spouse; when the house leaves the trust, it becomes exempt and the spouse gets to keep all the liquid assets, depending upon the amounts involved.

Q 14:44 What limits are placed on the value of an exempt home?

Although homestead laws (which vary from state to state) may place a limit on the value of a house that can be protected from creditors, no such limit is set by Medicaid regulations. As long as the house is occupied by the applicant (or the applicant intends to return), his or her spouse and/or dependent child, the value of the house is not taken into consideration in the eligibility process. Keep in mind that a large or multiple-family home can be rented to provide a source of income to the community spouse that will not be tapped for the institutionalized spouse's care under MCCA.

Q 14:45 What assets, although not exempt, may not be counted as available for purposes of asset eligibility determinations?

In addition to the exempt property items previously listed, two other categories of assets may be ignored in making the eligibility calculation, depending on the state's precise implementation of federal rules.

First, jointly held real estate may well be treated as being "inaccessible." If the other (nonspouse) owners refuse to sell their shares, and also refuse to buy out the applicant's share, *and* it can be shown that there is no market for the applicant's share, then the applicant's share will not be considered available even if it is a nonexempt asset. Evidence to back this up includes the written opinion of a local real estate agent and a written refusal by the co-owners. Generally, states have not taken the step of requiring an applicant to bring a partition action to access interests in real estate, although this is theoretically possible. In some states, it may also be necessary to claim that selling the asset would be considered a hardship to the co-owner (e.g., he or she would have to move if jointly held real property were sold) in order for the asset to be considered unavailable. Similarly, a "life use" in real estate may also be treated as inaccessible/not considered a "resource," if the other owners refuse to "buy out" the applicant's life estate. However, the agency may require the property to be rented and the income paid to the nursing home.

One major caveat: In some states, the existence of unmarketable or jointly owned property may lead to "conditional" eligibility, requiring continuing efforts to liquidate the interest. If the property actually is sold, the terms of the conditional eligibility may require that the proceeds be applied toward the accumulated cost of care paid by the Medicaid program. Although the family will be careful not to sell, the problem is that this conditional eligibility may result in a lien being placed on the property to secure the applicant's (and agency's) interest in the event of sale, and this may be hard to discharge on the applicant's death. Even if the property passes outside probate, the lien may remain.

The second category of non-counted assets is residential property in which a relative owns an interest where the sale of the property would cause the relative to lose his or her residence will also be excluded. In other words, a home jointly owned with a child, who lives in the home, need not be sold before eligibility can be obtained. This exception, which applies in "SSI" states, is grounded in Section SI 01130.130 of the Social Security Program Operations Manual System or "POMS" dealing with SSI eligibility.

Overall, the category of "unavailable" or "inaccessible" assets is one that can be explored. If the practitioner finds that the applicant is inadvertently over-asset—for example, finds out that there is an insurance policy previously unknown—it may work to argue that the asset is then "inaccessible" and should not be counted until cashed —at which point it will be treated as income in the month in which the proceeds are received under SSI rules (see Q 14:46). This has also been applied to interests in limited partnerships, restricted stock, non-assignable annuities, and promissory "balloon" notes with non-acceleration provisions. To the extent that the inaccessibility is the result of the applicant's (or spouse's) own legal planning, however, these arrangements may be found to be transfers of assets.

Q 14:46 What happens where there are "after-discovered" assets?

It is not impossible for an applicant (or spouse) to discover only later an asset that was innocently overlooked. The concern is that the person exceeded asset limitations prior to discovery of the asset. At least in SSI states, this concern is unfounded. POMS Section SI 01110.117 provides that the asset is not a "resource" during the period in which the individual was unaware of his or her ownership. When discovered, it is treated as "income" in the month of discovery and a resource only in the following month. A similar approach is sometimes applied when assets are treated by a state as "unavailable."

Protection from Spousal Impoverishment

Q 14:47 What provisions protect the income and resources of the community spouse?

Prior to the adoption of the Medicare Catastrophic Coverage Act of 1988 (MCCA), all assets and income of either spouse were considered available to an institutionalized spouse, and the eligibility limits were only slightly higher for an institutionalized married person whose spouse remained in the community. The consequence of this policy approach was to encourage divorce (the only means by which a spouse in the community could retain any significant portion of the couple's combined assets). This approach also resulted in substantial hardship occasioned by the requirement that both spouses be impoverished before one spouse could be eligible for care. In addition, because community spouses were (and are) vulnerable to the possibility of institutionalization, the then-existing financial eligibility system made it even more likely that a community spouse would soon become a Medicaid-subsidized institutional resident.

MCCA adopted a sweeping new approach to spousal impoverishment. It also adopted a new prescription drug benefit that was promptly repealed by Congress in the face of widespread dissatisfaction among elderly beneficiaries. When those provisions were repealed, the MCCA spousal impoverishment provisions were left intact. As a result, the community resident whose spouse becomes institutionalized is somewhat protected, although the protection is limited.

The resources of both spouses, whether owned separately or jointly, are scrutinized when one spouse is applying for Medicaid benefits. Separately held property is treated as available to the institutionalized spouse, despite prenuptial agreements, state community and separate property laws, and even property of both spouses settlement agreements in marital separation proceedings. On the other hand, the community spouse is entitled to retain some significant amount of assets while the institutionalized spouse qualifies for Medicaid benefits: The community spouse is permitted to retain his or her own income (see Q 14:51) and even (in some cases) some of the income of the institutionalized spouse (see Q 14:49), and the community spouse is protected against estate recovery claims made by the Medicaid agency (see Q 14:100).

Q 14:48 What is the minimum monthly maintenance needs allowance?

The community spouse whose institutionalized husband or wife has qualified for Medicaid subsidies is permitted to retain all of his or her *own* income, including Social Security or other pension benefits in the community spouse's name, investment and other income received only in the community spouse's name (and, in community property states, one-half of all income received in both spouses' names). In addition, the community spouse may be entitled to receive additional support from the institutionalized spouse in order to ensure that the community spouse receives at least a minimum income level. This minimum level is referred to as the minimum monthly maintenance needs allowance (MMMNA), and is set by federal law. It can be increased, however, if the spouse's shelter expenses are high, up to a set maximum (without recourse to a hearing). These numbers are changed annually and set federally.

If the community spouse's income is less than the MMMNA, then the institutionalized spouse's income can be used by the community spouse to bring the community spouse's income up to MMMNA. The amount of the MMMNA that exceeds the community spouse's actual income is added to the community spouse's income and subtracted from the institutionalized spouse's income.

The MMMNA is composed of a basic allowance and an excess shelter allowance. The basic allowance is equal to 150 percent of the poverty level for a family of two. [42 U.S.C. § 1396r-5(d)(3)] The excess shelter allowance is the amount by which the community spouse's shelter expenses exceed 30 percent of the poverty level for a family of two. Shelter expenses include rent or mortgage, taxes and insurance, maintenance fees for a cooperative or condominium, and utilities. [42 U.S.C. § 1396r-5(d)(4)] The figure is adjusted annually. As of July, 2003, if the community spouse's shelter costs are greater than $454.50 per month, the community spouse is entitled to an excess shelter allowance to make up the difference.

The MMMNA actually varies somewhat, as it can be increased by several factors such as the excess monthly shelter allowance and the heating and utility allowance, and the threshold amount is adjusted annually. As of July, 2003, the MMMNA threshold is $1,515. After adjustments, the maximum MMMNA (as of January, 2003) can go as high as $2,267 without need for any hearing; in some states, the maximum is automatically used as the presumptive amount. The MMMNA for the spouse can be further increased, at a hearing, under certain circumstances.

Q 14:49 How is the community spouse's income increased to reach the MMMNA?

In some states, the community spouse is permitted to retain income-producing assets (over and above the community spouse resource allowance—the CSRA) sufficient to guarantee the additional income necessary to raise his or her income level to the MMMNA. (See Qs 14:51–14:53 for a discussion of the CSRA.) This approach is known as "asset first" and in many states has been the rule for years. In some states this is known as an "enhanced" CSRA.

Most states now, or soon will, instead apply the so-called "income first" rule—allowing the community spouse to receive a portion of the institutionalized spouse's separate income to reach the MMMNA level. The income first approach has consistently been upheld as a permissible method for states to implement, and was validated by the decision of the U.S. Supreme Court in *Wisconsin Department of Health and Family Services v. Blumer* [534 U.S. 473 (2002)].

> **Example 14-2.** Mrs. Ballam's husband is a Medicaid patient in a skilled nursing facility. Income in her name totals $1,100; her husband's net pension and Social Security income totals $1,600. Mrs. Ballam is entitled to receive at least $415 from her husband's income (in order to bring her to the $1,515 figure). Her state does not automatically allow her the full MMMNA amount of $2,267 (which would permit her to receive a total of $1,167 from her husband's income), but her monthly mortgage and utility expenses total $654.50, so she will be entitled to an additional $200 (the amount by which those expenses exceed the annually adjusted $454.50 figure) as part of her MMMNA. In other words, Mrs. Ballam will receive $615 ($415 MMMNA plus $200 excess monthly shelter allowance) from her husband's income. Mr. Ballam is also entitled to receive $82.80 (in 2003) in personal needs allowance because his state utilizes the personal needs calculation of 15 percent of the maximum SSI benefit of $552 (see Q 14:14), and his Medicare Part B premium will also continue to be paid. This means that the monthly payment to the skilled

nursing facility will be $843.50 (his Social Security income of $1,600, minus his Part B premium of $58.70, minus his personal needs allowance of $82.80, minus Mrs. Ballam's MMMNA payment of $615).

Example 14-3. Same as previous, except that Mr. Ballam's income is only a $200 pension he receives from the city government, which had operated outside the Social Security system as a state subdivision. Mrs. Ballam's needed $615 cannot be met by her husband's $200 income. Instead, assets must be retained to generate the additional $415. The prevailing interest rate is 2 percent. In theory, this would mean that to generate $415 per month, or $4,980 per year, Mrs. Ballam could retain $249,000 in assets. However, since $249,000 exceeds the maximum allowable of $90,660, she will have to go to an administrative hearing to make her case.

Some states have followed a hybrid of "income first" and "resource first" rules. Iowa permits the community spouse to retain resources to guarantee that he or she has sufficient income, but the amount of resources so retained is computed by applying an annuity rate calculation. This methodology has been upheld despite the fact that it effectively returns a portion of the principal amount with each "payment." [Ford v. Iowa Dep't of Human Services, 500 N.W.2d 26 (Iowa 1993)] Connecticut applies a four-factor test to decide whether or not to apply income or resources first to reach the MMMNA. [Connecticut Uniform Policy Manual § 1570.25 (Transmittal UP-01-04) (although proposals to switch to 100 percent income first are pending)]

Q 14:50 Is there any income of the institutionalized spouse that cannot be required to be applied to the community spouse first, before protecting assets?

Yes. The Second Circuit Court of Appeals has held that the anti-assignment provisions of Social Security forbid the state Medicaid agency from requiring assignment by the institutionalized spouse of Social Security benefits to the community spouse. [Robbins v. DeBuono, 218 F.3d 197 (2d Cir. 2000)] The case should not affect the ability of the institutionalized spouse to voluntarily make the assignment, however. The effect of this decision is potentially enormous: for many seniors, Social Security is the vast majority of the family income, and the institutionalized spouse is far more likely to have the lion's share of that income. By precluding an obligatory assignment of Social Security to a community spouse, the *Robbins* case means that it is far more likely that the couple will be able to prevail when seeking to preserve assets from the spend-down requirement.

> **Example 14-4.** If Mr. Ballam's income in Example 14-3 were Social Security and not assignable to Mrs. Ballam, she could keep resource sufficient to generate not only $415/month, but the entire $615/month. Assuming her state uses a "prevailing interest rate" methodology, and the rate is 2percent, this means preservation of $369,000.

Q 14:51 What portion of the couple's combined assets may the community spouse retain while the institutionalized spouse still qualifies for Medicaid long-term care benefits?

The resources of both the husband and the wife are considered in determining whether the institutionalized spouse satisfies the resource limitation; however, the community spouse is allowed to retain a certain amount of resources. The amount of resources that the community spouse is permitted to retain is called the community spouse resource allowance or "CSRA." The CSRA is composed of countable assets only; the community spouse is also permitted to retain the residence, automobile, and other exempt assets (see Q 14:42). The institutionalized spouse is permitted to retain the same $2,000 (or less in a few states) in available resources allotted to an unmarried Medicaid applicant. Medicaid regulations allow transfers of property between the spouses to change title to the community spouse (see Q 14:61), although there may be logistical difficulties if the institutionalized spouse is incompetent but has not executed a durable power of attorney.

In some states, the CSRA is set at a fixed amount by reference to federal figures (in the year 2003, that figure is $90,660), without regard to the assets held by the couple at the time of institutionalization. The states utilizing the presumptive maximum figure for all couples include Alaska, California, Colorado, the District of Columbia, Georgia, Louisiana, Maine, Massachusetts, Mississippi, North Dakota, Vermont, and West Virginia.

In some other states, the community spouse is allowed to retain (or receive via transfer) half of the combined non-exempt marital assets, with a minimum of $18,132 and a maximum of the same $90,660 (year 2003 figures) in non-exempt assets. (In a community property state, this is expressed by saying that the community spouse is deemed to own that one-half.) These figures are adjusted annually. The states calculating the CSRA as having a minimum and maximum set by federal calculations include Arizona, Arkansas, Connecticut, Idaho, Indiana, Kansas, Maryland, Michigan, Montana, Nebraska, Nevada, New Jersey, Ohio, Oregon, Pennsylvania, Tennessee, Texas, and Virginia.

The two approaches briefly described here are not the only techniques employed by the states, even though federal law limits the states to those two choices. Some states have simply failed to update the maximum allowable community spouse figure for several years; others have set an arbitrary or differently computed minimum that is considerably higher than the federal minimum.

Q 14:52 How is the CSRA determined?

As of the beginning of the first period of continuous institutionalization a "snapshot" is taken of the assets of both spouses. [42 U.S.C. § 1396r-5(c)(1)(B)] This snapshot calculation may actually be made months or years after the institutionalization began, but must be calculated as of the date of institutionalization (or eligibility for institutionalization). The CSRA is based on this assessment of the couple's resources. The CSRA is calculated at the beginning of the period of continuous institutionalization or medical eligibility for institutionalization, even if application is not made for Medicaid at that time. The resource assessment is made by the state Medicaid agency at the request of the community spouse or the institutionalized spouse, whether at the time of institutionalization or at the (later) time of application for Medicaid benefits.

Resources acquired between the date of the first institutionalization and Medicaid eligibility will not increase the CSRA. Because of this, the snapshot amount (and the resultant CSRA) is fixed at the time of institutionalization even though no Medicaid application is made. Resources acquired by the community spouse after Medicaid eligibility is determined do not affect the Medicaid eligibility of the institutionalized spouse.

Q 14:53 Is it possible to increase the community spouse's CSRA?

Yes. Although regulations and practices differ tremendously by state, Medicaid law permits the CSRA to be increased at a "fair hearing," whether through administrative agencies or appropriate courts. In some states, that mandate is interpreted as permitting either the agency or a court of competent jurisdiction to increase the CSRA to a sufficient level to ensure that the community spouse's income will at least reach a minimum level (the MMMNA) [42 U.S.C. § 1395r-5(e)(2)] (see Qs 14:48–14:49). Other states apply the "income first rule" and instead direct that the institutionalized spouse's income be assigned to the community spouse to reach the MMMNA. In some states "fair hearing" practice provides a regular opportunity for useful advocacy, while other states seldom increase the CSRA. Examples 14-3 and 14-4 show the benefit for the community spouse in proceeding to a hearing. Hearings may also be used to increase the *maximum* MMMNA for reasons of "exceptional circumstances" or "hardship." States differ in the strictness of their approach to these exceptions. Examples might be the unusual expense of caring for a disabled adult child, inordinately high shelter expenses for a home that was otherwise impossible to sell or where relocation would cause hardship. "Exceptional circumstances" may or may not include high health costs for the community spouse; in Connecticut, these are now treated as the inevitable problems of old age that were considered by Congress in establishing the standard MMMNA figures. [Burinskas v. Dept. of Social Services, 240 Conn. 141 (1997)]

Spending Down

Q 14:54 What is a spend down?

"Spend down" can be applied to either income or assets, and therefore has two disparate meanings. The first is the requirement in a medically needy state that the beneficiary spend or incur debt for medical expenses the amount by which income exceeds the "categorically needy income limit" before receiving benefits. The second meaning is the amount by which the Medicaid applicant's allowable resources (whether a single or married applicant) must be reduced before eligibility can be obtained. One way of reaching Medicaid's allowable level of resources (and the method favored by state Medicaid agencies) is to spend the "excess" resources for the benefit of the applicant—usually for the costs of long-term care. This approach is usually referred to as the "spend down."

Q 14:55 What types of expenditures are permissible while spending down the assets of the institutionalized spouse and the community spouse's assets?

As long as funds are spent for the benefit of the applicant or his or her spouse, and not for the benefit of third parties, such expenditures will not affect eligibility. Even travel and entertainment are allowed. The applicant and spouse would, however, be well-advised to apply such funds toward exempt assets, such as paying off the mortgage on the home, purchasing a wheelchair-accessible van, remodeling, or paying off debts and other liabilities. If they have not done so already, they can purchase a burial plot and funeral contract (or purchase a small life insurance policy to cover burial costs), and purchase other assets considered exempt under Medicaid laws. (The insurance cash value can always be tapped later as if it were an extra savings account.) Considering looming cuts in Medicaid benefits, it is also highly advisable for any individual expecting a long nursing home stay to spend funds on a thorough dental examination and dental work, procuring glasses and other hardware that may be unavailable through Medicaid, purchasing orthopedic shoes, and generally attending to any health care needs that may be unmet from government benefits. Even though this process will result in expenditures (and loss of financial flexibility and freedom), it may remove substantial burdens from the community spouse, who already faces a loss of income and a reduction of assets because of the institutionalization of the spouse.

For most people, purchase of exempt assets will require the active involvement of an elder law attorney or other adviser familiar with Medicaid eligibility principles. Moreover, clients schooled in scrimping and saving will have trouble coming to grips with the reality of impending poverty and will require encouragement to take theses steps. Depending on the generosity of the state's Medicaid program, it may be absolutely critical to attend to the often-ignored health needs of the soon-to-be impoverished institutionalized individual. For example, if dental care in the nursing home is inadequate and there is any already existing decay, this can quickly escalate into a painful condition that causes tooth loss and a system unwilling to pay for dentures or any restorative dental work. The resident is doomed to spend his or her last days eating creamed corn, which might have been prevented by thorough dental care when there were still funds to pay for it. Obviously, this is care that should be provided through the Medicaid system itself, but in the meantime, attention to these needs can prevent future anguish for the family and the resident.

Expenditures need not only be spent on items of "value," moreover, but also for items that will improve the quality of life for resident and spouse. Examples would be purchase of a television, VCR, stereo, computer (assuming appropriate access), books, videos, tapes, subscriptions, toiletries, clothing, and/or snacks. This will be contingent upon the standards the Medicaid agency uses when determining what items are "personal effects" and which may be converted to cash. Televisions are usually disregarded; state of the art laptops possibly may not be. Too often families are encourage to purchase the most expensive funeral contract available rather than planning for the quality of life of the institutionalized person and spouse.

In appropriate circumstances and subject to careful review of the state agency's approach to such matters, it may be possible to "purchase" in advance a care contract, particularly if the individual(s) providing services are not related to the resident, such as a friend. This will help to defray the cost and burden of attending care conferences and running errands in the future.

Last but not least, it is critical for the elder law attorney to make sure that legal fees are paid in full, up-front and in advance. Better that these are paid from the "spend down" amount than from the community spouse's share. If the elderly client is single, there will be no more source of payment for legal fees once the client qualifies for Medicaid. (Funds put aside in the attorney's "trust account" are likely to be counted as "resources" should the agency become aware that they are there, even if they are said to be non-refundable.)

The timing of the "spend down" may be critical. There is a time for saving and a time for spending. Expenditures made before the first institutionalization will reduce the total available resources as of the date of institutionalization—the "snapshot" amount. That, in turn, will reduce the amount the community spouse is permitted to retain in those states utilizing any number other than the maximum CSRA as the state's minimum CSRA figure.

Example 14-5. Mr. and Mrs. Carlson have $250,000 in available resources (consisting of investment securities, cash, and certificates of deposit). Mr. Carlson has been diagnosed as suffering from early-stage Alzheimer's type dementia, and the couple would like to receive Medicaid coverage for his anticipated long-term care at the earliest possible moment. The Carlsons live in a state that utilizes the federal maximum CSRA as the minimum, so that if Mr. Carlson is admitted to a long-term care facility in 2003 Mrs. Carlson will be permitted to retain $90,660 (regardless of the level of assets at the time of first institutionalization) while still qualifying Mr. Carlson for Medicaid assistance. In order to hasten Medicaid eligibility, the Carlsons might choose to spend money now to visit their children (who live in three different states) while Mr. Carlson will still be able to interact with his grandchildren—but not to pay to have the children make the visits, as such a payment will be viewed as a gift for the benefit of the children. They might also pay off outstanding debts (including their mortgage) because debts are not counted against assets in determining Medicaid eligibility; this has the effect of reducing their available resources without affecting net worth.

If, however, Mr. and Mrs. Carlson live in a state that used the $18,132 figure for the minimum CSRA calculation, they should consider delaying at least some expenditures until after Mr. Carlson becomes institutionalized. If the total available resources are less than twice the maximum CSRA figure at the time of institutionalization, early spend-down will have had the perverse effect of reducing the amount that Mrs. Carlson can retain. Careful balancing of the amount to be spent, the categories of "spend down" to utilize, and timing are factors to be contemplated by Mr. and Mrs. Carlson and all others considering a similar course of action. (With appropriate timing, they could use credit cards to visit the grandchildren; the CSRA calculation does not factor in liabilities.)

Asset Transfers

Q 14:56 May a Medicaid applicant simply give away assets to become eligible for Medicaid?

Uninformed Medicaid applicants often believe that they can qualify for Medicaid by simply giving away assets before the Medicaid application is filed. This is a mistake commonly made by many individuals facing long-term care. In fact, such gifts will probably cause the applicant to lose eligibility, at least for a time. Medicaid agencies believe (and most taxpayers would probably agree) that welfare benefits should not be made available to those who can well afford to pay but deliberately impoverish themselves in order to become eligible. (The policy debate rages over whether or not this is ethical conduct when paying for all anticipated care expenses is clearly impossible, and the question is not if, but only when, the individual will be impoverished; many elder law attorneys feel that this conduct is at least as ethical as prudent tax planning to minimize estate tax for the more affluent.) In order to discourage people from giving away assets, Medicaid law imposes a "penalty period" of ineligibility for Medicaid on non-exempt transfers made during the "look-back" period. *The penalty period and the look-back period are not the same.* Many clients confuse the two. The "look-back" period simply describes how far the agency must "look" to find transfers. Transfers further "back" are ignored. Only if the transfer falls within the look-back does a penalty apply. This is known as the "transfer penalty."

Q 14:57 What is the look-back period for gifts by an applicant or spouse?

The "look-back" period describes how far back in time the agency will "look" to find transfers of assets by the applicant or spouse. The "look-back" period is 36 months, with a longer "look-back" period for transfers of assets to a trust, or from a trust established by the applicant and/or spouse. In most states, such gifts made during this 36 month look-back period prior to the application for Medicaid benefits and institutionalization of the benefits recipient must be declared by thc applicant. In addition, most (but all) states, acting in accordance with federal law, use a "look-back" period of 60 months with respect to transfers to or from a trust. [State Medicaid Manual (HCFA Transmittal 64) § 3258.4E]

Prior to the Omnibus Budget Reduction Act of 1993 (OBRA '93), the maximum penalty period of ineligibility was 30 months. OBRA '93 *repealed the cap on the penalty period*. This is of paramount importance. If a gift is made within the "look-back" period, there is no cap on the penalty. If the gift is made "outside" the look-back period, for eligibility purposes it simply never happened.

The attorney should pay close attention to the state regulations governing such transfers, as states vary in their actual implementation of federal transfer penalty rules. For example, as of this writing California still has not implemented the 36-month look-back period and uses only 30 months, the period that was in effect prior to the effective date of OBRA '93. Conversely, as of this writing, the State of Connecticut has asked for a "waiver" under Section 1115 of the Social Security Act (see Q 14:9) to extend the look-back period for all transfers of real estate to 60 months.

The significance of the look-back period is critical to the Medicaid applicant. Eligibility workers are entitled to inquire about transfers made within, but not about those made before, the applicable look-back period. In other words, an outright gift of millions of dollars made more than 36 months before the Medicaid application will not prevent eligibility for Medicaid long-term care coverage, even though the ineligibility period (calculated as described in Q 14:58) might be many years beyond the 36 months.

Example 14-6. Mrs. White made a $1,010,000 gift to her only son in January 2001, for the purpose of fully utilizing her federal transfer tax exemption equivalent amount. Shortly thereafter she entered a skilled nursing facility, where she has since resided. In February 2004, her assets dropped below $2,000 and she applied for Medicaid assistance. How far back must she disclose gifts she has made? Only as far back as February, 2001. She cannot be required to disclose any gift made more than 36 months ago (i.e., before February 1, 2001), and so the large gift in January 2001 will have no effect on her current eligibility. However, if Mrs. White had applied for Medicaid assistance in January, the result might have been very different. In that case, she would have been required to disclose any gift made in January, 2001, and as a result, the gift would have generated a penalty period of ineligibility. Her state's "average cost of care" figure or "divisor" is currently (at time of application) $4,000. Mrs. White's ineligibility period for the January, 2001 gift would therefore have been 252.5 months, or 21 years and 2 weeks. She would have been ineligible for Medicaid until mid-February 2026. Although applications of this analysis have not been reported, it would be catastrophic for Mrs. White if she had made an early application and been penalized in this fashion. A graphic outline illustrates this proposition:

Assuming "divisor" of $4,000 and "look-back" of 36 months:

Example 1:	Gift of $40,000, made within 3 years of applying for Medicaid.	(1) Made within the "look-back" period, so the gift affects eligibility. (2) The gift results in a "penalty period" of 10 months. (3) After 10 months have passed, the gift no longer affects eligibility.
Example 2:	Gift of $400,000 made within 3 years of applying for Medicaid.	(1) Made within the "look-back" period, so the gift affects eligibility. (2) The gift results in a "penalty period" of 100 months, or 8.33 years. (3) The person making the gift is NOT ELIGIBLE for Medicad unitl 8.33 years has passed.
Example 3:	Gift of $400,000 made 3 years + 1 day before applying for Medicaid.	Outside the "look-back" period, so the gift does not affect eligibility.

Note also that if instead of Mrs. White making a $1,010,000 gift to her son, Mr. White had made a $1,010,000 gift to his mistress and then left for South America, in theory Mrs. White would be similarly ineligible. States do, however, have "hardship" provisions that in theory should step in to protect Mrs. White in that situation.

Q 14:58 For gifts occurring within the look-back period, how is the "penalty period" calculated?

The Medicaid agency will determine the exact amount of the gift. In community property states, the agency may also value whether the gift was made by the applicant alone or by the marital community, although under MCCA, transfers by *either* spouse will cause the imposition of a penalty period on *both* spouses (unless both are receiving institutional care, in which case the penalty period may be divided between them).

The penalty is based on the fair market value of the asset. The amount of the gift will then be divided by the average monthly private pay rate for nursing home care for that geographical location, as set by the Medicaid agency. This rate, known in some places as the "average monthly cost of care," usually does not fully reflect the actual private pay rate for the community.

The penalty period begins with the first day of the month in which the gift is made (in which case all gifts made in one month are aggregated), or in some states, the first day of the following month. [42 U.S.C. § 1396p(C)(1)(D)] In the case of multiple gifts made within a penalty period that is "running," however, successive penalty periods are "tacked on" to the end of the currently active penalty period, or put another way, the next penalty period begins to "run" only after the preceding penalty period has expired. (In states where the penalty otherwise starts on the first day of the month of gift, this arrangement causes a slightly longer penalty period.)

Example 14-7. If the applicant makes a $20,000 gift to a child on January 12th and applies for benefits during the 36 months prior to his application for benefits, and the private pay rate in his community has been set at $4,000 per month by the state Medicaid agency, he will be ineligible to receive benefits for five months. The five months may begin to "run" on January 1st (expiring June 1st) or it may begin to "run" on February 1st (expiring July 1st), depending on the state's methodology.

This may change. Currently, one state (Connecticut) has filed an application with the Centers for Medicare and Medicaid for a waiver under Section 1115 of the Social Security Act that would delay the start of the penalty period until the individual was "otherwise eligible" for benefits—in theory, until the individual had no more than $1,600 in assets (the Connecticut limit). Should this actually take effect, the results will be dramatic.

> **Example 14-8.** A Connecticut resident makes a $24,000 gift to a child on January 12, 2004 and applies for benefits 35 months later, in December, 2006, when her assets are only $1,600 (Connecticut's limit on assets). The private pay rate in Connecticut is then $8,000 and the penalty period is therefore three months. Because the penalty would not start to run until December, 2006, she would be ineligible for Medicaid for three months and without any means to pay for care. Also under the proposed Connecticut waiver and proposed implementing "transferee liability" legislation, the state and/or nursing home could sue the child for the cost of her care during that time, up to the amount of the $24,000 gift.

The Connecticut example is extreme and as of this writing, hypothetical.

Q 14:59 How can one find out the "divisor" used to compute the penalty period?

"Average private pay rates" used to determine ineligibility penalties are set by the individual state agencies, and are not required to be adjusted on a fixed schedule, nor are they reliably published in any centralized location. The elder law practitioner will have to find out through contacting the state Medicaid agency, state bar association elder law section, or National Academy of Elder Law Attorneys chapter, in order to remain up-to-date on the particular state's annual "divisor" for computing penalty periods.

This is particularly problematic when planning for someone who might move to a different state. It is extremely difficult to maintain an accurate, up-to-date list of private pay rate figures for all states. Table 14-1 at the end of this chapter makes an attempt; other resources maintained by the authors are *www.elder-law.com/lawyers.htm and www.sharinglaw.net/elder/divisor.htm.*

However, this may be of limited utility. The real question is: how much would the actual (not hypothetical) client have to pay for his or her actual (not hypothetical) costs during the penalty period? This may involve computations that are more complicated than a simple comparison of nursing home cost to assets, and must factor in other sources of income and additional care costs such as home care for those not already in a nursing home. Even then, it is more useful to determine the actual nursing home costs of those facilities in which the client might become interested when nursing home care is imminent, rather than a statewide average.

Q 14:60 Besides gifts, does anything else constitute a "transfer"?

Yes, under 42 USC Section 1396p(c)(1)(A), penalties are imposed whenever an applicant or MCCA spouse "disposes of assets for less than fair market value." "Disposes" has been broadly read to include:

- Purchase of an annuity that is not "actuarially sound," that is, is not computed to distribute completely to applicant or spouse within their lifetimes actuarially determined;
- In some states, purchase of an actuarially sound annuity if the result is increasing the community spouse's income above the MMMNA;
- Disclaiming an inheritance or other right to property (assuming even that state law does not prohibit disclaimers by benefit recipients or former recipients (see, for example, *Department of Income Maintenance v. Watts*, [211 Conn. 323 (1989)]; Massachusetts Statutes Section 1918.A (insolvency bars disclaimer));
- Failing to make the statutory election "against the will" of a deceased spouse (see, for example, *Perna ex rel. Bekus v. Department of Public Welfare*, [807 A.2d 310 (Pa. Cmwlth. 2002)]; *Estate of Dionisio v. Westchester Dept. of Social Services* [665 N.Y.S.2d 904 (Mem), 244 A.D.2d 483 (1997)]); Tannler v. Wisconsin Dept. of Health & Social Services, [564 N.W.2d 735 (Wisc. 1997)];
- Failure to exercise a "Crummey power' withdrawal right in a trust;
- Sale of an asset below a supposed "market value"; and
- Withdrawal by another joint owner of jointly held bank accounts.

The concept of uncompensated transfers may be limited only by the creative thinking of state Medicaid agencies.

Q 14:61 Can assets be transferred between spouses without incurring a penalty?

Yes. There is no penalty for transfers between spouses. [42 U.S.C. § 1396p(c)(2)(B)] In fact, after eligibility has been obtained any resources not transferred to the community spouse may be deemed available to the institutionalized spouse and can affect his or her continued eligibility, so that transfer can be vitally important. Medicaid eligibility is calculated based on the assets available to either the institutionalized or the community spouse, so transfers of assets to the community spouse before the eligibility application will not ordinarily make initial eligibility any easier to obtain (see Q 14:51).

One possible exception to this rule is the different treatment states accord to purchases of annuities for the benefit of a community spouse or transfers in trust for the benefit of a community spouse. These are discussed in Q 14:73.

Q 14:62 Are there some types of assets that may be given away without incurring a penalty?

Yes. Assets that can be transferred without penalty include:

1. Assets transferred to a third party but for the sole benefit of the spouse [42 U.S.C. § 1396p(c)(2)] (see, however, Q 14:73);
2. Assets transferred to the applicant's blind or disabled child [42 U.S.C. § 1396p(c)(2)];
3. Transfers into a trust for the sole benefit of a spouse, blind or disabled child or individual [CMS State Medicaid Manual §3257.6];
4. Transfers of assets belonging to a disabled individual into a so-called "payback" or "OBRA '93" trust for a disabled individual under age 65 [42 U.S.C. § 1396p(d)(4)(A), (C)];
5. Asset transfers to a qualified income assignment trust ("Miller trust") for the benefit of an institutionalized spouse [42 U.S.C. § 1396p(d)(4)(B)] (see Q 14:91);
6. A home transferred to a spouse, child under the age of 21, sibling of the applicant who lived in the home for one year

prior to the applicant's institutionalization and who had some ownership interest in the home, or an adult child who lived in the home at least two years before the institutionalization of the applicant and provided sufficient care to that person to allow him or her to remain in the home [42 U.S.C. § 1396p(c)(2)(A)]; and

7. Transfers to third parties of income-producing assets currently used in a trade or business owned by the applicant or his or her family or the liquid assets of such trade or business.

In addition, a transfer of assets technically will not affect Medicaid eligibility if:

1. The individual intended to receive fair market value or some other valuable consideration [42 U.S.C. § 1396p(c)(2)(C)];
2. The asset was disposed of exclusively for a purpose other than obtaining Medicaid eligibility [42 U.S.C. § 1396p(c)(2)(C)]; or
3. Denial of eligibility would work an undue hardship [42 U.S.C. § 1396p(c)(2)(D)].

These "exceptions" are difficult to obtain in many states, while in others (notably California), transfers "for a purpose other than obtaining Medicaid eligibility" may include transfers of any exempt asset, even the home.

Assets transferred to an OBRA '93 or "payback" special needs trust for a disabled person under 65, or to a Miller trust for the benefit of an institutionalized spouse will also be allowed, although the requirements for these trusts must be strictly observed (see Qs 14:85, 14:91). Moreover, each state applies these exemptions differently, and may or may not have published its approach in a written rule or regulation.

Q 14:63 What is meant by the "half-a-loaf" strategy of Medicaid planning?

The applicant can take advantage of the ineligibility rules by transferring approximately half of his or her non-exempt assets to a third party and retaining the other half to support himself or herself during the resulting period of ineligibility. This strategy is referred to as the "half-a-loaf" strategy (and sometimes as "the rule of halves") for the obvious reason: For the Medicaid applicant who wishes to save all of his or her assets for later generations, this approach will at least allow half of his or her preference. Of course, when transfer of half of the prospective applicant's assets results in ineligibility for the maximum look-back period (ordinarily 36 months), there is no additional disincentive to transfer more than that half. In other words, the client who can comfortably cover three years of private pay at whatever level of care he or she desires may transfer as much additional wealth as the client possesses, without fear of losing Medicaid eligibility after the three years runs out. If the client is not wealthy enough to retain funds sufficient to cover three years, however, a "half-a-loaf" calculation should be used.

Example 14-9. If Helen, a nursing home resident, transfers half of her $50,000 in assets to a child and the penalty "divisor" in her area is $2,500 per month, she has triggered an ineligibility period of 10 months. She can use her remaining $25,000 in assets to support herself for that 10 months until she becomes eligible. Helen has the satisfaction of knowing that she has kept at least some of her assets protected from the nursing home.

However, counsel is cautioned that the calculations must be made carefully to ensure that the applicant does not run out of funds before the period of ineligibility expires.

Example 14-10. Helen is living at home and gives her child half of her $50,000, because she is afraid that she will "lose everything to the nursing home." She is told the penalty divisor is $2,500 and believes the remaining $25,000 will be sufficient for her, as she is supporting herself on her income and will only need the $25,000 "in case" she is in the nursing home. Unfortunately, she needs two root canals and further uncovered dental or medical work costing her $5,000; she has a minor accident with an uninsured driver and pays for car repairs; next month she has a stroke and requires first hospital and then nursing home care but loses Medicare coverage within 30 days, and it turns out that although the divisor was $2,500, the nursing home she and her family prefer actually charges $5,000 per month. She is out of money within four months, not ten. Hopefully her daughter still has the $25,000 and can spend some of it on her care, but if the $25,000 went to a grandchild's tuition payment, this may not be possible.

As should be evident, the precise calculation of the transfer amount is slightly more complicated than simply dividing the remaining assets in half. In addition to the "what-ifs" expressed in Example 14-10, on the bright side there may be adjustments for Social Security and other income received during the ineligibility period; on the dark side, anticipated increases in the cost of nursing care (because of both inflation and the progressive need for higher levels of care). In some cases, refinements to the "half-a-loaf" calculation would permit the transfer of substantially more than half of the applicant's assets.

Example 14-11. Mr. Harris is about to enter a skilled nursing facility. His assets are all in cash, and total $200,000. He determines that he would like to make a large gift to his children, but retain sufficient assets to pay for his care until the penalty period expires. His monthly income from Social Security and retirement benefits totals $1,500. Care at the facility he is entering will run $4,500 per month. The average cost of care (penalty divisor) figure for Mr. Harris' state is $4,000.

If Mr. Harris simply gifts half of his assets, he will have $100,000 remaining. His pension and retirement income will fall short of paying for his long-term care by $3,000 each month (not counting return on his assets). Allowing for a 6 percent return on his invested funds, but compensating for the fact that they will be steadily reduced, he will have actually spent his remaining $100,000 in a little more than three years; however, his penalty for the transfer will have expired in 25 months ($100,000 divided by the $4,000 penalty divisor figure), so Mr. Harris will have missed out on an opportunity to make a slightly higher gift. By making a gift of, say, $115,000, Mr. Harris will have added three months to the penalty period, and simultaneously reduced his ability to pay privately by another five months. Under this scenario, he will be eligible within a month or so of running out of funding for private care.

Of course, the calculation of Mr. Harris' "half-a-loaf" strategy makes several unreasonable assumptions. Key among those is that his care will not become significantly more expensive for the next three years, and that he will not incur any extraordinary medical or other costs. Adjustments will need to be made to the formula for Mr. Harris' personal situation. This calculation also does not account for the need to enter the nursing home of his choice with "key money" to ensure a private room and to get a good placement on the waiting list if the home already has filled sufficient "Medicaid beds" to permit it to discriminate.

Q 14:64 Are "post-eligibility" transfers treated differently?

Yes, if made by the community spouse. Because the resources of the community spouse are not attributable to the institutionalized spouse after eligibility has been determined, the community spouse may transfer almost anything without penalty after the institutionalized spouse has been awarded eligibility. [42 U.S.C. § 1396r-5(c)(4)]. This means that even the home may be sold and the proceeds transferred.

The federal statute specifically states that the home may not be transferred post-eligibility without a resulting penalty. [42 U.S.C. § 1396r-5 (c)(5)(A)](This prohibition would seem to apply even if there is no "community spouse," for example, if both were institutionalized at the time of application.) In California, however, the home may also be transferred—without regard to federal law—presumably applying the SSI terminology to declare that the home was not a "resource" and since only transfers of "resources and income" are penalized, the transfer of the home should not result in a penalty.

Of course, a transfer by the community spouse can affect that person's own eligibility for benefits.

Finally, transfers by the beneficiary will cause the imposition of a penalty. For example, if the institutionalized beneficiary receives an inheritance and transfers it to another, it will be considered a transfer of assets that causes imposition of a penalty.

Liability for Eligibility-Related Asset Transfers

Q 14:65 If a prospective Medicaid applicant makes gifts, might he or she face criminal liability?

Congress has become increasingly frustrated with the ability of the moderately and very wealthy (and their attorneys) to figure out ways to impoverish applicants for the sake of Medicaid eligibility, yet still ensure that their wealth passes intact to third parties. The Health

Insurance Portability and Accountability Act of 1996 (HIPAA) tried to address this problem by applying criminal penalties to individuals making false statements related to transfers made for the purpose of becoming Medicaid-eligible. [Pub. L. No. 104-91, §217 amending 42 U.S.C. § 1320a-7b(a)] This law, immediately dubbed "Granny Goes to Jail," was universally recognized as both badly written and unenforceable, and Congress revisited the problem the following year (see Q 14:67).

Q 14:66 Will the recipient of gifts from a Medicaid applicant be criminally liable for participating in the transfers?

There is no current law that penalizes a recipient of gifts from an applicant in any way, although the applicant who makes gifts may thereby become ineligible for benefits. Of course, a recipient who was involved in securing the gift by tortious or criminal means may be either civilly or criminally liable (or both) for those acts.

In addition, at least one state, Connecticut, is attempting to impose a lien or debt status on any transferred property of a person who later applies for Medicaid during the look-back period. The analogy may be to the "preference" items under bankruptcy law, whereby payments to a creditor within nine months of declaring bankruptcy may be recoverable by the bankruptcy trustee. In the Medicaid context, however, this seems highly problematic and subject to legal challenge if it is ever effectuated. Nevertheless, other states, looking at ways to trim Medicaid expenditures, may become persuaded that such a law would be an effective deterrent.

Other liabilities may accrue, however. In 1993 Connecticut adopted a gift tax law that was really intended to discourage transfers for Medicaid planning. The law is not "unified" with the estate or inheritance tax law, so that individuals unlikely to have federally taxable estates are still subject to the tax. Conceivably, other states may adopt a similar approach. Gift tax, if it is applicable, must be taken into account when making a transfer to avoid future liability on the recipient of the property.

Q 14:67 Is there any criminal liability for an attorney or other adviser who is involved in asset transfer planning?

Rather than making the client criminally liable, the Balanced Budget Act of 1997 (BBA '97) targeted advisers (i.e., lawyers and financial planners) counseling applicants about transfers geared toward attaining Medicaid eligibility. [Pub. L. No. 105-35, § 5755 amending 42 U.S.C. § 1320a-7b(a)] Like its predecessor, "Granny Goes to Jail," the new law was immediately criticized as unenforceable and unconstitutional, and was given a catchy nickname: "Granny's Lawyer Goes to Jail." Once again, the law was so badly written that it attempted to apply criminal penalties even to those who did nothing more than discuss the current law with their clients. The Federal District Court for the Northern District of New York enjoined the federal government from enforcing the criminalization provision, despite the protestations of the Attorney General's office that the law was admittedly unconstitutional and no prosecutions were contemplated or anticipated. [New York State Bar Association v. Reno, 999 F. Supp. 710 (N.D.N.Y. 1998)] Attorney General Janet Reno issued a letter in March, 1998 stating that in her opinion the law is unconstitutional under the First Amendment and is thus not subject to prosecution.

Asset Transfer Techniques

Q 14:68 How can resources be spent down?

In disposing of resources, one planning device is simply to convert them to "exempt" assets (e.g., home, furnishings, automobiles) that are not considered resources, or in other words, are exempt from being counted as available (see Q 14:38). Transfer available resources into those exempt categories. This might be accomplished, depending on the situation, by one or more of the following:

1. Purchase of a home, or sale of an existing home and purchase of a new, more expensive home.
2. Home improvements, including roof repair, room addition, wheelchair accessibility work, completion of deferred maintenance.

3. Purchase of new furniture, appliances, furnishings (floor coverings, window coverings, etc.).
4. Purchase of a new automobile (sometimes coupled with the gift of the previous, exempt, vehicle, as described here).
5. Payment of the existing home mortgage. To maximize the value of this technique in a marital situation, it may even be advantageous to acquire a mortgage or secured line of credit immediately before institutionalization, and to pay off the indebtedness immediately after institutionalization. In many states, this technique has the effect of increasing the community spouse resource allowance, because even secured indebtedness is not used in the calculation. Once the CSRA is fixed (by institutionalization or documented eligibility for institutionalization), the debt can be retired, leaving a larger net amount in the hands of the community spouse.

For other suggestions, see Q 14:55.

Q 14:69 Is any mechanism available to protect the Medicaid recipient's home from having to be sold?

"Saving" the family residence from nursing home costs (and Medicaid estate recovery) is actually a much more complicated question than it at first appears. First it must be asked: Protect the residence for whom? For the Medicaid recipient, who will likely never return home? Or for the spouse? Or for children and others who expected (but have no legally enforceable right) to receive the residence upon the parents' deaths?

Medicaid eligibility rules exempt the applicant's residence from being counted as an available resource, so the problem is usually not determining how legally to protect the residence during the recipient's life (although a handful of states have sought to impose an objective test to determine whether the recipient is likely to return home, and declare the residence a non-exempt asset once that objective standard has been met) or even the life of the recipient's spouse (since the property remains exempt as long as a spouse resides in the home). [42 U.S.C. § 1396p (a)(2)]

More important, in most cases, is the economic reality: Although the residence may be legally protected, the recipient's required contributions to the cost of nursing care make it impossible to maintain the residence, or to pay taxes, utilities, or upkeep. Although most states permit the residence to be rented during the Medicaid recipient's nursing home stay, any net rental income usually must be paid to the nursing home as part of the recipient's share of the cost of care, so there is no incentive to manage the family home in a businesslike fashion. The upshot is frequently that children or other family members live in the home, paying utilities and maintenance costs but no rent, until the death of the Medicaid recipient, although the Medicaid agency might have the power, at least theoretically, to assert the recipient's right to receive fair rental value for the use of the property. If no such arrangement is possible, it is likely that the residence will be sold regardless of Medicaid rules, for the practical reason that there are insufficient resources to maintain the property. *However*, if held until the institutionalized spouse attains eligibility, the community spouse can sell the house thereafter and if desired, transfer the proceeds, without penalty.

Although California permits the gift of the exempt residence of a Medicaid recipient or applicant, in other states such a transfer will trigger a penalty unless the recipient is a disabled or minor child. Transfer of a partial interest may reduce the penalty period, and permit the property to pass to others automatically on the death of the Medicaid recipient (thereby avoiding the estate recovery program described later). To accomplish this result, the prospective Medicaid recipient may choose to give the home to children (or others) while retaining a life estate, or to create a joint tenancy between himself or herself and one child, for example. Either transfer will create a period of ineligibility; the retention of a life estate will trigger a period of ineligibility calculated by reference to actuarial tables (which will not be adjusted for the donor's actual life expectancy based on medical condition). Moreover, there may be other drawbacks to such a transfer: gift tax; loss of the step-up in basis that would otherwise occur at the client's death if there is no retained life use; if there is a life use retained, inability to sell the property because the "life use" has value that must be transferred to the nursing home or otherwise spent down, and because some of the capital gains exclusion for sale of a home will be lost to the extent that the remainder interest is now owned by children; possible loss of the elderly property tax exemption that had kept the maintenance costs low.

Q 14:70 What advanced techniques might be employed to preserve the residence?

Although the effectiveness of the technique may vary by state, one common suggestion is for the Medicaid applicant or recipient to gift the residence while retaining both a life estate and the power to dispose of the property during his or her life. Such an arrangement is sometimes effected by retaining a life estate and either a special power of appointment or a power to sell the asset and receive the proceeds. These transfer instruments are sometimes referred to as a "deed with retained power of sale," a "deed with retained power of appointment," or (at least in Florida) "Lady Bird deeds." At least one state (Arizona—see Arizona Revenue Statutes Section 33-405) has formally adopted a similar arrangement by statute, described as a "beneficiary deed" and analogized to POD or TOD title designations. On the other hand another state, California, has held that deeds with retained powers are subject to estate recovery claims. [Bonta v. Burke, 120 Cal. Rptr. 2d 72 (Cal. App. 2002)]

In any such case, the Medicaid agency may agree that there was no transfer, because the "donor" retains all of the essential powers over the property. Provided that the special power of appointment or power to sell is not actually exercised, upon the donor's death the holder of the remainder interest will then receive the property outside of probate (and without subjecting it to the estate recovery program). Before attempting such an approach, it is advisable to determine both the state Medicaid agency's view of the transaction and the ultimate marketability of the property.

Q 14:71 Can the residence be transferred into a revocable living trust?

The effect of a retained life estate coupled with a special power of appointment is tantamount to a beneficiary designation as to real property, akin to the pay-on-death provision commonly available for bank and other financial accounts. Of course, it is possible to effect the same result more directly, simply by transferring the property into a revocable trust; however, in many states, the property held by a trust is treated as non-exempt—apparently on the questionable theory that because the "owner" of the property is no longer the individual, then it cannot be a personal residence. Consequently, in those states at least (e.g., Arizona, Oklahoma, Ohio, and others), trust ownership is not a reasonable approach to resolving the problem. In one state, Connecticut, a special "trust-busting" statute would make any such trust vulnerable to termination if the grantor or spouse applied for benefits within five years. [Conn. Gen. Stat. § 45a-486] This law has not yet been challenged.

Q 14:72 Is it a mistake to transfer the residence into a living trust in those states treating trust assets as non-exempt?

Not necessarily. Precisely because the trust's assets are counted as available use of a living trust may be a clever and powerful Medicaid planning technique. If the residence is owned by the trust at the time one spouse first becomes medically eligible for Medicaid, the value of the property will be included in the calculation of available resources. Because that calculation is in turn used to determine the community spouse's maximum allowance in many states, trust ownership of the residence effectively inflates the amount that the community spouse is permitted to retain. By the simple expedient of transferring the residence out of the trust and into the spouses' names (or, if permitted by the trust's terms, into the community spouse's name alone), the couple's assets may be reduced below the eligibility level. As a consequence, long-time trust ownership of the family residence is highly beneficial, at least in those states that both treat trust assets as non-exempt and calculate the community spouse resource allowance by dividing the total available resources (rather than adopting a presumptive CSRA for all applicants). This benefit will, of course, be insignificant for the wealthy couple, whose assets easily exceed two times the maximum CSRA without considering the family residence.

> **Example 14-12.** Mrs. and Mrs. Danielson live in Oklahoma, which treats a home titled to a trust as an available resource. In addition to their home (valued at $125,000), they also own $80,000 of available resources. Neither is presently institutionalized or even ill. If one of them should enter the nursing home with their current asset situation, the home would be exempt and the community spouse would be permitted to retain $40,000 of the remaining assets; eligibility would be obtained when the total available resources reached $42,000 (allowing for the institutionalized spouse's $2,000). The community spouse will have to spend, gift, or otherwise dispose of $38,000 of cash.

If, however, Mr. and Mrs. Danielson establish a revocable living trust and transfer their home to the trust, their circumstance changes. Upon the later institutionalization of one spouse, the other (community) spouse will be permitted to retain the CSRA maximum of $90,660 (in 2003) because the home will have been treated as an available resource. By simply transferring the home from the trust to the name of both spouses (or to the community spouse alone, if the trust permits such a transfer) *after* institutionalization, the institutionalized spouse will immediately qualify for Medicaid assistance. The cost of establishing a trust will have been repaid many times; in the meantime, in spite of their relatively modest estate size and Oklahoma's relatively liberal probate rules, Mr. and Mrs. Danielson will also have received protection from the (modest) cost of probate if neither is ever institutionalized.

Q 14:73 How can annuities be used in planning for eligibility for long-term care Medicaid?

One popular and successful asset-limitation strategy is the purchase of an immediate payment, single-premium annuity. An annuity purchase is a transfer for value and therefore is not subject to the Medicaid transfer penalties. Usually annuities are used to secure eligibility for the institutionalized spouse while preserving wealth (now in the form of community spouse income) for the comparatively healthier community spouse, although the strategy has some limited application in the case of unmarried applicants. By purchase of an immediate (and irrevocable) annuity, assets are liquidated, but without the problem of a gift having been made (as the stream of income is necessarily "worth" the purchase price of the annuity). Effectively, assets are converted into income with no resulting penalty period.

Example 14-13. Mr. and Mrs. Rigby (ages 75 and 70, respectively) have $200,000 in available resources. Mr. Rigby has just been admitted to the nursing home, and it is unlikely that he will return home. Mrs. Rigby may retain $90,660 (2003 figure) in available resources, but the remaining assets (except for Mr. Rigby's $2,000 allowance) must be spent (or gifted, if the penalty period is not a concern) before Mr. Rigby will qualify for Medicaid.

One choice for Mrs. Rigby would be to purchase an annuity with as much as $113,000 of the couple's funds. The annuity should name her as annuitant and beneficiary; she may wish to have payments made to the couple's children upon her death before the annuity ends. The annuity can be established for her life or for a term of years, provided that the term of years does not exceed her life expectancy. According to CMS tables, her life expectancy is 14.66 years.

After checking price figures with several insurance companies Mrs. Rigby purchases a single-premium immediate annuity for $115,000. Her monthly payments for 176 months will be approximately $800; if she dies before the final payment is received, succeeding payments will be divided among her children. Mr. Rigby is immediately eligible for Medicaid, although the amount of his monthly income that will be given to Mrs. Rigby is reduced because the annuity provides a significant increase in her monthly income.

Annuities must be carefully thought out, so that the income generated does not exceed monthly income limits when combined with that of the institutionalized spouse, or simply convert an asset into a stream of income that must be paid to the nursing facility. Usually the community spouse will be the beneficiary (otherwise the income goes straight to the nursing home), and this can be an extremely effective arrangement when the community spouse has significantly less income than does the institutionalized spouse, or when one of the assets to be "spent down" is an IRA that could not be liquidated without causing income tax but can purchase individual retirement annuity instead. A word of caution: a few states, notably Connecticut, will treat purchase of an annuity that raises the community spouse's income *above* the MMMNA to be a disqualifying transfer of assets. In the example, if Mrs. Rigby's income before the annuity were $2,500, and the annuity raised it to $3,300, Connecticut would almost certainly claim that this was a disqualifying transfer.

Q 14:74 How should an annuity be structured for a married Medicaid applicant?

Immediate annuities must be designed carefully to avoid causing irreparable problems for the applicant and spouse. Because the annuity must (in order to qualify) be an irrevocable purchase and fully annuitized, failure to plan effectively can create an insoluble problem for future Medicaid applications. The following factors must be considered in purchasing the annuity (be sure to review state regulations—many states have adopted counter-intuitive rules regarding annuities and Medicaid applications):

1. *Amount of annuity purchase.* Typically, the appropriate value of the annuity will be set after all other planning steps have been undertaken (purchase of new home, investment in home repairs and automobiles, limited gifts to children, etc.). The amount of the annuity will often, but not always, be the difference between remaining resources and the community spouse resource allowance (the amount permitted to the community spouse), plus an appropriate allowance for annuity income in the first month(s), undervalued assets, and similar adjustments. Thus, after all other planning opportunities have been undertaken, the institutionalized spouse can be made eligible almost immediately.
2. *Term of annuity.* There are competing considerations in setting the term of the annuity. For some purposes (e.g., minimizing the couple's total income, delaying the growth of the couple's assets, and providing for an ultimate benefit for children or other beneficiaries), a longer term is desirable. For others (e.g., total investment return and access to cash), shorter terms are better. In addition, the Medicaid agency's interpretation must be contended with—most states treat annuities as uncompensated transfers to the extent that the term exceeds the life expectancy of the annuitant (the primary beneficiary of such an arrangement, not the annuitant, is the ultimate recipient of the funds). Most states do not penalize transfers by the community spouse nor look at the community spouse's assets after eligibility has been obtained (or, in some states, one year or some other fixed period after eligibility), so the use of a shorter-term annuity may be a fine planning technique.
3. *Commercial versus private.* In many states, there is no need to purchase annuities through commercial (insurance) companies—they can be established by contract between the community spouse and children or other family members. In some states attention will be paid to whether the annuity is commercially reasonable (e.g., whether it provides an ade-

quate rate of return), but annuity agreements among family members will be permitted. Still other states prohibit private annuities, or treat the transfers into private annuities as uncompensated transfers (gifts), as discussed in Q 14:73.

Q 14:75 When is an annuity useful in Medicaid planning for an unmarried person?

Although annuities are far more common (and more useful) when used in connection with Medicaid eligibility for a married applicant, there are some limited circumstances in which they might be considered for an unmarried potential Medicaid recipient. If the applicant is in ill health, for example (a common circumstance, of course, among nursing home residents), the Medicaid agency's actuarial tables may predict an unlikely longevity. In such a case, the purchase of an annuity for a fixed term of years (set at the applicant's actuarial life expectancy) can effectively transfer assets to a later generation without incurring a transfer penalty.

Even if the Medicaid recipient actually lives to the actuarial life expectancy, there may be value in an annuity. Although the applicant's assets will have been converted into income, and then applied to his or her nursing care, the result will have been use of the Medicaid agency's superior purchasing power to procure those services at a discount from the private pay rate. Across the country, Medicaid payment rates run at 85 percent or less of the private pay rate; if the purchase of an annuity permits the applicant to pay Medicaid rates and either make monthly gifts (of less than the posted private pay rate) or purchase extra services with the balance, he or she may still benefit from the annuity strategy.

Q 14:76 Are there problems with annuity planning?

Yes. One common problem is the purchase of an annuity too early in the planning process. In general terms, short-term immediate annuities are not particularly attractive when viewed only for their investment value. In other words, purchase of a too-large annuity will cause the applicant (and spouse) to forgo better investment opportunities; more concretely, the liquidation of assets used to purchase the annuities may cause tax and other problems for the applicant and spouse.

The most common problem with annuity planning is the growing cottage industry of financial planners, accountants, and insurance agents marketing annuities to a poorly informed populace. It is increasingly common for clients to have been sold nonqualifying annuities (usually deferred, rather than immediate, annuities) with promises that Medicaid eligibility will follow automatically. Even though a pre-purchased deferred annuity can be annuitized (converted into an immediate annuity), there may be undisclosed costs for the transfer, or the wrong spouse may have been chosen as the annuitant at the time of the initial purchase. The investment value of the deferred annuities may be questionable, and the level of sophistication and understanding displayed by the client-purchaser may be minimal.

Q 14:77 How can a self-canceling installment note be used to hasten Medicaid eligibility?

The self-canceling installment note (SCIN) was originally used as a tax-minimization device. By loaning money to family members and taking back a SCIN, a parent could effectively transfer assets to the next generation at less than the face value, particularly if the parent did not anticipate living to his or her actuarial life expectancy.

In Medicaid planning, a SCIN works much like an annuity. Like an annuity it is a transfer for value and should not be subject to the Medicaid transfer penalties. A SCIN converts an available asset into a stream of income, which ends upon the death of the parent. Unlike an annuity, the parent's death simply ends the SCIN relationship. In an annuity, the payee shifts automatically to the successor, but the stream of income continues and the remaining value of the asset is unreachable. On the other hand, if the parent is still living at the end of the term the payments stop.

> **Example 14-14.** Mr. and Mrs. Rigby (see Example 14-13) face the same circumstances, except that Mrs. Rigby decides to explore a SCIN rather than a single-premium immediate annuity. Mrs. Rigby loans $115,000 to her three children, who give her a nonassignable, noncallable note bearing 10 percent interest; the interest figure is computed at the then-prevailing rate of 8 percent plus a 2 percent increase to compensate for the other benefit of the note—its self-canceling provision. Upon Mrs. Rigby's death, the remaining balance of principal and any accumulated income will

be forgiven. Mrs. Rigby's children make regular payments to Mrs. Rigby on the note. The loan is not a gift (Mrs. Rigby received something of value), and even the self-canceling provision was compensated by the additional 2 percent interest premium. Mr. Rigby should immediately be eligible for Medicaid, although (as with the annuity approach) Mrs. Rigby's receipt of income payments from the note may affect her entitlement to a portion of Mr. Rigby's income.

Q 14:78 What are the advantages of using a SCIN rather than an annuity?

SCINs offer two advantages over annuities, at least in appropriate cases: (1) they permit the transaction to be completely private (in those states limiting or prohibiting private annuities), and (2) they permit the successors (children, or other borrowers) to use the parent-applicant's assets immediately upon the transfer, rather than having to wait until the parent-applicant's death.

Q 14:79 What risks are associated with using SCINs for Medicaid planning?

Although the theory of SCINs seems perfectly logical, not every state Medicaid agency has been sanguine about approving the technique. In some states SCINs have become widespread, and have been aggressively constructed. Some practitioners, for example, construct SCINs with payments of less than the current interest accumulation, with large balloon payments scheduled for the end of the Medicaid applicant's life expectancy (despite the reality that he or she is unlikely to survive for the life expectancy period). Such SCIN arrangements are likely to be seen as abusive, and not treated as arm's-length transactions equally benefiting both parties. When so viewed, SCINs (perhaps including less-aggressive SCINs) will be rejected by Medicaid agencies. [See Ptashkin v. Department of Public Welfare, 731 A.2d 238 (Pa. 1999)]

Q 14:80 How can a long-term care Medicaid applicant use a family limited partnership or limited liability company to hasten Medicaid eligibility?

In estate tax planning, family limited partnerships (FLPs) and limited liability company (LLCs) are often used to reduce the value of a parent's assets, thereby reducing the estate tax liability on the parent's death. This works by virtue of the reduction in value occasioned by the combination of loss of control of the asset and the resultant lack of marketability; although the original asset may have been valued at one price, 90 percent ownership of that asset is not valued at 90 percent of the original price.

The same logic and mechanism works for Medicaid planning as well. In fact, FLPs and LLCs may work even better for Medicaid than estate tax planning purposes precisely because of the loss of control. By establishing an FLP and transferring all or substantially all of his or her assets to it, a potential Medicaid recipient not only reduces the value of the underlying asset but also establishes the possibility of having the FLP interest ignored for eligibility purposes because it is unmarketable.

Q 14:81 What is the practical difference between an FLP and an LLC for Medicaid planning purposes?

While family limited partnerships were widely utilized in estate tax planning through much of the 1980s, their use has diminished somewhat with the adoption in many states of statutes authorizing creation of limited liability companies. LLCs have the modest advantage because they are treated as corporations for liability and record-keeping purposes, but as partnerships for income tax purposes. As a result, in states with favorable LLC legislation LLCs are more commonly used. As a practical matter, either kind of entity leads to the same result: loss of marketability and reduction in value of the assets held by the FLP or LLC.

Q 14:82 Will FLPs and LLCs work in every jurisdiction?

Not necessarily. Although practitioners in some states (notably Colorado) regularly utilize FLPs to attain Medicaid eligibility, other state agencies analogize FLPs and LLCs to trusts and treat the assets held by the separate entity as if they were available to the applicant.

Before attempting to establish an FLP or LLC, the elder law practitioner should check local practice and experience. In the absence of regulation or prior decisions, it may be appropriate to expand local practice by the use of such techniques.

Q 14:83 What are some specific Medicaid planning techniques permitted in individual states?

Although the variation from state to state is tremendous, a number of specific practices merit attention. In some cases, local state practice may be based on an interpretation not previously considered in another state; in other cases, it may be important to be able to advise clients who are moving to or arriving from another state, or who have ill parents or other relatives in another state. Of course, the Medicaid rules vary so significantly among states that no elder law practitioner should expect to be able to give specific advice in a state in which he or she has not actually become familiar with local rules and practices. A list of the more common (and interesting) state variations would include:

1. *Transfer of home (California).* California permits the transfer of the (exempt) home to third persons, reasoning that any transfer of an exempt asset must necessarily be motivated by a purpose other than to qualify for benefits. Given the value of California real estate, this opens a tremendous opportunity.
2. *Spousal refusal (New York).* The community spouse's assets can be made unavailable by simply declaring an intent not to support the institutionalized spouse. The institutionalized spouse's right to support must then be assigned to the Medicaid agency (unless he or she is unable to make the assignment because of impairment). [42 U.S.C. § 1396r-5 (c)(3)(A)] Medicaid law then limits the amount of the community spouse's income that can be required to support the institutionalized spouse. Coupled with the exemption for interspousal transfers, this creates a powerful planning opportunity unique to New York. [Shah v. DeBuono, 711 N.Y.S.2d 824 (N.Y. 2000), aff'g, 694 N.Y.S.2d 82 (N.Y. App. Div. 1999)]
3. *Annuity analogized to irrevocable trust (Kansas and Alabama).* Kansas treats all annuities as if they were transfers to

an irrevocable trust, imposing a transfer penalty and thereby making the annuity an unusable plan in most circumstances. Alabama apparently adds a good-faith test: An annuity purchased during the look-back period is suspect, while an annuitized retirement account is not. In Connecticut, annuities that cause the community spouse's income to exceed the MMMNA are treated as transfers.

4. *No asset recovery (Georgia, Michigan, and Texas).* Although 1993 federal Medicaid amendments mandated that every state adopt an estate recovery program (see Q 14:97), these states have yet to implement a plan. As a result there is no pressure to transfer homes during the Medicaid recipient's life, nor to change the recipient's estate plan.
5. *Rental real estate exempt (Indiana).* Apparently on the theory that rental real estate is an illiquid investment and that the income can be used to subsidize nursing care in any case, Indiana simply exempts all rental real estate. Medicaid planning may be as simple as purchasing a family member's home and renting it back to the family member.

Medicaid Trust Planning

Q 14:84 How can trusts be used as a Medicaid planning device?

Since the adoption of the Omnibus Budget Reconciliation Act of 1993, the usefulness of trusts in Medicaid planning has been dramatically reduced. Although practice differed from state to state, trusts (and especially irrevocable trusts) frequently were used to secure eligibility while retaining some interest in or control over the trust principal. OBRA '93 changed that practice, while simultaneously introducing a handful of new, although sharply circumscribed, trust possibilities.

Under current rules (adopted as part of OBRA '93), a revocable trust is treated as fully available to the beneficiary. [42 U.S.C. § 1396p(d)(3)(A)] An irrevocable trust established by a Medicaid applicant, his or her spouse, or someone acting on his or her behalf (including a fiduciary or court) will be treated as an available resource and its distributions as income if (or to the extent that) there is any discretion in the trustee to make any distributions whatsoever to the applicant. [42 U.S.C. § 1396p(d)(3)(B)] In other words, "self-settled" discretionary trusts will not protect assets or preserve eligibility for Medicaid. There are, however, four important exceptions to this bright-line rule, all discussed in Q 14:85.

The effect of this strong statutory language is to make trust planning—other than the exceptions previously mentioned—all but useless for Medicaid applicants (or prospective applicants). This point is made more powerfully by the different treatment of transfers to individuals and those to or *from* a trust: Transfers involving trusts carry a 60-month look-back period, while transfers to individuals will incur a maximum penalty period of 36 months. [42 U.S.C. § 1396p(c)(1)(B)(i)]

Q 14:85 What types of trusts are still useful for Medicaid planning since the adoption of OBRA '93?

OBRA '93 added three new exceptions to the new harsh treatment of trusts:

1. Irrevocable trusts for the benefit of a disabled individual under age 65 that provide for payback of Medicaid expenses upon the death of the beneficiary [42 U.S.C. § 1396p(d)(4)(A)] (see Q 14:88);
2. Trusts (only in income cap states) utilized solely to handle the applicant's income and to make him or her eligible, [42 U.S.C. § 1396p(d)(4)(B)] (see Q 14:91); and
3. Trusts established as accounts for a disabled individual under age 65 (or if not under age 65, the applicant's child) in a pooled trust held by a nonprofit organization, [42 U.S.C. § 1396p(d)(4)(C)]. (see Q 14:90).

In addition, OBRA '93 added another trust concept. It exempted from transfer penalty rules (but not resource availability rules) transfers in trust made to spouses and disabled children, each time invoking the language "to or for the sole benefit of" the respective favored beneficiaries. [42 U.S.C. § 1396p(c)(2)(B)] This has given rise to discussion and use of so-called "sole benefit of" trusts to handle those transfers (see Q 14:93). (Transfers to disabled children were already exempt; transfers in trust were added.)

These trusts and their implications are discussed in more detail in Sections 3257 through 3259 of the Centers for Medicare and Medicaid State Medicaid Manual, issued originally as (and still referred to collectively as) "Transmittal 64."

In addition to these special exceptions, there is another, sometimes very important exception, the testamentary trust.

Q 14:86 What is the "testamentary trust" exception to the trust rules?

OBRA '93 states at 42 USC Section 1396p(d)(2)(A) that:

> (2)(A) For purposes of this subsection, an individual shall be considered to have established a trust if assets of the individual were used to form all or part of the corpus of the trust and if any of the following individuals established such trust other than by will:
>
> (i) The individual.
>
> (ii) The individual's spouse.
>
> (iii) A person, including a court or administrative body, with legal authority to act in place of or on behalf of the individual or the individual's spouse.
>
> (iv) A person, including any court or administrative body, acting at the direction or upon the request of the individual or the individual's spouse.

The essential term in this paragraph is "other than by will." The rules that treat as available any discretionary trust established by applicant or spouse do *not* apply to testamentary trusts. This means that one spouse can name the other in his or her will as beneficiary of a discretionary trust that gives the trustee the right to withhold payments, without affecting the surviving spouse's benefits, *and* without the trust being vulnerable to a state lien on the surviving spouse's death. In states where other planning devices to protect a spouse are weak, this can be an important choice for the spouse likely to die first—statistically, the husband. As a planning technique, this requires either a guess as to which spouse may die first versus who may require long-term care first, or a decision to split the odds and have assets evenly divided between the parties. (In community property states, presumably there is no need to make the choice, unless of course it is possible to first convert community property to separate property.) It also requires a deliberate choice to go through probate, depending upon one's state law respecting the establishment of a testamentary trust outside the probate process. For example, in a common law state the home's joint tenancy must be severed so that one-half will pass to the testamentary discretionary trust under the will of the first to die. This step is so counterintuitive to clients schooled in probate avoidance that it may be overlooked. Of course, it is best used where the first spouse's death appears imminent.

The utility of the technique must be tempered by state law governing the surviving spouse's statutory share. Where that share is large, failure to elect against the will that instead sets up a discretionary trust, may well be treated as a disqualifying transfer by the surviving spouse, to the extent of the value of the statutory share at the time. If the surviving spouse has no imminent need for long-term care, it may be worthwhile to accept that risk. On the other hand, where the statutory share is more modest, the surviving spouse can make the statutory election but leave the balance of the property protected (provided the will preserves that right against a state law that would deprive the party making the election of any other interest under the will). In some states, the presence of a trust in the will that approximates the statutory share, a "statutory share trust," may eliminate the right of election entirely. Finally, it may be possible to argue that the failure to elect was made for consideration, in that the spouse would have had to forego the discretionary trust in order to receive the elective share. If the discretionary trust contains the entire estate, and the statutory share is a more limited portion, this may be an effective approach.

There has been some attempt to argue that although the trust might not be available, the testamentary creation of the trust was still a disqualifying transfer by an applicant's spouse and should cause ineligibility. This reasoning was soundly defeated in *Skindzier v. Com'r of Social Services* [258 Conn. 642 (2001)].

Q 14:87 Are any variations on the testamentary trust concept permitted?

Some practitioners have suggest that a "pour-over" bequest to an unfunded trust should also be considered a "testamentary" trust, since the transfer only occurs upon death. Most states have so far taken a hard line, however, and require the terms of the trust to be set forth in the decedent's will in order to meet this exception. Other practitioners, (e.g. from California), insist that provided the terms of the trust are included in a will, a testamentary instrument, it is permissible to distribute from a probate-avoiding living trust directly to the testamentary trust but bypassing any statutory rights of election or other claims of creditors. This may work in some states, but in others, the distributive act, from the *inter vivos* trust, will be sufficient to trigger a penalty period, unless it is a complete "pour-back." [See, e.g., Bezzini v. Department of Social Services, 49 Conn. App. 432, 715 A.2d 791 (1998)]

Q 14:88 What is an "OBRA '93" or "payback" trust for a Medicaid applicant under age 65?

Normally receipt of assets by a person receiving need-based government benefits would render that individual ineligible, at least temporarily, for those benefits; however, federal law after OBRA '93 now requires states to allow such funds to be transferred to a special needs trust for a disabled person under the age of 65. [42 U.S.C. § 1396p(d)(4)(A)] (See chapter 17 for a discussion of special needs trusts.) The trust language must be carefully written to ensure that government benefits will continue, and the distribution provisions usually make it clear that the disabled person is the sole beneficiary of the trust and that the funds are to be spent on extraordinary medical care, travel, entertainment, and other benefits not provided through government programs.

One requirement of federal law regarding such trusts is that any trust assets remaining at the time of the beneficiary's death must be first applied to repay state Medicaid benefits; the repayment requirement is limited by the actual amount paid by the state (in states utilizing capitated Medicaid programs, this may mean the state's premium payments, not the actual cost of services provided). As a result, this kind of trust is frequently referred to as a "payback" trust. More commonly, such special needs trusts are referred to as "(d)(4)(A)" trusts, after the section of Medicaid law requiring states to recognize them.

The additional benefit of the payback trust, as noted above, is that a transfer to such a trust, even by a third person, is not a disqualifying transfer on the part of the transferor. [42 U.S.C. § 1396p(c)(3)(A)]

Q 14:89 When might a payback trust be an effective Medicaid planning device?

Transfers to payback trusts for disabled persons under age 65 are allowed by Medicaid without affecting eligibility; thus, the applicant making the transfer can move assets out of his or her estate without jeopardizing his or her own application for benefits. Additionally, such third-party trusts put assets out of the reach of Medicaid-generated liens. Special needs trusts must be established by a parent, grandparent, legal guardian, or court. (See chapter 17 for a discussion of special needs trusts.) Typically the state is named the remainder beneficiary of the trust, or another party is named the remainder beneficiary with the understanding that the state has a lien against the trust to the extent and in the amount that it provided care to the disabled person.

Q 14:90 What is a pooled trust?

Pooled trusts allow the income and assets of a number of disabled persons to be managed by a nonprofit association, with the property not counted as a resource to the individual person who holds an account with the trust. [42 U.S.C. § 1396p(d)(4)(C)] There must be a separate account for each beneficiary. As with "payback" trusts, the "pooled" trust account must be established by the disabled person, his or her parents or grandparents, legal guardian, or the court. Although there is no transfer penalty for assets transferred into a pooled trust by persons under age 65, transfer penalties apply for persons over age 65 in most states (excluding Michigan and Tennessee). Upon the death of the individual beneficiary, the trust must provide for repayment to the Medicaid program "[t]o the extent that amounts remaining in the beneficiary's account upon the death of the beneficiary are not retained by the trust." [42 U.S.C. § 1396p(d)(4)(A)(iv)] This seems to permit the remaining principal to be accumulated for the benefit of other pooled trust beneficiaries, although the requirement that the trust maintain separate accounts for each beneficiary [42 U.S.C. § 1396p(d)(4)(A)(ii)] is difficult to reconcile with this provision. The New Jersey pooled trust provides that 50 percent will be retained and 50 percent repaid to the state; the Michigan pooled trust retains the entire balance; and the newly established Connecticut pooled trust retains the assets but is currently being litigated.

Because the pooled trust under USC Section 1396p(d)(4)(C) must be managed by a nonprofit association, few such trusts existed for many years. One leader in developing pooled trusts in various states has been The ARC (formerly the Association for Retarded Citizens), with pooled trusts operating in (at least) California, Florida, Indiana, Kansas, Maryland, New York, North Carolina, Pennsylvania, Rhode Island, Tennessee, Texas, and Virginia.

One concern expressed by some states has been the extent to which the "separate accounts" rule conflicts with the "pooling" requirement. If the arrangement is in effect an aggregate of separate trusts with assets pooled for management purposes only, does this qualify under USC Section 1396p(d)(4)? How are the income taxes assessed for these trusts? New York and Connecticut have taken a particularly rigorous approach to the "pooling" requirement.

Some have viewed the nonprofit association management as a way to help disabled individuals place in trust relatively modest amounts that would be of little interest to a traditional corporate fiduciary. However, some pooled trusts require minimum amounts for each account, which to some extent may reduce the utility of this technique.

Q 14:91 What is a Miller trust?

In income cap states an applicant may be unable to qualify for Medicaid assistance yet have insufficient income to pay for long-term care (see Q 14:28). The U.S. District Court in Colorado addressed this conundrum in *Miller v. Ibarra* [746 F. Supp. (D. Colo. 1990)], by permitting the establishment of a trust that consisted solely of an "assignment" of the beneficiary's income (Social Security and pension income) and that directed payment from the trust of just less than the maximum income amount. The trust also provided that any accumulated income remaining at the death of the beneficiary would be used to repay the state for Medicaid costs.

OBRA '93 codified a variation of the "Miller" trust. [42 U.S.C. § 1396p(d)(4)(B)] Now available in all income cap states, the Miller (or "qualified income") trust must meet two standards:

1. It must consist solely of pension, Social Security, and other income, plus the accumulated income on those trust amounts; and

2. It must provide that any sums remaining in the trust on the death of the beneficiary will first be used to repay the state for Medicaid expenditures.

Q 14:92 How does a Miller trust work in practice?

Although the rules governing Miller or qualified income trusts are simple, they are deceptively so. Once established, the trust becomes the assignee of all periodic income of the beneficiary (despite the difficulty that Social Security benefits, for example, are nonassignable pursuant to 42 USC Section 407). The income so assigned does not count toward Medicaid income eligibility, but is still treated as available income for purposes of calculating the beneficiary's duty to contribute to the cost of care as required under 42 CFR Section 435.725(c). The same regulation directs that the cost of care contribution be reduced by a personal needs allowance, payments to a community spouse (to the extent necessary to bring the community spouse's income to the MMMNA level; see Q 14:49), and Medicare Part B premiums, among other items.

Mechanically, a Miller trust should be operated so that each month it receives all the beneficiary's income, and immediately makes payments to the nursing facility or care provider, the beneficiary (or his or her personal needs account), and the spouse. Within a few days of the receipt of monthly income, the trust account should be emptied. There is no requirement that personal needs be paid for directly from the trust account, nor that any unused personal needs accumulate. Because the trust must provide for repayment of the state's Medicaid contributions at the beneficiary's death, there is good reason to maintain the trust balance at the lowest possible level. It may be practical to leave a small amount in the trust account to prevent the imposition of bank service charges; otherwise, the Miller trust should almost always be empty.

Q 14:93 What are "sole benefit" trusts?

A transfer "to or for the sole benefit of" a spouse or disabled child may be permissible without invoking a transfer penalty. [42 U.S.C. § 1396p(c)(2)(B)] Unfortunately, the statute does not include a precise description of the meaning of "sole benefit." State interpretations may differ, for example, on whether a trust "for the sole benefit of" an individual must provide for distribution of the trust principal to the estate of the beneficiary upon his or her death. Section 3257.B.6 of the State Medicaid Manual (Transmittal 64) states:

> a trust is considered to be established for the sole benefit of a spouse, blind or disabled child, or disabled individual if the trust benefits no one but that individual, whether at the time the trust is established or any time in the future. ... In order for a transfer or trust to be considered to be for the sole benefit of one of these individuals, the instrument or document must provide for the spending of the funds involved for the benefit of the individual on a basis that is actuarially sound based on the life expectancy of the individual involved.

When might a "sole benefit" trust be appropriate? In addition to situations in which the couple wishes to raise the community spouse's income by using the technique, there are other times it could be used not so much to enhance income as to prevent its diminution. For example, if the couple's assets are highly appreciated, there might be a significant capital gains tax if they had to be liquidated to purchase an annuity or otherwise spent. Moreover, if those assets could be held in the name of the community spouse until death, they would qualify for the step-up in basis. Nonliquid assets that the agency insists in treating as available might also be included. Finally, even where annuities are permitted, the community spouse might prefer a trustee to invest the funds rather than receive the potentially lower yield (and negative income tax consequences) of a permanent commercial annuity.

As with annuities, however, the utility of this technique varies depending on the state. If the state, applying its own "availability" rules, determines that a "sole benefit" trust for a spouse will nevertheless be included in the couple's "resources," there may be little benefit to making the change. Moreover, while the spouse can transfer resources after the institutionalized spouse's eligibility, he or she will have no such ability to dispose of "sole benefit" trust assets. Only if the sole benefit trust will be treated as the functional equivalent of an annuity (i.e., beyond his or her control and thus not a resource) does this technique seem useful. The technique is apparently routinely used in the state of Washington.

Q 14:94 What is a "Medicaid qualifying trust"?

Under Medicaid law prior to the adoption of OBRA '93, some trusts were characterized as "Medicaid qualifying trusts" or MQTs. Oddly, the effect of treatment as an MQT was to disqualify the beneficiary from Medicaid eligibility, because the trust principal was treated as an available resource. With the enactment of OBRA '93 the MQT provisions were repealed, but subsequent court decisions have consistently held that trusts established before OBRA '93's effective date (August 10, 1993) may still be MQTs and subject to those earlier rules. [National Bank of Detroit v. Department of Social Services, 614 N.W.2d 655 (Mich. App. 2000)]

Under prior law, any trust established by a Medicaid applicant or his or her spouse that provided for any discretionary distributions of income or principal would be treated as an MQT, and the maximum amount of discretion would be deemed to have been executed. [(former) 42 U.S.C. § 1396a(k)(2), repealed Aug. 10, 1993] As a consequence, that maximum discretionary amount would be an available resource and would, in all but the most restrictive trusts, result in ineligibility for Medicaid. This result was reached whether or not the discretion was actually exercised.

Because of the repeal of 42 USC Section 1396a(k)(2), the significance of "MQT" as a term is lost for any trust created since August 10, 1993; however, preexisting trusts must always be scrutinized for possible treatment as MQTs.

Moreover, OBRA '93 effectively confirmed the basic approach of the MQT provisions. Under 42 U.S.C. Section 1396p(d)(3)(B),

> (B) In the case of an irrevocable trust—
>
> (i) if there are any circumstances under which payment from the trust could be made to or for the benefit of the individual, the portion of the corpus from which, or the income on the corpus from which, payment to the individual could be made shall be considered resources available to the individual, and payments from that portion of the corpus or income—
>
> (I) to or for the benefit of the individual, shall be considered income of the individual, and

(II) for any other purpose, shall be considered a transfer of assets by the individual subject to subsection (c); and

(ii) any portion of the trust from which, or any income on the corpus from which, no payment could under any circumstances be made to the individual shall be considered, as of the date of establishment of the trust (or, if later, the date on which payment to the individual was foreclosed) to be assets disposed by the individual for purposes of subsection (c), and the value of the trust shall be determined for purposes of such subsection by including the amount of any payments made from such portion of the trust after such date.

Q 14:95 What is a trigger trust?

Prior to OBRA '93 one common planning technique was to create and fund a revocable trust that provided that the assets would become completely unavailable to the beneficiary upon the happening of some future event—usually institutionalization. By the operation of this "trigger" device, the trust principal could be made unavailable without incurring a transfer penalty (at least arguably), because the beneficiary would have taken no steps to make the assets unavailable. OBRA '93 effectively ended the use of trigger trusts by providing that such a trust would be treated as having been a transfer of assets as of the date of the triggering event. [42 U.S.C. § 1396p(d)(3)(B)(ii)] Even before OBRA '93, New York (the state in which the use of trigger trusts had been most widespread) had moved by statute to foreclose the use of trigger trusts. [N.Y. Estates, Powers and Trusts Law § 7-3.1(c)]

A "trigger" may still be used, however, where a person other than an applicant or spouse establishes the trust. For example, if a child wished to leave funds in trust for a parent, but was concerned about the parent's future long-term care needs, the trust in the child's will could include a trigger that would convert the trust to a supplemental needs trust at such time as the parent required long-term care.

Q 14:96 What is an "income only" trust?

Only the amounts that *could* be paid to an individual are counted as available. If the individual establishes a trust that absolutely prohibits any payments of principal to the individual under any circumstances, the principal is not counted as available, but the income is even if the trustee refuses to pay it out. An individual may still, therefore, transfer assets into a trust, incurring an ineligibility period, but retaining the use of the income only on the trust for lifetime. This is most attractive to those who have much to lose and plenty of time to get past the look-back period. The grantor does not cede the assets to a third party during his or her lifetime, the survivors receive a step-up in basis provided that a special power of appointment is reserved in the instrument, and (similarly) no gift tax is due.

On the other hand, it seems hardly prudent for most people to lock principal away for life where it can benefit neither the grantor, nor any of the grantor's near and dear, receiving only such pathetically low income as is currently available, anywhere from 1 percent to 4 percent. (OBRA '93 precludes any opportunity for the trustee to transfer the principal to third persons without creating a new penalty.) The most likely candidate may be the house, assuming that the life use by the grantor will be treated as "income" and not as the use of principal.

Estate Recovery

Q 14:97 What is "estate recovery"?

In 1993 Congress mandated that every state adopt a program to recover Medicaid expenditures from the estates of recipients. [42 U.S.C. § 1396p(b)(1)(B)] This is known as "estate recovery." The states can attach liens to personal or real property [42 U.S.C. § 1396p(a)] or seek to recover from the Medicaid recipient's estate [42 U.S.C. § 1396p(b)(1)(A)]. The states may also apply an expanded definition of "estate" that will encompass more than the probate estate. Because eligibility is based on financial criteria, it might seem unproductive to seek reimbursement; in fact, a tiny fraction of the costs of Medicaid has been recovered by the states. Nonetheless, the ramifications of the estate recovery program are serious, even for the modest estates of most Medicaid recipients.

The asset most often affected by estate recovery programs, of course, is usually the family home, the only substantial asset permitted to most Medicaid recipients. While Medicaid rules do exempt the home during the recipient's life (depending on whether the subjective test of "intent to return" is applied), estate recovery programs usually target that very asset, leading to circumstances in which the recipient (and family) have been lulled into the false expectation that the home is untouchable until it is too late to take any protective action. One state, West Virginia, actually filed suit on constitutional grounds, refusing to practice estate recovery against the family home, but lost. [West Virginia v. U.S. Department of Health and Human Services, 281 F.3d (4th Cir. 2002)]

The practitioner must keep in mind that the individual states may have their own "estate recovery" policies for other benefit programs that are not federally funded, and that these rules may be far more severe.

Q 14:98 When is estate recovery allowed?

Each state's estate recovery program is required to seek reimbursement from the probate estate of any Medicaid beneficiary; however, the state plan may not seek recovery from the estate of a recipient until after the death of the recipient's spouse. [42 U.S.C. § 1396p(b)(2)] No recovery may be initiated against the estate of a recipient who is survived by a disabled child or a child under age 21. [42 U.S.C. § 1396p(b)(2)(A)] The Medicaid recipient's home is also exempt from estate recovery programs if either (1) a sibling lives in the home, and lived there for one year prior to the recipient's institutionalization, or (2) a child lives in the home, lived there for at least two years prior to the recipient's institutionalization, and provided care that helped keep the recipient out of the institution. [42 U.S.C. § 1396p(b)(2)(B)]

Notice of the estate recovery program must be given both at the time Medicaid is applied for and at the time of estate recovery. [CMS State Medicaid Manual § 3810.G]

Q 14:99 How is "estate" defined for purposes of each state's estate recovery program?

Under federal law, all states must recover from the "estate" of the recipient. [42 U.S.C. § 1396p(b)(4)(A)] While federal law specifically permits the states to expand the definition of estate and make claims against joint tenancy interests, life estates, and other interests that automatically lapse at death, it does not provide any new mechanism to do so. [42 U.S.C. § 1396p(b)(4)(B)] Faced with the difficulty of creating, defining, and administering a program that seeks to recover such assets, most states have demurred; nearly all of the states define "estate" to mean the Medicaid recipient's probate estate. Few Medicaid recipients have estates that will be subject to the probate process, so the estate recovery program perhaps has a more terrorizing than financial effect, assuming that title to an institutionalized spouse's assets (including the home) are transferred to the community spouse.

Q 14:100 Are there limitations on the estate recovery program?

Yes. By federal law, no state estate recovery program can provide for claims against the estate of a Medicaid recipient if a spouse, a child under age 21, or a blind or disabled child survives him or her. [State Medicaid Manual § 3810A4] It is irrelevant whether the recipient actually left anything to the spouse or disabled child, and the claim cannot be reasserted after the (later) death of the spouse or disabled child. [But see Idaho Department of Health and Welfare v. Jackman, 132 Idaho 213, 970 P.2d 6 (1998), which permitted recovery after the death of the surviving spouse to the extent of the predeceasing recipient-spouse's community interest acquired after institutionalization]

Every state is also required to implement a hardship program. [42 U.S.C. § 1396p(b)(3)] Although hardship principles vary tremendously by state, they typically will exempt small estates, or estates consisting only of a home resided in by a family member who is unable to secure alternate housing. Vermont, for example, has requested a specific federal waiver for its version of hardship: It seeks to forgo estate recovery for modest homesteads when family income is below minimum poverty levels.

Recently, some have challenged estate recovery where the deceased was a tobacco smoker, arguing that the proceeds of a settlement reached by many states with the tobacco companies were actually payment to the states to reimburse for the coverage, and that estate recovery would be double-dipping. While such challenges are new, at least one has been successful. [In re Estate of Raduazo, 148 N.H. ____, 814 A.2d 147 (N.H. 2002)]

Practically speaking, where the beneficiary's "estate" really consists only of an account with $2,000 or less (depending on the state), recovery can be avoided by making the account joint with a family member. The account then passes automatically to the family member at death, unless of course the state has opted to include jointly held accounts as the recoverable estate. (A 1998 North Carolina Department of Health and Human Services survey indicates that at that time, California, Iowa, Nevada, South Dakota, and Washington recovered against jointly held property.) If, however, the account is held in the nursing home's "residents' trust account," or in a separately titled account at a bank, most likely the state will take the money through estate recovery.

Q 14:101 When can a lien be filed against the property of a Medicaid recipient?

States may (but are not required to) adopt a plan for the imposition of liens against the homes of Medicaid recipients, to be foreclosed only upon the death of the recipient or sale of the residence. The state plan may not provide for a lien in any case in which a spouse, a disabled or blind child, or a child under age 21 occupies the home, or by a sibling who lived with the recipient in the home for one year prior to the recipient's institutionalization. The lien must be dissolved if the recipient returns home. Any lien program must include a notice provision, advising Medicaid recipients of the nature and limitations of the lien and reassuring them that the lien will not result in the forced sale of the home during the recipient's life. [42 C.F.R. § 433.36(g)(2)]

Liens may also be imposed by a state plan on both real and personal property for the recovery of payments improperly made. [42 U.S.C. § 1396p(a)(1)] Such a lien may be imposed only upon an entry of judgment in a court proceeding. [42 C.F.R. § 433.36(g)(1)]

For jointly held property, where the joint owners do not meet the criteria above, the lien means that probate avoidance may be ineffective. Although title may transfer to the joint owners automatically upon the Medicaid recipient's death, the title will be subject to the lien, and the agency will refuse to release the lien unless the lien is paid (to the extent of the value of the proportionate share of the property).

Q 14:102 Will the state Medicaid agency be permitted to take the Medicaid recipient's home away?

This is perhaps the greatest fear of Medicaid applicants and their spouses, and it is a fear that is usually unfounded. During the Medicaid recipient's life, the home remains exempt; as long as a spouse or disabled child is living in the house, no lien or other encumbrance can be attached for the benefit of Medicaid. If a lien is placed on the home, estate recovery is permitted only if:

1. There is no sibling of the individual residing in the home, who has resided there at least one year immediately prior to the date of the individual's admission to the institution, and has resided there on a continuous basis since that time; and
2. There is no son or daughter of the individual residing in the home, who has resided there for at least two years immediately before the date of the individual's admission to the institution, and has resided there on a continuous basis since that time, and can establish to the agency's satisfaction that he or she has been providing care so that the individual could reside at home rather than in an institution.

[State Medicaid Manual § 3810A4]

If the Medicaid recipient owns the home at the time of death, a claim in probate—not a lien—may be made against it for the reimbursement of Medicaid payments. Although states are permitted to impose liens on the Medicaid recipient's property, few do. The result is that the Medicaid reimbursement claim is simply a claim (albeit a large one) made against the probate estate, which may include the family residence and no other assets. In such a case the Medicaid agency does not actually "take" the residence, although the result may be the same: the forced sale of the residence in order to satisfy the Medicaid claim. While this result is usually viewed with horror, it is important to note again that it applies only where the Medicaid recipient is not survived by a spouse or disabled child, and has not made any prior arrangements for the protection of the residence. In most circumstances and in most states, a competent elder law practitioner should permanently protect all or most of the family homestead.

Medicaid Planning-Related Practice Issues

Q 14:103 How might an elder law attorney assist a typical client in Medicaid planning?

While the individual scenarios differ widely, clients interested in Medicaid planning can be roughly grouped into types. A review of several of the more common planning scenarios may help to make the Medicaid planning process somewhat more understandable. Remember that techniques and regulations vary widely from state to state; in the scenarios that follow, practitioners in some states may have simple solutions not available in other states, so the proposed resolution may be completely inappropriate in some states (and even localities).

Q 14:104 How might an elder law attorney assist a married couple in Medicaid planning?

Mr. and Mrs. Jones are both in their 70s. Mr. Jones was recently admitted to the hospital for respiratory problems, and his discharge is pending. He will be released to a nursing facility, and Mrs. Jones has been assured that Medicare will pay for up to 100 days of care in that facility. Once his Medicare benefits run out, she fears that he will be unable to return home and his nursing care is likely to cost about $4,000 per month. They have accumulated a small estate, consisting of their home (worth about $150,000, and with a secured line of credit with a balance of about $10,000), their automobile (an older model sedan), household effects, and bank and stock accounts worth about $200,000. In addition, Mr. Jones receives $1,200 per month in Social Security benefits, and Mrs. Jones receives $600. The couple has three children, and Mrs. Jones expresses her wish that there be something to leave those children after she and her husband pass away. She wonders whether there is anything she can do to plan for the likely long-term institutionalization of her husband.

The first question must be whether Medicaid assistance should be sought for Mr. Jones' care at all. If he is able to return home with some assistance, it may be better for his care (and Mrs. Jones' peace of mind) to provide that care in the home rather than keeping him institutionalized. In states with limited community-care alternatives through Medicaid, it may be problematic to secure the appropriate level of assistance even if Mr. Jones can qualify for Medicaid. This can result in the paradox that, because of Medicaid's preferential treatment of nursing home care, the higher level of care is actually less expensive for Mr. and Mrs. Jones. If Mrs. Jones chooses to provide care in the home in such a situation, she will likely exhaust both their financial resources and her personal caregiving ability by providing home care for even a fairly short period of time. Even at low hourly rates full-time nurses' aides will cost $6,000 to $10,000 per month, and additional costs (food, medications, operating the household, etc.) can push those figures substantially higher.

Assuming that Medicaid eligibility is desirable (either because Mr. Jones will require nursing home care anyway, or because their state provides sufficient home care services through Medicaid), Mrs. Jones should consider how to qualify for Medicaid assistance at the earliest possible time. This is particularly important because, despite assurances Mrs. Jones has received, Medicare coverage for the full 100 days of potential eligibility is actually quite unlikely. Once Mr. Jones is determined to need institutional-level care for the rest of his life, Medicare coverage will end quite abruptly.

Whether the Jones' state calculates the CSRA as one-half of available resources at the time of first institutionalization or simply defaults to the maximum CSRA, the result should be the same. Mrs. Jones will be entitled to retain $90,660 (in 2003) of the available resources (in addition to the home, auto, and household effects), and Mr. Jones' "share" of the assets must be reduced to $2,000 (in that state) before he will be eligible for Medicaid assistance. Depending on state practices and Mrs. Jones' shelter expenses or other unusual expenses, it may be possible to increase the figure that Mrs. Jones may retain by use of the so-called "fair hearing" process, in either a court or an administrative proceeding. Advocacy will almost certainly be required to increase the CSRA figure, as few states make the calculations simple or routine.

Once the maximum CSRA figure has been calculated, Mrs. Jones will probably still need to dispose of assets. She may prefer to make gifts to her children; it may be possible to secure Medicaid eligibility fairly easily by doing so, although there will be a penalty period of ineligibility for any total gift in excess of the state's published figures for the actual cost of nursing home care. If, for example, that figure is $3,000, a gift to each child of $2,500 will trigger a total period of ineligibility of two months ($7,500 of total gift divided by the $3,000 average cost of care figure yields a two and one-half month period of ineligibility, which under federal law should be rounded down to two months—note that some states fail to round the ineligibility period down, and instead round up despite federal law, or in other cases, apply "partial months" of ineligibility). If Medicare continues to provide care during that ineligibility period, then eligibility for Medicaid may commence just as Medicare coverage expires. Of course, that level of planning would require being able to predict the length of Medicare coverage, and it is unlikely that it will be predictable.

Mrs. Jones can also hasten eligibility by maximizing the value of her home exemption. In other words, she can pay off the credit line and even improve the house (and/or furnishings and fixtures). The timing of these steps is important; in this scenario, she is free to pursue both payment of the mortgage and home improvements immediately, but if the facts were changed slightly, so that Mr. Jones' institutionalization had not yet occurred, she would be well-advised to delay these steps until after the CSRA has been calculated, at least in those states that do not simply default to the maximum CSRA. In fact, in those states, if Mrs. Jones was seeking assistance *before* Mr. Jones' hospitalization, it might sometimes be advisable actually to increase the amount of the mortgage (e.g., by borrowing money using the secured line of credit) and incur monthly mortgage payment obligations in order to increase the CSRA calculation just before institutionalization. After Mr. Jones' admission to the hospital or nursing home, the recently borrowed money can be repaid, thereby bringing Mrs. Jones' assets below the (increased) CSRA figure.

In addition to the home mortgage payoff and home repair, Mrs. Jones can purchase a new automobile (provided that it is used for medical purposes, including Mrs. Jones' visits to her own physician, or to pick up medications for either her or her husband) as a way of sheltering some of her liquid assets. She can also use money for travel (her own or, if he is able, her husband's), entertainment, therapy, medical treatment not covered by Medicare, or medical supplies. After all of those expenditures are completed, she may be able to bring the available resources below the CSRA figure. For example, beginning with the Jones' $200,000 of liquid assets, she might make the following expenditures:

$200,000	Available resources
$(10,000)	Payoff of secured credit line
$(15,000)	Roof repair; enlargement and handicapped accessibility of bathroom
$(28,000)	Purchase of new vehicle (after gift of old vehicle to one child)
$(3,000)	Wheelchair and medical supplies for Mr. Jones
$(5,000)	Travel (Mrs. Jones visiting her family)
$(4,000)	New appliances, carpeting
$135,000	Remaining balance
$(50,000)	Purchase of an immediate annuity OR set aside to ensure Mrs. Jones reaches the MMMNA (in "rcsouce first" states)
$(85,000)	Remaining available resources

If there are assets remaining, Mrs. Jones may choose to convert some of those assets into income by the purchase of an immediate annuity (for these purposes, investment in a family limited partnership or some types of unsecured loans to family members may have a similar effect). If she chooses the annuity route, she will purchase an annuity in her own name, with either herself or her husband as annuitant, and with payments made to her alone. If she chooses a term of years (instead of a lifetime benefit), she can make her children the alternate beneficiaries, but if she chooses a term of years longer than her current life expectancy (by reference to tables maintained by Medicaid in Transmittal 64, the State Medicaid Manual) she will in most states be deemed to have made a gift of at least some of the purchase price of the annuity. In most states, she could at least consider purchasing the annuity from family members, but it may be easier to explain and defend the purchase if a commercial annuity is purchased from an insurance company.

By some combination of these techniques, Mrs. Jones can probably make her husband eligible for Medicaid assistance without too much difficulty (of course, it becomes more challenging as the size of their joint estate increases); however, his eligibility does not end the discussion, as there are at least two remaining issues with which she must contend. In addition, she must consider any overriding concern she may have about the quality of care provided under the Medicaid system: Nationwide, Medicaid is currently paying something less than 85 percent of the private-pay rate for nursing care, and so there will be some inevitable pressure on the care provider to minimize the expense of Mr. Jones' care. Other shortfalls in the care provided by Medicaid are discussed in Q 14:8, and Mrs. Jones may try to ensure that certain services are provided to him with some of the "excess" resources before all is gone.

In addition to the quality-of-care issues, Mrs. Jones must be concerned about the potential estate recovery program and the contribution to care required from Mr. Jones' income. As for the estate recovery program, if Mrs. Jones survives her husband there will be no problem (at least in most states—a handful of states have attempted to pursue estate recovery against surviving spouses despite the clear federal prohibition, and some state court opinions are less than clear about whether such efforts might be permitted). If Mrs. Jones passes away after her husband qualifies for Medicaid there may be some difficulty, particularly with a Medicaid claim against the family home. She may be able to forestall this problem by transferring the home into her own name (either before or after Mr. Jones' eligibility) and simply disinherit her husband by will, although most states will create a statutory right to elect against the will (or some substitute mechanism), and treat Mr. Jones' failure to make that election as a gift in his own right, thereby disqualifying him from continued Medicaid coverage for some period of time after her death. Other than the family home, most of the remaining assets can be transferred to Mrs. Jones' name and then to the children without invoking any ineligibility period if she should predecease her husband. If she is in California, or otherwise can risk a period of ineligibility for herself and her husband as a result, she can transfer the home first to herself and then to the children or to a trust naming the children as beneficiaries, or add the children's names to the deed to avoid probate. Otherwise, however, she may be "stuck" with the home, *unless* she sells it after her husband is eligible, as transfers of non-home property by the community spouse, after the institutionalized spouse's eligibility, do not cause the imposition a penalty period.

After Medicaid eligibility has been obtained, Mrs. Jones will still be required to pay some portion of Mr. Jones' income to the nursing home for his care. She should be able to retain all of her own income (including her Social Security, even if paid under his earnings, the proceeds from the annuity she purchased to reduce assets, and the investment income from the remaining assets transferred into her own name). In addition, she will be entitled to retain a sufficient portion of his income to bring her total income to the MMMNA level (up to $2,267 in 2003). Finally, Mr. Jones himself can retain a personal needs allowance set by the state to offset his minor personal expenses. After those deductions (and payment of the Medicare Part B premium), the remaining income received in Mr. Jones' name must be turned over to the nursing home. Obviously, this makes the annuity choice somewhat less attractive in the Jones' situation: Even though the annuity neatly solves the asset eligibility problem (up to an unlimited amount), it can reduce the total amount available to Mrs. Jones by reduction of the nonannuity income she is permitted to retain. As a consequence, the annuity option is usually most attractive when the lower-earning spouse is institutionalized, although it may still be a workable solution in the Jones' situation after careful consideration of the options.

In the Jones' case, Mrs. Jones has pension income of $600. She also has at least some remaining assets, which will earn additional income. If she has purchased an immediate annuity or increased her CSRA to ensure more income, her income will have risen accordingly. Assuming that her investment and annuity income totals $1,100 per month, she will be entitled to receive at least $415 per month from her husband's pension and Social Security income (to bring her level to at least the threshold MMMNA amount of $1,515 for 2003). Depending on her state and her costs of shelter, that figure may actually be higher. In addition, Mr. Jones is entitled to a personal needs allowance of between $30 and $79.50, depending on the state. In other words, Mr. Jones' Social Security and pension income will be distributed as follows each month:

$58.70	deducted for Medicare Part B premium
$79.50	to Mr. Jones, to his personal needs account, or to Mrs. Jones for his use
$415	to Mrs. Jones
$646.80	to the nursing home for Mr. Jones' care

Q 14:105 How might an elder law attorney assist an unmarried person with a disabled child in Medicaid planning?

Mrs. Smith, age 85 and a widow, has just been admitted to the hospital for treatment of a broken hip sustained in a fall in her home. Her children are concerned about the likelihood that she will remain in the nursing home after discharge from the hospital, and do not want to see her estate depleted by the cost of that care. This is particularly problematic because one of her children, her 55-year-old developmentally disabled son, has lived with her in the home since birth, and the remaining children fear the effect of placing him outside the home if it must be sold. One of the other children is prepared to move into the home and provide care for the disabled son, but the son's only income is SSI of $388 per month and there is concern about whether it can adequately provide for his needs. Mrs. Smith's other assets include bank accounts of $400,000, her automobile, and household effects.

Mrs. Smith can easily obtain Medicaid eligibility by simply gifting her entire estate to her disabled son. Gifts to (or for the sole benefit of) disabled children do not incur a transfer penalty. Unfortunately, there are at least two other problems with this approach: Mrs. Smith's ability to understand or make the gift may be questionable, and her son's ability to handle the resultant gift may be problematic.

Assuming that Mrs. Smith can make the gift (or that a power of attorney with appropriate gifting powers was executed before Mrs. Smith's current disability), the transfer to her son may solve her eligibility problems. In some states, a transfer into a trust for his benefit (with one or more of the remaining children as trustees) may have the same result, although some states insist that a transfer into a trust is not "for the sole benefit" of the income beneficiary, at least unless it is a "payback" trust. If the son has the ability subsequently to transfer the received assets into a trust for his own benefit, her eligibility should not be affected (after her transfer to him, she loses the ability to control, or be affected by, his retransfer). If he is unable to make that transfer, it may require a conservatorship (or guardianship of the estate) proceeding to provide effective management of the money and property transferred to him.

Paradoxically, the transfer of the house to the son should result in an increase in his current SSI benefits. Because Mrs. Smith has been providing shelter, his benefits have been reduced (by one-third the benefit he would otherwise be entitled to receive ($552) plus $20). If he owns the home in his own name, or in the name of an OBRA '93 trust, that reduction should cease (because no one is now providing in-kind shelter for him). In fact, if the caretaker sibling pays utilities as part of his or her "rent" obligation, it may be possible to maintain the maximum SSI benefit while reducing or eliminating the cost of maintenance of the home.

If the remaining assets are also transferred to Mrs. Smith's disabled son, he may be disqualified from receiving SSI benefits. After December 14, 1999, any transfer by him of the money he receives from his mother will result in a period of ineligibility for continued SSI benefits *unless* the money is transferred into a "payback" OBRA '93 trust with provisions for repayment of any Medicaid benefits he may have received as of the time of his subsequent death, and keeping in mind that any payments for food, clothing, and shelter from the trust will be treated as in-kind support and maintenance, thereby reducing his benefits. Assuming that he has modest medical needs, such a trust may still be an excellent choice for his eligibility planning, and so a two-step transfer (Mrs. Smith to disabled son, disabled son to supplemental benefits trust), or even Mrs. Smith direct to "payback" trust, may be a viable planning choice.

Q 14:106 How might an elder law attorney assist a moderately wealthy unmarried Medicaid applicant in Medicaid planning?

Mr. Johnson, a widower age 75 and in poor health, has been turned down on his application to purchase long-term care insurance. He anticipates that he may soon require nursing home care. He is concerned about maintaining his assets for his own use and also wishes to maximize what he can leave to his children upon death. Like Mrs. Smith, his assets include a home, automobile, personal effects, and $400,000 in bank accounts and stocks (the financial accounts are mostly held in joint names with one or another of his three children). None of his children is disabled, although one daughter has lived with him since her divorce three years ago.

First, of course, Mr. Johnson must consider whether he wishes to adjust his assets and his plans to accommodate Medicaid eligibility. That question will be intensely personal and will depend on the quality of local Medicaid care, Mr. Johnson's desire to maintain control over his assets as long as possible, and his relationship with his children. Assuming that he chooses to plan for Medicaid eligibility, Mr. Johnson's choices are considerably narrower than in either of the preceding examples.

As in the other cases, in most states Mr. Johnson's home will remain an exempt asset as long as he intends to return home (in most states, intent to return home is determined solely by reference to the applicant's answer on the Medicaid application form itself). He may shelter additional assets by investing them in the home: by paying off any mortgage, adding onto or remodeling the home, or replacing furnishings, appliances, and fixtures. Of course, in his situation the state's estate recovery program may make the value of sheltering home assets problematic, because the home may need to be sold upon his death to repay benefits rather than transferred to his children.

Even if the effect of sheltering assets in his home is solely to delay payment of his nursing home costs, Mr. Johnson may consider taking such steps. By doing so, he not only avoids the interest costs on his nursing home care, but also takes advantage of Medicaid's strong purchasing power: The 15 percent (or more) savings his state's Medicaid agency can save in nursing home costs will ultimately be passed on to his estate even if it fully repays the cost of nursing home care.

Furthermore, in many states Mr. Johnson can consider transferring his home to his children while retaining both a life estate and the power to sell the property (and retain the proceeds) during his life. This may avoid the transfer penalty altogether, and prevent his estate from owning any interest in the property at his later death. If the "power of sale' is not recognized in his state, at least he can retain the life estate, incurring a shorter ineligibility period and keeping the home from his estate at death, thereby escaping the state's repayment claim. Finally, even though none of his children is disabled Mr. Johnson may be able to take advantage of another exception to the transfer penalty rules: transfer of a home to a child who resided with the Medicaid applicant for a period of three years and who provided care that prevented the applicant from requiring nursing care will not invoke a transfer penalty. In other words, if Mr. Johnson can show that his daughter provided care that kept him out of the nursing home, he may be able to give the house to her without incurring any period of ineligibility.

Even if Mr. Johnson can transfer his home to his daughter, or to all of his children while retaining a life estate (and the power to sell), problems remain. First, he must also dispose of the remaining (liquid) assets before becoming eligible. Second, once institutionalized he will be unable to afford the cost of maintaining the home (because nearly all of his income must be paid to the nursing home, even after Medicaid eligibility), so any plan must take into consideration the need for other family members to take over (and to be able to bear) the cost of maintenance.

Of course Mr. Johnson can simply give away both his home and his liquid assets, and incur the ineligibility penalty. Even though it will almost certainly exceed 36 months (depending on the average cost of care in his estate), the look-back period is limited to that 36-month period (provided, of course, that the transfer is not made out of a trust). Assuming that no application is made during that 36-month period, and that family members can pay any actual costs of care incurred, Mr. Johnson may be made eligible a great deal more quickly than he would if he simply paid for his own care until his money was exhausted. As his attorney, however, it will be important to point out that his family members could predecease him leaving "his" assets to others (by choice or by law); could be subject to the claims of creditors or divorcing spouses, and that it may be far too risky to put his future well being so completely in the hands of others, no matter how well intentioned. The attorney will also want to point out that at least as long as he owns his home he may be able to forestall the moment of relocation to a nursing home by obtaining a reverse mortgage on the home to increase liquid assets and thereby pay for home care.

Mr. Johnson may also consider an annuity, although it is likely to be beneficial only if his real life expectancy is considerably less than his actuarial life expectancy. In such a case, he might purchase an annuity, naming himself as annuitant, for the period of years of his remaining life expectancy, naming his children as alternate beneficiaries. Upon his earlier death, payments would flow to them without being subject to the Medicaid estate recovery program. Of course, in the meantime all of the annuity income would be used to pay for his care. That may not be a completely objectionable result if the total income (Social Security and annuity income) barely exceeds Medicaid's payments to the nursing home, because Mr. Johnson will have benefited from the purchasing power of Medicaid and still left something to his children upon his anticipated early demise. He may also purchase an annuity with a term certain longer than his life expectancy, and hope that the state agrees that his ineligibility is based only upon the difference between the price of the annuity with and without the additional term certain. [Hill v. Wilson-Coker, No. CV 02 0513538 (Conn. Sup. Ct. Feb. 18, 2003)]

Mr. Johnson might also consider entering into a personal services contract with one or more of his children. Under such an arrangement, he could pay a flat amount now for a promise of services (medical case management, transportation, respite care, etc.) for the rest of his life. Assuming that the purchase price is reasonable (so that no implication of gift is raised), it should not incur a transfer penalty and should permit his children to receive adequate compensation for the care they anticipate providing for their father. Personal service contracts have been easily accepted by some state Medicaid agencies, and resisted by others; proof of the reasonable value of the services may be problematic if the Medicaid agency challenges the arrangement.

Transfer Penalties—Data current to 2002–2003*

State	*Medicaid penalty divisor ($ = 1 month ineligibility)*
Alabama	$3,500.00
Alaska—north	community average (est. $10,000)
Alaska—south	community average (est. $12,000)
Arizona—Maricopa, Pima and Pinal counties (including Tucson and Phoenix)	$3,898.95
Arizona—other counties	$3,624.18
Arkansas	$1,700.00
California	$4,415.00
Colorado	$4,065.00
Connecticut	$7,602.00
Delaware	$4,245.60
District of Columbia	facility average
Florida	$3,300.00
Georgia	$3,131.00
Hawaii	$7,314.00
Idaho	$4,520.00
Illinois—north	facility average (est. $2,000.00)
Illinois—south	facility average (est. $5,000.00)
Indiana	$3,598.00
Iowa	$3,111.69
Kansas	$3,000.00
Kentucky	$2,560.00
Louisiana	$3,000.00
Maine	$3,917.00
Maryland	$4,300.00
Massachusetts	Est. $6,420.00 ($214/day)
Michigan	$5,043.00
Minnesota	$3,702.00
Mississippi	$3,100.00
Missouri	$2,625.00

Transfer Penalties—Data current to 2002–2003* *(cont'd)*

State	Medicaid penalty divisor ($ = 1 month ineligibility)
Montana	$3,684.00
Nebraska	facility average
Nevada	$4,583.00
New Hampshire	$5,627.00
New Jersey	$5,402.00
New Mexico	$4,188.00
New York—Central	$5,127.00
New York—Long Island	$8,272.00
New York—NE	$5,769.00
New York—Northern Metropolitan	$7,138.00
New York—NYC	$7,894.00
New York—Rochester	$5,745.00
New York—W	$5,393.00
North Carolina	$4,200.00
North Dakota	$3,945.00
Ohio	$3,903.00
Oklahoma	$2,000.00
Oregon	$4,300.00
Pennsylvania	$5,313.18
Rhode Island	$5,516.00
South Carolina	$3,719.65
South Dakota	$3,474.83
Tennessee	$3,394.00
Texas	$2,908.00
Utah	$3,118.00
Vermont	$4,927.00 (also uses $165/day for additional periods)
Virginia—North (DC suburbs)	$4,684.00
Virginia—South	$3,517.00
Washington	Est. $4,890.00 ($163/day)

Transfer Penalties—Data current to 2002–2003* *(cont'd)*

State	*Medicaid penalty divisor ($ = 1 month ineligibility)*
West Virginia	$3,380.00
Wisconsin	$4,542.00
Wyoming	$4,061.00

*Most "expensive" (highest divisor), starting at the top: Alaska, New York (Long Island), New York (Manhattan), Hawaii, New York (northern metropolitan), Connecticut, and Massachusetts.

**Lowest divisor (not necessarily least expensive), starting at the lowest end: Arkansas, Oklahoma, Kentucky, Missouri, and Texas.

Chapter 15

Social Security

Social Security refers to a form of social insurance wherein taxes collected from the employed are used to provide benefits to retired and disabled persons, and their dependents. Social Security covers retirement, disability, dependents, and survivor's benefits. This chapter discusses the various kinds of benefit programs, the application process, and issues a practitioner may encounter.

Overview

Q 15:1 What is Social Security?

Social Security was created during the post-Depression years in part to bring the income of senior citizens and disabled persons above the poverty line. Through Social Security and the Retirement (Old Age), Survivors, and Disability Insurance (OASDI) programs the federal government provides assistance to retired and disabled workers and their families. Social Security is not need-based, but rather is a benefit directly tied to a citizen's work history. Workers who pay FICA (Federal Insurance Contributions Act) taxes on minimum annual earnings during a minimum number of quarters are entitled to Social Security retirement and disability benefits, and will qualify their dependents for survivor's benefits.

Resources for researching Social Security law include:

- Social Security Act: *http://www.ssa.gov/OP_Home/ssact/*
- Social Security Regulations, 20 CFR: *http://www.ssa.gov/OP_Home/cfr20/cfrdoc.htm*
- Social Security Handbook: *http://www.ssa.gov/OP_Home/handbook/ssa-hbk.htm*
- Social Security administrative rulings: *http://www.ssa.gov/OP_Home/rulings/rulings.html*
- Social Security Program Operations Systems Manual or "POMS": *http://policy.ssa.gov/poms.nsf/poms?OpenView*
- Social Security Forms: *http://www.ssa.gov/online/forms.html*
- Claimant representatives' page: *http://www.ssa.gov/representation/*

Q 15:2 What Social Security benefits are available?

Social Security is actually a collection of different but related programs and benefits, including retirement and disability coverage, survivor's benefits, and the "lump-sum death benefit." In addition, spouses, dependent children, and parents may be eligible to receive benefits under an individual worker's coverage.

Q 15:3 What is the difference between Social Security and SSI?

Supplemental Security Income (SSI) is funded by tax revenues. Eligibility is based on age or disability *and* lack of income and assets. Work history is not relevant to an individual's entitlement to SSI benefits. In other words, SSI is a federal welfare program for the aged, blind, and disabled. Another way to say this is that SSI is "needs-based" (see chapter 16).

Social Security, on the other hand, is not a welfare program and is not "needs-based." Instead, it is a combination insurance and retirement savings program operated by the federal government. Qualification and amount of benefits are based on a worker's history of participation in the program and level of contributions. One portion of the Social Security program, Social Security Disability Insurance (SSDI), provides benefits to the disabled under rules similar to those of SSI. Eligibility for SSDI depends, however, on the work history of the disabled individual (or for those disabled prior to age 22, the work history of his or her retired or deceased parents).

Q 15:4 Can Social Security benefits be garnished or assigned?

No. The Social Security Act specifically provides that "the right of any person to any future payment ... shall not be transferable or assignable ... and none of the moneys paid or payable or rights existing under this statute shall be subject to levy, attachment, garnishment, or other legal process." [42 U.S.C. § 407(a)] Social Security payments held in a segregated account remain inviolate. [See, e.g., NCNB Financial Services v. Shumante, 829 F. Supp. 178 (W.D. Va. 1993)] They may or may not be protected if deposited to a joint account or commingled with other funds.

Because of the "non-assignment" provision, it has been successfully argued that a state Medicaid agency cannot require the spouse in an institution to assign income to the community spouse in order for him or her to meet the monthly maintenance needs allowance, or MMNA. [Robbins v. DeBuono, 218 F.3d 197 (2d Cir. 2000)]

Eligibility

Q 15:5 How does one qualify for Social Security benefits?

In general, the precondition for Social Security benefits is (1) having earned sufficient "quarters of coverage" (QC) or (2) having a specified family or dependent relationship with someone who has sufficient quarters of coverage (see Q 15:6).

The primary benefit goes to the worker who has "earned" the coverage. However, Social Security also provides some level of benefits to the following classes of individuals:

Spouses of insured retired, disabled, or deceased workers, if (1) at least age 62 (for retirement) or 60 (for survivor's benefits), or (2) disabled, or (3) widowed and not remarried, or (4) caring for the minor or disabled children of the worker.

Ex-spouses can have benefits the same as spouses if married to the worker for 10 years, and either not remarried, or remarried but only after turning 60.

Unmarried minor children (under age 18), or if age 19, are attending high school.

Disabled children who are over 18 but disabled from a disability that begin prior to age 22.

Grandchildren in some cases are treated as children (if the child is deceased and the grandchild is dependent).

Parents who were dependents of a deceased worker.

Note that a child includes a biological child, adopted child, and stepchild. [20 C.F.R. § 404.354]

Q 15:6 What is a "quarter of coverage"?

A quarter of coverage (or QC) is a calendar quarter of a year in which a worker received employment (or self-employment) income of a minimum amount, and as to which FICA was paid. [20 C.F.R. § 404.140] In 2002 the minimum quarterly income to qualify for a QC was $870. [20 C.F.R. § 404.110] For current benefit and qualification levels, including the earnings necessary for crediting a QC, see the Social Security Administration website (see *http://www.ssa.gov/cola/cola2002.htm*).

Eligibility for benefits depends on the number of quarters of coverage the worker has accumulated. Having 40 "quarters of coverage" makes one "fully insured." Having 6 quarters out of the 13 prior to application makes one "currently insured." [20 C.F.R. § 404.115] Either way, one can receive retirement benefits. However, for a worker to qualify for Social Security disability benefits on his or her own work record, the worker must be fully insured and must have worked 20 of the 40 quarters preceding the onset of the disability (see Q 15:17). [20 C.F.R. § 406.421] In other words one must work more to be eligible for Social Security Disability benefits than Social Security Retirement benefits. Farm workers, servicemen, employees of nonprofit organizations, and citizens working abroad are paid according to special regulations.

Provided a worker has the requisite number of quarters and is otherwise eligible, the worker will be entitled to a primary insurance amount (see Q 15:7), upon which the benefits of others will also be based.

Q 15:7 What is the "primary insurance amount"?

The basis for all calculations of Social Security benefits is the worker's primary insurance amount (PIA). The PIA is calculated based on Social Security contributions made by the worker during the entire work history, with more weight given to more recent contributions (so that a retiree's last earnings—presumably higher than earlier earnings—are given extra weight in the calculation). The PIA determines the amount of benefits that will be paid, although in the case of a retiree the PIA may be reduced for early retirement or enhanced for late retirement.

Q 15:8 What is the difference between employees and self-employeds for Social Security purposes?

Generally speaking, self-employed individuals are required to contribute to and are covered by Social Security just as if they were employees. [42 U.S.C. § 411] "Self-employment" is defined to exclude most passive investment income such as dividends and capital gains, rental income, and partnership income. [42 U.S.C. § 411(a)] Employees contribute 6.2 percent of their income to the Social Security program, and their employers contribute an equal amount. Self-employed individuals must pay both portions, and so their contribution is 12.4 percent of self-employment income. (The tax shows up as 15.3 percent rather than 12.4 percent due to the additional 2.9 percent Medicare tax; the payment on the self-employed's tax return is for 15.3 percent "self-employment tax.")

Q 15:9 What can affect a beneficiary's continued eligibility for benefits??

The Social Security Handbook Section 133.2 indicates that a recipient of benefits *must* notify the Administration of the following changes:

- A beneficiary (other than a disabled individual) is working and has, or expects to have, more earnings than the amount exempted under the earnings test;
- The marriage of a person who is entitled to child's, widow(er)'s, mother's, father's, parent's, or divorced spouse's insurance benefits;
- A beneficiary under age 62 entitled to spouse's, mother's, or father's insurance benefits who no longer has in care a child under age 16 or disabled that is entitled to benefits;
- A person entitled to benefits because of disability has either (1) returned to work; or (2) the condition has improved so that he or she is able to work;
- A non-disabled child beneficiary age 18 or over no longer attending elementary or secondary school full-time;
- The death of a beneficiary;
- A beneficiary works outside the United States for more than 45 hours in a calendar month;
- A person under age 65 who is entitled because of disability becomes entitled to compensation benefits, or there is a change in the public disability payment rate;
- Imprisonment for a conviction of a criminal offense that carries a sentence of more than one year;
- Individuals confined by court order to an institution at public expense following a verdict or finding that an individual has been found guilty by reason of insanity or similar verdict;
- A person begins to receive a governmental pension or annuity, or there is a change in a present pension amount and the person receives a spouse's Social Security benefit;
- A beneficiary leaves the United States;
- A beneficiary's citizenship or alien status changes; or
- A retirement or disability beneficiary is divorced from the parent of an entitled stepchild.

Not all of these may actually eliminate or affect benefits, but a failure to report a relevant change can result in a determination of overpayment that can lead to reduction in future benefits payments until the overpayment is recouped. Although the notice of these obligations is provided to every recipient, they are easily forgotten, and the attorney assisting the beneficiary should be alert for changes.

Retirement Benefits

Q 15:10 How does one qualify for Social Security retirement benefits?

The general rule is that a worker must earn a minimum amount for each of 40 quarters, or 10 years, before he or she can qualify for retirement benefits. [20 C.F.R. § 404.115] The quarters do not have to be consecutive. [20 C.F.R. § 404.110]

Thus, not everyone is entitled to Social Security retirement benefits. As explained in Q 15:6, "quarters" can only be earned by those who are (1) employees or self-employed persons, and (2) pay in to the FICA system their share of Social Security or self-employment tax. If taxes are not paid, quarter's are not earned. Stories abound of self-employed persons or workers paid "under the table," such as domestics or farm laborers, who become disabled or reach retirement age and cannot qualify for Social Security benefits. In addition, prior to 1986 most state and municipal employees were not covered by Social Security, and those who retired prior to that time may have negligible, if any, Social Security retirement benefits. (There is still a government pension offset for many such employees.)

Those who do not qualify for Social Security benefits will not receive automatic Medicare coverage and will have to "buy in" if he or she desires. The elder law attorney should include in the initial interview of all clients a determination of their eligibility or potential ineligibility for Social Security benefits.

Q 15:11 What is the amount of the Social Security retirement benefit?

Retirement benefits were always intended to provide supplemental income, and not be the sole source of income for retirees. The annual benefit averages only about $10,500 per year for a single retired person, and $17,450 for couples; the highest benefit in 2002 was $19,392 per year. Those who earned more during their lifetime will receive a larger check, but because the benefit is designed to offset poverty, low-income workers might get as much as 56 percent of their pre-retirement salary, while high-income workers could get as little as 28 percent (the average is 42 percent). Approximately 65 percent of those collecting benefits are senior citizens. Benefits are adjusted each year based on inflation.

Q 15:12 When can Social Security retirement benefits be collected?

A qualified worker can collect retirement benefits beginning at the age of 62, but he or she will pay a penalty for early participation. As of 2000, the full retirement age began increasing by two months every two years, and will reach the age of 67 by the year 2022. For example, in 2003 Social Security full retirement age is 65 years and two months. That is, while the earliest a person can start receiving Social Security retirement benefits will remain at age 62, the earliest a person can receive full retirement benefits is age 65 years and two months. The rule applies to persons born in or after 1938 (i.e., those turning 65 in 2003). For every month before the age of full retirement that the retiree begins collecting benefits, the benefits are cut five-ninths of 1 percent, up to a maximum of 20 percent. The longer an individual waits, the higher the income payment (by about 8 percent per year after 2008), until he or she attains age 70. The benefits do not continue increasing after the applicant reaches age 70. [20 C.F.R. § 404.313]

Although not directly related to Social Security benefits, Medicare eligibility is often confused with Social Security eligibility. It is important to realize that Medicare coverage does not begin until age 65 (Medicare's eligibility ages do not increase with the increase in Social Security's normal retriement age—at least not yet) regardless of retirement status.

Q 15:13 Can one defer collecting Social Security retirement benefits beyond the normal retirement age?

Yes. Social Security benefits can be delayed until age 70, and the monthly benefit amount will increase (in 2002) by thirteen twenty-fourths of 1 percent for each month retirement is delayed. [20 C.F.R. § 404.313] The increase in benefits for delayed retirement will increase every two years until 2008, at which time it will have reached two-thirds of 1 percent. [20 C.F.R. § 404.313] Social Security counselors will often recommend that the retiree not wait to collect, theorizing that the loss of benefits during the years of delay will not be offset by the increased figure unless the retiree lives an unusually long time. It is also important to remember that Medicare eligibility will not be delayed with delayed retirement.

Q 15:14 What Social Security benefits are available to an insured retiree's spouse and children?

Spouses of covered retired workers may be eligible for benefits if they are at least age 62, disabled, widowed, or caring for the minor or disabled children of the worker. [20 C.F.R. § 404.330] If age 62 or older, the spouse of a retiree is eligible to receive one-half of the living retiree's benefits (but if the spouse has a separate work history yielding greater benefits, he or she would receive the latter amount). [20 C.F.R. § 404.330] Children under age 18, children under age 19 who are enrolled in high school, and children over age 18 who are disabled (with a disability that commenced prior to age 22) are also eligible for benefits under the retirement program. Benefits are calculated on the basis of the retired parent's contribution and eligibility, and are one-half of the primary insurance amount. [20 C.F.R. § 404.350]

Spouses and minor children of an early retiree can collect as soon as the retiree begins collecting and thus boost the retiree's monthly family income by as much as 180 percent. If the worker waits until age 70, the spouse who is not covered by his or her own work history and any minor children must wait with the worker.

Q 15:15 What is the Senior Citizens' Freedom To Work Act of 2000?

Retirees receiving Social Security income were traditionally discouraged from earning significant outside income. This has generally been considered an anachronistic provision of the program, dating to Depression days when millions were out of work. A healthy economy and low unemployment have spurred federal legislators to raise, and finally eliminate, the cap on earnings for persons aged 65 to 69, with total repeal of the cap effective in 2002. Confusingly enough, the penalty for work after retirement continues to apply to those who retire (and begin receiving Social Security benefits) before their normal retirement age. For every two dollars earned (in 2003) over $11,520, a Social Security retirement recipient under age 65 will experience a one dollar reduction in Social Security benefits. If the working retiree reaches age 65 in 2003, he or she will experience a one dollar reduction in Social Security benefits for every three dollars earned over $30,720—but the reduction in benefits ends in the month in which the beneficiary reaches normal retirement age (65 years and 2 months in 2003).

Disability Benefits

Q 15:16 How does one qualify for disability benefits under Social Security?

Disability benefits are available to workers who were fully insured and worked 20 of the 40 quarters preceding the onset of the disability. [20 C.F.R. § 404.130] In addition, blind workers are categorically eligible for Social Security disability. [20 C.F.R. § 404.130] The benefits convert to retirement benefits when the worker reaches age 65. Because disability benefits are not needs-based, they are not reduced if there is income or gain from sources such as investments or personal injury proceeds. [20 C.F.R. § 404.316]

Q 15:17 What is a "disability"?

For Social Security purposes, a "disability" is physical or mental disability that is terminal or is expected to prevent the worker from maintaining gainful employment for at least 12 months. In determining whether there is a disability the Social Security Administration (SSA) will look to the severity of the impairment and whether the individual can perform any other substantial gainful activity. It will also consider functional capacity, age, education, and work experience. [20 C.F.R. § 404.1505] (For SSI disability for a child under age 18 is defined as a medically determinable physical or mental impairment that results in marked and severe functional limitations. [20 U.S.C. § 1382c(a)(3)(H)] Of course, for a minor child disability would be relevant to SSI (see chapter 16) but irrelevant for Social Security benefits.)

Q 15:18 Who determines whether a person is disabled?

Field offices of the Social Security Administration determine disability. An application can be filed at the local office to begin the process. The Social Security office will obtain a release from the applicant, copies of his or her medical records, and may schedule an evaluation. However, if a qualified professional has previously evaluated the individual, and it is important to argue the case at the initial level, it is permitted and appropriate to provide documentation and a brief with the application.

Q 15:19 How is the disability evaluated?

Eligibility for Social Security Disability benefits is based on the applicant's inability to perform any "substantial gainful activity," or "SGA," a number that change annually and for 2002 was $780 per month. The SSA applies a five-step evaluation process in determining disability:

1. If the applicant is working and the work is substantial gainful activity, he or she will not be found to be disabled regardless of medical condition or age, education, and work experience.
2. The applicant must have a severe impairment, one that significantly limits one's physical or mental ability to do basic work activities.
3. The impairment must be listed in the SSA's "Listing of Impairments" (the listing for adult applicants is available online at *www.ssa.gov/disability/professionals/bluebook/AdultListings.htm)* or be equal to one listed, and must be expected to last (or have already lasted) for 12 months, or to lead to the applicant's death.
4. The impairment must prevent the applicant from doing past relevant work.
5. The impairment must prevent the applicant from doing any other work.

[20 C.F.R. § 404.1520]

In some cases an individual who is or has had SGA can still qualify if he or she can show that the compensation was more than the value of the work performed, because of a "benevolent employer," such as a sheltered workshop or family member. Moreover, SGA is measured as net income—if the applicant had expenses in getting to or staying at the workplace, for example, those would be deductible from the gross income to reach the true measure of the earnings.

A long-standing problem has been that the Social Security Administration applies a test that considers work available *nationwide*, rather than work available in the individual's residential area. [Heckler v. Campbell, 461 U.S. 458 (1983)] The Administration uses a "grid" that matches age, disability, skill set, etc. against available work anywhere in the country.

Q 15:20 When can a person apply for disability benefits under Social Security?

The worker must wait at least five months before applying for disability benefits, and will be examined by an independent physician through a state agency subcontracted by the SSA called the Disability Determination Service. [42 U.S.C. § 425(a)(1)(A); 20 C.F.R. § 404.1503(a)] However, up to 12 months of benefits are available retroactively to the approved disabled worker, and up to six months for spouses or dependents. [20 C.F.R. § 406.421]

Q 15:21 What should the applicant do if the application is denied?

Initial applications are frequently denied, and as frequently appeals are successful. Elder law attorneys should encourage clients to take advantage of the appeals process, preferably by consulting an attorney who specializes in such cases. The Social Security Administration limits fee awards available to attorneys, so in most cases the specialist will not bother to become involved until the appeals stage. Applicants should maintain complete records of all communications, oral and written, and send all letters and applications by certified mail. The client will have only 60 days to file an appeal (see Q 15:33).

Q 15:22 What is the amount of the disabled worker's Social Security disability benefit?

The monthly benefit for a disabled worker is equal to the primary insurance amount. Benefits may be reduced if the worker also receives worker's compensation before age 62. Benefits may also be reduced if the applicant is entitled to other retirement-age benefits before age 65. [20 C.F.R. § 404.317]

Q 15:23 What Social Security benefits are available to the retiree's family members?

A qualified spouse entitled to benefits based on the record of a disabled worker is eligible to receive up to 50 percent. A qualified child who is entitled to benefits based on record of a disabled worker is eligible to receive up to 50 percent of the worker's PIA. (See Q 15:5.)

The amount paid may be limited by the family maximum amount (FMA). The amount that a family can be paid is limited depending on the amount of the worker's benefit and the number of family members qualifying on the worker's record. The total amount of benefits is approximately 150 to 180 percent of the worker's disability benefit.

Q 15:24 How does drug addiction or alcoholism affect the applicant's ability to receive Social Security Disability benefits?

Social Security disability benefits coverage periods may be shortened or eliminated if drug addiction or alcoholism are the *primary* disabling conditions. [20 C.F.R. § 404.316] Benefits will be paid to disabled persons with addictions or alcoholism only if they can prove that their disabling condition would continue even if their substance abuse stopped. Therefore, benefits are paid to those suffering permanent and terminal organ damage resulting from drug addiction or alcoholism.

Q 15:25 Is a person receiving Social Security Disability benefits required to undergo certain types of treatment?

Social Security Disability benefits are conditioned on the beneficiary's continued cooperation with treatment that might restore the beneficiary's ability to work. If the beneficiary's physician prescribes treatment that could restore the beneficiary's ability to work, the beneficiary is required to pursue the treatment. Limited exceptions are made if the beneficiary has moral or religious objections to the prescribed treatment, or if surgery has already been tried and is now being recommended again, or if the proposed treatment includes amputation of a limb or part of a limb. [20 C.F.R. § 404.1530] If, however, the condition is congenital, treatment is not likely to be required.

Q 15:26 Will returning to work affect disability benefits?

A Social Security Disability recipient is permitted to earn a nominal amount without affecting eligibility. The disability program is based on total disability: Any ability to engage in substantial gainful activity (SGA) is disqualifying and the amount of earnings is not completely determinative of the status of disability. There are, however, some guidelines in determining how income affects the continued status of disability:

1. Earnings of less than $560 per month (2002 figure) will ordinarily be presumed not to be substantial gainful employment (but note that the ability to earn more employment income will disqualify the beneficiary).
2. Earnings of over $780 per month (2002 figure) will ordinarily be presumed to be evidence of substantial gainful employment.
3. Earnings between those two figures will require the Social Security eligibility worker to evaluate all of the circumstances of the disability and employment.
4. Earnings in a "sheltered workshop" environment are treated specially, and will not disqualify the worker from eligibility. (See Q 15:19 for a discussion on "net" earnings and benevolent employers.)
5. Social Security disability recipients are usually entitled to a single lifetime nine-month trial work period to determine whether they are able to return to work. During the trial work period, income of less than $560 per month (2002 figure) will not count as substantial gainful employment. Income over that amount will not result in ineligibility, but will use one of the nine months of trial work eligibility. If at the end of the trial work period the individual is still unable to engage in SGA, he or she will continue to receive benefits.
6. Note that a disabled worker whose disability ends will lose Social Security benefits immediately, regardless of the trial work period rules. [20 C.F.R. § 404.430]

"Ticket to Work" Program

Q 15:27 What is the Ticket To Work and Self Sufficiency Program?

The Ticket to Work and Self Sufficiency Program (Pub. L. No. 106-170) became effective January 28, 2002; regulations may be found at 66 Fed. Reg. 67,369–67,442 (Dec. 28, 2001). The program provides beneficiaries with disabilities expanded options for access to employment services, vocational rehabilitation services, or other support services. The objective is to assist beneficiaries in obtaining, regaining, or maintaining employment in order to reduce dependency on Social Security and Supplemental Security Income benefits. Participation in the program is voluntary.

Q 15:28 Why was the Ticket To Work and Self Sufficiency Program created?

According to the National Organization on Disability/Harris Survey of 1998, only 29 percent of individuals with disabilities were employed in full- or part-time jobs. From 1986 to 1999, the number of people receiving disability benefits rose by 80 percent (half receiving Social Security, the other half Supplemental Security Income). This increase has been attributed to the aging of the work force as well as the outreach of the Social Security Administration. Furthermore, according to the U.S. General Accounting Office, less than 1 percent of beneficiaries leave the Social Security and Supplemental Security Income rolls each year as a result of employment.

Due to these circumstances resulting in heightened cost to the government, the Ticket to Work and Self Sufficiency Program was created. The goal of the program is to lessen the dependency of beneficiaries on Social Security and Supplemental Income benefits.

Q 15:29 How does the Ticket To Work and Self Sufficiency Program work?

In February of 2002, the Commissioner began issuing tickets to Social Security disability beneficiaries. Each beneficiary will have the option of using these tickets to obtain services from providers in the employment network. The ticketholder is to give the ticket to an employment network who will then work with the ticketholder in designing an employment plan outlining services that will be provided to help the beneficiary reach employment goals. Participating employment networks can be found online at *http://www.ssa.gov/work.*

Q 15:30 Is the ticketholder required to become employed as a result of the program?

No. The beneficiary/ticketholder is not required to work but may use their ticket to attempt to go to work.

Q 15:31 Has the Ticket to Work and Self Sufficiency Program begun operation?

Yes. The Commissioner started issuing tickets in February 2002. From February to July 2002 approximately 2.4 million beneficiaries (SS and SSI) in 13 states will receive a ticket to work. By 2004, all beneficiaries nationwide will have received tickets.

The tickets are being distributed in three issuing phases. The first phase, which began February 2002, will provide tickets to 13 states: Arizona, Colorado, Delaware, Florida, Iowa, Illinois, Massachusetts, New York, Oklahoma, Oregon, South Carolina, Vermont, and Wisconsin. The second phase will issue tickets in late 2002. The states in phase two are: Alaska, Arkansas, Connecticut, Georgia, Indiana, Kansas, Kentucky, Louisiana, Michigan, Mississippi, Missouri, Montana, New York, New Hampshire, New Jersey, New Mexico, North Dakota, South Dakota, Tennessee, Virginia, and the District of Columbia. The last ticket-distributing phase is scheduled to occur in 2003. The states in the last phase are: Alabama, California, Hawaii, Idaho, Maine, Maryland, Minnesota, Nebraska, North Carolina, Ohio, Pennsylvania, Rhode Island, Texas, Utah, Washington, West Virginia, and Wyoming as well as American Samoa, Guam, Northern Mariana Islands, Puerto Rico, and the Virgin Islands.

Q 15:32 Can a beneficiary receive a ticket sooner?

Yes. A beneficiary may request to receive a ticket to work immediately. To make this request, call 1-866-968-7842 (1-866-YOUR-TICKET) or for TDD/TTY users the number is 1-866-833-2967 (1-866-TDD2WORK). Ticket to Work program information can be found at *http://www.ssa.gov/regulations/rin0960_af11f.htm* or *http://www.ssa.gov/work/Ticket/ticket_info.html.*

Appeals

Q 15:33 What appeal rights do Social Security Disability applicants have?

Once denied benefits, claimants only have 60 days to request an appeal. [20 C.F.R. § 404.909] If the appeal is denied, they can request a hearing, at which documentation and testimony can be presented before a hearing officer (not a judge, and usually not even a lawyer). [20 C.F.R. § 404.914] Claimants who have been denied disability benefits have the right, when preparing for the hearing, to review the Social Security Administration file, and to be represented. The hearings are usually informal, and adherence to the rules of evidence is not required.

If the applicant does not file an appeal within 60 days of the initial denial and cannot present a good reason for the delay, the applicant may wait until the 6-month or 12-month retroactive benefits period passes, file a new application and request the reopening of the prior application before an administrative law judge (ALJ). [20 C.F.R. § 404.930] This is especially important when there is new medical or other evidence.

The ALJ's decision can be appealed to the SSA Appeals Council, in Arlington, Virginia, which reviews the case in its entirety to determine whether there has been an abuse of discretion of the ALJ or hearing officer, or legal, procedural, or policy issues that have been resolved incorrectly. [20 C.F.R. § 404.970] Finally, the Appeals Council decision can be appealed to federal court through a civil complaint, which must be filed within 60 days after the date notice of the Appeals Council's action is received. [20 C.F.R. § 404.981]

Q 15:34 How are attorneys involved in Social Security Disability determinations and appeals?

Social Security Disability is a complicated and highly focused practice, and most who work in the area specialize or limit their practices. Attorneys (including elder law attorneys in some cases) are limited by Social Security law as to what they can charge for their services. First, to appear as a representative, they must file SSA-Form 1696 and indicate whether they will or will not be requesting a fee award. In general, to have a fee paid directly to the attorney from the applicant's award, the attorney must agree to accept the lesser of $4,000 or 25 percent of the award (usually including the lump sum for retroactive benefits). [42 U.S.C. § 406] If instead the attorney has a fee agreement with the applicant, the agreement must be filed with and approved by the Social Security Administration. The alternative is for the attorney to submit a fee petition to the Office of Hearings and Appeals, where it is decided by the administrative law judge who reaches a determination on the appeal. [20 C.F.R. §§ 404.1720–404.1735] However, if the matter is heard in federal court, the judge may approve a higher fee. Fees for any representation before the court must be approved by the court. [42 U.S.C. § 406(b)] (Note that an attorney who is serving as fiduciary, and therefore subject to oversight and approval by a court with respect to the fees assessed, is not subject to these requirements.)

A troubling issue is whether this limit also applies if a third party, such as a family member, gratuitously chooses to pay the attorney. It is fairly well established that the fee is limited if the attorney is paid by someone acting on behalf of the applicant, such as an insurance company or employer. Practitioners report mixed conclusions about the limitations on fees where a grandparent hires the attorney, who then charges the applicant nothing. This is particularly questionable when the attorney is asked to assist at the initial application level so that the request for approval does not go to the Office of Hearings and Appeals, which ordinarily rules on fee requests. Even the Social Security Administration Form SSA-1696 includes in its remarks, "Even when someone else will pay the fee for you, for example, an insurance company, your representative usually must get our approval."

Survivor's Benefits

Q 15:35 What are Social Security survivor's benefits?

Social Security "survivor's benefits" might also be viewed as a form of life insurance. Survivor's benefits are benefits that are payable to the widowed spouse, ex-spouse (marriage of 10 years or more and not remarried), minor or disabled (disability commencing prior to age 22), or dependent parent of a deceased worker who was insured at the time of death. The purpose of the survivor's benefits program is to provide support that the worker had provided to the family members when the worker dies. To be entitled to survivor's benefits, the deceased worker must have earned a sufficient amount of credits. The number of credits varies depending on the age of the decedent, and the maximum number of credits is 40.

Q 15:36 How long must the worker have been employed before his or her survivors may be entitled to benefits?

Before survivor's benefits can be paid to a worker's "survivors," the worker must have enough quarters of coverage to qualify as either "fully insured" or "currently insured." A worker is "fully insured" so that his or her family members can collect dependents' benefits, if he or she has either 40 total quarters of coverage or one quarter of coverage for each calendar year since turning 21—provided that there are at least six quarters of coverage. [42 U.S.C. § 414(a)] A worker is "currently insured" if, at the time of death, disability, or reaching retirement age, he or she had six quarters of coverage in the 13 quarters immediately preceding death, retirement, or disability. [42 U.S.C. § 414(b)]

Q 15:37 What is the amount of the survivor's benefit?

The amount of survivor's benefits is based on the average lifetime earnings of the deceased worker. The higher the worker's earnings, the higher the benefit will be. The amount received is a percentage of the deceased worker's Social Security benefit that varies depending on the age and type of benefit for which the family member is eligible. The amount that a family can be paid is limited depending on the amount of the worker's benefit and the number of family members qualifying on the worker's record. [20 C.F.R. § 404.304] An estimate of the survivor's benefits can be obtained from the Social Security Administration by filing a Form SSA-7004, Request for Personal Earnings and Benefit Estimate Statement.

The spouse's benefit will usually be 100 percent of the deceased worker's benefit, with some exceptions (see Q 15:43).

In addition, there is a special one-time death benefit payment of $255 that can be made to the surviving spouse or minor children. [20 C.F.R. § 404.390]

Q 15:38 Who is eligible to receive survivor's benefits?

Survivor's benefits are available for dependents of a worker who has qualified for Social Security status, including spouses (and ex-spouses of 10-year or more marriages), children who are minor or disabled (from a disability commencing prior to age 22), and dependent parents. Children receive benefits until they marry or turn age 18 (age 19 if they are full-time students), except that disabled children receive benefits throughout their lifetimes. Mothers who care for disabled children can collect survivor's benefits immediately, rather than wait until the usual required age of 60 years. [20 C.F.R. § 404.339] Survival and spousal benefits are especially important for full-time housewives who never paid into the FICA system, because they would not otherwise be eligible for retirement or Medicare benefits.

Dependent's Benefits

Q 15:39 Can others receive Social Security benefits on the account of a retired or disabled worker, while the worker is living?

Social Security benefits may be payable to the retired or disabled worker's spouse (including divorced spouses), the worker's children, the parent of the worker's children and even the worker's parents, depending on the circumstances. Eligibility for dependent's and survivor's benefits will depend not only on the relationship of the claimant to the worker, but also on the type of benefits available to the worker.

Q 15:40 Are spouses of disabled and retired workers eligible for Social Security benefits?

Yes. The spouse of a disabled or retired wage earner [42 U.S.C. § 402(e)(2)(A)] or a disabled surviving spouse of a wage earner is eligible for Social Security benefits [42 U.S.C. § 423(d)(2)(B)]. The spouse is entitled to spouse's benefits based on the earnings record of the worker if the claimant:

1. Filed an application for spouse's benefits;

2. Is age 62 or older, or has in his or her care a child entitled to child's benefits; and
3. Is not entitled to retirement or disability benefits or is entitled to retirement or disability benefits based on a PIA that is less than half of the PIA of the worker.

Q 15:41 What benefits will the spouse of a living retired or disabled worker be entitled to receive?

The spouse's benefit is one-half of the worker's PIA. [42 U.S.C. §§ 402(b), 402(c)] The spouse who is entitled to benefits on his or her own account will receive whichever benefit is greater but will not receive both benefits. [42 U.S.C. §§ 402(b) (for wives), 402(c) (for husbands)]

Q 15:42 What benefits will the spouse of a deceased worker be entitled to receive?

Upon the death of a retired worker, the eligible surviving spouse (or ex-spouse; see Q 15:43) generally will receive 100 percent of the worker's PIA.

There are several exceptions to this rule. If the surviving spouse's own PIA is greater, he or she will not receive any additional benefit from the deceased worker's account. If the surviving spouse is over 60 years old but has not yet reached full retirement age, his or her survivor's benefit will be reduced. [42 U.S.C. §§ 402(e) (for widows), 402(f) (for widowers)] If the surviving spouse is under age 60 and has the worker's children in his or her care, he or she will be entitled to a "mother's" or "father's" benefit of 75 percent of the worker's PIA. [42 U.S.C. § 402(g)]

> **Example.** Mary, who is 70, has a Social Security retirement benefit of $800 per month. John, her husband, who is 75, has a benefit of $1,200 per month. (If Mary's own benefit were only $200, she would instead receive $600, one-half of John's benefit amount.) Together, they have $2,000 per month. When John dies, Mary receives John's $1,200 and no longer receives her own. Her check will have John's Social Security number as the "claim number."

Q 15:43 Can a divorced spouse receive "spouse's" retirement or disability benefits based on the earnings record of a living worker?

Yes. The divorced spouse is entitled to spouse's benefits based on the earnings record of the worker if the claimant:

1. Filed an application for spouse's benefits;
2. Is age 62 or older, or has in his or her care a child entitled to child's benefits;
3. Was married to the worker for at least 10 years prior to the date when the divorce became final;
4. Is not married; and
5. Is not entitled to retirement or disability benefits or is entitled to retirement or disability benefits based on a PIA that is less than half of the worker's PIA.

Divorced persons can collect (even if the former spouse is not) if they were married 10 years to a covered worker, the marriage terminated at least two years prior to the application, and the applicant has not remarried. [20 C.F.R. § 404.331]

Q 15:44 What benefits will the ex-spouse of a deceased worker be entitled to receive?

Divorced spouses of *deceased* workers can receive spouse's or survivor's benefits if previously married to the covered worker for at least 10 years, the applicant is at least age 60, and is unmarried. [42 U.S.C. § 416(d); 20 C.F.R. § 404.336] If the divorced spouse is caring for the deceased worker's child who is under age 16 or disabled, and who is also getting Social Security benefits under the worker's record, the 10-year marriage requirement does not apply. Divorced spouses cannot receive survivor's benefits if they remarry. [42 U.S.C. §§ 402(b), 402(c); 20 C.F.R. § 404.332(b)(3)] One important exception: Survivor's benefits (but not wife's or husband's benefits) can continue after remarriage provided that the marriage occurs after the surviving spouse has reached age 60 (or age 50 if disabled). [42 U.S.C. §§ 402(e)(3), 402(f)(4); 42 C.F.R. 404.336]

Q 15:45 When do a spouse's or ex-spouse's benefits end?

The spouse's benefits generally end if the spouse dies, if a divorced spouse remarries (unless the remarriage is after age 60), or if the spouse—divorced or otherwise—becomes entitled to a larger benefit from another source (including his or her own Social Security benefits, or in the case of the remarried ex-spouse over age 60, from his or her spouse's benefits). [20 C.F.R. § 404.332]

Q 15:46 What benefits will the deceased worker's parents be entitled to receive?

Parents of a deceased retired worker may be entitled to benefits based on the deceased worker's account in some circumstances. It is important to distinguish the "parent's" benefit from the "mother's" and "father's" benefits payable to the mother or father of the deceased worker's children (see Q 15:43). In order to qualify for a "parent's" benefit, the parent or parents of the deceased worker must be at least age 60 and have relied on the worker for at least half of his, her, or their support prior to the worker's death, and not be entitled to a higher benefit on his, her, or their own Social Security account. A single parent will be entitled to a benefit of 82.5 percent of the PIA; if both parents qualify they will each receive 75 percent of the PIA. The parent's benefit will cease if the parent remarries after the worker's death. [42 U.S.C. § 402(h)]

Q 15:47 What benefits may the child or children of a *living* retired or disabled worker receive?

Children under age 18 (or under age 19 and attending elementary or high school) are entitled to benefits under the retired parent's account. In addition, a child over age 18 who became mentally or physically disabled prior to reaching age 22 may also qualify for children's benefits. Social Security includes adopted children and children born out of wedlock within the definition. The benefit payable to the child of a retired or disabled worker who is still living is generally one-half of the PIA. [42 U.S.C. § 402(d)]

Q 15:48 What benefits will the child of a *deceased* worker be entitled to receive?

Upon the death of a covered worker the child's benefit increases to 75 percent of the PIA. [42 U.S.C. § 402(d)(2)]

Q 15:49 Can stepchildren receive survivors benefits?

Stepchildren can collect survivor's benefits if the worker was providing at least half the child's support.

Q 15:50 Are there any reductions in dependents' or survivors' benefits based on multiple beneficiaries?

Yes. The benefits payable to dependents (but not the worker's own benefits) are reduced as necessary to keep the total payment at a family maximum amount. This maximum total benefit amount is calculated as a series of percentages, beginning with 150 percent of an initial share of the PIA and varying at four different levels, with the percentage ranging as high as 272 percent of portions of the PIA. The precise adjustment points for the four percentage values are changed each year according to changes in Social Security's cost-of-living adjustments, so it is difficult to calculate the actual family maximum for any worker in a given year. Thus, if one or more spouses (remember that a "spouse" can be one who is divorced from the worker but was married for more than 10 years), one or more children, one or more parents of the worker's children, and one or more parents all qualify for benefits, their benefits will be reduced proportionally so that the total amount paid to the worker and dependents will not exceed the family maximum amount. [42 U.S.C. § 403]

Q 15:51 How much must a wage earner pay toward Social Security each year?

Employees and their employers each contribute 6.2 percent of gross salary to the Social Security system, and another 1.45 percent each to Medicare. In other words, FICA contributions will total 15.3 percent of earnings, with half paid by the employer and half paid by the employee. FICA tax is due on the first $80,900 (2002 figure) of an employee's earnings; earnings in excess of that amount are not taxed for Social Security. [42 U.S.C. § 409] Current cost-of-living figures are available online at *http://www.ssa.gov/cola/cola2002.htm.*

Q 15:52 Do the self-employed pay more in Social Security taxes?

Yes, but only because no employer makes payments on behalf of the self-employed. Those who work for themselves contribute 15.3 percent of earnings, with the same $80,900 cap on covered income for 2002.

Q 15:53 Is Social Security income taxed?

Federal income tax is due on up to 50 percent of Social Security benefits when the recipient's adjusted gross income plus one-half of Social Security benefits exceeds $25,000 for a single person or $32,000 for a married couple (in 2002). [20 C.F.R. § 404.430] If the same calculation yields an amount greater than $34,000 for a single person or $44,000 for a married couple, 85 percent of the Social Security income over those second threshold amounts is subject to income taxation.

Q 15:54 What happens if the benefits recipient is overpaid?

The Social Security Administration periodically reviews its cases and may discover overpayments, which are calculated strictly on applicable eligibility requirements, not the circumstances of the error. Social Security is especially unforgiving with regard to overpayment.

Overpayment determinations may be appealed, but an appeal must be made within 30 days of the determination. [20 C.F.R. § 404.506] The SSA considers three factors in determining appeals:

1. whether a claimant was actually overpaid,
2. whether the overpayment amount was correctly computed, and
3. whether the recipient is entitled to a waiver of the overpayment.

A request for reconsideration and request for waiver can be made at the same time. To be eligible for a waiver, the individual must show (1) that he or she was "without fault," and (2) that either (a) he or she is unable to pay (recovery of the overpayment would reduce funds necessary for living expenses of the recipient) or (b) repayment would be "against equity and good conscience"—typically, when the recipient adversely relied on the overpayment to a point where recovery would be unjust. [20 C.F.R. § 404.506] A factor in determining "fault" is whether the beneficiary accepted benefits he or she knew to be incorrect. [20 C.F.R. § 404.507(c)] A factor in determining whether repayment would be "against equity" will be whether or not the individual was worse off as a result of the overpayment [20 C.F.R. 404.509(a)], for example, because he or she was overpaid from one worker's account at a time when he or she might have received more had he or she claimed on another person's account.

While a waiver may be hard to achieve, it is not uncommon to reach an accommodation with Social Security whereby repayment is made through a modest reduction in the benefit check payable over a period of time until the entire overpayment has been recovered. [20 C.F.R. § 404.515(e)] A scheduled repayment will be made available where the individual "does not have the present or prospective ability to pay the full amount of the claim within a reasonable time." [20 C.F.R. § 404.515(a)]

Q 15:55 What if the Social Security benefits are not enough to live on?

Social Security recipients who meet Supplemental Security Income eligibility requirements may receive benefits from both programs, although the total received will not exceed the SSI maximum benefit rate ($552 per month in 2003). (See chapter 16 for a discussion of Supplemental Security Income.)

Application for Benefits

Q 15:56 How does one apply for benefits?

To receive benefits an applicant or designated representative must complete, sign, and file a formal application. Some forms, such as the appointment of representative form, may be obtained online at *http://www.ssa.gov/online/forms.html;* others, such as Form 3368A, the form required with a disability application, can only be completed by a Social Security Administration officer at an office visit, but may be completed in draft using the sample available online.

An application is considered filed the day it is received by a Social Security Administration representative, although an earlier informal written communication received by SSA may be sufficient proof of initiation of the application for purposes of retroactive benefits, if a formal application is eventually submitted as well. [20 C.F.R. § 404.630]

Q 15:57 Must the applicant have an interview in person with the representative?

For retirement benefits, no. One can apply for SS retirement online at *www.ssa.gov/applytoretire.htm*, or over the phone. For disability benefits, an interview may be required at some point, although a duly appointed representative may appear at the initial interview. A field representative who can assist with and accept the application will visit disabled applicants who cannot travel from home. If, however, the applicant is incompetent and has an appointed conservator, the conservator may attend the interview.

Q 15:58 Where are Social Security offices located?

The Social Security Administration, which separated from the Department of Health and Human Services in 1995, is divided into 10 regions and has more than 1,300 district offices throughout the country. Social Security office locations can be obtained online at *http://s3abaca.ssa.gov/pro/fol/fol-home.html*, or by calling the Administration toll-free number, 1-800-772-1213.

Q 15:59 How does one know if he or she is covered by Social Security?

As of October 1999, the Social Security Administration is required to provide all persons age 25 and older with an annual Earnings and Benefit Estimate Statement, which includes their earnings history and the expected rate of payment at retirement. Anyone may request this statement at any time, either by calling (800) 772-1213 or going through the SSA web page: *www.ssa.gov*. The site includes a program to help calculate the primary insurance amount (monthly benefit) and other benefits. The website also includes statistical tables and actuarial information and the Social Security Handbook, which provides detailed answers to innumerable questions about Social Security benefits and procedures.

Q 15:60 What if there is a mistake on the Earnings and Benefits Statement?

SSA will accept corrections to the worker's record up to April 15 of the fourth year after the year in which the incorrectly listed earnings were paid. This deadline will be extended under special circumstances, and an employee can sue an employer for failing to comply with income reporting and withholding requirements.

Receipt of Benefits

Q 15:61 Must all Social Security benefits be received by direct deposit to the recipient's bank account?

As of January 1, 1999, all Social Security and SSI recipients must have direct deposit for their monthly income benefits. Exceptions are based on hardship, certain kinds of checks, and whether the individual can certify that he or she does not have a bank account. The bank account must be in the individual's own name or in joint names, not into the name of a third party.

Q 15:62 What if the Social Security benefits recipient is under guardianship or conservatorship?

The Social Security Administration believes it has its own protective regime when it comes to Social Security beneficiaries. It will deal only with (1) the beneficiary himself or herself, or (2) the "Representative Payee" that has been appointed by the Administration pursuant to a formal application on a Social Security form. Court appointment as guardian of the person or conservator of the estate may or may not qualify the appointee as Representative Payee. Social Security may choose not to accept the state court's determination of incapacity (especially where state law avoids any requirement of finding of legal incompetence), and even if Social Security agrees that the beneficiary is incompetent the agency may determine that a caretaker or family member should have priority for appointment as Representative Payee over the court-appointed fiduciary. Usually, however, the Social Security Administration will appoint a guardian or conservator as Representative Payee.

Q 15:63 What are the obligations of a Representative Payee?

Social Security reporting requirements are different from (and usually considerably less exacting than) state court reporting requirements imposed on guardians and conservators. However, the report is required no matter how small the amount of funds, and will be required even after the beneficiary's death. Moreover, the Representative Payee is required to expend the Social Security benefit exclusively on the beneficiary. This can be problematic if the benefits are accumulated in an account and it becomes desirable to make a gift of the benefits. Furthermore, as commingling is not permitted, the account required for the funds may result in probate (or affidavit requirements) that would not otherwise have been required. If the beneficiary is married, the check may be deposited to the couple's joint account without need for Representative Payee, which may be significantly easier to cope with. Many practitioners urge clients and attorneys to avoid being appointed Representative Payee if at all possible.

When a beneficiary is a nursing home resident on title XIX, it is common practice for the nursing home to seek appointment as Representative Payee. On the plus side, this saves trouble for the family and there is no danger of the beneficiary's bank account exceeding the $2,000 or lower asset limit for benefits. On the negative side, there is then no opportunity to use the "applied income" towards medical expenses not otherwise provided, as might be possible depending on state law. In an analogous situation, the U.S. Supreme Court has held that a state agency serving as Representative Payee for foster children could apply the Social Security benefit against the costs of the foster children's care. [Washington State Department of Social and Health Services v. Guardianship of Keffeler, 123 S. Ct. 1017 (2003), *reversing,* 145 Wash. 2d 1, 32 P. 3d 267 (2001)].

Q 15:64 What happens when the primary wage earner dies?

If the wage earner was a retiree or disabled and collecting benefits, the decedent's Social Security checks will not be paid for the month in which he or she dies. Benefits are paid retroactively on the third day of the following month, so Social Security must be notified of the death; if the check is actually paid (or more commonly, automatically deposited in the decedent's bank account), it will be deducted from that account. A small lump-sum death payment will be paid to the spouse or other dependent person.

Usually, the funeral director will notify Social Security of the death, or possibly the town Vital Records department when issuing the death certificate. If this is not done, the family must notify the Administration.

Practice-Related Issues

Q 15:65 How do Social Security issues typically arise in an elder law practice?

Following is a discussion of some Social Security-related issues typically encountered in an elder law practice:

1. *Taxation of Social Security Income.* Richard and Susanna are married. They retired in late 2000, and both now receive Social Security benefits. Their total Social Security income in 2001 is $16,000. In addition, their adjusted gross income for the year totals $40,000. They wonder whether they will have to pay income taxes, and what they can do to minimize any tax problems in future years.

   To calculate Richard and Susanna's income tax liability, their adjusted gross income and one-half of Social Security income must be compared to the two figures that determine tax liability: $32,000 and $44,000. Their "modified adjusted gross income" (adjusted gross income plus one-half of Social Security receipts) totals $48,000. That figure is more than the $32,000 threshold for taxation of Social Security, and so at least one-half of their Social Security income is subject to taxation. In addition, their modified adjusted gross income exceeds the second threshold by another $4,000. Up to 85 percent of that excess amount will be subject to income taxation. In Richard and Susanna's case, they will pay tax on one-half of the first $12,000 of Social Security income, and on 85 percent of the remaining $4,000.

There is little Richard and Susanna can do about taxation of their 2001 income. In future years they might consider deferring non-Social Security income by, for example, purchasing annuities, or investing for growth rather than income.

2. *Remarriage of a Social Security recipient.* Meredith, a widow, receives Social Security benefits based on her late husband's account. She has met an elderly gentleman, himself retired, and is considering marrying him. Several of her friends have advised her to just move in with her gentleman friend, because marrying him might affect her Social Security benefits.

   Remarriage will terminate Meredith's entitlement to her late husband's Social Security benefits unless she is over age 60 (age 50 if she is disabled). She would still be entitled to receive benefits on her own account (although those benefits would apparently be lower than her late husband's benefit), and she would be entitled to receive one-half of the amount of her new husband's Social Security benefit after nine months of marriage. If her new husband dies, she would be entitled to the greater of her own benefit or 100 percent of his benefit.

3. *Losing Social Security Disability benefits.* Roger has received SSDI payments for two years, based on a disabling injury he suffered in an accident. He has been trying to build up his strength and skills and to re-enter the job market. He started a part-time job several months ago, but is not sure he will be able to continue to work. He is now concerned that his SSDI benefits might be cut off, despite the fact that his doctor still lists him as disabled.

A disability finding relies heavily on medical evidence but is not solely determined by the physician's work recommendation. The ability to perform any substantial gainful activity disqualifies the SSDI recipient. Roger's ability to hold a job may be evidence of the end of his disability period—and his SSDI coverage.

Roger is permitted up to nine months of work during his current disability as a "trial" work period. After he successfully works for nine months, he will no longer be considered disabled and his benefits will end. His benefits might end before that date if the Social Security Administration decides that he is no longer disabled.

If Roger does not earn $530 during a given month, he is not considered employed for purposes of the nine-month trial work period. He can reduce the likelihood of problems by holding his monthly earnings below that level, but if he is able to earn more he may lose his benefits even though he does not actually earn the higher amount.

Chapter 16

Other Benefit Programs

Medicaid, Medicare, or Social Security provide at least some benefits for the vast majority of elderly Americans. Although less common, several other government benefits programs touch the lives of at least some elders. This chapter discusses the Supplemental Security Income (SSI) program, veteran's benefits, and the Railroad Retirement program.

Supplemental Security Income

Q 16:1 What is the Supplemental Security Income program?

Supplemental Security Income (SSI) [42 U.S.C. §§ 1381 et seq.] benefits are payable to elderly, blind, or disabled individuals who qualify financially. It is a federal welfare program, with both financial and categorical eligibility requirements. SSI benefits may be paid to children as well as adults.

Q 16:2 How is SSI different from Social Security benefits?

Social Security Disability and Retirement benefits are essentially a contribution-based insurance and annuity program operated by the federal government. In other words, the benefits due to a participant are calculated based on his or her contributions, and eligibility is determined by having met minimum contribution levels. Supplemental Security Income, on the other hand, is a government welfare program, with benefits payable to anyone who is both disabled and poor—with poverty defined according to complex and stringent financial eligibility rules.

Q 16:3 Who administers SSI?

SSI is administered by the Social Security Administration. Funding for SSI is separate from the Social Security trust fund, and comes from annual appropriations.

Q 16:4 How can one contact the Social Security Administration?

The Social Security Administration has 10 regional and 1,300 offices throughout the United States. They can be contacted toll free at 1-800-772-1213. The hearing impaired may call toll free 1-800-325-0778. The SSA also has a valuable and fact-filled website at *www.ssa.gov*.

Q 16:5 What is the maximum SSI benefit?

SSI benefits are set at a maximum amount, which increases annually (in January) in concert with the increase in Social Security benefits (based on increases in the cost of living). For 2002, the maximum federal benefit rate is $545 for a single disabled SSI recipient, and $817 for a married couple.

In addition, some states pay a supplemental amount administered by the Social Security Administration. SSI recipients living in California, Delaware, Hawaii, Iowa, Massachusetts, Michigan, Montana, Nevada, New Jersey, New York, Pennsylvania, Rhode Island, Utah, Vermont, Washington (state), or Washington, D.C. will receive a supplement that may take their total benefits higher than the federal maximum. The additional benefit varies widely, from Utah's $4.60 supplement paid only to couples to California's $182 for an elderly or disabled individual or $475 for married couples (2001 figures in each instance).

Twenty-eight other states administer a separate state subsidy program, providing generally small additional payments to at least some SSI recipients. Such state benefits must be applied for separately from SSI benefits. State-administered supplements are available in Alabama, Alaska, Arizona, Colorado, Connecticut, Florida, Idaho, Illinois, Indiana, Kentucky, Louisiana, Maine, Maryland, Minnesota, Missouri, Nebraska, New Hampshire, New Mexico, North Carolina, North Dakota, Ohio, Oklahoma, Oregon, South Carolina, South Dakota, Texas, Virginia, Wisconsin, and Wyoming. This information is available at *www.ssa.gov/notices/supplemental-security-income/text-understanding-ssi.htm.*

Q 16:6 What is the maximum SSI benefit?

SSI benefits are set at a maximum amount, which increases annually (in January) in concert with the increase in Social Security benefits (based on increases in the cost of living). For 2003, the maximum federal benefit rate is $552 for a single SSI recipient, and $829 for a married couple.

In addition, some states pay a supplemental amount administered by the Social Security Administration. SSI recipients living in California, Delaware, Hawaii, Iowa, Massachusetts, Michigan, Montana, Nevada, New Jersey, New York, Pennsylvania, Rhode Island, Utah, Vermont, Washington (state), or Washington, D.C. will receive a supplement that may take their total benefits higher than the federal maximum.

Twenty-eight other states administer a separate state subsidy program, providing generally small additional payments to at least some SSI recipients. Such state benefits must be applied for separately from SSI benefits. State-administered supplements are available in Alabama, Alaska, Arizona, Colorado, Connecticut, Florida, Idaho, Illinois, Indiana, Kentucky, Louisiana, Maine, Maryland, Minnesota, Missouri, Nebraska, New Hampshire, New Mexico, North Carolina, North Dakota, Ohio, Oklahoma, Oregon, South Carolina, South Dakota, Virginia, Wisconsin, and Wyoming.

Q 16:7 For what other benefits will an SSI recipient qualify?

In addition to the monthly SSI benefit, in most states an SSI beneficiary will automatically qualify for both food stamps and

Medicaid coverage. Medicaid, of course, covers both urgent care needs and long-term nursing care; because SSI benefits are suspended during periods of institutionalization at state or federal expense, SSI recipients will not normally automatically receive institutional nursing care services. General medical coverage through Medicaid is often the most important element of the SSI recipient's benefits, because doctor's visits, hospital and outpatient care, prescription medicines, and in-home services may be worth many times the direct SSI benefit amount each month in at least some cases.

Q 16:8 Who is eligible to receive SSI benefits?

SSI is available to applicants who meet two separate sets of eligibility standards. The recipient must be either blind, elderly, or disabled *and* must qualify financially. The recipient must also be a citizen of the United States or a qualified alien and resident of the United States. [42 U.S.C. § 1382(f)] (See Q 14:15.) Residents of a public institution are not eligible for SSI. [20 C.F.R. § 416.211] A public institution is "an establishment that makes available some treatment or services in addition to food and shelter to four or more persons who are not related to the proprietor." [20 C.F.R. § 416.201]

Q 16:9 Who is not eligible to receive SSI benefits?

Fugitive felons and those housed in public institutions (including prison or jail) will have benefits suspended during their incarceration or fugitive status. A beneficiary who makes gifts may be disqualified from receiving SSI benefits for a period of months calculated by dividing the total amount of gifts by the maximum SSI benefit.

Q 16:10 When may a noncitizen be eligible for SSI?

Beginning August 22, 1996, noncitizens must meet two requirements to be eligible for SSI. The noncitizen must be a "qualified alien" and meet an exception condition that allows qualified aliens to get SSI. There are eight categories of "qualified aliens" (details can be found at *http://www.ssa.gov/notices/supplemental-security-income/text-understanding-ssi.htm*). (See also Q 14:16 (because Medicaid rules are to a considerable extent dependent on SSI regulations, many questions of SSI eligibility are also treated in any discussion of Medicaid eligibility).)

Q 16:11 What are the categorical requirements for SSI eligibility?

An SSI recipient must fit into one of three categories: blind, elderly, or disabled. [42 U.S.C. § 1382c(a)(1)(A)] For SSI purposes, those categories are defined as follows:

1. *Blind.* Vision must be limited to 20/200 or less in the better eye *after correction* or the field of vision must be less than 20 degrees. Note that a person with poor vision who does not meet these criteria may nonetheless qualify as disabled if the vision impairment is sufficient to prevent any substantial gainful employment.
2. *Elderly.* Age 65 or older.
3. *Disabled.* Physical or mental impairment that prohibits the applicant from performing any substantial work and that is expected to last at least 12 months (or lead to the applicant's death). In the case of a child, the test requires the applicant to have "marked and severe functional limitations" as a result of a physical or mental impairment.

[42 U.S.C. § 1382c(a)]

Q 16:12 What are the financial requirements for SSI eligibility?

Because SSI is a means-tested program, SSI recipients must meet income and resource requirements. Long-term care Medicaid eligibility rules (discussed at length in chapter 14) are actually based on SSI financial eligibility requirements, and most of the specifics contained in that discussion apply here as well.

Q 16:13 What are the SSI resource eligibility requirements?

SSI resource eligibility requires that a single applicant have no more than $2,000 in countable resources. A married applicant and his or her spouse must have less than $3,000 of countable resources (even if only one spouse is applying for SSI eligibility). [20 C.F.R. § 416.1205(c)] Resources are defined as "cash or other liquid assets or any real or personal property that an individual (or spouse, if any) owns and could convert to cash to be used for his or her support and maintenance." [20 C.F.R. § 426.1201(a)]

Noncountable resources include:

- Applicant's home
- Tools of trade or business
- Automobile used for employment or medical purposes (if not used for employment or medical purposes, only up to $4,500 in equity)
- Ordinary household furnishings and furniture up to $2,000
- Burial plots for individuals and immediate family
- Burial funds up to $1,500
- Life insurance with a face value of $1,500 or less
- One wedding ring and one engagement ring

[20 C.F.R. § 416.1210]

Q 16:14 What kind of trusts will not count as a resource for an SSI beneficiary?

Under SSI policy, two types of trusts will not be counted: (1) a so-called "Medicaid" trust (i.e., a trust that meets the qualifications for not being counted for Medicaid) described in 42 USC Section 1396p(d)(4), and (2) a third-party "discretionary" trust. Specifically, the Social Security Administration Program Operations Manual Systems Section SI 01120.200.D.1.a. states:

> If an individual (claimant, recipient, or deemor) has legal authority to revoke the trust and then use the funds to meet his food, clothing or shelter needs, or if the individual can direct the use of the trust principal for his/her support and maintenance under the terms of the trust, the trust principal is a resource for SSI purposes.
>
> Additionally, if the trust provides for mandatory disbursements to the beneficiary and the beneficiary is not prohibited from anticipating, assigning or selling the right to future payments, the current value of these payments may be a resource to the beneficiary. For example, if the trust provides for payment of $100 per month to the beneficiary for spending money, absent a prohibition to the contrary, the beneficiary may be able to sell the right to future payments for a lump-sum settlement.

In sum, "If an individual does not have the legal authority to revoke the trust or direct the use of the trust assets for his/her own support and maintenance, the trust principal is not the individual's resource for SSI purposes." [POMS § SI 01120.200.D.2] A discretionary trust with supplemental needs language, established by a third party, should not be considered a resource for SSI purposes, *whether or not* expenditures for food, clothing and shelter are explicitly prohibited.

Q 16:15 What are the SSI income eligibility requirements?

Income eligibility is a little easier to calculate for SSI purposes than for Medicaid long-term care purposes. For SSI, the total income from all sources must not exceed the applicable maximum SSI benefit (including state supplements, where appropriate). If the income is lower than that level and the applicant is otherwise eligible, SSI will pay the difference between an individual's income and the SSI maximum benefit level.

Countable income is defined as anything received in-cash or in-kind that can be used to meet the need for food, clothing, and shelter. Sometimes the income calculated for SSI purposes includes more or less than is actually received. In-kind income is food, clothing, or shelter, or something that can be used to get one of these. [20 C.F.R. § 416.1102] Income can be earned or unearned and there are different rules for counting each type of income. In 2002 countable income must be less than $552 a month for a single adult and less than $829 a month for married couples. [42 U.S.C. §§ 1382(a)(1), 1382f] As previously mentioned, countable income can be higher in states that pay SSI supplements.

Q 16:16 What happens to an SSI recipient's benefits if he or she leaves the United States?

Eligibility will be lost if an individual leaves the United States for 30 consecutive days. Upon returning, one must be back in the United States for 30 consecutive days to be considered "back in the United States" for eligibility purposes. Eligibility for SSI benefits will begin in the month in which the 30 days end if all other eligibility requirements are met. [20 C.F.R. § 416.215]

Q 16:17 What is the difference between earned and unearned income?

SSI eligibility depends on the applicant's income level, and counts both "earned" and "unearned" income. Earned income includes wages and self-employment income, whether paid in cash or by in-kind payments of goods or services. For SSI eligibility purposes, some earned income is excluded from consideration:

- The first $20 per month of most income
- $65 per month of wages and one-half of wages over $65
- Food stamps
- Home energy and housing assistance

[20 C.F.R. § 416.1112]

Unearned income includes interest, dividends, rent receipts (after deduction of expenses), annuity and pension payments, insurance proceeds, and even lottery or prize winnings. Unearned income is calculated at its value as gross income—in other words, Medicare premiums, garnishments, and automatic withholdings are counted as income even though not actually received by the applicant.

Q 16:18 What are the rules for in-kind support and maintenance?

In-kind support and maintenance is any food, clothing, or shelter that is given to an individual by a third party. [20 C.F.R. § 416.1130] In-kind gifts of necessities (food, clothing, or shelter) are treated as income although the calculation of benefit reductions may be different depending on the recipient's living arrangements. Rather than crediting the applicant with the fair-market value of in-kind contributions, the value is determined by the "presumed value" rule when the recipient lives in his or own household. This rule fixes the value of the support at one-third of the maximum SSI benefit (or, if it is lower, the fair market value). [20 C.F.R. § 416.1131] This computation has the effect of reducing the SSI benefit by one-third of the maximum monthly SSI benefit, minus the $20 permitted without causing any effect on beneficiaries, for most SSI recipients who receive in-kind support and maintenance. Clearly, if the gift is sufficiently valuable, it may be better to receive the gift and reduce the benefit by one-third. Note also that the gifts are in effect aggregated.

Example 16-1. John receives $552 SSI. In January, he receives $100 of clothing from his mother. his benefit should be reduced by $80. (One hundred dollars is less than one-third multiplied by $552 or $184.) In February, his grandmother says she will pay the landlord if he moves to a better apartment with a $800/month rent. His benefit will be reduced by $164 every month that she does this.

Q 16:19 Can an SSI recipient receive gifts?

Gifts of *cash* to or for the benefit of an SSI recipient or applicant will be counted as income. In other words, while an SSI recipient may receive cash gifts from, for example, a family member, SSI benefits will be reduced accordingly. Once the $20 "disregard" threshold is reached, cash gifts will reduce the SSI benefit dollar-for-dollar.

In-kind gifts of non-necessities are ordinarily not counted as income, and are therefore completely permissible. Gifts of entertainment, travel, education, therapy, or other treatment can be freely given to SSI recipients. One proviso: An in-kind gift that could be converted into food, clothing, or shelter will be treated as a cash gift. In other words, providing refundable airline tickets may result in a reduction or loss of SSI benefits, but providing nonrefundable tickets will not. Similarly, coupons for movie theaters technically would cause SSI reductions (provided they exceed the $20 threshold), but the direct payment of movie tickets will not.

In-kind gifts of necessities (food, clothing, and shelter) are treated as income. The benefit reduction is not, however, calculated dollar-for-dollar, but instead, at the lesser of fair market value or one-third of the maximum monthly benefit (see Q 16:18).

Q 16:20 What are the income deeming rules for SSI?

In some circumstances an SSI applicant will be "deemed" to have income available from other individuals living in the household. Three different considerations will apply in calculating the deeming of income in a specific case:

1. *The relationship of the individual whose income is deemed available.* Only the income of certain household members will be deemed available, including that of parents, spouses,

spouses of parents, and sponsors of aliens. In addition, the income of "essential persons" can be deemed available to the applicant, but the "essential persons" category invokes pre-1973 rules and requires that the applicant and the essential person have lived together continuously since the 1973 change in rules.

2. *The allocation of income.* Once the income of the applicant's parent, spouse, etc., has been calculated, the amount deemed available will be reduced according to the number of ineligible persons living in the household. This calculation varies depending on the ages and relationships of the applicant, the individual whose income is deemed available, and the other household residents.
3. *The calculation of deemed income.* A portion of the income of the individual is then deemed available to the applicant. This portion depends, again, on the relationship of the parties. Parents' income, for example, is deemed available to the extent that it exceeds the applicable maximum federal benefit rate (remembering that the available income is reduced by any allocation to, say, other children in the household from the previous step). [20 C.F.R. § 416.1165] A spouse's income is deemed available to the extent that it exceeds the difference between the maximum federal benefit rate for a single person and the rate for a married couple.

[20 C.F.R. § 416.1163]

Q 16:21 May an SSI applicant or recipient make gifts of assets in order to become financially eligible for the program?

Prior to 1988, SSI eligibility was affected by uncompensated transfers of assets (e.g., gifts). Between 1988 and late 1999, SSI recipients or applicants could make unlimited gifts without affecting their SSI eligibility. As of December 14, 1999, uncompensated transfers again result in a penalty for eligibility purposes. [42 U.S.C. § 1382b(e)]

Current SSI transfer penalties are similar in design and effect to the transfer penalties imposed on Medicaid applicants. Ineligibility for most uncompensated transfers will extend for a period of months calculated by dividing the amount of the gift by the applicable maximum SSI benefit rate. Some transfers are exempted from this effect, including transfers to disabled children or spouses, and transfers into qualifying "special needs" trusts for the benefit of the SSI recipient or applicant. Transfers of assets in the month in which they are received may still be exempted from the penalty rules, because SSI defines any asset as income in the month of receipt and an asset only to the extent that some portion of the "income" remains at the beginning of the next month. [20 C.F.R. § 416.1207]

Transfers into "special needs" trusts for the benefit of the SSI recipient-applicant will not be penalized *if* the trust meets the same criteria as those applied to Medicaid long-term care applicants. (See chapter 14 for Medicaid eligibility rules and chapter 17 for more discussion of special needs trusts.) [Social Security Administration Program Operations Manual Systems ("POMS") § SI 01150.121] For most individuals, that means transfers into a trust that:

1. Does not provide any enforceable right to payments for necessities (food, clothing, and shelter); any payments for these items will, however, reduce the SSI benefit (see Q 16:18); and
2. Provides for repayment to the state(s) for any *Medicaid* payments made on behalf of the SSI recipient on the recipient's death. Oddly, SSI rules do not require the repayment of SSI benefits received, but rather that of Medicaid benefits received by the SSI beneficiary. Thus, the POMS refers to the special needs trust as a "Medicaid" Trust. Keep in mind that there is no estate recovery for Medicaid received "in the community," which is the living situation of SSI recipients. Transfer of assets to a "payback" trust of this kind will therefore have a tradeoff for the SSI recipient who had hoped to leave some of the funds behind for loved ones.

Veterans Benefits

Q 16:22 What kinds of benefits are available for veterans and their families?

Cash, health care, dental care, pharmacy services, life insurance, and burial benefits are available for eligible veterans and their dependents. Those veterans partially or totally disabled through injury or disease incurred during active training or active duty may be entitled to monthly compensation benefits. Pensions are available to veterans who served during wartime, with benefits varying according to need and degree of disability. Medical benefits, including outpatient and home care services, respite and hospice care are provided to veterans, although with significant limitations on eligibility. Finally, the dependents and survivors of veterans may be eligible to receive compensation, pensions, death benefits, and medical care. The federal statutes governing veterans benefits can be found at 38 USC Sections 101 et seq.

Q 16:23 How does the Department of Veteran's Affairs determine eligibility for benefits?

Veterans' benefits are not entitlements, and the availability of benefits depends on the amount of funding allotted by Congress in any given year and the availability of facilities. For this reason, a priority system has been developed for veterans who have performed active service in the military and who were not dishonorably discharged. [38 U.S.C. § 101(2)] A priority list of veterans entitled to benefits ranks them according to disability level, service experience, need, and ability to pay. The list, in priority order, includes:

- Veterans determined to have service-connected disabilities of 50 percent or greater
- Veterans with service-connected disabilities between 30 percent and 50 percent
- Former POWs, veterans with 10 percent to 30 percent service-connected disabilities, those with active-duty discharges for compensable conditions, and those injured by negligent care in the Veterans Administration (VA) system
- Veterans receiving aid and attendance benefits
- Veterans meeting income and asset standards
- All other veterans not required to make any copayments for their care
- Veterans above income and asset standards, if they agree to make copayments

[38 U.S.C. §§ 1705 et seq., 1151 for provisions regarding injury by VA negligence]

In each budget year, the Veterans Administration determines how far down the priority list the actual enrollment of veterans will progress.

Q 16:24 Can otherwise eligible veterans be precluded from receiving benefits because of misconduct?

Veterans whose disabilities result from their own willful misconduct, or "deliberate or intentional wrongdoing with knowledge of or wanton and reckless disregard of its probable consequences," may be ineligible for benefits. [38 C.F.R. § 3.1(n)] Interestingly, the Veterans Administration perceives alcoholism, drug addiction, venereal disease, and suicide (precluding benefits for survivors) as examples of willful misconduct. [38 C.F.R. § 3.1(m)] But if alcoholism or drug abuse were caused by a service-connected disability (e.g., post-traumatic stress disorder), then any organic disease caused by the alcoholism or drug abuse can be deemed service-connected. [38 C.F.R. § 3.301(c)(2)]

Q 16:25 What cash benefits are available to disabled veterans?

Veterans can receive either compensation, which is a cash benefit for service-related disability [38 U.S.C. § 1110], or pension benefits for non-service-related disabilities [38 U.S.C. §§ 1521, 1522; 38 C.F.R. § 3.3].

Q 16:26 What is a service-related disability?

A service-related disability is a disability incurred during the veteran's term of service (including attendance with service obligations at a military academy), or as a direct result of VA-provided health care. The injury does not have to be related to combat. Veterans may also be eligible for compensation if a pre-existing condition was significantly aggravated during service, or if the disability resulted from another service-related disability, disease, or injury. [38 C.F.R. § 3.303] Certain conditions are presumed by statute to be service-related. These include:

- Certain chronic diseases
- Certain tropical diseases
- Diseases specific to former POWs

- Diseases specific to radiation-exposed veterans
- Diseases associated with exposure to certain herbicide agents

[38 C.F.R. § 3.309]

Q 16:27 What benefits are available for service-related disability?

A disability is compensable as long as it was service-related. Once the VA has determined that the disability is service-connected, it then sets a disability rating in 10 percent increments based on the effect the disability has on the veteran's earning ability. [38 U.S.C. § 1114] A 100 percent disability rating will be given when an individual is unable to secure or follow a substantially gainful occupation as a result of service-connected disabilities. This is called "individual unemployability" (IU). A veteran who is at least 60 percent disabled may also be considered for individual unemployability status, when there are factors other than the disability itself that may affect the veteran's ability to find work. [38 C.F.R. § 4.16] Level of education and work history are typical IU variables.

Disabilities may be periodically rerated based on changes in the law, increased medical knowledge and technology, and changes in the disability itself. Compensation ranges from approximately $100 per month for a 10 percent disability to nearly $2,000 per month for a 100 percent disability. [38 U.S.C. § 1114] Compensation is generally not subject to income tax, garnishment, or attachment.

Additional compensation is provided for those veterans who are housebound or need nursing or other regular assistance. [38 U.S.C. § 1114]

Q 16:28 Can veterans with non-service related disabilities receive pension benefits?

Pensions may be available for veterans with non-service-connected disabilities if they are totally and permanently disabled and financially needy. The VA applies stringent eligibility requirements for pensions. The veteran must:

1. Have served 90 days during a period of war.
2. Not have been discharged dishonorably. [38 U.S.C. § 5303(a)]

3. Be disabled, but not as a result of either a service-connected injury or the veteran's own willful conduct.
4. Not have assets so large that it would be "reasonable" that some part of the assets would be consumed by the costs of care. While the level of assets that raise this "reasonableness" test has not been codified, it is usually assumed to be $50,000. [38 C.F.R. §§ 3.274–3.276]

The pension program guarantees a minimum income to the veteran, so that a qualified veteran with no countable income will receive the maximum annual pension amount. Those with income less than the maximum allowable pension rate may still be eligible. [38 C.F.R. §§ 3.271–3.272.] There are three VA pension programs:

1. *Old-Law Pension.* Available to veterans who became eligible prior to July 1, 1960, and does not count spousal income to determine income eligibility;
2. *Section 306 Pension.* Covers veterans eligible between July 1, 1960 and December 31, 1978, and counts the spouse's Social Security income but not spousal income to determine income eligibility; and
3. *Improved Pension.* Covers veterans eligible after January 1, 1979. This is the only pension program open to new enrollees. Current enrollees must be under 55 and totally and permanently disabled. All income—including spousal income—is counted. A home, burial expenses, and certain other assets are exempt from consideration for need-based benefits, and transfers of property will not be acknowledged by the VA as reducing the countable resources of the applicant.

[38 C.F.R. § 3.3]

Both the Old Law Pension and the Section 306 Pension can be converted to the Improved Pension.

Q 16:29 What is "financially needy" for pension qualification?

Any veteran receiving countable income less than the maximum applicable annual pension rate may be deemed needy. Among those sources excluded from consideration as income are welfare payments, other VA pension benefits, profit from sale of property, burial expenses, educational expenses, Department of Defense survivor benefit annuities, and cash surrender values of life insurance.

Q 16:30 What is "permanently and totally disabled" for pension qualification?

The veteran must have a physical or mental impairment sufficient to make it impossible for the average person with that disability to obtain and maintain gainful employment. The disability will be deemed permanent if it is reasonable to assume that the disability will continue throughout the veteran's life.

Q 16:31 How is eligibility and the amount of the Improved Pension determined?

The Improved Pension Plan, the current pension program now available to all qualified veterans, deems a veteran eligible if he or she was in active military service for 90 days (continuous or interrupted) during a period of war or was discharged because of a service-connected disability sustained while serving during a period of war. The discharge cannot have been dishonorable. Veterans will also be deemed eligible if they are permanently and totally disabled from a non-service-connected disability, the disability did not result from the veteran's own willful misconduct, and the veteran does not have sufficient income or resources to sustain himself or herself. Generally a veteran will be deemed eligible if he or she has less than $50,000 in assets (not counting a home and ordinary personal effects) and income less than the maximum applicable annual pension rate.

Q 16:32 Are surviving spouses and children of veterans eligible for compensation benefits?

Eligible family members include spouses who are legally married to the veterans (legally separated but still married spouses are eligible); children who are minors, in school (up to age 23), or dependent; and parents, either natural or adoptive. In order to receive benefits, children must be unmarried, and may be natural, adoptive, or illegitimate. Stepchildren may also qualify for benefits.

Spouses, children, and parents may be eligible for monthly dependency and indemnity compensation (DIC) benefits if the veteran died as a result of a service-connected disability incurred while on active duty, or if the death was not service-connected but the veteran was totally and permanently disabled for at least 10 years as a result of a service-connected condition. [38 U.S.C. § 1318] Pension benefits are available but at a much lower rate than for the veterans themselves, and survivors of veterans who died prior to 1957 must file a special election to receive DIC benefits.

The surviving spouse may be entitled to $935 per month in DIC benefits plus $202 per month if the veteran had a service-connected disability for at least eight years prior to his or her death. An additional $224 per month is provided for each minor child of the veteran, or if there is no surviving spouse, $397 for the first child, $571 for two children, and $742 for three children.

Q 16:33 Are veterans entitled to medical care through the VA?

VA benefits are not entitlements, and the VA is required to provide medical care only to veterans with service-connected conditions, former prisoners of war, veterans exposed to radiation or other toxic substances during their service, and World War I veterans. [38 U.S.C. § 1705(a)] Veterans with non-service-connected disabilities receive medical care only if they are financially needy, and even then hospital, nursing home, and hospice care are available only to the extent that facilities can be provided.

In response to increasing demand, the VA has begun to institute various programs in geriatric assessment and long-term care, including community service programs. Few veterans qualify, however, and the programs are restricted by the availability of facilities.

Under a new rule adopted in 2002, the VA will grant priority to "severely disabled" veterans, even if the immediate health problem needing attention is unrelated to their military service, and to "moderately disabled" veterans who seek care for disabilities stemming from their service. The new policy would not affect emergency treatment. Prior to the rule, services were provided more on a "first-come, first-served" basis.

Q 16:34 How does the Veterans Administration determine eligibility for medical services?

The Veterans Administration has instituted an enrollment incentive for all veterans in its move to managed care. As of October 1998, most veterans must be enrolled to receive medical benefits, including inpatient and outpatient treatment, home health, respite care, and hospice care. A veteran can apply for enrollment at any time. The following veterans do not have to enroll, although they are encourage to do so:

1. Veterans who have a service-connected disability of 50 percent or more;
2. Veterans who want care for compensable disability during the 12-month period following discharge; or
3. Veterans who want care for a service-connected disability.

[38 U.S.C. § 1705(c)(2)]

Not all enrolled veterans will receive benefits, and the priority requirements may be adjusted from year to year depending on funds made available by Congress. Veterans discharged within the preceding 12 months who have a service-connected disability are given the highest priority. Veterans injured in the line of duty, former prisoners of war, those catastrophically disabled, and those without sufficient income or resources have higher priority for benefits than those who are not disabled or can afford to pay or make copayments.

Q 16:35 How is financial ability to pay the cost of care determined?

The priority order of veterans awaiting access to Medicare under the VA system is correlated directly with how extreme the respective disability and impoverishment of the veteran is, and the administration is given fairly broad discretion to consider extenuating circumstances in individual cases to qualify or disqualify the veteran for benefits. The statute [38 U.S.C. § 1722] states that a veteran shall be considered to be unable to defray the expenses of necessary care if he or she is eligible to receive medical assistance under a state plan approved under Title XIX of the Social Security Act [42 U.S.C. §§ 1396 et seq.], the veteran is currently receiving a disability-related pension, or the veteran's attributable income is not greater than $17,240 in the case of a veteran with no dependents; or $20,688 in the case of a veteran with one dependent, plus $1,150 for each additional dependent (and a formula is provided in the statute to adjust these figures proportionately to increases in pensions since 1990).

Q 16:36 How are copayments determined?

Veterans who have sufficient income or resources to disqualify them from hardship eligibility may still receive medical benefits if they agree to pay copayments. Hospital care copayments are equivalent to the lesser of the cost of care, or the sum of the Medicare hospital deductible for the first 90 days of care plus half of the deductible for each subsequent 90-day period plus $10 per day. Nursing home copayments equal the lesser of the cost of care, or the sum of the Medicare deductible for the first 90 days plus $5 per day of care. Outpatient copayments equal 20 percent of the cost of an average outpatient visit, and prescriptions require a $2 copayment for every 30-day supply.

Q 16:37 Does the VA's medical service benefit include nursing or other long-term care?

The Veterans Administration operates nursing homes in every region of the country, and qualified veterans *may* receive nursing home care in one of these facilities. [38 C.F.R. § 17.47(a)] Most of the care actually provided to veterans is short-term, rehabilitative care, although long-term institutionalization is occasionally provided. Unless the need for institutionalization is occasioned by a service-connected disability, it is increasingly difficult to secure VA care for veterans in need of nursing services. Veterans with service-related disabilities are given priority. Veterans who do not have a service-connected disability must be unable to defray the expenses of necessary care. The ability to defray the expenses of care is determined by an income test. For purposes of determining nursing home eligibility, a veteran with a non-service-related disability will be determined eligible for necessary care if the veteran's attributable income does not exceed $20,000 if the veteran has no dependents, $25,000 if the veteran has one dependent, plus $1,000 for each additional dependent. [38 C.F.R. § 17.47(d)(2)]

Veterans who may be provided nursing home care without an income eligibility assessment include:

- Veterans with service-connected disabilities
- Veterans exposed to herbicides while serving in Vietnam
- Veterans exposed to radiation

- Veterans with a condition related to an environmental exposure in the Persian gulf
- Former POWs
- Veterans on a VA pension
- Veterans of the Mexican Border period or WWI
- Veterans eligible for Medicaid

[38 U.S.C. § 1710]

In some regions, the VA provides short-term nursing home care by contracts with outside providers. If the patient is being released from a VA hospital to the nursing home, he or she may qualify for such a short-term contract—usually for a total of no more than six months of care for veterans with non-service-related disabilities. The benefit is unlimited if the veteran has a service-related disability. Where VA nursing home contracts are utilized, the patient is usually not required to contribute to the cost of care. [38 C.F.R. § 17.51]

Q 16:38 If the disability results from medical care provided in a VA facility, what is the liability of the VA?

Prior to October 1997 claimants did not have to prove negligence on the part of the VA, or that the death or the injury leading to the disability was accidental; however, for all claims filed after September 1, 1997, the disabled veteran must prove that the injury or death occurred in a VA facility and was proximately caused by carelessness, negligence, lack of skill on the part of the VA in its provision of medical, training, or vocational rehabilitation services. [38 U.S.C. § 1151] The VA in turn must prove that it exercised the degree of care expected of a reasonable health care provider.

Claims should be filed within a year of the injury or death in order to qualify for retroactive benefits or compensation, and can be processed either through the Section 351 compensation procedure or under the Federal Tort Claims Act. Veterans should apply for both, although they can receive compensation from only one of the two proceedings.

Q 16:39 What are the eligibility requirements for medical benefits for families of veterans?

The VA Civilian Health and Medical Program (CHAMPVA) provides medical care for dependents and survivors of veterans. The following individuals are eligible for CHAMPVA:

1. Spouses and children of veterans who were permanently and totally disabled through service-connected injury or disease;
2. Spouses and children of veterans who died of service-connected injuries or diseases or who were totally disabled from service-connected condition at the time of death; and
3. Spouses and children of veterans who were killed in the line of duty within 30 days of entry into active service.

[38 U.S.C. § 1713; 38 C.F.R. § 17.84]

Generally those who qualify for benefits under the Department of Defense (CHAMPUS) or Medicare (both Parts A and Part B) will not qualify for CHAMPVA benefits, although the latter can be a secondary payor.

Q 16:40 What other benefits are available to veterans?

The VA will authorize the burial of veterans in national cemeteries and will provide a headstone or marker. On December 27, 2001, President Bush signed the Veterans Education and Benefits Expansion Act. Included in this law is a provision that allows the VA to furnish and appropriate markers for the graves of eligible veterans buried in private cemeteries, whose deaths occurred on or after December 27, 2001, regardless of whether the grave is already marked with a non-government marker. If the veteran died while in active service or as a result of a service-connected disability, the VA may pay up to $1,500 for burial expenses. [38 U.S.C. §§ 2302, 2303, 2304, 2307] Life insurance is also available to veterans. Servicepersons in active duty receive automatic coverage of $200,000; upon discharge, they are offered various life insurance options. Veterans are expected to pay premiums except if they are totally and permanently disabled, in which case premiums on the first $10,000 of coverage are waived. [38 U.S.C. § 1922A] In addition, pharmacy services are provided free to veterans requiring medication for the treatment of service-connected conditions and to veterans whose income does not exceed the maximum VA pension. All other veterans may be charged $2 for each 30-day supply of medication. [38 U.S.C. § 1722A(a)]

Q 16:41 What are the procedural requirements for filing a claim for veteran's benefits?

Payment of claims is retroactive to the filing of the claim, not the incurring of the disability itself or dates of service. [38 C.F.R. § 3.400] All that is required to set the filing date is written notification to a VA regional office, although eventually a formal claim must be submitted. The VA has a duty to assist claimants, such as by providing medical records and medical examinations. An intricate system of appeals has been established for claims disallowed at the regional office level, leading to the Board of Veterans' Appeals (BVA) (independent of the VA) and, in some cases, the U.S. Court of Veterans' Appeals and the federal circuit court system.

Attorneys are not permitted to charge fees for service in VA matters prior to the final decision of the Board of Veterans' Appeals, and in fact the VA is obligated to assist claimants. Once the claim has been denied by the BVA, any representative of the claimant may charge fees not exceeding 20 percent of the benefits awarded through the claim for service after the claim is denied. [38 U.S.C. § 5904(d)(1)] Fee agreements may be reviewed by the BVA and by the Court of Appeals for Veterans' Claims, and either entity may reduce the fees if they are considered unreasonable. [38 U.S.C. § 5904(c)(2)]

Railroad Retirement Benefits

Q 16:42 What is the Railroad Retirement program?

The Railroad Retirement program [45 U.S.C. §§ 231 et seq.], begun in the depth of the Great Depression in 1934, preceded the Social Security program by a year. At the time of establishment of the program, Railroad Retirement benefits were relatively widespread and more generous than those in other industries, but the Depression challenged the vitality of the pre-existing programs. Because the railroad industry was widespread and because it was viewed as essential to national security, railroad workers could successfully argue that their retirement program should remain separate from the new Social Security Administration. Although the railroad industry has shrunk considerably in the intervening decades, Railroad Retirement remains a separate program.

Q 16:43 Who qualifies to receive Railroad Retirement benefits?

The basic requirement for Railroad Retirement benefits is 120 months of creditable railroad service. [45 U.S.C. § 231a(a)(1)] The 120 months need not be consecutive; in some cases, military service can be credited toward the 120-month requirement. Since 1974, a creditable month has usually meant any month in which the employee receives at least $25 in wages from a covered employer. Covered employers include all railroads engaged in interstate commerce (and some subsidiaries), railroad associations, and national railway labor organizations. In 2002, 297,000 railroad retirees received benefits from Railroad Retirement, together with 150,000 spouses and 193,000 survivors. [See *http://www.rrb.gov/act/pdf/stat_qbs1202.pdf*] Retirees were clustered in California, Florida, Illinois, Missouri, New York, Ohio, Pennsylvania and Texas, with over 10,000 covered retirees in each of those states.

Railroad Retirement will become less important to the aging population over time. Although nearly 300,000 retirees currently receive benefits, only 227,300 current employees were still covered by Railroad Retirement in 2002—down by more than 10 percent in the previous two-year period. [See *http://www.rrb.gov/act/pdf/statedata.pdf*]

Q 16:44 Who administers the Railroad Retirement program?

The Railroad Retirement Board (RRB), a three-member board of directors, administers the Railroad Retirement program. The President of the United States appoints all three members; one must be recommended by railroad management, one by railroad labor interests, and the third (who always serves as Chair of the Board) represents the public interest. The Railroad Retirement Board has offices at 844 North Rush Street, Chicago, Illinois 60611-2092, phone: (312) 751-4500. The RRB also operates a toll-free automated answering service at (800) 808-0772. Local field offices are located in 53 cities in 35 states. More information about the RRB, and addresses and telephone numbers for its field offices, can be obtained online at *www.rrb.gov*.

Q 16:45 How does Railroad Retirement differ from Social Security?

Although Railroad Retirement operated completely separately from Social Security until the mid-1970s, administration of the two programs was gradually coordinated beginning in 1974. Today, most Social Security rules apply to Railroad Retirement beneficiaries as well, including the scheduled increase in the normal retirement age to 67 by 2022, the reduction in benefits for early retirement (as young as 62), and the enhanced benefits for retirement as late as age 70, the five-month waiting period for disability benefits, and other provisions. Benefits are calculated by the Railroad Retirement Board, but in concert with the Social Security Administration for those railroad employees who might be entitled to dual benefits.

One important difference between Social Security and Railroad Retirement requires explanation. The "Tier I" portion of Railroad Retirement benefits (see Q 16:46) increases pursuant to the same automatic cost-of-living adjustment as that of Social Security; however, the "Tier II" portion increases annually at 32.5 percent of the consumer price index adjustment. [45 U.S.C. § 231b(g)] In other words, the enhancement of Railroad Retirement benefits is marginally reduced each year by the operation of inflation.

Q 16:46 What happens when a Railroad Retirement beneficiary also qualifies to receive Social Security benefits?

Railroad Retirement operates a two-tier benefit structure. "Tier I" benefits are calculated to approximate what the railroad employee would have received had he or she been covered by Social Security, and "Tier II" benefits are the enhanced benefits paid only to Railroad Retirement beneficiaries. [45 U.S.C. § 231b(b)] If a railroad employee has a work history covered by Social Security, and retired after 1974, the Tier I benefits are reduced by the amount of Social Security benefits. Because the Tier I benefit levels are computed using both Railroad Retirement and Social Security work history, the effect is to prevent double benefits from being paid because of coverage in both retirement systems. Tier II benefits, on the other hand, are computed solely on the basis of Railroad Retirement-covered employment.

The same computations are applied to spousal benefits. In other words, a Railroad Retirement beneficiary whose spouse has work history covered by Social Security will not be able to benefit from both programs: His or her spousal Railroad Retirement benefit will be reduced by the amount of Social Security benefit to which he or she is entitled. [45 U.S.C. § 231c(b)]

For some Railroad Retirement beneficiaries who worked in Social Security-covered employment before 1975 (and whose rights vested before that date), an additional retirement benefit may be available. After 1974, congressional changes to the Railroad Retirement program attempted to prevent dual benefit payments. Funding for the pre-1975 dual benefits is based on separate annual appropriations by Congress, and may be reduced proportionally if budget appropriations are insufficient to cover all vested benefits. [45 U.S.C. § 231n(d)]

For most Railroad Retirement beneficiaries (and spouses), the practical result will be that they will receive a single retirement check from the Railroad Retirement Board that will be calculated in concert with the Social Security Administration. In order to facilitate this process, Social Security records are reviewed by Railroad Retirement Board administrators.

Q 16:47 How are Railroad Retirement benefits determined?

Railroad Retirement is, as mentioned before, a two-tier benefit system. Tier I is calculated similarly to Social Security benefits. Tier II benefits are the enhanced portion of Railroad Retirement, and are calculated based solely on covered railroad employment. The Tier II benefit consists of 0.7 percent of the employee's average earnings during the 60 highest-earning months of employment, multiplied by the number of years in railroad service. [45 U.S.C. § 231b(b)] This amount is reduced both for early retirement and for vested dual-benefit rights (by 25 percent of the vested rights). [45 U.S.C. § 231b(b)]

Q 16:48 What survivor's benefits are available through the Railroad Retirement program?

Like Social Security, the Railroad Retirement program offers benefits to surviving spouses and dependent children of deceased Railroad Retirement beneficiaries. Unlike Social Security, eligibility for survivor's Railroad Retirement benefits requires that the deceased beneficiary's last employment (before death or retirement) must have been in the railroad industry. [45 U.S.C. § 231a(d)] Survivor's benefits also include a portion of the employee's Tier II benefits.

Q 16:49 What Railroad Retirement benefits are available for spouses?

Again like Social Security, spouses are eligible to receive benefits on the work history of covered Railroad Retirement beneficiaries. Spouses receive benefits calculated on the same two-tier system, and the spouse's own or spousal Social Security benefits (if any) will reduce the Tier I portion of the Railroad Retirement benefits. [45 U.S.C. § 231c(c)]

Practice-Related Issues

Q 16:50 How might an elder law attorney encounter issues involving the Veterans Administration, the Railroad Retirement Board, or the Supplemental Security Income program?

Although most elder law attorneys will have few cases involving these programs, they do occasionally arise. Representation of clients in Veterans Administration matters is particularly problematic, and might include:

1. *Representation in VA claims.* A client whom the attorney has represented in other matters contacts the attorney and asks for help in filing a VA disability claim. The attorney is eager to help this client and the client is willing to pay. What should the attorney know about representation of clients in VA matters?

   Unless willing to represent the client *pro bono,* the attorney should encourage the client to go as far as he or she can on his or her own. Attorneys are not permitted to charge fees for service in VA matters prior to the final decision of the Board of Veterans' Appeals, and in fact the VA is obligated to assist claimants. Once the claim has been denied by the BVA, any representative of the claimant may charge fees not exceeding

20 percent of the benefits awarded through the claim for further efforts on his or her behalf. Fee agreements may be reviewed by the BVA and by the Court of Appeals for Veterans' Claims, and either entity may reduce the fees if they are considered unreasonable.

2. *SSI recipient receiving large inheritance or personal injury settlement.* One common scenario encountered in the elder law practice is the SSI recipient who inherits money, or receives a substantial personal injury settlement. In the case of the personal injury settlement, the injury may even be the cause of the disability leading to SSI benefits.

In either case, the SSI recipient must first analyze the importance of continued SSI eligibility. In most cases, the real issue will be categorical eligibility for Medicaid care—particularly in the case of personal injury settlements, where the cost of care may be overwhelming and the settlement amount comparatively modest.

Of course, in the case of inheritance the problem is easily solved by planning on the part of the donor. Establishment of a "pure" discretionary trust (one in which the trustee has the discretion to pay no benefits to the SSI recipient, and the authority to provide nonnecessities directly) will ordinarily prevent the loss of SSI benefits and Medicaid coverage. Too often, unfortunately, donors fail to make such plans in advance, and the resultant intestate or outright inheritance will require legal repair work.

Even though the SSI recipient's cost of care may be substantial, if the funds to be received can provide for an extended period of care some consideration must be given simply to receiving the funds and ending benefits. If, for example, the recipient's life expectancy is short, or immediate needs are great, it may be advisable to receive the funds and anticipate that there may come a time when SSI and Medicaid benefits will be available once again—after the funds have been exhausted.

Assuming that continued SSI eligibility is important, the beneficiary will have two basic options (although he or she may mix the two options in an appropriate case):

1. spend the proceeds quickly, or
2. establish a special needs trust.

Spending the money can include one or more of the following (this list is not intended to be exhaustive, but to suggest common expenditures):

- Purchase of a residence
- Adaptation of an existing residence (e.g., for wheelchair accessibility, or to permit live-in caretakers)
- Home repairs (e.g., replacement of appliances, carpeting, drapes, whether for medical or cosmetic purposes)
- Purchase of a single vehicle (e.g., wheelchair-equipped van or other special transportation)
- Acquisition of medical equipment (motorized wheelchair, specialized bed, etc.)
- Special therapy or treatment programs (e.g., experimental procedure not covered by Medicaid and requiring travel to another city)

While special needs trusts are discussed more fully in chapter 17, the general concepts are straightforward. If the SSI recipient is under age 65, and the continued receipt of SSI (and Medicaid coverage) is important, a special needs trust should be considered. The recipient, with the lawyer's help, must weigh the administrative costs and the restrictions on use of the money (food, clothing, and shelter cannot be provided without affecting benefits) against the continued SSI eligibility benefits. Frequently, the SSI recipient may elect to take a significant portion of the funds received and, in the same month, purchase food, clothing, and several of the exempt items suggested previously, placing the remaining amounts in a special needs trust immediately upon completion of those steps. Note that the amount received, though treated as income in the month of receipt for SSI purposes and not otherwise treated as an asset until the month after receipt, will probably be treated as an asset if transferred for less than full value during the month of receipt.

Of course, SSI recipients are frequently incapable of handling the funds, regardless of the effect on benefits. Persons acting for the benefit of the SSI recipient may be family members, payees designated by the Social Security Administration, or a duly appointed conservator. Throughout the discussion of alternatives, the attorney must be mindful of the different roles played by the individuals involved, and the inherent conflicts of interest. For example, family members may have been providing room and board, and may now be considering payment for continued services, or purchase of a residence for the SSI recipient (and, perhaps, the family member in question). While family involvement is important and should usually be encouraged, careful consideration (and occasional reconsideration) of those roles and conflicts must be undertaken.

Part V

Health Care Decision-Making and Protection of the Elderly

Chapter 17

Special Needs Trusts

With the rising cost of care (particularly medical care, but also nursing and personal care), the increase of government involvement in that care, and the maturation of government benefits programs, the problem of providing extra benefits for disabled individuals has spawned a whole cottage industry of legal, social, medical and care management experts in the past two decades. The problem of providing for disabled children is not new, but the effect on government benefits is, and can be devastatingly important. Continued eligibility for government benefits is critical to their continued well-being. Most commonly, continued eligibility is important primarily for the medical benefits offered by Medicaid (particularly in long-term care, whether institutional or home-based) or as an adjunct to Supplemental Security Income benefits (SSI recipients usually qualify categorically for Medicaid eligibility, including acute and chronic medical care as often as long-term nursing care).

"Special needs" and "supplemental benefits" trusts provide for the disabled individual's special needs without jeopardizing his or her public benefits. This chapter discusses self-settled and third-party special needs trusts, requirements for establishing them, permissible distributions, and trustee selection.

Overview

Q 17:1 What is a special needs trust?

Outright distribution of assets to an individual who is disabled and receiving Supplemental Security Income (SSI) or Medicaid benefits may cause that person to lose those need-based benefits. The central purpose of a special needs trust (SNT) is to provide for supplemental needs without disrupting public benefits. In most cases, that means protecting Supplemental Security Income and Medicaid benefits, although veteran's, Section 8 housing ("public" housing), and other benefits may be involved for some beneficiaries. Because Medicare and Social Security Disability benefits are not means-tested, they are not affected by the expenditures from the SNT.

Special needs trusts can be set up to allow recipients to receive money without jeopardizing their benefits, but they must be drawn up with care to conform with state and federal guidelines. Any trust providing for the special (or extra) needs of the trust beneficiary can be said to be a special needs trust. In common usage, a SNT is any trust established for the benefit of an individual who receives (or may later receive) government benefits. The commonly used term ("special needs") reflects that the trust's primary purpose is to provide for those needs—other than necessities—that are special to the beneficiary's disability with minimal effect on the entitlement to government benefits.

Q 17:2 What is the difference between a self-settled special needs trust and a third-party special needs trust?

SNTs can be third-party or self-settled. A third-party SNT is established by one person, using his or her own funds, for the benefit of another, disabled, person. A self-settled SNT is established by the disabled person (or by a court or surrogate acting on behalf of the individual) for his or her own benefit, using his or her own assets. Not surprisingly, the treatment of these two kinds of trusts and the benefits flowing from them may be radically different within the appropriate government benefits program; however, for purposes of defining these trust types, both are "SNTs."

Q 17:3 Is there a difference between a "special needs trust," a "supplemental needs trust," and a "discretionary trust"?

Not exactly. The linguistic difference primarily reflects the feelings of draftspersons concerning the true scope of the Trustee's discretion. "Special needs" focuses on the beneficiary's needs and does not preclude the possibility of expenditures that might conceivably reduce a benefit, after weighing the pros and cons for the beneficiary of such a choice. "Supplemental needs" focuses on the benefit programs to which the beneficiary is entitled. "Discretionary trust" focuses on the Trustee's ability to decide when and if to make or withhold payments. This being said, the law of many states will infer a "support" motive for a trust that is otherwise silent on the standard to be applied by the Trustee. This can be fatal for the beneficiary's entitlements. Therefore, the typical "special needs trust" is a discretionary trust that indicates clearly an intention *not* to provide support or otherwise interfere with the beneficiary's entitlements, in order to rebut such an inference.

Some observers use yet another term, "supplemental benefits trusts" ("SBTs"), which they apply to third-party trusts, using "special needs trust" only for self-settled trusts. There is not, however, any widespread agreement on this convention to distinguish the titles.

Finally, another way to approach the dilemma is to use SNT for third-party trusts and "OBRA '93 Trust" (or, more prosaicly, "payback trust") for self-settled special needs trusts, since only those self-settled trusts that comply with the provisions of the Omnibus Budget Reconciliation Act of 1993 ("OBRA '93"), enacting 42 USC Section 1396p(d)(4), will serve the purpose of supplementing, and not replacing, benefits; the most noticeable of the OBRA '93 requirements, of course, is that the trust must repay state Medicaid expenditures on the death of the beneficiary.

Q 17:4 Why should an elder law practitioner know about special needs trusts?

Special needs trusts are generally prepared for beneficiaries who are not, in fact, elderly, and who expect to rely on needs-tested government entitlements for most of their lives. There are three reasons why an elder law attorney should be familiar with the concepts in spite of that reality: first, SNTs may also exist under the terms of a spouse's will, or be created by a child for a parent, and it is important to know how trusts will affect the senior's eventual Medicaid benefit. Second, as a practical matter familiarity with entitlement law is the cornerstone of an elder law practice, and few attorneys other than elder law attorneys will be as qualified to prepare SNTs; thus, as a matter of practice and business development, it is prudent for the elder law attorney to take advantage of his or her general knowledge of Medicaid and apply it to the potentially large field of clients who require this service. And third, elderly clients have special needs children and grandchildren.

Q 17:5 What provisions should be included when drafting a special needs trust for a disabled beneficiary?

The central purpose of an SNT is to permit the use of trust funds for the extra or supplemental needs of a public benefits recipient. Most SNTs will include language explicitly referring to that purpose. The choice of language, and the importance of including such language, will differ depending on whether the trust is established with assets owned by the disabled person or assets from a parent or other source. Because trusts established with the disabled person's own assets (including personal injury settlements and outright inheritances) must comply with the provisions of 42 USC Section 1396p(d)(4), the language of such "self-settled" trusts must be much more precise and carefully crafted; trusts established by persons other than the beneficiary, using money the beneficiary is not otherwise entitled to receive, may need only to include language making distributions discretionary with the trustee in order to prevent the trust (and its distributions) from being treated as available to the beneficiary—always depending on state law. If state law presumes that a trust for a single beneficiary is intended for "support" unless explicitly stated otherwise, the trust *must* still include some language as to its supplementary intent. It is probably not enough even to explicitly reserve the right in the Trustee to withhold any payments in the Trustee's "absolute" discretion, since that discretion must be exercised reasonably and for the benefit of the beneficiary.

The assets in the trust must not be considered available resources or the beneficiary will be disqualified from means-tested benefits programs. The trust language should state that it is the intent of the grantor to set up a special needs trust that will *not* jeopardize the recipient's government benefits and that the funds must be used solely for the benefit of the recipient-beneficiary. A self-settled trust must include language requiring repayment to the state for Medicaid benefits provided during the recipient's lifetime. Ideally, trust language will allow for some flexibility in case the laws of the jurisdiction or the Medicaid or Social Security rules change. As long as the intent of the settlor *not* to jeopardize benefits is clearly stated, the trust can be modified to conform to those statutes and rules, provided the right to amend for these purposes has been included in the document.

Even though specific language may not be necessary for a third-party trust to qualify as an SNT, it is advisable for the draftsperson to include in all SNTs provisions that:

1. Make distributions of income and principal purely discretionary;
2. Specifically prohibit the trustee from making cash distributions directly to the beneficiary (although in some circumstances it may be advisable to permit occasional cash distributions, resulting in periods of ineligibility managed by the trustee);
3. Direct the trustee to consider the effect of distributions on public benefits eligibility; and
4. Express the settlor's intention that the trust be used for to supplement rather than replace public benefits (preferably including some specific examples of trust uses).

There has been an important shift in one feature of SNTs for beneficiaries receiving SSI. Prior to the promulgation of provisions concerning SNTs in the POMS, it was widely believed that a trust, to avoid being considered a resource, had to expressly forbid expenditures for food, clothing, and shelter. The POMS, which are the Social Security Administration's manual governing these matters, do *not* require any such language. Instead POMS Section SI 01120.200.D.2 (available on-line at *http://policy.ssa.gov/poms.nsf*) provide that "[i]f an individual does not have the legal authority to revoke the trust or direct the use of the trust assets for his/her own support and maintenance, the trust principal is not the individual's resource for SSI purposes." The importance of this distinction can be great. Many SSI beneficiaries can cope with their food and clothing expenditures out of the tiny SSI stipend. However, shelter is quite another matter. If the trust forbids use for shelter, the result may be a trust intended to improve the beneficiary's quality of life, with no ability to keep the beneficiary from relying on a homeless shelter for a place to sleep. In many cases a contribution for shelter will be worth more to the beneficiary than the reduction in benefits caused by application of the "in-kind support and maintenance" rules (see Q 17:31).

Self-Settled Special Needs Trusts

Q 17:6 What is a "self-settled" special needs trust?

A self-settled special needs trust, also often referred to as a "(d)(4) trust," "OBRA '93 trust" or "payback trust," is established with a disabled person's own assets. [42 U.S.C. § 1396p(d)(4)(A)] To qualify for exclusion from being counted as a resource available to the beneficiary the trust must:

1. Be established for the benefit of one individual who is (a) disabled and (b) (for d(4)(A) trusts only) under age 65 at the time the trust is funded;
2. Be established by the parent, grandparent, or guardian of a disabled person or by the court;
3. Be an irrevocable inter vivos trust;
4. Give the trustee sole and absolute discretion over the use of trust income and property (not explicitly included in the statute, but required by implication); and
5. Provide for repayment to the state of money paid for the benefit of the beneficiary pursuant to the state's Medicaid plan (or if more than one state, pro rata).

If these requirements are met, the transfer will not be considered a resource to the grantor/beneficiary, nor will the transfer of funds to the trust (for a child or beneficiary under age 65) result in a penalty period. This is the case only for a "payback"/"OBRA '93" trust, *not* other self-settled trusts. As a general rule, self-settled trusts are a problem for SSI or Medicaid eligibility. Unlike the property of a third-party trust, the principal of a revocable (self-settled) trust established by an SSI or Medicaid beneficiary will be treated as an available resource as if no trust existed. A self-settled irrevocable trust that does not meet the "payback" requirements of OBRA '93 will ordinarily be treated as an available resource or income to the extent that the trustee has any discretion to transfer principal or interest to or for the benefit of the beneficiary. In essence, any discretion will be treated as fully exercised whether it is exercised or not. (Creation of a trust that prohibits distributions to the settlor and/or distributions by the Trustee to third parties from a trust created by the settlor will also be treated as disqualifying transfer by the settlor or spouse.) By contrast, a third-party trust may give the trustee absolute discretion to withhold payments, and this discretionary power will be honored.

Since the Omnibus Budget Reconciliation Act of 1993 ("OBRA '93"), however, SSI and Medicaid regulations permit self-settled irrevocable trusts to be treated as unavailable and therefore not a resource (both as to undistributed income and principal) *if* they comply with either 42 USC Section 1396p(d)(4)(A) or 1396p(d)(4)(C). Otherwise, any attempt to restrict the availability of principal or income while retaining any benefit for the settlor will be ineffective under eligibility rules, leading to the worst possible result: If a restrictive trust is effective under state trust laws, the trust may not actually be available to the transferor, but the desired goal of attaining public benefits eligibility will be lost. Furthermore, a transfer of assets from the individual beneficiary to a trust other than a (d)(4)(A) or (d)(4)(C) trust will result in a period of ineligibility (calculated differently for Medicaid and for SSI eligibility purposes).

Q 17:7 What types of self-settled special needs trusts will not affect Medicaid or SSI?

The Omnibus Budget Reconciliation Act of 1993 (OBRA '93) authorized the use of two types of self-settled special needs trusts: (1) the (d)(4)(A) or "payback trust" and (2) the (d)(4)(C) or "pooled trust." Not only are these trusts *not* counted as resources, transfers to them should be exempt from the transfer penalty rules (except that a transfer to a pooled trust, which may be established for someone who is over 65, will not escape penalty unless the beneficiary is under 65 or the transferor's child). [42 U.S.C. § 1396p(c)(2)(iii), (iv); State Medicaid Manual §§ 3258.10.B,3529.7.B)] The self-settled SNT will require specific language in order to qualify under these provisions. (See discussion of 42 USC Section1396p(d)(4) at Qs 17:8 and 17:9.) The trust assets will continue to be treated as available to the settlor unless the "special needs" restrictions are properly described and the appropriate "payback" provision included. These trusts may be referred to as "(d)(4)" trusts, "OBRA '93" trusts, "payback" trusts, or "self-settled SNTS."

In addition, OBRA '93 created a third type of self-settled trust, the "qualified income," "Miller" or "(d)(4)(B)" trust. The utility of this type of trust is limited to those circumstances in which a long-term care Medicaid applicant has income in excess of his or her state's income cap, and a (d)(4)(B) trust is not usually considered a "special needs" trust at all. (See chapter 14 for more detailed discussion of the (d)(4)(B) trust.)

Q 17:8 What is a "(d)(4)(A)" trust?

The first type of self-settled special needs trust [codified at 42 U.S.C. § 1396p(d)(4)(A)] exempts transfers made to a trust that:

1. Is established for the benefit of an individual (only one) who is (a) disabled under Social Security standards, and (b) is under age 65 at the time the trust is funded; if the beneficiary later attains age 65, the trust corpus continues to be treated as unavailable);
2. Is established by the parent, grandparent, guardian, or a court for the benefit of the disabled individual; and
3. Provides for repayment to the state of money paid for the benefit of the beneficiary pursuant to the state's Medicaid plan. Repayment must be made from the assets remaining in the trust on the beneficiary's death up to an amount equal to the total medical assistance paid on behalf of the individual. (Moreover, if more than one state has provided assistance, should the trust remainder prove insufficient, repayment must be made *pro rata*. [State Medicaid Manual § 3259.7]).

This type of trust is usually referred to as a "(d)(4)(A)" trust, an "under 65" trust, or "a payback trust." Such trusts are sometimes referred to as "Zebley" trusts after the named plaintiff in *Sullivan v. Zebley* [493 U.S. 521 (1990)], a class action that generated a substantial SSI back payment for a group of developmentally disabled plaintiffs in the mid-1980s. The proceeds from those settlements were placed in an early prototype of the modern special needs trust. Although the term "special needs trust" was first coined to describe third-party trusts, and although 42 USC Section 1396p(d)(4)(A) does not expressly require "special needs" limitations, both SSI and Medicaid rules will still treat *distributions* from a (d)(4)(A) trust as income to the extent that they comprise or can be converted into food, clothing, or shelter, and the State Medicaid Manual accordingly uses the term. Common usage of the term "special needs trust" has, as a result, come to include trusts established pursuant to 42 USC Section 1396p(d)(4)(A). Although 42 USC Section 1396p(d)(4)(A) provides that the trust must "contain the assets of the individual," the State Medicaid Manual permits contribution of trust assets by third parties. [State Medicaid Manual § 3259.7.A] As a practical matter it is possible to have a third-party funded OBRA '93 Trust unless one feels it necessary to make a gift to the disabled person who can then contribute the asset to the trust; presumably, contributions for the individual's benefit can be considered assets "of the individual" once they enter the trust. Unless the donor will soon require Medicaid, it is difficult to imagine very many circumstances in which a third party's assets should be contributed to a (d)(4)(A) trust; it will usually be far preferable to separately create a third-party SNT with no payback provision and, generally, more lenient treatment by state Medicaid agencies and the Social Security Administration.

Q 17:9 What is a "(d)(4)(C)" or "pooled" trust?

The second type of self-settled special needs trust exempted from transfer penalty rules under both SSI and Medicaid is a "pooled trust," also described and discussed in Q 14:90. [42 U.S.C. § 1396p(d)(4)(C)] This type of trust must:

1. "Contain the assets of" (i.e., be established for the benefit of) a disabled individual;
2. Be both established and managed by a nonprofit association;

3. Be treated as a separate trust for accounting purposes, but be pooled with assets held for other beneficiaries for investment and management purposes;
4. Include a separate account established for the individual beneficiary by his or her parent, grandparent, guardian, or a court, or (unlike (d)(4)(A) trusts) by the beneficiary himself or herself; and
5. Provide for repayment to the state for Medicaid payments to the extent that money remains in the account upon the beneficiary's death.

The fifth provision is somewhat ambiguous, as it provides that repayment is required only to "the extent that amounts remaining in the beneficiary's account upon the death of the beneficiary are not retained by the trust." In practice, most pooled trust accounts provide that some or all of the trust assets remaining at the beneficiary's death will be added to the accounts held for other beneficiaries; some states take the position that the Medicaid agency must be repaid first, while others do not. The pooled trust in at least one state, New Jersey, has interpreted this by requiring that up to 50 percent be used to repay the state and retaining the other 50 percent of trust assets.

42 USC Section 1396p(d)(4)(C) was enacted to permit pooled trust arrangements common in Illinois. Since its adoption as part of OBRA '93, pooled trust arrangements have been established in many other states, including, at least, California, Connecticut, Florida, Indiana, Kansas, Maryland, Michigan, New York, North Carolina, Pennsylvania, Rhode Island, Tennessee, Texas, and Virginia.

Q 17:10 Must a self-settled special needs trust be irrevocable?

Yes. Any self-settled trust must be irrevocable in order to qualify under 42 USC Section 1396p. Any power to amend or revoke retained by the settlor will almost certainly cause the self-settled SNT to fail.

Q 17:11 Can a self-settled special needs trust be amended?

Yes, at least in some states. Although a self-settled SNT must be irrevocable (in order to qualify as a (d)(4)(A) or (d)(4)(C) trust), federal law does not require it to be unamendable. Some state Medicaid agencies will permit such a trust to be amendable (by the trustee, a "trust protector," or some other person or group other than the beneficiary), although they may limit amendments to those necessary to ensure compliance with public benefits rules. Of course, if the beneficiary retains any right to amend, that right itself may be marketable, leading to treatment of the trust as an available resource; however, a power to amend given to a third person (perhaps including the trustee) may not interfere with the trust's ability to qualify.

Different states may treat a power to amend differently. Before including a power to amend, review state regulations (if any) and determine whether there will be any adverse consequences. Many states allow trusts that include a power to amend, particularly if that power is limited to amendments required to ensure continued compliance with Medicaid or SSI regulations.

Q 17:12 What is a trust protector?

Trust "protectors" have been used by some drafters even before the advent of special needs trusts. Although specifics vary depending on trust provisions, a trust protector may be given the power to amend the trust (to conform to changed regulations or circumstances), remove the trustee and name a successor, require or waive accountings, and take other actions to help ensure that the trust continues to be effective. Typically, a trust protector is also empowered to name his or her own successor. The trust protector can also help families resolve the dilemma of siblings who care about their special needs sibling but are not really inclined to serve as Trustee, if only because they will then be in the position of having to reject a sibling's demands. Serving as Trust Protector helps the sibling maintain contact and ensure that the trust is being properly carried out by the Trustee at a time when the beneficiary may be disabled from taking those steps on his or her own.

Q 17:13 Will transfers of assets into a self-settled special needs trust (other than a payback trust) result in a penalty period of ineligibility for public benefits?

In addition to treatment of trust assets or income as available to the beneficiary, transfer penalties may be imposed upon the establishment (or funding) of a self-settled trust. Both SSI and Medicaid law specifically exempt transfers into an under-65 [42 U.S.C. § 1396p(d)(4)(A)] trust. These transfers are not subject to the look-back and transfer penalties. Transfers by a person 65 years of age or older into a pooled trust are, however, subject to a 36-month look-back period in most states. [42 U.S.C. § 1396p(c)(2)(B)]

Transfers into other types of trusts may invoke a penalty period, but still provide useful planning opportunities; if the discretion of the trustee is appropriately limited, and the settlor is prepared to weather the transfer penalty period, a self-settled SNT may still be constructed to protect trust principal for children or other beneficiaries (without complying with Section 1396p). For example, an individual might transfer substantial assets into an irrevocable trust that provides that income is available to the settlor at the discretion of the trustee, but that no principal invasions are permitted under any circumstances. This transfer will result in a penalty period (which may be as long as 60 months, because the transfer is into a trust) during which the settlor will be ineligible to receive Medicaid benefits. After expiration of that period, the trust's income will be treated as available, but the principal may have been made unavailable to the settlor. This will result in income being used to supplement the Medicaid contribution for current care, but will preserve the principal for the residual beneficiaries. Such a trust is sometimes referred to as an "income only" trust. Properly speaking, however, "income only" trusts are not SNTs.

In some states, the use of such "income only" trusts is widespread —although they should not be confused with the similar-sounding but quite-different trusts provided for in 42 USC Section 1396p(d)(4)(B) (sometimes called "Miller," "qualified income" or, confusingly, "income only" trusts). The latter type of trust has limited value, because its only function is to make a Medicaid applicant with income over the state income eligibility limit nonetheless qualify for Medicaid long-term care benefits. The term "income only" trust in those states with Medicaid income caps almost always refers to what would better be described as a "qualified income" trust. (See chapter 14 for a discussion of Medicaid trusts.)

Q 17:14 Must existing Medicaid expenditures be reimbursed before funding of a self-settled special needs trust?

Repayment of Medicaid expenses before establishment of an SNT is an issue not of SNT administration *per se* but of Medicaid's lien recovery rights. When Medicaid expenses are incurred by virtue of a compensable injury (as in the case of an automobile accident caused by someone other than the Medicaid patient), Medicaid is subrogated to the individual's rights. Federal regulations require a state Medicaid plan to require "cooperation" by a Title XIX applicant in obtaining payment from third parties, including "paying to the agency any support or medical care fund received that are covered by an assignment of rights." [42 C.F.R. § 433.147] "Third party" coverage has been held to include tortfeasors who are liable for the cost of services under negligence principles. [Gooch v. Edelman, 398 F. Supp. 723 (D. Ill. 1974)] Therefore, if there is a recovery, Medicaid has a lien against the recovery. In general, this lien must be satisfied before any proceeds are distributed to or for the benefit of the Medicaid recipient. [42 U.S.C. § 1396k(a)(1)(A)] This is true when an SNT is not established, and most courts have held that the rule is the same when an SNT will be set up to receive the settlement (or judgment). [See Calvanese v. Calvanese, 93 N.Y.2d 111 (1999); Criccio v. Pennisi and Link v. Town of Smithtown, 90 N.Y.2d 296, 683 N.E.2d 301, 660 N.Y.S.2d 679 (1997); Waldman v. Candia, 317 N.J. Super. 464, 722 A.2d 581 (1999); S.S. v. State, 972 P.2d 439 (Utah 1998); Cargill v. State Department of Health, Division of Health Care Financing, 967 P.2d 999 (Wyo. 1998); Cuello v. Valley Farm Workers Clinic, Inc., 91 Wash. App. 307, 957 P.2d 1258 (1998); Herstberg Inter Vivos Trust v. Department of Mental Health, 578 N.W.2d 289 (Mich. 1998)]

Although some early decisions held that 42 USC Section 1396p(d)(4)(A) permitted funding of an SNT without the necessity of paying back the Medicaid lien, more recent decisions are uniform in ordering that lien recovery must precede the settlement. [Criccio v. Pennisi and Link v. Town of Smithtown, 90 N.Y.2d 296, 683 N.E.2d 301, 660 N.Y.S.2d 679 (1997)] A shrinking number of states may still permit the beneficiary to bypass lien recovery. For example, in one case, California allowed postponement of the lien when it would cause "financial hardship" to the plaintiff. [Garcia v. County of Sacramento, 103 Cal. App. 4th 67, 126 Cal. Rptr. 2d 465 (2002)] The vast majority, however, do not, and the trend favors the majority approach.

Remember, however, that the Medicaid payback is a function of that program's lien rights. In cases other than personal injury recoveries (such as inheritance, or lottery winnings, or even personal injury recovery for an injury not requiring medical care covered by the Medicaid program) there is no lien recovery right, and therefore no payback provision required before the funding of the trust.

It is also important to remember that state Medicaid agencies are required to adopt and implement hardship procedures. As a result, and in practice, there is always room to negotiate with the state Medicaid agency. 42 USC Section 1396p(d)(4) was enacted in part to cure the disincentive for Medicaid beneficiaries to bring lawsuits if they would lose all use of the funds. Where the lien may exceed the settlement proceeds, it may be possible to negotiate with the agency to postpone repayment of the lien or reduce the amount to be paid currently. Where the outcome of a case is uncertain, it may be possible to negotiate with the state before obtaining a settlement, on the grounds that without state leniency there would be no incentive to settle the case, but that settlement will provide a surer source of funds for the State.

Q 17:15 What portion of a recovery compensates the disabled person's attorney?

Suppose a disabled person has a $300,000 personal injury settlement. The person had entered into a one-third contingent fee arrangement with the attorney. The Medicaid lien is $200,000. Does the person get nothing? Or does the Medicaid agency get allocated $200,000, the plaintiff $100,000, and the $100,000 fee get allocated pro rata to each share? In at least one recent case the court held that it was allocated pro rata, on the theory that the claim was really subrogated to the state, which could have proceeded to collect but had not done so, and that accordingly the attorney was collecting a common fund for both the state and the plaintiff. [Roberts v. Sanders, 2002 WL 256740 (Tenn. App. 2002)] A New York court has reached the opposite result. [Mitchell v. Coney Island Site 4A-1 Houses, Inc., 2002 N.Y. Slip Op. 40239U, 2002 N.Y. Misc. LEXIS 650 (Sup. Ct. May 20, 2002]

Q 17:16 Must existing *Medicare* expenditures be reimbursed before funding of a self-settled special needs trust?

Although it is often viewed as similar to Medicaid's lien provisions, Medicare instead has adopted a "secondary payor" approach that recognizes Medicare's right of recovery from insurance coverage available to an injured Medicare beneficiary. [42 U.S.C. § 1395y (b)(2)(B)(iii); 42 C.F.R. § 411.26] Medicare's claim for reimbursement, however, may not extend to most personal injury recoveries. The secondary payor statute limits its application to "primary plan" payments, and those are in turn defined as group health insurance, liability or other insurance plans which can be expected to "promptly" (i.e., within 120 days) pay the medical costs; in such a case, the Medicare payment for services can be "conditional," requiring repayment. In *Thompson v. Goetzmann* [315 F.3d 457 (5th Cir. 2002)], the Fifth Circuit Court of Appeals held that the secondary payor statute did not permit Medicare to seek reimbursement from a products liability settlement, and strongly castigated the agency for seeking to expand its recovery rights beyond the limits of the statute —suggesting the possibility of judicial sanctions for any repeat efforts.

There is, independent of the problem defining the concept of secondary payors, an additional problem with Medicare: where a special needs trust is to be funded with a workers' compensation settlement, Medicare requires an "offset" going forward of any proceeds intended to compensate for future medical expenses, and will deny coverage until those proceeds are exhausted. It may be important to establish a "Medicare set-aside trust" to segregate such proceeds from other compensation, such as "scar awards" for permanent disability or disfigurement, in order to prevent Medicare from treating the entire award as being available for medical expenses.

Q 17:17 Who should consider establishing a self-settled special needs trust?

In many cases the self-settled SNT is an attractive option. This will often be true where medical needs are great, where the assets are modest (but not so modest as to be expended in a "pull out the stops" effort), or where the beneficiary has limited ability to appreciate the different consequences of the choices. In such cases, the individual (or guardian, parent, or other surrogate) should strongly consider establishing an SNT.

A self-settled SNT involves several trade-offs. Not every disabled individual who receives substantial assets will benefit from establishing an SNT. Although the SNT will permit the individual's assets to be extended (particularly where there are significant medical needs), the restriction on availability of the assets and income may be unattractive in individual cases. Particularly where the assets are modest, the administrative costs associated with maintaining the SNT (coupled with the nuisance of dealing with agency reporting requirements) may make it an even less attractive option. If the beneficiary is likely to continue living in the community, so that there would otherwise be no payback requirement on his or her death, it may be better to purchase housing than put funds in trust. In other cases, payment of existing debts, or purchase of a handicap-equipped vehicle or other adaptive devices, may prove to be a more administratively efficient use of funds than establishing an SNT (see Q 17:19).

Q 17:18 Who should *not* consider establishing a self-settled special needs trust?

In some cases, continued eligibility for public benefits is not important enough to subject the beneficiary to the limitations of an SNT. In other cases, the public benefits will not be affected by direct receipt of assets or income, so an SNT places an unnecessary limitation on the beneficiary's access to funds. Some public benefits are not "means tested." For example, Social Security Disability beneficiaries will not have their benefits affected by the acquisition of assets or income. After 24 months of SSD coverage such individuals will qualify for Medicare benefits as well, and those benefits will also be unaffected by receipt of assets or income. Of course, Medicare benefits may not be sufficient to cover all medical needs: Medicare fails to cover medications (except for hospice patients) and some other important medical care. If the trust is large, it will be able to afford payments for a quality Medigap policy and otherwise to pay for the "gaps" in Medicare. Thus, for many SSD/Medicare beneficiaries the value of an SNT will be limited. Those SSD recipients whose benefits are less than the maximum SSI benefit ($552 in 2003) may also qualify for SSI and Medicaid. Although it may not be critical for such an individual to continue to qualify for Medicaid coverage (after all, Medicare will pay for most of the acute medical needs), in some cases dual coverage will be important.

Q 17:19 What alternatives are there to self-settled special needs trusts?

In some cases rather than establish a special needs trust the disabled beneficiary will prefer to adopt one of these alternate approaches:

1. The assets may be used to purchase exempt property (home, handicap-equipped transportation, etc.). If the purchases can be made quickly, the loss of benefits may be short and the beneficiary's quality of life will be enhanced.
2. Assets can be spent quickly on therapy, treatment programs, or food, clothing, and shelter. The beneficiary might reasonably determine that "pulling out all the stops" for a brief period may result in some medical or physical improvement; if not, the beneficiary will return to the same circumstance as he or she was in prior to receipt of the assets.
3. The beneficiary might calculate that, with careful management of the money, he or she will be able to enjoy the benefits from the money for an extended period. Particularly where medical needs are modest, simply accepting the money, foregoing the public benefits, and managing the assets for maximum longevity may be the most attractive choice.

Third-Party Special Needs Trusts

Q 17:20 What is a third-party special needs trust?

A third-party special needs trust is a special needs trust established by one person for the benefit of another, and funded exclusively with assets not belonging to the disabled beneficiary. These trusts are usually established by a parent for the benefit of a disabled child (but could also be established by a child for a disabled parent). A properly drafted third-party special needs trusts allows the grantor to provide for the disabled beneficiary without jeopardizing the beneficiary's public benefits. The principal of a third-party SNT is not an available resource to the beneficiary. Distributions from the third-party SNT will not be treated as income unless either (1) the beneficiary is entitled to receive income distributions or (2) distributions are actually made directly to the beneficiary, or are made in a manner that would permit the beneficiary to convert them into food, clothing, or shelter. As is true with in-kind gifts to a beneficiary receiving SSI, in-kind provision of shelter from a third-party SNT may result in a proportional reduction in benefits without eliminating the benefits altogether.

Q 17:21 Must a third-party SNT repay the State upon the beneficiary's death for assistance paid to the beneficiary during his or her lifetime?

In general, no. The only exception under federal law is the situation when a d(4)(A) trust that is not directly self-settled, but was funded by someone who was a Medicaid applicant also—the parent going into the nursing home who instead of giving funds directly to a disabled child (exempt from penalty) chose to give them to a d(4)(A) trust. In a sense, this is a third-party funded OBRA '93 Trust.

The other possible exception may be in a State that decides that SNT provisions are void as against public policy unless there is a repayment obligation. To date, the only state that has taken this stance is Ohio. Ohio's HB 178, effective October 2001, amends Section 1339.51 of the Ohio Revised Code to provide:

> (G) Once a trustee takes action on a trust created by a settlor under this section and disburses trust funds on behalf of the beneficiary of the trust, then the trust may not be terminated or otherwise revoked by a particular event or otherwise without payment into the services fund created pursuant to section 5119.17 or 5123.40 of the Revised Code of an amount that is equal to the disbursements made on behalf of the beneficiary for medical care by the state from the date the trust vests but that is not more than fifty percent of the trust corpus.

Although the Ohio courts have seemed prepared to consider the invalidity of laws or regulations treating third-party trusts *without* a payback provision as "available," the implication in *Metz v. Ohio Department of Human Services* [145 Ohio App. 3d 304, 762 N.E.2d 1032 (2001) (dealing with a discretionary "support" trust)] was that a reimbursement right could be imposed by the legislature.

Q 17:22 What language should be used when drafting a third-party special needs trust?

In theory, a third-party trust should be able to function as an SNT without specific language, provided that the trustee has discretion as to whether to distribute or accumulate income and principal and meets any other state law requirements for a "spendthrift trust" to be immune from claims of the beneficiary's creditors. Because the beneficiary has no right to anticipate benefits from such a purely discretionary trust, it should not be counted as either an available asset or income to the beneficiary *except* to the extent that trust assets or income are actually distributed to the beneficiary (or expended on in-kind distributions that could be converted to necessities). Of course, if the trust requires the distribution of income to the beneficiary, or gives the beneficiary the power to compel distributions of principal, it will be treated as available [POMS § SI 01120.200.D.2]

However, even though specific special needs language may not technically be necessary for a third-party trust to qualify as an SNT, in the absence of such language state case law may create a presumption that the grantor had intended the trust to provide for the beneficiary's support, particularly where the trust is large and there is only one beneficiary. Therefore, it is always advisable for the draftsperson to include provisions that:

1. Make distributions of income and principal purely discretionary;
2. Specifically prohibit the trustee from making cash distributions directly to the beneficiary (although in some circumstances it may be advisable to permit occasional cash distributions, resulting in periods of ineligibility);
3. Direct the trustee to consider the effect of distributions on public benefits eligibility; and
4. Express the settlor's intention that the trust be used for supplemental benefits (preferably including some specific examples of trust uses) and not for necessities.

More important, perhaps, is what the trust language should *not* include. For example, Connecticut has recently adopted a statute that will treat as "available," for Medicaid purposes, any trust that is established for the beneficiary's "general or medical support."

[Public Act No. 01-02, amending Conn. Gen. Stat. § 17b-261] Even if the language described above were included, inclusion of offending language about "support" would cause the entire trust to be available. "Support" language is particularly dangerous, even if the Trustee retains discretion and no distributions are required. [See, e.g., Metz v. Ohio Department of Human Services, 145 Ohio App.3d 304, 762 N.E.2d 1032 (2001); Kryzso v. Ramsey County Social Services, 2000 N.D. 43, 607 N.W.2d 237 (2000)] Similarly, in Ohio a discretionary third-party trust that permits distributions for "welfare" or "general well-being" will still be considered available *even if* it prohibits distributions that would reduce or replace benefits. [Ohio Admin. Code 5101:1-39-271(C)(4)(b), (c)]

Some professionals advocate the use of a two-trust system, in which the trustee of the first trust has discretion to make payments only to the other trust. The second trust's distribution provisions are limited, in turn, to extra or supplemental benefits. This device retains the full discretion of the first trust's trustee, and the limitations against in-kind distributions that could be used for food, clothing, or shelter are imposed on the second trust's trustee. This approach is also being advocated in Ohio in light of the new restrictions on third-party trusts.

Finally, it will be important to review the particular state's laws even when drafting a third-party SNT. In some states, express prohibition on distributions that might affect benefits may be an essential term to refute any claim that the trust is for "support." In other states, such as Ohio, this language may be considered "against public policy" and explicitly void, unless the trust either requires termination if it is treated as available, or complies with the limits of Ohio Rev. Code Section 1339.51, including a cap on the amount that can fund the trust ($218,000 in 2003). [Ohio Adm. Code 5101:1-39-271(A)(2)(e), (C)(4)(b), (c)] In Ohio, the case law is undecided on the public policy issue. [See, e.g., Carnahan v. Ohio Dept. of Human Serv., 139 Ohio App.3d 214, 743 N.E.2d 473 (2000); Young v. Ohio Dept. of Human Serv. 76 Ohio St.3d 547, 668 N.E.2d 908 (1996)] It cannot be overemphasized that the practitioner *must* review current laws, even those not yet codified, to be sure that any statutory requirements have been met.

Q 17:23 Must a third-party special needs trust be irrevocable?

A third-party trust can be revocable, provided that the beneficiary does not hold the power of revocation. Even if a beneficiary's power of revocation is limited in time, the Medicaid agency or Social Security Administration will likely treat the future power of revocation as having a current value, causing inclusion of some or all of the trust principal in the beneficiary's available resources. Consequently, any power to revoke or amend should be retained by the grantor or granted to the trustee, a trust protector, or a suitable third person. Revocability (along with limited powers of appointment and other retained powers) may have either an income or estate tax effect —or both—so it is important to coordinate the different treatment of such trusts under public benefits and tax regulations.

One related technique might be to make a present transfer in trust, retaining the power (in the third-party grantor) to revoke the trust. This should cause the trust to be treated as a grantor trust for income tax purposes, resulting in income tax liability to the grantor. In an appropriate circumstance, this might permit larger transfers to the benefit of the disabled beneficiary without incurring gift tax liability (or, incidentally, reducing the grantor's estate for tax purposes—except by the amount of the income tax liability itself). The same result can be reached in any case in which the original grantor retains other powers that cause the trust to be treated as a grantor trust under I.R.C. Code Sections 671 through 675. Such a trust is often referred to as an "intentionally defective" irrevocable trust (see Q 5:111).

Q 17:24 Who should consider establishing a third-party special needs trust?

Every parent or grandparent of a disabled child should strongly consider special needs trust planning. This is true whether the anticipated inheritance is large or small, and even when the inherited assets might include exempt resources (such as the family home, which the disabled beneficiary could own while still qualifying for continued benefits). By providing for the child's extra or supplemental needs, while retaining government benefits, the child's life can actually be enhanced by the inheritance. If the child's "share" of the parent's estate is large, it can provide useful benefits for the child's life and still provide for an ultimate inheritance for grandchildren (including, where they exist, the disabled child's children). If the "share" is smaller, it can be stretched over an extended period of time, providing meaningful enhancements to the child's quality of life throughout that time period. This is clearly more beneficial than the traditional approach of simply disinheriting the disabled child. When the client says "but his brother will look after him," it is the lawyer's job to gently suggest that the disabled child's brother may (a) want to live his own life; (b) resent such a burden being placed upon him; (c) marry someone who feels the same; (d) have a future of uncertain financial stability; or (e) fail to outlive the disabled sibling, leaving nieces, nephews and in-laws responsible for "looking after" their disabled relative.

Q 17:25 How and when should a third-party special needs trust be funded?

Usually, it is most convenient *not* to fund a third-party special needs trust during the grantor's lifetime. A gift to a special needs trust will not qualify for the annual exclusion from gift taxes, because it is not a gift of a present interest. Typically, the trust is simply substituted for the child in the family member's estate planning documents, beneficiary designations, etc. Some additional funding options and issues:

1. Include the trust as one of several beneficiaries of a separate life insurance trust. The special needs trust should not itself hold a "Crummey" power over the life insurance trust, and if the special needs trust simply owns the policy, there are potential gift tax problems (relevant to those with ultimately federally taxable estates or those in a state that does not tie gift tax to the unified credit, for now, only Connecticut.) Some practitioners suggest limiting the Crummey withdrawal right to a right to special needs payments. Far preferable is to give other parties a minor but non-*de minimis* benefit upon the settlor's death, and let those individuals hold the Crummey powers. For example: if there are three children, only one of whom has special needs, the two healthy children might each be entitled to 5 percent plus $1 of the trust upon the grantor's death, and also hold the Crummey powers.

The special needs trust would receive effectively 90 percent on the grantor's death, but hold no Crummey powers during lifetime.

2. Consider making gifts to a 529 Plan that then names the special needs trust as beneficiary. Gifts to a Section 529 Plan are automatically exempt from gift tax. The gifts to the plan would be exempt, and, moreover, would grow tax-free. Upon distribution for educational needs—including those relating to accommodating the individual's disability—there should be no income tax. If the distribution is for non-qualified purposes, there would be both tax on any gains or income, and a 10 percent penalty—but this may be far preferable than the alternative, that is, paying income tax at trust rates from funding until the date of distribution.

3. Name a trust as an IRA beneficiary (carefully). If the trust is likely to receive IRA distributions, the trust should be drafted to avoid any charitable or non-human vested remainderman. With a vested remainder in a charity, the trust will not qualify as a trust which may be "looked through" to the beneficiary's life expectancies when computing distributions. This means that if an IRA owner who has passed age 70½, and names the trust as a beneficiary, on the owner's death, distribution to the trust must be made over the IRA owner's remaining actuarial life expectancy; if the IRA owner is under age 70½, the IRA will have to be distributed within five years. By contrast, if the beneficiaries are identifiable individuals, and the charity as beneficiary is only contingent upon the premature death of another named individual remainderman, the life expectancies of the individual beneficiaries may be used, for a longer distribution and reduced income tax burden.

In addition to gift tax issues, the drafter must also be aware of generation-skipping tax issues, because the special needs trust is a lifetime trust and the remainder may pass ultimately to more remote heirs. The drafter will have to consider whether the grantor's/testator's GST exemption should be allocated more substantially to the special needs trust than to other trusts established as part of the overall process, perhaps by making a reverse election on a timely filed gift tax return with respect to gifts made to *other* trusts.

Q 17:26 Can the court establish or convert an existing trust to a special needs trust?

Early development of special needs trusts focused on the imagined distinction between trusts established by the beneficiary on the one hand and trusts established by court order on the other. In the states that expressly permit courts to establish trusts for the benefit of wards under conservatorship, the argument was made that those trusts were not self-settled but were actually third-party trusts —with the "third party" being the court. This legal fiction was eliminated with the adoption of 42 USC Section 1396p(d)(2)(A)(iii) and (iv), which expressly include any trust established by a court or administrative body when acting "on behalf of" or "at the request of" the individual or his or her spouse.

Practically speaking, courts may be very reluctant to serve in the role of "grantor" and thereby to "establish" a special needs trust. They may, depending on state law, be permitted but not required, to establish such trusts. [See, e.g., Matter of the Guardianship of Scott G.G., 2003 Wisc. App. 52 (2003), which read authority to establish an SNT into the statute directing guardians (of the estate) to "exchange property of the guardianship estate ... for the purpose of ... providing for the ward's care."]

Recently, the Social Security Administration threw practitioners into confusion by stating that *only* a guardian or court could establish such a trust, because a parent or grandparent had no authority to dispose of the person's assets. [POMS § SI 01120.203 B.1.e] This logic is hard to fault, except that the federal law provides otherwise. The SSA apparently distinguishes between the statutory authority to act as grantor and the legal power to transfer assets; this problem may be resolvable in some cases by having a competent beneficiary give a power of attorney to a parent or grandparent. In this fashion the trust can be "established" by one of the individuals listed in the statute, but utilizing the beneficiary's authority to effect the transfer by the power of attorney. This distinction may seem foolish and elevates form over substance; nevertheless, it is clearly preferable to use an approach that will satisfy the SSA if the beneficiary is an SSI recipient.

Depending on state law it may be possible, upon a court petition, to reform an existing trust that no longer will pass muster, into an appropriate third-party self-funded trust, as the case may be. It will, however, be necessary to educate the court as to the reason why such a reformation is necessary. In the case of a third-party trust it will be important to ensure that the petition indeed reforms the trust, including evidence of the original grantor's intent, to avoid having the transaction treated as creating a new, self-settled trust.

Q 17:27 What alternatives are there to establishing a special needs trust for a disabled child?

Traditionally, parents of disabled children faced three choices in estate planning dealing with their child's disability:

1. Disinherit the child, on the theory that he or she would be provided for by government benefits;
2. Leave the child his or her "share" of the estate, anticipating that public benefits would thereby be lost, at least until the inheritance was consumed; or
3. Leave the disabled child a greater share of the estate, anticipating that his or her needs would be greater—particularly after the loss of government benefits.

Special needs trust planning permits a much more satisfying (for most parents) choice: Leave the disabled child his or her "share," but in an SNT that will allow the child to retain government benefits.

Distributions from Special Needs Trusts

Q 17:28 What payments may a special needs trust make without interfering with the beneficiary's government benefits?

The central purpose of an SNT is to provide for supplemental needs without disrupting public benefits. In most cases, that means protecting SSI and Medicaid benefits. Because Medicare and Social Security Disability benefits are not means-tested, they are not affected by the expenditures from the SNT.

Both Medicaid and SSI rules are similar: Any "income" received or considered "available" to the beneficiary will reduce or eliminate the benefits received. [42 U.S.C. § 1382(b)] Cash will affect benefits dollar for dollar (after the occasional $20/month gift). Payments not to the beneficiary, but to pay for "food, clothing or shelter" will reduce benefits by approximately one-third of the maximum benefit (for 2003, $552, so the reduction will be $184), with or without a $20 adjustment depending on living situation. Payments not to the beneficiary, and for something that could not reasonably be converted to food, clothing, or shelter (a new furnace; a television that cannot be returned for cash), do not count at all. And finally, all other payments not to the beneficiary but that could be readily converted to cash, count as cash, measured by the fair market value of the item.

Q 17:29 How do payments of cash by the special needs trust affect the beneficiary?

"Income" that reduces benefits includes periodic payments made by anyone, even though the beneficiary may not be entitled to those payments or any future payments. [42 U.S.C. § 1382(b)] In other words, any payment of benefits directly to the trust beneficiary will directly affect Medicaid and SSI eligibility. They will reduce SSI dollar for dollar (after the first $20 unless received regularly); they will affect Medicaid eligibility to the extent that they cause the recipient to exceed an income cap or cause the recipient to have a greater "spend-down" of income requirement in a medically needy state (see Q 14:18).

Q 17:30 How do payments by the special needs trust for (but not to) the beneficiary affect benefits?

Both Medicaid and SSI permit in-kind distributions by third parties (including trusts) to beneficiaries. Only if the distributions or payments are either food, clothing or shelter, or convertible into one of those categories of necessities, do they reduce benefits.

In other words, an SNT trustee who purchases clothes for the trust beneficiary will reduce public benefits. So will the trustee who purchases gift certificates and delivers them to the beneficiary, but only if the gift certificates are for a store that sells food, clothing, or shelter, or if the store permits the gift certificates to be cashed in or transferred. In the last case, the beneficiary could sell the certificates to others, then use the proceeds to purchase necessities; as a consequence, the certificates themselves will be disqualifying (even if the beneficiary actually uses them to purchase non-essentials). Usually, other kinds of in-kind distributions, such as the gift of a television, are not considered convertible to food, clothing or shelter, even though presumably the recipient could sell or pawn the television for that purpose.

The SSI program does have one important exception to these rules. Small gifts are ignored; the first $20 received by the beneficiary in any month will not reduce or otherwise affect the SSI benefit. [42 U.S.C. § 1382a(b)(2)(A)]

Q 17:31 Are in-kind distributions of food, clothing, or shelter treated like distributions of cash?

No. In-kind distributions of food, clothing, or shelter invoke special rules. In-kind contribution of food, clothing, or shelter may reduce, but should not usually eliminate, benefits.

The Social Security Administration has different rules for different living arrangements. First, when a beneficiary is living with family, or generally living with others but not in an institution, and is provided with not only shelter but "maintenance," SSI rules reduce benefits by one-third of the maximum SSI benefit, known as the "value of the one-third reduction" (VTR). [POMS § SSI 00835.001] This is the rule as set out in 42 USC Section1382a(a)(2)(A).

When, on the other hand, the beneficiary receives in-kind support and maintenance (food, clothing, or shelter) but does not receive both food and shelter from the household in which the beneficiary lives, a slightly different rule applies—benefits are reduced by the lesser of the actual value (or if unknown the market value) or the "presumed maximum value," which is once again, the one-third of the maximum SSI benefit. [POMS § SI 00835.300] The difference is that in this case, the additional $20 that was disregarded for the person living in another's household is not disregarded and the reduction will be $20 higher. [See, e.g., § SI 00835.900 Values for In-Kind Support and Maintenance]

In either case, the benefit is not reduced by more than one-third or at the most, one-third of the maximum plus $20. This is a tremendously important benefit for SSI and Medicaid recipients (SSI beneficiaries categorically qualify to receive Medicaid benefits), both in the realm of SNTs and in general practice. Many SSI beneficiaries live with family members, who provide extensive care in addition to the shelter; those beneficiaries will experience a reduction in their benefits, but the SSI check will not be eliminated. In turn, for SSI states categorical Medicaid eligibility will be extended so that medical care (which may be the most important component of the public benefits scheme) will be provided. Finally, if the beneficiary is living in an apartment for which another family member provides rental assistance paid directly to the landlord, benefits will not be lost. [POMS § SI 00835.350]

Q 17:32 What kinds of expenses are considered "shelter" and what are not?

The Social Security POMS lists 10 items that constitute "food and shelter" or "household expense" items, and makes clear that the list is exclusive:

1. Food
2. Mortgage (including property insurance required by the mortgage holder)
3. Real property taxes (less any tax rebate/credit)
4. Rent
5. Heating fuel
6. Gas
7. Electricity
8. Water
9. Sewer
10. Garbage removal

Note. Condominium fees in themselves are not household costs. However, condominium fees may include charges which are household costs (e.g., garbage removal). To the extent that such charges are identifiable, use them in the computation of inside and outside ISM. [POMS § SI 00835.465]

Q 17:33 How can this treatment of "ISM" be used to benefit an SNT beneficiary?

Because in-kind distributions will usually not eliminate the SSI and Medicaid benefits, it may be appropriate in some circumstances to permit the trust to provide food, clothing, or shelter directly—particularly shelter, which will likely cost more than the "one-third."

This can be done by purchasing a residence for the beneficiary (and titling it in his or her name) or by purchasing or renting a residence and providing it to the beneficiary without cost. Depending on individual circumstances, either approach may be appropriate in at least some cases. In preparing the trust's language, the SNT draftsperson should consider the possibility that shelter at least will be provided in the future.

For public benefits purposes, "shelter" includes not only the beneficiary's residence but also those services necessary for the maintenance of the residence. Taxes, repairs, and necessary utilities (water, sewer, electricity, gas) will be included in the definition of shelter. Telephone, cable television, and other non-essential utilities may be provided without being treated as in-kind distributions of shelter.

Q 17:34 How might the provision of shelter be structured to benefit the SNT beneficiary?

Assuming the trust permits the provision of shelter for the beneficiary, and that the trustee determines it to be in the beneficiary's best interests, there are a number of methods available to secure shelter:

1. *Purchase of a residence in the trust's name.* Occupation of the home by the special needs trust beneficiary will not give rise to "in-kind support and maintenance" by a third party, because the beneficiary has a "beneficial interest" in the trust. [POMS § SI 01120.200F] Of course, a home owned by a (d)(4)(A) trust will be subject to that trust's payback requirement on the death of the beneficiary.
2. *Purchase of the residence in the beneficiary's name.* This approach will not reduce the continuing benefits, although it may result in one month's ineligibility (the transfer of the residence into the beneficiary's name is "income" under SSI rules). Although the effect on benefits is minimized, this does leave the residence unprotected if there is any likelihood that the beneficiary could encumber it, and subjects the home to any estate recovery rights the State may have if the beneficiary is over age 55. Furthermore, if the trust continues to pay utilities and taxes, the SSI benefit will be reduced at least periodically.

3. *Rental by the trust for the beneficiary*. Rather than purchasing a residence outright, the trust could pay the rent (and utilities) for a home for the beneficiary. This approach will have the same effect as outright purchase; the benefits will be reduced but should not be eliminated. Meanwhile, the trust's assets may be more productive than the growth in real estate values, and flexibility is retained for the frequently unpredictable circumstances of the beneficiary's life.
4. *Fractional interests*. The trust could purchase a residence in the name of the beneficiary and another person as joint tenants (assuming that there are no fiduciary issues—either because the joint tenant contributes to the purchase or is also a trust beneficiary). In this fashion, the ability of the beneficiary to encumber the asset is limited, and the effect on benefits is minimized.
5. *Taking back a secured interest*. Finally, the trustee might choose to purchase the beneficiary a residence, deeded to the beneficiary, but with a lien in the trust's favor for the full value of the property. This will minimize the loss of benefits and protect the trustee from concerns about owning real property, but still restrict the beneficiary's ability to encumber the property.

Q 17:35 What other kinds of distributions might be made from the SNT?

The SNT Trustee might distribute the following to the beneficiary without affecting benefits:

1. *Vehicle*. A single vehicle (quaintly, the list of acceptable vehicles includes cars, trucks, boats, snowmobiles, animal-drawn vehicles, and even animals) is excluded from available resources regardless of its value (so long as it is modified for a handicapped person, necessary for employment or medical treatment, or necessary because of climate, terrain, etc.). Otherwise, the vehicle may not have more than $4,500 in equity. (The trust could presumably arrange so that the car's equity never exceeded $4,500.) Modifications for the handicapped may cost $30,000 or more; a new handicapped-modified van may be at least $50,000. Since distribution of a vehicle from the SNT to the beneficiary is not a distribution of

food, clothing, or shelter (and therefore not ISM), no income will be attributed to the beneficiary in a month in which a vehicle is purchased by the trust for the beneficiary, nor will income be attributed when the trust pays the auto insurance. On the other hand, if the trust *owns* the vehicle, the trustee puts the trust assets at risk in the event of an accident by the beneficiary as driver.

2. *Burial space, prepaid funeral arrangements and irrevocable burial trusts.* As with purchase of a vehicle, purchase of burial and funeral arrangements in the name of the beneficiary will not be penalized in any way if the resultant asset is not an available resource. In other words, the SNT can purchase a burial plot and casket, prepay the costs of burial, and set aside $1,500 in funeral expenses (or more, if it is possible under state law to create an irrevocable burial trust). For an OBRA '93 "payback" trust, this is particularly important, as the state's claim must be paid *before* any funeral has been paid for.
3. *Personal effects.* Purchase of items worth less than $2,000 (other than food, clothing, or shelter) will not result in any penalty. Because the fair market value of personal items delivered to the beneficiary may be less than the purchase price, it should be permissible to purchase substantial quantities of furniture, furnishings and the like—including computers, televisions, stereo equipment, etc.
4. *Travel.* Airline tickets (and other travel tickets) given to an SSI beneficiary are not income if they are for domestic travel (travel within the 50 states, the District of Columbia and U.S. possessions and protectorates). Tickets for non-domestic travel must be non-refundable—if they are refundable they will be treated as ISM because the recipient could cash them in and purchase food, clothing and/or shelter. This is true even if the tickets are not cashed in but are actually used for the intended travel. [POMS § SI 00830.521]
5. *Loans to the beneficiary.* A loan to an SSI recipient is not treated as income—provided that the transaction is a bona fide loan. [POMS § SI 00815.350] If the loan is not bona fide, the proceeds are income in the month received. Clearly, any loan should be carefully documented and evidenced by a written note signed by the recipient. Whether or not the

borrowing beneficiary is credit-worthy does not apparently affect the bona fide status of the loan. Here again, however, it is desirable to include language expressly authorizing such loans which may otherwise violate the trustee's duties towards other beneficiaries.

6. *Medical care.* Payments for medical and dental care and insurance are not income to the beneficiary. [20 C.F.R. § 416.1103(a)] Even if the beneficiary is on Medicaid, dental insurance would be a highly prudent expenditure.
7. *Educational, vocational, social, and personal services.* So long as payments are not for food, clothing or shelter, none of the listed distributions will result in ISM treatment [20 C.F.R. § 416.1124] Note, however, that dorm fees (because they are for room and board) will be treated as income to the recipient.

Q 17:36 Are there any required restrictions on distributions from an OBRA '93 Trust?

Nothing in federal law prohibits the Trustee of an SNT from expending some or all of the trust principal for the benefit of the beneficiary, leaving nothing behind for the state's claim of repayment. A major issue with Medicaid agencies is whether the "payback" requirement should be treated as if the agency were a beneficiary—in which case the Trustee may owe a duty of impartiality to make sure there is enough remaining to pay the State—or simply a creditor. Some states have gone so far as to require pre-authorization by or advance notice to the agency before a distribution has been made for the distribution not to affect benefits. Whether or not this attitude is legally well founded, the Trustee would be advised to become familiar with the state law requirements rather than risk upsetting benefits needlessly.

A further issue for an OBRA '93 Trust may be the "sole benefit" requirement of 42 USC Section 1396p(d)(4). Inevitably, expenditures may be proposed that will benefit family members as well as the beneficiary. It may be possible to characterize these appropriately: to pay a family member to escort the beneficiary on a vacation; to refurbish the house that the beneficiary shares with the family; to purchase an item for the beneficiary that it is likely may also be used by third parties. On the other hand, the Trustee should be ready for a challenge and may wish to seek prior approval for particularly difficult expenditures.

Q 17:37 What else should the Trustee consider when making distribution decisions?

Eligibility and fiscal prudence aside, there are intra-family and emotional issues to consider in managing the distributions from a special needs trust.

1. *Relative wealth of the family*. One of the thorniest problems of all is how to treat the relatively "wealthy" SNT beneficiary who lives with his or her poor family. On one hand, the SNT should not be seen as support for the entire family. On the other hand, the beneficiary should not be constrained to live in poverty despite available resources just because he or she comes from a poor family. On the other hand again, it can be important not to encourage family members to either become dependent on SNT money or resentful of the beneficiary's relative wealth. This balance can be extremely difficult to maintain—and especially when family members act as trustee.

2. *Effect on family members*. If the proposal is for a therapy pool that other family members will know as a hot tub, how important is the therapy pool to the beneficiary's care? If, on the other hand, the proposed expenditure is for a computer that will be housed in the beneficiary's room, and especially if other children in the household have their own computers already, a favorable decision may be easier to make.

3. *Beneficiary's wishes*. A competent (or marginally competent) beneficiary should be given every opportunity to identify his or her preferences and desires. Whether the original source of money was first-party or third-party, the beneficiary's happiness and autonomy should be the primary goal.

Taxation

Q 17:38 How is a special needs trust treated for income tax purposes?

Trusts (except for "grantor" trusts, as described later) must file federal and state income tax returns. The trust may have available deductions (e.g., for costs of administration) that reduce the taxable income just as for individual taxpayers. In addition to more familiar deductions, the trust will be entitled to deduct distributions made to or for the benefit of the trust's beneficiary. Those deductions will (to the extent of net trust income) result in the reporting of income to the beneficiary, which will result in the tax ultimately being paid by the beneficiary.

If the trust is a grantor trust, no tax return is required. Federal tax law recognizes that trusts created by (or on behalf of) the grantor for the grantor's benefit should not alter the income taxation of income received by the trust, and so it ignores the existence of the trust. Thus, a grantor trust does not file any separate income tax return, and all of the trust's income is taxable directly to the grantor/beneficiary.

This is important for two reasons. First, treatment as a grantor trust saves the administrative expense of preparing a separate trust income tax return. Second, and more importantly, treatment as a grantor trust will almost always result in a lower federal tax liability, because trust income is taxed at the highest marginal rate of 39.6 percent after taxable income has reached $7,500 (2001 tax year figure), instead of at the $250,000 level, as it is for most single taxpayers. [I.R.C. § 1] In other words, to the extent that income is not actually distributed to or for the benefit of the beneficiary, grantor trust treatment can save nearly 15 percent in federal taxes for much of the trust's income.

Q 17:39 Must a special needs trust have a separate employer identification number (EIN)?

Third-party special needs trusts will almost always be separate taxpaying entities (unless the SNT is an intentionally defective grantor trust, and taxed as income to the donor) and therefore require a separate EIN. With regard to self-settled SNTs, however, the rules are less clear.

Assuming that care has been taken to ensure that the self-settled SNT is a grantor trust, the tax treatment of the trust's income will be entirely on the beneficiary's income tax return. There are, however, at least three ways to accomplish this result, with any one being acceptable. In the first, the self-settled SNT applies for and receives an EIN and then files an annual return. On each return the trustee notes that the filing is informational only (no actual income or deduction figures need be included on the return) and that trust income and expenses will be reported on the individual's individual income tax return.

In the second approach, no EIN is obtained at all. Although many accountants (and bank officers) believe that any trust in which the grantor is not the beneficiary must have a separate EIN, even though treated as a grantor trust, the regulations do not require that treatment. 26 CFR Section 301.6109-1(h)(2)(i) provides: "Except as otherwise provided in regulations or other guidance, a single owner entity that is disregarded as an entity separate from its owner under Sec. 301.7701-3, must use its owner's taxpayer identifying number (TIN) for federal tax purposes." The difference of opinion relates to whether or not a trust with a trustee, representing both the grantor/beneficiary, and the remainder interests, is properly a "single owner entity."

Finally, some practitioners prefer a hybrid approach. The trustee can apply for an EIN for the SNT and file single return, marked as the final return. Attached to that return the trustee can indicate that the trust is a grantor trust, that all income and expense amounts will be reported on the beneficiary's individual return, and that there will be no further filings by the trust as a separate entity.

Q 17:40 Is a special needs trust always a "grantor" trust for income tax purposes?

A self-settled special needs trust will almost always be a grantor trust, even if it is actually established by a court or someone acting on the beneficiary's behalf (as, for example, in the case of a personal injury settlement assigned to the trust). This will be true because the trustee usually is given the power to make distributions of income for the benefit of the beneficiary without requiring the approval of a person who holds a remainder interest in the trust. [I.R.C. § 677] Even if the trust is constructed so that distributions for the benefit of the grantor/beneficiary require the approval of an adverse party (e.g., one who will receive the trust's corpus upon the beneficiary's death [I.R.C. § 672(a)]), a reversionary interest may be included to ensure treatment as a grantor trust. [I.R.C. § 673]

Third-party special needs trusts may not qualify as "grantor" trusts quite so easily. In order to gain treatment as a grantor trust, it may be advisable to give the beneficiary a power to borrow from the trust without having to give adequate security [I.R.C. § 675(2)], or to purchase trust property for less than adequate consideration [I.R.C. § 675(1)], or one of the other powers described in Code Sections 671 through 675. The benefit of a "grantor" type third-party special needs trust may well be offset by the possibility that these powers could open the door to state claims that the beneficiary seek to exercise them in order to access the trust principal.

Q 17:41 Won't the treatment of the special needs trust as a grantor trust result in disqualification of the beneficiary from public benefits?

Once the special needs trust has obtained grantor trust status, it need not file income tax returns. The beneficiary, on the other hand, will then be taxed on the trust's entire income, even though the income is not received directly. As a result that income will have to be reported for the beneficiary, ultimately causing that income tax to come to the attention of the public benefit program administration (e.g., SSI or Medicaid).

"Income" for tax purposes is not "income" for public benefit programs purposes. However, this fine distinction may be over the heads of some functionaries. The beneficiary's income tax return will now show all of the trust's income as if it were the beneficiary's own. Because many benefit programs require the beneficiary to produce income tax returns, which in some cases are the basis for an award of benefits, one has to expect at least an initial problem. Anyone who has tried to get an agency to understand that this year's income will not be the same as last year's, and so the income tax return should be disregarded, will understand the bureaucratic problems that may arise. Therefore, the practitioner should be ready to help explain the situation to the agency so that there is no sudden discontinuation of benefits on the theory that the beneficiary is over assets. Assuming adequate records are kept, it should be easy to demonstrate that the taxable income was not in fact received by the beneficiary, and that the trust provided no food, clothing, or shelter (or, as described previously, that they were provided in-kind, and that the resultant reduction in benefits was calculated at the time). The sooner this can be explained, the better, preferably prior to any need to submit income tax returns.

Q 17:42 What are the estate and gift tax consequences of funding a special needs trust *inter vivos*?

Once again the answer will differ for self-settled and third-party special needs trusts. Transferring the beneficiary's interest in trust property into an irrevocable trust in which he or she retains an income interest will not result in removing the asset from his or her estate, and so the entire trust corpus will be taxable upon the death of the grantor/beneficiary. [I.R.C. § 2036(a)]

Gift tax liability is somewhat more complicated, because the special needs trust will be irrevocable. Some practitioners feel that in order to avoid incurring a gift tax, the self-settled special needs trust should include a testamentary power of appointment. [Rev. Rul. 54-342, 1954-2 C.B. 315] There are some alternative theories for avoiding adverse gift tax consequences for a self-funded special needs trust, which include: (a) the payback requirement in effect means that for all intents and purposes the trust is payable to the beneficiary's estate at death, or at any rate, is likely to be wiped out in order to pay the creditors of the beneficiary's estate i.e., the beneficiary/grantor has retained a reversion over more than the greater of $5,000 or 5 percent of the trust; or (b) the gift is incomplete because of the trust's vulnerability to claims of the settlor/beneficiary's creditors generally as a self-settled discretionary trust. [Holtz v. Commissioner, 38 T.C. 37 (1962), acq., 1962-2 C.B. 4; discussed and clarified in Rev. Rul. 77-378, limiting the reach of Rev. Rul. 62-13 and applying Commissioner v. Vander Weele, 254 F. 2d 895 (6th Cir. 1958) and Gramm v. Commissioner, 17 T.C. 1063 (1951), acq., 1962-1 C.B. 4]

A third-party trust, on the other hand, will be taxable in the beneficiary's estate only to the extent that the beneficiary has sufficient incidents of ownership, such as a general power of appointment. [I.R.C. § 2041(a)] Ordinarily, the drafter of a third-party special needs trust will want to avoid inclusion of the trust assets in the beneficiary's estate, and so will choose to limit any power of appointment. There is some worry that the power of appointment will in some way cause the agency to suggest that it must be exercised (notwithstanding its terms) in favor of the agency. Although at least one court has defeated such a claim [Ahern v. Thomas, 248 Conn. 708, 733 A.2d 746 (1999)], the issue is less clear in New York. Inclusion of a power of appointment not limited to issue may also cause problems if the trust is to serve as the beneficiary of an IRA.

Trust Administration

Q 17:43 Who should be trustee of a special needs trust?

Although the beneficiary of an SNT should not be the trustee (and, in most cases, the beneficiary's spouse should also be foreclosed, as "deeming" rules can complicate calculations when spouses have discretion with regard to distributions), almost anyone else can be named. Among the choices in most cases:

- A parent or other family member
- A bank, trust department, or other corporate trustee
- A trusted family friend, financial adviser, or accountant
- In states where the industry is established, a professional private fiduciary or case management agency
- A lawyer

Q 17:44 What are the advantages and disadvantages of selecting each type of trustee for an SNT?

Selecting any of the common choices of trustee for an SNT has both advantages and disadvantages, which are detailed further here. Also provided are some suggestions for selecting specific persons or entities as trustee for an SNT.

1. *Family members*. Although they may seem like the logical choice, family members are seldom equipped to deal with the details of trust accounting (including tax preparation) and the

special requirements of distributions inherent in SNT administration, and at the very least will have to farm out these duties to paid professionals anyway. Most practitioners with substantial SNT experience have also learned that even the best-intentioned family members seem to be unable to resist the temptation of SNT assets, and will frequently misuse trust assets (either for their own benefit or for food, clothing, or shelter for the beneficiary, leading to suspension of public benefits). On the other hand, family members are more likely to know the immediate needs of the SNT beneficiary, to appreciate the real-world value of proposed expenditures, and to monitor the effectiveness of treatment, equipment, and discretionary spending for the benefit of the beneficiary. Family members are likely to be less expensive trustees; in fact, family members will usually not charge any fee, and may be precluded from charging fees if they are themselves recipients of public benefits.

2. *Corporate trustees.* Few corporate trustees are familiar with SNT requirements or public benefits rules, although a handful of banks have begun to "specialize" in SNT administration. Most SNT beneficiaries require at least some case management or social work from the trustee, which corporate officers are ill-equipped to provide. Banks and other corporate trustees are likely to be the most expensive alternative, as well. Corporate trustees, on the other hand, will be proficient at trust (and tax) accounting techniques, and offer stability, reliability, and continuity. Especially for larger SNTs (which require substantial investment experience and, at the same time, offer the possibility of negotiated trustee's fees), corporate trustees may be the only choice reasonably available in some areas.

3. *Financial advisers.* Accountants, brokers, financial planners, and others may hold themselves out to be SNT trustees. Unless the individual has particular experience with both public benefits and trust administration—and many do—such individuals are usually poor choices to act as trustee, unless they are ready, willing and able from the outset to consult both with family, and with legal professionals. Fees are likely to be lower than corporate trustees, but substantially higher than family members' fees. When considering a

non-professional trustee, look for personal experience; often the proposed trustee's exposure to public benefits and special needs comes from caring for a disabled child, parent, or sibling. Alternatively, endeavor to establish a "team" whereby the accountant or other such person at least keeps costs down but is trained to seek legal advice when issues arise.

4. *Case managers*. Professional case management agencies have grown in number and caseload in recent years, and many states have a well-developed case management industry. In some (but not all) of those states, case management agencies may act as trustees of SNTs. When this option is available, it is peculiarly well-suited for many beneficiaries; management of the SNT funds and the social, medical, and personal needs of the beneficiary often go hand in hand. Case managers may charge almost as much as corporate trustees, but the beneficiary may be receiving much more direct benefit for a slightly lower total cost; in fact, a growing number of corporate trustees are turning to the very same case management industry to provide the needed social service component of trust administration (but at an additional cost to the trusts). On the other hand, case managers tend to come from social service backgrounds, and may or may not be equipped to handle financial, investment, and accounting requirements. When considering case managers or professional private fiduciary organizations as trustee, look for continuity, depth of experience, bonding experience, and positive recommendations from prior beneficiaries. In a growing number of states, professional fiduciaries are being subjected to state regulation; make sure the proposed trustee has complied with state registration requirements.

5. *Lawyers*. Lawyers typically enjoy several exemptions from applicable laws governing trustees: They may not be required (by state law) to qualify as trust companies, or to register as private fiduciaries, and they arguably are exempted from federal registration as investment advisers. A growing number of lawyers have begun to act as trustees for SNTs. Usually, the cost to the trust is higher than the fees charged by family members but lower than corporate trustee fees; some lawyers provide case management services akin to those of

professional case management agencies, and some may employ professional agencies to perform those functions. Typically, lawyers will find it easier to secure bond (if it is required), and will be subject to state disciplinary proceedings for their actions as trustee. On the other hand, lawyers (and even law firms) may be unable to guarantee longevity and consistency over time. Many lawyers act as trustee in Massachusetts (where a sizeable practice has been under way for over a century) and Arizona (where the practice is much more recent, but growing); other states have followed suit gradually if at all.

6. *A nonprofit trustee.* In some states, the nonprofit organization that manages the local "pooled" trust may also have the power to act as trustee of special needs trusts. This can be particularly useful when the beneficiary has no other family members to watch over him but the trust is not large enough to attract much interest from an institution.

7. *The team approach.* Some attorneys prefer a trust that has an arrangement between different members of a team: the "Trustee," which may be a corporate fiduciary, which invests and manages the funds; and a "committee" of family members, case workers, etc. who can establish guidelines for expenditures, or even a budget, and can resolve discretionary issues. Some will even include a financial advisor, with the "Trustee" acting more as a custodian. Alternative teams might involve a trustee to make discretionary decisions and a different trustee to handle investments.

Q 17:45 Should an elder law attorney act as trustee of a special needs trust?

While law school training probably did not include exposure to trustee duties, accounting principles, or special needs, the special relationship lawyers enjoy under federal and state law makes acting as trustee an attractive concept for many elder law attorneys. The elder law attorney who has some experience in Medicaid administration, SSI and social security rules, and the needs of disabled (and elderly) clients may be able to provide real value to beneficiaries of SNTs by agreeing to act as trustee.

There are several concerns any lawyer proposing to act as trustee should keep in mind. Among the most pressing items are the need to secure investment advice, the importance of case management/ social work for the trust beneficiaries, and the effect of acting as trustee on malpractice insurance and office administration.

Any individual who gives investment advice is required to register (and maintain that registration) with the Securities and Exchange Commission as a registered investment adviser (RIA). A trustee arguably gives investment advice, and that conclusion may be more likely where the trustee also has a current or prior lawyer/client relationship with a trust beneficiary. One key provision of the registration requirement does exempt a lawyer who gives investment advice "solely incidental to the practice of his profession." [See 15 USC Section808b-2(a)(11)(B)] As a consequence, some commentators believe that the lawyer/trustee has no obligation to register as an RIA, although the effect of that exemption is not undisputed.

Nothing in legal training or the usual law practice particularly suits a lawyer to make investment decisions, and so when acting as trustee he or she should be careful to secure competent investment advice. In Massachusetts, where lawyers are extensively relied upon to act as trustees, such law firms commonly employ an investment adviser on a regular basis. Other lawyer/trustees would be well advised to seek outside professional investment advice on individual trusts as the need arises. When securing investment advice, it is usually preferable to utilize "fee for service" advisers, rather than having to deal with the inherent conflict associated with investment advisers who will earn commissions from the sale of the products they recommend.

Similarly, social service and case management are not skills learned by most lawyers in law school or practice. It will be necessary either to contract out for such services when acting as trustee, or to employ individuals with social service training in the law office. A number of lawyer/trustees have turned to hiring social service/case management staff, and once that step is taken it seems logical to expand the trust administration practice.

Q 17:46 Why would a lawyer want to act as trustee?

As has previously been noted, neither the investment nor the case management functions of a trustee are the subject of training or experience for most lawyers. Given that the lawyer is unlikely to be trained or experienced in either of the primary functions of an SNT trustee, it must be questioned whether the lawyer who chooses to act as trustee is making an appropriate choice. There are at least three reasons why lawyers may nonetheless be suitable trustees of SNTs:

1. *The lawyer is probably more familiar with trust eligibility rules, restrictions, and procedures than most of the other potential trustees are.* Particularly in the case of SNTs, the significance of this fact can hardly be overstated; SNTs regularly cause difficulties with the continued eligibility of their beneficiaries not through drafting mistakes or financial errors, but through the simple failure of the trustee to recognize the SNTs limitations or, even worse, failure to provide timely and complete information to permit continued eligibility.

2. *As described in Q 17:44, lawyers enjoy special exemptions from some of the regulations governing other professional trustees.* While this can create a dangerous situation (regulations, after all, are intended to protect beneficiaries and the public), it can also create an opportunity for lawyers who actually discharge their duties and respect their fiduciary responsibilities. Lawyers are also likely to be able to secure bond, and are more likely to be familiar with court accounting practices, both of which may be important to SNT administration in many states.

3. *Acting as trustee is personally rewarding, and dealing with disabled individuals (and helping to ensure better care for those individuals) is especially rewarding.* Most lawyer/trustees quickly describe the satisfaction received from individual cases when asked why they act as trustee: while financial rewards may be significant, personal satisfaction is more often cited as the reason for acting as trustee.

Q 17:47 What are the lawyer's responsibilities when advising SNT trustees?

Most lawyers will find that their involvement in SNT administration is as counsel to the trustee, rather than acting as trustee. Advising the trustee also creates both risks and opportunities. Particularly where family members are acting as trustee, the lawyer/adviser's role will usually be to monitor the trustee's performance for signs of difficulties. Those difficulties may arise when the trustee deals improperly with the trust (as by self-dealing, or outright theft), when the trustee fails to honor the trust's limitations (as by distributing cash to the beneficiary), or when the trustee fails to discharge the duties inherent in acting as trustee in any case (as when he or she fails to account adequately, or fails to file tax or court documents in a timely fashion).

Q 17:48 How can the lawyer advising an SNT trustee minimize the risk of damage to either the trust or to the lawyer personally?

The most important step for the lawyer advising the SNT trustee is to make sure the necessary information and instructions have been provided to the trustee. Obviously, this is both easier to document and more effective if instructions are in writing. The lawyer representing an SNT trustee should prepare a comprehensive letter of instructions and send it to the trustee; it probably makes good sense to repeat the letter periodically—perhaps annually, in conjunction with a review of the accounting.

SNT trustees may be required to account to a court on an annual basis, but general trust law requires that annual accounts be provided to all beneficiaries. In order to keep the trustee on a narrow legal path, the attorney should schedule periodic reviews with the trustee for the purpose of looking over the trust's books and records, checking that tax filings are current, and discussing upcoming court or beneficiary accounting requirements.

Q 17:49 What must the attorney do when he or she learns that a client has breached the fiduciary duty owed by a trustee?

The lawyer who learns of ethical or legal breaches by a trustee is in a different position from other lawyers who learn of client wrongdoing. Because of the nature of the trustee's relationship, the likely incapacity (or limited capacity) of the beneficiary, and the lawyer's status as a court officer with duties to the supervising court, it is almost always inappropriate to ignore or cover up the client's wrongdoing. In most cases, the lawyer will be required to report at least some information to an appropriate official; that duty can usually be discharged by either alerting the appropriate court of the possibility of wrongdoing, or by requesting the appointment of counsel to represent incapacitated (and injured) beneficiaries.

Many lawyers argue that the duty after learning of fiduciary lapses is to withdraw from representation of the defalcating trustee. While this may be personally satisfying to the lawyer, it may not be sufficient to discharge his or her responsibility to the beneficiary, to the legal system, and to any tribunal overseeing administration of the trust. Indeed, the lawyer continues to owe a duty to the trustee, even after learning of the breach; withdrawal as counsel neither satisfies that duty nor alerts the proper authorities to the problem that must be addressed. Uncomfortable as it may be, the lawyer in most cases should remain involved until the details of the breach can be determined, and the interests of the client protected as much as possible in the circumstances. Of course, if the client/trustee persists in a course of prospective action in violation of law, the lawyer's ethical duty may be different.

Practice-Related Issues

Q 17:50 How do special needs trusts issues arise in the elder law practice?

Although 42 USC Section 1396p(d)(4)(A) trusts (the most common variant of SNTs) are necessarily restricted to beneficiaries under age 65, elder law attorneys frequently become involved in SNT planning because of familiarity with Medicaid, SSI, and public benefit programs. Third-party SNTs may be drafted for elderly clients to protect their younger (but perhaps still elderly) children or other beneficiaries. With formal federal recognition of SNTs in 1993 (in OBRA '93), the SNT planning arena is fairly young and actively growing. Some typical SNT scenarios encountered by elder law attorneys are described here:

1. *Disabled personal injury recipient.* Gilbert is 34 and was injured in a motorcycle accident 18 months ago. He is a quadriplegic, will not recover use of any motor skills and requires total care. He is mentally competent. Since the accident, he has been cared for first in the hospital (most of the costs covered by his private insurance, but totaling around $250,000) and for the past six months in a nursing home. Because Gilbert had limited savings and no long-term care or private disability insurance, the entire nursing home care period has been covered by Medicaid. The current Medicaid contribution totals $75,000. Gilbert does receive Social Security Disability Insurance payments of $450 per month.

   At the time of the accident, Gilbert was separated from his wife. The couple's divorce was finalized thereafter, and his wife retains custody of the couple's two minor children. At the time of the accident, Gilbert had substantial child support arrearages, and he has been unable to make payments since that time.

   Gilbert's medical condition is now stable. He can take food and fluids orally, but must be spoon-fed, turned, and catheterized. He can be moved to a wheelchair, but has been effectively confined to his nursing home bed by a lack of transportation.

   Gilbert's personal injury lawyer has negotiated a settlement that, after payment of attorney's fees but before satisfaction of any liens, will amount to a net distribution to Gilbert of $3 million. Medicaid and the private insurance company have paid a total of $800,000 for his care.

   Gilbert's situation is not atypical. Given his high and continuing cost of medical care, he would deplete his remaining settlement proceeds quickly if he were to pay privately for his care. Gilbert may be a good candidate for a special needs trust.

First, Medicaid (and private insurance) liens must be handled. Medicaid is required to engage in negotiations for the reduction of its lien, but is not required actually to agree to a reduction.

Gilbert's personal injury lawyer or the lawyer preparing the SNT should contact Medicaid and begin the negotiation process.

Once the settlement value has been maximized, the benefit to Gilbert (and his family) should be considered. If the original litigation was brought in Gilbert's and his children's names then the proceeds could be attributed partially to the children (for loss of consortium or support, as state law permits). This division is as much art as science, so Gilbert might consent to a larger-than-usual distribution to his children, depending on his continuing relationship with them and their mother. Similarly, he may choose to use a portion of the settlement proceeds to satisfy his child support arrearages.

Gilbert may wish to transfer his remaining settlement proceeds into an SNT. But he may choose not to do so. Because he receives some Social Security Disability benefits, he will soon qualify for Medicare coverage (after 24 months of SSDI benefits). While that will provide significant benefits for Gilbert, it will not pay for his medications or personal care—two of the items most likely to require considerable expenditures over time.

The first barrier to an SNT is a technical one: Gilbert cannot establish the trust himself, as 42 USC Section 1396p(d)(4)(A) requires that step to be undertaken by a guardian, the court, or Gilbert's parents or grandparents. If either of Gilbert's parents is available to execute the trust, this problem may be easily overcome (although even that could be problematic if Gilbert were only able to obtain SSI rather than SSDI—the Social Security Administration takes the position that only someone with "authority" to make the transfer of a person's assets can establish the trust). If not, and because Gilbert is mentally competent, it may be difficult to utilize state guardianship law to establish the trust. If the state does permit a "voluntary" conservatorship proceeding, with no finding of incapacity required, that process may be the appropriate solution.

Before transferring settlement proceeds into the trust, Gilbert might choose to expend a significant portion on assets that will benefit him immediately. He might, for example, arrange for the purchase of a wheelchair-equipped van, and for clothing and food to last for a period of time. Because the personal injury settlement will cause at least one month of ineligibility for SSI anyway, he can receive food, clothing, and shelter benefits during that month without increasing his penalty. The trust must, however, be fully funded before the end of the month in which it is received, or another month of ineligibility will be incurred; Medicaid benefits might also be suspended and Gilbert might be required to go back through the application process once he requalifies—in most states, Medicaid eligibility applications are a notoriously unpleasant process.

Assuming that Gilbert decides to transfer the remaining settlement proceeds into an SNT, it might yield substantial improvement in his quality of life. The SNT can provide aides to care for Gilbert and take him out in his wheelchair-equipped van. It might even provide a suitable handicap-equipped home (plus continuing upkeep, taxes, and utilities). (If Gilbert is receiving SSI rather than SSD, there may be a reduction in his SSI benefit but continued Medicaid eligibility.)

2. *Misbehavior by the SNT trustee.* Some years later, Gilbert's trust is in place and providing benefits. He continues to receive SSDI, Medicare, and Medicaid benefits (and SSSI or the state supplement if receiving them initially); the loss of any of those benefits could be catastrophic for his continued care. Unfortunately, his trustee has made gifts to other family members from trust assets, and has paid for Gilbert's clothing (because of his condition, he requires special—and expensive—clothing with hook-and-loop closures) throughout the term of the trust. She (the trustee) has not disclosed those expenditures to Social Security and has not given Gilbert any accounting for the trust's administration. The lawyer who originally drafted the SNT has now learned of these problems because the trustee has consulted the drafter about how to proceed.

Setting aside the problem of conflicting representation, and assuming that the lawyer owes a duty only to Gilbert, it is important that Gilbert be given complete information about the current situation. While the lawyer does not have a similar obligation to inform Social Security of the problematic payments, it is probably in Gilbert's best interest to do so promptly.

It may be possible to argue that the "clothing" provided to Gilbert was actually medically necessary. If Gilbert's physician will prescribe the use of special clothing, its provision will probably be permitted. Otherwise, the improper purchases may result in a determination that benefits were overpaid, and a reduction in SSI benefits to recover that overpayment. Even if the payments are ultimately determined to have been inappropriate, they should not result in the trust corpus being treated as available. Any reduction in benefits might not affect continued eligibility for Medicaid; if it does, the trust should be able to repay the SSI overpayment without affecting current eligibility. It may even be possible to negotiate a schedule for repayment rather than reimbursing Social Security all at once.

The trustee's other improper expenditures may require appropriate court proceedings to enforce Gilbert's rights. If the trustee was not bonded, it may be impossible as a practical matter to recover any of the lost assets. The trustee can, however, be removed, ordered formally to account, and even surcharged in an appropriate trust proceeding; the special nature of the SNT will not affect Gilbert's state-law rights as a beneficiary.

Chapter 18

Patient Autonomy and Self-Determination

In the past half-century medical advancements have made it possible to extend some lives well past the time when the individual is able to communicate or likely to recover any substantial abilities. Particularly in the past quarter-century the conflict between the treatment imperative on the one hand and the patient's right to autonomy and a dignified death on the other has become especially pronounced. Although the law on patient self-determination has mostly developed in recent years it has developed quite rapidly. It is already possible to describe the patient's right to self-determination with some certainty; the statutory development of advance directives and the case law on the right to refuse treatment both proceeded quickly once undertaken by the states. This chapter discusses informed consent, the patient's right to refuse medical treatment, do not resuscitate orders (DNRs), health care powers of attorney, living wills, and physician-assisted suicide.

Overview

Q 18:1 What is the basis for an individual's right to refuse medical treatment?

Competent patients have the right to refuse medical treatment even if that refusal may be against the weight of medical opinion and will inexorably lead to the death of the patient. Although the mechanism for exercise of the right varies by state, incompetent patients retain at least some right to refuse treatment. The right to refuse treatment is predicated on some combination of common law ideas of informed consent, federal constitutional principles, and state constitutional provisions regarding a right to privacy.

Informed Consent

Q 18:2 What is informed consent and when is it required?

Patient self-determination has a well-developed history in American civil law. As early as 1891 the Supreme Court recognized the right of every individual to "possession and control of his own person, free from all restraint or interference of others, unless by clear and unquestionable authority of law." [Union Pacific Rwy. v. Botsford, 141 U.S. 250 (1891)] The famous and eloquent justice Cardozo wrote: "Every human being of adult years and sound mind has a right to determine what shall be done with his own body." [Schloendorff v. New York Hospital, 105 N.E. 92 (N.Y. 1914)] From the beginning of the 20th century, medical malpractice actions established that "informed consent" is required from a patient (or an appropriate surrogate) before treatment can begin. Failure to obtain informed consent results in a battery. [Cruzan v. Director, 497 U.S. 261, 269 (1990)] Courts have also held that operating without obtaining informed consent is the basis of a claim of malpractice against a physician. [Lambert v. Stovell, 205 Conn. 1 (1987)]

The doctrine of informed consent requires the physician to disclose material information to the patient so that the patient can make an informed decision. The elements of informed consent are:

1. Information provided to the patient about the risks of the proposed procedure, the alternatives, and the likely outcome if the procedure is not performed;
2. A patient sufficiently competent to understand the risks and likely outcomes; and
3. Actual consent to treatment.

[Schloendorff v. Society of N.Y. Hospital, 105 N.E. 92 (N.Y. 1914); Logan v. Greenwich Hospital Assn., 191 Conn. 282 (1983)]

There are limited exceptions to the requirement for obtaining informed consent. In a medical emergency consent may be presumed. In extremely rare circumstances, informed consent may not be required where the full disclosure of diagnosis, prognosis, and treatment options may itself be medically harmful to the patient. This is referred to as the "therapeutic privilege."

Q 18:3 What information is the physician required to disclose to the patient?

The physician must disclose the risks and benefits of any proposed course of treatment as well as any treatment alternatives. The patient must be given enough information to understand the consequences of the decision and to make an intelligent choice. [See, e.g., Matthies v. Mastromonaco, 733 A.D.2d 456 (N.J. 1999)] Under the reasonable physician standard, the physician must disclose those risks of treatment that a reasonable physician would disclose. In jurisdictions that apply the reasonable patient standard, the physician must disclose those risks and alternative treatments that a reasonable patient would find material to making a decision to undergo treatment. [See, e.g., Gemme v. Goldberg, 31 Conn. App. 527 (1993)]

Q 18:4 What capacity must the patient have in order to be able to consent?

In order to give informed consent a patient should be able to understand the information being supplied about the proposed course of treatment, understand its consequences, and be able to communicate a meaningful decision regarding the issue. An assessment of a patient's capacity should take into account whether the patient's choice is based on rational reasons or personal values, and not resulting from depression, reaction to medications, panic, or phobia.

Q 18:5 What if the patient does not have the capacity to consent?

Most patients will have some ability to comprehend and communicate on some level; however, in the case of a patient who is comatose or who has insufficient capacity to make an informed decision medical professionals must rely on substitute decision-makers such as an agent under a health care power of attorney, a guardian or, in states where they are authorized, a statutory surrogate.

Right to Refuse Medical Treatment

Q 18:6 Is the right to refuse treatment constitutionally protected?

Yes. Although many state and federal appeals courts have found the right to refuse treatment implicit in the U.S. Constitution's right to privacy [See, e.g., In re Quinlan, 70 N.J. 10, 38–42, *cert. denied sub nom.* Garger v. New Jersey, 429 U.S. 922 (1976), *overruled in part* In re Conroy, 98 N.J. 321 (1985)], the U.S. Supreme Court has not specifically concurred. In the only U.S. Supreme Court case on the subject [Cruzan v. Director, 497 U.S. 261 (1990)], the Court analyzed the right to die as a liberty interest under the due process clause of the Fourteenth Amendment, not under the right to privacy.

Many states have explicit state constitutional provisions protecting the right to privacy. In most of those states, appellate opinions have relied on those provisions to find a right to refuse treatment. [In re Farrell, 108 N.J. 335, 529 A.2d 404 (1987); Corbett v. D'Alessandro, 487 So.2d 368 (Fla. App.), *review denied* 492 So.2d 1331 (1986)]

Q 18:7 Does state law on living wills and other advance directives modify or limit the power of a competent patient to refuse treatment?

Every state has adopted some form of legislation recognizing the power of individuals to execute durable powers of attorney for health care purposes, "living wills," or both. Most states have adopted laws governing both kinds of advance directives, and a few have also regulated "do not resuscitate" orders, physician-assisted suicide, or other related concerns.

Because the right to refuse treatment is rooted in both common-law and constitutional principles, even without state legislation a patient's advance directives should control treatment choices. While in *Cruzan v. Director* [497 U.S. 261 (1990)], the Supreme Court did allow a state to require evidence of the patient's wishes by clear and convincing evidence, and arguably even to limit that evidence to written documents, even under *Cruzan*, a written expression of the patient's wishes should always control.

Q 18:8 What effect does the Federal Patient Self-Determination Act have on state law or patients' rights?

Effective December 1, 1991, under the Patient Self-Determination Act (PSDA) [Omnibus Budget Reconciliation Act of 1990, Pub. L. No. 101–508, §§ 4206, 4751 (codified at 42 U.S.C. §§ 1395cc(a)(1)(Q), 1395cc(f), 1395mm(c)(8), 1396a(a)(57), 1396a(w))] all hospitals, nursing homes, and health maintenance organizations receiving federal (e.g., Medicare and Medicaid) funds are required to notify patients of their right to make medical treatment decisions. Each state is also required to develop a written description of the applicable state law and the availability of living wills, durable powers of attorney, and other advance directives. The Patient Self-Determination Act did not change the existing law of any state, nor does it compel any state to develop laws or regulations. All that it requires is that patients be provided about the current status of state laws. The Act explicitly prohibits health providers from requiring patients to sign advance directions.

Q 18:9 Can a patient refuse treatment even though the refusal will certainly lead to the patient's death?

Yes, the right to refuse treatment does not require an evaluation of the advisability or appropriateness of the decision itself. In a number of highly publicized cases, the right of a patient to refuse treatment has been recognized even if the refusal will inevitably lead to the patient's death. Three examples from the case law serve to demonstrate the depth of that commitment:

1. *Bouvia v. Superior Court* [225 Cal. Rptr. 297 (Ct. App. 1986]. Elizabeth Bouvia, a cerebral palsy patient, admitted herself for treatment in a California public hospital. Although she sought treatment for pain, she specifically refused tube feedings even after she was advised that failure to accept tube feedings would almost certainly lead to her death. After her refusal, the treating physicians determined that her consent to *some* treatment (pain medication) should be treated as acceptance of their preferred treatment. The California Court of Appeals eloquently established that Ms. Bouvia had the right and power to refuse individual treatment options, and that her refusal was not tantamount to suicide. Ironically, though Ms. Bouvia's right to refuse life-sustaining treatment was twice upheld in the California Court of Appeals, she continues to lecture on the right to die more than a decade after her brush with fame.

2. *McKay v. Bergstedt* [801 P.2d 617 (Nev. 1990]. Kenneth Bergstedt, a total-care quadraplegic dependent on his father for his every need, had accepted tube feeding since the swimming-pool accident that had led to his incapacity as a child. When his father was diagnosed as terminally ill (with cancer), Mr. Bergstedt sought approval for his decision to disconnect his feeding tube, knowing that without it he would die. The Nevada Supreme Court agreed that refusal of medical treatment, even though the refusal would lead to death and even though the treatment was long-standing and not unduly burdensome, was not tantamount to suicide and was within the patient's right of self-determination. Mr. Bergstedt ordered the removal of his feeding tube, and died shortly before his father.

3. *Shine v. Vega* [709 N.E.2d 58 (Mass. 1999]. Catherine Shine, a lifetime asthma sufferer, went to a Massachusetts hospital during a particularly difficult attack. Although her attack had lessened by the time she reached the hospital, and she attempted to leave, the emergency room physician, Dr. Vega, insisted on treating her. He physically restrained her and held her overnight over her vehement objections. She developed a fear of hospitals and doctors, and when she suffered another attack some time later she refused hospitalization. After she lapsed into a coma, family members had her admitted for

emergency treatment; she did not survive. Her father (himself a physician) brought a wrongful death action against Dr. Vega on the theory that his wrongful treatment was the proximate cause of her later death. The Massachusetts court held that the wrongful death claim stated a cause of action and remanded the case for trial on Ms. Shine's father's claim.

As these cases illustrate, the right to refuse treatment is very powerful even though not absolute. The power of medical providers and state agencies to limit the right to refuse treatment is itself limited to steps necessary to prevent suicide, protect the rights of innocent third persons, or regulate the administration of health care industry.

Q 18:10 Where the patient is no longer competent and does not have an advance directive, is there a mechanism to exercise his or her right to refuse treatment?

In most states, a substituted decision-maker may speak for an incompetent individual who has not executed a living will or health care proxy. The incompetent individual will not lose the right to have unwanted life-sustaining treatment withheld or withdrawn. The individual's competency must first be determined, which may involve consultation with his or her physician and family. Absent a spouse, close family member, or close friends, a substitute decision-maker will be appointed in a guardianship proceeding.

In addition, at least 28 states and the District of Columbia have statutes that authorize surrogate decision-makers in the absence of advance directives: the District of Columbia, Alabama, Arizona, Arkansas, Colorado, Connecticut, Delaware, Florida, Hawaii, Illinois, Indiana, Iowa, Kentucky, Louisiana, Maine, Maryland, Mississippi, Montana, Nevada, New Mexico, North Carolina, Ohio, Oregon, South Carolina, Texas, Utah, Virginia, West Virginia, and Wyoming. Statutory surrogates are categories of persons listed in order of priority who, if available or reasonably available, are to be consulted by health care providers for patients who lack sufficient capacity to provide informed consent.

Regardless of whether the substitute decision-maker is a court-appointed guardian, or a statutory surrogate, he or she is generally required to follow the patient's wishes if they are known. Courts have developed two standards to guide surrogate decision-making: "substituted judgment" and "best interests." Under the more modern substituted judgment standard, the surrogate attempts to reach the decision that the incapacitated person would make if able to choose. [See In re Fiori, 673 A.2d 905 (Pa. 1996); Eichner v. Dillion, 420 N.E.2d 64 (N.Y. 1981)] This can be accomplished only if a patient has articulated intent to refuse or pursue treatment choices in the past while still competent. If there is no reliable evidence of such intent, the surrogate then follows the more traditional best interest standard. [See Ramussen v. Fleming, 741 P.2d 674, 688-89 (Ariz. 1987)] Under the best interest standard, the surrogate decision-maker assesses what medical treatment would be in the patient's best interests as determined by such objective criteria as relief from suffering, preservation or restoration of functioning, and quality and extent of sustained life.

Advance Directives

Q 18:11 What is the difference between a living will, a health care proxy, and a health care power of attorney?

Although the statutory terms may vary from state to state, most states recognize two different kinds of advance directives. An advance directive is a document outlining the patient's wishes to be carried out in case of incapacity. One type, frequently but not always called a living will, sets forth the patient's treatment choices, including the possible withholding or removing of life-sustaining treatment, in the event that the person is in a terminal condition or vegetative state, or some similar formulation. The "living will" was widely promulgated beginning in the mid 1960s by the organization Choice in Dying (now Partnership for Caring, Inc.) and distributed throughout the country. Today, Partnership for Caring's website includes living will and other advance directives forms from every state. [See *www.partnershipforcaring.org*]

The second type of advance directive may be called a health care proxy, or a durable power of attorney for health care. This type of directive appoints a surrogate to make health care decisions during the patient's incapacity. The proxy may or may not also have the power to execute a "do not resuscitate" order, or to decide when life-sustaining treatment should be removed; a separate designation is sometimes required for that particular proxy.

In states that specifically recognize these types of documents, most patients will benefit from executing both. Taken together, the two advance directives describe the kind of care the patient prefers and designate a trusted family member or friend to make those wishes known to health care providers. Sometimes a patient will be unable to identify a person to act as surrogate, but still can make treatment choices; a living will without a health care proxy can still ensure the patient's wishes are carried out. More frequently, a patient may be unwilling or unable to deal with particular treatment choices in advance, but wish to designate a trusted family member or friend to rely upon to make health care decisions in the best interest of the patient when the time comes; such patients may choose to execute a health care proxy without signing a living will.

Q 18:12 Is an advance directive effective in a state other than the state in which it is executed?

State laws in about two-thirds of the states expressly provide for the recognition of living wills, durable health care powers of attorney, or both, even though the documents are prepared in accordance with the law of another state. Alabama, Arizona, Arkansas, California, Delaware, Florida, Hawaii, Iowa, Maine, Maryland, Minnesota, Nebraska, New Hampshire, New Jersey, New Mexico, North Dakota, Ohio, Oklahoma, Oregon, Rhode Island, South Carolina, Tennessee, Texas, Utah, Virginia, Washington, and West Virginia all expressly provide for the recognition of both living wills and durable health care powers of attorney. Colorado, Indiana, Kansas, Massachusetts, Michigan, New York, and Vermont all recognize out-of-state documents naming a health care agent, but do not make any provision for out-of-state living wills (Massachusetts, Michigan, and New York do not have living will statutes for their own residents). Alaska, Delaware, Illinois, Louisiana, Montana, Nevada, and South Dakota recognize out-of-state living wills but make no provision for health care powers of attorney from another state (Alaska does not explicitly recognize health care powers of attorney at all). Connecticut, the District of Columbia, Georgia, Idaho, Kentucky, Mississippi, Missouri, North Carolina, Pennsylvania, Wisconsin, and Wyoming laws are all silent as to the validity or effect of an out-of-state advance directive, but may have relatively modest requirements for their own advance directives that are likely to be met by the laws of other states as well. In a number of states, for example, the only requirement of formality may be a signature and two witnesses; if no specific state form is not required, the form approved and/or executed under the laws of another state may be honored.

Table 18-1. State Provisions: Out-of-State Advance Directives

State	*Recognizes Out-of-State Living Wills*	*Recognizes Out-of-State Health Care Agency*	*No Provisions Regarding Reciprocity*
Alabama	X	X	
Alaska	X		
Arizona	X	X	
Arkansas	X	X	
California	X	X	
Colorado		X	
Connecticut			X
Delaware	X	X	
District of Columbia			X
Florida	X	X	
Georgia			X
Hawaii	X	X	
Idaho			X
Illinois	X		
Indiana		X	
Iowa	X	X	
Kansas		X	
Kentucky			X
Louisiana	X		
Maine	X	X	
Maryland	X	X	
Massachusetts		X	

Table 18-1. State Provisions: Out-of-State Advance Directives (*cont'd*)

State	*Recognizes Out-of-State Living Wills*	*Recognizes Out-of-State Health Care Agency*	*No Provisions Regarding Reciprocity*
Michigan		X	
Minnesota	X	X	
Mississippi			X
Missouri			X
Montana	X		
Nebraska	X	X	
Nevada	X		
New Hampshire	X	X	
New Jersey	X	X	
New Mexico	X	X	
New York		X	
North Carolina			X
North Dakota	X	X	
Ohio	X	X	
Oklahoma	X	X	
Oregon	X	X	
Pennsylvania			X
Rhode Island	X	X	
South Carolina	X	X	
South Dakota	X		
Tennessee	X	X	
Texas	X	X	
Utah	X	X	

Table 18-1. State Provisions: Out-of-State Advance Directives (*cont'd*)

State	*Recognizes Out-of-State Living Wills*	*Recognizes Out-of-State Health Care Agency*	*No Provisions Regarding Reciprocity*
Vermont		X	
Virginia	X	X	
Washington	X	X	
West Virginia	X	X	
Wisconsin			X
Wyoming			X

Q 18:13 Who can make an advance directive?

In most states advance directives may be executed only by competent adults. Some states permit guardians of the person to sign at least some types of advance directives for their minor or incapacitated wards; since guardians of the person generally have authority over health care matters anyway this power really amounts to an administrative authority rather than a substantive addition to the guardian's powers.

Q 18:14 How long does an advance directive remain valid?

Although early advance directive law (as in the case of the pioneering law in California) provided for automatic expiration of advance directives, those limitations have since disappeared from statutes. In most cases an advance directive will remain valid until the principal revokes it, unless it is time-limited by its terms.

Q 18:15 Can an individual have several advance directives, differing in form to comply with separate states?

Yes, although it may make better sense to have one single advance directive that complies with the law of several states. Assuming that neither state law nor the terms of the later documents require revocation of earlier documents, and assuming that the health care agents or proxies named in the documents are coincident, separate advance directives to comply with peculiarities of state law may make sense.

Q 18:16 Which is more powerful: a living will or a health care power of attorney proxy?

In states where both kinds of advance directives are permitted, the common view is that the health care proxy or power of attorney is a more powerful document than a living will. While a living will expresses the patient's wishes, the designation of a health care agent creates an advocate who can demand further information, seek confirming medical opinions, discharge noncooperative physicians, and aggressively insist that the patient's wishes be carried out. In addition, the health care power of attorney provides more flexibility than a living will because it covers situations that may not be anticipated in the living will.

Q 18:17 Does giving the attorney-in-fact power to initiate litigation give additional weight to the power of attorney?

Many practitioners believe that a health care power of attorney should include specific language empowering the agent to bring civil litigation to enforce the provisions of the advance directive. There is no empirical evidence to suggest that such language increases the likelihood that the patient's wishes will be followed, but there is anecdotal evidence to support that argument. The principal objection to such a provision would be that it encourages an adversarial (rather than supportive) relationship with health care providers; still, it is probably advisable to give the agent such powers in the majority of cases.

Q 18:18 Will an advance directive effectively prevent extraordinary treatment in all situations?

Recent studies have raised serious questions about the efficacy of advance directives. In the most widely publicized of those, the so-called "SUPPORT" Study conducted by the Robert Wood Johnson Foundation [The SUPPORT Principal Investigations, "A Controlled Trial to Improve Care for Seriously Ill Hospitalized Patients: The Study to Understand Prognoses and Preferences for Outcomes and

Risks of Treatments (SUPPORT)," 274 Journal of the American Medical Association (JAMA) 1591 (Nov. 22/29, 1995)], researchers reported a disturbingly low rate of compliance with advance directives by physicians. The study also points out another problem with advance directives: The number of patients with advance directives recorded in their medical charts remains low. Before the adoption of the federal Patient Self-Determination Act, only about 1 percent of hospital patients had advance directives in their medical charts. More recent studies show that even with extensive media coverage of the issue and large-scale federal intervention, the frequency of advance directives has increased only to about one in four.

When family members, health care providers, and the courts persist in ignoring the clear wishes of the patient, advance directives can become ineffective. In one reported example a Jehovah's Witness executed a health care power of attorney explicitly prohibiting the transfusion of blood or blood products and naming an agent who was not a family member. After she became comatose her husband sought appointment as temporary guardian for the express purpose of authorizing blood transfusions. Although the patient's wishes were ignored (and her designated agent was not even given notice of the proceedings), the appellate court opinion rendered after the fact —and after her death—made clear that the principal's wishes should have been paramount and that the guardianship court exceeded its authority in authorizing treatment she had refused. [In re Maria Isabel Duran, 2001 Pa. Super. 52 (2001)]

Despite the limitations of advance directives, properly executed documents can and do help ensure that patient's treatment choices are followed. Increasingly, medical providers are eager to comply with patient (and family) wishes, and are looking only for legal authority to do so. Sometimes the mere act of considering and signing an advance directive will generate discussion among patient, family, and health care providers, which will help inform all participants of the patient's wishes and the limitations the patient feels are important.

Q 18:19 How will health care providers know if a patient has an advance directive?

The Federal Patient Self Determination Act requires that all health care facilities receiving Medicare, Medicaid, or other federal monies must inquire about patients' advance directives upon admission to service. Emergency admissions need not be held up by the absence of an opportunity to ask about directives, however, and most reports indicate that a minority of patients have advance directives completed and on file with the health care provider.

Q 18:20 What is a do not resuscitate order?

A do not resuscitate (DNR) order is one, written by a physician, prohibiting resuscitation of a patient by health care professionals in the event of cardiac or respiratory arrest that ordinarily would require resuscitation efforts.

Q 18:21 Are there steps a patient can take to prevent resuscitation by emergency medical technicians and emergency room physicians?

In most jurisdictions paramedics and emergency medical personnel have limited authority to withhold resuscitation. Resuscitation is usually mandated by emergency medical protocols unless the patient's death is unequivocally established. For a patient whose death is imminent, to both patient and family the prospect of undergoing resuscitation may be especially alarming.

Family members of terminally ill patients who are at home may be specifically instructed not to call 911 upon the death of a patient to avoid unwanted resuscitation attempts. In most jurisdictions funeral home operators can transport the body, if the attending physician is willing to declare death and the medical examiner's office has no interest. Family members may nonetheless feel compelled to call 911 during the overwhelming moment when death occurs.

In a growing number of states, new legislation attempts to address this issue. Forty-three states have statutes that authorize some form of nonhospital DNR order, although the District of Columbia and seven states (Delaware, Iowa, Mississippi, Nebraska, North Dakota, Pennsylvania, and Vermont) have failed to address the issue specifically. In those states with DNR statutes the approach varies, but statutes usually provide for the formal execution of a DNR order by the patient's attending physician. If the legal requirements are followed precisely, the resulting DNR order permits paramedics and emergency medical personnel to refrain from attempting resuscitation.

Q 18:22 Can a DNR order be included in an advance directive?

Because in most states the do not resuscitate order is a physician's prerogative, it cannot simply be incorporated into an advance directive document by the patient. The patient can, however, express his or her preference regarding resuscitation in an advance directive. While that is not a DNR order, the patient's surrogate decision-maker should follow it.

In Arizona [Ariz. Rev. Stat. §§ 18.12.035–18.12.100] and Montana [Mont. Code Ann. § 50-10-101-107], a patient can personally direct the withholding of resuscitation. By strict compliance with the statutory provisions, the patient can execute a specialized advance directive upon which paramedics can rely. Physician confirmation of the patient's wishes may be required, but the decision remains the patient's.

Q 18:23 Why would a patient direct the withholding of resuscitation, especially in the home or the community?

While most people view cardiopulmonary resuscitation as a benefit, some disagree. Medical studies point to a surprisingly low success rate for resuscitative efforts, particularly among women and the elderly. In fact, the risk of debilitating injuries (such as broken ribs, pierced lungs, and anoxia leading to brain damage) may be higher than the likelihood of successful resuscitation in many patients.

Advanced cardiopulmonary resuscitation efforts may make it possible to treat many patients aggressively. Those who worry about the possibility of being resuscitated for a longer life, but with no guarantee of the quality of that life, should address the question in advance to the extent permitted by local law.

Language of Directives

Q 18:24 Where there are statutory advance directive forms, should they be used?

Frequently state laws establishing the validity of advance directives will also provide a sample form for ease of preparation and execution. At least in Oregon the use of the statutory advance directives forms may even be mandated, or the validity of forms restricted to those complying with the statutory format. [Or. Rev. Stat. § 127.531] Because they are generic, statutory forms in other states may not be as detailed, specific, or personalized as patients would want.

Even in those states where statutory forms are not mandated, a cogent argument can be made for using the provided format. Physicians and hospital staff members will be familiar with those forms, and will not be required to interpret the meaning. If the statutory form accurately reflects the patient's wishes, using the commonly recognized version of the advance directives may be preferable.

Usually, however, the patient's unique wishes should be reflected in the document. By avoiding checklists or canned forms, the attorney can more accurately capture the client's concerns, fears, and desires about medical treatment. A more personalized statement is also more likely to be honored by health care professionals in that the patient intended the wishes expressed in the document.

In a number of states, the statutory forms have been carefully crafted to limit patients' choices. Frequently, for example, statutory forms assume that all patients would want the administration of food and fluids, or the forms may define food and fluids as "comfort care." Where statutory forms are used, care should be taken to amend or supplement the forms as needed.

Q 18:25 Are standardized forms for advance directives readily available?

Besides statutory forms provided by individual state statutes, there are many potential sources for form documents. Every state is required by the federal Patient Self-Determination Act to describe the availability and enforceability of advance directives; the result in some states has been the creation of a widely recognized form that accompanies that description. Hospitals, HMOs, physicians, and nursing homes, all of which are required to provide information about advance directives to their patients, frequently give form documents upon request. If those forms are not the statutory forms, they are usually the product of work by a state hospital, medical, or legal association. The Uniform Health-Care Decisions Act [9 Uniform Laws Annotated, Master ed., pt. I] which has been adopted in whole or in part by four states (Delaware, Maine, Mississippi, and New Mexico) also provides a sample form that an individual can use to create an advance health care directive.

Of course, patients can purchase forms for advance directives from almost any book or stationery store. Most Area Agencies on Aging will provide forms at no cost (or for a nominal fee). Partnership for Caring, Inc. (Formerly known as Choice in Dying, Inc.), originally a New York-based nonprofit organization that now has its headquarters in Washington, D.C., has prepared a set of forms acceptable in each state and will provide copies for a nominal fee or permit download from the website (*www.partnershipforcaring.org*). Partnership for Caring, Inc., is located at 1035 30th St. N.W., in Washington, D.C. 20007, and can be reached at (202) 338-9790. In New York, the address for this organization is 475 Riverside Dr., Room 1852, New York, NY 10115, and the phone number is (212) 870-2003.

Q 18:26 Who should have a copy of the advance directive?

Although clients may choose to keep their estate plans generally confidential, advance directives should be given the widest possible distribution. Clients should be instructed to provide copies to their primary care physician, any hospital where they have recently been treated, all clinics and HMO offices, family members, religious advisers, and anyone named in the document itself. In addition the original document should be maintained readily available rather than secured in a safe deposit box or other inaccessible venue.

Q 18:27 Do advance directives typically need to be notarized or witnessed?

State law differs on the technical requirements for execution and witnessing, but no state invalidates documents simply because they have been notarized and/or witnessed. In order to satisfy the highest level of witnessing that may be required (now or in the likely future), it may make sense to have advance directives witnessed by two individuals and notarized. In most states, a document that was valid when and where it was executed will be valid even if it does not comply with the local requirements for execution, but it is probably a poor tactical choice to rely on that standard, especially since it may be difficult to determine what the law is (or was) in a distant state while a medical emergency develops. It is also worth noting that an advance directive that is credible and reliable, but does not comply with technical requirements, may nonetheless be a valid and enforceable expression of the patient's wishes.

Q 18:28 How detailed should health care directives be?

To lawyers, advance directives with more detail are usually preferable. A detailed directive will be more likely to address the illness and circumstance actually confronted by the signer. Going through the process of developing a more detailed directive will also be useful and enlightening for the client, and may increase the likelihood that the document will be honored.

From the medical perspective, detail is not always preferable. Many medical providers will insist that patients cannot realistically assess all of the possible conditions, prognoses, and future treatment choices that they might someday confront, and that there is value in maintaining flexibility. A cynical view might be that physicians are interested in maintaining primacy in the patient-physician relationship, but it is undoubtedly important to recognize the possibility of changed (and unanticipated) circumstances.

Most commentators resolve the conflict by favoring more detailed directives. At the extreme, the directive developed for JAMA by the husband and wife team of Emmanuel and Emmanuel requires the patient to complete a complex grid of mental conditions, diagnoses, and treatment options. Most clients will find the Emmanuel and Emmanuel document too intimidating, but the concept of more detail certainly has value. [Emmanuel, "The Medical Directive. A New Comprehensive Advance Care Document," 261 JAMA 3288-3293 (June 9, 1989)] There is also a "toolkit" of 10 worksheets, with a set of advanced directives on disk, offered by the American Bar Association Commission on Law and Aging (*http://www.abanet.org/aging/toolkit/home.html*). The Joint Center for Bioethics at the

University of Toronto (*http://www.utoronto.ca/jcb*) has formulated living wills that address different illnesses such as HIV or cancer.

Some clients may appear hesitant out of concern about the strictures of their religious faith. Many religious organizations have tailored living wills to address their concerns and show how to explain them to health care providers and agents. The Massachusetts Catholic Conference; the Mormons; Conservative Judaism; Muslims; orthodox Judaism; presbyterians; Baptists, have all developed special language to include in living wills.

Q 18:29 Should an advance directive nominate a guardian of the person?

Some states expressly permit the signer of an advance directive to nominate a desired guardian in the event court intervention is required. Because one of the principal reasons to execute an advance directive is to prevent the need for court intervention, the use of a nomination is itself an indication of the failure of the client's plan. Although most clients will be interested in avoiding the court system, they will usually prefer some control over the selection process. Even if there is no clear authority for the nomination of a guardian, most advance directives should include such a nomination; in most states (and in the Uniform Probate Code and the Uniform Guardianship and Protective Proceedings Act promulgated by the National Conference of Commissioners on Uniform State Laws) the incapacitated person's nominee has one of the highest priorities to serve as guardian. Of course, if the guardianship is sought because of the misfeasance, malfeasance, or nonfeasance of the agent or surrogate, the court may bypass the nominee in favor of another suitable guardian. Sometimes merely nominating the agent or surrogate as guardian will forestall any move by dissatisfied family members to substitute a different guardian.

Q 18:30 How should a patient's desire for physician-assisted suicide be handled?

Although Oregon has adopted a statute permitting competent, terminally ill patients to request physician assistance with suicide [Death with Dignity Act, Or. Rev. Stat. §§ 127.800–127.897], no other state has followed Oregon's lead, and Oregon's statute is under administrative challenge from the U.S. Department of Justice. In fact, voter initiatives intended to adopt an Oregon-style physician-assisted suicide law have failed in other states even since Oregon began its program. In addition, the U. S. Supreme Court has held that there is no constitutional right to suicide and the state's interest in preventing assisted suicide is a legitimate state interest. [Washington v. Glucksburg, 117. S. Ct. 2258 (1997); Vacco v. Quill, 117 S. Ct. 2293 (1997)] Although this area is experiencing rapid change in both law and public opinion, it is unlikely that physician-assisted suicide will be widely available in the near future.

Even Oregon's law unequivocally draws the line at patients requesting the administration of "assisted suicide" (which would really then be more akin to euthanasia) after loss of mental capacity. In other words, there is no jurisdiction in the country (or for that matter in the world) in which assistance with suicide could be obtained by a proxy or agency declaration. Furthermore, it is highly unlikely that the development of the law in any jurisdiction will lead to such a position in the foreseeable future.

Given those constraints, a reasonable argument can be made that there is no point in including assistance with suicide in an advance directive (which, after all, ordinarily speaks only after incapacity). It might even be argued that the inclusion of such language risks invalidating other desirable provisions of a well-drafted advance directive. At this stage in the development of the law, clients should probably be discouraged from including assisted-suicide language in their advance directives. On the other hand, it might be argued that the law is rapidly developing in this area, and there may be a time within the life expectancy of some clients when assisted suicide would be perfectly legal even after incapacity. If a client, after having been properly advised, still wishes to execute a document, even though there is only a slight likelihood of it being effective, that may be the client's choice to make. Prudence would suggest that there be carefully crafted language and full disclosure to the client, and that the document be separate from any other advance directive (to minimize the likelihood such a provision would have a negative effect on the other advance directive).

Enforcement

Q 18:31 What practical effect does an advance directive have on health care?

Recent studies (including the famous SUPPORT study) have indicated that medical professionals frequently do not rely on or accede to the provisions of health care directives. While most elder law practitioners might disagree, the available literature suggests that physicians are familiar with the provisions of advance directives and willing to honor them in a small minority of cases.

Q 18:32 What steps can the principal take to increase the likelihood that his or her wishes will be carried out?

By far the most important step for the principal to take is to circulate the document widely. Family members, friends, neighbors, religious advisers, physicians, hospitals, and anyone else who may be involved in the administration of health care should be aware of the existence of the directive, and most should have copies. Providing copies of the directive to the agent and any alternatives is particularly important well in advance, to give them an opportunity to ask questions, challenge assumptions, and develop an understanding of the role of the agent and wishes of the principal. Also important is that the agent realize he or she may be required to act on short notice, without complete information.

Besides providing copies of the advance directives to the primary physician, the patient should discuss with the physician the meaning and effect of the directive. Some forms provide a space for the signature of the attending physician; such an acknowledgment may be helpful in securing the physician's later cooperation in following the patient's wishes, and can lead the patient to recognize in advance when the physician's own biases conflict with the patient's desires and concerns.

Q 18:33 What steps can the attorney-in-fact take to improve the effectiveness of an advance directive?

Too often principals assume that the person selected as agent will know the principal's wishes, without taking the time to confirm that assumption. An agent should, upon learning of his or her designation as such, take the time to discuss care considerations with the principal, and attempt to gain an understanding of the values and choices that govern the principal's exercise of discretion. The agent should also encourage the principal to reduce some or all of those values to writing, to be used as evidence of the principal's wishes in any future disagreement with caregivers or family.

As important as it is for the principal to widely circulate advance directives, it too often happens that the contents, and even the existence of the documents remain unknown. The first duty of a health care agent in actually implementing an advance directive should be to determine whether copies have been given to the principal's primary care physician, specialists, nurse practitioner, HMO, hospital, facility director, religious adviser, and family.

During any period of incapacity or limited capacity of the principal, the health care agent should expect to be actively involved in decision-making. Care providers need to be consulted and challenged, second opinions considered, and the burdens and benefits of proposed treatment balanced. Although the relationship of principal and agent is less formal than that of ward and guardian, the powers and duties are similar; the principal expects active participation and advocacy from the agent, and should be entitled to receive exactly that.

As in other substitute decision-making models, the wishes of the principal should be paramount. In other words, the agent should not have as a first consideration the best interests of the principal, but rather the expressed or implied direction of the principal from the document itself, from prior conversations, or from other reliable sources. Unless the principal has completely failed to give direction in any form, the first duty of the agent is to determine what the principal would choose if not disabled by the condition under treatment.

Where the agent knows that the principal would refuse treatment, and the refusal is likely to result in the death of the principal, the agent may not choose to allow treatment in spite of the principal's wishes. Although the agent may feel this will cause the death of the principal, he or she should recognize that instead the inevitable death of the principal is thereby permitted on the terms chosen by the principal personally.

Q 18:34 Who has a duty to decide whether the attorney-in-fact is following the principal's wishes?

The health care agent's duty is to follow the wishes of the principal. Unfortunately, it often happens that the agent is unable to make the decision to withhold treatment, even when he or she knows the principal's preference. When that situation occurs other persons, such as the health care providers, may realize that the agent is not acting in accordance with the principal's wishes.

In such a situation the health care provider has at least an ethical, and (depending on state law) perhaps a legal, duty to take appropriate steps. Such steps might start with insisting on a consultation with an institutional ethics committee, the involvement of other family members or the state's adult protective services, or even initiation of a guardianship or other court proceeding. Some states have provided specific procedures for interpretation or enforcement of advance directives, which may be quicker, less expensive, and less confrontational than full guardianship proceedings.

Q 18:35 What is an action for wrongful life?

Some practitioners have suggested that a cause of action might lie against a health care provider for the injury sustained by a patient kept alive despite advance directives clearly refusing life-sustaining treatment. Philosophically, it is difficult to determine how to calculate damages in such a situation; clearly, the undesired medical expenses might be part of the damages, but it is not so clear that the pain and suffering of a patient in such a case would be compensable.

Many state advance directive statutes include specific provisions exonerating health care providers from all liability as long as actions are undertaken in good faith. [See, e.g., Ariz. Rev. Stat. § 36-3205] While it is not impossible to imagine a facility demonstrating bad faith in its refusal to honor an advance directive, there are few cases in which evidence of any improper motivation is clear.

In fact, the handful of cases against facilities for refusal to honor advance directives have mostly focused on the cost of the unwanted care, and the success of litigation has been spotty. [Estate of Taylor v. Moncie Medical Investors, 2000 WL 424306 (Ind. App. 2000); Grace Plaza of Great Neck, Inc. v. Elbaum, 82 N.Y.2d 10 (1993)] It is usually fairly easy for the facility to show that the validity, meaning, or even availability of the advance directive was in question at the time. In some cases, state law has arguably been unclear, and refusal to remove life-sustaining treatment prior to a court order has been excused on that basis. There is no reported case in which the liability of a physician or facility was determined at trial and upheld on appeal.

Practice-Related Issues

Q 18:36 How do patient self-determination issues arise in the elder law practice?

The following examples illustrate the kinds of patient self-determination issues that might arise in a typical elder law practice. Issues explored relate to: (1) the preparation of a living will, (2) selection of a health care agent, and (3) refusal of medical treatment.

1. *Living will preparation.* In the course of preparing wills for Husband and Wife, an attorney offers them health care powers of attorney and living wills as part of the package. Husband says, "Oh, yeah, I don't want to be hooked up to any machines," and Wife echoes, "Me neither, I'd rather be dead and we've told the kids that too." Attorney prepares boilerplate health care directives, which are executed with the wills. Was there any need for further discussion?

   One of the reasons many doctors are hesitant about honoring living wills is that circumstances are never as black-and-white as those envisioned by healthy persons. Withdrawal of artificial life-sustaining aids from a terminally ill cancer patient who is in great pain is seen as a relief by family members and doctors alike. But what of patients who have multiple strokes? Often they make significant recoveries, and pain may not be an issue. Sometimes prejudices about disability enter into the picture—"I'd rather be dead than spend my life in a wheelchair"—but, in fact, people may make the necessary mental and physical adjustments if living in a wheelchair is their fate. An AIDS patient told one of the authors years ago that he was virtually comatose on several occasions, to the point where he could not move or communicate, yet the sound of footsteps in the hallway was a source of interest and joy to him. For this reason, he refused to authorize do not resuscitate orders. The attorney should take a moment to discuss with his or her clients specific scenarios to give the health care agent better guidance for this most momentous decision.

2. *Family versus friends as agents.* A 73-year-old widow meets with the attorney to discuss health care directives. She is in good health now, but is concerned about the future. She has one son, a born-again Christian, who she fears will oppose her wishes regarding the artificial prolonging of her life. She has a personal horror of being dependent and helpless in her latter years, and particularly abhors the thought of being "a vegetable" hooked up to machines in a nursing home. She has discussed her concerns at length with her best friend, who has agreed to be her agent. Is there advice that the attorney could give that will help the client make this decision?

   The client can and should draw up health care directives that name her preferences, and some explanatory language in this case would probably help. For example:

   My only child, Robert Jones, and I do not agree about choices regarding end-of-life issues. My wish is that my life not be artificially prolonged under the circumstances detailed elsewhere in this document; my son may request that artificial aids be kept in place indefinitely. For this reason I have named my good and trusted friend, Jane Doe, to advocate on my behalf regarding health care decisions.

   The attorney should explain to the client, however, that most doctors would prefer to honor the wishes of a member of the immediate family. In this instance it is extremely important for the client to discuss her decision with her primary care physician to determine where he would stand. Also, there are documented instances of physicians refusing to "pull the plug" when only one family member opposes it, even when the patient has a living will in place and the other family members support it.

3. *Refusal of medical treatment as evidence of incapacity.* The attorney is retained to assist the client in her petition for temporary (emergency) guardianship. The client's father, a

77-year-old veteran who has a history of cantankerous behavior and signs of early Alzheimer's, has refused to allow surgery to remove a malignant tumor. There are no health care directives. The client has a letter from the surgeon stating that he believes the patient lacks the capacity to understand the consequences of his decision. The surgeon has told the patient and his daughter that while there was no guarantee, the surgery would probably extend the patient's life at least six months and, with radiation, might even cure the patient.

The attorney should alert the client to the fact that even with evidence of dementia, the patient may have sufficient capacity to refuse medical treatment. If and when the patient is assigned his own attorney or guardian *ad litem* for the guardianship proceedings, his objection may prevail in court. The daughter has a dilemma: If she delays filing the petition, her father may lose enough mental capacity so that her petition will likely succeed, but the delay may also cause his physical condition to worsen. The daughter's attorney may wish to bring in another attorney to represent and meet with the father even before filing the petition, so that the daughter can get a better idea of the nature and validity of an objection to the petition by the patient.

Chapter 19

Elder Abuse, Neglect, and Exploitation

Abuse, neglect, and exploitation of the elderly are all increasing, despite state and federal efforts to combat the problem. In response to federal initiatives, most states have adopted mandatory reporting laws (usually modeled on pre-existing statutes requiring reports of abuse or neglect of children); adult protective services are also widespread. Although specifics of mandatory reporting requirements will vary from state to state, the behaviors of abusers and their victims often follow the same patterns. Elder law attorneys are peculiarly well situated to see, diagnose, prevent, and remedy abuse, neglect, and exploitation. This chapter discusses the types of abuse, recognizing abuse and neglect, reporting abuse and neglect, and the warning signs of abuse and neglect.

Overview

Q 19:1 How are abuse, neglect, and exploitation defined?

The National Center on Elder Abuse in a study prepared for the Administration on Aging (AOA) and the Administration for Children and Families [a full copy of the report is available on the Internet at *http://www.aoa.gov/abuse/report/default.htm*] identifies the following seven types of abuse of the elderly:

1. *Physical abuse.* The use of physical force that may result in bodily injury, physical pain, or impairment. Physical abuse may include but is not limited to such acts of violence as striking (with or without an object), hitting, beating, pushing, shoving, shaking, slapping, kicking, pinching, and burning. The unwarranted administration of drugs and physical restraints, force-feeding, and physical punishment of any kind also are examples of physical abuse.
2. *Sexual abuse.* Nonconsensual sexual contact of any kind with an elderly person. Sexual contact with any person incapable of giving consent also is considered sexual abuse; it includes but is not limited to unwanted touching, all types of sexual assault or battery such as rape, sodomy, coerced nudity, and sexually explicit photographing.
3. *Emotional or psychological abuse.* The infliction of anguish, emotional pain, or distress through verbal or nonverbal acts. Emotional or psychological abuse includes but is not limited to verbal assaults, insults, threats, intimidation, humiliation, and harassment. In addition, treating an older person like an infant; isolating an elderly person from family, friends, or regular activities; giving an older person a "silent treatment"; and enforced social isolation also are examples of emotional or psychological abuse.
4. *Financial or material exploitation.* The illegal or improper use of an elder's funds, property, or assets. Examples include but are not limited to cashing checks without authorization or permission; forging an older person's signature; misusing or stealing an older person's money or possessions; coercing or deceiving an older person into signing a document (e.g., contracts or a will); and the improper use of conservatorship, guardianship, or power of attorney.

5. *Neglect.* The refusal or failure to fulfill any part of a person's obligations or duties to an elderly person. Neglect may also include a refusal or failure by a person who has fiduciary responsibilities to provide care for an elder (e.g., failure to pay for necessary home care service, or the failure on the part of an in-home service provider to provide necessary care). Neglect typically means the refusal or failure to provide an elderly person with such life necessities as food, water, clothing, shelter, personal hygiene, medicine, comfort, personal safety, and other essentials included as a responsibility or an agreement.

6. *Self-neglect.* The behaviors of an elderly person that threaten his or her health or safety. Self-neglect generally manifests itself in an older person's refusal or failure to provide himself or herself with adequate food, water, clothing, shelter, safety, personal hygiene, and medication (when indicated). The definition of self-neglect excludes a situation in which a mentally competent older person (who understands the consequences of his or her decisions) makes a conscious and voluntary decision to engage in acts that threaten his or her health or safety.

7. *Abandonment.* The desertion of an elderly person by an individual who has physical custody of the elder or by a person who has assumed responsibility for providing care to the elder.

Most state statutes use similar definitions, though they are typically limited to the three broad categories of abuse (physical, sexual, or emotional), neglect (usually by caregivers who are required to provide care), and (financial) exploitation.

The U.S. Senate's Special Committee on Aging [102d Cong., An Advocate's Guide to Laws and Programs Addressing Elder Abuse 3, 4 (1st Sess. 1991)] further breaks down neglect into active neglect, or "the intentional failure to fulfill a caretaking obligation necessary to maintain the elder's physical and mental well-being," and passive neglect, which is the "unintentional failure to fulfill a caretaking obligation."

Q 19:2 What standard applies when the alleged abuse is not physical or financial, but psychological or verbal?

This can be a difficult question, and the law is unsettled. In a recent case of alleged abusive and inappropriate language used by a nursing home aide to a patient (resulting in the aide's discharge), the Connecticut Supreme Court held that an "objective" rather than "subjective" standard should apply in determining whether the conduct was abusive, and that abuse requires evidence of improper motivation. [Salmon v. Dept. of Public Health, 259 Conn. 288 (2002)]

Q 19:3 Why are the elderly especially vulnerable to abuse?

Like the very young, the elderly have few defenses. They may be physically weak and often mentally incapacitated. They can become increasingly dependent on family members, friends, and neighbors for assistance with shopping, housekeeping, trips to the doctor, etc. Most elderly Americans live at home; at least 5 million of them could not remain in their homes without assistance in the tasks of daily living. Spouses, daughters, or daughters-in-law are usually the ones providing such assistance; it has been estimated that 20 percent of persons over 45 provide help to an elderly relative. [Shilling, 83 Family Caregiving: New Insights, Elder Law Advisory 1 (West Group, Feb. 1998)] Children of ailing parents often resent the role reversal, especially because the time and effort spent may not prevent the deterioration of the parents' health. Adult children may find themselves caring for their parents while still raising their own children.

More than 60 percent of abusers of the elderly are family members (spouses, adult children, other relatives) [Tatara & Kuzmaskus, National Center on Elder Abuse, Elder Abuse Information Series #2, Elder Abuse in Domestic Settings, at 2 (May 1996 & Nov. 1997 Supp.)]; the rest include opportunistic neighbors, acquaintances, or strangers, and, of course, caretakers hired by family members (particularly adult children who live out of state) with little or no supervision, who subsequently find it hard to resist the temptations of exploiting their charges. The elderly are often lonely, and are eager to entrust their financial affairs to or share their homes with anyone willing to spend some time with them.

Caring for an elderly person, particularly one with dementia, is not an easy task. Changing the diapers of an infant is difficult enough; dealing with the incontinence of an adult who is mobile and often unwilling to wear proper garments can be extremely frustrating. A demented individual may ask a family member or caretaker the same questions 20 times in the course of the day, and be upset and tearful for days at a time for no apparent reason. Caretakers who would never characterize themselves as abusive may lose their tempers under such difficult circumstances, and be too ashamed to seek help.

Unlike the very young, elderly individuals may have financial resources, which can be tempting targets for con artists and unethical caretakers. We are all familiar with the vulnerability of the elderly to phone scam artists; victims are encouraged to write dozens of checks for foreign lotteries, investments in worm farms, and fake charities, perhaps even exhausting their life savings. Despite improvements in law enforcement technology, phone exploiters are rarely caught.

Q 19:4 What is the Older Americans Act?

The Older Americans Act (OAA) was originally adopted in 1965. The Act created the Administration on Aging and authorized grants to states for community planning and services programs, research, demonstration projects, and training in the field of aging.

Q 19:5 What is the effect of amendments to the Older Americans Act adopted in 2000?

The Older Americans Act Amendments of 2000 established the National Family Caregiver Support Program [Older Americans Act Amendments of 2000, Pub. L. No. 106-501, § 373(a)], modeled in large part after successful state long-term care programs in California, New Jersey, Wisconsin, and Pennsylvania. The program requires states, working in partnership with area agencies on aging and local community-service providers, to have five basic services for family caregivers, including:

1. Information to caregivers about available services;
2. Assistance to caregivers in gaining access to services;

3. Individual counseling, organization of support groups, and caregiver training to assist caregivers in making decisions and solving problems relating to their caregiving roles;
4. Respite care to enable caregivers to be temporarily relieved from their caregiving responsibilities; and
5. Supplemental services, on a limited basis, to complement the care provided by caregivers.

Q 19:6 What groups are eligible to receive services under the Older Americans Act and the OAA Amendments of 2000?

The Older Americans Act Amendments of 2000 require states and Area Agencies on Aging (AAA) to provide services to:

1. Family caregivers of older adults; and
2. Grandparents and relative caregivers, age 60 years or older, of children no older than age 18 (including grandparents who are sole caregivers of grandchildren and those individuals who are affected by mental retardation or who have developmental disabilities).

[Older Americans Act Amendments of 2000, Pub. L. No. 106-501, § 373(c)(2)]

The statute also requires states to give priority consideration to:

1. Persons with the greatest social and economic need (with particular attention to low-income, minority individuals); and
2. Older individuals providing care and support to persons with mental retardation and related developmental disabilities.

[Older Americans Act Amendments of 2000, Pub. L. No. 106-501, § 373(c)(2)]

Q 19:7 Who can a family caregiver contact for information or assistance?

Every area of the country is required by the Older Americans Act to have an Area Agency on Aging, and the local AAA is usually an excellent resource for caregivers and seniors. Local AAAs are generally listed in the city or county government sections of the telephone directory under "Aging" or "Social Services," and can also be located through a "lookup" website at *http://www.aoa.dhhs.gov/aoa/pages/state.html.* The Administration on Aging also supports a nationwide, toll-free information and assistance directory called the Eldercare Locator, which can be contacted by telephone at (800) 677-1116. The Eldercare Locator can also be accessed online at *http://www.eldercare.gov/*. The Eldercare Locator will assist a caregiver or senior looking for the appropriate AAA.

Q 19:8 How widespread are problems of abuse, neglect, and exploitation?

It would be extremely difficult to pinpoint the actual number of cases of elder abuse each year, because it is underreported. Estimates range from 700,000 to 2 million victims per year, with neglect being the most common form of abuse. [Tatara, "Understanding the Nature and Scope of Domestic Elder Abuse with the Use of State Aggregate Data: Summaries of the Key Findings of a National Survey of State APS and Aging Agencies," 5 J. Elder Abuse & Neglect 35, 37 (1993)] The Subcommittee on Health and Long-Term Care of the House of Representatives Select Committee on Aging reported in 1990 that one out of 20 elderly Americans (a total of 1.5 million persons) may be victims of abuse annually. [Subcommittee, etc., Elder Abuse: A Decade of Shame and Inaction, Comm. Pub. No. 752, 101st Cong., 2d Sess. (Apr. 1990)] The Subcommittee found that while one in three cases of child abuse is reported, only one in eight cases of elder abuse is reported. There are multiple reasons why the reporting rate is so low. The victim may feel powerless, fearful of retaliation, unaware of the legal remedies, or may even believe that abusive treatment is a normal part of the aging process. There also may be instances where the victim is protective of the abuser. [45 S.D. L. Rev. 655, A Call to Legislative Action: Protecting our Elders From Abuse, Heath R. Oberloh] The growth of the elderly sector in proportion to the rest of the population (and the increase in sheer numbers, as a result of improved medical care and, arguably, greater affluence) has led to the formation of advocacy groups and law enforcement task forces with the specific purpose of targeting elder abuse. Unfortunately, longer-lived individuals are more likely to suffer from dementia—an estimated 50 percent of all individuals over age 80 have Alzheimer's disease—and are thus more vulnerable as targets.

According to a report of the American Bar Association Commission on Legal Problems of the Elderly (since renamed the "Commission on Law and Aging") ["Elder Abuse and Domestic Violence: What Is the Elder Law Attorney's Role in Recognition and Prevention?," National Academy of Elder Law Attorneys 11th Annual Symposium, May 1999], elder abuse experts warn that cut-backs in welfare and social service programs will create a larger population of potential abusers. Adult children who lose welfare benefits, for instance, may be more likely to exploit and abuse their elderly parents.

The National Elder Abuse Incidence study sponsored by the Administration on Aging reported approximately 450,000 elderly persons in domestic settings were abused or neglected during 1996. Of this total, 70,942 (16 percent) were reported and the claims substantiated by Adult Protective Services agencies, but the remaining cases represent a serious problem of underreporting of abuse and neglect. When cases of self-neglect are added, the number increases to approximately 551,000 in 1996. This report can be found at *http://www.aoa.gov/abuse/report/default.htm*.

Q 19:9 What seniors are most likely to be victims of abuse?

Female elders are abused at a higher rate than males, after accounting for their larger proportion in the aging population. Our oldest elders (80 years and over) are abused and neglected at two to three times their proportion of the elderly population. In almost 90 percent of the elder abuse and neglect incidents with a known perpetrator, the perpetrator is a family member, and two-thirds of the perpetrators are adult children or spouses.

Q 19:10 What is the Elder Justice Act?

In December 21, the National Center on Elder Abuse held a National Policy Summit on Elder Abuse, funded by the U.S. Administration on Aging, supported by the Office for Victims of Crime of the U.S. Department of Justice, and in which the ABA Commission on Legal Problems of the Elderly was a partner. As a result of the summit, the Elder Justice Act (S. 333) was introduced in the Senate on Monday, February 10, 2003. The proposed law would: (1) establish an Office of Elder Justice within the U.S. Department of Health and Human Services under the Assistant Secretary for Aging; (2)

establish an Office of Elder Justice within the U.S. Department of Justice; (3) amend the Social Security Act to require background checks for all nursing facility workers; and (4) establish an Office of Adult Protective Services within the U.S. Department of Health and Human Services, Administration for Children and Families Center and legislative initiatives. As of this writing, the bill has been sent to the Finance Committee, but if the bill fails to gain passage it is likely to be resubmitted in the future.

Reporting Requirements

Q 19:11 What legal requirements exist to report abuse, neglect, and exploitation?

Forty-three states and the District of Columbia have statutes requiring reporting by certain professionals of suspected elder abuse. Reporting is voluntary in the other seven states: Colorado, Illinois, Iowa, Kentucky, North Dakota, South Dakota, and Wisconsin. [ABA Elder Abuse Report]

States vary somewhat regarding the individuals with a statutory duty to report elder abuse, but generally health care practitioners, mental health professionals, clergymen, nursing home administrators and staff, social workers, and law enforcement officers are required to report abuse. Attorneys, accountants, trustees, guardians, and conservators may also be statutorily required to report exploitation or abuse. Sanctions against those who fail to report include fines or even jail time. In some states, such as Nevada and Rhode Island, a reporter who is mandated to report but does not do so may be determined to be personally liable for damages incurred by the victim.

In recognition of the fact that the social services approach is not an adequate remedy, most states are beefing up laws to provide criminal and civil remedies for victims. Every state in the union has enacted legislation directed toward elder abuse and has established adult protective service (APS) programs that investigate reports of abuse and make the necessary referrals to social services. Adult protective services have been defined as a system of prevention, support, and surrogate services set up to enable the elderly to maintain independent living and avoid abuse and exploitation. Many law enforcement agencies have set up elder abuse hot lines or established special task forces trained to address elder abuse, and usually the identity of the reporter is kept confidential.

State initiatives have been driven to some extent by federal incentives, including federal funding. [42 U.S.C. § 3058b(a)(2)(C)(ii)] The federal Center on Elder Abuse, governed and funded by the Administration on Aging, serves as a clearinghouse for elder abuse research and programming, and works with participating states to compile information and statistics. According to the House Subcommittee on Health and Long-Term Care, only $3.80 is allocated for each elderly victim by the states, compared to $45.03 per child abuse victim.

In most jurisdictions reports of elder abuse are handled on a confidential basis by local adult protective service agencies, which make a preliminary investigation. State statutes generally give APS services total access to bank accounts, medical records, and other confidential sources to help them determine whether elder abuse exists in a specific case. APS then refers the case to the appropriate health or social agency or, if necessary, local law enforcement officials. Many jurisdictions also have public agencies (public guardians or public conservators) that will assume responsibility for an incapacitated elderly person when there are no family members or friends willing to take on that person's care.

Q 19:12 What criticisms have been leveled at mandatory reporting laws?

Most mandatory reporting laws have been modeled after child abuse reporting laws, an integral part of which is the legal incompetence of the minor child. Critics observe that this approach patronizes and infantilizes the elderly and further promotes ageist attitudes. Whereas age alone can determine the incompetence of the child, no such concrete measure exists for the elderly individual. Many states have thus reworked guardianship and conservatorship statutes to address the inability of the ward to make decisions in his or her best interest, rather than to determine legal incapacity or incompetence. For instance, Virginia defines an incapacitated person as "any adult who is impaired by reason of mental illness, mental retardation, physical illness or disability, advanced age or other causes to the extent that the adult lacks sufficient understanding or capacity to make, communicate, or carry out responsible decisions concerning his or her well-being." [Va. Code Ann. § 63.1-55.2] By contrast, other states have expressly deleted language referring to "advanced age" out of concern that age alone may be treated as a justification for the imposition of a guardianship or conservatorship. Many statutes use a medical approach, defining mental illnesses or conditions that would indicate incapacity or incompetence. The Indiana Code, for example, includes among its definitions of an incapacitated individual one who is unable to manage his or her property or provide self-care "because of mental illness, dementia, physical illness, infirmity, habitual drunkenness, excessive use of drugs, confinement, detention, fraud, undue influence of others on the other individual." [Ind. Code § 12-10-7-1] Critics suggest that rather than categorize wards by mental diagnoses which may or may not be relevant, the concept of incompetence should instead be based on functional abilities or disabilities. [See Walsh, Mental Capacity, Legal and Medical Aspects of Assessment and Treatment 2-4 (Shepard's McGraw-Hill Inc. 2d ed. 1994)] Specific behaviors should be the defining criteria, they argue, such as management of Social Security checks, payment of bills, ability to monitor heating and cooling in the home, preparation of meals, and safety issues.

Mandatory reporting laws may also make it impossible to acknowledge decisions made by an elderly individual that may not appear to be in his or her best interests, but that in fact indicate a reasoned-out preference. For instance, an elderly person may be willing to put up with verbal abuse and exploitation by an adult child if it means remaining at home, with easy access to familiar neighbors and shops, rather than being institutionalized. An elderly person's decision to refuse medical treatment should be scrutinized with extra care, because it may indicate a preference for a quick death over prolonged illness or pain.

Finally, attorneys and physicians argue that mandatory reporting may violate privileged communications between professionals and their clients. Elderly individuals may hesitate to seek medical or legal help if they believe that doing so will set in motion an investigation that may lead to their institutionalization, or the punishment of a close family member. Professionals prefer having some flexibility in the laws so that they can do what they can to defuse the situation without bringing in law enforcement or adult protective services. On the other hand, social service agencies point out that mandatory reporting laws force professionals to become involved in situations they might otherwise ignore. Adult protective services and other agencies are often willing to cooperate with the families and the professionals to work out solutions that do not require institutionalization or the involvement of law enforcement.

Recognizing Abuse or Neglect

Q 19:13 What are some of the warning signs of elder abuse?

Attorneys may not have access to the most obvious warning signs, such as physical injuries or the ransacking of bank accounts. They can and should be alert to signs of bruising or malnutrition, mental fragility and paranoia, unusual financial activities, an unhealthy dependence on others, especially nonrelatives, and evidence of alcoholism or drug abuse in either the potential victim or the suspected abuser.

A common red-flag situation arises when an adult child or caretaker requests an attorney to draft a financial power of attorney for an elderly person, naming that person as the agent. If the client is reluctant to bring in the elderly person for execution of the document, offering instead to take the document to the principal for signature, the attorney may reasonably suspect exploitation. Discussion with the client-caretaker may reveal that he or she obtained sizeable financial gifts or title to real estate. While some might argue that the attorney has no obligation other than to prepare the requested documents and warn the client of the consequences of abuse, the general consensus is that in preparation of a document such as a will or power of attorney, the signatory is the true client and must be consulted in person by the attorney. The attorney should insist on meeting the elderly person and determine his or her wishes and ability. If the attorney then has reason to suspect past or intended exploitation, he or she may have a duty (legal, or if not, moral) to make a report to the appropriate agency, provided that such a report can be made without violating duties of confidentiality. However, it may be going too far to make such a report based solely upon the refusal to bring in the elderly person. A well-intentioned child, concerned about "what will happen" if the parent becomes unable to handle his or her affairs, may be unable to persuade the parent that the time has come to ask for help.

Q 19:14 How might the elder law attorney determine whether a client is a victim of abuse?

The most basic requirement is that the attorney meet alone with the elderly client. A second important step is for the attorney to clearly explain that the elderly person is the client, that the elderly person's statements are kept confidential unless he or she authorizes to the contrary and that the elderly person's decisions control. This should also be made explicitly clear to any other person involved in the representation, especially one who may have initiated the relationship with the lawyer by making the appointment or suggesting the need for legal services. Finally, the attorney must be alert for signals, verbal or physical, suggesting fear, excessive deference, or anxiety.

One elder law practitioner has devised a checklist of interviewing strategies that can facilitate determination of possible abuse once suspicion is aroused. [Lehrman, "Client Interview, The Impact of Domestic Violence on Your Legal Practice," The American Bar Association Commission on Domestic Violence, 1996] Her suggestions include:

- Discussing client confidentiality with the client
- Screening for a history of domestic violence
- Assessing the level of danger and developing a safety plan
- Asking for names of witnesses to the abuse
- Validating statements by the client

The victim of abuse should be discouraged from rationalizing the behavior of the abuser and from maintaining that such behavior is acceptable.

The investigator should use broad, open-ended questions that become progressively more specific; there should be no one else present during the interview (and the suspected abuser should be nowhere near the premises). The investigator should note information presented nonverbally as well as verbally, along with the general physical condition and lucidity of the victim. Without laying blame, the investigator should allege abuse to determine the victim's response.

A dilemma for many attorneys can be how to respond to accusations made by persons suffering from dementia against caregivers. It is not unusual for a delusional person to accuse caregiver of anything from "taking all my money" (perhaps because the child has taken over bill-paying, or confiscated the checkbook after finding that the parent was being victimized by scam artists) to "poisoning me" (perhaps because the child has insisted that the delusional person take prescribed medication). Certainly a person with increasing dementia may say "she thinks I'm crazy" after overhearing conversations with medical personnel. This may be complicated further because such delusions may arise not from a progressive dementia such as Alzheimers, but a more temporary condition such as a dementia derived from an infection or meningitis. Other forms of dementia, such as Lewy Body disease, may cause intermittent periods of dementia interspersed by long periods of clarity. This is not to suggest that any apparently "paranoid" statements should be dismissed lightly, even coming from an obviously demented person. Any suggestion of abuse is worthy of investigation. This is only to point out that it is important to look for factual evidence of abuse or exploitation rather than relying upon emotional "gut reactions."

Responsibilities in Cases of Abuse, Neglect, or Exploitation

Q 19:15 What ethical duties might an elder law attorney have when he or she knows of or suspects abuse, neglect, or exploitation of a client?

When the client is the abused person and there is strong evidence of mental incapacity, the attorney's responsibility is usually quite clear. The attorney with no statutory duty to report may investigate solutions to the problem without forcing the victim to change his or her living situation. At the other extreme, the attorney can take immediate steps to remove the abuser through an injunction or restraining order. If the abuser is an employee of the victim's care facility, either the employee, or the victim should be removed immediately. More commonly the attorney can "call protective services" who will then use personnel skilled in evaluating the possibility of abuse and taking appropriate action without further involvement by the attorney. Adult protective services can assist in locating family members or trustworthy individuals who can petition for guardianship and conservatorship, or the victim can be referred to the local public fiduciary, if one exists. In most jurisdictions the attorney can also petition for guardianship or conservatorship—provided the attorney does not seek his or her own appointment, and does not represent a third party seeking appointment (see chapter 9).

When the victim is not mentally incapacitated, but merely afraid and vulnerable, the attorney may have a difficult time convincing the victim to report the abuser, especially if the abuser is an adult child of the victim. Drafting powers of attorney naming trustworthy individuals as agents is one option, but the elderly client cannot be expected to enforce such documents while still vulnerable to the abuser. The attorney may, however, seek permission of the client to provide the documents to the agents and to assist the agents in enforcing the client's wishes. The attorney should become familiar with the statutes in his or her jurisdiction. Some states, such as Connecticut, exempt attorneys from reporting requirements based on the attorney-client privilege, but this is not the case in every state. In Arizona, for instance, attorneys, accountants, or fiduciaries who are responsible for the preservation of an incapacitated person's property are required immediately to report any suspected exploitation. [Ariz. Rev. Stat. § 46-454] At the very least the attorney should refer the client for counseling and psychological testing in order to determine capacity and help convince the client of the need for action.

The victim's attorney should also investigate all past transfers and have them reversed where there is evidence that the victim did not know of the transfer or did not understand the consequences. Bank accounts and credit card statements should be reviewed to determine whether the victim has been exploited by phone scam artists and other thieves.

Q 19:16 What if the client is the abuser?

The lines are less clear when the attorney suspects that a client is exploiting or abusing an elderly person. If the attorney tries to discuss his or her suspicions with the client, the client may well disappear. In a state where attorneys are not exempt from reporting requirements, does this create a conflict—that is, does the attorney have a duty to report the abuse? Is the conflict removed or reduced if the attorney makes an anonymous report?

Most attorneys are extremely uncomfortable with the idea of making an anonymous report on their clients, and in fact most would regard this as extremely unethical. The acts of the client would be put in the worst possible light, whereas an attorney's active and open assistance may put those same acts in a context that might not appear quite so heinous, for instance, where the alleged abuser also needs medical or psychological assistance. The attorney can best serve the client by convincing him or her to go to the appropriate authorities as a demonstration of good faith, and working with them on a solution, such as counseling for the client or repayment of the alleged theft. An anonymous call, on the other hand, would doom the client to almost certain investigation and possible indictment.

Sometimes the abuser is remorseful and eager to discuss solutions, in which case the attorney can be of invaluable assistance, especially if he or she has already developed a good relationship with local authorities. Because federal and state guidelines emphasize confidentiality, often social service and adult protective programs are willing to work with all parties toward a goal of permanent protection of the victim. Depending on the capacity of the victim, guardianship or conservatorship can be established to prevent further exploitation or abuse, and the abuser can make amends to the satisfaction of the victim and of adult protective services.

The attorney should assume that any caregiver of an elderly person is under stress and may be suffering from exhaustion. Materials should be routinely provided to caregivers (whether or not they are the clients) regarding such community services as Meals on Wheels, day care for the elderly, respite care, and transportation assistance.

Q 19:17 What if the elderly victim refuses intervention?

Often the victim refuses to move from home, or even refuses to meet with health care or adult protective service representatives. He or she may fear being placed in a nursing home or losing control of day-to-day activities. If there is strong enough evidence of mental incapacity in conjunction with abuse or neglect, emergency intervention may be needed. Typically an adult protective service representative will first determine whether there is such a need, and local law enforcement may need to be brought in to remove the elderly person physically from home. Less intrusive methods should be tried first, such as having a family member accompany the visitors. Elderly individuals who no longer have the capacity to prepare adequate meals may be eager to open the door for a health care worker or attorney who has brought along fast food or a bag of groceries.

The victim may then be escorted to a psychiatric ward or similar facility where professionals can determine whether he or she is a danger to him or herself or others. It can be a mistake to assume incapacity and compel the "victim" to enter a psychiatric ward against his or her expressed wishes; not only can this be a gross violation of the person's own rights, but it may also be counterproductive if the individual is humiliated by having been taken to the "nuthouse" and accused of being "crazy"; alternatives to any such involuntary removal, whether forcible or through pretext, should be preferred whenever possible. Moreover, if such a removal is unavoidable, the attorney should have nothing to do with it and leave that decision to the protective services authorities. If there is to be any attempt to accommodate the client's view of reality and obtain the claim's assent, the attorney must not be associated with any coercive action.

A court proceeding may be the next step, resulting in involuntary commitment or some other monitored situation until the emergency has passed. Often proper nutrition, social interaction, and the administration of medication will restore some level of capacity to the victim, so that less drastic measures such as guardianship or conservatorship can be put in place. Here again, however, administration of medication against the client's expressed wishes can raise serious issues of personal self-determination and invoke its own due process requirements (see Q 9:53).

Because removal from the home and involuntary commitment are such serious intrusions on one's constitutional rights, at least some jurisdictions mandate the appointment of an attorney or a guardian *ad litem* to represent the rights of the incapacitated individual. For example, in Alabama the court will appoint a guardian *ad litem* and an attorney (and they can be the same person) to represent the incapacitated individual [Ala. Code §16-61-108]; in Arkansas, the court has the power to appoint a guardian *ad litem* to represent an incompetent person not already represented by a guardian or next friend, but will appoint an attorney *ad litem* only when notice is required to a nonresident parties [Ark. Code Ann. §28-1-111]; Colorado sends a visitor to interview the alleged incapacitated person and empowers the visitor to make the decision as to whether a guardian, attorney, or medical examiner should be appointed [Colo. Rev. Stat. § 15-14-303]; Kansas guarantees legal representation if abuse, neglect, or exploitation has already occurred [Kan. Stat. Ann. § 39-1408]; and Michigan requires the appointment of a guardian *ad litem*, but not of an attorney [Mich. Comp. Laws § 700.5406]. In any case, the rules of professional responsibility state that a lawyer may suggest the appointment of a guardian *ad litem* to the court or family members if the lawyer feels it would be in the elderly client's best interest. [American College of Trust and Estate Counsel (ACTEC), Commentaries on the Model Rules of Professional Conduct 134 (2d ed. 1991)] Medical examiners or independent investigators may also be brought in to assess capacity and determine the circumstances that brought the victim before the court.

Q 19:18 Do the same rules apply to guardians, conservators, and other fiduciaries?

A fiduciary has an even higher ethical duty to the ward than other individuals have. Court appointment subjects them to special statutory obligations to do their utmost to protect and provide for their charges. (See chapter 9 for a discussion of guardianship.) Guardians who abuse, or at the very least neglect, their wards may be removed from guardianship and, depending on the extent of the abuse or neglect, may be subject to criminal charges. Conservators who exploit the wards will also be removed by the court and may be personally liable for the mismanagement or theft of funds.

Attorneys have also been known to take advantage of elderly individuals, and risk suspension or disbarment if they improperly spend their clients' funds.

Q 19:19 What assistance can health care professionals provide to the attorney in assessing elder abuse?

The attorney's best option when representing a victimized client may be to seek the assistance of health care professionals who are trained to recognize and treat psychological and physical abuse. The health care professional may be subject to stricter reporting regulations than the attorney is, and may have more familiarity with the community agencies best equipped to deal with the victim's particular needs. An attorney who deals regularly with guardianship, conservatorship, and elder abuse issues should make it a priority to become familiar with the agencies and health care professionals in his or her area.

Progressive communities have established multidisciplinary task forces, involving representatives of law enforcement, the medical field, family members, adult protective services and other social service programs, and elder advocates.

Q 19:20 How are nursing home residents protected from abuse?

States receiving financial assistance under the Older Americans' Act [42 U.S.C. § 3058g] are required to establish long-term care ombudsman programs, administered on the federal level by the Department of Economic Security, Aging and Adult Administration. The focus of the program is to address the needs and rights of residents of long-term care facilities, and to provide a reporting resource for federal programs. The ombudsman is legally entitled to full access to medical records and to the residents themselves, and has the authority to intervene on behalf of a resident, even when the resident is under legal guardianship. Ombudsmen educate residents of long-term care facilities about their rights and help them develop the assertiveness necessary to enforce their rights. Complaints from residents typically include the unjustified or unexpected discharge or eviction from the facility, poor food quality, personal hygiene, loss or theft of personal property, verbal and mental abuse from staff, accidents and falls, mismanagement of personal funds, roommate conflicts, shortage of staff, and unattended symptoms. Ombudsmen are less useful in protecting residents who are incapable, however, as the ombudsman plays more of a mediating and counseling role than advocacy. The ombudsman does not, for example, file criminal charges or lawsuits on behalf of a resident who has been victimized.

Medicaid Fraud Control Units (MFCUs), established by federal mandate [Omnibus Reconciliation Act of 1993, Pub. L. No. 103-66, 42 U.S.C. § 1396p(d) (Aug. 10, 1993)], are designed to prosecute complaints of abuse and neglect of patients of residential care facilities that receive Medicaid funds. They are permitted to investigate the care of both Medicaid and non-Medicaid patients at these facilities. [State v. Thomason, 33 P.3d 930 (Okla. App. 2001)] The state

MFCU must operate independently of the state Medicaid program and should be housed or otherwise linked with the state attorney general's office. However, prosecutorial discretion by such units, or the attorney general's office, may result in problems being ignored until a tragedy occurs.

At a minimum, the family should if possible choose a facility carefully. The Centers for Medicare and Medicaid Services (CMA) (formerly the Health Care Financing Authority or HCFA), the agency that oversees Medicare and Medicaid, maintains a database that includes, among other things, reports of deficiencies in the quality of care. Such deficiencies are reported in more than a fourth of nursing homes in the country. The most frequent violations reported by CMS include the failure to prevent bed sores and accidents and the failure to assess patients' needs.

CMS has broad authority to penalize nursing homes that are in violation, including imposing $10,000-a-day fines, but in fact it rarely does so. [See the U.S. General Accounting (GAO) Report HEHS-99-46 at *http://www.gao.gov/archive/1999/he99046.pdf*; other reports may be found at *http://www.gao.gov/*] This is true on the state level as well; in 1998, a study issued by the General Accounting Office of the U.S. Congress noted that one in three California nursing homes had been cited for severe violations, but were not fined or otherwise sanctioned. One nursing home had been fined $30,000 within a 15-month period, but none of the fines had been collected by the state. [State v. Thomason, 33 P.3d 930 (Okla. App. 2001)]

Unfortunately, as with most things, budgetary constraints can imperil nursing home residents despite the existence of protective laws. Ombudsmen's may find their hands tied from lack of funding, or incorporated into state departments that for reasons of funding, staffing, or corruption discourage action. State Health Departments may be unwilling to enforce state regulations that require the imposition of penalties on already financially strapped facilities, for fear of accelerating a closure. Such financial concerns can imperil nursing home residents as surely as abuse. In Connecticut, a 2002 fire at the Greenwood Health Care Center nursing home caused when a mentally ill resident smoked in bed resulted in the death of at least 11 elderly individuals. Had the state required sprinkler systems in place in nursing homes as a licensure requirement, the tragedy might have been avoided. (Legislation to institute such a requirement was proposed following the incident.)

A March 6, 2002 report of the General Accounting Office, "Nursing Homes: More Can Be Done to Protect Residents From Abuse" (online at *http://www.gao.gov/new.items/d02312.pdf*) concludes that more needs to be done to ensure quality of care to nursing home residents and to protect them from abuse. Texas and Maryland have passed laws allowing cameras, nicknamed "grannycams," to be installed in nursing home rooms; other states are considering or may have passed similar measures.

Remedies

Q 19:21 What are some of the criminal penalties for perpetrators of elder abuse, neglect, or exploitation?

Half of the states do not include penalties for abusers in their adult protective service statutes, and many of those that do generally label the crime as a felony or misdemeanor and call for fines or limited jail time. For example, Missouri law classes "elder abuse in the first degree," which involves an attempt to kill or cause serious physical injury to an individual age 60 or over, as a Class A felony carrying a prison term of 10 years to life [Mo. Rev. Stat. §§ 565.180, 558.011], "elder abuse in the second degree," committed by one who knowingly or purposely causes or attempts to cause physical injury to a person over age 60, as a Class B felony carrying a term of up to seven years [Mo. Rev. Stat. §§ 565.182, 558.011], and "elder abuse in the third degree," which entails causing emotional distress to an older person through physical contact, threats, or intentional failure to provide care, goods, or services, or acting or failing to act in a manner that results in grave risk to the person of an older adult [Mo. Rev. Stat. §§ 565.184, 558.011], as a Class A misdemeanor, which may incur up to one year of prison time. Those who have a statutory duty to report and do not may be convicted of a Class A misdemeanor, and those who file false reports may be convicted of a Class D misdemeanor, which may involve a prison sentence of one to two years. [Mo. Rev. Stat. §§ 565.188, 558.011RS] California is another state that has taken action specifically to protect the elderly, imposing a prison sentence of one to four years for persons convicted of willfully causing or allowing the physical or mental suffering by an elder or dependent adult, or otherwise endangering the health of an elder. [Cal. Welf. & Inst. Code § 15656] Caretakers of elderly or dependent adults who steal or embezzle more than $400 may be sentenced to one to four years in prison and a $1,000 fine. [Cal. Welf. & Inst. Code § 15656]

Federal sentencing guidelines provide for increased penalties for crimes against vulnerable victims such as the elderly. [U.S. Sentencing Guidelines Manual § 3A1.1(b)] It has been argued that one cannot impose a penalty on a caretaker for neglect, when most states do not impose a duty of care on nonprofessional caretakers for the elderly. Fiduciaries who have been found guilty of or liable for abuse may lose their fiduciary status and, in the case of professionals, their licenses.

All states require a preliminary investigation, which leads to assignment of the case to a specific agency. Most state APS laws do not allow for the elderly victim to refuse to consent to an investigation, which may be in the victim's best interests but again diminishes the victim's personal rights and assumes incapacity. A coordinated plan is then established that is designed to keep the victim living independently and free from abuse, if possible, with a range of health, social, psychological, and legal services in place.

Q 19:22 What civil remedies are available to victims of elder abuse, neglect, or exploitation?

Civil remedies have always been available to the victims, although an increase in public awareness about abuse and exploitation of the elderly has given the victims greater credibility. Victims may be awarded compensatory damages, costs, attorney's fees, and even punitive damages in some states. If the abuse takes place in a care facility, and particularly if the abuser is an employee, the facility can be held liable for damages. Many states are putting in place statutes that mandate special penalties for abusers of elderly persons, or as an alternative allow the defendant to make restitution.

Unfortunately, most individual perpetrators are judgment-proof, having long spent their own funds and funds they have illegally or unethically obtained from the exploitation victim. The attorney who decides to go after the perpetrator anyway may be hampered by the incapacity and frailty of the chief witness, the victim.

After the victim's death, the victim's estate may be able to pursue a claim for damages. Of course, if the victim was a Medicaid recipient, such a claim may only inure to the benefit of the State, and family members who do not stand to gain may not be willing to undertake such an enterprise. Relatives have tried to pursue claims on their own behalf for "infliction of emotional distress." However, "bystander" emotional distress claims of this nature may not be available under state law; even if available, they may only be available to a spouse or perhaps a child, not a concerned friend or relative. [See, e.g., Moon v. Guardian Postacute Services, Inc., 116 Cal. Rptr. 2d 218 (Cal. App. 2002) (claim by son-in-law dismissed)]

An important issue in determining the financial feasibility of such a suit will be the state's punitive damages laws. In some states, there is no cap on punitive damages, and egregious conduct may be "punished" by an award commensurate with the financial resources of the defendant in order to "send a message." For example, in a 2001 case, the jury awarded a verdict of $21 million in a case of nursing home abuse that resulted in death. [Phillip Lavalis, Individually and as Representative of the Estate of Rose Bonton, et al. v. Copperas Cove LLC (Texas Dist. 2001) (the case, which is not officially reported, was apparently settled, as the defendant withdrew its appeal in 2002)] In other states, such as Connecticut, there are caps on punitive damages. In addition to the punitive damages availability, recent movements in Congress and around the country to cap "non-economic" damages should also make it harder to enforce anti-abuse laws through civil suits, as by definition an elderly person in his or her last years of life, with no resources or means of income, is unlikely to have any economic damages at all.

Q 19:23 What can a practitioner do to prevent abuse of a client who is in a nursing home?

The most important factor in ensuring quality of care for a nursing home resident is active involvement and oversight by friends of family. For this reason, relocation to a facility near the family may be critical. If there are no friends or family in the area, friends or family should be urged to engage a care manager or advocate to visit the resident periodically and attend care conferences, and of course, to report any abuse.

For those involved in such oversight, whether friends, family, or other third parties, the attorney can provide information and guidelines:

1. Provide a checklist to guide the client through the process of selecting a long-term care facility. When long-term care seems likely, such a checklist might be included as part of the client's package. Some checklists are available at the Medicare website, at *http://www.medicare.gov/Nursing/Checklist.asp;* many others are listed on the national Agency on Aging website and/or published by the state ombudsman's office.
2. Explain to the client and family about resident rights, quality of care, and the care planning process, and provide copies of relevant laws to assist the family in enforcing these rights.
3. Explain how the inspection process works and how to find information about the facility's record of care.
4. Provide the client with telephone numbers for licensing agencies, state ombudsman, and others; at least, advise the client to talk to the local agency on aging and direct the client to appropriate websites.
5. Develop brochures or reference materials for clients to take home and consult at later dates.
6. Revise and provide copies of the "Elder Abuse Prevention Toolkit" available online from the National Association of Adult Protective Services Administrators and the National Center on Elder Abuse, *http://www.elderabusecenter.org/basic/speakers.pdf*.
7. Loan to clients, or urge them to purchase, the National Coalition for Nursing Home Reform book "Nursing Homes: Getting Good Care There," which may be ordered online at *http://www.nccnhr.org*.
8. Network with geriatric care managers, case managers, and other persons to whom you can refer clients who need help with nursing home or other placements, and who may be hired to act as "watchdogs" on behalf of absent children.
9. Consider adding geriatric social services to services your office will provide, or include a paralegal with some social

work training who can be engaged to make periodic checkup visits on clients in institutions.

Practice-Related Issues

Q 19:24 How do cases of abuse, neglect, or exploitation arise in an elder law practice?

From concerns about the lawyer's own duty to report abuse to methods of recovering a client's losses to exploitation, the problems of abuse, neglect, and exploitation are diverse and common in an elder law practice. A few illustrations demonstrate how the issues might arise, and what steps the elder law attorney might take in response:

1. A 35-year-old man calls the attorney and asks her to prepare financial and health care powers of attorney for his 70-year-old mother, who was recently widowed. The attorney explains that the mother would then be her client, not the son, and asks to meet with her alone. The son brings his mother to the appointment and waits obediently in the lobby while the attorney meets with the client. The attorney notices that the woman is quiet and passive, and learns during the interview that she is deeply depressed about her husband's death. After further questioning, the woman discloses that her son, an only child, has had difficulty finding work and lives at home, but he has been a strong source of support and comfort. "I don't know what I would do without him," she says. The son had suggested the powers of attorney to her because they had not had them for her husband and it did create some logistical problems on occasion. Should the attorney prepare the documents?

   A dozen attorneys would probably respond in a dozen different ways to this scenario. Some might argue that the son will just go somewhere else for the powers (or use a do-it-yourself kit), and in fact an only child who has the trust and affection of the parent is the ideal choice for a financial and health care agent. Others would argue that there are too many red flags, and that even a normally trustworthy person under these circumstances might be tempted to abuse a financial power of attorney. Cautious attorneys might advise the mother and son to wait at least until she had dealt with the depression and could make a more rational decision. There should also be some discussion of the alternatives to powers of attorney, such as guardianship and conservatorship proceedings if and when the mother becomes truly incapacitated. Finally, the power of attorney may be prepared, but expressly excluding any gifting provisions, while the attorney makes a calendar entry to check up on the client, as a client, at regular intervals.

2. Daughter calls an attorney and asks what she can do to prevent her alcoholic mother from spending all her money on sweepstakes and psychics. The attorney explains that addictive behavior alone is not sufficient to obtain guardianship or conservatorship, and the daughter wails, "But it's like throwing it in the parking lot!" The attorney tells the daughter to find out if utilities and other bills are being paid. The daughter does some snooping, which is difficult because her mother is guarded about her finances, and learns that she is behind two months on her mobile home lot rent and the electricity was turned off once. The daughter also discloses that her mother keeps herself and her home neat and clean, except for the piles of sweepstakes mail on every available surface. Does the attorney have enough information to initiate conservatorship?

   This is one situation where it might be advisable to bring in an adult protective services or some other government agency, which could do a far more thorough investigation of the woman's financial status and assess her mental status. The attorney may simply suggest to the daughter that this is the daughter's appropriate recourse. People are allowed to make bad decisions, even to the point of bankruptcy, but if a physician (preferably a mental heath expert) can determine that the client-patient is oblivious to the consequences of these bad decisions because of some form of mental disorder or dementia, then the attorney may well have enough to go to court with. He should be prepared to deal with an objection from the mother and her attorney. More problematic, some protective services units are understaffed and will not investigate financial abuse unless physical abuse is also involved.

This may throw the dilemma back to the daughter. Provided there is no prior attorney-client relationship with the parent, provided the attorney does not believe the petition is genuinely unfounded, and provided there is no basis to suspect abuse by the daughter, the attorney may assist with the petition, knowing that a physician's evaluation and report is required to support the petition and that it is the court, not the attorney, who must make the ultimate decision as to whether the conservatorship is appropriate.

Chapter 20

Age Discrimination

Age discrimination is frequently encountered by elderly clients, but difficult to prove in most cases. Although the laws prohibiting discrimination on the basis of race, religion, national origin, and disability are well developed and broadly applied, the only national prohibition against discrimination on the basis of age exists in the context of employment rights. This chapter discusses the Age Discrimination in Employment Act, coverage under the act, and its requirements for bringing suit, proving age discrimination, and remedies. This chapter also discusses protection from discrimination based on employee benefit plans under the Older Workers Benefit Protection Act of 1990. While the typical elder law attorney may lack the competence to prosecute a federal discrimination case without assistance from a more experienced litigator, it is important for an elder law attorney to recognize situations that are appropriate for litigation.

Overview

Q 20:1 What is age discrimination

Age discrimination, at least in the legal sense, is the practice of ageism in the employment context. During the 1960s, when minorities were finding their voices and the federal government tried to respond, "gray power" advocates pointed out that productive, experienced, well-trained employees were losing promotions and even their jobs solely on the basis of age. The Age Discrimination in Employment Act (ADEA) [29 U.S.C. §§ 621 et seq.], *http://www.eeoc.gov/laws/adea.html,* was passed in 1967 to "promote employment of older persons based on their ability rather than age; to prohibit arbitrary age discrimination in employment; [and] to help employers and workers find ways of meeting problems arising from the impact of age on employment." [29 U.S.C. § 621(b)]

Q 20:2 How do demographics figure into the importance of ageism in the workplace?

One hundred years ago only 4 percent of the population lived past age 65, while 40 percent of the population was under age 18. In 1990 one in eight was 65 or older, and by the year 2030 at least 22 percent of the population will be 65 or older; only 21 percent will be under 18. [United States Senate Special Commission on Aging, American Association of Retired Persons, Federal Council on the Aging, U.S. Administration on Aging, Aging America—Trends and Projections, 1991 ed., at xix] In 1950 there were about 14 percent as many Americans over age 65 as there were working-age Americans (aged 20 to 64); by 2030, the ratio is expected to increase to over 35 percent. [2000 Annual Report of the Board of Trustees of the Federal Old-Age and Survivors Insurance and Disability Insurance Trust Funds, March 30, 2000] In other words, there are strong social incentives to keep older Americans in the workplace, particularly skilled employees.

Q 20:3 Who is the typical ADEA plaintiff?

One study found that about 80 percent of all those who file ADEA suits are male, most are middle-level managers or professionals, and more than half are between the ages of 50 and 59. [Eglit, Age

Discrimination (2d ed., Clark Boardman Callaghan, 1997), citing Schuster & Miller, "An Empirical Assessment of the Age Discrimination in Employment Act," 38 Indus. & Lab. Rel. Rev. 64, 68 (1984)] Experts explain that blue-collar workers often have unions to represent their interests, and younger workers have a relatively easier time of finding similar employment. As female employees continue to break through the glass ceiling, these statistics are expected to change.

Coverage

Q 20:4 What practices does the ADEA specifically prohibit?

The ADEA prohibits employers from arbitrarily discharging, demoting, refusing to promote, or refusing to hire individuals based solely on their age. The act also extends to discrimination in compensation, terms, conditions, or benefits of employment, as well as advertisements for positions. In addition, employers cannot force employees into early retirement. [29 U.S.C. § 623]

Q 20:5 What are legitimate grounds for employee dismissal recognized by the ADEA?

Absent a written employment contract most employment is "at will." An employer may fire an "at will employee" for no reason or for a good reason, but not for an illegal reason. Termination on the basis of age alone is illegal, but the ADEA allows for "reasonable factors other than age," or RFOAs. [29 U.S.C. § 623(f)(1)] As a defense the employer can say that the worker did not get along with colleagues, was consistently late to work, did poor work, etc. The employer must then be able to back the RFOA up, preferably with past evaluations that put the employee on notice of problems with his or her work. If past evaluations are excellent, the employer may find it difficult to come up with a plausible RFOA.

Q 20:6 Does the ADEA preempt state age discrimination laws?

The ADEA does not preempt state age discrimination laws, either statutory or common law, except when local provisions directly conflict with ADEA provisions. [29 U.S.C. § 633] Where there is no conflict ADEA and state claims can be litigated and remedies sought in the same action, and the federal statute does not invalidate state statutes that impose tougher standards. [Simpson v. Alaska State Commission for Human Rights, 423 F. Supp. 552 (D. Alaska 1976), *aff'd*, 608 F.2d 1171 (9th Cir. 1979)] When there is a conflict with the ADEA, the employer cannot rely on state statutory or common law as a defense because the federal statute would supersede such law. [29 U.S.C. § 633(a)]

Q 20:7 Does the ADEA cover older employees in the hiring process?

Yes, in fact its initial impetus came from a congressional study that indicated that discrimination in hiring was a significant problem. [29 U.S.C. § 621(a)] In fact, only about one in 10 complaints reported to the ADEA stems from a hiring incident. The problem is that the plaintiff cannot bring a complaint based solely on the fact that a younger person was hired; the plaintiff must prove that but for his or her age, he or she would have been hired. The plaintiff must have some way of finding out whether the candidate hired was better qualified, and if there were other, non-age-related factors that caused him or her not to be hired. [See Armbruster v. Unisys Corp., 62 F.E.P. 395 (E.D. Pa. 1993), *aff'd in relevant part*, 32 F.3d 768, 65 F.E.P. 828 (3d Cir. 1994); Allen v. Park-Ohio Indus., 66 F.E.P. 1153 (N.D. Ohio 1992)] If the plaintiff believes that the employer has a history of ageism in hiring, he or she may be able to interest a public reporting agency, such as the Equal Employment Opportunity Commission (EEOC) or the State Attorney General's Office, in obtaining the necessary documentation to assemble a class action case.

Q 20:8 Who is protected by the ADEA?

The ADEA initially protected employees from the ages of 40 to 65. In 1978 the upper age limit was raised to 70 [former 29 U.S.C. § 631(a) (1984)], and in 1986 it was removed altogether [29 U.S.C. § 631(a)]. The ADEA not only prohibits preferential treatment because of age for people under 40, but also prohibits discrimination based on age between two employees who are over 40. [29 C.F.R. § 1625.2(a); O'Connor v. Consolidated Coin Caterers Corp., 517 U.S. 308 (1996)]

Q 20:9 How is "employee" defined under the ADEA?

The ADEA (as with some other federal statutes) defines an employee only as "an individual employed by an employer." [29 U.S.C. § 630(f)] The U.S. Supreme Court has adopted a common law test that distinguishes employees from independent contractors (who are not covered under the ADEA) by considering the hiring party's right to control the time, place, and manner of work, the skill required, who furnishes the tools and equipment, the method of payment, who hires assistants, and the tax treatment of the hired party. Partners, directors, or owners of businesses are not considered employees. [Nationwide Mutual Insurance Co. v. Darden, 503 U.S. 318 (1992)]

Q 20:10 Which employers are required to comply with the ADEA?

All federal, state, and local government agencies with 20 or more employees are covered, as well as private-sector employers of 20 or more workers. To meet the 20-employee requirement, the employer must have at least that many full-time workers every working day of the week for 20 weeks. [29 U.S.C. § 630(b)] If the employer meets the requirement, then all full-time, part-time, and temporary employees are covered.

Employment agencies are covered under the ADEA if they regularly procure employees for at least one covered employer. [29 U.S.C. § 630(c); 29 C.F.R. § 1625.3] If this criterion is met then the employment agency is covered with respect to all of its activities. The ADEA applies not only to the employment agency's referral activities, but also the agency's own employment practices regardless of the number of employees the agency employs. [29 C.F.R. § 1625.3]

Unions that maintain a hiring hall or serve as exclusive bargaining agents for 25 or more members are also subject to the ADEA. [29 U.S.C. § 630(e)]

Establishing and Proving an ADEA Claim

Q 20:11 What is the difference between liability based on "disparate treatment" and that based on "disparate impact"?

Age discrimination claims may be based on "disparate treatment" or "disparate impact" theories of liability. The U.S. Supreme Court in *Hazen Paper Company v. Biggens* distinguished these two theories of liability. [507 U.S. 604 (1993)]

To prove disparate treatment, the employee must show that the employer treated the employee differently from other employees based on that employee's protected characteristic. The employee's protected trait must have actually motivated the employer's adverse actions. Disparate treatment cases may involve a single-motive or mixed-motives basis for an employer's discriminatory action. In *Lovelace v. Sherwin-Williams Company* [681 F.2d 230 (4th Cir. 1982)], for instance, the plaintiff, lacking direct evidence, claimed that he was demoted because of his age, thus creating a presumption of discrimination. The defendants were able to produce other reasons for the demotion—for example, that the plaintiff's store lost money. The plaintiff did not effectively refute these arguments and lost the case on appeal.

Disparate impact cases, on the other hand, involve employment practices, including tests or promotion policies, that are neutral on their face but have a discriminatory effect on one protected group where the difference cannot be justified by business necessity. The *McDonnell Douglas* approach (see Q 20:12) does not apply, and in fact courts often rely on statistical evidence to show the impact of the neutral policy on a protected group. [See Griggs v. Duke Power Co., 401 U.S. 424, 431 (1971)] Courts have questioned the validity of this approach, because of the sheer number of policies and tests that affect older workers only because of their seniority or level of experience. [See Larson, 8 Employment Discrimination (2d ed. Lexis Publishing 2000)] In *Hazen Paper Company v. Biggins* [507 U.S. 604 (1993)] the Supreme Court undermined the disparate impact approach in a fact pattern where an older employee was fired just prior to the vesting of his pension benefits. The Court acknowledged that vested or almost-vested employees were likely to be older than other employees of the company, and framed its examination of the issues on "whether an employer violates the ADEA by acting on the basis of a factor, such as an employee's pension status or seniority, that is empirically correlated with age." [Id. at 608] In the wake of *Hazen Paper* some courts have begun to back off from the disparate impact approach.

In April, 2002 the U.S. Supreme Court dismissed (on the basis of certiorari improvidently granted) a case that would have decided the validity of disparate impact claims under the Age Discrimination in Employment Act (ADEA). [Adams v. Florida Power Corp., 255 F.3d 1322 (11th Cir. 2001), *cert. granted,* 534 U.S. 1054, *dismissed,* 535 U.S. 228 (2002)] In the underlying case, the Eleventh Circuit Court of Appeals held that disparate impact was not a basis for an ADEA action. As of 2002, the First, Seventh, Tenth, and Eleventh Circuits have not allowed disparate impact claims under the ADEA, while the Second, Eighth, and Ninth Circuits have allowed them.

Q 20:12 What are the elements necessary to prove a disparate treatment case of age discrimination?

The Supreme Court in 1973 in *McDonnell Douglas Corporation v. Green* [411 U.S. 792 (1973)] provided a four-part test to establish a prima facie discrimination case. As adapted to ADEA criteria, that test requires the plaintiff to prove he or she:

1. Belongs to the protected group of those aged 40 or over;
2. Applied for, was qualified for, or worked in a job for which the employer was seeking applicants;
3. Was not hired, promoted, or maintained in a job for which he or she was qualified; and
4. Was not hired, and a younger person (even if that person is over 40) was selected for the position instead. The ADEA's enforcement agency, the EEOC, interprets this to mean that age discrimination may occur even if the favored worker is within the protected class. [259 C.F.R. § 1625.2(a)] Some courts had disagreed with this interpretation, but in 1996 the U.S. Supreme Court laid the matter to rest in *O'Connor v. Consolidated Coin Caterers Corporation* [517 U.S. 308 (1996)], in which the court ruled that a prima facie case can be established even when the favored person is older than 40. The court stated: "[T]here can be no greater inference of *age*

discrimination (as opposed to '40 or over' discrimination) when a 40-year-old is replaced by a 39-year-old than when a 56-year-old is replaced by a 40-year-old." [Id.]

If other workers assimilated the plaintiff's duties, then he or she does not have the necessary element of being replaced by a younger worker.

If the plaintiff thereby demonstrates prima facie discrimination, the burden then shifts to the employer, who must prove that the plaintiff was rejected for legitimate nondiscriminatory reasons. If the employer can produce a non-age-related reason, the burden shifts back to the plaintiff, who argues that the reason given is a pretext, and that but for his or her age the plaintiff would have been hired. [McDonnell Douglas Corp. v. Green, 411 U.S. 792 (1973). See also St. Mary's Honor Center v. Hicks, 509 U.S. 502 (1993)]

Q 20:13 Is salary a legitimate nondiscriminatory reason for replacing an older worker?

The replacement of an older, higher-paid employee with a younger, lower-paid one may be in violation of the ADEA, even though the employer's sole motivation was to save costs. This applies whether the employer replaces one older worker or a group of older workers. [Leftwich v. Harris-Stowe State College, 702 F.2d 686 (8th Cir. 1983); Metz v. Transit Mix, Inc., 828 F.2d 1202 (7th Cir. 1987)] The "prospect of imminent bankruptcy" may constitute a valid defense. [EEOC v. Chrysler Corp., 733 F.2d 1183 (6th Cir. 1984)]

Q 20:14 What elements are necessary to prove a disparate impact claim of age discrimination?

As explained by the Eleventh Circuit Court of Appeals in its decision in *Adams v. Florida Power Corp.* [255 F.3d 1322 (11th Cir. 2001), *cert. granted,* 534 U.S. 1054, *dismissed,* 535 U.S. 228 (2002)], "disparate impact" as a basis for a discrimination claim is borrowed from Title VII discrimination suits because of the similarity in language between Title VII and the ADEA. Courts that have accepted this disparate impact theory thus far are the Second, Eighth, and Ninth Circuits. [See Criley v. Delta Air Lines, Inc., 119 F.3d 102, 105 (2d Cir. 1997) (per curiam); Lewis v. Aerospace Cmty. Credit Union,

114 F.3d 745, 750 (8th Cir. 1997); Frank v. United Airlines, Inc., 216 F.3d 845, 856 (9th Cir. 2000); E.E.O.C. v. Local 350, 998 F.2d 641, 648 n. 2 (9th Cir. 1993)]

The Supreme Court has yet to decide whether the disparate impact theory of liability is available under the ADEA. The Court's decision in *Hazen Paper Company v. Biggens* [507 U.S. 604 at 610 (1993)] seems to cast doubt on the transferability of the theory from Title VII to the ADEA. In April, 2002 the U.S. Supreme Court dismissed a case, on the basis of certiorari improvidently granted, in a case that would have decided the matter. [Adams v. Florida Power Corp., 255 F.3d 1322 (11th Cir. 2001), *cert. granted,* 534 U.S. 1054, *dismissed,* 535 U.S. 228 (2002)] In *Adams,* the Eleventh Circuit Court of Appeals had joined the circuits rejecting or strongly questioning the availability of a disparate impact theory, others being the First, Third, Sixth, Seventh. [See Mullin v. Raytheon Co., 164 F.3d 696, 700-01 (1st Cir.), *cert. denied,* 528 U.S. 811 (1999); E.E.O.C. v. Francis W. Parker School, 41 F.3d 1073, 1076–77 (7th Cir. 1994); Ellis v. United Airlines, Inc., 73 F.3d 999, 1006–07 (10th Cir. 1996); DiBiase v. SmithKline Beecham Corp., 48 F.3d 719, 732 (3d Cir. 1995); Lyon v. Ohio Educ. Ass'n and Prof'l Staff Union, 53 F.3d 135, 139 n. 5 (6th Cir. 1995)]

In any case, in order to establish a prima facie case of disparate impact (presumably in circuits other than the First, Third, Sixth, Seventh, Tenth, or Eleventh), the plaintiff must:

1. Describe the policy, activities, or criteria practiced by the employer that allegedly has had a negative impact on older employees;
2. Demonstrate the disparate impact upon protected employees; and
3. Prove causation between the practice and the effects on the older employees. [See, e.g., EEOC v. McDonnell Douglas Corp., 191 F.3d 948 (8th Cir. 1999)]

While statistics are usually irrelevant to individual ADEA actions, they would make or break a disparate impact case. After the plaintiff has established a prima facie case the burden would then shift to the employer, who as a defense will either discredit the statistics or prove that the practice is job-related for the position in question and consistent with a legitimate business necessity. [42 U.S.C. §

2000e-2(k)] Once the employer meets this burden, the burden shifts back to the plaintiff to show that the proffered business reason is a pretext for illegal age discrimination (see Q 20:15).

Q 20:15 What is the difference between a mixed-motives case and a pretext case?

An ADEA case can be proved by direct evidence of discrimination; however, in most cases discrimination is inferred. In a pretext case under the ADEA, the plaintiff has no direct evidence of discriminatory intent; he or she must instead present facts that permit an indirect inference that ageism was the impetus behind the employer's action. Once the plaintiff establishes a prima facie case of age discrimination, the employer counters with its nondiscriminatory reasoning for the action. The employee argues that the reason given is pretextual. The employer may have several reasons, all supported, for the dismissal, but if the fact-finder determines that but for his or her age the employee would not have been dismissed, the employer will lose.

In a mixed-motives case, the defendant can argue as an alternative that it would have made the same decision to dismiss, and in fact would have dismissed, even if ageism were not a factor. [Price Waterhouse and Co. v. Hopkins, 490 U.S. 228 (1989)] Both the plaintiff and the defendant have a greater burden of proof in a mixed-motive case than in a pretext case; the plaintiff, because he or she must have direct evidence of the discrimination sufficient for a jury to agree that age played a substantial part in the discriminatory decision; the defendant, because it must raise the affirmative defense that it would have made the same decision even if it had not taken age into account, and must convince the jury that the absence of improper motives with regard to age would not have changed its decision.

Q 20:16 Is the bona fide occupational qualification defense based on age recognized by the ADEA?

Yes. Employers are also allowed to hire and fire in situations "where age is a bona fide occupational qualification (BFOQ) reasonably necessary to the normal operation of the particular business." [29 U.S.C. § 623(f)(1); 29 C.F.R. § 625.6] This exception is given a narrow interpretation. The employer asserting the BFOQ defense must prove:

1. The age limit is reasonably necessary to the essence of the business; and
2. Either (a) all or substantially all individuals excluded from the job involved are disqualified or (b) some of the excluded individuals possess a disqualifying trait that cannot be ascertained except by reference to age.

[29 C.F.R. § 625.6]

The employer may, for example, successfully argue that physical strength or perfect eyesight is needed to perform the job properly. The plaintiff may counter that rather than set age limits, the employer should test candidates individually to make sure they do not meet the criteria. The employer must then prove that individual testing is not possible or would not be adequate.

Q 20:17 What is the bona fide executive exception?

The ADEA exempts employers with respect to the mandatory retirement of "bona fide executives" or "high-level policymakers" who have reached age 65 and who for the two-year period immediately before retirement are employed as a bona fide executive or top level policymaker and are entitled to retirement benefits totaling at least $44,000 annually. [29 C.F.R. § 1625.12] The "bona fide executive" exception applies only to "very top level employees who exercise substantial executive authority over a significant number of employees and a large volume of business." [29 C.F.R. § 1625.12(d)(2)] It does not apply to middle-management employees. High-level policymakers are individuals who "have little or no line authority but whose position and responsibility are such that they play a significant role in the development of corporate policy and effectively recommend the implementation thereof." [29 C.F.R. § 1625.12(e)] The executives must have the authority to hire and fire, or be in a high policy-making position.

The ADEA does not apply to firefighters and law enforcement officers who are forced to retire on the basis of age. [29 U.S.C. § 623(i)(1)] In 1986 a temporary amendment to the ADEA was enacted to allow state and local governments to mandate retirement ages for law enforcement personnel and firefighters. The temporary amendment expired in 1993, but was reinstated in 1996 and applies retroactively to the intervening years. Occasionally this is still litigated, but usually over such issues as the definition of "law enforcement officer" or whether the characterization of "state or local government applies." [See Larson at 131-19]

Q 20:18 What is the first step in making a claim against the employer?

The ADEA requires victims alleging ADEA violations to report them to the appropriate state agency before or at the same time as they report them to the federal Equal Employment Opportunity Commission (EEOC). [29 C.F.R. § 1614.105(d)] The EEOC enforces Title VII of the Civil Rights Act of 1964, the Equal Pay Act, the Americans with Disabilities Act (ADA), and, as of 1980, the ADEA.

Some states have age discrimination laws (these are referred to as deferral jurisdictions) with broader provisions or stronger remedies than those of the ADEA. Other states have no age discrimination laws at all. If the state has no discrimination law, then a report must be made with the EEOC within 180 days of the alleged discriminatory act. [29 U.S.C. § 626(d)(1)] In deferral jurisdictions the employee must file a report with the EEOC within 300 days of filing the report with the state agency; often the state agency can assist with the filing of both reports simultaneously. The claimant must then wait 60 days before filing a private lawsuit, to give the state or EEOC agency sufficient time to make a preliminary investigation. [29 U.S.C. § 626(d)(2)] If the EEOC or (depending on state law) the state agency files a lawsuit against the employer based on the complaint, the claimant cannot file a private lawsuit. A lawsuit must be filed within 90 days after receiving notice that the administrative proceeding has been terminated. [29 U.S.C. § 626(e)]

Although nearly 20,000 age discrimination charges were filed with the EEOC in each of the three years from 1992 to 1994, the number of filings has dropped off briefly in 1994 to 2000, but with the economic downtown since 2000, filings are on the rise. In fiscal year 2002 the EEOC reported just over 19,921 age discrimination cases filed, the highest since 1994.

Table 20-1. Age Discrimination Cases Filed with EEOC (FY 1992–2002)

	FY 1992	FY 1993	FY 1994	FY 1995	FY 1996	FY 1997
Receipts	19,573	19,809	19,618	17,416	15,719	15,785
	FY 1998	FY 1999	FY 2000	FY 2001	FY 2002	
	15,191	14,141	16,008	17,405	19,921	

(Figures from EEOC Office of Research, Information and Planning Charge Data System at *http://www.eeoc.gov/stats/adea.html.*) Of these filings, over half are dismissed as being without reasonable cause; the EEOC files an average of only about 50 ADEA lawsuits per year. [EEOC Litigation Statistics, FY 1992 through FY 2002 Summary Report, Feb. 2003, online at *http://www.eeoc.gov/stats/litigation.html*]

Q 20:19 What is the EEOC's Mediation Program?

The EEOC's Mediation Program is a voluntary program offered by the EEOC allowing for an option to mediate charges of discrimination. The mediation program is an alternative to the traditional investigation and litigation process. The EEOC provides a trained mediator to assist parties in reaching a negotiated solution to a charge of discrimination. During mediation, parties have an opportunity to discuss issues raised in the charges, clear up misunderstandings and thereby narrow the issues, determine underlying concerns and wants, find areas of agreement, and incorporate those areas into a resolution. The mediation process is at no cost to the employer or the employee (although the parties are permitted to hire an attorney to accompany them). The process is informal and takes place prior to an investigation of a charge. Further information on the EEOC Mediation Program can be found online at *http://www.eeoc.gov/mediate/index.html.*

Q 20:20 What documentary evidence might the EEOC or the private claimant seek from the employer?

Employers will typically be asked to produce the employee's complete file, including all evaluations, memoranda, and incident reports. The plaintiff should carefully review the file to determine whether positive reports have been removed, and should be alert to such suggestive words as "overqualified" or any references to appearance. Policy manuals and employee handbooks may also be useful, if only to prove the employer's knowledge of ADEA requirements. The agency or plaintiff should also request a complete list of all employees employed by the defendant for at least a year prior and a year subsequent to the discriminatory incident at issue. This list should include the employees' birth dates, hire dates, termination dates, and job description. While statistics alone are usually not helpful in an ADEA suit, the plaintiff may note a pattern of discriminatory treatment against older individuals. The list may also shed light on circumstances surrounding the termination of the plaintiff—for instance, although the worker who now occupies the desk of the terminated employee is the same age as the victim, a 35-year-old is actually performing the tasks performed by the terminated employee.

The EEOC, as the enforcement agency for the ADEA, requires employers to retain for at least three years each employee's name, address, date of birth, occupation, rate of pay, and weekly compensation. Job applications, résumés, records of promotions, demotions, transfers, training, test results, and advertisements must be kept for one year. [29 C.F.R. §§ 1627.1–1627.7]

Remedies

Q 20:21 What remedies are available to a victim of age discrimination?

The ADEA does not specify the remedies available, but rather incorporates by reference the remedies provided in the Fair Labor Standards Act. [29 U.S.C. § 626(b); 29 U.S.C. § 216(b)] The successful plaintiff can be awarded back pay (past lost wages) and reinstatement to the position. He or she is also entitled to front pay (future loss of earnings) if he or she does not wish to return to work for the employer. In fact most employers are not eager to take back these employees and are willing to come up with front pay, but this is a heavily negotiated item—it is difficult to prove how long an employee would have stayed with a particular employer. Out-of-pocket expenses and attorney's fees are also recoverable.

Damages for pain and suffering are not available and while injunctions may be sought to prevent future violations, punitive damages are not allowed. Liquidated damages, in an amount equal to the back pay award, may be recovered if the plaintiff proves that the employer willfully violated the ADEA by knowing yet showing reckless disregard for its provisions. [29 U.S.C. § 626; see, e.g., Nance v. Maxwell FCU, 186 F.3d 1338 (11th Cir. 1999); Whittlesey v. Union Carbide Corp., 567 F. Supp. 1320 (S.D.N.Y. 1983), *aff'd,* 742 F.2d 724 (2d Cir. 1984)]

Q 20:22 Is the plaintiff required to mitigate the damages?

The plaintiff is required to mitigate damages by using reasonable diligence in finding other suitable employment. [See, e.g., Smith v. Great Am. Restaurants, Inc., 969 F.2d 430 (7th Cir. 1992); Real v. Continental Group, 627 F. Supp. 434 (N.D. Cal. 1986)] It is assumed that older workers have greater difficulty finding work after being terminated, and the plaintiff's failure to mitigate damages has generally not been a significant factor in ADEA cases. In general, failure to mitigate will result in reduced recovery only if the defendant employer can show that the employee actually refused reasonable employment opportunities. [See, e.g., Pierce v. F. R. Tripler & Co., 955 F.2d 820 (2d Cir. 1992); Starceski v. Westinghouse Elec. Corp, 54 F.3d 1089 (3d Cir. 1995); Thorkildson v. Insurance Co. of N. Am., 631 F. Supp. 372 (D. Minn. 1986)]

Q 20:23 Are ADEA damages taxable?

Damages received under the ADEA, including back and future wages and liquidated damages, are not excludable from gross income and are taxable. This has been confirmed by the U.S. Supreme Court in *Commissioner v. Schleier* [515 U.S. 323 (1995)]. In addition, awards of attorney's fees are also likely to be taxable. [Sinyard v. Commissioner, 76 T.C.M. (CCH) 654 (2001), *aff'd,* 268 F.3d 756 (9th Cir. 2001), *cert. denied,* Sinyard v. Rossotti, 536 U.S. 904 (2002)] Depending on the amounts involved and the offset of expenses to income, in the *Sinyard* case, alternative minimum tax resulted in a net tax to the Sinyards that the court found regrettable but unavoidable.

Older Workers Benefit Protection Act

Q 20:24 What is the Older Workers Benefit Protection Act?

The ADEA was amended by the Older Workers Benefit Protection Act of 1990 (OWBPA) to protect workers from discrimination in employee benefit plans. [29 U.S.C. §§ 626 et seq.] In 1990 Congress passed OWBPA, in response to a Supreme Court decision [Public Employees Retirement System of Ohio v. Betts, 492 U.S. 158 (1989)] that held that the ADEA did not forbid age discrimination in the area of employee benefits except in unusual circumstances. Section 4(a)(1) of the ADEA now forbids discrimination in employee benefits as well as in every other aspect of employment that is not protected by some specific exemption from coverage of the act. The act also codified the "equal benefit or equal cost" concept, which requires a company to provide to its older workers benefits that are at least equal to those provided to younger workers, unless the company can prove that the cost of providing an equal benefit is higher for an older worker than for a younger one. The only exception to this equal benefit or equal cost rule is a voluntary early retirement incentive plan.

Q 20:25 Can an employer fire or refuse to hire a protected person based on benefit plan costs?

Employers are allowed to thin the ranks of middle management because it would be cost-effective to do so—even if those "thinned" were mostly in the protected group. Employers also argue that cost-effectiveness was behind their refusal to hire or keep older workers who cost more in benefits than younger workers. Now the employer is not allowed to use this as an RFOA, although the employer may spend the same amount in benefits on each employee even if this has a negative impact on older workers.

Employers have found another solution to the problem of expensive benefit programs by encouraging older workers to retire early. If the worker can be persuaded by bonuses, the employer has not violated the ADEA; however, if direct or implied threats of termination are the "stick" accompanying the "carrot," the employee may have an ADEA complaint. If the employer requires the employee to sign a waiver promising not to sue, the employee must sign such a waiver voluntarily and with full knowledge of his or her rights under the ADEA. [29 U.S.C. § 626(f)]

Q 20:26 What are the OWBPA requirements for voluntary early retirement incentive plans?

The OWBPA sets out the following rules and requirements for voluntary early retirement incentive plans:

1. When such a plan is challenged in court, the burden is on the employer to prove that its conduct does not violate the OWBPA.
2. The company may set a minimum age as a condition of eligibility for either a normal or an early retirement benefit.
3. The company may provide pension subsidies to subsidize regular pension benefits.
4. No discrimination based on age is permitted with respect to severance pay when employees are terminated; however, a company may offset severance payments, including up to 52 weeks of supplemental unemployment compensation benefits paid until the employee is eligible for a pension, by the value of any retiree health benefits that the pensioner is entitled to as well as any immediate and unreduced pension benefits that the terminated employee can get.
5. The company may reduce long-term disability benefits by a like amount of pension benefits that the retiree elects to receive or that he or she is eligible to receive after attaining the latter of age 62 or normal retirement age.
6. The company may implement a new disability plan that reflects the OWBPA's requirements, and then give employees the option of being covered under either the old or the new plan.

[29 U.S.C. § 626(f)]

Q 20:27 Are waivers and releases of age discrimination claims valid under the OWBPA?

Under the OWBPA the following requirements must be met in order for a waiver to be valid under the ADEA:

1. The waiver of ADEA claims must be part of an overall agreement between employer and employee, written in plain, everyday English that can be understood by the employee.

2. The waiver section of the agreement must specifically refer to rights or claims arising under the ADEA.
3. The waiver cannot be prospective; that is, it cannot seek to waive rights or a cause of action that may arise as a result of the company's actions or behavior after the date the agreement is signed.
4. The employee must receive good consideration for executing the waiver, and that consideration must be given by the company in addition to anything of value (such as severance benefits under a pre-existing severance policy) that the employee would have been entitled to without signing the waiver.
5. The employee must be advised in writing that he or she should consult an attorney before signing the agreement.
6. The employee must be given reasonable time in which to decide whether or not to execute the waiver. This reasonable time can range from 21 to 45 days, depending upon the circumstances under which the agreement is signed.
7. There must be a seven-day revocation period.
8. If the waiver is requested in connection with an employment termination program, the employer must provide written disclosure of the class of persons who are eligible and any time limits, and the job titles and ages of all the individuals eligible or selected for the program, and the ages of all individuals in the same job classification or organizational unit who are not eligible or selected.

[29 U.S.C. § 626(f)]

Q 20:28 Can attorneys' fees be recovered in ADEA cases?

The ADEA, like other anti-discrimination laws, provides for an award of attorney's fees to a prevailing plaintiff. [29 U.S.C. § 626(b), incorporating by reference 29 U.S.C. § 216(b)] Attorneys' fees are not, however, available at the administrative level. [Lowenstein v. Baldridge, 38 Fair Empl. Prac. Cas. (BNA) 466 (D.D.C. 1985); 29 C.F.R. § 1614.501(e)(1)] A fee award must be sought and contemporaneous time records provided; the court will then award fees using a rate that factors in prevailing rates in the region, the difficulty of the case, the results achieved, and other such factors. Attorney's fees will be computed first by determining the "lodestar," with adjustments thereafter. The "lodestar" is the number of hours reasonably expended multiplied by a reasonable hourly rate. [Hensley v. Eckerhart, 461 U.S. 424, 434 (1983)] Prevailing rates shall also be awarded to legal services attorneys and private attorneys who had opted to charge a reduced rate.

For the boutique firm that routinely files ADEA cases, and which selects clients able to pay the out-of-pocket expenses while litigation is pending, this can be a lucrative field. (Job discrimination cases can be expensive to litigate, requiring multiple depositions, lengthy discovery, and a well-financed opponent in the corporate employer defendant.) Otherwise, however, given the low success rate, high costs, and limited damages (unless additional claims may be made), an attorney may not get his or her full fees out of most ADEA cases, and will take an ADEA case for more altruistic reasons, because the clients find it almost impossible to find other work at their age.

Practice-Related Issues

Q 20:29 What age discrimination scenarios might an attorney deal with in an elder law practice?

An example serves to illustrate the issues involved when an attorney is considering the potential merits of an age discrimination-related employment termination case. A 68-year-old woman meets with an attorney (the fourth she has met with so far) to discuss her recent firing from a cafeteria catering to seniors, where she had worked for eight years. Because she receives a widow's Railroad Retirement pension, she was limited in her income-earning ability, and was planning to retire at age 70 anyway. The damages will probably not amount to more than $10,000, but this money would mean a great deal to the client, who still owes $2,000 on her car and can barely make ends meet on her pension alone. What should the attorney tell her about representation?

The attorney should first determine whether the client has exhausted her administrative remedies, specifically a complaint to the EEOC or the equivalent state civil rights agency. This procedure must be undertaken before litigation can begin, and is something the client can do without legal representation. Just as important, it may furnish some crucial information: (1) the level of commitment the client has to her own case, (2) initial discovery that may support or hurt the claim, and (3) some indication of how the client will handle herself in a deposition, because the investigators usually tape the initial interview with the client. If the government agency agrees to take on the case—which is extremely unusual—then the client will not need legal representation. The attorney should not expect to get his full fees out of this case.

Chapter 21

Grandparents' Rights

The concept of nuclear family has undergone significant changes in recent decades. Divorce, separation, children born out of wedlock, and remarriages—all relatively unusual occurrences a century ago—now have dramatic effects on families. As conflicts have arisen and families have become more separated by geography, ideology and circumstance, grandparents, stepparents, and other family members and caretakers increasingly find themselves with no legal rights to see the children in their lives. Legal intervention has increasingly come about when grandparents have been denied visitation and guardianship rights by one or both parents, and state legislatures (and often state courts) have been eager to provide some help to anxious grandparents and other significant adults in the child's life. This chapter discusses the legal response to this conflict.

Grandparent Visitation Rights

Q 21:1 What are grandparent visitation rights?

Grandparent visitation rights are much like the rights granted to non-custodial parents. The court grants a grandparent (or step-parent, or other caretaker depending on the state) visitation rights when one or both parents limit or deny visitation with the grandchildren. State statutes vary greatly in terms of who is permitted to petition for visitation rights and under what circumstances.

Q 21:2 What is meant by reasonable or fixed visitation?

Courts either grant "reasonable visitation" or order visitation based on a "fixed schedule." When granted "reasonable visitation," the custodial parent(s) determine dates, times, and duration of visitation. This requires that both parties communicate and cooperate with one another. When a court orders visitation based on a "fixed schedule," the dates, times, and duration of visitation are fixed by the court.

Q 21:3 What factors do courts consider in determining grandparent visitation rights?

Many states only permit a grandparent to petition for grandparent visitation rights when the grandchild's parents are divorced, deceased, or unmarried. Some states do not grant grandparent visitation rights following a stepparent's adoption of the grandchild.

In deciding whether to grant a petition for grandparent visitation rights, courts look at whether grandparent visitation is in the "best interests of the child." At least one state requires the grandparent to prove that significant harm will come to the child unless grandparent visitation rights are granted. [Ga. Code Ann. § 19-7-3] This high bar is often difficult to overcome.

Q 21:4 What is the status of state law on grandparent visitation rights?

All states currently have some form of a "grandparent visitation" statute, though appellate courts have struck some. Furthermore, state laws vary greatly. Detailed information on current state law status is maintained by AARP online at *www.aarp.org/litigation/table.html*, and at *www.grandparenting.org/Grandparent%20 Visitation.htm*; because this information is in rapid flux it is important to check current developments in each state.

Note also that in Alabama, Florida, Iowa, Missouri, Oregon, Rhode Island, and Utah petitions are permitted only when the nonparent is denied visitation altogether. Also, statutes in Minnesota, New Mexico, Pennsylvania, and Texas only permit visitation if the child previously resided with the grandparent.

Q 21:5 How is "best interests of the child" established?

What constitutes the "best interests of the child" depends on the state. Included in most states' definition of "best interests of the child" are the following factors:

- The strength of the relationship between the child and the grandparents;
- The relationship between each of the child's parents or person with whom the child is residing and the grandparents;
- The nature and reason for the objection to the grandparents' request for visitation;
- The effect that granting or denying the visitation will have on the child;
- The capacity and disposition of the grandparents to provide necessities during the time of such grandparents' visitation;
- The moral, mental, and physical health of the grandparents, as it relates to caring for a grandchild during visitation; and
- The reasonable preference of the grandchild to have grandparents' visitation.

[Richard Victor, "Grandparent Visitation Rights in the 21st Century," 2000 L. Rev. M.S.U.-D.C.L. 793 (2000)]

These factors play a significant role in deciding whether visitation rights will be granted. Therefore, much is dependent on the specific facts of the case. Courts have wide latitude in considering any other relevant factors.

In addition, expert witnesses are often used to determine whether it is in the "best interests of the child" to receive visitation from the petitioning grandparents. Often these expert witnesses are psychologists or psychiatrists.

Q 21:6 Are grandparents' visitation rights Constitutional?

In light of all of the variation among state statutes and the uproar from parents resisting the implementation of them, the Supreme Court granted certiori to review a grandparents' visitation rights statute. In June of 2000, the Supreme Court handed down a decision in the case of *Troxel v. Granville* [530 U.S. 57 (2000)]. In *Troxel*, paternal grandparents sought visitation with their granddaughters, who were born out of wedlock following the death of their son. Granville, the children's mother, permitted a short visit once per month. The grandparents petitioned for more visitation time. Washington State's highest court struck down that state's permissive grandparent visitation statute as unconstitutional. Section 26.10.160(3) of the Revised Code of Washington permits "any person" to petition for visitation rights "at any time" and authorizes stat superior courts to grant visitation whenever it is in the "best interests of the child." The Supreme Court affirmed this decision, ruling that the statute violated parents' fundamental right to make decisions concerning the care, custody, and control of their children. The Court stated that the Fourteenth Amendment gave parents this fundamental right, although it is not absolute. The Court took note of the fact that the state may limit these parental rights in certain ways, including prohibiting abuse or neglect of children, regulating child labor, requiring children to be vaccinated, requiring school attendance, and requiring that children be restrained while riding in motor vehicles. [See *Troxel*, 530 U.S. at 66–67]

The Court reasoned, however, that the Washington statute was "breathtakingly broad," and it violated the fundamental rights of parents. [Id. at 66] The statute has the effect of "permit[ing] a court to disregard and overturn any decision by a fit custodial parent concerning visitation whenever a third party affected by the decision files a visitation petition, based solely on the judge's determination of the child's best interests." [Id. at 67] In *Troxel*, this induced a violation of the Due Process Clause for several reasons. First, it was not alleged that the parent was unfit. There is a presumption that fit parents act in the best interests of their children. [Id. at 67, citing Parham v. J.R., 442 U.S. 584 (1979)] The lower court gave no special weight to the parents' determination. The Court noted "The problem here is not that the Washington Superior Court intervened but that when it did so, it gave no special weight at all to Granville's determination of her daughter's best interests. More importantly, it appears that the Superior Court applied exactly the opposite presumption." [See *Troxel,* 530 U.S. at 66–67] Second, the lower court did not give significant weight to the mother's offer of visitation. The court pointed out that this is a significant factor "because many state statues do not even allow a visitation order for a nonparent unless a parent has denied or unreasonably denied visitation." [Id. at 71] These factors combined provided no protection for Granville's fundamental parental rights. Although the Washington Supreme Court held the statute to be unconstitutional, the U.S. Supreme Court narrowed their reasoning and ruled that the Washington statute was held to be unconstitutional as applied to Granville. Furthermore, it is important to note that the *Troxel* decision was upheld only by a plurality, or less than a majority. Two Justices concurred, and three others dissented.

Q 21:7 Is a nonparent seeking visitation rights required to show harm or potential harm?

The Supreme Court in *Troxel* made clear that they were not deciding whether the Due Process clause requires a petitioning nonparent to make a showing that harm or potential harm will result if the child is not allowed visitation.

Q 21:8 Did the Supreme Court in *Troxel* declare specific nonparent visitation state statutes unconstitutional?

In *Troxel v. Granville* [530 U.S. 57 (2000)], the Supreme Court refrained from declaring any specific state statute unconstitutional. The Court stated,

> We do not, and need not, define today the precise scope of the parental due process right in the visitation context. In this respect, we agree with Justice Kennedy that the constitutionality of any standard for awarding visitation turns on the specific manner in which that standard is applied and that the constitutional protections in this areas are best 'elaborated with care.' Because much state-court adjudication in this context occurs on a case-by-case basis, we would be hesitant to hold that specific nonparental visitation statutes violate the Due Process Clause as a per se matter. [Id. at 73]

Q 21:9 What effect does *Troxel* have on specific state statutes?

Many states have had the opportunity to review their nonparental visitation statute following the *Troxel* decision. In light of *Troxel*, state courts have determined the constitutionality of their statutes. As pointed out by the Indiana Court in *Crafton v. Gibson* [752 N.E.2d 78 (Ind. App. July 21, 2001)] states have handed down decisions that fall into three categories: states that found their statute constitutional, states that found their statute unconstitutional as applied, and states that found their statute unconstitutional on its face. States such as Arizona, Maine, Missouri, Texas, and Louisiana have found their statutes to be constitutional, mainly due to the fact that their statutes are narrower than the Washington statute. Those states' statutes, the courts have reasoned, provide for heightened constitutional protection. Other states such as Kansas, Maryland, and California have ruled that their statutes *as applied to particular cases* are unconstitutional. These state courts found their lower courts to have improperly applied *Troxel*, or to have misconstrued the significance of the custodial parent's right to make parenting decisions. A handful of states have ruled their grandparent visitation statute to be patently unconstitutional; the Illinois Supreme Court, for example, has held that its state law on grandparent visitation is facially unconstitutional in *Wickham v. Byrne* [2002 Ill. LEXIS 313 (April 18, 2002)], as has the Florida Fifth District Court of Appeal in *Belair v. Drew* [776 So. 2d 1105 (Fla. Dist. App. 2001)].

There are significant differences in how states have applied *Troxel* to their own statutes. Law in this area is rapidly developing, and it is advisable to check current information on the status of individual state statutes. Sites such as *www.grandparenting.org* and *www.aarp.org* contain updated case law and statutes.

Q 21:10 If visitation is granted in one state, will it apply in other states?

The Visitation Rights Enforcement Act, signed into law by the President in November of 1998, guarantees that grandparents can visit their grandchildren anywhere in the United States if they have visitation rights in any one state. [Visitation Rights Enforcement Act of 1998, Pub. L. No. 105–374, 112 Stat. 3383, amending 28 U.S.C. § 1738A] Although this law does not establish a federal right to grandparent visitation, it eliminates the problem of a grandparent having to relitigate visitation if the grandchild's custodian moves to another state.

Q 21:11 What are the "cons" to filing for grandparents' visitation rights?

Litigation, of course, can be costly, and paying for litigation over custody and visitation issues may be difficult or impossible for some grandparents. There may be emotional costs as well. Litigation is likely to produce strain on the relationship between the opposing parties—grandparent and parent. If the grandparents are not successful in the litigation it may result in a complete termination of contact, or the imposition of impossible barriers to a positive relationship between grandparents and grandchild. Not only will this have an effect on the entire family, it may have damaging effects on the grandchildren, who will find themselves in the middle.

Q 21:12 Are there alternatives to litigation?

Mediation is an alternative to litigation. Litigation differs from mediation, as litigation is an adversarial tool. Mediation is a more peaceful and cooperative means to reaching a solution with which both parties can be pleased. The process of mediation involves bringing in a neutral third party to help resolve disputes. Each side will have the opportunity to explain their points of view. The parties can then create a legally binding agreement through compromise. For more information about mediation and what is available in a particular area, see the American Bar Association website at *www.abanet.org/dispute*, the American Arbitration Association website at *www.adr.org*, and the Conflict Resolution Center website at *www.conflictres.org*.

Grandparent Caretakers

Q 21:13 How many children live in grandparent-headed households?

In the last 25 years, the number of children living in households headed by grandparents has increased by over 50 percent. According to the U.S. Census 2000, 6.3 percent of children under 18 live in grandparent-headed households. Approximately one-third of these children have no parent present in the grandparent-headed household. There are grandparent-headed households in every ethnic and socioeconomic group. More information can be found at *http://www.aarp.org/confacts/programs/grandraising.html.*

Q 21:14 Why has the number of children living in grandparent-headed households increased?

The number of children living in grandparent-headed households has increased due to a number of factors. There are more nontraditional families now than in the past. Other factors such as divorces, deaths, drug and alcohol addiction, teen pregnancy, and unemployment have contributed to the changing structure of the family.

Q 21:15 What options are available to caretaker grandparents who wish to obtain a formal legal relationship with their grandchild?

A lot of problems experienced by grandparents raising grandchildren arise from the lack of legal authority to make decisions for the child. It is possible to gain legal authority to make personal, medical, educational, and various other decisions for the child through written consent from one of the child's parents. Though this option exists, parents rarely give written consent. Furthermore, it would be cumbersome to frequently provide written consent on a day-to-day basis.

Grandparents may instead opt for several other legal avenues that would invoke more permanent legal authority to make decisions for their grandchild. These options include obtaining legal custody, guardianship, and adoption.

Q 21:16 What is custody of a grandchild?

A grandparent who has legal custody of a grandchild may determine the child's upbringing, including making decisions regarding the child's education and health care. States vary in their statutes regarding who may get custody of a child and under what circumstances. Courts will often require a finding that both parents are unfit or somehow unable to care for the child before permitting a third party to petition for custody. Furthermore, courts may require a showing that granting the grandparent custody is in the best interests of the child.

One potential downfall of legal custody is that a parent may return (perhaps years later) and request that the court return the child to the custody of the parent. This could severely interfere with the child's need for stability. States have had to weigh this need with the fundamental right of the parent to raise his or her own child. States vary on when and how a parent can return to regain custody. However, where the parent has appeared at the trial level or waived his or her appearance at the time custody is granted to the grandparent, most states require the moving parent to show a substantial change in circumstances. This is a substantial burden of proof on the moving parent. [See Carolyn Zisser, "Grandparents Have Rights After All," 76 Fla. Bar J. 53 (January 2002)]

Q 21:17 What is guardianship of a minor?

In general, a guardian is one who legally has the care and management of a person. Grandparents can seek guardianship of their grandchildren as a way of securing a formal legal relationship. Guardianships are usually conducted in the probate court, and the guardian is supervised by the court. Therefore, a grandparent/guardian must accept that the court is essentially a participant in parenting the child. Any interested party may intervene and contest the grandparents' actions regarding the child. For the same Constitutional reasons that court-ordered visitation is suspect, guardianship may be challenged (depending on the basis for the guardianship) by the natural parents, even after guardianship has been established. Furthermore, a guardian of a minor will be required to seek court approval prior to taking at least some actions, such as moving to another state with the minor, or changing the minor's name.

Q 21:18 What is adoption?

Adoption grants the grandparent the most complete legal right, acting to sever any parental right of the child's parents. Following adoption, parents no longer have rights, responsibilities, nor duties toward the child. Therefore, the grandparent is legally responsible for the child. One danger for the grandparent is loss of benefits for the grandchild that may be available if the grandchild lacks resources of his or her own, or is the child of a deceased parent and therefore entitled to Social Security benefits as a surviving minor child. If a child is living, it may also be traumatic for the parent to surrender all parental rights (unless those have already been terminated due to abuse).

Adoption proceedings are usually held in juvenile court or in some states, probate court. In some states and under some circumstances, there may be financial subsidies available to adoptive parents; such a subsidy may make adoption more attractive than guardianship.

Q 21:19 Should a grandchild apply to be a foster parent?

Depending upon the financial exigencies, in some cases a grandparent may wish to apply to the state as a foster parent. This will result in more state intervention, as technically the state will have custody of the child, but there may be sufficient financial remuneration to make the arrangement worthwhile. If the grandparent is relatively solitary, and the grandchild has "no one else," it may even be preferable to have state intervention in place in the event of the grandparent's death. However, many states will not provide the same financial subsidy to a relative acting as foster parent as they will to a stranger. This is changing; check local statutes.

Grandparents Raising Grandchildren

Q 21:20 Where can a grandparent raising a grandchild obtain legal assistance?

For legal assistance on issues such as custody, guardianship, adoption, and foster care, a grandparent can contact such agencies as the local or state bar association, legal aid, mediation services, or a family law lawyer. In addition, an elder law attorney may be consulted regarding the estate that may pass to the adopted grandchild.

Q 21:21 Where can a grandparent raising a grandchild obtain financial assistance?

Several states offer subsidies for grandparent caregivers. Furthermore, a grandparent may be able to receive assistance from the

Temporary Assistance to Needy Families (TANF) program. Other resources include Social Security or Supplemental Security Income, local grandparent support groups, and local social service agencies for the aging. The National Council On Aging has developed an easy to use website at *www.benefitscheckup.org*. The site includes a simple online questionnaire, used to identify federal and state assistance programs for older Americans.

It is also important to consider *why* the grandchild is residing with the grandparent in the first place. If the grandchild's parent is deceased, and had paid in to the Social Security system, the minor *grandchild* may be eligible for, and should be receiving, "survivor's" benefits which may defray support costs, as well as potentially receiving SSI and/or Medcaid. [20 C.F.R. § 404.339] A disabled grandchild may even be entitled to claim "child's" benefits on the earnings record of one deceased grandparent if the parent is deceased. [42 U.S.C. § 416(e)]

Q 21:22 What is TANF?

In 1996, the Personal Responsibility and Work Opportunity Reconciliation Act (PRWORA) created "Temporary Assistance to Needy Families" as a replacement for "Aid to Families with Dependent Children" and related assistance programs as the partially federally funded welfare program for families with children. Unlike AFDC, which shared costs on a basis similar to the Medicaid program, TANF is a block-grant program; some states even use the TANF block grants to finance the earned income credits. TANF is intended to encourage adult members of such families to seek work, therefore, the grandparent who is "on the grant" and receiving benefits to that will pay for childcare or to encourage the grandparent to work, will receive more benefits than if only the child in the family is a beneficiary. The maximum period for which the adult can receive benefits is five years, over his or her entire lifetime; the child can, however, continue to receive benefits for a longer period of time. State programs implementing TANF vary. The State of Connecticut maintains a website that includes information regarding many of the operating agencies for the TANF program in all 50 states. [See *http://www.dss.state.ct.us/pubs/TanfList.htm*]

Q 21:23 Is a grandparent raising a grandchild eligible to pay lower taxes?

There are ways in which a grandparent may be eligible to receive tax refunds or credits. First, a grandparent may be eligible for the Earned Income Tax Credit (EITC). The EITC provides a refund to families who do not have to pay federal income tax. In order to qualify, the grandparent must be employed and meet an income requirement. Also, filing a W-5 form may permit the grandparent to receive advance payments throughout the year thereby increasing the amount received per paycheck.

Some states have Earned Income Tax Credits. Of the 43 states that have personal income taxes (including the District of Columbia), 11 now have state EITCs. Those states are: Colorado, Iowa, Kansas, Maryland, Massachusetts, Minnesota, New York, Oregon, Rhode Island, Vermont, and Wisconsin.

A grandparent may also be eligible for the Child and Dependent Care Credit, designed to help families who must pay for childcare in order to work or look for a job. The credit lowers the amount of federal income tax. The credit amount is dependent on the number of children, family income, and the amount paid for care.

In addition, a grandparent raising a grandchild may be eligible to receive a Child Tax Credit. The credit operates like the Child and Dependent Care Credit in that it serves to reduce the federal income tax liability. "Qualified" dependents under the Child Tax Credit must be under the age of 17, a U.S. citizen or resident alien, and must have been claimed as a dependent of the previous year's federal income tax return. Grandchildren are identified as "qualified" dependents.

Finally, a grandparent may be able to claim an additional exemption because the grandchild is a "dependent." Five tests must be met to claim a person as a dependent:

1. Dependent has less than $3,000 (revised annually) of "gross income" for the calendar year (exceptions for students, etc., minors). Medicaid does not count as "gross income." Social Security disability does not count as "gross income."
2. Over half of the dependent's "support" must have been furnished by the taxpayer (some exceptions apply). "Support" includes "the fair rental value of lodging furnished to a depen-

dent," out of pocket expenses for the dependent, a share of household expenses such as food, but does not include a proportionate share of items that might make up the "fair rental value" such as household maintenance. In other words, you do not get to count it twice. Even though Social Security and SSI do not count as income, they are considered as being contributed by the recipient to his or her own support. Assistance from the state to pay for the training and education of handicapped children are not considered to constitute support unless the state assumes custody.

3. The dependent must fall within one of various relationships, specifically including a grandchild. (The relationship survives death: that is, if a grandmother has married someone not related to the grandchild, and claims the grandchild as dependent during her lifetime, her husband, if continuing to provide support, can continue to claim the grandchild as dependent.)
4. The dependent may not have filed a joint return with a spouse.
5. The dependent must be a U.S. citizen, national, or resident of the United States, a resident of Canada or Mexico at some time during the year in which the taxpayer's tax year begins, or an alien adopted by and living with a U.S. citizen of national as a member of the household for the entire year.

[I.R.C. § 152(b)(3); Reg. § 1.152-2(a)(2)]

AARP provides assistance for grandparents in preparing taxes. AARP can be contacted at 1-888-227-7669 (1-888AARPNOW).

Appendix A

Estate Planning Questionnaire

Date

Client's name

Client's address

Client's city, state ZIP

ESTATE PLANNING QUESTIONNAIRE

You have made an appointment to meet with us about your estate plan. In order for us to properly assess your estate and to evaluate tax, probate and other issues, we need to have a considerable amount of information. Please complete this questionnaire to the best of your abilities; do not be distressed if you are unable to provide all the detail we have requested. If you have prepared a financial statement (or description of your family), please feel free to refer to a copy of that statement where it is appropriate in this questionnaire. Some questions may not apply (if, for example, you are unmarried); please simply ignore the inapplicable items.

Please try to have this questionnaire completed prior to our appointment. If you need assistance, our staff will try to help you to prepare the information.

Family Information

	Name	*Date of Birth*	*Social Security Number*
You:	______	______	______
Your spouse:	______	______	______
(will you both be present for the interview?)	Yes ____	No ____	

Date of Marriage: ______

Address: ______

Home Telephone ______ Business Telephone: ______

Occupation (yours): ______

(your spouse's): ______

Children common to the marriage:

Name	*Date of Birth*	*Address*
______	______	______
______	______	______
______	______	______
______	______	______
______	______	______

Husband's children:

______	______	______
______	______	______

Wife's children:

______	______	______
______	______	______

Others important to your estate plan (grandchildren, siblings, etc.):

______	______	______
______	______	______

Is there anyone important to your estate plan (including you and your spouse) who is not a citizen of the United States?

______

Do any of your children (or potential beneficiaries) suffer from a disability or illness which should be considered in planning your estate? ______ If so, please describe:

____

____

____

Personal Information

(Please bring copies of all important documents)	*Husband*	*Wife*
Do you have a Will? (Yes/No)	________	________
Are you the beneficiary of any trust? (Yes/No)	________	________
Do you have a power of attorney? (Yes/No)	________	________
Are you a Veteran of the U.S. Military? (Yes/No)	________	________
Who should make financial decisions for you in the event of disability?	________	________
If that person were unavailable, whom would you choose?	________	________
Who should make medical decisions for you in the event of disability?	________	________
If that person were unavailable, whom would you choose?	________	________
Are you covered by Medicare? (Yes/No)	________	________
Supplemental Insurance? (Yes/No)	________	________
Do you have Long Term Care Insurance? (Yes/No)	________	________

Personal Information (*cont'd*)

Who referred you to our office? ______________ ______________

May we thank him or her for the referral? (Yes/No) ______________ ______________

What do you see as the most important issue to be dealt with in our meeting?

____

____

____

____

____

Financial Information

Please list your monthly income from the following sources (estimate if you are unsure or if the income varies):

Income Source	*Husband*	*Wife*
Social Security	______________	______________
Other pension income	______________	______________
(Describe pension source(s)) (for example"State Retirement")	______________	______________
Dividends and interest	______________	______________
Rental income	______________	______________
Employment	______________	______________
Other income	______________	______________

Describe your assets (explicit detail is not required, but it will help if you give us more information), and let us know how you believe each asset is held:

Real Estate—address	*How titled? (Joint tenancy, community property, etc.)*	*Estimated value*	*Mortgage balance*

Stock/Bonds—Company and number of shares	*How titled?*	*Estimated value*

Bank accounts—Bank name and type of account	*How titled?*	*Estimated balance*

IRAs and other Qualified Retirement Plans—List Institution and Account Type	*Owner*	*Beneficiary*	*Balance or value*

Automobiles—Describe by year and make	*How titled?*	*Estimated value*

Life Insurance—Company Name	*Insured*	*Cash value*	*Face amount*	*Beneficiary*

Prepaid burial and funeral arrangements—Name of plan, funeral home or cemetery	*Type of arrangement*	*Amount*

Other assets—List a brief description	*How titled?*	*Estimated value*

Do you expect to receive an inheritance or gift (from any source) which should be considered in planning your estate?

____

Have any of your assets appreciated in value (since you acquired them) such that capital gains taxes would make it difficult to liquidate them?

____

List any substantial debts (other than mortgages listed above):

____

Debt owed to (include short description)	*Estimated balance*

Thank you for taking the time to complete this questionnaire. Please bring the completed questionnaire to the interview with you. In addition, it will help us if you bring copies of the following documents:

1. Your existing will(s) (and trust documents, if any)
2. Deed to your residence and any other real estate
3. Recent statements from banks, brokerage houses and annuity companies
4. Insurance policies
5. Any other documents you think might be relevant

We look forward to meeting with you.

Appendix B

Engagement Letter

Dear [*client*]:

I enjoyed meeting with you to discuss your estate planning goals, and look forward to continuing to work with you to meet those goals. The estate planning process will include several separate steps. Once you have returned a signed copy of this letter of engagement, I will prepare drafts of [a will *or* health care power *or* attorney/proxy *or* financial power of attorney *or* revocable living trust, etc.] for your review. After you have received those drafts, you will need to let my office know what changes (if any) you would like to suggest. You may wish to schedule an appointment to further discuss the drafts, or the larger estate plan. After that review, you will probably be ready to sign the final documents.

[*Add the following paragraph if a living trust is being prepared*]

[Because your estate plan includes a living trust, we will not be completed when the documents are signed. In addition to establishing the trust itself, we will need to work together to complete the transfer of assets into the trust's name. My office will prepare some of the transfer documents (deeds for in-state real estate, for example), but some transfers will require that we work together. In addition, it may become necessary to retain separate legal counsel for transfers of real estate located outside of the state.]

My fee for preparing your estate plan will be [*describe fee arrangement, including whether it will be hourly, flat or some other basis; include the amount of flat fees and the hourly rate as appropriate*]. That fee will be payable [in full on the day documents are signed *or* in full in advance *or* on a monthly basis *or* as bills are mailed to you].

I encourage you to discuss your estate planning goals as questions arise, and to let me know if you are unclear about the documents, my fees or the timing or sequence of steps in preparing your plan. Please sign the copy of this letter which is enclosed, and return the signed copy to my office. I will undertake preparation of initial drafts as soon as I have received the signed copy.

Very truly yours,

[*Attorney*]

I have read the foregoing letter and understand its contents. I agree that it accurately reflects our fee agreement and my understanding of the estate planning process, and hereby retain __________________ as my attorney as set out in the letter.

Dated:________________ ____________________________

[*Client*]

Appendix C

Joint Representation Agreement

[Note: This joint representation agreement is adapted from a form promulgated by the American College of Trust and Estate Counsel (ACTEC), which publishes a pamphlet called "Engagement Letters: A Guide for Practitioners" (1999) including proposed engagement letters for joint representation of multiple family members]

Dear [*clients*]:

I enjoyed meeting with both of you to discuss your estate planning needs, and look forward to continuing our professional relationship. You have requested that I prepare [*describe scope of representation*]. We have agreed that my work will be billed [*describe fee agreement*].

It is common for a husband and wife to employ the same lawyer to assist them in planning their estates. You have taken this approach by asking me to represent both of you in your planning. Because I will be representing both of you I will have separate obligations to each of you. Accordingly, ethical considerations prohibit me from agreeing with either of you to withhold information from the other. In this representation, I will not give legal advice to either of you or make any changes in any of your estate planning documents without your mutual knowledge and consent. Of course, anything either of you discusses with me is privileged from disclosure to third parties.

If a conflict of interest arises between you during the course of your planning or if the two of you have a difference of opinion, I can point out the pros and cons of your respective positions or differing opinions. Ethical considerations prohibit me, as the lawyer for both of you, from advocating one of your positions over the other. Furthermore, I would not be able to advocate one of your positions versus the other if there is a dispute at any time as to your respective property rights or interests or as to other legal issues between you. If actual conflicts of interest do arise between you it may become impossible for me to perform my ethical obligations to both of you; in that event it would become necessary for me to withdraw as your joint lawyer. Because I would then have represented each of you individually, I would also be required to withdraw from continued representation of either of you in connection with the contested matters. I ask that you sign a copy of this letter to acknowledge that you understand the problems that might arise from my representation of both of you, and to indicate your consent to my withdrawal from representation of either of you if the need should arise in the future.

Once documentation is completed to effect the planning that you have hired me to implement, my engagement will be concluded and our attorney-client relationship will terminate. In the meantime, I will not begin preparation of the estate planning documents we have discussed unless and until I hear back from you.

After considering these choices if you consent to my representing both of you jointly, I request that you sign and return the enclosed copy of this letter. If you have any questions about anything discussed in this letter, please let me know. In addition, you should each feel free to consult with a lawyer outside of my firm about the effect of signing this letter.

Very truly yours,

[*Attorney*]

CONSENT

We have read the foregoing letter and understand its contents. We consent to having you represent both of us on the terms and conditions set forth. We agree that you may, in your discretion, share with both of us any information regarding the representation that you receive from either of us or any other source. We further understand that, in the event an actual conflict of interest should develop in the future, you would be required to withdraw from representation of either of us, and we consent to the withdrawal if such a need should arise.

Dated: ____________ ________________________
[*Spouse*]

Dated: ____________ ________________________
[*Spouse*]

Appendix D

Instruction to Counsel Regarding Original Power of Attorney

I hereby direct the law firm of ____________________ (the law offices) to hold the Durable Power of Attorney that executed today until either one of the following occurs:

1. The law offices receive an original letter or affidavit from a physician indicating that he or she has examined me, and that he or she believes that I am so incapacitated that I am no longer able to either make or communicate responsible decisions concerning my person or effectively manage my assets to meet my needs, or

2. The law offices determine that for another reason (such as my disappearance or extended unavailability, or as a result of some other disability), it would be in my best interests and consistent with the planning I have today undertaken that the Durable Power of Attorney should be released.

Upon occurrence of either of the circumstances described above, I instruct the law offices to release my original Durable Power of Attorney to the person named therein as my attorney-in-fact. In the event that the law offices determine that the named attorney-in-fact is unavailable, unwilling to act or precluded from acting for any reason, I instruct the law offices to release my original Durable Power of Attorney to the appropriate alternate attorney-in-fact named therein.

I expressly waive any physician-patient privilege to the extent that it may be necessary to permit a physician to provide the information required to authorize release of the Durable Power of Attorney. I also expressly waive any conflict of interest that might arise by reason of this instruction. I further authorize the law offices to provide such counsel and direction as may be necessary to assist my attorney-in-fact to discharge his or her duties in accordance with my wishes and directions as they may have been made known to the law offices.

Dated: ______________________________

[*Client*]

Index

[References are to question numbers.]

A

B

C

D

E

F

G

H

I

J

K

L

M

O

P

Q

R

S

T

U

V

W